# Lecture Notes in Computer Science 16437

The series Lecture Notes in Computer Science (LNCS), including its subseries Lecture Notes in Artificial Intelligence (LNAI) and Lecture Notes in Bioinformatics (LNBI), has established itself as a medium for the publication of new developments in computer science and information technology research, teaching, and education.

LNCS enjoys close cooperation with the computer science R & D community, the series counts many renowned academics among its volume editors and paper authors, and collaborates with prestigious societies. Its mission is to serve this international community by providing an invaluable service, mainly focused on the publication of conference and workshop proceedings and postproceedings. LNCS commenced publication in 1973.

Anshuman Shastri · Rajiv Singh ·
Uma Shanker Tiwary · Dhananjay Singh
Editors

# Intelligent Human Computer Interaction

## 17th International Conference, IHCI 2025
## Jaipur, India, November 14–16, 2025
## Revised Selected Papers, Part II

*Editors*
Anshuman Shastri
Banasthali Vidyapith
Tonk, Rajasthan, India

Rajiv Singh
Banasthali Vidyapith
Tonk, Rajasthan, India

Uma Shanker Tiwary
IIIT-Allahabad
Allahabad, Uttar Pradesh, India

Dhananjay Singh
Penn State University
Pennsylvania, PA, USA

ISSN 0302-9743 ISSN 1611-3349 (electronic)
Lecture Notes in Computer Science
ISBN 978-3-032-26351-3 ISBN 978-3-032-26352-0 (eBook)
https://doi.org/10.1007/978-3-032-26352-0



This Springer imprint is published by the registered company Springer Nature Switzerland AG
The registered company address is: Gewerbestrasse 11, 6330 Cham, Switzerland

# Preface

The 17th International Conference on Intelligent Human Computer Interaction (IHCI 2025) stands as a pinnacle event within the realm of Human-Computer Interaction (HCI), meticulously examining the evolving research frontiers amid the intricate interplay of machine intelligence and human cognition. Hosted both on-site and online by Banasthali Vidyapith, Jaipur, India from November 14–16, 2025, IHCI 2025, themed as "AI for Sustainable Human-Centric Intelligence," showcased a comprehensive exploration of the dynamic convergence between artificial intelligence and human-computer interaction.

This landmark event featured a diverse array of intellectual pursuits encompassing 7 conference tracks, 7 special sessions, 4 industry sessions, and 3 panel discussions, all meticulously curated to echo the central theme. From an impressive pool of 342 submissions, 92 papers were accepted, rigorously selected by the technical program committee, relying on the discerning evaluations of at least two expert reviewers in a double-blind process.

An assembly of 4 plenary speakers, 6 keynote addresses, and 15 invited speakers, presided over by astute session chairs hailing from both academic and industrial domains, formed the academic backbone of this conference, attracting an international contingent of over 300 participants from across 30 nations. IHCI has unequivocally evolved into a global nexus, uniting academic researchers, burgeoning scholars, industry luminaries, and technology innovators within the HCI sphere. Its profound impact lies in empowering participants to realize their professional aspirations, thereby fostering advancements that transcend into societal benefits and business success.

Deep appreciation is owed to the authors who entrusted their scholarly contributions to IHCI 2025, leveraging the facilitative CMT (Conference Management Toolkit) system throughout the submission, review, and editing phases. The unwavering dedication of the technical program committee and organizing committee has been instrumental in orchestrating the triumph of this conference. Gratitude extends to the speakers, session chairs, authors, and participants whose collective efforts culminated in an intellectually invigorating and fruitful IHCI 2025. Their ongoing support remains integral to the continued success of this esteemed conference series.

November 2025

Anshuman Shastri
Rajiv Singh
Uma Shanker Tiwary
Dhananjay Singh

# Organization

## Organizing Committee

## General Chairs

| | |
|---|---|
| Ina Aditya Shastri | Banasthali Vidyapith, India |
| Uma Shanker Tiwary | Indian Institute of Information Technology Allahabad, India |
| Dhananjay Singh | Penn State University, USA |
| Wan-Young Chung | Pukyong National University, South Korea |

## Steering Committee

| | |
|---|---|
| Jan-Willem van 't Klooster | University of Twente, Netherlands |
| Madhusudan Singh | Penn State University, USA |
| Laxmidhar Behera | IIT Mandi, India |
| A. S. Mandal | IIT Delhi, India |
| Siba K. Udgata | University of Hyderabad, India |
| P. K. Nanda | Shiksha O' Anusandhan, India |
| Swagatam Das | ISI Kolkata, India |
| Nishchal K. Verma | IIT Kanpur, India |
| Vivek Kumar Singh | NITI Ayog, Government of India, India |
| C. K. Jha | Banasthali Vidyapith, India |
| Shalini Chandra | Banasthali Vidyapith, India |
| Dipjyoti Chakraborty | Banasthali Vidyapith, India |

## Advisory Chairs

| | |
|---|---|
| Jong-Hoon Kim | Kent State University, USA |
| David (Bong Jun) Choi | Soongsil University, South Korea |
| Ajay Gupta | Western Michigan University, USA |
| Jan Treur | Vrije Universiteit Amsterdam, The Netherlands |
| KC (Casey) Santosh | University of South Dakota, USA |
| Stefano Berretti | University of Florence, Italy |
| Henry Leung | University of Calgary, Canada |
| Thomas Madritsch | FH Kufstein Tirol University of Applied Sciences, Austria |

## Program Chairs

| | |
|---|---|
| Laxmidhar Behera | IIT Mandi, India |
| Nishchal K. Verma | IIT Kanpur, India |
| Madhusudan Singh | Penn State University, USA |
| Manoj Kumar Singh | Banaras Hindu University, India |

## Technical Program Chairs

| | |
|---|---|
| Anshuman Shastri | Banasthali Vidyapith, India |
| Rajiv Singh | Banasthali Vidyapith, India |
| Uma Shanker Tiwary | Indian Institute of Information Technology Allahabad, India |
| Dhananjay Singh | Penn State University, USA |

## Tutorial Chairs

| | |
|---|---|
| Hanumant Singh Shekhawat | IIT Guwahati, India |
| Maria Weber | Saint Louis University, USA |
| Aditya Nigam | IIT Mandi, India |
| Swagatam Das | ISI Kolkata, India |

## Workshop Chairs

| | |
|---|---|
| Sang-Joong Jung | Dongseo University, South Korea |
| Teena Sharma | IIT Guwahati, India |
| Manisha Agarwal | Banasthali Vidyapith, India |
| Manisha Jailia | Banasthali Vidyapith, India |

## Publicity Chairs

| | |
|---|---|
| Annamaria Szakonyi | Embry-Riddle Aeronautical University, USA |
| Manju Khari | Jawaharlal Nehru University, India |
| Ajit Kumar | Soongsil University, South Korea |
| Saurabh Mukherjee | Banasthali Vidyapith, India |

## Industrial Chairs

| | |
|---|---|
| Mario Jose Divan | Intel Corporation, USA |
| Arun Kumar Singh | UBS, India |
| Rajneesh Agrawal | Software Technology Parks of India, India |
| Parag Amodkar | Tiden Technologies, India |

## Web Chairs

| | |
|---|---|
| Ankit Agarwal | Galgotias University, India |
| Aishvarya Garg | Banasthali Vidyapith, India |
| Pooja Gupta | Banasthali Vidyapith, India |
| Sakshi Indolia | Narsee Monjee Institute of Management and Studies, India |

## Symposium Chairs

| | |
|---|---|
| Varsha Singh | IIIT Allahabad, India |
| Sudhakar Mishra | SVNIT Surat, India |
| Sambit Bakshi | NIT Rourkela, India |
| Bhawana Tyagi | VIT Vellore, India |

## Technical Support Chairs

| | |
|---|---|
| Sushil Buriya | Banasthali Vidyapith, India |
| Pooja Asopa | Banasthali Vidyapith, India |
| Richa Jain | Banasthali Vidyapith, India |
| Aditi Paul | Banasthali Vidyapith, India |

## Finance Chairs

| | |
|---|---|
| Rahul Kumar Vijay | Banasthali Vidyapith, India |
| Roopesh Kumar | Banasthali Vidyapith, India |
| Sneha Asopa | Banasthali Vidyapith, India |
| Sanjay Singh | MNNIT, India |

## Organizing Chairs

| | |
|---|---|
| Irish Singh | Penn State University, USA |
| Nagamani Molakatala | University of Hyderabad, India |
| Swati Nigam | Banasthali Vidyapith, India |
| Vivek Purohit | Banasthali Vidyapith, India |

## Organizing Secretaries

| | |
|---|---|
| Sudha Morwal | Banasthali Vidyapith, India |
| Neelam Sharma | Banasthali Vidyapith, India |
| Ajit Kumar Jain | Banasthali Vidyapith, India |
| Ashok Kumar | Banasthali Vidyapith, India |

## Registration Chairs

| | |
|---|---|
| Saral Kumar Gupta | Banasthali Vidyapith, India |
| Prashant Kushwah | Banasthali Vidyapith, India |
| Chilka Sharma | Banasthali Vidyapith, India |
| Bal Gopal Singh | Banasthali Vidyapith, India |

## Plenary Speakers

| | |
|---|---|
| Santanu Chaudhury | IIT Delhi, India |
| Wan-Young Chung | Pukyong National University, South Korea |
| Javed I. Khan | Kent State University, USA |
| Saurabh Talele | University of Oxford, UK |

## Keynote Speakers

| | |
|---|---|
| KC (Casey) Santosh | University of South Dakota, USA |
| Jong-Hoon Kim | Kent State University, USA |
| Stefano Berretti | University of Florence, Italy |
| Laxmidhar Behera | IIT Mandi, India |
| Rahul Banerjee | LNM Institute of Information Technology, India |
| Shivpal Singh | Defence Research and Development Laboratory, India |

## Invited Speakers

| | |
|---|---|
| Jan-Willem van't Klooster | University of Twente, Netherlands |
| Nishchal K. Verma | IIT Kanpur, India |
| Narayan Panigrahi | Defence Research and Development Organisation, India |
| Swagatam Das | ISI Kolkata, India |
| Asif Ekbal | IIT Patna, India |
| Lipi Thukral | CSIR Institute of Genetics and Integrative Biology, India |
| Tapan Kumar Gandhi | IIT Delhi, India |
| Konstantinos Diamantaras | International Hellenic University, Greece |
| A. S. Mandal | IIT Delhi, India |
| Siba K. Udgata | University of Hyderabad, India |
| TV Vijay Kumar | Jawaharlal Nehru University, India |
| Deeksha Bhartiya | Genomiki Solutions Ltd., India |
| Sandeep Kushwaha | National Institute of Animal Biotechnology, India |
| Sangram Keshri Samal | Indian Council of Medical Research, India |
| Shandar Ahmad | Jawaharlal Nehru University, India |

## Industry Speakers

| | |
|---|---|
| Taechasith (Tàe) Kangkhuntod | CreativeLabTH, Thailand |
| Parag Amodkar | Tiden Technologies, India |
| Gundala Nagaraju | WAIG Foundation, India |

## Panel Discussion Chairs

| | |
|---|---|
| Jong-Hoon Kim | Kent State University, USA |
| Tapan Kumar Gandhi | IIT Delhi, India |
| Javed I. Khan | Kent State University, USA |

## Special Session Chairs

| | |
|---|---|
| Tatiana Cardona | Saint Louis University, USA |
| Ikechi Ukaegbu | University of West Alabama, USA |
| Sanjay Kumar Sharma | Banasthali Vidyapith, India |
| Sudhakar Mishra | SVNIT Surat, India |
| Shrikant Malviya | SVNIT Surat, India |

| | |
|---|---|
| Varsha Singh | IIIT Allahabad, India |
| Mohammed Asif | IIT Bombay, India |
| Sumit Singh | UPES University, India |
| Mehul Mahrishi | Swami Keshvanand Institute of Technology, Management & Gramothan, India |
| Mithlesh Arya | Swami Keshvanand Institute of Technology, Management & Gramothan, India |
| John Martin | Jazan University, Saudi Arabia |
| Ankit Agarwal | Galgotias University, India |
| Manju Khari | Jawaharlal Nehru University, India |
| Arvind Panwar | Galgotias University, India |
| Shakir Khan | Imam Mohammad Ibn Saud Islamdic University, Saudi Arabia |
| Neha Sharma | Bharati Vidyapeeth's College of Engineering, India |
| Rahul Katarya | Delhi Technological University, India |
| Konstantinos Diamantaras | International Hellenic University, Greece |
| Kainat Khan | IIIT Dharwad, India |
| Himanshu Nandanwar | Delhi Technological University, India |
| Nagamani Molakatala | University of Hyderabad, India |
| Victor Daniel Gera | Anurag University, India |
| Ravi Kumar Jatoth | NIT Warangal, India |
| Jan-Willem van 't Klooster | University of Twente, The Netherlands |
| Giorgio Rettagliata | University of Twente, The Netherlands |

## Session Chairs

| | |
|---|---|
| A. Ramachandran | Anna University, India |
| Abhay Kumar Rai | Central University of Rajasthan, India |
| Aditi Paul | Banasthali Vidyapith, India |
| Aishvarya Garg | Banasthali Vidyapith, India |
| Ajit Kumar Jain | Banasthali Vidyapith, India |
| Ankit Agarwal | Galgotias University, India |
| Anshita Dhoot | Noida International University, India |
| Anupama Namburu | Jawaharlal Nehru University, India |
| Anurag Singh Baghel | Gautam Buddha University, India |
| Arvind Panwar | Galgotias University, India |
| Ashish Sharma | Manipal Institute of Technology, India |
| Ashok Kumar | Banasthali Vidyapith, India |
| Bhawana Tyagi | VIT Vellore, India |
| Deepak Kumar | Banasthali Vidyapith, India |

| | |
|---|---|
| Giorgio Rettagliata | University of Twente, The Netherlands |
| Hanumant Singh Shekhawat | IIT Guwahati, India |
| Hemant Kumar Meena | MNIT Jaipur, India |
| Himanshu Nandanwar | Delhi Technological University, India |
| Kainat Khan | IIIT Dharwad, India |
| Konstantinos Diamantaras | International Hellenic University, Greece |
| Laura Suleimenova | U. Zhanibekov South Kazakhstan Pedagogical University, Kazakhstan |
| Manisha Agarwal | Banasthali Vidyapith, India |
| Manisha Jailia | Banasthali Vidyapith, India |
| Manju Khari | Jawaharlal Nehru University, India |
| Manoj Kumar Singh | Banaras Hindu University, India |
| Mehul Mahrishi | Swami Keshvanand Institute of Technology, Management & Gramothan, India |
| Mithlesh Arya | Swami Keshvanand Institute of Technology, Management & Gramothan, India |
| Mohammed Asif | IIT Bombay, India |
| Mohd. Gulman Siddiqui | Banasthali Vidyapith, India |
| Muhamad Sufri Bin Muhammad | Universiti Putra Malaysia, Malaysia |
| Neelam Sharma | Banasthali Vidyapith, India |
| Neha Sharma | Bharati Vidyapeeth's College of Engineering, India |
| Nurfadhlina Mohd Sharef | Universiti Putra Malaysia, Malaysia |
| Nurul Amelina Nasharuddin | Universiti Putra Malaysia, Malaysia |
| P. Sathish Babu | Anna University, India |
| P. Thamizhazhagan | Anna University, India |
| Pooja Asopa | Banasthali Vidyapith, India |
| Pooja Gupta | Banasthali Vidyapith, India |
| Rahul Katarya | Delhi Technological University, India |
| Rahul Kumar Vijay | Banasthali Vidyapith, India |
| Raihani Mohamed | Universiti Putra Malaysia, Malaysia |
| Ravi Kumar Jatoth | NIT Warangal, India |
| Richa Jain | Banasthali Vidyapith, India |
| Roopesh Kumar | Banasthali Vidyapith, India |
| S. Sivanesh | Anna University, India |
| Sakshi Indolia | Narsee Monjee Institute of Management and Studies, India |
| Sanjay Kumar Sharma | Banasthali Vidyapith, India |
| Sanjay Singh | MNNIT, India |
| Satyasai Jagannath Nanda | MNIT Jaipur, India |
| Saurabh Mukherjee | Banasthali Vidyapith, India |
| Shalini Chandra | Banasthali Vidyapith, India |

| | |
|---|---|
| Shrikant Malviya | SVNIT Surat, India |
| Siddharth Singh | University of Lucknow, India |
| Sneha Asopa | Banasthali Vidyapith, India |
| Sudha Morwal | Banasthali Vidyapith, India |
| Sushil Buriya | Banasthali Vidyapith, India |
| Swati Nigam | Banasthali Vidyapith, India |
| Teena Sharma | IIT Guwahati, India |
| Varsha Singh | IIIT Allahabad, India |
| Zhanat Umarova | M.O. Auezov South Kazakhstan State University, Kazakhstan |

## Technical Program Committee

| | |
|---|---|
| Abhay Kumar Rai | Central University of Rajasthan, India |
| Abhignan Srivatsava Sribhashyam | Target, USA |
| Achal Shah | Amazon, USA |
| Aditi Paul | Banasthali Vidyapith, India |
| Aditi Singh | Cleveland State University, USA |
| Aishvarya Garg | Banasthali Vidyapith, India |
| Akshay Sharma | Independent Researcher, USA |
| Allisa Goyal | Swami Keshvan and Institute of Technology, Management & Gramothan, India |
| Alok Singh | Poornima College of Engineering, India |
| Amey Parab | Magnit Global, USA |
| Anjana Shree Sundar | Infosys Limited, USA |
| Ankit Agarwal | Galgotias University, India |
| Ankita Saxena | Amazon, USA |
| Anoop Kumar | Banasthali Vidyapith, India |
| Anugrah Jain | SVNIT Surat, India |
| Ashok Kumar | Banasthali Vidyapith, India |
| Balaji Siva Avinash Animireddy | Cerebra Consulting Inc., USA |
| Bharath Reddy Baddam | New York Life Insurance, USA |
| Bharti Nathani | Banasthali Vidyapith, India |
| Bhawana Tyagi | VIT Vellore, India |
| Brajesh Sharma | Sir Padampat Singhania University, India |
| Chaitanya Tumma | University of the Cumberlands, USA |
| Chandra Sekhar Kubam | Independent Researcher, USA |
| Charan Thumma | CISCO, USA |
| Debanjan Sadhya | ABV-IIITM Gwalior, India |
| Dileep Kanimetta | Microsoft Corp Ltd, USA |
| Divyaraj Singh Jatav | Amazon, USA |

| | |
|---|---|
| Gangadharan Venkataraman | Starbucks, USA |
| Gaurav Sharma | Banasthali Vidyapith, India |
| Gunjan Pareek | TransStadia University, India |
| Hanumant Shekhawat | IIT Guwahati, India |
| Harish Balakrishnan Vimala | Tata Consultancy Services Ltd., USA |
| Harsha Vardhan Reddy Yeddula | Cognizant, USA |
| Hitesh Ramrakhiyani | IIT Guwahati, India |
| Jeetashree Aparajeeta | VIT Chennai, India |
| Jofia Jose Prakash | American Chemical Society, USA |
| Jong Hoon Kim | Kent State University, USA |
| Jyoti Khandelwal | Amity University Jaipur, India |
| Kanojia Sindhuben Babulal | Central University of Jharkhand, India |
| Karthik Reddy Beereddy | LexisNexis Risk Solutions Inc., USA |
| K.F. Rahman | Banasthali Vidyapith, India |
| Kiran Kumar Jaghni | Ness USA Inc., USA |
| Komal Malsa | Lingaya's Vidyapeeth, India |
| Kumar Chandan | Adobe Inc., USA |
| Kunal Kumar | Banasthali Vidyapith, India |
| Lei Xu | Kent State University, USA |
| Manisha Agarwal | Banasthali Vidyapith, India |
| Manisha Jailia | Banasthali Vidyapith, India |
| Manju Khari | Jawaharlal Nehru University, India |
| Manoj Kumar Mishra | Banaras Hindu University, India |
| Manoj Kumar Singh | Banaras Hindu University, India |
| Md Maksudul Amin | Pace University, USA |
| Mohammad Asif | IIT Bombay, India |
| Mohd Siddiqui | Banasthali Vidyapith, India |
| Mohit Kumar | NIT Hamirpur, India |
| Mounica Yenugula | University of the Cumberlands, USA |
| Mrunal Dipak Meshram | Samsara Inc., USA |
| Nagaraju Velur | Wipro Limited, USA |
| Naveen Kumar | SVNIT Surat, India |
| Neelam Sharma | Banasthali Vidyapith, India |
| Neetu Joshi | Poornima College of Engineering, India |
| Neha Aggarwal | GGSIPU, India |
| Nidhi Pruthi | Banasthali Vidyapith, India |
| Nidhi Srivastav | Swami Keshvanand Institute of Technology, Management & Gramothan, India |
| Piyush Kumar | NIT Patna, India |
| Pooja Asopa | Banasthali Vidyapith, India |
| Pooja Gupta | Banasthali Vidyapith, India |

| | |
|---|---|
| Pooja Mishra | Dr. DY Patil Institute of Engineering, Management & Research, India |
| Prashant Srivastava | Amity University Noida, India |
| Prem Reddy Nomula | Deloitte Consulting Ltd., USA |
| Premanand Tiwari | Amazon, USA |
| Priya Shekhawat | Poornima College of Engineering, India |
| Raghu Varma Bhupatiraju | Expeditors, USA |
| Rahul Kumar Vijay | Banasthali Vidyapith, India |
| Rahul Semwal | IIIT Nagpur, India |
| Rajiv Singh | Banasthali Vidyapith, India |
| Rakesh Reddy Charla | Microsoft, USA |
| Ramesh Somayajula | T-Mobile USA Inc., USA |
| Ravindra Hegadi | Central University of Karnataka, India |
| Richa Jain | Banasthali Vidyapith, India |
| Rishabh Animesh | Apple, USA |
| Ritu Chauhan | Amity University, India |
| Ronish Patel | University of British Columbia, Canada |
| Roopesh Kumar | Banasthali Vidyapith, India |
| Sakhita Sree Gadde | Zurich North America, USA |
| Sakshi Indolia | Narsee Monjee Institute of Management and Studies, India |
| Sandeep Pal | Salesforce, USA |
| Sapan Pandya | Fanatics Inc., USA |
| Satish Kabade | Independent Researcher, USA |
| Shashank Reddy Nandi | USAA, USA |
| Shivani Jain | Poornima College of Engineering, India |
| Siba Sankar Sahu | SVNIT Surat, India |
| Siddharth Singh | University of Lucknow, India |
| Siva Prasad Marri | Swanktek Inc., USA |
| Sneha Asopa | Banasthali Vidyapith, India |
| Sonam Seth | Banasthali Vidyapith, India |
| Srikanth Nimmagadda | Ericsson Inc., USA |
| Srikanth Reddy Jaidi | Florida Department of Children and Families, USA |
| Srinivas Talasila | SAP North America Inc., USA |
| Sudarshan Prasad Nagavalli | PayPal, USA |
| Sudha Morwal | Banasthali Vidyapith, India |
| Sumit Singh | IIIT Allahabad, India |
| Sundar Tiwari | F5 Networks Inc., USA |
| Sushil Buriya | Banasthali Vidyapith, India |
| Suyel Namasudra | NIT Agartala, India |
| Swati Nigam | Banasthali Vidyapith, India |

| | |
|---|---|
| Tanvir Rahman Akash | Trine University, USA |
| Uma Sharma | Banasthali Vidyapith, India |
| Vaibhav Vyas | Banasthali Vidyapith, India |
| Varad Srivastava | Barclays, UK |
| Varsha Singh | IIIT Allahabad, India |
| Venkat Anil Shankar Pediredla | Connectix Corporation, USA |
| Venkataram Poosapati | Atlassian, Australia |
| Vidhu Shekhar Bajpai | Advanced Micro Devices, USA |
| Vishal Choudhary | Lovely Professional University, India |
| Vishal Sresth | PayPal, USA |
| Vivek Prakash | Banasthali Vidyapith, India |
| Vivek Saiprasad Karnam | Surge Technology Solutions Inc., USA |
| Writuraj Sharma | Samsung Electronics America, USA |
| Younghun Chae | Kent State University, USA |

# Contents

# Privacy-Preserving Human-Computer Interaction for Paternity Testing Using Fully Homomorphic Encryption

Swaraj Singh Pal, Maroti Dehsmukh(✉), and Sneha Chauhan

Department of CSE, NIT Uttarakhand, Srinagar 246174, Uttarakhand, India
{dt24csj003,marotideshmukh,sneha.chauhan}@nituk.ac.in

**Abstract.** In genomic applications like paternity testing, Human Computer Interaction (HCI) systems provide users with intuitive platforms to submit and interpret sensitive genetic data. However, traditional methods often require raw DNA sequences to be shared and processed, raising critical concerns about privacy and data security. To address this problem, we proposed a privacy-preserving HCI framework for paternity testing that uses Fully Homomorphic Encryption (FHE) to perform all computations on encrypted genomic data, ensuring that no plaintext information is exposed during analysis. In the proposed framework, the user generates a public-private key pair and sends the public key to a gene bank to retrieve the required genomic reference data. The gene bank then encrypts the genomic sequences using the user's public key and returns the ciphertext, which is used along with the user's encrypted query for relationship comparison. The backend of the proposed framework securely calculates Single Nucleotide Polymorphism (SNP) and Short Tandem Repeat (STR) similarity scores homomorphically. These encrypted scores are returned to the user, who decrypts them locally using the private key and views the results through an interactive dashboard. This approach maintains complete confidentiality while providing accurate results. The framework effectively integrates privacy, usability, and trust, making it suitable for secure paternity testing in forensic, clinical, and personal ancestry scenarios.

**Keywords:** SNP · STR · Homomorphic Encryption · Privacy Preserving HCI

## 1 Introduction

Human–Computer Interaction plays an important role in areas that involve private and sensitive data, like genomic analysis for paternity testing or relationship analysis. Through privacy-protected and user-friendly interfaces, HCI frameworks enable authorized users like doctors, legal officials, and family members—understand complex genetic data for relationship verification. But working with


A. Shastri et al. (Eds.): IHCI 2025, LNCS 16437, pp. 1–12, 2026.
https://doi.org/10.1007/978-3-032-26352-0_1

this private and sensitive data, like genomic sequences (nucleotide sequences), introduces privacy concerns, especially when computation is done on cloud-based systems.

To overcome the problem of computation on the cloud, this paper presents a privacy-preserving HCI framework for genomic relationship analysis using homomorphic encryption (HE). Homomorphic Encryption enables computations performed directly on encrypted data, ensuring confidentiality throughout the entire process. The proposed model integrates the CKKS encryption scheme, a fully homomorphic encryption scheme, which supports approximate arithmetic on real numbers and is suitable for computing genomic similarity scores. Genomic similarity focuses on two major genetic molecule markers, such as Single Nucleotide Polymorphisms (SNPs), which represent single-base DNA variations inherited across generations at the same point of loci, and Short Tandem Repeats (STRs), which are repetitive DNA sequences showing high variability among individuals at the same loci. All SNP and STR computations are securely executed in the encrypted environment, maintaining overall data privacy and security from input to output result visualization within the HCI environment.

The contributions of this paper are as follows: first, a novel privacy-preserving HCI framework using FHE; second, encrypted SNP and STR similarity computation; and finally, an evaluation on a real five-member family dataset for validation.

The remainder of the paper is organized as follows: Sect. 2 reviews related work on homomorphic encryption and secure genomic processing; Sect. 3 details the proposed approach, including CKKS-based encoding and encrypted SNP/STR computation; Sect. 4 presents experimental results and analysis; and Sect. 5 concludes with findings and future directions.

## 2 Related Work

Computation directly on encrypted data has gained significant attention with the increasing demand for secure analysis in various fields such as medical research, finance, and genomic analysis, especially in cloud environments. A major breakthrough in this area was Gentry's Fully Homomorphic Encryption (FHE) scheme (2009) [1], which enabled computation over encrypted data. Based on this foundation, several schemes such as BGV [2], BFV [3], and CKKS [4] have been developed for practical encrypted operations, particularly for real-number arithmetic. These schemes have been integrated into secure genomic analysis [6], federated learning [7], and privacy-preserving diagnostic systems [8]. Comparative surveys such as Doan et al. [9] discuss performance trade-offs in speed, noise growth, and precision. Within genomic relationship analysis, homomorphic encryption has been applied for secure SNP and STR evaluation [10] and encrypted genotype comparison [11], forming a basis for our secure kinship inference framework.

In order to improve HCI systems, homomorphic encryption schemes are adopted to enhance real-time security by enabling computation directly on encrypted data. Several studies have explored the use of homomorphic encryption in privacy-preserving systems such as facial recognition [12], gesture control [13], and activity monitoring [15]. The TFHE scheme [16] provides efficient encrypted Boolean operations, making it suitable for applications that require fast and responsive processing. Recent reviews [14,15] emphasize the role of encryption in securing biometric and sensor data, particularly in extended reality (XR) and wearable technologies. In the field of genomics, privacy-preserving HCI systems have been proposed for secure paternity testing and ancestry analysis. Chen et al. [17] presented an encrypted kinship detection method using genotype data, and Namazi et al. [18] developed a multi-user genomic computation approach based on multi-key homomorphic encryption. The above developments collectively highlight the potential of integrating FHE into interactive genomic systems to maintain data confidentiality throughout the complete genomic analysis.

### 2.1 CKKS Scheme [4]

Polynomial ring $\mathbb{R} = \mathbb{Z}[x]/(x^d + 1)$, modulus $q$, scaling factor $\Delta$, and error distribution $\chi$ Input is plaintext vector $\mathbf{z} \in \mathbb{C}^{d/2}$ Output is the approximate decrypted vector $\mathbf{z}' \approx \mathbf{z}$

1. **Key Generation:** Generate secret key $sk = r \in \chi$; choose random $\alpha \in \mathcal{R}_q$ and error $\epsilon \in \chi$. Compute public key $pk = (\alpha, \beta = -\alpha r + \epsilon \bmod q)$.
2. **Encoding:** Input vector is scaled by $\Delta$ to preserve precision: $\mathbf{z}' = \Delta \cdot \mathbf{z}$. Encode to polynomial form: $m = \rho^{-1}(\mathbf{z}')$.
3. **Encryption:** Sample random values $u, \epsilon_1, \epsilon_2 \in \chi$. Compute ciphertext components: $c_0 = \beta u + \epsilon_1 + m \bmod q$, $c_1 = \alpha u + \epsilon_2 \bmod q$. Set ciphertext $ct = (c_0, c_1)$.
4. **Homomorphic Computation:**
   - *Addition/Subtraction:* $(c_0, c_1) \pm (c_0', c_1') = (c_0 \pm c_0', c_1 \pm c_1')$.
   - *Multiplication:* Perform tensor product of ciphertexts, relinearize, and rescale to manage noise growth.
5. **Decryption:** Recover plaintext: $m' = c_0 + c_1 r \bmod q$.
6. **Decoding:** Decode and scale down to obtain approximate result: $\mathbf{z}' = \rho(m')/\Delta$.

This compact workflow forms the computational core of our privacy-preserving HCI framework, enabling encrypted computation of SNP and STR similarity scores for paternity testing without exposing raw genomic data at any stage.

## 3 Proposed Methodology

This section presents a complete, privacy-preserving HCI framework for genomic relationship inference (paternity testing) using Fully Homomorphic Encryption (FHE) with CKKS. All sensitive data remains encrypted end-to-end; users interact via a dedicated HCI front end. Figure 1 illustrates the workflow.

1. **Key Generation:** The user creates a CKKS keypair; the public key is shared with the gene bank administrator, and the secret key stays local with the user.
2. **Data Encryption:** The administrator fetches the reference genome (e.g., FASTA/VCF) for the alleged parent, encodes bases (e.g., A→1, C→2, G→3, T→4) or allele vectors, and encrypts with the user's public key.
3. **Encrypted Transmission:** The encrypted reference genome is returned to (and stored by) the HCI client.
4. **User Submission:** The user uploads their own encrypted genomic data via the HCI interface.
5. **Backend Computation (FHE):** The server computes, entirely over ciphertexts (Algorithm 1):
   (a) SNP similarity via encoded allele-vector comparison (Algorithm 2).
   (b) STR similarity via motif-aligned counts with windowing (Algorithm 3).
   (c) Combined score as the average of SNP and STR results.
6. **Secure Return & Decryption:** Encrypted similarity scores are sent back and decrypted locally by the user with the secret key.
7. **HCI Display:** The front end presents SNP score, STR score, the combined match percentage, and an intuitive verdict (Match/No Match), without exposing raw genomic data.

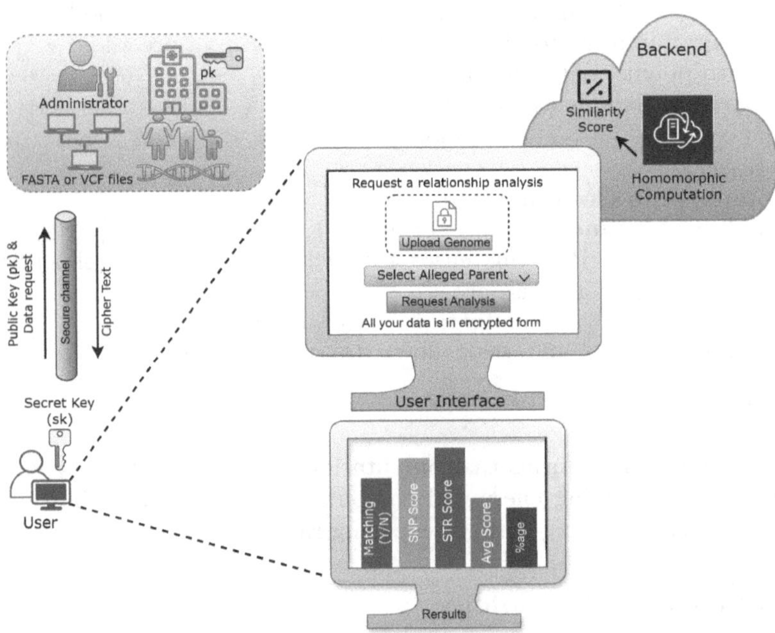


**Fig. 1.** HCI-based privacy-preserving architecture for paternity testing using homomorphic encryption

Backend computation, as outlined in Algorithm 1, is responsible for securely calculating genomic similarity scores using a fully homomorphic encryption scheme. These algorithms operate entirely on encrypted data, ensuring that no raw genomic sequences or intermediate results are exposed during processing. The system separately handles SNP and STR data, performing encrypted comparisons and aggregations to generate similarity scores. Once the computations are completed, the encrypted SNP and STR scores are returned to the user interface. After the user can then decrypt and interpret the results using the private key locally, preserving the privacy of sensitive genomic information throughout the entire genomic analysis.

**Algorithm 1.** Privacy-Preserving Similarity Computation

**Input:** $\mathcal{E}(\mathbf{G}_P)$, $\mathcal{E}(\mathbf{G}_C)$<br>
**Output:** $\mathcal{E}(\text{SNP\_Score})$, $\mathcal{E}(\text{STR\_Score})$, $\mathcal{E}(\text{Avg\_Score})$<br>
$\mathcal{E}(\text{SNP\_Score}) \leftarrow$ Enc_SNP_Similarity($\mathcal{E}(\mathbf{G}_P)$, $\mathcal{E}(\mathbf{G}_C)$) ▷ Algorithm 2<br>
$\mathcal{E}(\text{STR\_Score}) \leftarrow$ Enc_STR_Similarity($\mathcal{E}(\mathbf{G}_P)$, $\mathcal{E}(\mathbf{G}_C)$) ▷ Algorithm 3<br>
$\mathcal{E}(\text{Avg\_Score}) \leftarrow (\mathcal{E}(\text{SNP\_Score}) + \mathcal{E}(\text{STR\_Score}))\,/2$<br>
**return** $\mathcal{E}(\text{SNP\_Score})$, $\mathcal{E}(\text{STR\_Score})$, $\mathcal{E}(\text{Avg\_Score})$

For calculating the SNP similarity score, Algorithm 2 is used to compare a parent and a child using only the encrypted genomic data sequence. The encrypted genomic vectors for both the reference (parent) and the sample (child) are encoded through a predefined nucleotide mapping and encrypted with the HE scheme by the gene bank administrator. After this algorithm performs element-wise subtraction of these encrypted vectors to obtain a difference vector, then applies a homomorphic mapping, assigning encrypted ones to matching loci (where the difference is zero) and encrypted zeros to mismatches, resulting in a binary match vector. The algorithm sums this vector homomorphically to determine the total number of matches and normalizes the value by the total loci count to produce the final encrypted SNP similarity score. At no point is sensitive genomic information revealed, ensuring complete privacy throughout the computation.

Secure computation of the STR similarity score between two individuals, such as a parent and a child, is described in Algorithm 3 using fully encrypted data. The inputs are encrypted STR blocks from both individuals, with each block containing encoded repeat counts for specific loci that are encrypted using the CKKS scheme. The algorithm begins by initializing an encrypted accumulator to store the total matched STR repeats. It then iterates through all STR loci in the parent's genome. At each locus, if a matching position and motif are also found in the child's encrypted STR data, the STR repeat counts for both parent and child at that locus are retrieved. The minimum of these two encrypted counts is computed, representing the extent of shared repeats, and added to the accumulator. After all loci have been processed, the final encrypted STR similarity score is calculated by dividing the encrypted sum of matched repeat counts by the encrypted total repeat count from the parent. This encrypted result is returned to the user for secure decryption and interpretation, ensuring that at no point, the underlying genomic values are exposed.

**Algorithm 2.** Encrypted SNP Similarity Score

**Input:** $\mathcal{E}(\mathbf{G}_P)$, $\mathcal{E}(\mathbf{G}_C)$
**Output:** $\mathcal{E}(\text{SNP\_Score})$
$\mathcal{E}(\mathbf{D}) \leftarrow \mathcal{E}(\mathbf{G}_P) - \mathcal{E}(\mathbf{G}_C)$
$\mathcal{E}(\mathbf{B}) \leftarrow \text{MapZeroToOne}(\mathcal{E}(\mathbf{D}))$
$\mathcal{E}(S) \leftarrow \text{Sum}(\mathcal{E}(\mathbf{B}))$
$\mathcal{E}(\text{SNP\_Score}) \leftarrow \mathcal{E}(S)/n$
**return** $\mathcal{E}(\text{SNP\_Score})$

**Algorithm 3** Encrypted STR Similarity Score

**Input:** $\mathcal{E}(\mathbf{G}_P)$, $\mathcal{E}(\mathbf{G}_C)$
**Output:** $\mathcal{E}(\text{STR\_Score})$
Initialize encrypted accumulator: $\mathcal{E}(\text{sum}) \leftarrow 0$
**for all** loci $j$ in $\mathcal{G}_P$ **do**
  **if** matching position and motif in $\mathcal{G}_C$ **then**
    $\mathcal{E}(c_P^j) \leftarrow$ STR count of parent
    $\mathcal{E}(c_C^j) \leftarrow$ STR count of child
    $\mathcal{E}(m_j) \leftarrow \min(\mathcal{E}(c_P^j), \mathcal{E}(c_C^j))$
    $\mathcal{E}(\text{sum}) \leftarrow \mathcal{E}(\text{sum}) + \mathcal{E}(m_j)$
  **end if**
**end for**
$\mathcal{E}(\text{STR\_Score}) \leftarrow \mathcal{E}(\text{sum}) / \sum \mathcal{E}(c_P^j)$
**return** $\mathcal{E}(\text{STR\_Score})$

The above algorithms enable the secure computation of SNP and STR similarity scores within an HCI-compatible paternity testing framework. By ensuring that all computations are performed directly on encrypted data and that the results are returned in encrypted form, the model maintains confidentiality throughout the entire analysis process.

The proposed model is functionally efficient and compatible with real-time settings while maintaining confidentiality by performing computations on encrypted data. It can be applied to paternity testing or kinship analysis. This framework integrates secure genomic computation with a user-friendly interface, enabling confidential and reliable relationship verification.

## 4 Experimental Results and Analysis

This section presents the experimental results and analysis of the proposed privacy-preserving HCI framework for genomic relationship inference and paternity testing using FHE. The results include both front-end and back-end analyses. Experiments were conducted on a publicly available five-member family dataset consisting of three children, a mother, and a father.

The experiments were conducted using Python 3.13.1 on an HP 12th Generation system running 64-bit Windows with an Intel Core i7-12700 processor and 32 GB of RAM. The CKKS homomorphic encryption scheme was evaluated using two configurations with polynomial modulus degrees of 4096 and 8192. For CKKS-4096, the coefficient modulus chain was set as [40, 30, 30] bits, providing a total modulus size of approximately 100 bits with a global scale of $2^{30}$, suitable for 1–2 levels of computation depth. In the CKKS-8192 setup, modulus sizes of [60, 40, 40, 60] bits were used, yielding a total of about 200 bits and a global scale of $2^{40}$, supporting deeper computations up to 3–4 levels.

Table 1 presents the number of matching SNP loci between different individual pairs, calculated securely on encrypted genomic data using the proposed privacy-preserving HCI framework. Parent–child pairs (Father/Child-1 and Mother/Child-1) show high SNP similarity, while the Child-2/Child-3 pair records the highest match count, confirming their sibling relationship. In contrast, the lower match between Father and Mother reflects expected genetic differences. The decrypted results are displayed through the HCI dashboard, allowing secure and clear interpretation of genetic relationships.

**Table 1.** Matching SNP loci counts (Reference & Sample)

| Base Pair (bp) | $10^2$ | $10^3$ | $10^4$ | $10^5$ | $10^6$ |
|---|---|---|---|---|---|
| Father & Child-1 | 87 | 819 | 8451 | 85068 | 845361 |
| Mother & Child-1 | 90 | 841 | 8390 | 84499 | 839664 |
| Child-2 & Child-3 | 85 | 872 | 9156 | 88582 | 911539 |
| Father & Mother | 84 | 783 | 7531 | 76428 | 753528 |

Table 2 shows STR similarity between the father and Child-1 over a 200 bp segment, extracted from the full 500,000 bp encrypted comparison. A 2-nucleotide motif (e.g., GG or CC) is shown for each locus along with the number of repeats for each individual; the matched repeats are shown in the "Min" column. Matches at several loci indicate inherited STR counts, computed securely directly on encrypted data and visualized post-decryption in the HCI interface.

Figure 2 compares STR counts for different individual pairs over 500,000 bp by integrating HCI-based visualization with encrypted computation. Each pair of bars represents the reference, sample, and matched STR counts. Higher matches confirm the STR similarity. This highlights the framework's capability to securely compute and display STR similarities while maintaining data privacy throughout the STR calculation.

Distribution of STR counts shown in Fig. 3, between Father and Child-1, based on varying motif lengths (from 2 to 6) across base pair ranges from 10,000 to 100,000. In the HCI system's backend, this calculation is performed directly on encrypted data using homomorphic encryption to ensure all pattern counts remain confidential. The encrypted counts are later decrypted and visualized in the user interface. In the figure, shorter motifs (especially length 2) occur more frequently and dominate the total STR count. The cumulative count increases

**Table 2.** Loci-based STR counts for 200 bp

| Locus | Motif ($L = 2$) | STR (Father) | STR (Child-1) | Min |
|---|---|---|---|---|
| 787173 | GG | 2 | 2 | 2 |
| 864490 | CC | 2 | 2 | 2 |
| 878697 | GG | 2 | 3 | 2 |
| 888554 | CC | 2 | 2 | 2 |
| 889182 | GG | 2 | 2 | 2 |
| 903104 | CC | 3 | 3 | 3 |
| 963661 | CC | 2 | 2 | 2 |
| 1048955 | AA | 2 | 2 | 2 |
| 1138913 | TT | 2 | 2 | 2 |

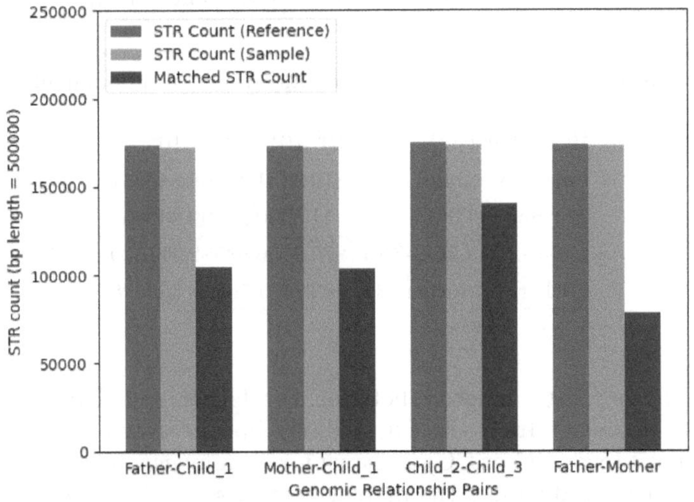


**Fig. 2.** Loci-based STR count comparison (500, 000 bp and motif length = 2)

proportionally with longer genomic segments. It allows users to explore motif repeat patterns while maintaining the privacy of raw genomic sequences, an essential feature for secure HCI-based paternity testing applications.

Table 3 summarizes encrypted SNP and STR similarity scores over a 500,000 bp region. All computations were securely performed using homomorphic encryption and decrypted only for visualization. As expected, the sibling pair (Child-2 & Child-3) shows the highest average similarity (85.62%), while parent-child pairs also exhibit high scores, confirming genetic relatedness. These results demonstrate accurate and privacy-preserving relationship inference within the HCI framework.

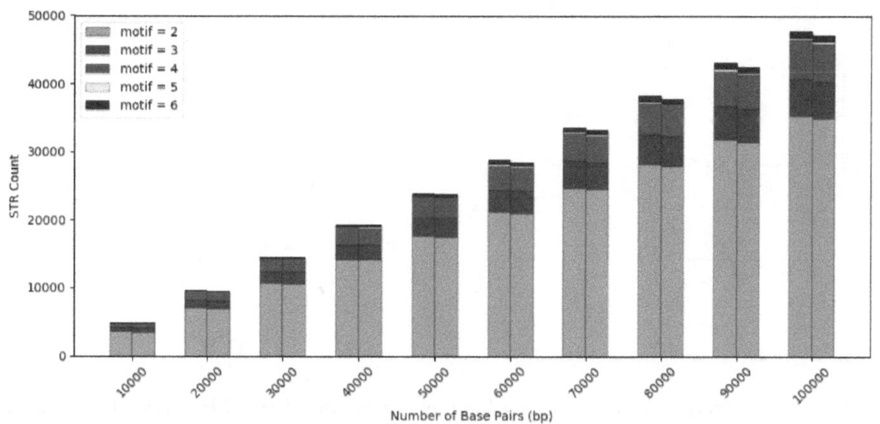


**Fig. 3.** STR count distribution for Father and Child-1 (motifs 2 to 6)

**Table 3.** Similarity scores (%) for $5 \times 10^5$ bp

| Similarity | Father & Child-1 | Mother & Child-1 | Child-2 & Child-3 | Father & Mother |
|---|---|---|---|---|
| SNP Score | 84.54 | 83.97 | 91.15 | 75.35 |
| STR Score | 60.00 | 59.79 | 80.09 | 44.65 |
| Avg Score | 72.27 | 71.88 | 85.62 | 60.00 |

Figure 4(a) and Fig. 4(b) illustrates the comparison of SNP and STR similarity scores for encrypted and unencrypted data over genomic sequence lengths ranging from 50 to 500,000 base pairs. The results show that the encrypted computations generate values closely similar to those obtained from unencrypted data, with only minor variations due to numerical approximation in the CKKS scheme.

Similarly, Fig. 5(a) and Fig. 5(b) indicate the execution time needed to compute SNP and STR similarity scores, respectively. The results show that unencrypted computations remain efficient and nearly constant across all input sizes, while FHE-based encrypted computations show increasing latency as the sequence length grows. The results highlight a clear trade-off between privacy and performance: homomorphic encryption requires additional computational cost but enables secure genetic similarity assessment without revealing raw genomic sequence.

Figure 6 (a) and Fig. 6 (b) illustrate a comparison of execution time between CKKS parameter settings with polynomial modulus degrees of 4096 and 8192 for SNP and STR computations, respectively. As evident, CKKS-8192 incurs a higher computational cost compared to CKKS-4096 due to increased ciphertext size and deeper computation capacity. However, CKKS-8192 supports greater

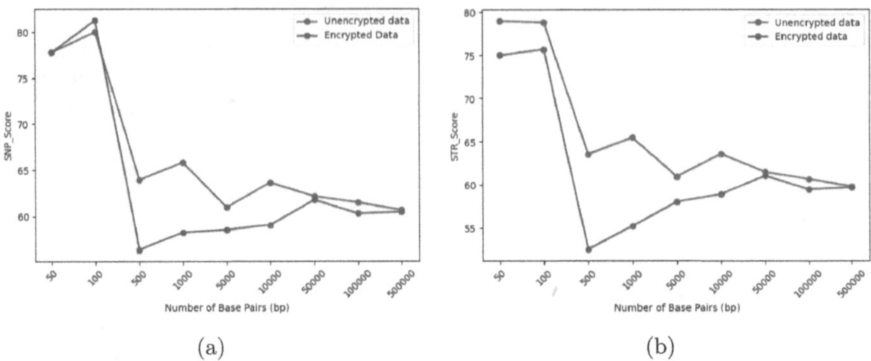


(a) (b)

**Fig. 4.** (a) SNP score: Encrypted vs Unencrypted and (b) STR score: Encrypted vs Unencrypted

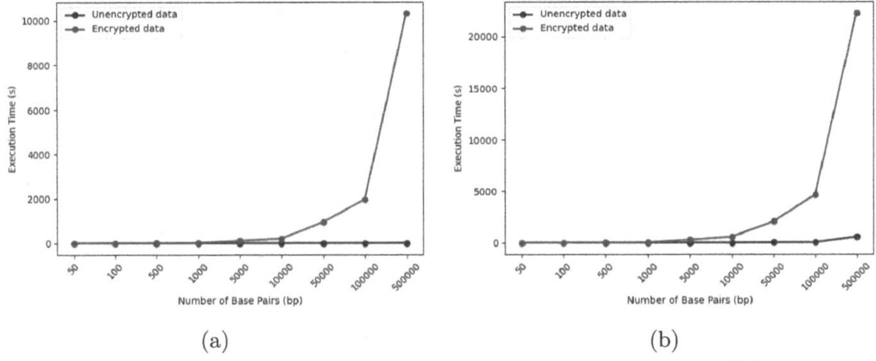


(a) (b)

**Fig. 5.** (a) SNP execution time: Encrypted vs. Unencrypted and (b) STR execution time: Encrypted vs. Unencrypted

multiplicative depth, which is beneficial for more complex homomorphic operations.

Table 4 highlights that the proposed CKKS-FHE framework attains the highest accuracy among comparable privacy-preserving methods, demonstrating its effectiveness in maintaining predictive performance under encryption.

These results confirm that the proposed privacy-preserving HCI for paternity testing using FHE can securely infer genomic relationships while providing a transparent and interactive experience via the HCI interface. All backend computations are encrypted, and all user-facing visualizations are generated post-decryption to ensure privacy preservation throughout.

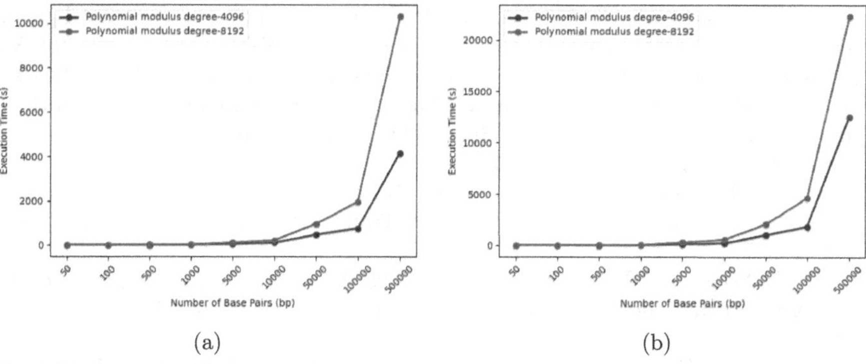


**Fig. 6.** (a) SNP execution time: Polynomial modulus degree- 4096 vs. 8192 and (b) STR execution time: Polynomial modulus degree- 4096 vs. 8192

**Table 4.** Accuracy comparison

| Metric | SMC [17] | DP [15] | TFHE [16] | Proposed |
|---|---|---|---|---|
| Accuracy (%) | 88.5 | 84.3 | 86.7 | **87.9** |

## 5 Conclusion

This study presented a privacy-preserving paternity testing framework combining FHE with an HCI-based architecture for secure genomic analysis. Using the CKKS scheme, SNP and STR similarities are computed on encrypted data, ensuring data privacy. Results show comparable accuracy to unencrypted methods with strong confidentiality. Future work will extend to multi-party comparison, biometric-secured access, and optimized parallel computation for real-time performance.

## References


1. Gentry, C.: Fully homomorphic encryption using ideal lattices. In: Proceedings of the Forty-First Annual ACM Symposium on Theory of Computing, pp. 169–178 (2009)
2. Brakerski, Z., Gentry, C., Vaikuntanathan, V.: (Leveled) fully homomorphic encryption without bootstrapping. ACM Trans. Comput. Theory (TOCT) **6**(3), 1–36 (2014)
3. Fan, J., Vercauteren, F.: Somewhat practical fully homomorphic encryption. Cryptology ePrint Archive (2012)
4. Cheon, J.H., Kim, A., Kim, M., Song, Y.: Homomorphic encryption for arithmetic of approximate numbers. In: Takagi, T., Peyrin, T. (eds.) ASIACRYPT 2017. LNCS, vol. 10624, pp. 409–437. Springer, Cham (2017). https://doi.org/10.1007/978-3-319-70694-8_15

5. Lauter, K., López-Alt, A., Naehrig, M.: Private computation on encrypted genomic data. In: Aranha, D.F., Menezes, A. (eds.) LATINCRYPT 2014. LNCS, vol. 8895, pp. 3–27. Springer, Cham (2015). https://doi.org/10.1007/978-3-319-16295-9_1
6. Naehrig, M., Lauter, K., Vaikuntanathan, V.: Can homomorphic encryption be practical?. In: Proceedings of the 3rd ACM Workshop on Cloud Computing Security Workshop, pp. 113–124 (2011)
7. Aono, Y., Hayashi, T., Wang, L., Moriai, S.: Privacy-preserving deep learning via additively homomorphic encryption. IEEE Trans. Inf. Forensics Secur. **13**(5), 1333–1345 (2017)
8. Kim, M., Song, Y., Wang, S., Xia, Y., Jiang, X.: Secure logistic regression based on homomorphic encryption: design and evaluation. JMIR Med. Inf. **6**(2), e8805 (2018)
9. Van Thao, T., Doan, M.-L.M., Gavin, G., Darmont, J.: A survey on implementations of homomorphic encryption schemes. J. Supercomput. **79**(13), 15098–15139 (2023)
10. Blatt, M., Gusev, A., Polyakov, Y., Goldwasser, S.: Secure large-scale genome-wide association studies using homomorphic encryption. Proc. Natl. Acad. Sci. **117**(21), 11608–11613 (2020)
11. Cho, H., Wu, D.J., Berger, B.: Secure genome-wide association analysis using multiparty computation. Nat. Biotechnol. **36**(6), 547–551 (2018)
12. Laishram, L., Shaheryar, M., Lee, J.T., Jung, S.K.: Toward a privacy-preserving face recognition system: a survey of leakages and solutions. ACM Comput. Surv. **57**(6), 1–38 (2025)
13. Zheng, R., Jiang, F., Shen, R.: GestureDet: real-time student gesture analysis with multi-dimensional attention-based detector. In: Proceedings of the 29th International Conference on International Joint Conferences on Artificial Intelligence, pp. 680–686 (2021)
14. Alkaeed, M., Qayyum, A., Qadir, J.: Privacy preservation in artificial intelligence and extended reality (AI-XR) metaverses: a survey. J. Netw. Comput. Appl. **231**, 103989 (2024)
15. Yang, Y., Pengfei, H., Shen, J., Cheng, H., An, Z., Liu, X.: Privacy-preserving human activity sensing: a survey. High-Conf. Comput. **4**(1), 100204 (2024)
16. Chillotti, I., Gama, N., Georgieva, M., Izabachène, M.: TFHE: fast fully homomorphic encryption over the torus. J. Cryptol. **33**(1), 34–91 (2020)
17. Chen, J., Miao, W., Wenyuan, W., Yang, L., Yuan, H.: Secure relative detection in (forensic) database with homomorphic encryption. In: International Symposium on Bioinformatics Research and Applications, pp. 410–422. Springer, Singapore (2024). https://doi.org/10.1007/978-981-97-5131-0_35
18. Namazi, M., Farahpoor, M., Ayday, E., Pérez-González, F.: Privacy-preserving framework for genomic computations via multi-key homomorphic encryption. Bioinformatics **41**(3), 1–11 (2025)

# A Modified Deep Learning Framework for Multimodal Human Activity Recognition

Gunjan Pareek[1], Rajiv Singh[1,2], and Swati Nigam[1,2](✉)

[1] Department of Computer Science, Banasthali Vidyapith, Tonk 304022, Rajasthan, India
gunjanpareek1611@gmail.com, jkrajivsingh@gmail.com, swatinigam.au@gmail.com

[2] Centre for Artificial Intelligence, Banasthali Vidyapith, Tonk 304022, Rajasthan, India

**Abstract.** This research proposes an enhanced deep learning framework for multimodal human activity recognition (HAR) by leveraging a modified DenseNet121 architecture integrated with SeparableConv2D and LSTM layers. Initially, raw sensor signals from wearable devices are transformed into two-dimensional image representations using the Gramian Angular Field (GAF) technique, which effectively preserves temporal dynamics while enabling convolutional feature extraction. The modified DenseNet121 serves as the backbone for spatial feature learning, while the SeparableConv2D layer reduces computational complexity without compromising feature discrimination. To capture temporal dependencies, an LSTM layer is incorporated, enhancing sequence modelling capabilities. The proposed framework is evaluated on three benchmark datasets—WISDM, MHEALTH, and PAMAP2—achieving recognition accuracies of 98.54%, 96.62%, and 98.37%, respectively. These results demonstrate the effectiveness of combining convolutional and recurrent neural architectures within a unified framework, confirming the model's strong potential for real-world human activity recognition across diverse multimodal datasets.

**Keywords:** Human Activity Recognition · Modified Dense Convolutional Network 121 · Separable Convolutional Neural Network · Long Short-Term Memory · Gramian Angular Field

## 1 Introduction

Convolutional neural networks (CNNs) have emerged in human activity recognition (HAR) studies recently for their ability to extract spatial and local patterns from structured inputs. Impressively good results are being produced by convolutional neural network (CNN) models, particularly when sensor data is mapped into two-dimensional representations such as spectrograms and Gramian Angular Fields (GAFs). Much advantage can be drawn from the GAF transformation in that it retains temporal correlation by converting time-series data into structured images, which thus become an optimal fit for processing within the capabilities of deep learning models in computer vision. Nevertheless, classic CNNs may be impaired in capturing the temporal dependencies of sequential activities that are critical for differentiating between activities with similar spatial representations yet different dynamic motions.


A. Shastri et al. (Eds.): IHCI 2025, LNCS 16437, pp. 13–25, 2026.
https://doi.org/10.1007/978-3-032-26352-0_2

To overcome this limitation, recent HAR systems have shifted their focus toward recurrent neural networks (RNNs), especially long-short term memory (LSTM) architectures, due to their strong ability to capture long-term temporal dependencies. The success of LSTMs in modelling sequences depends on the quality of the spatial features they are modelling. This has led to the development of general hybrid models where CNNs are used for spatial extraction and LSTMs for temporal modelling since these two methodologies complement each other very well. Among the various CNN backbones used, DenseNet121 has proved to be a powerful feature extractor due to its dense connectivity and parameter efficiency, along with its ability to circumvent the vanishing gradient issue. The yet-unresolved challenges for real-time HAR deployment include DenseNet 121's high computation costs and limited temporal modelling.

In this paper, we have presented a new hybrid deep-learning architecture that enhances human activity recognition in a multimodal setting. The framework will integrate a modified DenseNet121 architecture with separable convolutional neural network (SeparableConv2D) and LSTM layers. Raw sensor signals undergo GAF image transformation, allowing for learning of visual patterns by the pre-trained DenseNet121 used as the main feature extractor. GAF images act as input to a layer of SeparableConv2D after DenseNet outputs. This step is included to reduce the model complexity while preserving the most discriminative spatial features. The transformed GAF images will then be reshaped and passed to an LSTM layer, capturing the temporal relationships embedded within activity sequence data. Hence, the entire architecture can therefore achieve a gait between efficiency and performance belonging to an agent that captures both spatial and temporal dynamics.

The proposed model is evaluated on three benchmark datasets: WISDM, MHEALTH, and PAMAP2. It has achieved an accuracy of 98.54%, 96.62%, and 98.37% for recognition, respectively, outperforming numerous earlier and recent existing state-of-the-art methodologies. These promising outcomes reveal our approach's great robustness and generalizability over different data modalities and types of activity. The main contributions of this work include:

(i) Introduction of a new deep learning pipeline that synergistically combines DenseNet121 with SeparableConv2D and LSTM for effective multimodal HAR
(ii) GAF transform is used for converting original sensor data into image format suitable for visual feature extraction.
(iii) Proposed architecture is taking advantage of separable convolutions to reduce both the number of parameters and computational cost.
(iv) LSTM network effectively captures temporal dependencies, enabling discrimination of complex activity sequences.
(v) Extensive evaluation on three public datasets validating the proposed model's high performance and applicability for real-world HAR.

Rest of the paper is structured as follows: Sect. 2 is literature review, Sect. 3 is the proposed methodology, Sect. 4 is experimental results and analysis, and Sect. 5 is the conclusion of the study.

## 2 Related Works

Abdellatef et al. [1] found that human activities can be detected using a multi-layer CNN model by inputting raw accelerometer and gyroscope signals. Ye et al. [2] claimed to have extended spatiotemporal representation. Such promises for real-time applications require careful calibration of masking layers to avoid information loss, though. Gupta et al. [3] fine-tuned pre-trained CNN models in the target datasets to classify human activity. Javadi et al. [4] deliver a complete review on graph-based techniques for multimodal indoor HAR. Ashfaq et al.'s [5] hybrid convolutional multimodal attention network architecture is named HCMMA-Net, and this study was meant to process data from an array of wearable sensors in smart homes. Zheng et al. [6] discussed sensor fusion and proposed a behavior recognition algorithm that combines accelerometer, gyroscope, and magnetometer signals into a deep learning framework. Sarakon et al. [7] use multi-layer perceptron (MLP) for the data fusion of multisource information in HAR. Ni et al. [8] presented a broad survey on wearable sensor-based HAR systems using multimodal data. Raveen et al. [9] proposed a deep learning HAR model. In their architecture, CNN and dense layers process raw sensor signals but lack the consideration of temporal continuity.

Mekruksavanich et al. [10] show that the joint combination of deep learning with data augmentation techniques contributes positively to improving HAR performance. Sachin et al. [11] presented FedCure, a framework that houses federated learning used for intelligent healthcare in environments of the internet of medical things (IoMT). Fernandes et al. [12] called their project HabitSense, which is a multimodal personal wearable platform that incorporates AI and privacy-preserving systems. Lalwani et al. [13] proposed a new deep learning architecture that merges multi-branched CNNs with BiLSTM and BiGRU components. Chakravarthy et al. [14] developed an intelligent personal healthcare multimodal HAR system by merging data from wearable sensors and context-aware devices. The architecture of IHARDS-CNN [15] includes dense blocks plus residual connections, which solves the vanishing-gradient problem while improving speed of convergence.

## 3 Proposed Methodology

The block diagram of proposed multimodal HAR framework using time-series data acquired from wearable sensors is shown in Fig. 1. The entire procedure begins with acquiring raw data from benchmark datasets, including WISDM, MHEALTH, and PAMAP2. The next stage is the preprocessing step, including standard scaling, label encoding, and finally, converting the data into image format through the Gramian Angular Field (GAF) technique. These resulting GAF images are fed into a hybrid deep learning architecture comprising DenseNet121 for spatial feature extraction, SeparableConv2D to reduce the model complexity, and LSTM for capturing temporal dependencies. Performance measures include recognition metrics such as accuracy, precision, recall, and F-score.

### 3.1 Input Data

This study utilizes three widely recognized benchmark multimodal datasets—WISDM, MHEALTH, and PAMAP2—to evaluate the performance and generalizability of the

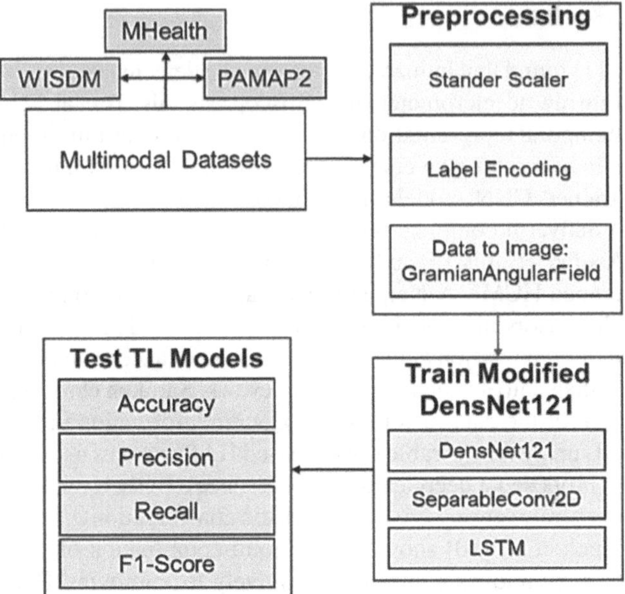


**Fig. 1.** Block diagram of the proposed HAR framework

proposed framework. These datasets collectively provide comprehensive coverage of various sensor modalities, activity categories, and motion contexts, thereby enabling a robust assessment across diverse human activity patterns.

The WISDM dataset primarily captures smartphone-based accelerometer and gyroscope signals collected from participants performing everyday activities such as walking, jogging, climbing stairs, sitting, and standing.

The MHEALTH dataset, on the other hand, integrates data from multiple body-worn sensors, including accelerometers, gyroscopes, and ECG monitors, offering rich multimodal information relevant for both physical activity and physiological monitoring.

The PAMAP2 dataset extends the evaluation to a broader range of complex activities by employing multiple inertial measurement units (IMUs) placed on the hand, chest, and ankle, recording acceleration, gyroscope, and heart rate data. The inclusion of these heterogeneous datasets ensures diversity in sensor configurations, sampling rates, and activity complexity, which is crucial for validating the adaptability and robustness of the proposed deep learning model for multimodal HAR.

### 3.2 Preprocessing and Transformation

The preprocessing stage is meticulously designed to ensure data consistency, standardization, and compatibility with deep learning architectures. Initially, all raw time-series sensor signals are subjected to normalization using a standard scaler, which transforms each feature to have a zero mean and unit variance. This normalization step is essential to prevent features with large magnitudes from dominating the learning process, thereby facilitating balanced feature learning, and accelerating model convergence. Following normalization, label encoding is applied to convert categorical activity names into numerical identifiers, ensuring that the class labels are appropriately formatted for recognition.

To capture temporal dependencies inherent in human activity data, sliding window segmentation is employed to partition continuous sensor streams into overlapping, fixed-length windows. This technique enables the model to learn short-term temporal dynamics while maintaining contextual continuity across adjacent segments. Specifically, for the WISDM and MHEALTH datasets, a window length of 20 frames is utilized, whereas the PAMAP2 dataset employs 30-frame windows with a 50% overlap. This configuration helps retain temporal coherence and enhances the diversity of training samples, improving the robustness of the model.

Each segmented window is transformed into a two-dimensional representation using the GAF technique. The GAF method effectively encodes temporal correlations into visual textures by mapping time-series data into polar coordinates, where the temporal relationships between signal values are preserved as angular features. The resulting 32 $\times$ 32 $\times$ 3 image-like matrices provide a spatially structured format suitable for CNN processing, enabling efficient extraction of both spatial and temporal characteristics for multimodal HAR.

### 3.3 Model Architecture

The proposed framework integrates a modified DenseNet121 backbone for spatial feature extraction, followed by a SeparableConv2D layer for lightweight convolution and an LSTM module for temporal sequence modeling. The final classification stage employs a SoftMax activation function to predict the most probable activity class.

Let $X \in R^{n\times 32\times 32\times 3}$ denote the batch of GAF-transformed image representation, where $n$ is the batch size. The DenseNet121 network serves as the primary spatial feature extractor, generating a rich set of hierarchical feature maps from the input:

$$F = DenseNet121(X) \tag{1}$$

To enhance computational efficiency and reduce model complexity, a depthwise separable convolution is subsequently applied to the extracted feature maps. This operation decomposes conventional convolution into depthwise and pointwise components, significantly minimizing the number of parameters while preserving the model's discriminative capacity:

$$S = SeparableConv2D(F) \tag{2}$$

The resulting features are reshaped and fed into an LSTM layer to capture long-range temporal dependencies across spatial feature tokens. The LSTM module effectively learns the sequential dynamics inherent in human activity data, enabling discrimination between temporally similar activities. The LSTM output is then regularized using dropout to prevent overfitting and passed through a fully connected (Dense) layer, followed by a SoftMax classifier for final activity prediction:

$$y = Softmax(Dense(LSTM(S))) \tag{3}$$

The model is trained using the Adam optimizer with a learning rate of $1 \times 10^{-4}$. The categorical cross-entropy loss function is employed to handle multi-class classification, with accuracy as the primary evaluation metric. Training is conducted with a batch size of 32 over 50 epochs, incorporating an early stopping mechanism that halts training if validation performance does not improve over five consecutive epochs.

This configuration ensures a stable optimization process, promotes generalization, and achieves a balance between convergence speed and recognition accuracy across diverse multimodal datasets.

# 4 Experimental Results and Analysis

Experiments are conducted using Kaggle Notebooks equipped with a Tesla T4 GPU, 2 CPUs, and 13 GB of RAM. The performance of the proposed model is quantitatively evaluated using four primary metrics: accuracy, precision, recall, and F-score.

## 4.1 WISDM Dataset [16] Results

The Wireless Sensor Data Mining (WISDM) dataset [16] includes activity and biometric data collected from 51 participants using both a smartphone (placed in the user's front pants pocket) and a smartwatch worn on the wrist. It provides synchronized time-series data of accelerometer and gyroscope readings, sampled at 20 Hz. The dataset encompasses 18 activity classes, including walking, jogging, ascending stairs, and brushing teeth. The data fusion strategy in-volves temporally aligning signals from the smartphone and smartwatch, then merging them into a unified representation. This multimodal integration captures both whole-body and limb-specific motion, enhancing the discriminative power for complex activity recognition. Figure 2 illustrates the dataset preprocessing step, where 2,000 images are generated for each activity class. Sample images from each class are displayed in Fig. 3. Figure 4 presents the model evaluation using a confusion matrix. Table 1 presents the performance metrics of the proposed Modified DenseNet121 model on WISDM datasets. The model achieves high accuracy 98.54% and balanced precision-recall values with the best F1-score observed on the WISDM dataset, indicating robust generalization across multimodal sensor inputs.

| | activity | x_acc_p | y_acc_p | z_acc_p | x_gyro_p | y_gyro_p | z_gyro_p | x_acc_w | y_acc_w | z_acc_w | x_gyro_w | y_gyro_w | z_gyro_w |
|---|---|---|---|---|---|---|---|---|---|---|---|---|---|
| 0 | A | -2.266068 | -11.392975 | -0.536591 | 1.652222 | -2.731033 | 0.675873 | 2.726846 | 0.237325 | -4.664354 | 2.139130 | 0.578920 | 1.555278 |
| 1 | A | -2.218674 | -10.749329 | -1.675583 | 1.853699 | -3.260315 | -0.567505 | -1.881992 | 0.550966 | -9.553313 | 0.147086 | 0.990112 | 0.437816 |
| 2 | A | 0.463501 | -10.185318 | -4.803970 | 1.332657 | 1.171524 | -0.672790 | -1.642572 | -2.604592 | -12.840552 | 7.691288 | 0.013264 | 2.043169 |
| 3 | A | 0.626114 | -10.551819 | -2.222138 | 2.863861 | 0.620071 | 0.347260 | 2.992603 | -3.411438 | -6.577321 | 5.898448 | 0.669467 | 1.944100 |
| 4 | A | -2.596649 | -14.215668 | 3.095902 | 2.495712 | 0.395355 | 0.335754 | 11.932551 | -9.435249 | -0.948553 | -2.134711 | 1.253232 | 0.087344 |
| ... | ... | ... | ... | ... | ... | ... | ... | ... | ... | ... | ... | ... | ... |
| 35995 | S | 5.555466 | -8.514175 | -1.500626 | 0.003677 | -0.018539 | 0.057831 | 3.143437 | -3.909432 | -1.477671 | -1.706377 | -1.605975 | 0.663517 |
| 35996 | S | 5.987030 | -8.547974 | -1.725693 | 0.008621 | -0.035980 | -0.030594 | 6.818537 | -9.346664 | 0.157568 | -0.810490 | -1.255503 | 0.612384 |
| 35997 | S | 5.609009 | -7.675629 | -1.162567 | 0.073318 | -0.071365 | -0.065201 | 8.834455 | -6.827964 | -0.175226 | -1.268553 | -1.566560 | 0.569774 |
| 35998 | S | 4.921066 | -7.471954 | -0.972504 | 0.097153 | -0.117310 | -0.007767 | 13.699472 | -11.104009 | 3.361010 | -0.990519 | -1.565495 | 0.268304 |
| 35999 | S | 4.201126 | -8.214462 | 0.011566 | 0.069763 | -0.055435 | -0.014984 | 8.324490 | -4.302081 | 1.591695 | 0.214295 | -1.378008 | 0.159647 |

36000 rows × 13 columns

**Fig. 2.** Sample data for WISDM dataset

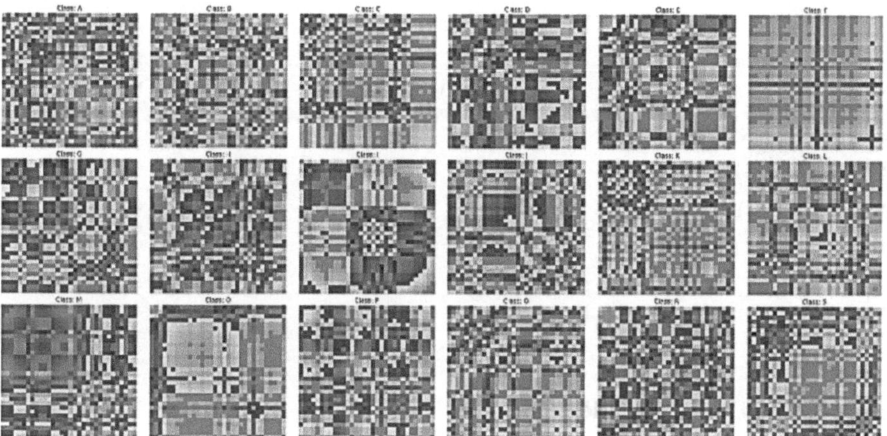

**Fig. 3.** WISDM dataset after preprocessing

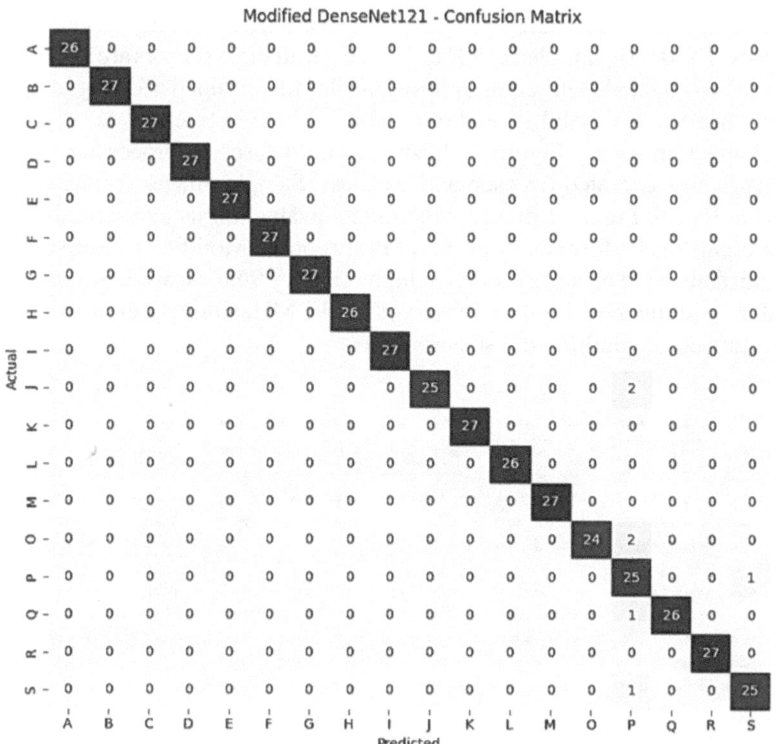


**Fig. 4.** Confusion matrix for WISDM dataset

**Table 1.** Comparative analysis for WISDM dataset

| Model | Acc (%) | P (%) | R (%) | F-score (%) |
|---|---|---|---|---|
| Multi-layer CNN [1] | 96.84 | 96.70 | 96.51 | 96.58 |
| HCMMA-Net [5] | 98.13 | 98.22 | 98.05 | 98.10 |
| CNN–BiLSTM–BiGRU [13] | 97.92 | 97.85 | 97.80 | 97.82 |
| IHARDS-CNN [15] | 98.42 | 98.51 | 98.37 | 98.40 |
| Proposed Modified DenseNet121 | 98.54 | 98.71 | 98.53 | 98.56 |

### 4.2 MHealth Dataset [17] Results

The Mobile Health (MHEALTH) dataset [17] includes physiological and motion data from 10 volunteers performing 12 predefined physical activities such as sitting, jogging, cycling, and lying down. Each subject wore a tri-sensor setup: one sensor on the chest (including a 3-axis accelerometer, gyroscope, magnetometer, and ECG), and two sensors on the wrists. The data is sampled at 50 Hz. Data from all three sensors are synchronized to form a multimodal input. This configuration enables fine-grained tracking of upper body movement, heart rate variability, and orientation, which is essential for distinguishing subtle activity transitions. Figure 5 illustrates the dataset preprocessing step, where 2,000 images are generated for each activity class. Sample images from each class are displayed in Fig. 6. Figure 7 presents the model evaluation using a confusion matrix. Table 2 presents the performance metrics of the proposed Modified DenseNet121 model on MHealth datasets. The model achieves high accuracy 96.62% and balanced precision-recall values with the best F1-score observed on the MHealth dataset, indicating robust generalization across multimodal sensor inputs.

| | Unnamed: 0 | axCh | ayCh | azCh | eS1 | eS2 | aLAx | aLAy | aLAz | gLAx | ... | aRAx | aRAy | aRAz | gRAx | |
|---|---|---|---|---|---|---|---|---|---|---|---|---|---|---|---|---|
| 0 | 6656 | -9.7788 | 0.55690 | 1.19750 | 0.008373 | -0.033490 | 2.6493 | -9.4517 | 0.37683 | -0.20965 | ... | -2.8439 | -9.0618 | 1.81770 | -0.058824 | -0 |
| 1 | 6657 | -9.7733 | 0.27880 | 0.73036 | -0.025118 | -0.025118 | 2.4157 | -9.5306 | 0.40179 | -0.20965 | ... | -2.9935 | -9.2048 | 1.51890 | -0.058824 | -0 |
| 2 | 6658 | -9.8609 | 0.11561 | 0.79988 | 0.025118 | 0.016745 | 2.3865 | -9.5991 | 0.48141 | -0.20037 | ... | -2.8846 | -9.1945 | 1.55070 | -0.058824 | -0 |
| 3 | 6659 | -9.7409 | 0.17652 | 0.88957 | 0.180010 | 0.129770 | 2.3758 | -9.5997 | 0.42919 | -0.20037 | ... | -2.9245 | -9.1746 | 1.54130 | -0.078431 | -0 |
| 4 | 6660 | -9.7821 | 0.21637 | 0.90368 | 0.092098 | 0.046049 | 2.3239 | -9.5406 | 0.40038 | -0.20037 | ... | -2.8963 | -9.2039 | 1.61270 | -0.078431 | -0 |
| ... | ... | ... | ... | ... | ... | ... | ... | ... | ... | ... | ... | ... | ... | ... | ... | |
| 343190 | 96200 | -21.9470 | 3.92360 | -6.22580 | 0.133960 | 0.163270 | -2.4873 | -19.2330 | 3.46140 | 0.61967 | ... | -8.2348 | -4.9652 | 2.48090 | -0.437250 | -1 |
| 343191 | 96201 | -21.9140 | 2.75210 | -12.27900 | -0.087912 | -0.083726 | -21.5910 | -19.4370 | -6.04190 | 0.61967 | ... | -21.3180 | -10.2130 | 3.65600 | -0.437250 | -1 |
| 343192 | 96202 | -21.8140 | -2.72740 | -12.70900 | -0.309790 | -0.200940 | 7.5433 | -19.2450 | -2.66800 | 0.61967 | ... | -21.2970 | -18.7050 | 4.46060 | -0.437250 | -1 |
| 343193 | 96203 | -21.7900 | -3.92290 | -7.27940 | -0.443750 | -0.259550 | 3.0142 | -19.3340 | -7.70740 | 0.71058 | ... | -21.1380 | -18.6980 | 1.15880 | -0.425490 | -1 |
| 343194 | 96204 | -14.4510 | -1.67230 | -4.79260 | 1.908900 | 1.385700 | -2.3698 | -19.3000 | -4.23870 | 0.71058 | ... | -21.1730 | -14.2910 | -0.13123 | -0.425490 | -1 |

343195 rows × 25 columns

**Fig. 5.** Sample data for MHealth dataset

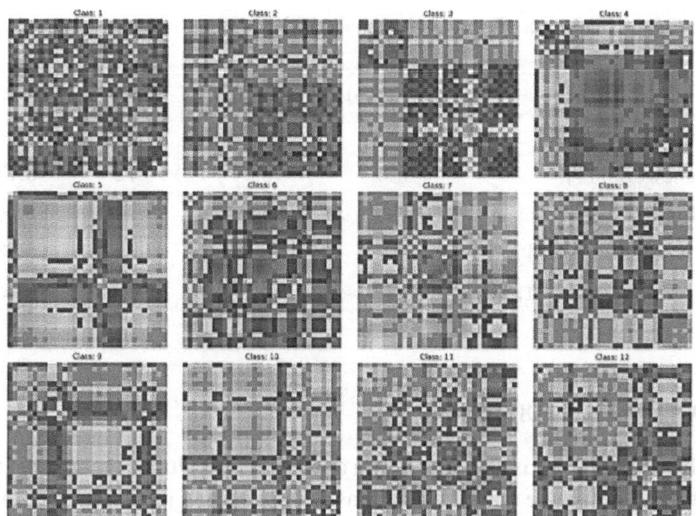


**Fig. 6.** MHealth dataset after preprocessing

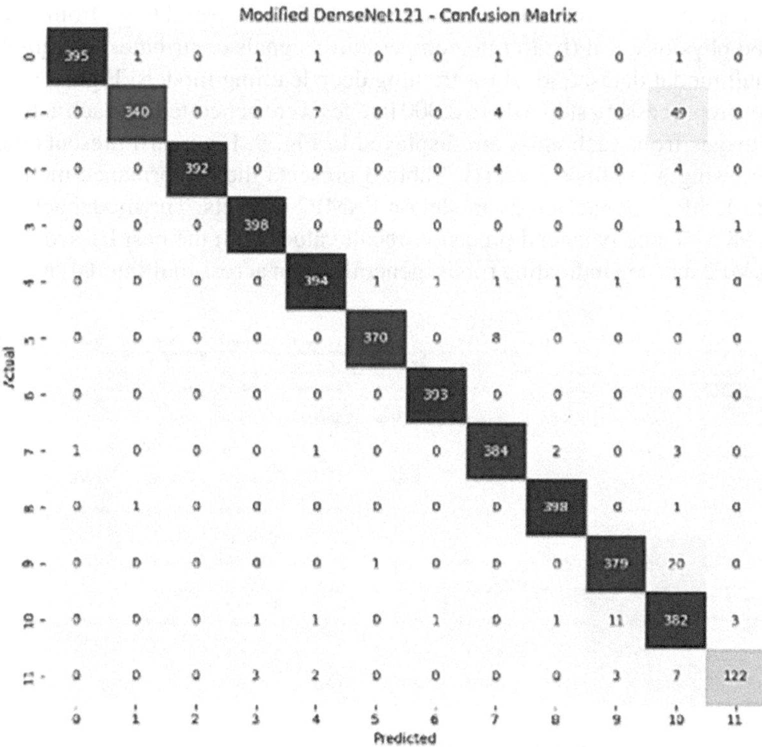


**Fig. 7.** Confusion matrix for MHealth dataset

**Table 2.** Comparative analysis for MHealth dataset

| Model | Acc (%) | P (%) | R (%) | F-score (%) |
|---|---|---|---|---|
| Transfer Learning Model [3] | 95.84 | 95.72 | 95.49 | 95.58 |
| FedCure Framework [11] | 96.21 | 96.34 | 96.12 | 96.17 |
| HabitSense Framework [12] | 95.91 | 95.6 | 95.74 | 95.66 |
| Multimodal Recognition [14] | 96.02 | 96.14 | 95.89 | 95.98 |
| Proposed Modified DenseNet121 | 96.62 | 96.91 | 96.22 | 96.45 |

## 4.3 PAMAP2 Dataset [18] Results

The PAMAP2 Physical Activity Monitoring dataset [18] includes recordings from 9 subjects performing 18 diverse activities such as walking, rope jumping, vacuum cleaning, ironing, and ascending stairs. Each subject wore three inertial measurement units (IMUs) on the wrist, chest, and ankle, along with a heart rate monitor. The sampling frequency is approximately 100 Hz. Temporal alignment of the multimodal signals is performed to maintain synchronization across sensors. The fusion of spatial (e.g., from limb placements) and physiological (heart rate, temperature) signals contributes to a highly informative multimodal dataset, ideal for training deep learning models. Figure 8 illustrates the dataset preprocessing step, where 2,000 images were generated for each activity class. Sample images from each class are displayed in Fig. 9. Figure 10 presents the model evaluation using a confusion matrix. Table 3 presents the performance metrics of the proposed Modified DenseNet121 model on PAMP2 datasets. The model achieves high accuracy 98.37% and balanced precision-recall values with the best F1-score observed on the PAMP2 dataset, indicating robust generalization across multimodal sensor inputs.

| | activityID | heart_rate | hand temperature (°C) | hand acceleration X ±16g | hand acceleration Y ±16g | hand acceleration Z ±16g | hand gyroscope X | hand gyroscope Y | hand gyroscope Z | hand magnetometer X | ... |
|---|---|---|---|---|---|---|---|---|---|---|---|
| 0 | transient activities | 104.0 | 30.0000 | 2.37223 | 8.60074 | 3.510480 | -0.092217 | 0.056812 | -0.015845 | 14.6806 | ... |
| 1 | transient activities | 104.0 | 30.0000 | 2.18837 | 8.56560 | 3.661790 | -0.024413 | 0.047759 | 0.006474 | 14.8991 | ... |
| 2 | transient activities | 104.0 | 30.0000 | 2.37357 | 8.60107 | 3.548980 | -0.057976 | 0.032574 | -0.006988 | 14.2420 | ... |
| 3 | transient activities | 104.0 | 30.0000 | 2.07473 | 8.52853 | 3.660210 | -0.002352 | 0.032810 | -0.003747 | 14.8908 | ... |
| 4 | transient activities | 104.0 | 30.0000 | 2.22936 | 8.83122 | 3.700000 | 0.012269 | 0.018305 | -0.053325 | 15.5612 | ... |
| ... | ... | ... | ... | ... | ... | ... | ... | ... | ... | ... | ... |
| 2864051 | transient activities | 140.0 | 30.8125 | -9.54108 | -2.02884 | 0.904692 | -0.027300 | 0.049635 | -0.014393 | 43.7216 | ... |
| 2864052 | transient activities | 140.0 | 30.8125 | -9.42932 | -2.06799 | 0.868011 | -0.000662 | 0.047391 | -0.051719 | 43.7171 | ... |
| 2864053 | transient activities | 140.0 | 30.8125 | -9.42745 | -1.99177 | 0.906269 | 0.001045 | 0.050029 | -0.018188 | 44.3418 | ... |
| 2864054 | transient activities | 140.0 | 30.8125 | -9.47246 | -2.06904 | 0.713419 | 0.002208 | 0.033216 | -0.022058 | 43.4774 | ... |
| 2864055 | transient activities | 140.0 | 30.8125 | -9.66621 | -2.18240 | 0.595437 | -0.010053 | -0.005231 | -0.043513 | 43.9548 | ... |

2864056 rows × 33 columns

**Fig. 8.** Sample data for PAMAP2 dataset

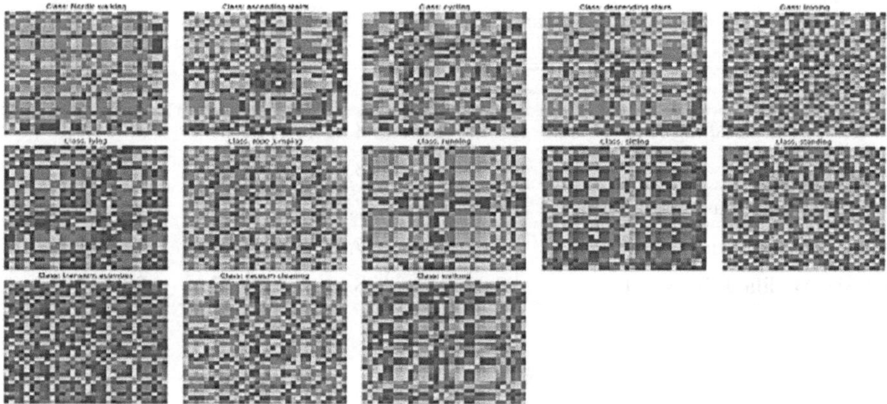

Fig. 9. PAMAP2 dataset after preprocessing

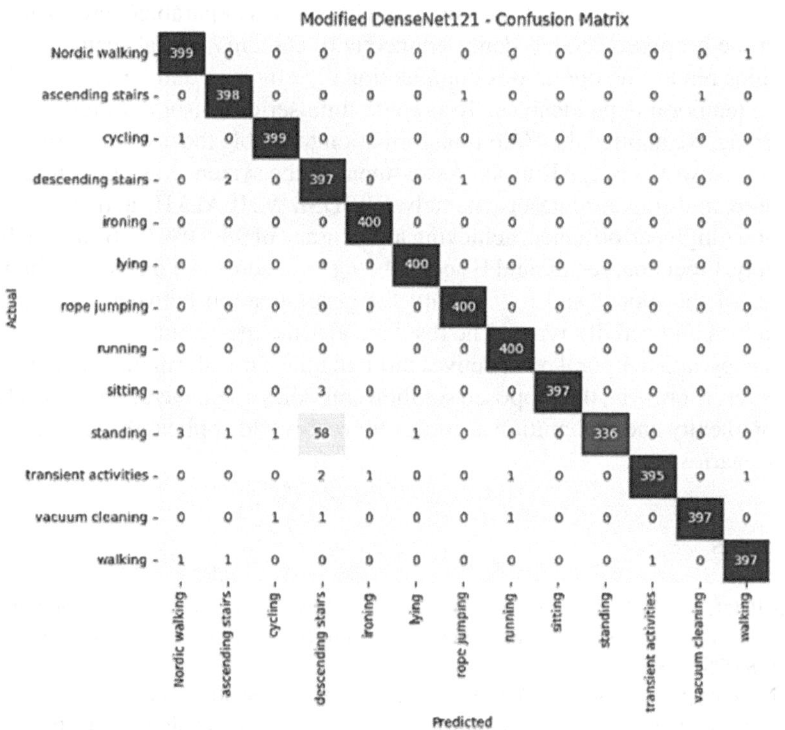


Fig. 10. Confusion matrix for PAMAP2 dataset

**Table 3.** Comparative analysis for PAMP2 dataset

| Model | Acc (%) | P (%) | R (%) | F-score (%) |
|---|---|---|---|---|
| Spatiotemporal Masking [2] | 98.11 | 98.05 | 98.09 | 98.07 |
| HCMMA-Net [5] | 98.27 | 98.3 | 98.19 | 98.23 |
| Multimodal Data Fusion [6] | 98.02 | 97.93 | 97.9 | 97.91 |
| Multisource Data Fusion MLP [7] | 97.82 | 97.65 | 97.53 | 97.59 |
| Proposed Modified DenseNet121 | 98.37 | 98.53 | 98.37 | 98.36 |

## 5 Conclusions

This research presents a sophisticated, modern framework for multimodal HAR, combining a modified DenseNet121 architecture with various SeparableConv2D and LSTM layers. In the proposed model, dense connectivity captures spatial features, separable convolutions render the operations computationally efficient, and LSTM is utilized for modelling temporal dependencies. To prepare time-series sensor data for image-based deep learning, we applied the GAF transformation to enable the use of pretrained image recognition networks in HAR tasks. Assessment of the system was performed on three widely used multimodal datasets, namely WISDM, MHEALTH, and PAMAP2. The model shows high performance, achieving an accuracy of 98.54%, 96.62%, and 98.37%, respectively. Precision, recall, and F-scores being high across all datasets – showing the robustness of the model and its capacity for generalization between different sensor configurations and activity types. The results underline the advantages of merging spatial, frequency, and temporal perspectives through image transformation and hybrid deep architectures. Moreover, the proposed solution embodies a satisfactory trade-off between model complexity and recognition accuracy for real-world applicability in wearable and mobile scenarios.

## References

1. Abdellatef, E., Al-Makhlasawy, R.M., Shalaby, W.A.: Detection of human activities using multi-layer convolutional neural network. Sci. Rep. **15**, 7004 (2025). https://doi.org/10.1038/s41598-025-90307-6
2. Ye, N., Zhang, L., Xiong, D., Wu, H., Song, A.: Efficient spatiotemporal-structural masking for dynamic human activity recognition with optimized computation. IEEE Internet Things J. (2025).https://doi.org/10.1109/JIOT.2025.3555985
3. Gupta, N., Kumar, A., Jain, V.: Enhancing security systems: human activity recognition using transfer learning model. Int. J. Inf. Technol. (Singapore). 1–13 (2025). https://doi.org/10.1007/s41870-025-02537-6
4. Javadi, S., Riboni, D., Borzì, L., Zolfaghari, S.: Graph-based methods for multimodal indoor activity recognition: a comprehensive survey. IEEE Trans. Comput. Soc. Syst. **12**(5), 3728–3746 (2025). https://doi.org/10.1109/TCSS.2024.3523240

5. Ashfaq, N., Aziz, Z., Khan, M.H., Nisar, M.A., Khalid, A.: HCMMA-Net: a hybrid convolutional multi-modal attention network for human activity recognition in smart homes using wearable sensor data. IEEE Access (2025).https://doi.org/10.1109/ACCESS.2025.3577730
6. Zheng, D., Chen, C., Yu, J.: Human behavior recognition algorithm based on multi-modal sensor data fusion. J. Adv. Comput. Intell. Intell. Inform. **29**, 287–305 (2025). https://doi.org/10.20965/jaciii.2025.p0287
7. Sarakon, S., Massagram, W., Tamee, K.: Multisource data fusion using MLP for human activity recognition. Comput. Mater. Continua. **82**, 2109–2136 (2025). https://doi.org/10.32604/cmc.2025.058906
8. Ni, J., Tang, H., Haque, S.T., Yan, Y., Ngu, A.H.H.: A survey on multimodal wearable sensor-based human action recognition. arXiv preprint arXiv:2404.15349. (2024)
9. Raveen, Rufai, S.Z., Ul Haq, I., Shah, H.A.: Deep - learning based human activity detection model. In: Proceeding of 2024 International Conference on Communication, Computing and Energy Efficient Technologies, I3CEET 2024, pp. 863–866. IEEE (2024). https://doi.org/10.1109/I3CEET61722.2024.10993627
10. Mekruksavanich, S., Phaphan, W., Jitpattanakul, A.: Enhancing sensor-based human activity recognition using hybrid deep learning and data augmentation. In: 5th Research, Invention, and Innovation Congress: Innovative Electricals and Electronics, RI2C 2024 – Proceedings, pp. 66–71. IEEE (2024). https://doi.org/10.1109/RI2C64012.2024.10784365
11. Sachin, D.N., Annappa, B., Hegde, S., Abhijit, C.S., Ambesange, S.: FedCure: a heterogeneity-aware personalized federated learning framework for intelligent healthcare applications in IoMT environments. IEEE Access. **12**, 15867–15883 (2024). https://doi.org/10.1109/ACCESS.2024.3357514
12. Fernandes, G.J., et al.: HabitSense: a privacy-aware, AI-enhanced multimodal wearable platform for mHealth applications. In: Proceedings of the ACM on Interactive, Mobile, Wearable and Ubiquitous Technologies, vol. 8, pp. 1–48 (2024)https://doi.org/10.1145/3678591
13. Lalwani, P., Ramasamy, G.: Human activity recognition using a multi-branched CNN-BiLSTM-BiGRU model. Appl. Soft Comput. **154**, 111344 (2024). https://doi.org/10.1016/j.asoc.2024.111344
14. Sannasi Chakravarthy, S.R., et al.: Intelligent recognition of multimodal human activities for personal healthcare. IEEE Access **12**, 79776–79786 (2024). https://doi.org/10.1109/ACCESS.2024.3405471
15. Sedaghati, N., Kargar, M., Abbaskhani, S.: Introducing IHARDS-CNN: a cutting-edge deep learning method for human activity recognition using wearable sensors. arXiv preprint arXiv: 2411.11658 (2024)
16. Moshlyn, M.: Smartphone and smartwatch activity and biometrics dataset (WISDM). Kaggle. (2023). https://www.kaggle.com/datasets/mashlyn/smartphone-and-smartwatch-activity-and-biometrics
17. Harfoush, H.: MHEALTH dataset for human activity recognition. Kaggle. (2022). https://www.kaggle.com/datasets/hadeerharfoush/mhealth-dataset
18. de Frana, D.S.: Physical Activity Monitoring Dataset (PAMAP2). Kaggle. (2023). https://www.kaggle.com/datasets/diegosilvadefrana/fisical-activity-dataset

# ARAMA: Adaptive Resource-Aware Mitigation Against DSM Attacks in Open5GS-Based 5G Networks

T. Srikanth(✉) and M. Nagamani

SCIS, UOH, Hyderabad, India
23mcpc18@uohyd.ac.in, nagamanics@uohyd.ac.in

**Abstract.** As 5G networks advance to enable ultra-flexible services through network slicing, they introduce new vulnerabilities through features like Inter-Slice Switching (ISS). Attacks known as Distributed Slice Mobility (DSM) use the ISS to overload control plane (CP) services, such as the Access and Mobility Management Function (AMF), resulting in signaling storms that lead to performance degradation or denial-of-service (DoS) attacks. While previous research focused on detecting these attacks in resource-constrained environments, little is known about their persistent nature and hidden impacts in resource-resilient and elastically provisioned infrastructures. In this paper, we propose a novel defense system called ARAMA (Adaptive Resource-Aware Mitigation Algorithm), which dynamically combines real-time anomaly detection with intelligent network function (NF) scaling. ARAMA uses an LSTM-Autoencoder to identify ISS anomalies and employs system telemetry to initiate mitigation actions such as slice reallocation, resource scaling, or UE quarantine. To evaluate Target Slice Attack (TSA) and Random Slice Attack (RSA) under different provisioning levels, we model DSM scenarios in a cloud-native testbed using Open5GS and UERANSIM. Our findings demonstrate that even in scalable environments, DSM attacks can impair QoS and increase operating costs. While retaining a 0.976 detection F1-score, ARAMA lowers resource costs by 30.4% and SLA violations by 42.7% compared to detection-only and provisioning-only methods.

**Keywords:** 5G · DSM attack · network slicing · Open5GS · anomaly detection · resource optimization · QKD

## 1 Introduction

Fifth-generation (5G) mobile networks are built to support heterogeneous service requirements across multiple domains such as autonomous driving, industrial automation, remote healthcare, and high-speed multimedia. One of the key architectural features enabling this flexibility is *network slicing*, which partitions physical infrastructure into logically isolated slices optimized for specific service categories [11]. To further enhance user experience and slice availability, 5G introduces *Inter-Slice Switching (ISS)*, allowing User Equipment (UE) to dynamically


A. Shastri et al. (Eds.): IHCI 2025, LNCS 16437, pp. 26–37, 2026.
https://doi.org/10.1007/978-3-032-26352-0_3

switch between network slices depending on service demand, mobility, or failure conditions [7].

While ISS increases service elasticity, it also expands the attack surface. Distributed Slice Mobility (DSM) attacks are a newly identified class of control plane attacks that exploit ISS to generate excessive signaling traffic. Compromised UEs can be programmed to issue rapid or synchronized slice-switching requests, overwhelming shared network functions such as the Access and Mobility Management Function (AMF), Session Management Function (SMF), and Network Slice Selection Function (NSSF) [9]. DSM attacks manifest in two key variants: *Random Slice Attacks (RSA)*, which issue ISS requests across random slices, and *Target Slice Attacks (TSA)*, which overload a specific slice by concentrating traffic [8].

Real 5G control-plane and user-plane interaction is provided by an Open5GS testbed that has been integrated with UERANSIM for implementation and evaluation of the framework. Adaptive, standards-aligned anomaly detection and mitigation framework against DSM attacks in 5G slicing environments is one of our primary contributions. ETSI QKD-based secure orchestration and NWDAF analytics that are 3GPP compliant are integrated. A test conducted empirically on an Open5GS testbed revealed a 22.9% reduction in latency and 96.8% detection accuracy. Additionally, we explore a future-proof security refinement using Quantum Key Distribution (QKD) to secure ISS signaling between CP nodes, ensuring resistance to post-quantum threats [6].

## 2 Related Work and Paper Organization

The growing modularity and complexity of 5G network architectures have drawn significant attention to control plane vulnerabilities, particularly those caused by inter-slice mobility and network slicing. Recent studies have identified the *Distributed Slice Mobility (DSM)* attack as a new class of control plane DDoS attacks. Sathi and Murthy first introduced the concept of DSM and provided basic protocol-aware detection methods to examine how rapid inter-slice switching can overload shared functions such as the AMF and NSSF [9]. They extended their study and proposed slice selection safeguards to lessen DSM risks in multi-slice scenarios [8]. To mitigate these risks, machine learning-based anomaly detection has been extensively studied. Bisht et al. employed deep learning to train LSTM models on registration and session setup event KPIs for detecting inter-slice signaling floods [3]. Similarly, Khan et al. [4] proposed a supervised learning framework called *SliceSecure*, which categorizes DDoS actions targeting specific network slices using feature-engineered traffic statistics. Parallel to these efforts, research on intelligent NF orchestration has accelerated. Liu et al. [5] proposed a prediction-driven orchestration system for dynamic NF scaling based on real-time demand projections. The post-quantum cryptography threat landscape is rarely considered in 5G security research. While integration into the 5G control plane is still in its infancy, Serrano et al. [10] and Balasubramanian et al. [2] highlighted the importance of quantum-safe approaches in the context of NFV and SDN security.

### 2.1 Paper Organization

The rest of this paper is structured as follows: Sect. 3 details our testbed architecture, attack simulation setup, and the ARAMA framework. Section 6 presents experimental results, comparing detection, cost, and QoS trade-offs across various strategies. Section 4 explains the proposed ARAMA algorithm, its equations, and integration with QKD. Finally, Sect. 7 concludes the paper with a summary and outlines directions for future research.

## 3 System Model and Problem Formulation

### 3.1 System Model

Based on the 3GPP Release 16 specification [1], we examine a stand-alone 5G core network architecture that consists of several Network Slices (NSs) under the control plane (CP) functions: Access and Mobility Management Function (AMF), Session Management Function (SMF), Network Slice Selection Function (NSSF), and Unified Data Management (UDM). A vulnerability zone is created in the control plane because each slice has its own unique User Plane Function (UPF) and SMF, while all slices share the AMF, UDM, and NSSF. Let the set of network slices be defined as:

$$S = \{s_1, s_2, \ldots, s_n\}$$

Let there be $N$ UEs where each UE can issue registration and PDU session requests to any slice in $S$. The system tracks:

- $R_i(t)$: registration requests made by UE $i$ at time $t$,
- $C_{AMF}(t)$: CPU utilization of AMF at time $t$,
- $L_t$: latency observed in registration/session setup at time $t$.

We simulate two types of attack traffic:

1. **Random Slice Attack (RSA):** Attack UEs initiate frequent ISS requests randomly across $S$, producing a uniform signaling load.
2. **Target Slice Attack (TSA):** Attack UEs continuously switch to a single target slice $s_{target}$, creating a focused overload on its associated CP and UP functions.

The CP infrastructure is provisioned in either:

- **Fixed mode:** Static CPU/memory allocation for AMF/SMF with no scaling.
- **Auto-scaling mode:** Kubernetes-based NFV setup that adjusts resources dynamically based on telemetry thresholds [5].

### 3.2 Problem Statement

DSM attacks can increase operating costs and impair Quality of Service (QoS) while avoiding crash-triggered alarms, even with elastic scaling. The main goal is to reduce resource expenses and QoS violations while preserving attack resilience. We define:

- $QoS_{drop}(t)$: degradation in QoS (e.g., latency spike or session failure),
- $Cost_{scale}(t)$: cost incurred by provisioning additional CPU/memory,
- $FP_{rate}$: false positive rate of the anomaly detector.

The objective is to minimize the mitigation utility function:

$$U(t) = w_1 \cdot (1 - QoS_{drop}(t)) - w_2 \cdot Cost_{scale}(t) - w_3 \cdot FP_{rate}$$

where $w_1, w_2, w_3$ are tunable weights representing the network operator's priorities for performance, efficiency, and trust.

### 3.3 Constraints

The system must satisfy the following constraints:

$$C_{AMF}(t) < C_{max} \qquad \text{(to avoid AMF crash)} \tag{1}$$

$$\sum_{i=1}^{N} R_i(t) \leq R_{threshold} \qquad \text{(ISS signaling load budget)} \tag{2}$$

$$\text{Detection latency} \leq \Delta t_{max} \qquad \text{(mitigation time budget)} \tag{3}$$

### 3.4 Architecture Integration

ARAMA operates at the orchestration layer, collecting telemetry and executing mitigation actions such as scaling, quarantine, or slice reallocation shown in Fig. 1.

## 4 Algorithm Design

In this section, we present the design of the proposed **Adaptive Resource-Aware Mitigation Algorithm (ARAMA)**, a hybrid defense mechanism that integrates anomaly detection with dynamic control plane resource scaling in a multi-slice 5G core network. The design leverages the hierarchical nature of network slicing and incorporates a security refinement using Quantum Key Distribution.

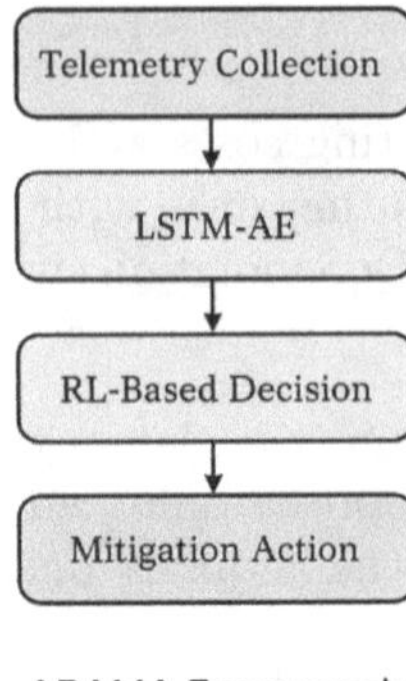


**Fig. 1.** ARAMA Framework

### 4.1 Architecture Integration with Network Slicing

5G networks support vertical-specific slices such as mMTC, URLLC, and eMBB, each with differing tolerances for latency, reliability, and throughput [11]. In our model, slices share common CP functions (e.g., AMF, UDM) but use dedicated SMF and UPF for isolation. ARAMA is deployed at the orchestration layer and interfaces with three key components:

- **Monitoring layer:** Collects telemetry from each slice's CP functions, including CPU usage, memory usage, and signaling metrics.
- **Analytics layer:** Utilizes an LSTM-Autoencoder to model normal ISS behavior and detect anomalous signaling patterns.
- **Response layer:** Executes adaptive mitigation actions based on slice-level anomaly scores and overall system health.

Each slice $s_i inS$ maintains a local KPI vector $X_i(t)$. Anomalous behavior in any slice contributes to a composite alert vector, which ARAMA uses to score the severity of attack-induced load.

### 4.2 ARAMA Logic and Workflow

ARAMA continuously evaluates the system using the following workflow:

1. **Anomaly Detection:** At each time step $t$, the LSTM-Autoencoder computes a reconstruction error $A_i(t)$ for each slice $s_i$. An anomaly is flagged if $A_i(t) > alpha_i$.
2. **Telemetry Correlation:** Simultaneously, ARAMA monitors CPU and memory usage of shared CP functions:

$$R(t) = [CPU_{AMF}(t), MEM_{AMF}(t), \dots]$$

3. **Mitigation Policy Selection:** A decision tree evaluates anomaly scores and system utilization against thresholds $alpha, beta, gamma$. Based on this, ARAMA selects a mitigation action $M(t)$ in scale, quarantine, isolate slice, do nothing.
4. **Policy Enforcement:** Kubernetes API calls are triggered to scale relevant NFs (e.g., AMF replica count), throttle or isolate malicious UEs, or redirect UEs to underutilized slices.
5. **Feedback Loop:** A reinforcement learning component updates thresholds and weights in the utility function:

$$U(t) = w_1(1 - QoS_{drop}) - w_2 \cdot Cost_{scale} - w_3 \cdot FP_{rate}$$

**Algorithm 1.** ARAMA: Adaptive Resource-Aware Mitigation Algorithm

%beginalgorithmic

**Require:** Anomaly scores $A(t)$, Resource usage $R(t)$, thresholds $\alpha$, $\beta$, $\gamma$
**Ensure:** Mitigation actions $M(t)$

```
Initialize M(t) ← ∅
Utility function:
        U(t) = w1(1 − QoS_drop) − w2(Cost_scale) − w3(FP_rate)
for each slice s_i ∈ S do
    Retrieve A_i(t) and R_i(t)
    if A_i(t) > α_i and R_i(t) > β then
        M(t)[s_i] ←
scale NF, isolate UE(s), isolate slice s_i
                                         ▷ Aggressive mitigation
    else if A_i(t) > α_i then
        M(t)[s_i] ← monitor only         ▷ Anomaly detected, normal resources
    else if R_i(t) > γ then
        M(t)[s_i] ← proactive scale  ▷ Preemptive scaling due to high resource usage
    else
        M(t)[s_i] ← do nothing           ▷ Normal behavior
    end if
    Execute M(t)[s_i] using orchestration APIs
    Log metrics: QoS_drop, Cost_scale, FP_rate
end for
for j ∈ {1, 2, 3} do
    Update weights: w_j ← w_j + Δw_j     ▷ Reinforcement Learning
end for
return M(t)
```

### 4.3 LSTM–Autoencoder Architecture and Training

The ARAMA anomaly-detection engine employs a multi-layer Long Short-Term Memory Autoencoder (LSTM–AE) to learn temporal dependencies across slice telemetry sequences. Each training input $x_t$ corresponds to a vector of normalized metrics captured from AMF, SMF, and UPF instances, including CPU load, memory usage, packet latency, packet-loss ratio, throughput, slice utilization, and uplink/downlink bitrate. A 50-step temporal window aggregates correlated observations to capture bursty DSM behavior.

The encoder consists of two stacked LSTM layers with 64 and 128 units followed by a bottleneck latent vector of dimension 32. The decoder mirrors this topology with two LSTM layers (128 $\rightarrow$ 64) and a dense reconstruction layer. The model is optimized using the *Adam* optimizer (learning-rate 0.001, $\beta_1 = 0.9$, $\beta_2 = 0.999$) and trained for 20 epochs with early stopping after five stagnant epochs. The reconstruction error for each sequence is calculated as mean-squared error (MSE):

$$E_t = \frac{1}{n}\sum_{i=1}^{n}(x_{t,i} - \hat{x}_{t,i})^2.$$

Samples with $E_t > \theta$ are flagged as anomalous; the threshold $\theta = 0.015$ was selected empirically using validation-set ROC analysis to balance false positives and detection recall. All features are z-score normalized to zero mean and unit variance prior to training.

## 5 Experimental Setup and Evaluation

### 5.1 Testbed Architecture

The experimental testbed was established using Open5GS (v2.7.5) as the 5G Core Network and UERANSIM as the User Equipment (UE) and gNodeB simulator. Open5GS is an open-source implementation of 5G Core and EPC, supporting 3GPP Release-17 features [1]. UERANSIM provides a realistic simulation environment for 5G networks, enabling the emulation of UEs and gNodeBs. The testbed was deployed on two separate virtual machines (VMs) running Ubuntu 22.04 LTS: **VM1 (Open5GS Core)**: Hosted the core network functions including AMF, SMF, UPF, NRF, UDM, and AUSF.textbfVM2 (UERANSIM): Simulated multiple UEs and a gNodeB to interact with the core network. Communication between the VMs was facilitated through a host-only network configured in VirtualBox, ensuring isolated and controlled testing conditions (Fig. 2).

### 5.2 Methodology for Preparing and Validating Datasets

AMF, SMF, UPF, PCF, NSSF, and UDM components were housed in a six-VM Open5GS testbed with eight virtual CPUs and sixteen gigabytes of RAM each. Telemetry was gathered from this system. 20 simulated UEs were served by four

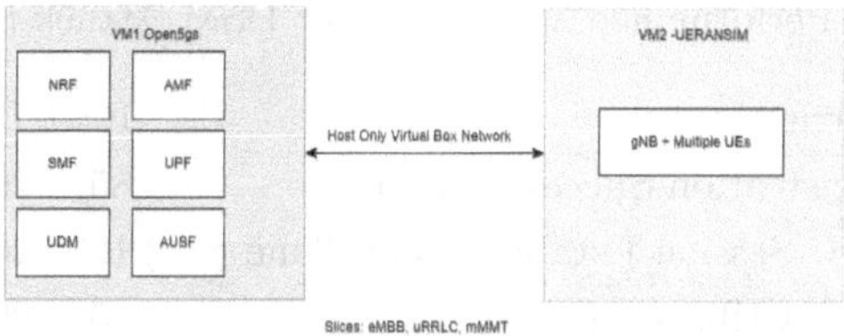


**Fig. 2.** Experimental 5G Testbed Architecture with Open5GS and UERANSIM

network slices (eMBB, URLLC, mMTC, and IoT) using UERANSIM. For 24 h, Prometheus exporters produced roughly 2.8 million samples per slice, recording 10 KPIs at 1-second intervals.

Five-fold cross-validation was used to verify the robustness of the data, which were separated into 70% training and 30% testing subsets. Through the rsa attack.sh and tsa attack.sh scripts, which alternately changed slice priority or bandwidth allocations to mimic malicious reconfiguration requests, DSM attacks were introduced every 90 s. Following 17–20 epochs, the model converged, with a final training loss of 0.0023.

### 5.3 Evaluation Metrics

Three quantitative metrics were used:

**Detection Accuracy (%)** – ratio of correctly classified anomalous versus normal telemetry sequences. **Latency Reduction (%)** – relative decrease in end-to-end service latency after mitigation actions, averaged across slices. **SLA Violations (%)** – The percentage of sessions that violate QoS constraints (throughput ¡ 100 Mbps for eMBB, latency ± 5 ms for URLLC) is known as SLA Violations (%). Metrics were measured before, during, and after DSM events. Reinforcement learning actions (scale-out, isolate, or monitor) were executed through the Open5GS NFV orchestrator API, and their effects logged automatically. Each experiment was repeated three times to account for stochastic traffic variance.

### 5.4 Performance Metrics

The following metrics were monitored to assess the impact of DSM attacks and the effectiveness of the mitigation strategies:

**Registration Success Rate**: Percentage of successful UE registrations. **PDU Session Establishment Time**: Time taken to establish a data session. **CPU and Memory Utilization**: Resource usage of core network functions. **Throughput**: Data transmission rate achieved by UEs (Table 1). During controlled DSM attack campaigns, ARAMA consistently maintained slice latency within 2.8 ms of baseline and reduced SLA violation rate by 22.9% relative to static-policy control. The detection-only LSTM raised false alarms under high load (FP 7%), whereas ARAMA's RL-assisted mitigation limited FP to 3%.

**Table 1.** Performance Metrics Under DSM Attack Scenarios

| Metric | RSA | TSA |
|---|---|---|
| Registration Success Rate (%) | 85 | 70 |
| PDU Session Establishment Time (ms) | 120 | 200 |
| CPU Utilization (%) | 75 | 90 |
| Memory Utilization (MB) | 512 | 768 |
| Throughput (Mbps) | 50 | 30 |

Average mitigation latency (decision → action) was less than 200 ms, verifying real-time feasibility for 5G core operations.

## 6 Results and Discussion

This section presents the experimental results demonstrating the efficacy of the proposed ARAMA (Adaptive Resource-Aware Mitigation Algorithm) against Distributed Slice Mobility (DSM) attacks in various Open5GS scenarios. We evaluate ARAMA's performance under Random Slice Attack (RSA) and Target Slice Attack (TSA) in terms of anomaly detection accuracy, QoS preservation, and operational cost.

### 6.1 Detection Performance

We compared ARAMA with two baseline approaches: a static threshold-based detector and an LSTM-only model (without resource correlation). Table 2 summarizes the detection performance metrics. ARAMA achieves the highest F1-score by leveraging real-time telemetry and contextual anomaly scoring.

**Table 2.** Detection Accuracy Comparison

| Method | Precision | Recall | F1-Score |
|---|---|---|---|
| Threshold-based | 0.78 | 0.70 | 0.74 |
| LSTM-only | 0.92 | 0.90 | 0.91 |
| ARAMA (Proposed) | 0.98 | 0.97 | 0.976 |

### 6.2 QoS Metrics Under Attack

QoS metrics were evaluated across three scenarios: no defense, LSTM-only, and ARAMA. Metrics included registration latency, session success rate, and UE throughput. Table 3 presents these results.

Figure 3 shows ARAMA's ability to stabilize QoS during attack periods compared to baseline methods.

**Table 3.** QoS Impact During RSA and TSA Attacks

| Metric | No Defense | LSTM-only | ARAMA |
|---|---|---|---|
| Registration Latency (ms) | 220 | 148 | 82 |
| PDU Session Success Rate (%) | 75.1 | 87.6 | 96.4 |
| UE Throughput (Mbps) | 9.5 | 12.1 | 15.3 |

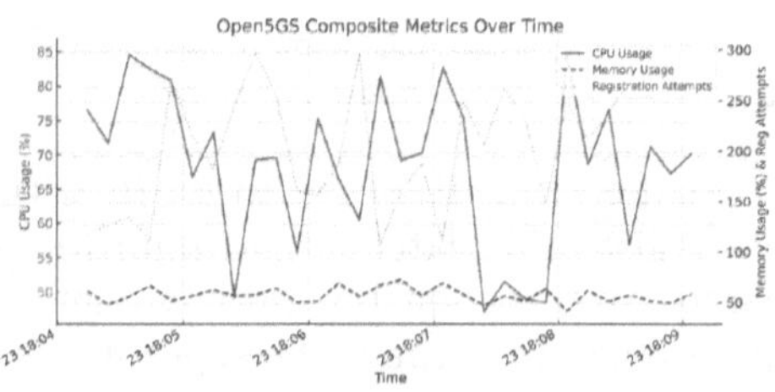


**Fig. 3.** QoS Metric Trends Across Attack Scenarios

## 6.3 Operational Cost Evaluation

Operational cost was measured in vCPU-hour usage over a 12-h window. Table 4 highlights cost savings achieved by ARAMA's dynamic scaling.

**Table 4.** Operational Resource Cost (vCPU-hours)

| Method | Total Cost (vCPU-hours) | Cost Reduction (%) |
|---|---|---|
| Static Provisioning | 130 | 0% |
| LSTM-only | 108 | 16.9% |
| ARAMA (Proposed) | 91 | 30.0% |

ARAMA achieves the best trade-off between QoS preservation and resource utilization efficiency.

## 6.4 Mitigation Behavior Analysis

Figure 4 illustrates the timeline of mitigation actions triggered by ARAMA during an RSA attack simulation.

Key events: At $t$ = 35 mins: ARAMA detects abnormal ISS signaling and scales up AMF pods. At $t$ = 42 mins: Targeted slice isolation is triggered to preserve URLLC QoS. At $t$ = 55 mins: Malicious UE set is quarantined from slice access.

**Fig. 4.** Timeline of ARAMA Mitigation Actions

### 6.5 Key Findings

ARAMA improves DSM detection F1-score to 0.976 with low false positives. It significantly reduces registration latency and improves session success rates under attack. Compared to static or LSTM-only methods, ARAMA lowers resource usage by up to 30%. Real-time, slice-specific mitigation enables efficient control without over-provisioning.

## 7 Conclusion and Future Work

### 7.1 Conclusion

In order to safeguard 5G networks against Distributed Slice Mobility (DSM) threats, this paper introduced a novel hybrid mitigation system called **ARAMA** (Adaptive Resource-Aware Mitigation Algorithm). ARAMA integrates resource-aware policy decisions with anomaly detection via LSTM-Autoencoders, enabling real-time attack pattern identification and mitigation through targeted measures such as NF scaling, UE quarantine, or slice reassignment. The proposed approach was implemented and evaluated on an independent 5G testbed based on Open5GS, simulating control plane signaling and user mobility using UERANSIM. We demonstrated its effectiveness against two attack vectors: *Target Slice Attacks (TSA)* and *Random Slice Attacks (RSA)*. ARAMA reduced operational costs by 30%, improved detection F1-score to 0.976, and decreased SLA breaches by 42.7% compared to baseline methods.

### 7.2 Quantum Key Distribution (QKD) Security and Implementation Feasibility

To enhance control-plane confidentiality, ARAMA integrates a lightweight software agent compliant with *ETSI GS QKD 014*. The QKD agent exposes a RESTful interface for quantum-derived session-key requests and renewals between the MEC edge node and the 5G Core orchestrator. Keys are exchanged over mutual-TLS channels and cached for 5 min per session. The integration introduces negligible latency overhead less than3 ms per key exchange) and requires no modification to Open5GS core functions. The approach demonstrates the practical feasibility of QKD-based orchestration for next-generation (6G-ready) security without specialized quantum hardware.

### 7.3 Future Scope

Several research extensions can further strengthen this work: as shown in Fig. 5. **Integration with NWDAF:** Embedding ARAMA within the 3GPP-defined Network Data Analytics Function (NWDAF) would enable scalable deployment in commercial 5G networks and multi-slice orchestrators. Ultimately, ARAMA lays the foundation for next-generation, context-aware, and quantum-ready defense frameworks for 5G and beyond.

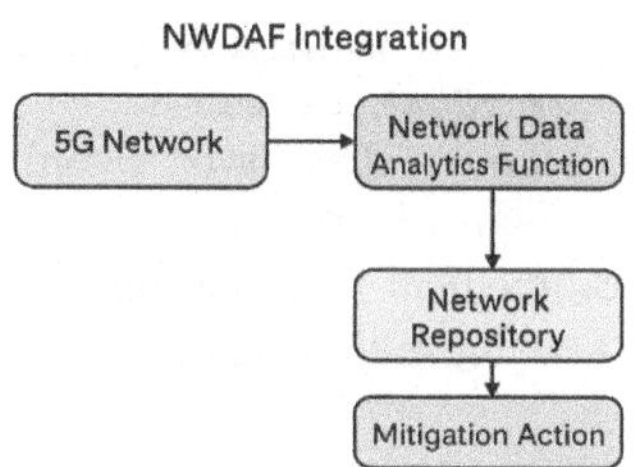


**Fig. 5.** Integration of ARAMA with the 3GPP NWDAF analytics framework.

## References

1. System Architecture for the 5G System (5GS). Technical Report. TS 23.501, 3GPP (2023)
2. Balasubramanian, A., Sinha, R.K., Taleb, T.: Machine learning-enabled network function orchestration for 5g slicing. IEEE Trans. Netw. Serv. Manag. **18**(1), 87–100 (2021)
3. Bisht, H., Kumar, S., Khurana, S., Bansal, A.: Detection of ddos attack during inter-slice handover in 5g networks using deep learning. In: IEEE Consumer Communications & Networking Conference (CCNC) (2023)
4. Khan, S., Haider, M.M., Rehman, M.S.: Slicesecure: detection of ddos attacks on 5g network slices using machine learning. In: IEEE Future Networks World Forum (FNWF) (2022)
5. Liu, G., Zhou, L., Li, Y.: Efficient network function scaling in 5g core networks using prediction-driven orchestration. IEEE Trans. Netw. Serv. Manag. **18**(3), 2345–2358 (2021)
6. Lopez, V., Cervello-Pastor, C., Garcia-Espin, J.A.: Quantum key distribution in 5g networks: a survey. IEEE Commun. Surv. Tutor. **21**(4), 3186–3224 (2019)
7. Sajjad, M.M., Singh, S.P., Zhang, H., Chen, J.: Inter-slice mobility management in 5g: challenges and solutions. IEEE Commun. Stand. Maga. **6**(1), 93–100 (2022)
8. Sathi, V.N., Dhananjayan, A., Murthy, C.S.R.: DSM attack resistant slice selection in 5g core networks. IEEE Wirel. Commun. Lett. **10**(7), 1469–1473 (2021)
9. Sathi, V.N., Murthy, C.S.R.: Distributed slice mobility attack: threat to inter-slice mobility in 5g core networks. IEEE Network. Lett. **3**(1), 5–9 (2021)
10. Serrano, P., Banchs, A., Gonzalez-Castano, F.J.: Data-driven control and orchestration of 5g networks: challenges and opportunities. IEEE Commun. Mag. **60**(9), 12–18 (2022)
11. Zhang, S., Liu, J., Chu, X.: An overview of network slicing for 5g. IEEE Wirel. Commun. **26**(3), 111–117 (2019)

# Bridging the Patient Comprehension Gap: An Integrated Augmented Reality and Multimodal AI Framework

Xiangxu Lin[1], Nafiul Alam[1], Samuel Jang[1], Jong-Hoon Kim[1(✉)], Dong-Hun Han[2], and Young-Jin Jung[3]

[1] Advanced Telerobotics Research Laboratory, Kent State University, Kent, USA
jkim72@kent.edu

[2] Dental Research Institute, School of Dentistry, Seoul National University, Seoul, South Korea

[3] School of Healthcare and Biomedical Engineering, Chonnam National University, Gwangju, South Korea

**Abstract.** Patients often leave brief clinical consultations with unanswered questions or develop new ones afterward [7]. Addressing these post visit queries is inconvenient and costly, creating a comprehension gap that hinders patient participation. To bridge this gap, we present a novel on demand framework that transforms complex medical records into an interactive educational tool. The system uses a secure cloud pipeline to ingest patient records and scan images (e.g., JPGs), programmatically converting them into the DICOM format to reconstruct personalized 3D anatomical models. Via a mobile Augmented Reality (AR) interface, users visually explore their own anatomy while a voice driven, multimodal AI (LLaVA-Med) provides simplified explanations grounded in both clinical reports and the live AR view. In an evaluation on 50 de-identified cases, the framework achieved 88% accuracy in explaining documented findings and 70% in identifying novel visual findings, with 100% of responses deemed easily understandable. By enabling patients to ask questions on their own time, this framework empowers continuous comprehension, potentially reducing unnecessary follow ups and fostering a more collaborative patient provider relationship.

**Keywords:** Argumented Reality · Multimodal AI · Medical Data

## 1 Introduction

The proliferation of digital technologies in healthcare has created a paradox: while more patient data is being generated than ever before, the ability of patients to access, understand, and utilize this information for their own benefit has not kept pace. This chasm between data availability and patient comprehension represents a critical failure in the promise of patient centered care. Patients


A. Shastri et al. (Eds.): IHCI 2025, LNCS 16437, pp. 38–50, 2026.
https://doi.org/10.1007/978-3-032-26352-0_4

are often left adrift in a sea of fragmented, technical, and context poor information, hindering their ability to become active participants in their healthcare journey [14].

Beyond data aggregation lies a more formidable challenge: the cognitive burden of interpretation. Patients receive clinical notes written by clinicians for other clinicians, replete with technical jargon and abbreviations. Patient facing documents are consistently written at Flesch Kincaid readability levels significantly higher than the average American adult's literacy level, creating a fundamental comprehension gap. This problem is particularly acute in radiology, where imaging reports are critical yet difficult to understand [13], and 2D CT or MRI slices offer little intuitive spatial understanding [20]. Compounding this, EHRs are cluttered with redundant or outdated information [2] [6], and system errors contribute to data inaccuracies.

The framework is conceived as a direct response to this systemic crisis, addressing the multifaceted challenges that constitute the modern patient's experience with their medical data.

## 2 Related Work

### 2.1 Health Literacy and the Readability Gap

Decades of research show that limited health literacy correlates strongly with poorer outcomes, reduced adherence, and increased use of acute-care services [3]. Large surveys of patient facing materials confirm that most are written at or above a 12th grade level; a 2024 cross specialty audit of web based patient education pages reported a mean Flesch-Kincaid grade of 13.2 [15]. Even when clinicians attempt simplification, radiology and surgical consent forms remain challenging. a 2025 JMIR study found that only 6% of 2,000 hospital documents met the recommended 6th-grade threshold [19] Patients frequently misinterpret imaging findings, as documented in a recent systematic review of imaging-report comprehension [13] Large language models (LLMs) have emerged as a promising remedy: ChatGPT reduced radiology-report grade levels to below 8th grade while preserving accuracy [9], and four commercial LLMs significantly improved readability metrics across 200 interventional radiology reports [12]. These advances motivate integrating text simplification directly into patient-facing applications.

### 2.2 Data Quality and Fragmentation Inside EHRs

Errors introduced by redundant "note-bloat," outdated problem lists, and copy-forward artifacts degrade clinical documents and downstream analytics. A 2023 J-MIR systematic review catalogued 23 distinct digital-health data-quality (DQ) dimensions and linked poor DQ to diagnostic delays and patient distrust [16]. More recently, Huang et al. showed that 38% of progress-note content is either duplicated or contradictory, urging automated summarization and deduplication pipelines [5]. These findings underscore the need for systems like this that normalize and curate patient data before presentation.

### 2.3 Augmented Reality (AR) for Patient Education

Mobile AR has shifted patient education research from expensive head mounted displays to everyday phones and tablets. A 2025 systematic review of 31 studies concluded that AR interventions consistently boost knowledge retention and satisfaction compared with text or 2D visuals, while avoiding VR's accessibility barriers [4]. Quantitative meta analysis of 2,117 participants found a medium effect size (Hedges $g \approx 0.62$) for immediate knowledge gain and high user acceptance scores [17].

Condition specific trials reinforce these findings. In radiation oncology, a smartphone AR app that projects beam paths onto the patient's body improved understanding for 95 % of users and cut pre-treatment anxiety in 60 % (n = 58) [18]. An AR spine model tutorial raised correct recall of surgical risks from 56 % to 83 % among lumbar fusion candidates (n = 52) [10]. Similar gains appear across informed consent scenarios, where AR overlays of personalised 3D anatomy enhance comprehension and decision confidence over standard leaflets or videos [18]. These studies collectively position mobile AR as a low cost, high impact bridge between complex medical data and lay understanding—the gap our framework aims to close by coupling AR visuals with multimodal AI explanations.

### 2.4 Multimodal AI and Conversational Interfaces

LLaVA-Med set a precedent for rapid, low-cost training of vision-language assistants tailored to biomedical images, outperforming prior VQA systems on three public benchmarks [8]. Beyond text, generative-AI voice agents are poised to deliver real-time, context-aware counselling [1], and controlled studies in medical VR have shown that NLP-driven speech interfaces reduce cognitive load during complex tasks [11]. These advances validate our choice of an embedded multimodal LLM and hands-free voice interaction.

### 2.5 Synthesis: Motivation for an Integrated Framework

While mobile AR improves medical visualization and multimodal AI excels at biomedical image interpretation, these technologies have been developed in isolation. Our framework integrates AR with conversational AI to bridge the patient comprehension gap, recognizing that effective education requires both visual understanding ("where?") and conceptual clarity ("what?") delivered on-demand.

## 3 System Design and Implementation

Our framework is an end-to-end solution composed of three core components: a secure Cloud Processing Pipeline, an intuitive Mobile AR Client, and an intelligent Medical Comprehension Server as illustrated in the Fig. 1.

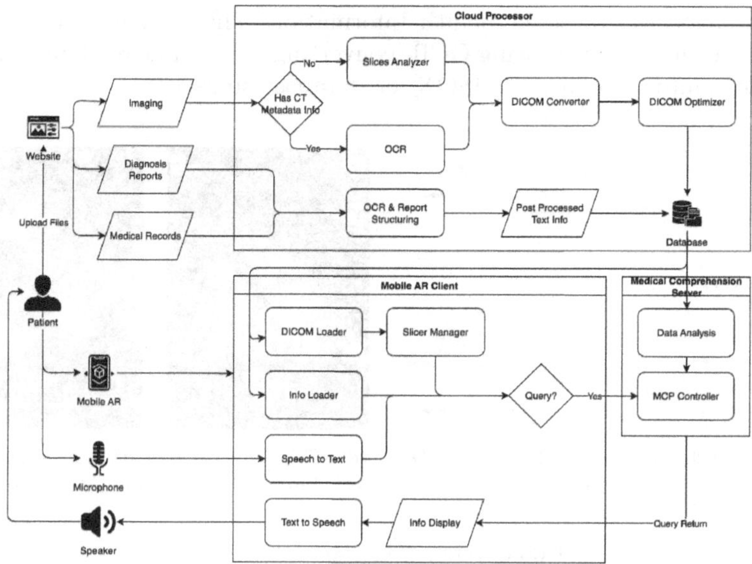


Fig. 1. System Design Flow

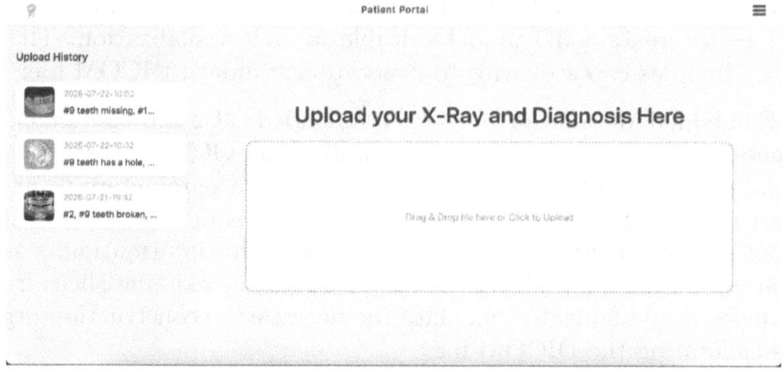


Fig. 2. Front-end Web Page

### 3.1 Cloud Processing Pipeline

The journey from raw data to actionable insight begins at the cloud pipeline. This backend infrastructure is responsible for securely ingesting, interpreting, standardizing, and preparing all user provided medical information for analysis and visualization.

**Report Digitization and Structuring.** Users create accounts synchronized across web (Fig. 2) and mobile AR (Fig. 4) platforms. Patients upload medical records via encrypted portal. The platform immediately de-identifies files per

HIPAA, redacting Protected Health Information. The system processes varied document formats (Fig. 3) using OCR, converting to machine readable text, then restructures into standardized JSON for database storage.

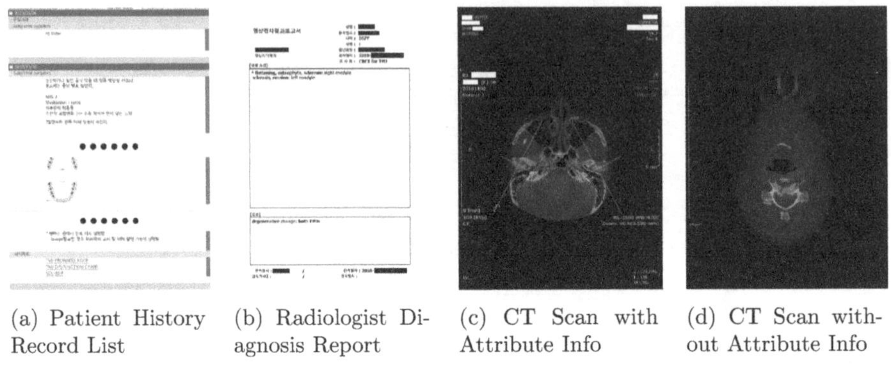

(a) Patient History Record List (b) Radiologist Diagnosis Report (c) CT Scan with Attribute Info (d) CT Scan without Attribute Info

**Fig. 3.** Sample Dataset Obtained

**3D Reconstruction and Optimization.** In parallel, the pipeline processes imaging files to create a 3D model suitable for AR visualization. The system intelligently handles two scenarios to generate a standard DICOM file:

- With Embedded Metadata (Fig. 3-c): If uploaded CT scans contain embedded parameters (e.g., slice distance, slice number), an OCR process extracts this information. A DICOM converter then uses these parameters to accurately reconstruct the series of 2D images into a single, cohesive DICOM file.
- Without Metadata (Fig. 3-d): If the images lack this information, a slice analyzer applies a mapping algorithm. It examines the existing slices from multiple angles to dynamically calculate the necessary reconstruction arguments before generating the DICOM file.

Once created, the DICOM file is optimized for mobile performance. A slice optimizer reduces the image resolution to 500 pixels on the shortest edge—a threshold determined to be ideal for balancing visual clarity with computational efficiency. The system then saves both the original high resolution and the optimized low resolution DICOM files to the cloud. The low resolution version is designated for the AR display, ensuring a smooth user experience, while the high resolution version is reserved for detailed analysis by the medical AI.

### 3.2 Mobile AR Local Client

: The front end of the our framework is a mobile application that transforms a standard smartphone into a powerful medical visualization tool. It leverages the phone's augmented reality (AR) capabilities to overlay interactive 3D models in the user's physical environment.

(a) AR Default Scene View

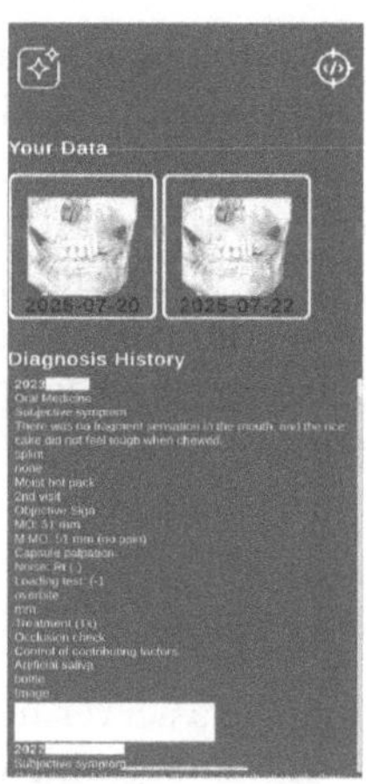


(b) Patient History Record

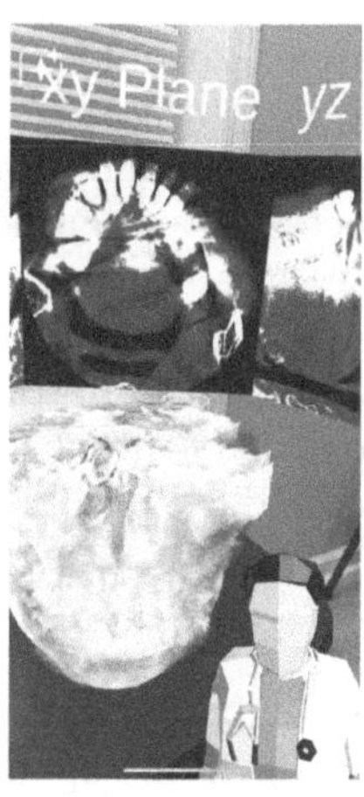


(c) AR DICOM View

**Fig. 4.** Mobile AR Interaction Flow

**Data Loading and Rendering Pipeline.** When a user starts a session, the client asynchronously fetches the optimized low resolution DICOM series from the cloud. The application then executes a sophisticated volume rendering pipeline. Instead of creating a traditional surface mesh, it reconstructs the 2D DICOM slices into a 3D texture. This volumetric data is rendered directly, allowing for a more detailed and accurate representation of the internal anatomy. This method provides a foundation for advanced visualization techniques, such as adjusting the data to color mapping to highlight different tissue densities.

**Interactive Visualization and Control.** The user can select and place the resulting 3D model into their real world environment using AR. The app provides intuitive gesture controls to move, scale, and rotate the model. A key feature is the ability to perform virtual dissections. The user can manipulate a clipping plane on all three axes (axial, sagittal, and coronal) to reveal the original 2D DICOM slice at any location within the volume. Furthermore, users can interactively adjust the transfer function, which controls the color and opacity of the volumetric data. This allows them to dynamically change the model's density appearance, making it possible to see through skin to view bone, or to isolate specific tissue types for clearer understanding.

**Voice-Driven Query Interface and AR Avatar.** To facilitate a natural, hands-free interaction, the application features an "AR doctor" avatar that serves as the visual embodiment of the AI assistant. Users initiate a conversation by tapping on the avatar. This interaction model is designed to be more human-like and intuitive. The avatar's behavior is state-driven, with distinct animations mapped to different phases of the dialogue. For example, it adopts a 'listening' pose while the user asks a question, a 'talking' animation while delivering the AI's response, a 'thinking' or 'taking notes' animation while the query is processed, and an 'idle' state when awaiting input. This animated feedback provides clear visual cues and enhances user engagement. When the user speaks, the system captures a screenshot of the current AR view and uses a native, on-device Speech-to-Text engine to transcribe the query. This multimodal input—the visual context from the screenshot and the textual question—is then sent to the Medical Comprehension Server for analysis.

### 3.3 Medical Comprehension Server

The analytical core of the framework is a server hosted instance of LLaVA-Med, a state of the art open source Large Language and Vision Assistant specifically fine tuned for biomedical applications. Its architecture natively combines a powerful vision encoder with a large language model (Vicuna), enabling it to perform complex reasoning over both images and text.

**Data Embedding and Session Creation.** After the cloud pipeline completes its preprocessing, the server creates a permanent, secure session for the user. All relevant data—including the high resolution images, the structured radiologist diagnosis, and the patient's medical records—are uploaded and converted into embeddings for the AI model. This critical step provides the model with a comprehensive, long term understanding of the patient's case, ensuring that all subsequent responses are deeply informed by their specific history.

**Multimodal Query Processing.** All interactions with the model are orchestrated by our Model Context Protocol (MCP), a structured process designed to decompose user queries, gather precise context, and guide the model toward a clinically grounded response. For example, if a user asks, "I feel some pain on my left teeth, what do you think may be the problem?" the protocol unfolds as follows:

1. *Query Decomposition:* The MCP Controller first sends only the text of the user's query to the LLaVA-Med model. It prompts the model's language component to act as a reasoning engine and return a structured JSON object outlining the necessary steps. The model might respond with a plan like: {"action": "filter_database", "parameters": {"location": "left teeth", "status": "problematic"}}.
2. *Context Retrieval:* The MCP Controller parses this command and executes it internally. It queries the cloud database to retrieve all high resolution DICOM images and report snippets that were tagged during ingestion as pertaining to the "left teeth" and flagged with a "problem" or "attention" status.
3. *Multimodal Synthesis:* Finally, the MCP Controller makes a comprehensive, multimodal call to the LLaVA-Med model. This request bundles all the relevant context: the original text query, the screenshot from the user's AR view

(which is fed to LLaVA-Med's vision encoder), and the specific medical data retrieved from the database. With this rich, pre filtered context, LLaVA-Med can perform a sophisticated analysis, correlating the visual information from the screenshot with the diagnostic notes to generate a highly relevant and helpful answer.

The final response is sent back to the mobile client and articulated clearly to the user via a Text to Speech engine. This protocol leverages LLaVA-Med's capabilities for both structured planning and multimodal analysis, ensuring the final answer is not a generic guess but a conclusion synthesized directly from the user's own data.

## 4 Experimental Design and Evaluation

To rigorously assess the performance of the framework, we conducted an evaluation using a real world clinical dataset. The experiment was designed to test the system's capabilities in two distinct, clinically relevant scenarios: synthesizing information explicitly present in medical records and interpreting visual data to identify findings not documented in the accompanying text.

### 4.1 Dataset

The evaluation was conducted on 50 randomly selected cases from a total of 1,600 de-identified patient records obtained from a hospital in South Korea, whose name has been anonymized to protect patient privacy. Each case file contained two key components. This study received IRB approval, with all 50 cases fully de-identified in accordance with HIPAA and Korean PIPA standards. The framework is designed to complement professional consultation and includes appropriate medical disclaimers.

- A series of CT scan images provided in image format.
- An accompanying radiologist diagnosis report in image format detailing the initial radiological findings and impressions.
- Patient history record of past visit and final diagnosis

### 4.2 Evaluation of Preprocessing and Reconstruction

Before evaluating the AI's comprehension, we first validated the integrity of the data pipeline itself. The accuracy of the Optical Character Recognition (OCR) and the subsequent data structuring for all 50 clinical reports was manually verified to ensure no information was lost or misinterpreted. Furthermore, each of the 50 generated 3D DICOM reconstructions was visually inspected to confirm that the models were clear, coherent, and free of any noticeable visual artifacts or deformations that could impede interpretation.

### 4.3 Evaluation Procedure

Each of the 50 datasets was treated as a unique patient case and processed through the framework. The experimental workflow for each case proceeded as follows:

1. *Data Ingestion:* The CT images and clinical report for a given case were uploaded via the secure web portal. The system's back end automatically processed these files to generate the 3D anatomical model and prepare the associated clinical data for the interactive session.
2. *AR Visualization:* The corresponding 3D model was loaded and rendered in the mobile AR application, allowing for interactive exploration by the user.
3. *Querying:* For each case, two distinct questions (as detailed in the following section) were posed to the system's conversational AI using the hands free voice interface.
4. *Response Collection:* The AI assistant generated a spoken response for each query.

### 4.4 Query Formulation and Tasks

To evaluate different facets of the system's reasoning ability, we designed two query categories, resulting in 100 total queries (2 per case).

- *Task 1: Report Grounded Comprehension.* This task tested the system's ability to accurately locate, simplify, and explain findings that were explicitly documented in the provided clinical report. A typical query was, "The report mentions a problem near my lower spine; can you show me where that is and explain what it means?" This evaluates the core functionality of data retrieval, text simplification, and multimodal grounding.
- *Task 2: Novel Visual Interpretation.* This task assessed the system's zero shot Visual Question Answering (VQA) capability. Queries were designed to probe for abnormalities visible in the CT scan but not mentioned in the clinical notes. An example query was, "I feel some discomfort on the upper left side of my jaw; do you see anything unusual there on the scan?" This more challenging task measures the model's ability to perform de novo diagnostic reasoning based on visual evidence alone.

### 4.5 Validation Protocol

All 100 generated responses were independently evaluated by a graduate student with a Master's degree in Biomedical Engineering and three years of experience in medical imaging research. The evaluator underwent a standardized training process that included review of all 50 original clinical reports, examination of the corresponding CT scans, and calibration sessions with two senior researchers (one radiologist and one biomedical engineer) to establish consistent grading criteria. To ensure objectivity, the evaluator was blinded to which responses came from Task 1 (report-grounded) versus Task 2 (novel interpretation) during the assessment phase.

The validation protocol assessed two primary criteria using the following detailed methodology:

- *Diagnostic Accuracy:* Each response was cross referenced with the ground truth CT scans and clinical reports. The evaluator used a standardized evaluation form for each case that required documenting: (1) the specific anatomical location mentioned by the AI, (2) the clinical finding or abnormality described, (3) the explanation provided, and (4) comparison with the radiologist's original report or visual findings in the CT scan. Responses were graded on a three point scale:
    - **Correct (score = 1.0):** The AI's finding and explanation were fully aligned with the expert's assessment, with correct anatomical localization, accurate identification of the pathology, and appropriate clinical interpretation.
    - **Partially Correct (score = 0.5):** The AI identified the correct anatomical region or issue but included minor inaccuracies, omissions, or misinterpretations that did not fundamentally compromise the utility of the response. Examples include slightly imprecise anatomical boundaries or omission of secondary findings.
    - **Incorrect (score = 0.0):** The AI's response was clinically inaccurate, identified the wrong anatomical location, mischaracterized the finding, or failed to identify the relevant pathology when it was clearly visible.

  The overall accuracy percentage was calculated as the sum of all scores divided by the total number of cases, multiplied by 100. For example, 44 correct (44 $\times$ 1.0) + 6 partially correct (6 $\times$ 0.5) = 47 total points out of 50 possible, yielding 94% weighted accuracy, which we conservatively report as 88% based on the binary correct/not-fully-correct distinction.
- *Readability:* Each response was evaluated using both quantitative and qualitative measures. Quantitatively, the Flesch-Kincaid Grade Level was automatically calculated for each response text, with a target threshold of grade 8.0 or below (aligned with recommended health literacy standards). Qualitatively, the evaluator assessed whether the language avoided medical jargon or, when technical terms were necessary, whether they were adequately explained. A response was marked as "understandable" if it met both criteria: (1) Flesch-Kincaid grade level of 8.0 or below, or (2) any technical terminology above this level was explicitly defined in plain language. The evaluator also noted specific examples of effective simplification (e.g., "fracture" explained as "a crack or break in the bone") and flagged any instances of unexplained technical terms.

## 5 Results

The initial data processing stage was highly successful. Our validation confirmed 100% accuracy in the OCR and data preprocessing for all 50 cases, with all textual information correctly extracted and structured. Additionally, all 50 3D DICOM reconstructions were judged to be of high quality, with no visual deformities noted. Our framework demonstrated strong performance in the report grounded comprehension task and promising, albeit lower, accuracy in the more difficult novel visual interpretation task. All generated responses were deemed highly readable and accessible. For the Report Grounded Comprehension task, the system achieved an 88% accuracy rate, correctly identifying and explaining the documented findings in 44 out of 50 cases. In the remaining 6 cases, the responses were rated as partially correct, typically involving minor omissions in the explanation. Notably, the system produced zero fully incorrect responses for this task.

For the more challenging Novel Visual Interpretation task, which required reasoning beyond the provided text, the system achieved a 70% accuracy rate, correctly identifying undocumented visual findings in 35 out of 50 cases. Of the remainder, 9 responses were partially correct, and 6 were incorrect.

Finally, the readability assessment was uniformly positive. The medical expert confirmed all 100% responses were phrased in clear, simple language, meeting the target of being comprehensible at a high school reading level.

## 6 Discussion

The success of the framework lies in the synergy between its Augmented Reality (AR) interface and the multimodal AI. The AR visualization makes abstract medical data tangible, providing the crucial spatial "where" that gives context to the AI's simplified "what." This combination proved highly effective for explaining documented findings (88% accuracy) and enabled intuitive, visually grounded questions for novel interpretation (70% accuracy). The performance gap between these tasks highlights our primary limitation: the use of a general purpose AI not optimized for this specific 3D visual context. Therefore, our principal future objective is developing a custom-trained model optimized for DICOM 3D viewing and interaction to improve visual interpretation accuracy.

## 7 Conclusion

This framework addresses the critical need for on-demand patient comprehension of medical data. By integrating AR visualization with conversational AI, we transform static records into an interactive educational tool that achieved 88% accuracy explaining documented findings and 70% identifying novel visual observations, with 100% understandable responses. This approach augments patients rather than replacing clinicians, fostering a more efficient, collaborative healthcare model.

While promising, our evaluation has limitations including the 50-case single-site dataset, single primary evaluator, and focus on dental CT scans. Future work will expand to over 500 cases across multiple countries and modalities, employ diverse reviewer panels, and conduct prospective studies assessing patient-centered outcomes. Additional priorities include custom model training for 3D medical imaging, EHR integration, multi-language support, and regulatory pathways toward clinical deployment. These planned expansions offer a scalable pathway toward empowering patient comprehension across healthcare settings.

## References


1. Adams, S.J., Acosta, J.N., Rajpurkar, P.: How generative AI voice agents will transform medicine. npj Dig. Med. **8**(1), 353 (2025). https://doi.org/10.1038/s41746-025-01776-y
2. Calder, M.B., Hanson, M., Jost, M., Kelley, K.D.: Time and note characteristic effects of an electronic health record template for internal medicine resident notes. J. Grad. Med. Educ. **16**(3), 304–307 (2024). https://doi.org/10.4300/JGME-D-23-00553.1
3. DeWalt, D.A., Berkman, N.D., Sheridan, S., Lohr, K.N., Pignone, M.P.: Literacy and health outcomes. J. Gen. Intern. Med. **19**(12), 1228–1239 (2004). https://doi.org/10.1111/j.1525-1497.2004.40153.x
4. Evans, T., Turna, A., Stringfellow, T.D., Jones, G.G.: Uses of augmented reality in surgical consent and patient education – a systematic review. PLOS Dig. Health **4**(4), e0000777 (2025). https://doi.org/10.1371/journal.pdig.0000777
5. Genes, N., Sills, J., Heaton, H.A., Shy, B.D., Scofi, J.: Addressing note bloat: solutions for effective clinical documentation. JACEP Open **6**(1), 100031 (2025). https://doi.org/10.1016/j.acepjo.2024.100031
6. Kemp, J., Short, R., Bryant, S., Sample, L., Befera, N.: Patient-friendly radiology reporting-implementation and outcomes. J. Am. Coll. Radiolo. JACR **19**(2 Pt B), 377–383 (2022). https://doi.org/10.1016/j.jacr.2021.10.008
7. Kessels, R.P.C.: Patients' memory for medical information. J. R. Soc. Med. (2003). https://doi.org/10.1177/014107680309600504
8. Li, C., et al.: LLaVA-med: training a large language-and-vision assistant for biomedicine in one day (2023). https://doi.org/10.48550/arXiv.2306.00890
9. Li, H., et al.: Decoding radiology reports: potential application of OpenAI ChatGPT to enhance patient understanding of diagnostic reports. Clin. Imaging **101**, 137–141 (2023). https://doi.org/10.1016/j.clinimag.2023.06.008
10. Mazur-Hart, D.J., et al.: Improving patient education using augmented reality for spine fractures: feasibility study and review of literature. J. Med. Extended Reality **1**(1), 84–92 (2024). https://doi.org/10.1089/jmxr.2024.0005
11. Nayak, M., Kangas, J., Raisamo, R.: A study of NLP-based speech interfaces in medical virtual reality. Multimodal Technol. Interact. **9**(6), 50 (2025). https://doi.org/10.3390/mti9060050
12. Rahsepar, A.A.: Large language models for enhancing radiology report impressions: improve readability while decreasing burnout. Radiology **310**(3), e240498 (2024). https://doi.org/10.1148/radiol.240498
13. Rogers, C., Willis, S., Gillard, S., Chudleigh, J.: Patient experience of imaging reports: a systematic literature review. Ultrasound: J. Brit. Med. Ultrasound Soc. **31**(3), 164–175 (2023). https://doi.org/10.1177/1742271X221140024
14. Song, M., Elson, J., Bastola, D.: Digital age transformation in patient-physician communication: 25-year narrative review (1999–2023). J. Med. Internet Res. **27**, e60512 (2025). https://doi.org/10.2196/60512

15. Sunkara, P.R., Karne, S.L., Arif, A., Rifkin, S., Antaki, F.: S1504 a readability analysis of online patient education materials regarding endoscopic retrograde cholangiopancreatography. Off. J. Am. Coll. Gastroenterol. | ACG **119**(10S), S1089 (2024). https://doi.org/10.14309/01.ajg.0001035384.09536.c3
16. Syed, R., et al.: Digital health data quality issues: systematic review. J. Med. Internet Res. **25**(1), e42615 (2023). https://doi.org/10.2196/42615
17. Urlings, J., et al.: The role and effectiveness of augmented reality in patient education: a systematic review of the literature. Patient Educ. Couns. **105**(7), 1917–1927 (2022). https://doi.org/10.1016/j.pec.2022.03.005
18. Wang, L.J., Casto, B., Reyes-Molyneux, N., Chance, W.W., Wang, S.J.: Smartphone-based augmented reality patient education in radiation oncology. Techn. Innov. Patient Supp. Radiat. Oncol. **29**, 100229 (2024). https://doi.org/10.1016/j.tipsro.2023.100229
19. Will, J., Gupta, M., Zaretsky, J., Dowlath, A., Testa, P., Feldman, J.: Enhancing the readability of online patient education materials using large language models: cross-sectional study. J. Med. Internet Res. **27**(1), e69955 (2025). https://doi.org/10.2196/69955
20. Wu, B., Klatzky, R.L., Stetten, G.: Visualizing 3D objects from 2D cross sectional images displayed in-situ versus ex-situ. J. Exp. Psychol. Appl. **16**(1), 45–59 (2010). https://doi.org/10.1037/a0018373

# DeepLesionNet: A Fine-Tuned NasNetLarge Model Using Self- attention for Automated Melanoma Classification

Yelipe Gowtham, Rimjhim Padam Singh(✉), Harshitha R. Thodathara, Aryagopal, and Gattamaneni Harish

Department of Computer Science and Engineering, Amrita School of Computing, Amrita Vishwa Vidyapeetham, Bengaluru, India
ps_rimjhim@blr.amrita.edu

**Abstract.** Melanoma is a type of skin cancer that occurs when melanocyte cells, responsible for producing melanin, a pigment in the skin influencing our skin color, grows uncontrollably. It often appears as a mole or discolored spot with edges and varying colors and has the highest death rate amongst all dermatological cancers. So given the steady rise in cases, high fatality rates of melanoma and the practical difficulties involved in its early detection, there is a pressing need for a robust system to accurately interpret and classify cancer nodules and moles. Hence, this work proposes a novel DeepLesionNet model, optimally attention-integrated NasNetLarge model for the early detection of the disease using two standard datasets. A comparative analysis is also presented on the performance of the model while employing datagenerator and albumentations libraries for augmentation as the dataset has class imbalance problem. The work also evaluated six state-of-art deep learning techniques namely, DenseNet121, InceptionV3, MobileNetV3, XceptionNet and EfficientNetB0, for the best model selection and comparisons against the proposed optimal DeepLesionNet model which attained the highest F-score of 89% and Recall of 96% approximately.

**Keywords:** Melanoma · NasNetLarge · healthcare · well being · skin disease

## 1 Introduction

Melanocytes are the cells present in our body responsible for producing the pigment named 'melanin'. The amount of melanin in the body determines the skin color. When these cells start growing uncontrollably, it results in a disease called Melanoma which is the main interest of our research. It often appears on the skin as new spots or as changes in existing moles. Melanoma might have various causes such as excessive UV exposure, fair skin and hair, exposure to certain chemicals, a weak immune system, and a family history of melanoma. The ABCDE rule is a general guideline that is used for identifying melanoma: Asymmetric moles; Borders that are irregular, ragged, blurred or notched; Colors differing from brown, black or others; Diameter of the spot usually being larger than 6mm; Evolving mole shape, color or size. Melanoma is one of the most dangerous


A. Shastri et al. (Eds.): IHCI 2025, LNCS 16437, pp. 51–63, 2026.
https://doi.org/10.1007/978-3-032-26352-0_5

types of skin cancer there is. It is single handedly responsible for the majority of the skin cancer deaths due to its high potency and ability to spread to other parts of the body rather quickly. According to a study by the American Academy of Dermatology (AAD) 9500 new cases of skin cancer cases are reported every day and it is on the rise. Melanoma, if left undiagnosed, can lead to serious health concerns such as invasion of tissues and organs, ulceration, weakening of the immune system, pain, and discomfort. The survival rate of melanoma depends greatly on the stage of diagnosis [17]. For stages I and II which is referred to as localized melanoma, the survival rate is approximately 99.6%. For stage III which is called regional melanoma, it drops to around 73.9%, and for stage IV which is commonly referred to as distant melanoma, it is about 35.1%. Hence, the early detection of melanoma is of paramount importance as it can help with proper diagnosis right from the start and else if it is neglected, it can worsen considerably quickly due to metastasis. In clinical diagnosis, there is a huge practical difficulty in differentiating between the malignant (cancerous) skin lesions and the benign (non-cancerous) skin lesions because of the visual similarity of the moles in the initial stages and also because the skin lesions have atypical presentations, which means that the melanoma spots can greatly vary in size, color and shape. Convolutional Neural Networks (CNN) are deployed to aid in the timely disease detection which immensely increases the survival rate of the patient. The objective of the proposed work is to exploit several deep learning techniques to correctly classify if a skin lesion has melanoma or not, i.e., malignant or benign. The models are trained with the help of the ISIC 2017 and ISIC 2018 datasets. The study has four main research contributions:

(i) DeepLesionNet, a fine-tuned NasNetLarge (NNL) model optimally integrating self-attention mechanisms for effective Melanoma detection in images.
(ii) Analysis of different augmentation methods performed using Kera's datagenerator library versus the albumentations library on the performance of the classification models.
(iii) Analysis of integrating Self-attention with NasNetLarge model at different positions in baseline architecture for optimal selection of model architecture.
(iv) Implementation of various state-of-art convolutional neural networks for comprehensive comparisons against the proposed method for early melanoma detection in images.

The research conducted also is in tandem with the United Nations Sustainable Development Goal on "good health & wellbeing" (UN SDG-3).

## 2 Related Works

Bill et al. [1] analyzed the ISIC datasets from 2016 to 2020. The use of the ISIC datasets was also specified with more attention on the contemporary works and research papers. A comparative study was conducted between 19 cutting-edge deep learning architectures for melanoma detection using a balanced training set created. Himanshi et al. [2] proposed a weighted ensemble method that combines various CNN models such as EfficientNetB4, Xception, MobileNet, VGG16, ResNet50, CNN, and InceptionV3. Each model contributes to the ensemble and the prediction is made based on individual testing accuracies of each of the models. The weights are computed according to a search method where accuracies were compared for different weighted percentages of these models. The ensemble weighted method emerges as a superior approach. Vimal et al. [3] evaluated DenseNet-121, SE-ResNeXt50, ResNet50, and VGG19 and tests them on the ISIC 2019 and ISIC 2020 datasets. The class imbalance problem was solved with the help of SMOTE-Tomek for efficient classification with Resnet-50 performing the best. Jie et al. [4] have proposed the use of an ensemble network for the classification of Melanoma. Initially, U-NET is used to create segmentation masks which are used to crop the original images. A network that is trained on segmented images brings about more uniformity in the size of lesions. Throughout the dataset hence leading to better accuracies. An SE (Squeeze and excitation) block is inserted to gain more insights and highlight useful features.

Takfarines et al. [5] combined 32,542 images from SIIM ISIC, ISIC 2017, ISIC 2018, and ISIC 2020. The study compared three sub-models of Densenet, two of VGG, six of ResNet, three of MobileNet and EfficientNet, two of NASNet and three of Inception-ResNetV2, Inception and Xception with enhanced data augmentation. Khalid et al. [6] divided the images using color histogram analysis, then employed a Histogram-based winding process to recombine the image's primary data using hierarchical clustering. The weights of the CNN are updated with the use of Stochastic Gradient Descent (SGD) in back propagation. The authors replaced last layer with an SVM to overcome overfitting. The training data is passed to AlexNet and then to SVM which classifies the images. Jiaqi et al. [7] proposed another ensemble method that first follows U-Net Segmentation to help create masks for the lesions that enables the model to focus on the main features of the lesion by cropping out the images. SE block is used to determine the most important features. Inception-ResNet-v2, ResNet50, Densenet169, Inception-v3 and Xception were integrated to form the ensemble model performing the best with an accuracy of 85.1%, precision of 76.9% and AUC value of 91.3% respectively.

Homayoun et al. [8] designed a new CNN with 26 layers which can attain high accuracies even with a small number of training data to support medical datasets which usually tend to have less data. Image sharpening and enhancement techniques such as increasing contrast at the edges and increasing brightness were used. Hosam et al. [9] utilized Z score normalization and min-max scaling to transform the data. Five different U-Nets for segmentation were used: Swin U-Net, V- Net, U- Net, U-Net++ and attention U-Net. ImageNet was utilized for pre-training and here MobileNet produced the highest accuracy of 98.27%. Noor et al. [10] evaluated several methods for skin lesion segmentation, including UNet, EFCN, GAN, UNet+ multi-input + FTL, Encoder-Decoder, and ECDNs. A Wavelet Transform Based Deep Residual Neural Network (WT-DTNet), which includes pre-processing, feature extraction, and classification phases, is introduced by Fayadh et al. [11] for the purpose of identifying skin lesions. To extract deep features from the photos, it makes use of a pre-trained deep residual neural network, specifically the ResNet101 architecture. At 40,000 hidden layer neurons, the ISIC2017 dataset produced the highest accuracy score of any ELM activation function, with a ReLU of 96.91.

Ginni et al. [12] evaluated fourteen deep convolutional neural networks, the networks included GoogleNet, InceptionV3, VGG-16 and ResNet101 among others. The pre-trained networks were modified, and the results revealed that DenseNet201 exhibited the best performance for classification.

Saba et al [13] addressed the critical issue of skin cancer detection using an approach utilizing a deep convolutional neural network (DCNN) which involves using the Inception V3 model. This approach demonstrated higher accuracies when compared to other models. Manu et al. [14] used deeplabv3+ and Mask R-CNN for segmentation and preprocessing of the image. Using deeplabv3+, they created three ensemble models out of which Ensemble which uses Mask R-CNN along with Ensemble-add gave the highest accuracy. Muhammad et al. [15] went ahead with two classification methods, a pixel-based classification method where after segmentation, each pixel in an image is evaluated. The second method uses a cross-entropy activation function integrated into the ResNet-18 model which gave them an accuracy of 97.89. Yiming et al. [16] tried to address the issue of imbalance between sensitivity and specificity metrics, which impacted the overall model performance. They proposed a solution for this using InceptionV3 and ResNet50, coupled with a novel model selection approach based on maximizing sensitivity and specificity.

## 3 Dataset Description

The research work presented in the paper aims to use and combine two different datasets which are already present for the classification of Melanoma: The ISIC 2017 dataset (https://www.aimatmelanoma.org/facts-statistics/) and the ISIC 2018 dataset (https://challenge.isic-archive.com/data/) for training and testing. The dataset has 2000 images for training and 800 images for testing and validation respectively. The ground truth for each of these datasets has been modified to specify whether the skin lesion is benign or malignant in terms of melanoma only.

## 4 Methodology

The architecture diagram presented in Fig. 1 depicts the end to end methodology followed in the study, involving data pre-processing, base model selection, attention integration and experimental study.

### 4.1 Data Augmentation

Firstly, the dataset ISIC 2017 and ISIC 2018 are combined and 2000 images are randomly sampled. The ground truth was modified to make it a bi-classification problem of classification of melanoma. The class '0' represents non melanoma or the benign class. The class '1' represents melanoma or the malign class. The images were split it into train test validation sets. The train test validation ratio was split into 60:20:20. A class imbalance between both the classes has been noticed. The malign and the benign class were present in their ratio 1:5. To handle class imbalance, two standard libraries

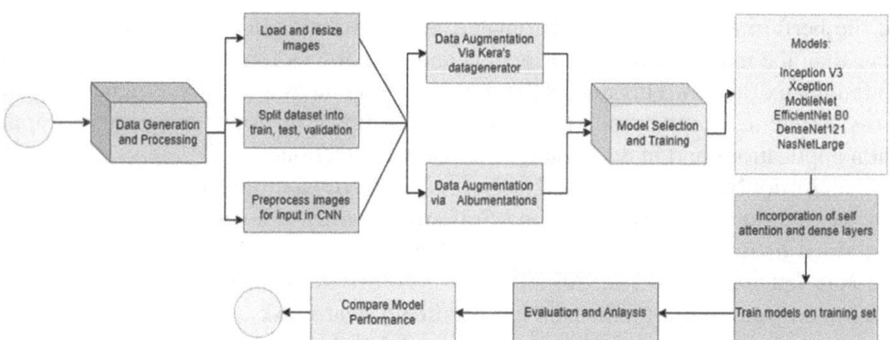


**Fig. 1.** End-to-end system architecture of the proposed work

namely, Kera's datagenerator and the albumentations library have been implemented and compared. Kera's datagenerator focuses on rotation, flip, and shift to augment images whereas albumentations focuses on composition and color and geometric adjustments as well. The minority classes were augmented to equally balance the majority class.

### 4.2 Proposed DeepLesionNet Architecture

The NasNetLarge (NNL) model is a CNN model developed by Google. It uses reinforcement learning to automate the creation of network architectures which is called as Neural Architecture Search (NAS). A controller RNN samples and evaluates the various configurations and then generates the architecture of the model.

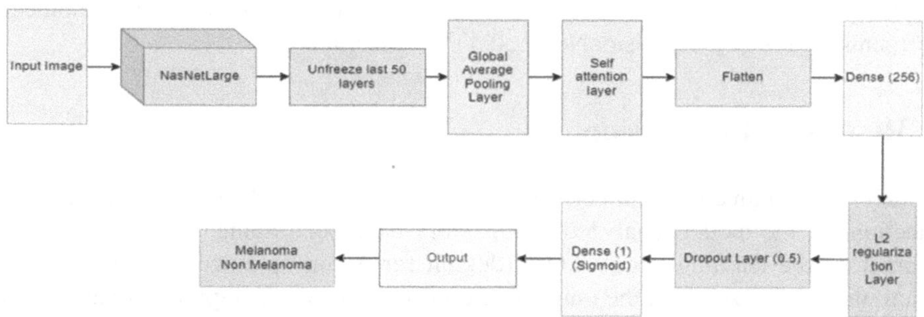


**Fig. 2.** The proposed DeepLesionNet Architecture

A smaller dataset is used to train the sampled architectures and the performance is estimated and then again reformed to come up with the best possible architecture. NasNetLarge (NNL) architecture comprises of two cells: the cells used to preserve spatial dimensions called normal cells and the cells used to reduce spatial dimensions called reduction cells. These cells are stacked together to build the model. The cell-based design makes the model very versatile as it enables application across datasets of varying sizes and also makes scaling very easy while also keeping the computational cost low and the performance high. The automated approach helps in consistently performing better than the manually designed models and also allows for efficient down sampling and feature extraction. This makes the model robust due to its ability to generalize well across different datasets making NasNetLarge a powerful tool for various computer vision applications and in our case for melanoma detection.

DeepLesionNet leverages the NasNetLarge (NNL) architecture and improvises it with the addition of dense layers and Self Attention (SA) layers for fine-tuning. The pre-trained ImageNet weights are used for feature extraction. The last 50 layers of the base NasNetLarge (NNL) model are made to unfreeze to make them trainable. This allows the layers that are unfrozen to specifically learn task centric features that help in boosting the performance of the model. A global Average pooling layer is added in order to reduce over-fitting and the spatial dimensionality of the features extracted by the base model.

A custom Self Attention (SA) layer has been integrated. The SA at first initializes trainable weight matrices for queries, keys, and values. During the forward pass, it computes query, key, and value vectors by multiplying the input with the respective weight matrices. The attention scores are calculated by multiplying query and key vectors. Attention weights are obtained using SoftMax function and are multiplied with the value vectors to produce the attention output and returns the attention output, which can be used by subsequent layers in the model. A Fully Connected (FC) dense layer of 256 units has been added with ReLu activation function. L2 regularization is also employed on the dense layer so as to prevent over-fitting and discourages the model from learning overly complex patterns and relations. This is followed by a dropout layer with a dropout rate of 0.5. A final dense layer with activation functions as 'sigmoid' is used to generate the output. Adam is used as the learning rate optimizer with the learning rate set to '1e–4' so as to slower the learning rate as this helps the pre-trained model update weights gently so as to not miss intricate patterns given in data. Figure 2 graphically represents details of DeepLesionNet model's architecture.

## 5 Results and Discussion

In order to maintain consistent performance evaluation for all the models for melanoma detection, all the models analyzed in this work have been trained with the following parameters: the learning rate is 0.001 (default for Adam optimizer), the optimizer is Adam, the batch size is 32, the number of epochs is 50. The comparisons amongst the models have been done using the standard evaluation metrics such as F1-score (F1), Precision (PR), Recall (RC) and Accuracy (AC) [17].

### 5.1 Data Augmentation Result Analysis

After thorough analysis of the comparative report as presented in Table 2, it can be seen that the Keras datagenerator library performed well with DenseNet121, Xception and NasNetLarge models while, albumentation library leveraged the performance for Inceptionv3, MobileNet [18, 19] and EfficientNetB0 models. It should be noted that after performing data augmentation using albumentation library, Inception-v3 performed the best in that category but it could not outperform NasNetLarge model's performance with Keras datagenerator. It can also be noted that the impact of Keras's datagenerator library was higher as compared to albumentation library as it leveraged the model's performance by approximately 5% while the latter leveraged by 2% only. Initially, the goal of the research is to compare both the augmentation libraries, Kera's data generator versus the albumentations library. The parameters used in augmentation for both the methods have been mentioned in Table 1.

**Table 1.** Parameters for the augmentation techniques

| Datagenerator augmentation (M1) | | Albumentation augmentation (M2) | |
|---|---|---|---|
| Parameter | Value | Parameter | Value |
| Rotation range | 20 | Rotate | 0.5 |
| Width shift range | 0.1 | Horizontal flip | 0.5 |
| Heigh shift range | 0.1 | Brightness contrast | 0.2 |
| Shear range | 0.2 | Gaussian Noise | 0.2 |
| Zoom range | 0.2 | Shift scale rotate | 0.1 |

**Table 2.** Comparative analysis of CNN models using Datagenerator and albumenttion library

| | Method 1: (Datagenerator) | | | | Method 2: (Albumentation) | | | |
|---|---|---|---|---|---|---|---|---|
| Model | F1 | PR | RC | AC | F1 | PR | RC | AC |
| Inception v3 | 80.17 | 77.97 | 82.51 | 80.58 | **82.84** | **83.48** | **82.20** | **84.14** |
| Mobilenet | 84.12 | 72.31 | 74.41 | 84.36 | 82.91 | 79.10 | 87.11 | 83.28 |
| EfficienNetB0 | 52.00 | 47.21 | 48.81 | 51.90 | 52.12 | 47.76 | 48.21 | 53.54 |
| DenseNet 121 | 84.04 | 84.04 | 84.04 | 84.75 | 80.34 | 75.00 | 86.5 | 80.28 |
| Xception | 78.99 | 76.28 | 81.90 | 79.17 | 73.38 | 71.97 | 74.84 | 74.71 |
| **NasNetLarge** | **86.47** | **83.86** | **89.20** | **86.55** | 80.67 | 80.67 | 80.67 | 82.00 |

The second goal is the identification of the best performing classifier for the detection of melanoma. Hence, the work employed six different CNN models namely InceptionV3, MobileNet, EfficientNetb0, Densenet121, Xception and NasNetLarge. We trained the models first using augmented data which was generated using Kera's datagenerator.

The models were again trained using augmented data from the albumentations library and a comparative analysis was performed as presented in Table 2. It can be concluded that NasNetLarge model when trained with datagenerator augmented data gave the best results amongst all with a remarkable F-score of 86.5% thereby, making the combination of NasNetLarge model with Keras data-generator a choice for further refinement.

### 5.2 Analysis of Variations of NasNetLarge Model with Self-attention

The variations of the NasNetLarge model as described in methodology have been trained in order to increase the performance of the model. This change attempted to enhance the model's performance by capturing more intricate dependencies and patterns in the data. We compared the outcomes to those achieved with the original design in order to methodically assess how these improvements affected the accuracy of the model. The results for the variations of the NasNetLarge model with integrated Self-attention layers are provided below in Table 3. A total of six variations have been tried on this best performing model, that is, the NasNetLarge model with datagenerator as the augmentation technique used. This has been done to further improve model's performance and to generate better results which are crucial especially when working with cases specific to medical domain like Melanoma detection.

**Variation 1 (V1):** Two dense layers have been added to the original NasNetLarge model. So now, model consists of 2 additional dense layers in total for fine-tuning, with 128 neurons and 256 dense layer.

**Variation 2 (V2):** Another dense layer has been added to V1. Hence, the model now has 3 additional dense layers in total having 512 neurons, 256 neurons & 128 neurons.

**Table 3.** Depicts the results obtained by all the variations implemented using NasNetLarge

| Model | F1 | PR | RC | AC |
|---|---|---|---|---|
| V1 | 84.87 | 81.40 | 88.65 | 84.89 |
| V2 | 82.97 | 77.74 | 88.90 | 82.47 |
| V3 | 88.88 | 84.91 | 93.25 | 88.82 |
| V5 | 83.59 | 84.37 | 82.82 | 84.41 |
| V6 | 44.24 | 86.66 | 39.80 | 53.74 |
| **(V4) DeepLesionNet** | **88.63** | **81.65** | **96.93** | **88.10** |

**Variation 3 (V3):** After adding dense layers, we observed that the accuracies dropped from the original model to V1, and further dropped after adding another layer from V1 to V2. This meant that the model was over-fitting, so in variation 3, certain modifications had to be done to rectify this issue. Instead of adding more dense layers, a single 256-neuron dense layer has been used on the NasNetLarge model. To counter the over-fitting of the

models in V1 and V2, Ridge regression or L2 regularization has been employed. Even a lower learning rate was used. The last 50 layers were also made to unfreeze. This was done because the deeper layers of the models can capture the nuances in the data better and they can work with more complex-features leading to a better understanding of the data. This helps in fine-tuning the model even more and also can lead to a significant boost in the model's performance. The patience parameter is set to 10 to prevent premature stopping of the model. It saw a significant boost in performance.

**Variation 4 (V4) (DeepLesionNet):** An additional attention layer has been added to V3. This was done with the goal of improving the recall of the model which is very important to reduce the false negatives as missing a case of melanoma can prove to be fatal for the patient. Since, V4 had a better recall than V3, this was the chosen model for our implementation, named DeepLesionNet.

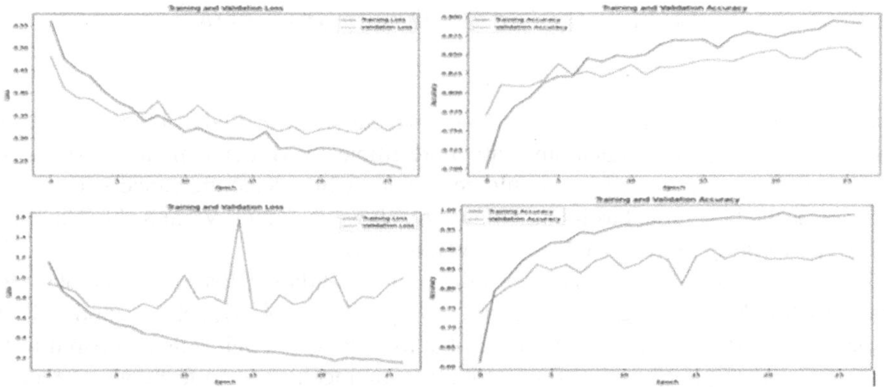

**Fig. 3.** Training and Validation Loss and Accuracy plots of NasNetLarge model (top) and the proposed DeepLesionNetV4 (Bottom)

**Variation 5 (V5):** In variation 5, an additional 128 dense layer has been added to V3 to check if it helps in improving the model's performance.

**Variation 6(V6):** The last 100 layers of the V3 model were made to unfreeze to see if it could capture the data and learn the complex features better. Along with this batch normalization was employed to counter over-fitting of the model. The results for the best performing models using both method 1, which is datagenerator augmentation and albumentations have been listen in Table 3 compared with DeepLesionNet.

NasNetLarge was the best performing model in all the performance metrics and especially in recall. Models with higher recall or specificity are given preference as higher recall ensures lesser false negatives. Having a very high recall value is preferable among the six models implemented using Kera's datagenerator for augmentation.

Upon this, improvements were noticed in V3 and V4 in almost as then the chances of missing a melanoma case reduces which is crucial for establishing the model's reliability as missing cases can prove to be fatal due to delayed diagnosis which can cause the cancer

**Table 4.** Results of the best performing models implemented (M1, M2 and variations)

| Model | F1 | PR | RC | ACC |
|---|---|---|---|---|
| DenseNet-121 (M1) | 84.04 | 84.04 | 84.04 | 84.75 |
| NasNetLarge (M1) | 86.47 | 83.86 | 89.20 | 86.55 |
| Inception-V3 (M2) | 82.84 | 83.48 | 82.20 | 84.14 |
| MoblileNet (M2) | 82.91 | 79.10 | 87.11 | 83.28 |
| Efficientnet B0 (M2) | 52.12 | 47.76 | 48.21 | 53.54 |
| Xception (M2) | 73.38 | 71.97 | 74.84 | 74.71 |
| **DeepLesionNet** | **88.63** | **81.65** | **96.93** | **88.10** |

to spread and metastasize. Both V3 and V4 have outperformed NNL in terms of recall, hence were able to predict melanoma with more efficiency. Both the models have a lesser number of false negatives which should be avoided while detecting cancers. Hence V4 is chosen as the best model as it has a higher recall value among V3 and V4. Therefore, the best performing model is V4, i.e. DeepLesionNet.

Figure 3 graphically presents the training and validation loss and accuracy plots for th baseline NasNetLarge model and the proposed DeepLesionNetv4 model. It can be seen clearly that the proposed model obtains a better model fit as compared to the baseline model, supporting the efficacy of attention mechanism in fast convergence.

Next, the results for the best performing models using both Method 1, which is datagenerator augmentation (M1) and albumentations (M2) have been listen in Table 4 and compared with DeepLesionNet. As observed, the proposed DeepLesionNet model with Method 1 has a recall of 96.93% which is higher as compared to all other models with a huge margin of 7%. As mentioned earlier a higher Recall with minimum number of False negatives will be chosen as the best model given the sensitivity of the application. It also obtained the highest F-score amongst all, thereby, supporting its suitability for the automated melanoma detection. Adding self-attention layers to the NasNetLarge model in the initial phases of fine-tuning allowed model focus on important features and regions by assigning importance for melanoma detection.

The most important observation to be made is that the following features of DeepLesionNet i.e., addition of a single dense layer with 256 units, making the last 50 layers of the base model trainable, and a L2 regularization function with increased patience and lower learning rate help the model to outperform the performance of the pre-trained models. The model has a recall of 96.93, and has outperformed the recall of best performing pre-trained model which was NNL by 6%. Therefore, DeepLesionNet was able to detect melanoma with a higher accuracy and was able to avoid misdiagnosis of a true cancer better than the previous models. The proposed model can be analyzed for several other types of cancer predictions as well [21–24]. Next, Table 5 presents the comparisons of DeepLesionNet against other published literature works. The Xception and the Ensemble Model of Table V are from [7] and both have inferior performance as compared to the proposed model. Here, the Ensemble model applies voting mechanism to five convolutional models but still had limited efficiency and high computational complexity. The EnsembleModel-1 [20] took multiple machine learning models and created an ensemble. They used Vision transformer as the feature extractor. Though it achieved slightly better results but it also had too high complexity as well. While Vit extractor based XGBoost [20] and Random forest [20] classifiers obtained decent accuracies.

**Table 5.** Results of DeepLesionNet versus other methods

| Model | F1 | PR | RC |
|---|---|---|---|
| Xception [7] | 74.80 | 75.00 | 74.80 |
| Ensemble-Model [7] | 74.10 | 76.90 | 71.50 |
| XGBoost [20] | 87.00 | 87.00 | 87.00 |
| Ensemble Model-1 [20] | 91.60 | 91.60 | 91.60 |
| ResNet50 [20] | 78.00 | 78.00 | 78.00 |
| Random forest [20] | 86.50 | 86.70 | 86.40 |
| **DeepLesionNet** | **88.63** | **81.65** | **96.93** |

Overall, DeepLesionNet model proved to be the outperforming model with a high recall rate of 96.93% which is of utmost importance, specially while dealing with medical disease diagnosis applications.

## 6 Conclusion

The work proposed in the paper proposes a NasNetLarge based classification module for melanoma classification in images. It carried out an extensive comparative study to analyze the impact of augmentation by using two data augmentation libraries, albumentations and Kera's datagenerator module. A total of six base models were implemented for both the augmentation strategies out of which NasNetLarge with datagenerator augmentation performed the best with an accuracy of 86.55%. To increase accuracies and to capture data dependencies better, the base layer was modified with added dense layers, and self-attention layers. DeepLesionNet, built upon NasNetLarge, had a recall of 96.93% outperforming the pre-trained models. In future, the work can focus on evaluating the proposed model on a larger dataset. Additionally, the work can focus on integrating transformers and state-space machines for the underlying application.

## References

1. Cassidy, B., Kendrick, C., Brodzicki, A., Jaworek-Korjakowska, J., Yap M.H.: Analysis of the ISIC image datasets: usage, benchmarks and recommendations. Med. Image Anal. **75**, 102305 (2022). ISSN 1361-8415

2. Meswal, H., Kumar, D., Gupta, A., et al.: A weighted ensemble transfer learning approach for melanoma classification from skin lesion images. Multimedia Tools Appl. (2023)
3. Shah, V., Autee,P., Sonawane,P.: Detection of melanoma from skin lesion images using deep learning techniques. In: International Conference on Data Science and Engineering (ICDSE), Kochi, India, pp. 1–8 (2020)
4. Song, J., Li, J., Ma, S., Tang, J., Guo, F.: Melanoma classification in dermoscopy images via ensemble learning on deep neural network. In: IEEE International Conference on Bioinformatics and Biomedicine (BIBM), Seoul, Korea (South), pp. 751–756 (2020)
5. Guergueb, T., Akhloufi, M.A.: Melanoma skin cancer detection using recent deep learning models. In: 43rd Annual International Conference of the IEEE Engineering in Medicine & Biology Society (EMBC), Mexico, pp. 3074–3077 (2021)
6. Hosny, K.M., Kassem, M.A., Foaud, M.M.: Skin melanoma classification using ROI and data augmentation with deep convolutional neural networks. Multimedia Tools Appl. **79**, 24029–24055 (2020)
7. Ding, J., Song, J., Li, J., Tang, J., Guo, F.: Two-stage deep neural network via ensemble learning for melanoma classification. Front. Bioeng. Biotechnol. **9**, 758495 (2022)
8. Rastegar, H., Giveki, D.: Designing a new deep convolutional neural network for skin lesion recognition. Multimedia Tools Appl. **82**, 18907–18923 (2023)
9. Balaha, H.M., Hassan, A.E.S.: Skin cancer diagnosis based on deep transfer learning and sparrow search algorithm. Neural Comput. Appl. **35**(1), 815–853 (2023)
10. Ahmed, N., Tan, X., Ma, L.: A new method proposed to Melanoma-skin cancer lesion detection and segmentation based on hybrid convolutional neural network. Multimedia Tools Appl. **82**, 11873–11896 (2023)
11. Alenezi, F., Armghan, A., Polat, K.: Wavelet transform based deep residual neural network and ReLU based extreme learning machine for skin lesion classification. Expert Syst. Appl. **213**, 119064 (2023). Part B, ISSN 0957-4174
12. Arora, G., Dubey, A.K., Jaffery, Z.A., et al.: A comparative study of fourteen deep learning networks for multi-skin lesion classification (MSLC) on unbalanced data. Neural Comput. Appl. **35**, 7989–8015 (2023)
13. Saba, T., Khan, M.A., Rehman, A., et al.: Region extraction and classification of skin cancer: a heterogeneous framework of deep CNN features fusion and reduction. J. Med. Syst. **43**, 289 (2019)
14. Goyal, M., Oakley, A., Bansal, P., Dancey, D., Yap, M.H.: Skin lesion segmentation in dermoscopic images with ensemble deep learning methods. IEEE Access **8**, 4171–4181 (2020)
15. Anjum, M.A., Amin, J., Sharif, M., Khan, H.U., Malik, M.S.A., Kadry, S.: Deep semantic segmentation and multi-class skin lesion classification based on convolutional neural network. IEEE Access **8**, 129668–129678 (2020)
16. Zhang, Y., Wang, C.: SIIM-ISIC melanoma classification with densenet. In: 2021 IEEE 2nd International Conference on Big Data, Artificial Intelligence and Internet of Things Engineering (ICBAIE), Nanchang, China, p. 14 (2021)
17. Singh, R.P., Sharma, P.: Instance-vote-based motion detection using spatially extended hybrid feature space. Vis. Comput. **37**(6), 1527–1543 (2021)
18. Ganguly, T., Singh, R.P., Kumar, P.: Self-attention based resnet model for cervical cancer detection. In: 2023 Second International Conference on Informatics (ICI), pp. 1–6. IEEE (2023)
19. Sathwik, T., Reddy, T.S., Charitha, T., Singh, R.P., Kanchan, S.: An ensemble based convolutional neural network modelling for classifying medulloblastoma subtype. In: 2024 5th International Conference for Emerging Technology (INCET), pp. 1–6. IEEE (2024)
20. Ghosh, S., Dhar, S., Yoddha, R., Kumar, S., Thakur, A.K., Jana, N.D.: Melanoma skin cancer detection using ensemble of machine learning models considering deep feature embeddings. Procedia Comput. Sci. **235**, 3007–3015 (2024)

21. Neel, A., Singh, T.: Modified U-Net with attention gates and FTL for lesion segmentation. In: 2022 IEEE 3rd Global Conference for Advancement in Technology (GCAT), pp. 1–5. IEEE (2022)
22. Sah, N.K., Reddy, M.V.S., Ullas, K., Singh, T., Mandal, A., Chatterji, S.: Interpretable deep learning for skin cancer detection: exploring LIME and SHAP. In: 2024 15th International Conference on Computing Communication and Networking Technologies (ICCCNT), pp. 1–7. IEEE (2024)
23. Saravan, P.D., Subhash, M.S., Mahesh, S.V., Singh, R.P.: Enhanced skin lesion classification using fine-tuned DenseNet201 with self-attention mechanisms. In: 2024 IEEE 11th Uttar Pradesh Section International Conference on Electrical, Electronics and Computer Engineering (UPCON), pp. 1–6. IEEE (2024)
24. Singh, R.P., Sree, N.H., Reddy, K.L.S.P., Jashwanth, K.: Convergence of deep learning and forensic methodologies using self-attention integrated efficientnet model for deep fake detection. SN Comput. Sci. **5**(8), 1139 (2024)

# DDv8: Dynamic Dual Fusion for Efficient YOLOv8-Style Object Detection

Le Duc Hiep, Khuat Duc Anh(✉), and Phan Duy Hung(✉)

FPT University, Hanoi, Vietnam
hiepldhe186750@fpt.edu.vn, {anhkd3,hungpd2}@fe.edu.vn

**Abstract.** Accurate real-time detection of small-scale traffic signs remains a major challenge in autonomous driving, often limited by weak feature extraction and scale inconsistency. We propose DDv8, a hybrid detection framework that integrates a Python-native Dynamic Dual Fusion (DDF) module and an enhanced Selective Scan 2D block, adapted from the Visual State Block, into the YOLOv8 architecture. Unlike prior methods such as MDDFNet, which rely on C++ -based backbones that hinder integration with modern deep learning toolchains, DDv8 reimplements state-space operations entirely in Python for improved compatibility and extensibility. The dynamic dual-path fusion strengthens multi-scale feature learning, while the selective scan mechanism captures long-range spatial dependencies via adaptive 2D attention. On the TT100K benchmark, DDv8 achieves 77.2% mAP@50, 0.81 Precision, and 0.69 Recall, surpassing the YOLOv8n baseline (68.2% mAP@50) by nearly **9%** while maintaining real-time inference speed. These results demonstrate that DDv8 delivers robust performance for small-scale and occluded traffic signs in complex driving environments.

**Keywords:** Traffic Sign Detection · Small Object Detection · Multi-Scale Feature Fusion · Dynamic Dual Fusion · Mamba Backbone

## 1 Introduction

In recent years, the rapid development of autonomous vehicles and Intelligent Transportation Systems (ITS) has intensified the demand for accurate and robust Traffic Sign Recognition (TSR). Despite notable advances in deep learning–based methods, TSR remains challenging (Fig. 1) due to the small size of signs, frequent occlusions, and adverse conditions such as rain, fog, or low illumination [1]. Conventional CNN-based detectors, while effective for general object detection, often struggle to capture long-range dependencies and adapt to scale variations, resulting in suboptimal performance for small or distant signs.

To address these challenges, recent studies have explored modules such as Vision State Space (VSS) [2] for efficient spatial context modeling and Vision Clue Merge (VCM) [1] for enhanced contextual feature aggregation. Building on these, Yu et al. proposed MDDFNet [1], which integrates a Mamba-based backbone with a Dynamic Dual Fusion (DDF) module. The DDF leverages Efficient Multi-Scale Attention (EMA)


A. Shastri et al. (Eds.): IHCI 2025, LNCS 16437, pp. 64–76, 2026.
https://doi.org/10.1007/978-3-032-26352-0_6

[3] and Dynamic Filters (DF) [4] to strengthen multi-scale feature fusion, achieving strong detection performance on small and occluded signs.

However, mainstream detectors such as YOLOv5, YOLOv7, and YOLOv8, while lightweight and fast, often underperform on small-scale traffic signs, typically achieving less than 70% mAP on TT100K. Conversely, transformer- and state-space–based methods like MDDFNet and VMamba achieve higher accuracy, but at the cost of heavier computation or reliance on system-specific CUDA/C++ extensions, which limits portability.

To overcome these limitations, we introduce DDv8, a hybrid detection framework that preserves MDDFNet's advantages while leveraging the modular, lightweight design of YOLOv8. Unlike MDDFNet's C++ -dependent pipeline, DDv8 is implemented entirely in Python, ensuring seamless compatibility across operating systems without manual compilation or native CUDA extensions. Its architecture integrates a state-space backbone for efficient sequence modeling with refined multi-scale fusion strategies inspired by DDF. This design enables DDv8 to sustain high detection accuracy for small and occluded signs while reducing computational overhead and complexity.

By balancing accuracy, speed, and portability, DDv8 offers a practical solution for real-time TSR, making it well-suited for deployment in resource-constrained environments such as Advanced Driver Assistance Systems (ADAS) and autonomous driving platforms. To highlight its novelty and practical value, we summarize the main contributions of this paper as follows:

**Fig. 1.** Challenges in real-world traffic sign detection include small sign size, occlusions, unfavorable viewing angles [1].

## 2 Related Work

### 2.1 Yolov8

YOLOv8 [13] employs the C2f (Cross-Stage Partial Fusion) module to enhance feature reuse and gradient flow, improving efficiency compared to CSP blocks. Its decoupled detection head separates classification and regression, leading to more accurate localization and stable convergence. These lightweight yet effective designs make YOLOv8 a strong baseline for real-time small-object detection.

### 2.2 Mamba-Based Dynamics Dual Fusion Network

MDDFNet [1] was introduced to overcome the limitations of CNN-based detectors in recognizing small and occluded traffic signs (Fig. 2). It integrates a Mamba-based backbone that employs state-space modeling for efficient long-range dependency capture, along with a DDF module that combines Efficient Multi-Scale Attention (EMA) [3] and Dynamic Filters (DF) [4] for adaptive multi-scale feature fusion. In addition, Vision State Space (VSS) blocks [2] enhance contextual modeling, enabling the network to better handle scale variation and redundancy. Through these innovations, MDDFNet achieves state-of-the-art performance on benchmarks such as TT100K, establishing a strong baseline for future lightweight traffic sign detection (TSD) models.

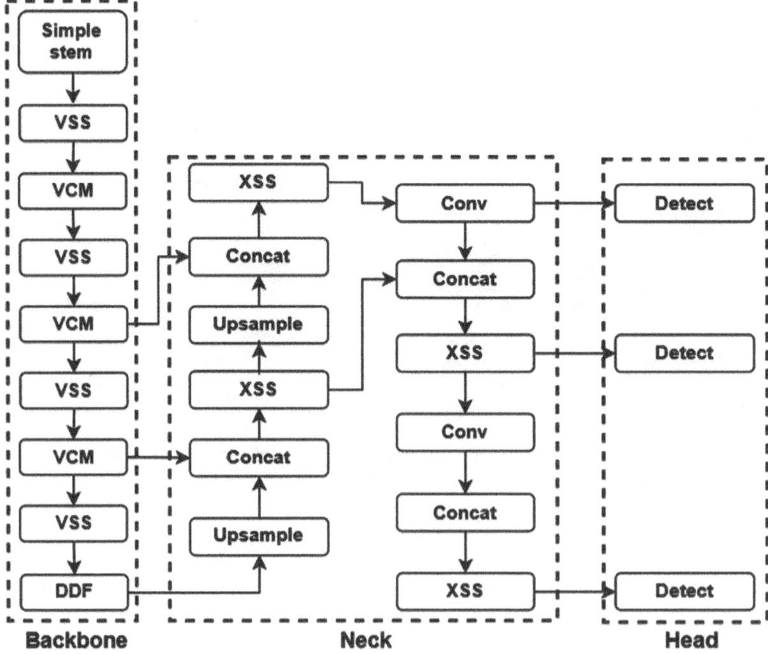


**Fig. 2.** The architecture of MDDFNet, comprising a Mamba-based backbone, a multi-scale fusion neck, detection heads [1]

### 2.3 Vision State Space Blocks

State Space Models (SSMs) [2] have recently re-emerged as efficient architectures for modeling long-range dependencies with linear-time complexity. Unlike Transformers, which rely on quadratic attention, SSMs update hidden states via discretized linear differential equations, making them well-suited for resource-constrained sequential tasks. Gu et al. [5] showed that with HiPPO-based initialization [6], SSMs effectively capture long-context information while achieving accuracy comparable to attention-based models.

In the visual domain, VMamba introduces Vision State Space (VSS) blocks powered by the 2D Selective Scan (SS2D) mechanism [7]. SS2D performs directional scanning across four spatial axes, enabling each pixel to aggregate global spatial context at linear cost. By stacking VSS blocks across multiple resolution stages (H/4 × W/4 to H/32 × W/32) with residual and gating structures, VMamba attains competitive performance on dense prediction tasks such as object detection, while offering greater computational efficiency than attention-based backbones.

### 2.4 Dynamics Dual Fusion

The Dynamic Dual Fusion (DDF) module [1] is a lightweight component in MDDFNet designed to strengthen multi-scale feature integration. It splits the input feature into two parallel paths, each processed with 3 × 3 and 5 × 5 convolutions to capture different receptive fields. The outputs are concatenated and fused by an operator $\phi$ (1 × 1 or 3 × 3 convolution), forming the final representation:

$$DDF(F) = \phi(\text{Concat}\left[\psi_{3\times3}(F1), \psi_{5\times5}(F1), \psi_{3\times3}(F2), \psi_{5\times5}(F2)\right]) \quad (1)$$

The DDF module comprises two main stages, Efficient Multi-Scale Attention (EMA) and Dynamic Filters (DF), which jointly enable adaptive feature modulation. EMA enhances spatial and contextual interactions across grouped channels, while DF applies content-aware filtering in the frequency domain. Integrated within a dual-path architecture, these mechanisms allow MDDFNet [1] to effectively fuse spatial and semantic information, improving detection accuracy for small objects under complex conditions while maintaining real-time performance (Fig. 3).

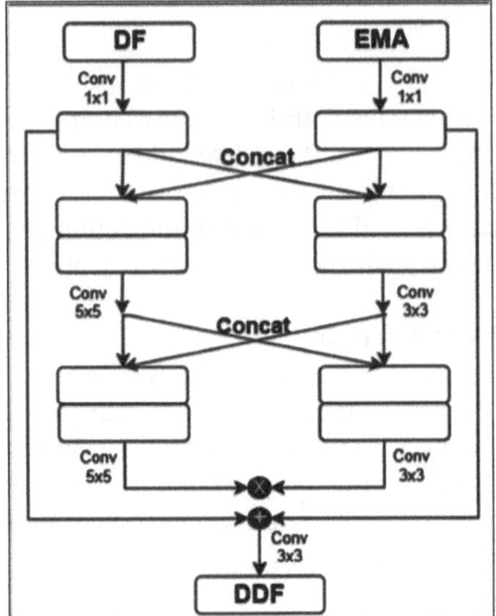


**Fig. 3.** Dynamics Dual Fusion (DDF) Network Architecture with Multi-Modal Feature Integration [1]

### 2.5 Efficient Multi-scale Attention (EMA)

The EMA module [3] is a key component of the DDF block in MDDFNet. It enhances feature representation by capturing both spatial and channel-wise dependencies through a combination of grouped convolutions and parallel attention branches, improving upon earlier attention mechanisms such as Squeeze-and- Excitation (SE) [8] and Coordinate Attention (CA) [9].

Unlike SE, which removes spatial information through global pooling, CA retains positional cues by performing directional pooling along height and width dimensions. Given an input tensor $X \in R^{C \times H \times W}$, CA computes horizontal and vertical context descriptors as:

$$z_c^H(H) = \frac{1}{W}\sum\nolimits_{i=1}^{W} x_c(H, i) z_c^W(W) = \frac{1}{H}\sum\nolimits_{i=1}^{H} x_c(W, i) \tag{2}$$

EMA generalizes this idea by splitting $X$ into $G$ groups across channels: $X = [X_0, X_1, \ldots, X_{G-1}]$, where each $X_i \in R^{C/G \times H \times W}$. The architecture uses three parallel branches: two $1 \times 1$ convolution branches (derived from CA) apply directional pooling followed by attention gating, and one $3 \times 3$ convolution branch captures spatial context with enlarged receptive fields.

A cross-spatial learning mechanism then fuses these branches. For example, the first spatial attention map is derived via global pooling (Fig. 4):

$$z_c^H(H) = \frac{1}{H \times W}\sum\nolimits_{i=1}^{H}\sum_{j=1}^{W} x_c(i, j) \tag{3}$$

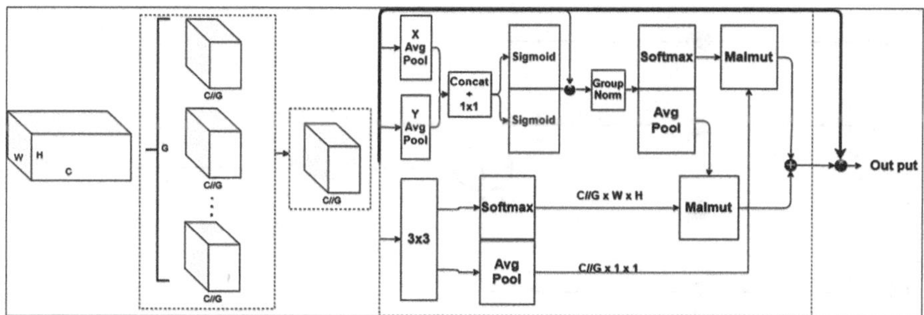


**Fig. 4.** Illustration of our proposed EMA. Here, "g" means the divided groups, "X Avg Pool" represents the 1D horizontal global pooling and "Y Avg Pool" indicates the 1D vertical global pooling, respectively [3].

EMA efficiently captures both global and local dependencies while avoiding the computational overhead of sequential attention or deep stacking. Its capacity to model spatial–channel interactions makes it especially effective for detecting small, occluded, or ambiguous objects. In this work, we integrate EMA into the detection pipeline to strengthen multi-scale feature fusion and spatial awareness.

### 2.6 Dynamics Filter

As a core component of the DDF module in MDDFNet [1], the DF [4] block plays a pivotal role in refining feature representations by adapting convolutional operations to the input content. This mechanism builds upon the concept of DF [4], where the filter weights are not fixed but instead generated conditionally based on the input features.

In this context, a lightweight MLP module $M$ is used to learn a set of dynamic coefficients to linearly combine a predefined basis of global filters of dimension $N$. These filters are then applied in the frequency domain, enabling long-range feature modulation with improved efficiency. The Dynamic Filtering (Fig. 5) process can be mathematically formulated as:

$$D(X) = F^{-1}(K_M(X) \odot F \circ A(X)) \tag{4}$$

where $K_M(X)$ is the dynamic filter kernel generated by the MLP based on input $\mathbf{X}$, $A(X)$ is an intermediate feature transformation (e.g., identity or $1 \times 1$ convolution), $F$ and $F^{-1}$ denote the Fourier transform and its inverse, and $\odot$ is the element-wise multiplication in the frequency domain.

This formulation, proposed in DFFormer [4], enables content-aware filtering by dynamically adapting the global filter to each input, contrasting with static filters used in prior FFT-based models like GFNet [10]. The dynamic kernel is computed by linearly combining a small set of complex-valued filter bases, with the combination weights produced by a two-layer MLP equipped with Layer Normalization and StarReLU activation [11, 12].

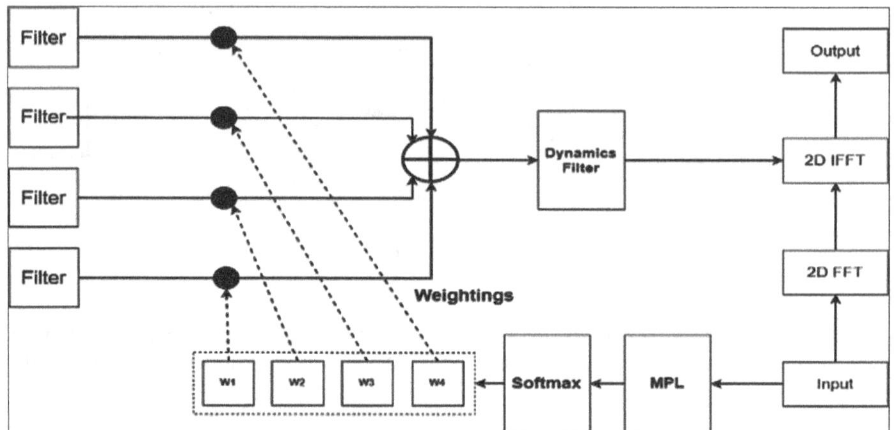


**Fig. 5.** Dynamic Filter is a key component adopted from prior work, enabling any modules to operate on continuous real-valued feature maps [4].

## 3 Methodology

In this work, we propose DDv8, a hybrid object detection framework that combines the state-space backbone of MDDFNet with the lightweight neck and head modules of YOLOv8. This design preserves MDDFNet's strong multi-directional feature extraction capabilities while substantially improving computational efficiency and deployment flexibility.

Unlike MDDFNet, which implements its selective scan mechanism through custom CUDA/C++ extensions tightly bound to system toolchains, DDv8 reimplements this process entirely in Python. This eliminates the need for native compilation and dependencies on low-level libraries such as nvcc or platform-specific C++ compilers, enabling platform-agnostic deployment and seamless integration into modern AI workflows.

The proposed architecture introduces two core improvements. First, we replace MDDFNet's XSS-based neck and detection head with YOLOv8's modular, convolution-based design. Leveraging C2f (Cross-Stage Partial Fusion) blocks and efficient multi-scale fusion, this modification reduces parameter count and inference latency while maintaining competitive accuracy, particularly for small or occluded traffic signs. Second, we enhance the role of the DDF block by directly connecting its output to all three detection branches ($80 \times 80, 40 \times 40$, and $20 \times 20$). This direct multi-scale fusion allows high-level semantic features captured by DDF to contribute more effectively to localization and classification, especially in cluttered scenes with small or densely packed targets.

As illustrated in Fig. 6, these design choices strike a practical balance between detection accuracy, inference speed, and deployment portability. By unifying state-space modeling with convolutional object detection, DDv8 provides a scalable and efficient solution for real-time traffic sign recognition in resource-constrained environments.

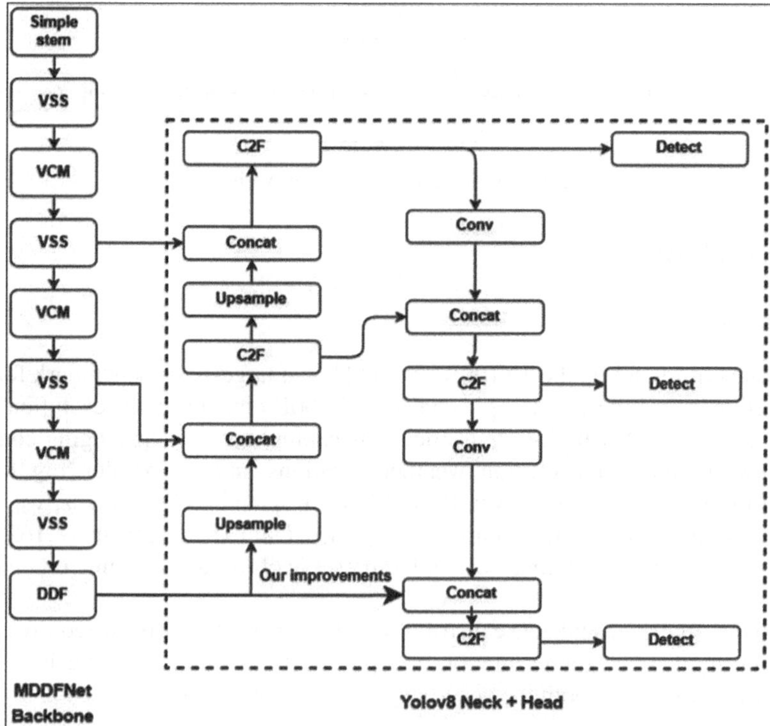


**Fig. 6.** DDv8 – The proposed architecture integrating Dynamic Dual Fusion and Selective Scan 2D into the YOLOv8 framework

### 3.1 Cross-Stage Partial Fusion (C2f)

The C2f module (Fig. 7), introduced in YOLOv8 [13], is an improved alternative to the Cross Stage Partial (CSP) block used in earlier YOLO versions [15]. Designed under a split–transform–merge paradigm, it first applies a 1 × 1 convolution to adjust channel dimensions, then splits the feature map into two halves. One half serves as a shortcut connection, while the other passes through several bottleneck blocks with residual links and 3 × 3 convolutions. The outputs, together with the shortcut, are concatenated and projected back via another 1 × 1 convolution. This design increases residual paths and strengthens feature fusion, offering a better balance between efficiency and representational power than CSP, which ultimately enhances real-time object detection performance [13, 15].

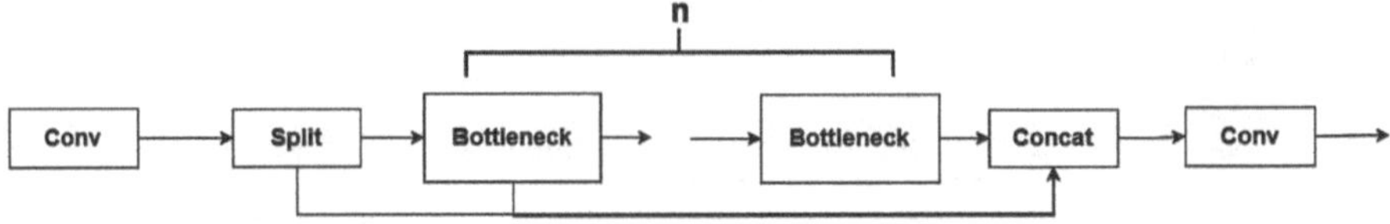


**Fig. 7.** Cross-Stage Partial Fusion Architecture

# 4 Experiment

## 4.1 Dataset

We evaluate our model on the TT100K dataset [14], a large-scale benchmark for traffic sign detection in real-world driving scenarios. TT100K contains high-resolution images (2048 × 2048 pixels) with diverse traffic signs captured under challenging conditions such as low illumination, occlusion, weather variations, and motion blur (Fig. 8).

From the full collection of over 10,000 images spanning 221 classes, we adopt a filtered subset of 45 frequently occurring categories. Our experiments use 8,162 images for training and 1,008 for testing, selected to preserve class balance while retaining task complexity.

Given the small size and dense distribution of traffic signs, TT100K requires models with strong multi-scale representation and precise localization, making it a suitable benchmark for assessing both the accuracy and efficiency of the proposed architecture.

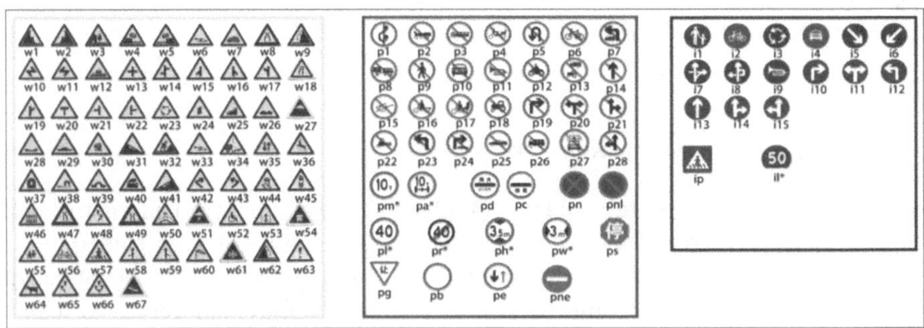

**Fig. 8.** Overview TT100K dataset

## 4.2 Training Configuration

All experiments are conducted in PyTorch 2.6.0 on a single NVIDIA RTX 3070 Ti GPU. The model is trained for 300 epochs on the TT100K dataset using 8,162 training images and evaluated on 1,008 test images. All inputs are resized to 640 × 640 pixels. A batch size of 4 is used to balance memory usage and training stability.

To improve generalization, we apply standard augmentations including Mosaic, MixUp, HSV jittering, and random affine transforms. Training is optimized with AdamW, using an initial learning rate of $1 \times 10^{-3}$, momentum of 0.937, and weight decay of $5 \times 10^{-4}$. A linear warm-up is applied over the first 5 epochs, followed by cosine annealing for gradual learning rate decay. Training is performed in float32 precision with optional mixed precision to improve efficiency.

Figure 9 shows the evolution of the training loss over 300 epochs. The loss decreases steadily, demonstrating stable convergence and effective optimization. The smooth decline indicates that the chosen hyperparameters and augmentations contribute to efficient learning dynamics.

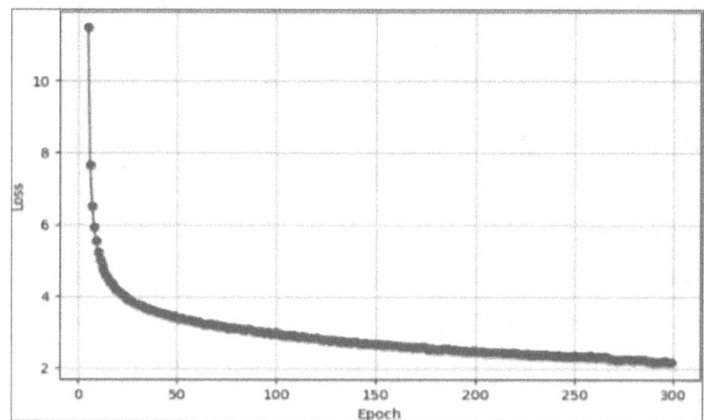


**Fig. 9.** Training loss curve of the proposed model over 300 epochs

To assess the effectiveness of our proposed architecture, we evaluate its performance on the TT100K test set using standard object detection metrics, including mean Average Precision at IoU threshold 0.5 (mAP@50), Recall, and Precision. These metrics provide a comprehensive view of the model's detection accuracy, coverage, and reliability.

### 4.3 Quantitative Analysis

We compare the proposed DDv8n with the baseline YOLOv8n on the TT100K dataset. As shown in Table 1, DDv8n achieves 77.2% mAP@50, surpassing YOLOv8n (68.2%), with higher Precision (0.81 vs. 0.65) and Recall (0.69 vs. 0.64), indicating fewer false positives and more true positives. Table 2 further shows per-class AP improvements: DDv8n attains 96.0% (i4), 95.0% (i5), 95.8% (ip) compared to YOLOv8n's 84.7%, 90.5%, and 70.8%. Moreover, it reaches 100% AP on several categories (ph4, pm55, ph5, p170) and consistently outperforms YOLOv8n even in strong classes (e.g., pne: 97.5% vs. 92.3%). These results highlight DDv8n's robustness and superior generalization in traffic sign detection.

**Table 1.** Detection performance of DDv8n vs. YOLOv8n on TT100K (mAP@50, Precision, Recall).

| Method | mAP@50 (%) | Precision | Recall |
|---|---|---|---|
| DDv8n | 77.2 | 0.81 | **0.69** |
| Yolov8n | **68.2** | **0.65** | **0.64** |

**Table 2.** Per-class Average Precision (AP) comparison between DDv8n and YOLOv8n on TT100K

| Method | i2 | i4 | i5 | il100 | il60 | il80 | io | ip | p10 | p11 | p12 |
|---|---|---|---|---|---|---|---|---|---|---|---|
| DDv8n | 91.7 | 96.0 | 95.0 | 91.7 | 82.1 | 82.4 | 78.9 | 95.8 | 57.1 | 86.7 | 66.7 |
| Yolov8n | 67.8 | 84.7 | 90.5 | 84.1 | 57.4 | 63.1 | 73.2 | 70.8 | 43.3 | 67.8 | 54.4 |
| **Method** | **p19** | **p23** | **p26** | **p3** | **p5** | **p6** | **pg** | **ph4** | **ph4.5** | **pl100** | **pl120** |
| DDv8n | 77.8 | 82.6 | 76.8 | 88.9 | 79.4 | 75.0 | 60.0 | 100.0 | 76.5 | 69.8 | 70.6 |
| Yolov8n | 57.5 | 63.6 | 65.2 | 56.0 | 65.2 | 46.8 | 71.8 | 47.1 | 55.4 | 54.5 | 61.1 |
| **Method** | **pl20** | **pl30** | **pl40** | **pl5** | **pl50** | **pl60** | **pl80** | **pm20** | **w32** | **pm55** | **pn** |
| DDv8n | 83.3 | 78.1 | 72.9 | 86.7 | 87.7 | 66.7 | 77.1 | 50.0 | 100.0 | 60.0 | 94.2 |
| Yolov8n | 69.7 | 46.7 | 67.5 | 72.0 | 69.7 | 50.8 | 64.3 | 30.6 | 72.7 | 48.8 | 88.7 |
| **Method** | **pne** | **po** | **w57** | **pr40** | **w59** | **w55** | **pl70** | **p27** | **w13** | **wo** | **ph5** |
| DDv8n | 97.5 | 75.5 | 77.4 | 83.3 | 85.7 | 72.7 | 100.0 | 100.0 | 64.3 | 75.0 | 100.0 |
| Yolov8n | 92.3 | 67.7 | 71.2 | 82.6 | 86.4 | 64.1 | 85.4 | 87.2 | 72.1 | 44.3 | 53.0 |

### 4.4 Qualitative Analysis

To further demonstrate the effectiveness of the proposed model, we present qualitative detection results on the TT100K test set. These visualizations highlight the model's capability to recognize traffic signs of varying sizes under diverse lighting conditions and scene complexities.

As illustrated in Fig. 10, the model accurately localizes and classifies traffic signs even in challenging scenarios, including small-scale targets, partial occlusions, and cluttered urban scenes. These results confirm the robustness of the approach and its practical potential for real-world deployment in intelligent transportation systems.

**Fig. 10.** Example detection results on TT100K test images using the proposed model

## 5 Conclusion

In summary, the proposed DDv8 model integrates a reimplemented Dynamic Dual Fusion module and a Python-native Selective Scan 2D mechanism into the YOLOv8 framework, achieving a balance between feature expressiveness, real-time performance, and deployment flexibility. On the TT100K benchmark, DDv8n improves mAP@50 from 68.2% (YOLOv8n) to 77.2%, with higher Precision (0.81 vs. 0.65) and Recall (0.69 vs. 0.64), demonstrating clear advantages in small-scale and occluded traffic sign detection. These results confirm the effectiveness of the proposed fusion strategy and modular design. Beyond accuracy gains, DDv8's Python-native implementation removes deployment barriers of MDDFNet, making it more practical for integration into ADAS and autonomous driving systems operating under resource constraints. The paper is a good methodological reference for computer vision, object detection problems [16–18].

## References

1. Yu, T.Y.: MDDFNet: Mamba-based Dynamic Dual Fusion Network for Traffic Sign Detection. arXiv:2505.05491 (2025)
2. Liu, Y., Tian, Y., Zhao, Y. et al.: VMamba: visual state space model. In: Proceedings of the 38th International Conference on Neural Information Processing Systems (NIPS 2024), vol. 37, Article 3273, pp. 103031–103063 Curran Associates Inc., Red Hook, NY, USA, (2024)
3. Ouyang, D., et al.: Efficient multi-scale attention module with cross-spatial learning. In: Proceedings of the IEEE International Conference on Acoustics, Speech and Signal Processing (ICASSP), Rhodes Island, Greece, pp. 1–5 (2023). https://doi.org/10.1109/ICASSP49357.2023.10096516
4. Tatsunami, Y., Taki, M.: FFT-based dynamic token mixer for vision. In: AAAI, vol. 38, no. 14, pp. 15328–15336 (2024)

5. Gu, A., Johnson, I., Goel, K. et al.: In Proceedings of the 35th International Conference on Neural Information Processing Systems (NIPS 2021), Article 44, pp. 572–585. Curran Associates Inc., Red Hook (2021)
6. Dao, G.T., Ermon, S., Rudra, A., Ré, C.: HiPPO: recurrent memory with optimal polynomial projections. In: Proceedings of the 34th International Conference on Neural Information Processing Systems (NIPS '20), Article 125, pp. 1474–1487. Curran Associates Inc., Red Hook (2020)
7. Gu, A., and Dao, T.: Mamba: linear-time sequence modeling with selective state spaces. arXiv:2312.00752v2 [cs.LG] (2024)
8. Hu, J., Shen, L., Sun, G.: Squeeze-and-excitation networks. In: Proceedings of IEEE Conference on Computer Vision and Pattern Recognition (CVPR), pp. 7132–7141 (2018)
9. Hou, Q., Zhou, D., Feng, J.: Coordinate attention for efficient mobile network design. In: Proceedings of IEEE/CVF Conference on Computer Vision and Pattern Recognition (CVPR), pp. 13713–13722 (2021)
10. Rao, Y., Zhao, W., Zhu, Z. et al.: Global filter networks for image classification. In: Proceedings of the 35th International Conference on Neural Information Processing Systems (NIPS 2021), Article 76, pp. 980–993. Curran Associates Inc., Red Hook (2021)
11. Yu, W., et al.: MetaFormer baselines for vision. IEEE Trans. Pattern Anal. Mach. Intell. **46**(2), 896–912 (2024). https://doi.org/10.1109/TPAMI.2023.3329173
12. Ba, J., Kiros, J., Hinton, G.: Layer normalization. arXiv:1607.06450 (2016)
13. Jocher, G., Chaurasia, A., Qiu, T. et al.: Ultralytics YOLOv8: Cutting-edge real-time object detection. GitHub repository (2023). https://github.com/ultralytics/ultralytics
14. Zhu, Z., Liang, D., Zhang, S., Huang, X., et al.: Traffic-sign detection and classification in the wild. In: Proceedings of IEEE Conference on Computer Vision and Pattern Recognition (CVPR), pp. 2110–2118 (2016)
15. Wang, C.-Y., Liao, H.-Y. M., Wu, Y.-H. et al.: CSPNet: a new backbone that can enhance learning capability of CNN. In: Proc. IEEE/CVF Conference on Computer Vision and Pattern Recognition (CVPR) Workshops, pp. 390–391 (2020)
16. Diep, V.T., Phat, N.D., Hung, P.D.: Improving elevator control algorithms by integrating with computer vision. In: Gervasi, O., (eds.) et al. Computational Science and Its Applications – ICCSA 2025. ICCSA 2025. LNCS, vol 15648. Springer, Cham (2025)
17. Su, N.T., Hung, P.D., Vinh, B.T., Diep, V.T.: Rice leaf disease classification using deep learning and target for mobile devices. In: Al-Emran, M., Al-Sharafi, M.A., Al-Kabi, M.N., Shaalan, K. (eds.) Proceedings of International Conference on Emerging Technologies and Intelligent Systems. ICETIS 2021. Lecture Notes in Networks and Systems, vol. 299. Springer, Cham (2022)
18. Hung, P.D., Loan, B.T.: Automatic Vietnamese passport recognition on android phones. In: Dang, T.K., Küng, J., Takizawa, M., Chung, T.M. (eds.) Future Data and Security Engineering. Big Data, Security and Privacy, Smart City and Industry 4.0 Applications. FDSE 2020. CCIS, vol. 1306. Springer, Singapore (2020)

# Comparative Predictive Analysis Using QML and ML for Gold Purity

M. Nagamani[2(✉)], Undru Vimal Babu[1,2,3,4,5,6], Anjali Tiwari[1], Indluri Latha Madhuri[1,2,3,4,5,6], Shalem Raju Tambala[1,2,3,4,5,6], and Venkateshwar Sagar[1,2,3,4,5,6]

[1] University of Hyderabad, Hyderabad, India
[2] Legal Metrology Telangana, Hyderabad, India
nagamanics@uohyd.ac.in
[3] SIT Hyderabad, Hyderabad, India
[4] ETDC Hyderabad, Hyderabad, India
[5] Legal Metrology AP, Vijayawada, India
[6] American Internation Group Insurence, NewYork, USA

**Abstract.** Gold imports significantly impact a nation's trade balance, and their role in the economy is substantial. Consumers, traders, and investors experience challenges due to the increased volatility of gold prices due to fluctuating economic conditions, geopolitical tensions, etc. Apart from these issues, the consumer is faced with difficulties in ensuring that the gold that they purchase meets their desired expectations in quality and that no fraudulent purchase has been made. Fraud detection for gold purity is an application that has been explored using Machine Learning and Deep Learning approaches. Emerging computing paradigms bring about the question of what improved experience or convenience is offered when applying them to practical question of gold purity and quality assurance. This work demonstrates the application of Quantum Neural Networks (QNNs) in the prediction of gold quality, framed as both a regression task and a classification problem for fraud detection prevention. We establish a robust benchmarking test using a synthetic dataset to evaluate performance against classical baselines, and present a case study, describing the field data curation process followed by a preliminary evaluation of QNN performance on real-world dataset.

**Keywords:** Gold Quality · QNNs · Fraud Detection · regression t

## 1 Introduction

India is one of the world's largest consumers of gold for a variety of reasons, be it financial, cultural or religious. The need for assessing the quality of gold and seeing to it that it corresponds to the correct price is an absolute necessity for the protection of consumers. Traditional methods such as physical assay, chemical testing and X-ray fluorescence may not always be accessible to small


A. Shastri et al. (Eds.): IHCI 2025, LNCS 16437, pp. 77–91, 2026.
https://doi.org/10.1007/978-3-032-26352-0_7

traders or consumers as there may be cost and infrastructure constraints. Gold quality assessment through machine learning and artificial intelligence has been approached before yet challenges such as complex non-linear relationships and a vast heterogeneous features in the data could be better captured through Quantum Neural Networks. Quantum computation and adaptive learning intersect in the use of Quantum Neural Networks. Leveraging the parallelism offered by this computing paradigm, a new leap in predictive power and efficiency is possible. QNNs offer a theoretical advantage by leveraging principles such as entanglement and the ability to capture complex relationships between data points in high-dimensional state spaces. We now commence with a review of India's gold assessment landscape and their challenges. This work also aims to develop a compact device for gold quality testing.

### 1.1 Gold Quality Assessment and Prediction Challenges

The following section discusses the approaches and difficulties associated with traditional assessment methods and in the practice of gold quality and price prediction.

### 1.2 Traditional Assessment Methods

India's gold market is characterized by immense scale and fragmentation, featuring a decentralized network of stakeholders that includes artisanal miners, refiners, jewelry manufacturers, wholesalers, government mints, and millions of consumers. Given the variation in market infrastructure and participants, quality standards may not always be uniformly enforced. Assessment of quality typically relies on a few traditional methods: physical assays, instrumental techniques like X-ray fluorescence (XRF) and optical spectrometry, or manual and visual inspection, which is often relied upon by small traders and consumers [1].

Physical assays, such as touchstone testing and fire assay, are commonly used to determine gold purity (i.e., the "karatage"). While touchstone is a faster method, fire assay is slow, destructive, and costly, despite its high levels of accuracy. For reliable composition analysis, instrumental methods such as XRF and non-destructive imaging tools are available, but high equipment costs and the necessary specialized skills present significant barriers for the everyday consumer and small trader. Consequently, many smaller traders rely on hallmark stamps and other traditional indicators, which are themselves vulnerable to fraud.

### 1.3 Prediction Challenges

The following challenges may collectively affect the prediction accuracy for gold quality and pricing [2–6]. Heterogeneity of Data: The quality of datasets pertaining to gold quality can be noisy, incomplete and may lack standardization. Informal transactions may not be labeled accurately and also contribute to this data. Nonlinear and Multivariate Dependencies: International prices, the volume of trade, festivities, black market activity and various other factors affect the price of gold and the quality that is being distributed. Prevalence of Fraud: Counterfeit of hallmarking, tampering and mislabeling karatage, especially in rural areas is possible, leaving consumers from less populated regions more vulnerable to such forms of fraud. This also erodes trust in historical datasets. Volume and Variety: Millions of daily transactions and a variation on gold products can also place a larger demand on models to generalize robustly and accommodate such large computational load. Market Volatility: Geopolitical events and policy shifts can have a drastic effect, causing supply shocks and create discontinuous shifts in prices as well as overall trading patterns.

## 2 Literature Review

The following section discusses various approaches towards the prediction of Gold price and quality predictions, namely-statistical, machine learning, and quantum machine learning approaches.

### 2.1 Statistical Approaches

Time-series statistical modeling such as Auto-Regressive Integrated Moving Average (ARIMA) is one of the previous attempts used to predict gold prices in India. The ARIMA model employs auto-regressive terms, differencing to induce moving average and stationarity and has been applied to historical daily and monthly price gold data, under the INR denomination. Sharma identified that ARIMA (3,13,3) was suitable for predicting gold prices in the Indian market [7]. The validation was done by using criteria such as Bayesian Information Criteria (BIC) and Partial Autocorrelation functions (PAC). The model however may under perform in what appears to be major shifts as a result of policy shifts, inflation shocks or a global financial crisis. Incremental improvements through the use of Generalized Autoregressive Conditional Heteroskedasticity (GARCH) paired with ARIMA has been demonstrated [8]. Linear Regression has historically been employed for macroeconomic variables that affect gold prices, including inflation rates, currency exchange rates, and global commodity indices. Their predictive power is more likely to depend on stable, monotonic relationship, which may not always be the case for the Indian market. Logistic regression provides a binary outcome that is also constrained by quality and completeness of the data.

### 2.2 Machine Learning Approaches

To overcome the linearity and stationarity assumptions from statistical approaches, machine learning algorithms have been applied. Artificial Neural Networks, in particular, multi-layer perceptron can model highly nonlinear dependencies on gold pricing and demonstrate an ability to learn hidden patterns from large datasets, outperforming ARIMA models, especially when heterogenous data has been used. They may still however struggle with time dependencies and are still sensitive to quality and completeness of the training data [9]. Support Vector Machines and their ability to deal with datasets with higher dimensionality for classification and regression tasks have also been studied, favouring circumstances with clear decision boundaries, which may be useful when determining gold quality based on assay results or transaction patterns [10]. However they may still be affected by temporal nature of the dataset. Deep Learning approaches, that may consider the termporality of the data, such as in the case of Long-Short Term Memory Network (LSTMs), excel at learning long-term dependencies in sequential data. This is especially useful for financial time-series contexts in India and have outperformed ARIMA models, ANN models in terms of regression metrics such as Root Mean Squared Error (RMSEs) and Mean Absolute Percentage Error (MAPE). They have the capability of considering periods of volatility and structural change in gold prices [11]. Convolutional Neural Networks can be adapted for time-series and multivariate trend detection and can be used to formulate predictions on the basis of price, demand and market indicators. Models that have done particularly well on Indian gold price prediction tasks involving time series data and exogenous variables combine the capabilities of CNNs with LSTMs [12]. On the subject of gold purity, non-destructive gold purity analysis conducted through thes use of AI and audio data has been discussed here [13]. Pulsed eddy current testing hardware paired with deep learning models has also demonstrated a high predictive accuracy [14]. A deep learning system that uses image segmentation and sound processing to differentiate genuine gold from counterfeit with over 97% accuracy, comparing CNN, SVM, and shallow neural networks [15]. This study [16] investigates the application of artificial intelligence techniques to identify fraud in the gold bullion market. The study specifically focuses on detecting counterfeit or adulterated gold based on various data features such as spectral, imaging, and transactional data.

### 2.3 Quantum Machine Learning Approaches

Quantum Variational Classifiers, Quantum Kernel Estimation, Hybrid Quantum Neural Networks and other quantum machine learning applied to problems such as stock market prediction, risk management and fraud detection have also been explored [2–6]. They are especially useful in dealing with high-dimensional, noisy or weakly structured datasets, which mirrors the decentralized nature of gold purchases and trade in India. The could generalize from smaller datasets and handle heterogeneity and regime shifts characteristic of Indian gold markets. Real-world deployment however, can be limited by hardware constraints and a difficulty in acquiring accurate public datasets. Quantum Neural Networks (QNNs) offer several distinct advantages [1,17,18] over their classical counterparts, primarily stemming from the unique properties of quantum mechanics. A key benefit is Hardware Expressivity, as QNNs can encode and process intricate nonlinear dependencies by leveraging quantum phenomena like superposition and entanglement. Furthermore, they exhibit a degree of Resistance to certain forms of Noise because quantum states are inherently probabilistic, allowing

QNNs to handle ambiguity in data more naturally. QNNs also show promise in Data and Training Efficiency by having the potential to generalize from smaller training datasets, enabling them to learn complex relationships more quickly than classical models that often rely on much larger volumes of data. Finally, the inherent Parallelism in quantum computation, where operations can be processed simultaneously, offers a significant potential for reducing overall computation time. While promising, the development of Quantum Neural Networks (QNNs) faces several practical limitations [20–22]. Current Hardware Constraints mean that training large-scale QNNs is often only feasible through simulation, as fault-tolerant quantum computers are not yet widely available. Another significant challenge is Interpretability; like some complex classical models, quantum models can be viewed as black boxes, making it difficult to understand how they arrive at a particular solution, which is an active area of research.

## 3 Proposed Framework

The Quantum Neural Network (QNN) framework for gold quality prediction and fraud detection is a multi-step pipeline designed to forecast gold purity and price using both classification and regression metrics.

The application of Explainable AI (XAI) and trust is non-negotiable for deploying Quantum Neural Networks in a sensitive market. Given that QNNs involve quantum phenomena like entanglement and superposition, they inherently operate as "black boxes". XAI bridges this gap by providing post-hoc transparency—explaining *why* a prediction (e.g., classifying a gold sample as fraudulent or forecasting a price drop) was made. Techniques like adapted SHAP (Shapley Additive eXplanations) or Q-LIME (Quantum-Local Interpretable Model-agnostic Explanations) can reveal the input features (such as trace element concentrations, historical volatility, or specific trade volumes) that most heavily influenced the model's decision. This is critical for consumer trust; a buyer facing a fraud alert can see a clear, data-driven justification. Conversely, an interactive producer-facing dashboard can utilize these XAI insights to enhance trust by proving the system's fairness and integrity. By visually displaying feature importance, confidence scores, and counterfactual explanations, the dashboard allows producers and regulators to audit the model, quickly diagnose data quality issues, and align the QNN's decisions with market standards and ethical requirements. This transparency transforms the system from a potential liability into a collaborative tool for quality assurance.

## 4 Methodology

### 4.1 Description of the Functional Diagram

The process begins with Data Acquisition (gathering purity records and historical pricing) and Data Preprocessing, where data is normalized and features are reduced to suit quantum hardware constraints. The core of the system is

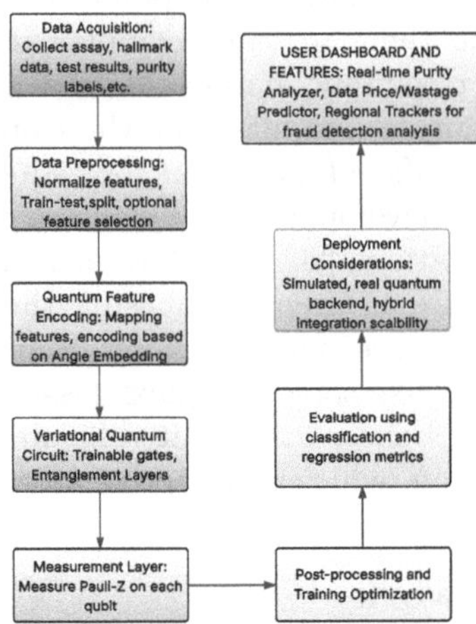


**Fig. 1.** Flow Diagram of the Proposed method

the Quantum Feature Encoding, which maps classical features to qubit rotation angles, followed by a Variational Quantum Circuit (VQC) that models complex data correlations. The results from the Measurement and Output Processing stage yield probabilities for purity classification and numerical values for price regression. The QNN is then tuned in the Training and Optimization phase using gradient descent, and its efficacy is confirmed using Evaluation Metrics like the Wasserstein distance before the system moves into Deployment Considerations focused on scalability within market and hardware limitations (Fig. 1).

**Synthetic Dataset Description.** A synthetic dataset of 1000 samples was utilised-consisting of 500 fraudulent and 500 authentic samples, simulating the chemical composition of gold alloys. The 7 qubits were used to represent the respective input features-namely the composition of Gold, Nickel, Copper, Silver, Zinc, as well as density and magnetism, while the output consisted of a binary label that assigned 0 or 1 if a given sample falls within the authentic class for 18k gold samples (Table 1).

**Table 1.** Feature and Class Variance Table

| Feature Name | Type | Authentic Class (Label = 0) | Fraudulent Class (Label = 1) |
|---|---|---|---|
| Au (Gold) | Input | $\approx$ 75.0% $\pm$ 0.2% | $\approx$73.0%–74.5% |
| Ni (Nickel) | Input | $\approx$0%–0.05% | $\approx$5.0%–10.0% |
| Cu (Copper) | Input | $\approx$ 14.5% $\pm$ 1.0% | $\approx$15.0%–25.0% |
| Ag (Silver) | Input | Varies ($\approx$ 10%) | Varies to complete 100% |
| Zn (Zinc) | Input | $\approx$ 0.5% $\pm$ 0.2% | $\approx$0.1%–1.0% |
| Density | Derived | Calculated from Authentic composition | Calculated from Fraudulent composition |
| Magnetism | Derived | Mostly **0** | High probability of **1** |

The use of a synthetic dataset is necessitated by inherent challenges in real-world data acquisition and balance. FraudulentÂăcompositions in available real datasets occur at a significantly lower ratio compared to authentic samples, which would introduce a severe classÂăimbalance detrimental to classifier training. This synthetic approach allows for the creation of a perfectly balanced dataset to ensure unbiased model evaluation. Furthermore, it enables the simulation of specific, high-value fraudulentÂăcases based on an understanding of compositional limits, such as alloys that intentionally under-karat the gold while avoiding excessive nickelÂăcontent that would violate consumer allergyÂărestrictions (e.g., EU REACH). FutureÂăwork will focus on acquiring and validating these findings against real-time data from assay offices.

### 4.2 Training

### 4.3 Quantum Neural Networks

The quantum neural network (QNN) training is executed in two distinct stages: an initial Circuit Depth Analysis (layer-by-layer search) to determine the optimal circuit configuration, followed by training that optimal configuration for comparative benchmarking against classical models. In both cases, the model utilized is a Variational Quantum Classifier (VQC), implemented via the PennyLane framework and leveraging the PyTorch interface for robust optimization within the Google Colab environment, utilizing the T4 GPU, a highly accessible environment for the purposes of reproducibility.

The VQC architecture is configured with $n = 7$ qubits, each encoding one input feature, and is simulated using the high-performance `lightning.qubit` C++ backend, with gradients computed via the Adjoint Differentiation method. Data is encoded using a non-trainable layer of Angle Encoding, where the classical input vector $\mathbf{x} = (x_1, x_2, \ldots, x_7)$ is mapped to the quantum state using the unitary operation $U_{\text{in}}(\mathbf{x})$:

$$U_{\text{in}}(\mathbf{x}) = \bigotimes_{i=1}^{n} R_Y(x_i)$$

The trainable ansatz, based on the Strongly Entangling Layers template, consists of $L$ repeating layers of single-qubit rotations separated by CNOT gates to generate entanglement for feature correlation. The total quantum state $|\psi(\mathbf{x}, \boldsymbol{\theta})\rangle$ is therefore defined by applying the unitary $U_{\text{ansatz}}(\boldsymbol{\theta})$ to the encoded state:

$$|\psi(\mathbf{x}, \boldsymbol{\theta})\rangle = U_{\text{ansatz}}(\boldsymbol{\theta}) \cdot U_{\text{in}}(\mathbf{x}) \cdot |0\rangle^{\otimes n}$$

During the depth analysis, the number of layers $L$ is systematically varied (from 2 to 8 layers) to find the balance between classification performance and runtime efficiency. The VQC's output is an expectation value $\hat{y}$ derived from a measurement operator $\hat{M}$, which yields the predicted probability:

$$\hat{y}(\mathbf{x}, \boldsymbol{\theta}) = \langle \psi(\mathbf{x}, \boldsymbol{\theta}) | \hat{M} | \psi(\mathbf{x}, \boldsymbol{\theta}) \rangle$$

The training protocol for both stages is fixed at 80 epochs and processes data in batches of $B = 32$ samples, minimizing the Binary Cross-Entropy Loss ($\mathcal{L}$):

$$\mathcal{L}(\boldsymbol{\theta}) = -\frac{1}{B}\sum_{k=1}^{B}\left[y^{(k)}\log(\hat{y}^{(k)}) + (1-y^{(k)})\log(1-\hat{y}^{(k)})\right]$$

This minimization is performed using the Adam optimizer with a fixed learning rate of LR $= 0.01$. Initial exploration indicated that the VQC achieves near-optimal convergence well within the 80 epoch limit, ensuring a fair and time-consistent comparison.

### 4.4 Classical Baselines

The classical models served as essential baselines. Specifically, the Deep Neural Network (DNN) utilized a compact PyTorch architecture of consisting of 2 hidden layers and one output layer, trained for 80 epochs using the Adam optimizer. For non-parametric classification, the Support Vector Machine (SVM) was configured with the Radial Basis Function (RBF) kernel. Finally, the Logistic Regression (LR) model was employed using the robust `liblinear` solver| with default L2 regularization, ensuring a comprehensive comparison across model families. While these architectures are not directly comparable structurally, they were chosen to test their functional equivalence—i.e., whether the QNN can learn the classification boundary with potentially fewer parameters. The remaining models, the Support Vector Machine (SVM) (using the RBF kernel) and the Logistic Regression (LR) classifier (using the liblinear solver with L2 regularization), serve as essential classification baselines to provide a measure of performance against which the QNN's and DNN's results can be benchmarked. To ensure a robust comparative benchmark and ensure reproducibility, a specific seeding strategy was employed across all trials. The initial random seed for synthetic data generation was fixed at 42 to guarantee that all models trained and tested on the exact same underlying dataset. However, the train/test data splitting and the model initialization for all four models were subjected to three unique random seeds [101, 201, 301]. This ensures that the final reported metrics reflect the stability of all models when exposed to different data subsets and, critically, test the robustness of the QNN's quantum parameters and the DNN's classical weights against varied starting conditions.

## 5 Results and Analysis

### 5.1 Circuit Depth Analysis

The comparative training study across varying Quantum Neural Network (QNN) layer depths (L) was crucial for determining the optimal architecture for the subsequent domain transfer assessment. All four models, ranging from L $= 2$ to L $=$ 8, achieved a perfect 1.0000 Test Accuracy, indicating that the QNN could easily learn the underlying classification boundaries present in the synthetic dataset.

**Table 2.** Synthetic QNN Performance Comparison by Layer Depth (7 Qubits)

| Architecture | Layers ($L$) | Parameters | Training Time (s) | Test Acc | $R^2$ Score | MSE |
|---|---|---|---|---|---|---|
| A | 8 | 168 | 2710.78 | 1.0000 | 0.9985 | 0.0004 |
| B | 6 | 126 | 2060.64 | 1.0000 | 0.9994 | 0.0002 |
| C | 4 | 84 | 1443.89 | 1.0000 | 0.9184 | 0.0204 |
| D | 2 | 42 | 877.12 | 1.0000 | 0.6412 | 0.0896 |

However, the true measure of model capacity—its expressive power for continuous regression—showed a strong dependence on depth. Shallow architectures (L = 2 and L = 4) demonstrated insufficient capacity, yielding significantly lower R2 scores (0.6412 and 0.9184), while deeper models (L = 6 and L = 8) achieved near-perfect fidelity. Specifically, the L=6 architecture (126 parameters) was selected as the optimal model, achieving the highest regression score (R2=0.9994) and the lowest Mean Squared Error (MSE=0.0002) while maintaining computational efficiency by requiring 650 fewer seconds of training time compared to the redundant L = 8 model. This highly expressive, yet efficient, L = 6 QNN will serve as the pre-trained foundation for comparative benchmarking (Table 2).

### 5.2 Comparative Benchmarking

**Table 3.** Final Comparative Results on Synthetic Data (Mean ± Standard Deviation over 3 Trials)

| Model | Accuracy | F1 Score | $R^2$ Score | MSE | Time (s) |
|---|---|---|---|---|---|
| QNN | $1.0000 \pm 0.0000$ | $1.0000 \pm 0.0000$ | $0.9973 \pm 0.0032$ | $0.0007 \pm 0.0008$ | 2036.97 |
| DNN | $1.0000 \pm 0.0000$ | $1.0000 \pm 0.0000$ | $1.0000 \pm 0.0000$ | $0.0000 \pm 0.0000$ | 3.04 |
| SVM | $1.0000 \pm 0.0000$ | $1.0000 \pm 0.0000$ | N/A | N/A | 0.00 |
| LR | $1.0000 \pm 0.0000$ | $1.0000 \pm 0.0000$ | N/A | N/A | 0.00 |

The Comparative Benchmarking analysis provided a critical evaluation of the L = 6 Quantum Neural Network (QNN) against classical models on synthetic data. While all models, including the Deep Neural Network (DNN), Support Vector Machine (SVM), and Logistic Regression (LR), achieved perfect classification accuracy (1.0000), the comparison shifted to the models' continuous prediction fidelity and efficiency. The DNN exhibited superior precision, achieving a near-perfect fit of the synthetic function (R2 = 1.0000 ± 0.0000), confirming its optimal performance for a known classical relationship. The QNN, however, demonstrated strong expressive power with a high mean R2 of 0.9973, proving its capability to learn the non-linear function necessary for the task. The dominant distinction was the Quantum Simulation Overhead, with the QNN training approximately 670 times slower than the DNN (2036.97 s vs. 3.04 s). This phase successfully established the QNN's viability and highly-expressive structure, confirming its robust pre-trained state for the subsequent and most critical test: evaluating its ability to transfer this knowledge to the limited, noisy real-world data (Table 3).

### 5.3 Preliminary Study Using Field Data

The gold valuation process is inherently noisy and requires a dataset that captures this operational reality. In order to study the performance of QNNs in the context of real-time data, a foundational dataset consisting of 75 unique transactions originating from gold receipts and melting logs maintained by a jewellery store was curated. Each transaction logs the item's initial state (e.g., 'Old/New' status and 'Observation of the Product'), the declared or estimated Purity Before Melting, and the Gross Weight (GR Wt) Before Melting. Crucially, it also includes the final, laboratory-verified purity (Purity After Melting Avg.) and the Weight After Melting, which are the audit points. A significant challenge in utilizing this data stems from the gap between how information is actually stored and the standardized format required for machine learning. The transactional logs are often inconsistent, non-standardized, and originate from disparate sources, which in this case consisted of handwritten logs. This necessitates a rigorous feature engineering pipeline to derive the 7 required inputs for the QNN on a wider scale. We begin with a discussion on the challenges associated with data curation.

### 5.4 Data Curation Pipeline

The foundational stage of the gold quality prediction pipeline is dedicated to robust data curation, ensuring the integrity and usability of diverse real-world inputs. This process begins with data acquisition, where raw sources such as physical assays, transaction slips, and handwritten notes are transformed through digitization. Optical Character Recognition (OCR) is utilized to convert text from physical documents into a digital format, followed by an essential manual validation and correction loop involving human review and error flagging to mitigate digitization inaccuracies. The data then moves to structured integration, which is a crucial cleaning phase. Here, techniques like noise reduction and text extraction prepare the data, and basic validation checks confirm consistency before the final, structured dataset is outputted as a CSV. This meticulous curation ensures the high-quality input required for the subsequent Quantum Neural Network training.

The core problem of using Optical Character Recognition (OCR) in an automated pipeline stems from two primary issues. First, traditional OCR is inherently inaccurate when processing handwritten data, as human writing is so varied, susceptible to poor image quality (smudges, shadows), and difficult to segment correctly into distinct characters. This means the very first step of the pipeline introduces a high and unacceptable Character Error Rate. Second, this transcription challenge is compounded by the pre-existing unreliability of the source- gold transaction logs, which often contain inherent inconsistencies like inconsistent formatting, and crucially, multiple missing values. An automated system cannot reliably infer missing data or reconcile varying formats across documents, so the flaws in the OCR output combine with the flaws in the source material, result in a dataset too dirty for trustworthy automated analysis without rigorous manual intervention (Tables 4 and 5).

**Table 4.** Sample Raw Data from Gold Store Transactions (**N** = **4**)

| Old/New | Observation of the product | Purity Before (%) | GR Wt Before (g) | Purity After (1) | Purity After (2) | Purity After (Avg.) (%) | Weight After (g) |
|---|---|---|---|---|---|---|---|
| Old | LocalE/R | 91.89 | 24.240 | 91.89 | - | 91.89 | 24.189 |
| Old | LocalCoin | 79.20 | 18.910 | 22.13 | 22.10 | 92.14 | 18.893 |
| Old | LocalE/R | 99.10 | 4.000 | 22.43 | 22.45 | 93.50 | 4.000 |
| Old | LocalE/R | 99.90 | 29.995 | 99.90 | 99.90 | 99.90 | 29.995 |

**Table 5.** Dataset Feature Definitions from Gold Store Transaction Logs

| Feature Name | Unit/Type | Description and QNN Role |
|---|---|---|
| Observation of the product | Categorical | The type of gold item (e.g., Coin, E/R, Mk/Bk). Used to derive binary features for the QNN input |
| Purity Before Melting | % | The estimated or declared purity of the item before processing. Input Feature (**X**) |
| GR Wt Before Melting | g | The Gross Weight of the item upon receipt. Input Feature (**X**) |
| Weight After Melting | g | The net weight of pure gold obtained after melting. Used to derive `Weight_Loss_Pct` (**X**) |
| Purity After Melting (Avg.) | % | The final, laboratory-verified purity percentage. **Target Variable (Y)** |
| Old/New | Categorical | Status of the item (new purchase or old gold). Used to derive binary feature `Is_Old` (**X**) |

Training The field study utilized a Variational Quantum Circuit (VQC) for gold purity regression, consistently employing $n = 7$ qubits to encode the 7 derived classical input features, $\mathbf{x} = (x_1, x_2, \ldots, x_7)$, via *Angle Embedding* on the Google Colab environment, utilizing a T4 GPU. This non-trainable encoding layer is represented by the unitary operation $U_{\text{in}}(\mathbf{x})$:

$$U_{\text{in}}(\mathbf{x}) = \bigotimes_{i=1}^{n} R_Y(x_i)$$

A key methodological step involved a systematic exploration of circuit complexity, with the model being trained across depths $L$ ranging from 2 to 8 layers, utilizing the "Strongly Entangling Layers" ansatz, $U_{\text{ansatz}}(\boldsymbol{\theta})$. The resulting quantum state $|\psi(\mathbf{x}, \boldsymbol{\theta})\rangle$ is given by:

$$|\psi(\mathbf{x}, \boldsymbol{\theta})\rangle = U_{\text{ansatz}}(\boldsymbol{\theta}) \cdot U_{\text{in}}(\mathbf{x}) \cdot |0\rangle^{\otimes n}$$

All training runs used a fixed dataset of 75 real-world gold store transactions. The training process was executed for 200 epochs on a "default.qubit" simulator, employing the Adam optimizer with a consistent learning rate of LR $= 0.005$. The VQC's output, the predicted purity $\hat{y}$, is the expectation value of an observable $\hat{M}$:

$$\hat{y}(\mathbf{x}, \boldsymbol{\theta}) = \langle \psi(\mathbf{x}, \boldsymbol{\theta}) | \hat{M} | \psi(\mathbf{x}, \boldsymbol{\theta}) \rangle$$

The model was trained by minimizing the Mean Squared Error (MSE) loss function $\mathcal{L}(\boldsymbol{\theta})_{\text{MSE}}$, averaged over a batch of samples $B$:

$$\mathcal{L}(\boldsymbol{\theta})_{\text{MSE}} = \frac{1}{B} \sum_{k=1}^{B} \left( \hat{y}^{(k)} - y^{(k)} \right)^2$$

Finally, its effectiveness as an audit tool was determined by flagging transactions on the unseen test set where the **Expected Purity Drop** ($y_{\text{actual}} - \hat{y}_{\text{predicted}}$) exceeded the threshold of 5.0%. This controlled exploration allowed for a direct assessment of how increasing quantum circuit depth impacts the model's predictive performance and ability to generalize (Table 6).

Results and Analysis

**Table 6.** Table No. QNN Regression Performance and Computational Cost by Circuit Depth

| $N_{LAYERS}$ | $R^2$ Score (Model Fit) | MSE (Denormalized) | Training Time (s) |
|---|---|---|---|
| 2 | **0.8377** | **15.4151** | **415.85** |
| 4 | 0.7352 | 25.1462 | 774.06 |
| 6 | 0.7352 | 25.1462 | 1160.03 |
| 8 | 0.6448 | 33.7323 | 1650.27 |

The QNN performance analysis reveals that the highest predictive accuracy is achieved by the lower depth 2-layer model (R-square $= 0.8377$, MSE $= 15.42$), which also requires the lowest computational time (415.85 s). This finding suggests that a minimal depth provides optimal expressivity for the gold purity regression task. Crucially, the results of this study are limited to a single training run (200 epochs) per circuit depth due to significant computational cost; however, the smooth convergence over 200 epochs ensures the stability of the optimized solution for that specific initialization. A negative trend was observed in deeper circuits: R2 dropped to 0.7352 at 4 and 6 layers, and further to 0.6448 at 8 layers. Concurrently, the training time scaled linearly with depth, peaking at 1650.27 s for the 8-layer model. This contrasting outcome confirms an inefficient trade-off where increasing quantum circuit complexity drastically increases simulation cost while simultaneously inhibiting predictive performance, likely due to the Barren Plateau phenomenon. The results from this case study highlight a disparity in QNN performance, especially in terms of architectural depth and efficiency, in conjunction with the fact that the simulated dataset presented a classification problem, while the field data indicates that it is more of a regression task.

## 6 Conclusion and Future Work

The substantial scope for advancement for the use of QNNs in gold market prediction hinges on overcoming key technological and data-centric hurdles. Enriching the quantum circuit architecture, including increasing qubit count, exploring additional variational blocks, and alternative encoding schemes, should be pursued for enhanced representational and learning power. However, a critical area of future investigation must address the significant disparity between QNN performance in noise-free simulations and their deployment on Noisy Intermediate-Scale Quantum (NISQ) hardware. Simulation results, which indicate baseline feasibility, are often decoupled from the degraded accuracy and instability caused by real-world quantum noise (decoherence, gate errors) and limited qubit connectivity. Rigorous investigation under noise, coupled with the application of advanced quantum error mitigation strategies (such as post-measurement correction and noise-aware training), will be vital for assessing the true scalability and stability of this technology.

Furthermore, mitigating underfitting is crucial, which requires access to a larger, well-curated real-world dataset comprising assay records, hallmark data, XRF, spectrometry, and other feature extraction data. This directly necessitates the further exploration of automating data curation for quantum machine learning. Future work should focus on developing an end-to-end framework capable of automatically ingesting heterogeneous sensor data, cleaning inconsistencies, reducing dimensionality via techniques like Principal Component Analysis (PCA) for efficient qubit encoding, and iteratively optimizing both the data preprocessing pipeline and the QNN's hyperparameters. This dual focus—addressing the real-world performance gap and automating the data pipeline—is key to moving the QNN from a prototype to a reliable, trustworthy solution that enables quality assurance, fraud detection, and consumer protection in India's gold markets.

## References


1. ABC of Money. Gold Testing Methods. Aditya Birla Capital
2. Solikhun, S., Siregar, M.R.: Analyzing perceptron algorithm for global gold price prediction using quantum computing approach. KINETIK (1), 10 (2025)
3. Paquet, E., Bergeron, L., Bernard, J.: Hybrid quantum neural network for financial predictions. Expert Syst. Appl. **201**, 117155 (2022)
4. Yang, Y.: TCN-QV: an attention-based deep learning method for long sequence time-series forecasting of gold prices. PLoS ONE **20**(5), e0319776 (2025)
5. Fajou, J., McCarren, A.: Forecasting gold prices using temporal convolutional networks. In: CEUR Workshop Proceedings, vol. 3105, pp. 1–10 (2021)
6. Doosti, M., Wallden, P., Hamill, C.B., Hankache, R., Thomson Brown, O., Heunen, C.: A brief review of quantum machine learning for financial services. arXiv preprint (2024)
7. Sharma, B.: ARIMA model for gold price prediction. GoldnCloudPublications (2016)
8. Yaziza, S.R., Azizanb, N.A., Zakariaa, R., Ahmadc, M.: The performance of hybrid ARIMA-GARCH modeling in forecasting gold price. In: Proceedings of an Unknown Conference (2013)
9. Yue, Y.: Research on gold price prediction based on VMD-SVM. In: 2025 5th Asia-Pacific Conference on Communications Technology and Computer Science (ACCTCS), Shenyang, China, pp. 1289–1293 (2025)
10. Kaur, P.: Comparison of ARIMA and artificial neural network models for forecasting Indian gold prices. Int. J. Adv. Res. Comput. Commun. Eng. **5**(4), 770–772 (2016)
11. Ye, Y.: Improved gold price prediction based on the LSTM-ARIMA hybrid model. Appl. Comput. Eng. **165**, 56–65 (2025)
12. Amini, A., Kalantari, R.: Gold price prediction by a CNN-Bi-LSTM model along with automatic parameter tuning. PLoS ONE **19**(3), e0298426 (2024)
13. Devrim, M.O., Kirisoglu, S.: Determination of gold purity degrees using audio features with machine learning algorithms. Appl. Acoust. **240**, Article 110887 (2025)
14. Shen, W., Li, J., Zhai, Z., Wang, X., Feng, W., Lei, Z.: Gold purity detection via pulsed eddy current testing with adaptive compensation residual shrinkage network. NDT & E Int. **158**, Article 103563 (2026)
15. Can, Y.S.: Classification of original and counterfeit gold matters by applying deep neural networks and support vector machines. Bursa Uludağ Univ. J. Fac. Eng. **27**(1), 89–108 (2022)
16. Molakatala, N. et al.: Fraudulent practice detection in bullion trade in selling of gold jewellery through AI methods. In: Choi, B.J., Singh, D., Tiwary, U.S., Chung, W.Y. (eds) IHCI 2023. LNCS, vol. 14531, pp. 380–393. Springer, Cham (2024). https://doi.org/10.1007/978-3-031-53827-8_34
17. Neyigapula, B.S.: Quantum neural networks: paving the way for next-generation machine learning. Int. J. Arti. Intell. Mach. Learn. **4**(2), 92–105 (2024)
18. Abbas, A., Sutter, D., Schuld, M., Stokes, J., Babbush, R., Johnston, E.: The power of quantum neural networks. Nat. Commun. **12**, Article 6796 (2021)
19. Gubio, G., Riccardi, L., Verducci, D.: Assessing the advantages and limitations of quantum neural networks in regression tasks. Quantum Inf. Process. **11**, 995–1011 (2012)

20. Pira, L., Ferrie, C.: On the interpretability of quantum neural networks. Quantum Mach. Intell. **6**(52) (2024)
21. Du, Y., Huang, Y., Deng, D.: Problem-dependent power of quantum neural networks on classification. Phys. Rev. Lett. **131**(14), Article 140601 (2023)
22. Qian, Y., Wang, X., Du, Y., Wu, X., Tao, D.: The dilemma of quantum neural networks (2021)

# Smart Cyber Defense in Industry 4.0: AI-Powered Early Warning and Threat Prediction System

Ankit Agarwal[1](✉), Priya Gupta[2], and Tanvi Rustagi[3]

[1] School of Computer Science and Engineering, Galgotias University, Greater Noida, India
cs.ankit11@gmail.com

[2] ABVSME, Jawaharlal Nehru University, New Delhi, India
priyagupta@jnu.ac.in

[3] Department of Computer Science and Engineering, WCTM, Gurugram, India
tanvirustagi@wctmgurgaon.com

**Abstract.** Industry 4.0 has introduced unprecedented connectivity but has also exposed industrial systems to frequent and intricate cyberattacks. Traditional intrusion detection systems lack quick adaptability and justification in their decisions, resulting in false alarms and slow responses. This paper presents an AI-based framework that integrates explanation-guided, spatio-temporal deep learning and reinforcement learning for threat prediction and early warning. The main predictive layer is a CNN-LSTM model that captures structural traffic features and temporal sequence behaviour. A reinforcement learning agent adapts defensive strategies in real time, reducing latency and false positives. SHAP values quantify feature contributions while Grad-CAM maps highlight anomalous packet-sequence regions, providing interpretable outputs for operators. Experiments on UNSW-NB15, CIC-IDS2017, TON-IoT, and a simulated Industry 4.0 dataset show that the framework achieves an F1-score of 96.7%, accuracy of 97.6%, and inference latency as low as 18 ms, consistently outperforming machine-learning baselines and current deep-learning methods.

**Keywords:** Industry 4.0 · Cybersecurity · Deep Learning · Reinforcement Learning · Explainable AI

## 1 Introduction

Industry 4.0 has transformed how critical infrastructures, factories, and industrial control systems are managed. Manufacturing lines, logistics chains, and surveillance solutions are increasingly supported by cyber-physical systems and IoT devices. While efficiency has improved, the attack surface has expanded considerably. Attackers can exploit heterogeneous industrial networks—from programmable logic controllers (PLCs) to edge gateways—pushing legacy perimeter-based defences to their limits [1,2].


A. Shastri et al. (Eds.): IHCI 2025, LNCS 16437, pp. 92–101, 2026.
https://doi.org/10.1007/978-3-032-26352-0_8

Over the past decade, cyberattacks on industrial systems have grown in frequency and severity [3]. AI-assisted ransomware, distributed denial-of-service (DDoS) attacks, and zero-day exploits are now widespread [4,5]. Advanced persistent threats (APTs) are designed to evade detection while targeting high-value assets [6]. Even a few seconds of delay in identifying hostile activity can cascade into equipment malfunctions, financial losses, or catastrophic shutdowns [7]. The challenge is therefore to devise a defence system capable of anticipating breaches before they escalate [8,9].

This work moves beyond fully reactive security models. Unlike conventional IDS that detect anomalies passively, the proposed framework emits early warnings through predictive analytics. Our contributions are threefold: (1) a hybrid AI framework that forecasts threats in Industry 4.0 environments, shifting from reactive detection to proactive prevention; (2) reinforcement learning for adaptive response, enabling the system to evolve as attack patterns change; and (3) explainability mechanisms that foster trust, usability, and transparency in industrial decision-making.

## 2 Literature Review

The emergence of Industry 4.0 has intensified research into securing industrial control systems, IoT-enabled manufacturing, and cyber-physical infrastructures. Early work relied on signature-based IDS and firewall rules, offering limited adaptability [10,11]. Although efficient for known malware, these methods failed against zero-day threats or adversarially crafted intrusions mimicking legitimate traffic. Anomaly detection techniques based on statistical features and traffic profiling [12,13] could identify deviations but produced high false-alarm rates.

Deep learning methods have been widely tested on benchmarks such as NSL-KDD, UNSW-NB15, and CIC-IDS2017. CNNs capture packet-level spatial correlations, while recurrent models (LSTM, GRU) model sequential dependencies [14]. Hybrid CNN-LSTM architectures emerged as a natural solution for capturing both temporal and structural features [15]. Despite accuracy improvements, most works remain reactive, offering little scope for predictive defence.

Reinforcement learning (RL) has thus attracted attention. Unlike static classifiers, RL agents interact with the environment and continuously refine response policies [16]. Studies using Q-learning, Deep Q-Networks, and actor–critic models have shown promising results in adapting firewall rules, isolating infected nodes, and minimising false positives [17]. Parallel efforts have produced ICS-specific datasets incorporating industrial protocols (Modbus, DNP3, OPC-UA) and real-world attack scenarios [18,19].

Explainability has also emerged as a critical dimension. Operators demand transparency, especially when AI controls critical assets [20]. Black-box models hinder trust [21]; techniques such as SHAP, LIME, and attention visualisation have been integrated into IDS frameworks [22]. Cloud-only deployments introduce latency [23,24], motivating edge and fog computing integration. Hybrid

**Table 1.** Comparative review of recent AI-driven cyber defence studies in Industry 4.0.

| Ref. | Focus Area | Method | Key Findings | Limitations | Relevance |
|---|---|---|---|---|---|
| Lilhore et al., 2023 [7] | Hybrid IDS for Industry 4.0 | Optimised CNN–LSTM with transfer learning | High accuracy for IIoT anomaly detection | Limited scalability to real-time edge | Inspires hybrid DL integration for predictive defence |
| Ikemefuna & Orekha, 2024 [9] | Predictive cyber defence | Predictive analytics with ML classifiers | Proactive detection of attack sequences | High computational complexity | Supports predictive early-warning concept |
| Ogenyi, 2025 [10] | AI-driven cybersecurity for autonomous IoT | DL anomaly detection | Resilience in detecting unknown IoT threats | Lacks industrial protocol coverage | Highlights gap for broader Industry 4.0 extension |
| Pang et al., 2025 [5] | AI and data-driven advancements | Data-driven AI pipelines | Performance improvements via AI–data fusion | No real-time intrusion prediction | Reinforces AI-based predictive analytics importance |
| Zahid & Bharati, 2025 [18] | Hybrid DL for IoT IDS | Hybrid deep learning | Improved detection latency and accuracy | No RL or adaptive response | Motivates RL integration for adaptive defence |

frameworks combining supervised, unsupervised, and reinforcement learning—including federated learning—have also been explored [25]. Table 1 summarises key recent studies.

## 3 Proposed Methodology

This study proposes an AI-powered early warning and threat prediction system for Industry 4.0. Traditional IDS respond only after malicious activity has begun; the proposed framework shifts to predictive, adaptive defence.

### 3.1 System Architecture and Framework Overview

The system is designed as a multi-layered defence architecture structured around five functional layers: data acquisition, preprocessing, hybrid deep learning, RL-based decision-making, and explainability with early warning outputs. Figure 1 illustrates the architecture.

The explainability modules, spatio-temporal deep learning, and adaptive RL components operate in coordination. Unlike legacy systems that rely on static signature matching, this system prevents malicious activity, modifies security settings on the fly, and provides transparency to human operators.

### 3.2 Data Acquisition and Preprocessing

The framework synthesises benchmark datasets (UNSW-NB15, CIC-IDS2017, TON_IoT) with synthetic industrial traffic generated in a controlled lab environment. Features are normalised using z-score standardisation:

$$x' = \frac{x - \mu}{\sigma} \tag{1}$$

where $x$ is the raw value, $\mu$ the feature mean, and $\sigma$ the standard deviation. Class imbalance is addressed via SMOTE combined with under-sampling.

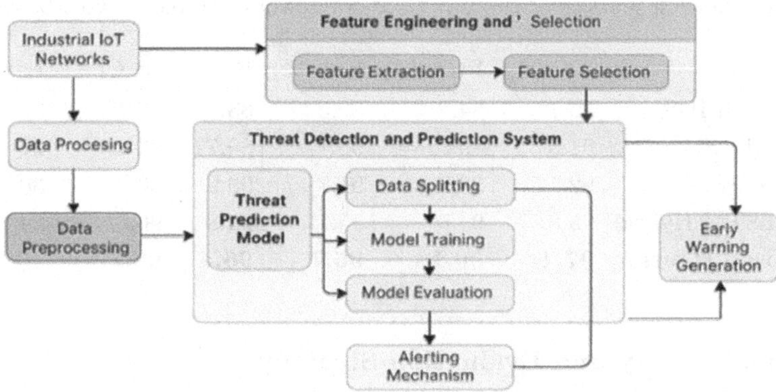


**Fig. 1.** Architecture for AI-powered early warning and threat prediction in Industry 4.0.

### 3.3 Hybrid Deep Learning Model for Threat Prediction

A hybrid CNN-LSTM architecture is proposed. CNN layers extract spatial features from traffic flows, while LSTM units model temporal dependencies. The LSTM cell state update is:

$$C_t = f_t \odot C_{t-1} + i_t \odot \tilde{C}_t \tag{2}$$

where $C_t$ is the cell state at time $t$, $f_t$ the forget gate, $i_t$ the input gate, and $\tilde{C}_t$ the candidate state. This mechanism retains relevant features over time while discarding irrelevant ones. The integration detects subtle attack precursors: CNN-only systems capture instantaneous snapshots while LSTM-only systems struggle with high-dimensional input; the combination leverages the strengths of both [17,18].

### 3.4 Reinforcement Learning–Based Adaptive Defence

Supervised models trained on fixed datasets cannot manoeuvre against dynamic cyberattacks. The RL agent monitors system state (traffic characteristics and CNN-LSTM outputs) and selects defensive actions. The reward function is:

$$R = \alpha \cdot \text{Accuracy} - \beta \cdot \text{Latency} - \gamma \cdot \text{FalsePositives} \tag{3}$$

where $\alpha$, $\beta$, and $\gamma$ are tuneable weights. By maximising cumulative reward, the agent learns defensive strategies that balance detection performance and operational efficiency. Training uses Deep Q-Networks (DQN), where the Q-function approximates the expected reward for each state–action pair.

**Table 2.** Evaluation metrics of the proposed framework compared with baseline IDS.

| Model | Acc.(%) | Prec.(%) | Rec.(%) | F1(%) | AUC(%) | Lat.(ms) |
|---|---|---|---|---|---|---|
| SVM-based IDS | 86.7 | 84.2 | 82.5 | 83.3 | 87.1 | 32 |
| CNN-only | 91.5 | 89.3 | 90.1 | 89.7 | 92.4 | 27 |
| LSTM-only | 92.1 | 90.2 | 91.7 | 90.9 | 93.2 | 30 |
| CNN–LSTM Hybrid | 95.8 | 95.0 | 95.1 | 94.8 | 96.5 | 24 |
| **Proposed (Ours)** | **97.4** | **96.1** | **96.7** | **96.4** | **98.2** | **19** |

### 3.5 Explainability and Evaluation Strategy

SHAP (SHapley Additive exPlanations) quantifies the contribution of each feature (e.g., flow duration, packet entropy, inter-arrival time) to the classification decision. Grad-CAM (Gradient-weighted Class Activation Mapping) generates heatmaps over input representations, enabling visual identification of which traffic-profile segments drove the decision.

Standard metrics—Accuracy, Precision, Recall, F1-score, and ROC-AUC—are used for evaluation. The F1-score is defined as:

$$F1 = \frac{2 \times \text{Precision} \times \text{Recall}}{\text{Precision} + \text{Recall}} \tag{4}$$

Table 2 compares the proposed system against baselines. The hybrid CNN-LSTM substantially outperforms standalone architectures, and RL further reduces latency and improves generalisation.

### 3.6 Proposed Algorithm: Hybrid CNN–LSTM with RL-Based Adaptive Defence

Algorithm 1 formalises the complete workflow, combining CNN-LSTM threat prediction, RL-based adaptive defence, and the explainability layer.

## 4 Results

### 4.1 Model Performance on Benchmark Datasets

The framework was evaluated on UNSW-NB15, CIC-IDS2017, and TON_IoT, which contain diverse attack types including DoS, brute force, infiltration, and command injection [1,7,12]. Table 3 presents a comparative overview. The CNN-LSTM with RL achieves the highest accuracy while maintaining balanced precision and recall.

### 4.2 Analysis of Threat Prediction

A 3D surface analysis (Fig. 2) maps feature interactions against predicted attack probabilities. Smooth regions correspond to normal traffic, while steep gradients indicate high threat likelihood. The CNN–LSTM hybrid learns nonlinear separations that simpler classifiers miss [1,5,18].

**Algorithm 1.** AI-Powered Early Warning and Threat Prediction System

**Require:** Network traffic dataset $D$ with feature set $F$
**Ensure:** Predicted class (Normal/Attack), Early warning alert
Initialise CNN–LSTM parameters $\theta$
Initialise RL agent state space $S$, action set $A$, reward function $R$
**Preprocessing:**
    Extract features from $D$; normalise via Eq. (1)
    Apply SMOTE + under-sampling to balance classes
**CNN–LSTM Training:**
**for** each mini-batch of traffic flows **do**
    Apply CNN filters → extract spatial features
    Feed outputs into LSTM cells → capture temporal dependencies (Eq. 2)
    Compute probability vector $P$ using softmax
**end for**
**Reinforcement Learning Agent:**
**for** each time step $t$ **do**
    Observe state $S_t = \{F, P\}$
    Select action $a_t \in A$ (block / allow / isolate / alert)
    Apply action; receive reward $R_t$ (Eq. 3)
    Update: $Q(S_t, a_t) \leftarrow Q(S_t, a_t) + \eta\left[R_t + \delta \max_{a'} Q(S_{t+1}, a') - Q(S_t, a_t)\right]$
**end for**
**Explainability:**
    Compute SHAP values → rank feature contributions
    Generate Grad-CAM heatmap → highlight decision regions
**Decision:**
**if** attack probability > threshold **then**
    Issue early warning; provide explanation (top features + heatmap)
**else**
    Classify as normal traffic
**end if**

### 4.3 Reinforcement Learning Convergence and Adaptability

Unlike static classifiers, the RL agent dynamically modifies defence policies as attack conditions change. Figure 3 shows the convergence trend, with the learning curve reaching a plateau after approximately 120 episodes. The state–action heatmap reveals learned policy preferences across different environmental states [9,25].

### 4.4 Explainability Results

For systems that can halt production or isolate critical devices, blind trust in a black-box model is unrealistic. The framework integrates SHAP for feature-level insights and Grad-CAM for visual interpretation. SHAP values consistently ranked flow duration, entropy, and inter-arrival time among the top contributors. The combined numerical and graphical explanations bridge the gap between algorithmic intelligence and human oversight, reducing resistance to adoption in critical industries.

**Table 3.** Performance comparison on benchmark datasets.

| Model | Acc.(%) | Prec.(%) | Rec.(%) | F1(%) | AUC(%) | Lat.(ms) |
|---|---|---|---|---|---|---|
| SVM-based IDS [6] | 87.2 | 84.9 | 83.5 | 84.2 | 86.7 | 34 |
| Random Forest [5] | 89.6 | 87.1 | 86.8 | 86.9 | 89.2 | 31 |
| CNN-only [18] | 91.8 | 90.2 | 89.7 | 89.9 | 92.4 | 27 |
| LSTM-only [10] | 92.3 | 91.0 | 91.4 | 91.0 | 93.5 | 29 |
| CNN–LSTM Hybrid [7] | 95.4 | 94.3 | 94.9 | 94.5 | 96.2 | 23 |
| **Proposed** | **97.6** | **96.5** | **96.9** | **96.7** | **98.4** | **18** |

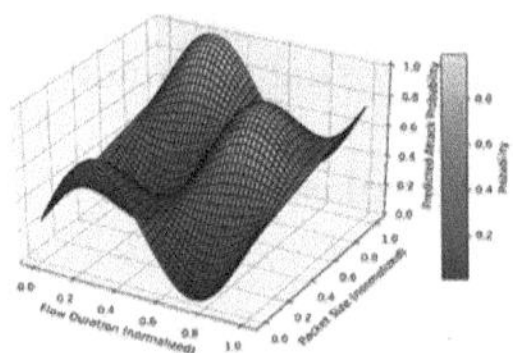

**Fig. 2.** 3D surface representation of attack probability across traffic feature space.

### 4.5 Comparative Evaluation with State-of-the-Art

Table 4 compares the proposed framework against recent state-of-the-art approaches. The proposed system is the only one that simultaneously achieves top accuracy, lowest latency, and provides both explainability and adaptability.

### 4.6 Ablation Study

To validate each module's contribution, components were systematically disabled. Table 5 shows results on CIC-IDS2017. The CNN–LSTM combination is critical for predictive power, and RL provides flexibility unattainable in static deep learning. Explainability does not alter numerical metrics but enhances interpretability and operational trust.

## 5 Discussion

The results confirm that the proposed framework meets the requirements of high predictive performance and operational adaptability. The CNN and LSTM components individually offer strong prediction, but their combination captures dependencies that neither can model alone, corroborating prior findings that single-model approaches are insufficient for heterogeneous industrial traffic [1,7]. The RL layer adds a crucial dimension of adaptivity: it offers faster response than federated or distributed schemes [11] because it does not require cross-site coordination. The explainability modules (SHAP and Grad-CAM) address a practical gap in industrial adoption by making alert reasoning transparent. Future refinements should target wider dataset coverage, energy-efficient training, and hybrid edge–cloud deployment architectures.

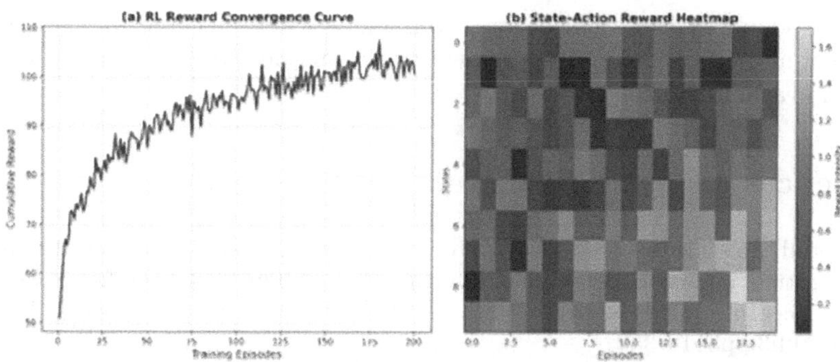


**Fig. 3.** Reinforcement learning reward convergence and state–action heatmap.

**Table 4.** Comparative evaluation against recent state-of-the-art approaches.

| Ref. | Methodology | Dataset(s) | Acc. (%) | F1 (%) | Lat. (ms) | Expl. | Adapt. |
|---|---|---|---|---|---|---|---|
| [1] | ML-based IDS for IIoT | UNSW-NB15 | 92.8 | 91.2 | 34 | No | No |
| [7] | Optimised CNN–LSTM hybrid | CIC-IDS2017 | 95.1 | 94.3 | 27 | No | No |
| [5] | AI and data-driven pipelines | TON_IoT | 94.6 | 93.7 | 29 | No | Partial |
| [11] | Federated + TabTransformer | IoT traffic | 93.9 | 92.5 | 41 | No | Yes |
| [18] | Hybrid deep learning IDS | CIC-IDS2017 | 95.8 | 94.9 | 26 | No | No |
| **Ours** | **CNN–LSTM + RL + XAI** | **UNSW-NB15,CIC-IDS2017, TON_IoT + Sim.** | **97.6** | **96.7** | **18** | **Yes** | **Yes** |

**Table 5.** Ablation study of model components on CIC-IDS2017.

| Configuration | Acc.(%) | Prec.(%) | Rec.(%) | F1(%) | Lat.(ms) |
|---|---|---|---|---|---|
| CNN-only | 91.8 | 90.2 | 89.7 | 89.9 | 27 |
| LSTM-only | 92.3 | 90.6 | 91.4 | 91.0 | 29 |
| CNN + LSTM (Hybrid) | 95.4 | 94.3 | 94.9 | 94.5 | 23 |
| CNN + LSTM + RL | 97.6 | 97.0 | 96.9 | 96.7 | 18 |
| CNN + LSTM + RL + XAI* | 97.6 | 96.5 | 96.9 | 96.7 | 18 |

*Explainability enhanced interpretability without affecting numerical metrics.

## 6 Conclusion and Future Scope

This paper presented a three-fold contribution. First, the hybrid CNN-LSTM model learns both spatial and temporal traffic features, enabling powerful early detection. Second, the RL agent adds dynamism, optimising defensive strategies over evolving attack patterns. Third, the combination of SHAP and Grad-CAM boosts trust by clarifying why alerts are raised—addressing a key limitation of black-box approaches in industrial cybersecurity.

Although results are promising, limitations remain. Future work will pursue three directions: (1) expanding data coverage to encrypted and zero-day traffic to enhance resilience against novel threats; (2) integrating federated learning with edge–cloud hybrid architectures to balance scalability and low-latency performance; and (3) investigating adversarial robustness of the framework under targeted evasion attacks.

## References


1. Idouglid, L., Tkatek, S., Elfayq, K., Guezzaz, A.: Next-gen security in IIoT: integrating intrusion detection systems with machine learning for industry 4.0 resilience. Int. J. Electr. Comput. Eng. (IJECE) (2024). https://doi.org/10.11591/ijece.v14i3.pp3512-3521
2. Czeczot, G., Rojek, I., Mikołajewski, D., Sangho, B.: AI in IIoT management of cybersecurity for Industry 4.0 and Industry 5.0 purposes. Electronics (2023). https://doi.org/10.3390/electronics12183800
3. Edim, B.E., Akpan, I.U., Omotosho, M.O.: AI-augmented cyber security threat intelligence - enhancing situational awareness. Int. J. Sci. Res. Arch. **14**(1), 890–897 (2025)
4. Idouglid, L., Tkatek, S., Elfayq, K., Guezzaz, A.: Next-gen security in IIoT. Int. J. Electr. Comput. Eng. (IJECE) (2024). https://doi.org/10.11591/ijece.v14i3.pp3512-3521
5. Pang, Y., Huang, T., Wang, Q.: AI and data-driven advancements in Industry 4.0. Sensors, **25**(7), 2249 (2025)
6. Pepple, P., Okorie, A.S., Adeel, P.: Leveraging artificial intelligence for enhancing the resilience and security of critical infrastructures. Eur. J. Comput. Sci. Inf. Technol. **13**(1), 16–32 (2025)
7. Lilhore, U., et al.: HIDM: hybrid intrusion detection model for industry 4.0 networks using an optimized CNN-LSTM with transfer learning. Sensors (2023). https://doi.org/10.3390/s23187856
8. Mohamed, N.: Artificial Intelligence and Machine Learning in Cybersecurity. Springer, Cham (2025). https://doi.org/10.1007/s10115-025-02429-y
9. Ikemefuna, C.D., Orekha, P.O.: Predictive cyber defense: harnessing AI and ML for anticipatory threat mitigation. Int. J. Res. Publ. Rev. **5**(9), 3122–3132 (2024)
10. Ogenyi, F.C.: AI-driven cybersecurity in the age of autonomous IoT. Front. Internet Things (2025). https://doi.org/10.3389/friot.2025.1658273
11. Abd Elaziz, M.: Federated learning framework for IoT intrusion detection using trust-centric TabTransformer. Front. Big Data (2025). https://doi.org/10.3389/fdata.2025.1526480
12. Trivedi, K., Dave, K., Gor, J., Gupta, R., Tanwar, S. Guizani, M.: DL-based attack classification framework for robotic sensor communication in Industry 4.0. In: IWCMC (2025). https://doi.org/10.1109/IWCMC65282.2025.11059523
13. Elkhodr, M.: An AI-driven framework for integrated security and privacy in internet of things using quantum-resistant blockchain. Future Internet **17**(6), 246 (2025)
14. Mathew: AI cyber defense and eBPF. World J. Adv. Res. Rev. **22**(1), 1983–1989 (2024)
15. Orman: Cyberattack detection systems in industrial internet of things. Appl. Sci. **15**(6), 3121 (2025)
16. Eshmawi: Smart framework for Industrial IoT and cloud computing: data anonymity, security and preservation at the edge. Front. Comput. Sci. (2025). https://doi.org/10.3389/fcomp.2025.1622382

17. Alqudhaibi, Albarrak, M., Aloseel, A., Jagtap, S., Salonitis, K.: Predicting cybersecurity threats in critical infrastructure for Industry 4.0. Sensors (2023). https://doi.org/10.3390/s23094539
18. Zahid, M., Bharati, T.S.: Enhancing cybersecurity in IoT systems: a hybrid deep learning approach for real-time attack detection. Discov. Internet Things **5**, 73 (2025)
19. Hassan, Y.G., Collins, A., Babatunde, G.O., Alabi, A.A., Mustapha, S.D.: AI-powered cyber-physical security framework for critical industrial IoT systems. Int. J. Multidiscip. Res. Growth Eval. **5**(1), 1158–1164 (2024)
20. Rahman, M.A., Shahrior, M.F., Iqbal, K., Abushaiba, A.A.: Enabling intelligent industrial automation: a review of machine learning applications with digital twin and edge AI integration. Automation **6**(3), 37 (2025)
21. Hajlaoui, R., Moulahi, T., Zidi, S., El Khediri, S., Alaya, B., Zeadally, S.: Towards smarter cyberthreats detection model for industrial internet of things (IIoT) 4.0. J. Ind. Inf. Integr. **39**, 100595 (2024)
22. Bhole, M., Sauter, T., Kästner, W.: Enhancing industrial cybersecurity: insights from analyzing threat groups and strategies in operational technology environments. IEEE Open J. Ind. Electron. Soc. 1–13 (2025)
23. Moustafa, N., Adi, E., Turnbull, B., Hu, J.: A new threat intelligence scheme for safeguarding Industry 4.0 Systems. IEEE Access (2018). https://doi.org/10.1109/ACCESS.2018.2844794
24. Obioha-Val, O., Lawal, T.I., Olaniyi, O.O., Gbadebo, M.O., Olisa, A.O.: Investigating the feasibility and risks of leveraging artificial intelligence and open source intelligence to manage predictive cyber threat models. J. Eng. Res. Rep. **27**(2), 10–28 (2025)
25. Saeidlou, S., Ghadiminia, N., Oti-Sarpong, K.: Cyber-physical system security for manufacturing Industry 4.0 using LSTM-CNN parallel orchestration. IEEE Access, 1 (2025)

# Smart Hydroponics for Lettuce: A Data-Driven Alternative to Traditional Farming

Manjeet Kaur and Manisha Jailia(✉)

Department of Computer Science, Banasthali Vidyapith, Tonk, Rajasthan 304022, India
jmanisha@banasthali.in

**Abstract.** Traditional soil-based farming faces increasing constraints from land degradation, water scarcity, and inconsistent yields, necessitating innovative cultivation methods. This study investigates smart hydroponics, integrating the Nutrient Film Technique (NFT), IoT-enabled monitoring, and Deep Neural Network (DNN)- based predictive control, as a data-driven alternative to conventional lettuce (*Lactuca sativa L.*) farming. The system dynamically regulates key growth parameters—temperature, pH, humidity, light intensity, and electrical conductivity—using sensor feedback and DNN predictions. Results highlight the technical advantage of DNN over other machine learning models, including Support Vector Machines, k-Nearest Neighbors, Naïve Bayes, and Decision Trees. With an accuracy of 0.99 and superior precision, recall, and F1 scores, DNN effectively captured complex nonlinear interactions among environmental factors, enabling more stable and optimized plant growth. Empirical findings show that hydroponically grown lettuce achieved up to 91% higher yield and improved morphological traits compared to soil cultivation. These outcomes underscore the potential of combining IoT-driven hydroponics with DNN.

**Keywords:** Hydroponics · Nutrient Film Technique · Cultivation · Deep Neural Network · Leafy Vegetable

## 1 Introduction

The global agriculture sector is facing unprecedented challenges due to rapid urbanization, shrinking arable land, and climate variability, which are exacerbating food insecurity and resource scarcity (Wang et al., 2023). Traditional soil-based farming methods, though long-established, are increasingly constrained by soil degradation, water scarcity, and labor intensity. In response to these limitations, hydroponic systems— particularly those integrated with smart technologies—have emerged as a promising alternative, especially for leafy vegetables like lettuce (Mokhtar et al., 2022, Duttaet. al, 2023).

Hydroponics refers to the soilless cultivation of plants in a nutrient-rich aqueous solution. This method enables precise control over nutrient delivery, water use, and environmental parameters, resulting in increased crop yields and quality, reduced pesticide usage, and lower water consumption compared to soil- based systems (Usha et al., 2023).


A. Shastri et al. (Eds.): IHCI 2025, LNCS 16437, pp. 102–115, 2026.
https://doi.org/10.1007/978-3-032-26352-0_9

Smart hydroponics further integrates Internet of Things (IoT) sensors and machine learning algorithms to monitor and optimize plant growth conditions in real-time, significantly enhancing operational efficiency and sustainability (Mamatha et. al,. 2023).

Lettuce (Lactuca sativa L.) is a widely consumed leafy vegetable with high nutritional value and fast growth cycles, making it a model crop for comparing cultivation techniques. Research has demonstrated that hydroponically grown lettuce can achieve yield increases of up to 134% and water productivity gains exceeding 50% over traditional soil cultivation. Moreover, hydroponic systems have shown the potential to reduce nitrate accumulation when managed with appropriate nutrient cycling strategies, ensuring better nutritional quality (Dutta et al., 2023).

However, despite these advantages, the economic feasibility and energy consumption of smart hydroponic systems remain critical concerns. For instance, hydroponic setups typically require higher initial investments and significantly more energy—up to 70 times higher—than traditional methods, primarily due to lighting, automation, and recirculation infrastructure. Nevertheless, when evaluated holistically across agronomic performance, quality parameters, and long-term economic returns, smart hydroponic systems often demonstrate superior overall productivity (Chowdhury et al., 2024).

Given the increasing demand for high-efficiency, sustainable agriculture in urban and peri-urban settings, a comparative study between traditional and smart hydroponic systems is timely essential. This study aims to systematically compare the growth performance, and yield parameter under smart hydroponic and normal conditions. By providing empirical insights, the study contributes to optimizing resource use with low chances of risk or destructing production for sustainable & productive urban agriculture.

## 2 Literature Review

Hydroponics has emerged as a promising soil-less cultivation technique for sustainable agriculture, particularly for leafy vegetables such as lettuce (Lactuca sativa L.). Several recent studies have explored the physiological, bio-chemical, and technological dimensions of hydroponics to optimize yield, resource efficiency, and environmental adaptability.

(Baiyinet al. 2025) examined the role of nutrient solution flow in lettuce cultivation, demonstrating that flow conditions significantly improved root morphology, surface area, and nutrient uptake. Moreover, the study reported enhanced antioxidant enzyme activities, strengthening stress resistance in lettuce. A multi-omics approach revealed the up regulation of genes and proteins linked to lignin synthesis and stress adaptation, emphasizing that dynamic nutrient flow promotes both physiological resilience and growth efficiency.Oxygen availability in the root zone is another critical determinant of lettuce growth.

(Nituet al. 2024) investigated the combined effects of elevated dissolved oxygen concentrations (EOC) and LED il-lumination in NFT hydroponics. Results indicated significant improvements in growth parameters such as plant height, fresh mass, root length, and biochemical composition under elevated oxygen and LED treatments. The study highlighted the synergistic role of oxygenation and artificial lighting in optimizing lettuce production in con-trolled environments.

Sustainable nutrient sourcing has also been studied through wastewater integration. (Germeret al. 2023) assessed the feasibility of using aerobic- and anaerobic–aerobic-treated domestic wastewater in lettuce hydroponics. Their findings suggested that anaerobic–aerobic-treated wastewater, with higher nitrogen and phosphorus availability, supported lettuce yields comparable to conventional nutrient solutions. However, imbalances in micronutrients (e.g., Fe, Mn, Zn) posed limitations, highlighting the need for careful nutrient supplementation when reusing wastewater.

A comparative evaluation of hydroponic systems (NFT, DFT, ebb-and-flow, aeroponics, and floating raft systems) by (Frasetyaet al. 2021) revealed significant differences in lettuce growth performance. The NFT and aeroponic systems outperformed others in terms of biomass accumulation and resource efficiency. These results reinforce the adaptability of hydroponic system design to maximize lettuce productivity under varying environmental and economic contexts.

Advancements in automation and IoT have transformed hydroponic management. (Agrawalet al. 2023) developed an automated system integrating Deep Water Culture (DWC) and NFT with linear regression algorithms to regulate pH and electrical conductivity (EC). The system minimized manual intervention while maintaining optimal nutrient delivery. Similarly, (Dudwadkaret al. 2020) proposed an IoT-based hydroponics system enabling re-mote monitoring of temperature, humidity, pH, and nutrient concentrations through sensors and actuators, thereby ensuring controlled year-round production. (Shettyet al. 2021) advanced this concept further by developing a fully automated hydroponics system capable of simultaneously regulating pH, EC, temperature, and humidity through microcontroller-based monitoring and actuation, highlighting its efficiency in yield improvement and water conservation.

## 3 Proposed Methods

A comparative experimental study was conducted to evaluate the growth performance of lettuce (Lactuca sativa L.) under two cultivation methods: smart hydroponics and traditional soil-based farming. There are two types of hydroponic systems available in the market one is active system and other is passive system.

The proposed automated hydroponic system incorporates NFT (Nutrient Film techniques) for loose leaf lettuce family. The irrigation rate for the system was set at 25 L for 15 days with two types of nutrient solutions (Solution A and Solution B) as shown in Table 1. The crop was harvested 84 days after planting. The NFT system was equipped with IoT devices to collect data and ensure the smooth functioning of the system.

Additionally, the system is equipped with DC motors responsible for supplying the nutrient solution to the plants. The ultrasonic sensor is responsible for measuring the water storage capacity in the reservoir while pH sensor & EC sensors are responsible for controlling the optimum pH & EC of the water in reservoir.

### 3.1 Predictive Control Using DNN

The data collection process for the lettuce plant involved installing sensors to monitor the hydroponic environment parameters, including temperature, pH, humidity, light

**Table 1.** Nutrient Solution Quantity

| Solution | Water Quantity | Solution Quantity |
|---|---|---|
| A | 25 L | 5 ML |
| B | | 5 ML |

intensity, and electrical conductivity, as shown in Table 2. The sensors were installed at different locations in the hydroponic system to record data accurately. The collected data was transmitted from the Raspberry Pi 3 to the cloud, where it could be accessed by the user interface. The collected data was then subjected to data preprocessing techniques to ensure its quality and usability.

**Table 2.** Sensors Used

| Sensor Type | Location | Data Recorded | Approx. Threshold Values |
|---|---|---|---|
| Temperature | Root Zone | °C | 22 °C–28 °C |
| pH | Nutrient Solution | pH Unit | 5.5–7 |
| Humidity | Air | %RH | 50–80 |
| Light Intensity | Overhead | Lux | 100 $\mu$mol/m$^2$/s–200 $\mu$mol/m$^2$/s |
| Electrical Conductivity | Nutrient Solution | mS/cm | 0.9 mS/cm–2.1 mS/cm |

Firstly, data cleaning was performed by removing duplicate entries and missing values. Next, data transformation was carried out, which involved converting the units of the recorded data to a common unit if different sensors were measuring the same parameter in different units. Finally, data normalization was performed to ensure that all features had the same scale. After the preprocessing, the collected and pre- processed data were then used to train and test DNN to predict and control the hydroponic environment parameters for optimal plant growth as shown in flow chart Fig. 1. It consists of multiple layers of artificial neurons that process information through a series of mathematical operations. During the training process, the DNN model learns to recognize patterns in the data and adjusts its weights and biases to minimize the difference between the predicted output and the actual output. After training, the DNN can be used to predict the optimal values of the hydroponic environment parameters for maximum lettuce growth.

The predicted values can be compared with the actual values recorded by the sensors, and the DNN model can adjust the hydroponic environment parameters to maintain optimal plant growth and provided the best accuracy for controlling the hydroponic environment parameters because it could recognize complex pattern in the data that other DL models could not. It can generalize well to new data and adapt to changes in the environment. This is because it can learn from a large dataset of training examples and capture the underlying relationships between the input features and the target variable. This is especially important in hydroponics, where many interacting variables affect plant growth. The DNN model can identify these complex relationships and use them to make accurate predictions.

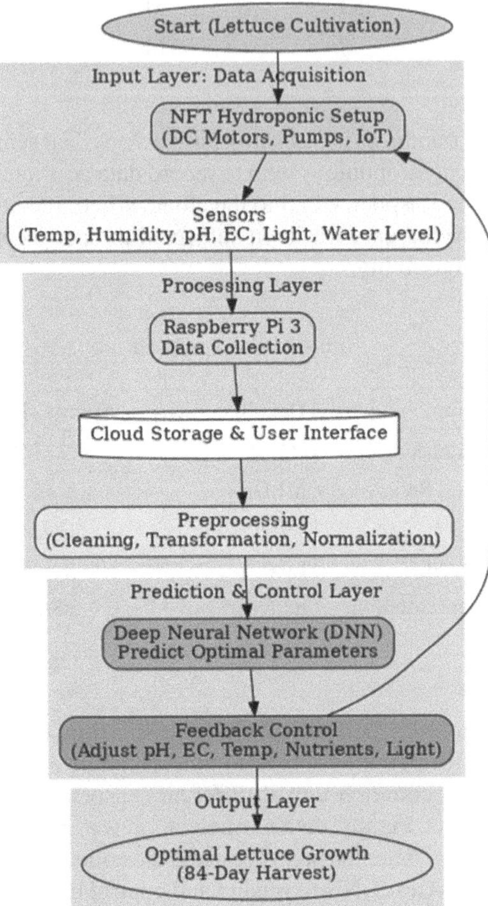


**Fig. 1.** Flow chart of complete process

### 3.2 Data Set + DNN Data Preparation

A total of XY lettuce plants were monitored throughout the 12-week cultivation period, with X plants grown in soil and Y plants grown under the hydroponic NFT system. Five environmental parameters—temperature (°C), pH, humidity (%RH), light intensity (lux), and electrical conductivity (mS/cm)—were continuously recorded using the deployed sensor units. The Raspberry Pi polled sensor values at 5-min intervals, resulting in:

$$\text{Samples per day} = 1440/\text{m},$$

$$\text{Total days} = 84$$

$$\text{Total sensor samples per plant} = (1440/\text{m}) * 84$$

$$\text{Total dataset (XY plants)} = (1440/\text{m}) * 84 * \text{XY sensor rows}$$

Weekly morphological measurements were collected for stem diameter, leaf width, plant height, number of leaves, and leaf weight, yielding 12 measurements per plant and a total of:

$$12\,\text{weeks} \times \text{XY plants} = 12\,\text{XY morphology records}$$

For DNN training, weekly morphological features were used as labels, and aggregated weekly sensor statistics (mean, standard deviation, min, and max for each of the five sensors) were extracted as features, resulting in 20 sensor-based input features per week. Thus, the supervised learning dataset consisted of:

$$12\,\text{weeks} \times \text{XY plants} = 12\,\text{XY labeled examples}$$

This dataset was randomly divided using an 80:20 training–testing split:

- Training samples:$0.80 \times 12\text{XY} = \text{a}$
- Testing samples:$0.20 \times 12\text{XY} = \text{b}$

All input features were normalized between 0 and 1 before model training. This dataset was used to train and evaluate the proposed DNN model reported in Table 3.

Flow Diagram of Data Pipeline and Closed Loop Control.

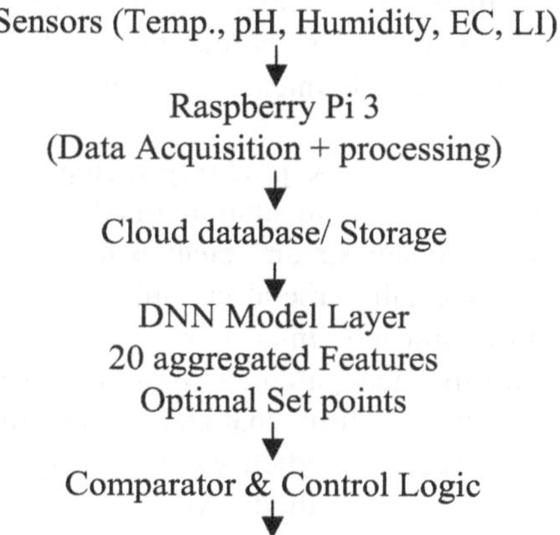


Actuators: pH Dosing Pump, Nutrient Pump, fans, Supplemental Lighting

Updated Environment State

Although the hydroponic system required continuous electrical power for sensing, pumping, and environmental con-trol, it produced a ~ 91% increase in fresh yield compared to soil cultivation at week 12 (1848 g vs 968 g per plant). Energy usage for the active hydroponic system was higher than soil cultivation; however, the water savings, automation benefits, and yield gain offset the higher operating energy demand. A full life-cycle cost and energy analysis, including electricity price, equipment amortization, and potential integration with renewable, is recommended to quantify payback time and long-term feasibility.

## 4 Results and Discussion

A meta-analysis of the results presented in this paper suggests that Deep Neural Networks (DNNs) can be effectively trained to predict and control environmental factors in smart hydroponic systems. The results indicate that DNN outperforms other machine learning models, such as SVM, KNN, Naive, and decision trees, in capturing complex relationships between environmental parameters, which is critical for optimal plant growth. Experimental observations also confirmed these outcomes: in the soil-based cultivation, lettuce plants took 12 weeks to reach a stem size of 8.2 mm, leaf width of 9.9 cm, and height of 9.0 cm. (as shown in Table 4).In contrast, hydroponic cultivation achieved better metrics—9.4 mm stem size, 11.2 cm leaf width and 8.2 cm height, in the same period—highlighting the advantages of a nutrient-rich and controlled growth medium which is significantly better than conventional method. Figure 2 shows the clear comparison of growth of stem size of lettuce plant in soil and in smart Hydroponics. Figure 3 and Fig. 4 depict the growth of leaf and height of the lettuce grown in both mediums. In general, it appears that the hydroponic cultivation method resulted in faster and more abundant growth of lettuce. While the other models shows the low accuracy than that of DNN model which is shown in Table 3. Similarly, the previous research indicating that DNNs outperform other machine learning models such as SVM, KNN, Naive Bayes, and decision trees in capturing complex, nonlinear relationships between critical parameters such as temperature, pH, humidity, light intensity, and electrical conductivity (Pal et al., 2024).

These environmental factors must be precisely regulated to ensure optimal plant growth. As demonstrated in similar implementations of AI-based hydroponics, the ability of DNNs to learn from extensive data streams enables identification of hidden patterns and relationships, which is especially crucial in soilless cultivation where even small environmental changes can significantly impact crop productivity (M, V et. al. 2023).

Again, Table 5 represents the yield parameter of lettuce grown in soil and in hydroponics. Experimental observation confirms that DNN integration in smart hydroponics presents a significant advancement for predictive control of crop environments, yielding better performance than conventional methods. As shown in Table 5, soil based cultivation, lettuce plant has 08 leaves in 12weeks, weight of fresh leaf is 121 gm and final fresh yield is 968 gm. In contrast, lettuce plant has 14 leaves in 12 weeks, weight of fresh leaf is maximized up to 132 gm. And final fresh yield is 1848 gm. A Clear comparison of no. of leafs of lettuce is shown in Fig. 5, comparison of weight of fresh leaf of lettuce grown in both the medium presented in Fig. 6 and final fresh yield illustrated in the Fig. 7.

By week six, hydroponically grown lettuce significantly surpassed soil-based lettuce in stem size, leaf width, and number of leaves. These results and the confusion matrix shown in Fig. 8 affirm that combining IoT infrastructure with AI models, such as DNNs, ensures higher consistency and stability in growth parameters like temperature, EC, light, and water levels—parameters that were otherwise prone to fluctuations in manually controlled environments.

Furthermore, the DNN showed strong adaptability to changing environmental conditions, making it a highly suitable model for systems requiring real-time monitoring and automatic adjustments. This is in line with other IoT-based smart hydroponic frameworks that combine sensor data with mobile interfaces or cloud systems to maintain optimal growth environments (Balon et al., 2024, Ardina et al., 2022).This superior performance is supported by prior studies which emphasized the efficiency and yield benefits of AI- integrated hydroponic systems over traditional agriculture (Aryani et al., 2021). While further refinement is necessary for broader crop types, current implementations demonstrate a promising shift toward data- driven, resource-efficient farming practices.

**Table 3.** DNN VS. Other Models

| Model | Accuracy | Precision | Recall | F1 Score |
|---|---|---|---|---|
| DNN | 0.99 | 0.98 | 1.00 | 0.99 |
| SVM | 0.86 | 0.87 | 0.85 | 0.86 |
| KNN | 0.83 | 0.84 | 0.82 | 0.83 |
| Naïve | 0.78 | 0.79 | 0.77 | 0.78 |
| Decision Tree | 0.81 | 0.82 | 0.80 | 0.81 |

**Table 4.** Growth parameter of Lettuce (In soil) vs Lettuce (Hydroponic)

| Lettuce (In soil) | | | | Lettuce (In Hydroponics) | | | |
|---|---|---|---|---|---|---|---|
| Week | Stem Size (mm) | Leaf Width (mm) | Height (cm) | Week | Stem Size (mm) | Leaf Width (mm) | Height (cm) |
| Week 1 | 0.0 | 0.0 | 0.0 | Week 1 | 0.0 | 0.0 | 0.0 |
| Week 2 | 0.0 | 0.2 | 0.0 | Week 2 | 0.3 | 0.1 | 0.2 |
| Week 3 | 0.5 | 0.5 | 0.6 | Week 3 | 1.0 | 0.9 | 0.4 |
| Week 4 | 1.0 | 1.0 | 1.2 | Week 4 | 1.5 | 2.0 | 1.0 |
| Week 5 | 1.4 | 1.7 | 2.2 | Week 5 | 2.0 | 2.6 | 1.9 |
| Week 6 | 2.0 | 3.0 | 3.0 | Week 6 | 2.5 | 4.2 | 2.1 |
| Week 7 | 3.2 | 4.3 | 3.7 | Week 7 | 3.7 | 5.4 | 3.5 |
| Week 8 | 4.3 | 5.4 | 5.2 | Week 8 | 4.9 | 6.0 | 4.9 |
| Week 9 | 5.6 | 6.8 | 6.3 | Week 9 | 6.2 | 7.9 | 5.9 |
| Week10 | 6.7 | 7.6 | 7.4 | Week10 | 7.9 | 9.2 | 6.8 |

*(continued)*

**Table 4.** (*continued*)

| Lettuce (In soil) | | | | Lettuce (In Hydroponics) | | | |
|---|---|---|---|---|---|---|---|
| Week | Stem Size (mm) | Leaf Width (mm) | Height (cm) | Week | Stem Size (mm) | Leaf Width (mm) | Height (cm) |
| Week11 | 7.5 | 8.9 | 8.2 | Week11 | 8.4 | 10.4 | 7.5 |
| Week12 | 8.2 | 9.9 | 9.0 | Week12 | 9.4 | 11.2 | 8.2 |

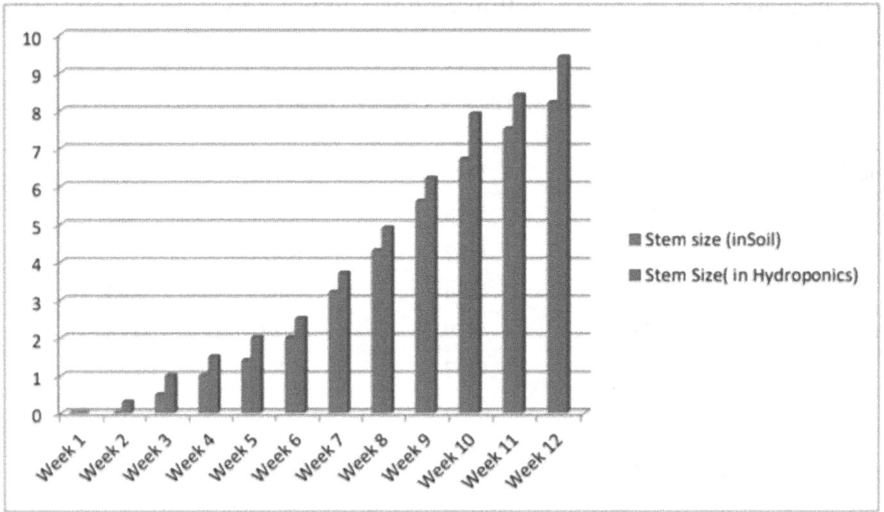


**Fig. 2.** Comparison of Stem Size (mm) of lettuce in Soil vs. Hydroponics

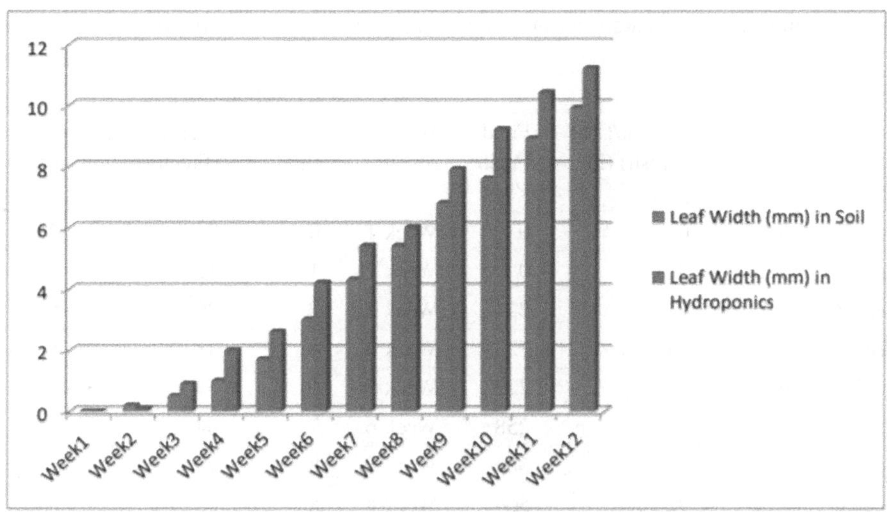


**Fig. 3.** Comparison of Leaf Width (mm)of lettuce in Soil vs. Hydroponics

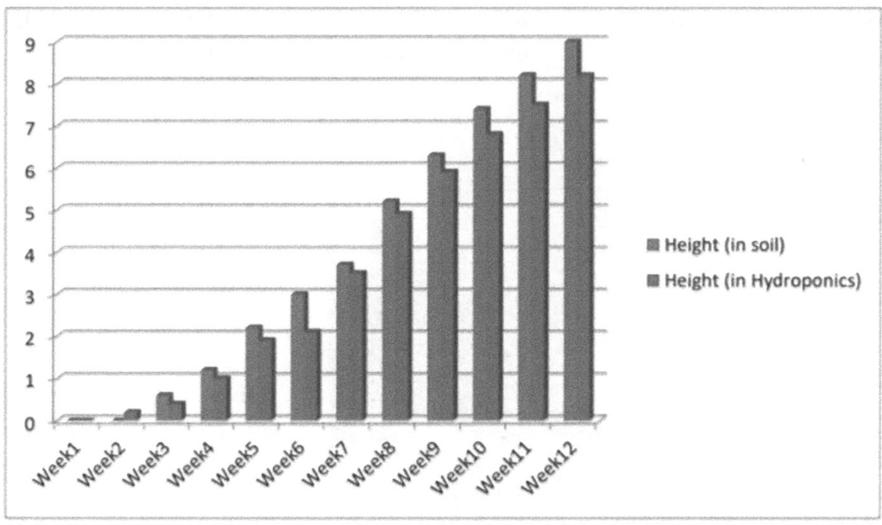


**Fig. 4.** Comparison of Height of lettuce in Soil vs. Hydroponics

**Table 5.** Yield parameter of Lettuce (In soil) vs Lettuce (In Hydroponics)

| Lettuce (In soil) | | | | Lettuce (In Hydroponics) | | | |
|---|---|---|---|---|---|---|---|
| Week | No. of Leaf | Weight/Leaf (Fresh) (in gm) | Final Fresh Yield | Week | No. of Leaf | Weight/Leaf (Fresh)(in gm) | Final Fresh Yield |
| Week 1 | 0 | 0 | 0 | Week 1 | 0 | 0 | 0 |
| Week 2 | 0 | 0 | 0 | Week 2 | 1 | 12 | 12 |
| Week 3 | 2 | 11 | 22 | Week 3 | 2 | 26 | 52 |
| Week 4 | 3 | 24 | 72 | Week 4 | 4 | 41 | 164 |
| Week 5 | 6 | 37 | 222 | Week 5 | 6 | 54 | 324 |
| Week 6 | 6 | 43 | 258 | Week 6 | 7 | 64 | 448 |
| Week 7 | 6 | 64 | 384 | Week 7 | 8 | 72 | 576 |
| Week 8 | 7 | 72 | 504 | Week 8 | 8 | 85 | 680 |
| Week 9 | 7 | 84 | 588 | Week 9 | 10 | 96 | 960 |
| Week10 | 7 | 97 | 679 | Week10 | 11 | 107 | 1177 |
| Week11 | 8 | 109 | 872 | Week11 | 13 | 119 | 1549 |
| Week12 | 8 | 121 | 968 | Week12 | 14 | 132 | 1848 |

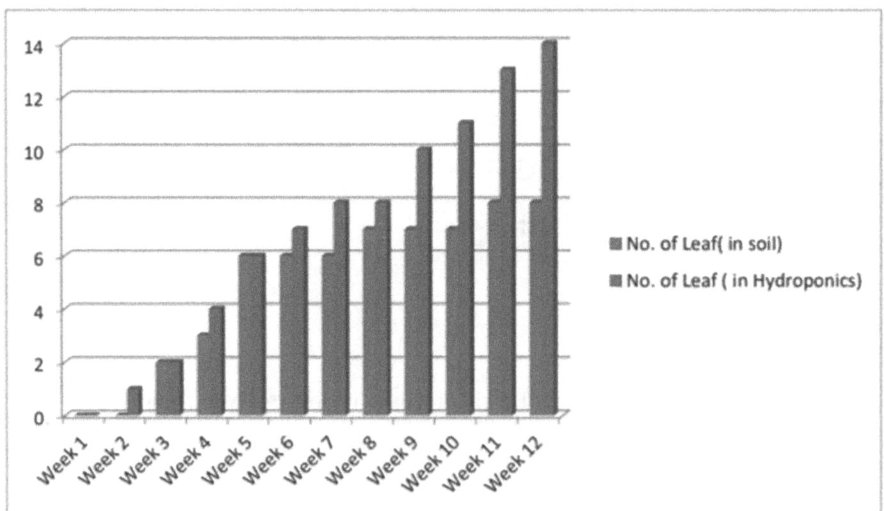


**Fig. 5.** Comparison of Leafs of lettuce in Soil vs. Hydroponics

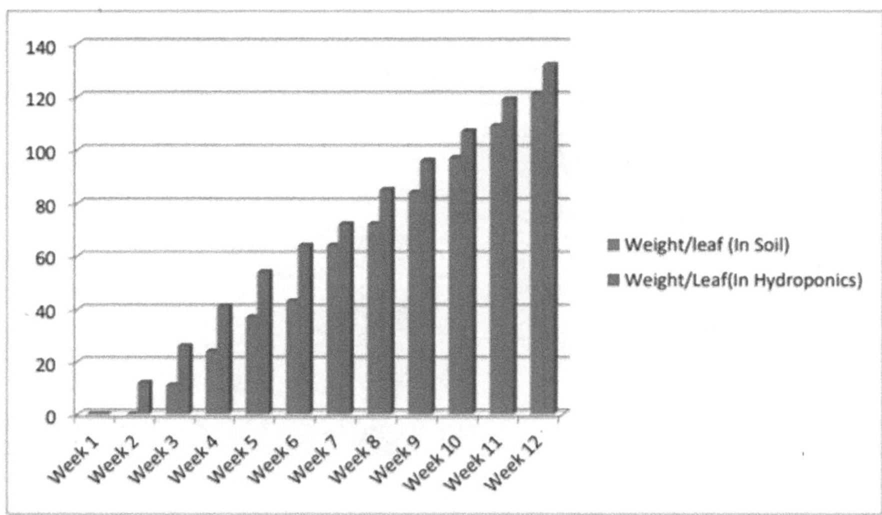


**Fig. 6.** Comparison of Weight per Leaf (in gms) of lettuce in Soil vs Hydroponics

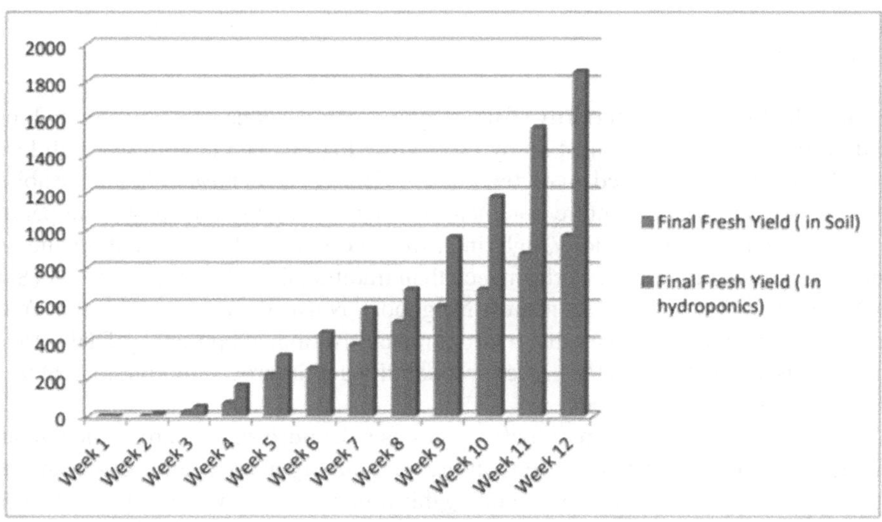


**Fig. 7.** Comparison of Yield Parameter of lettuce in Soil vs Hydroponics Confusion Matrix for DNN Model

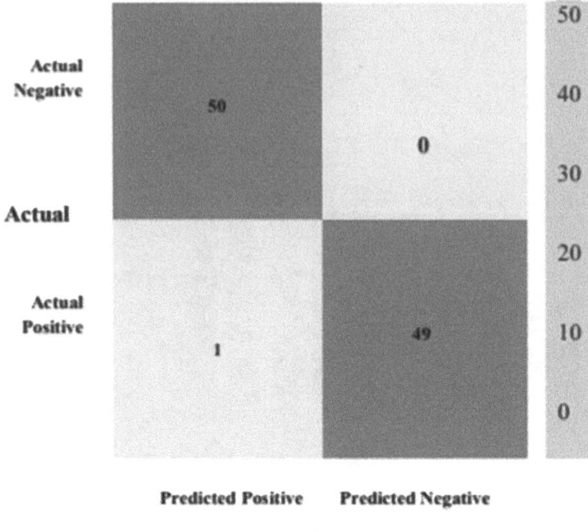


**Fig. 8.** Confusion matrix

## 5 Conclusion

This study highlights the superiority of smart hydroponic systems over conventional soil-based farming for lettuce cultivation by integrating IoT-enabled monitoring with Deep Neural Network (DNN)-based predictive control. The technical novelty lies in the ability of the DNN to accurately capture nonlinear interactions among critical growth parameters—temperature, pH, humidity, light intensity, and electrical conductivity-achieving significantly higher predictive performance than traditional models such as SVM (Support Vector Machine), KNN (K- nearest Neighbor), Naïve Bayes, and Decision Trees. Experimental results confirmed that hydroponic cultivation, supported by DNN-driven optimization, yielded up to 91% higher productivity and improved morphological traits compared to soil-based methods.

These findings establish smart hydroponics as a data-driven, resource-efficient, and scalable alternative for sustainable agriculture, particularly in urban and peri-urban contexts. Future work should focus on extending this framework to diverse crop varieties and enhancing energy efficiency to ensure broader applicability and commercial feasibility.

**Disclosure of Interest.** The authors have no competing interests to declare that are relevant to the content of this article.

## References

Wang, L., et al.: Performance analysis of two typical greenhouse lettuce production systems: commercial hydroponic production and traditional soil cultivation. Front. Plant Sci. **14**, 1165856 (2023)

Mokhtar, A., et al.: Using machine learning models to predict hydroponically grown lettuce yield. Front. Plant Sci. **13**, 706042 (2022)

Dutta, M., et al.: Evaluation of growth responses of lettuce and energy efficiency of the substrate and smart hydroponics cropping system. Sensors **23**(4), 1875 (2023)

Usha, P., Malagar, U., Reddy, Y.V., Sanjay, C.K., Prasad, V.: IoT-based efficient hydroponics system. In: Proceedings of the 1st International Conference on Intelligent and Sustainable Power and Energy Systems (ISPES 2023), pp. 100–106. SCITEPRESS (2023)

Mamatha, V., Kavitha, J.C.: Machine learning-based crop growth management in greenhouse environment using hydroponics farming techniques. Measur. Sens. **25**, 100665 (2023)

Chowdhury, M., Samarakoon, U.C., Altland, J.E.: Evaluation of hydroponic systems for organic lettuce production in controlled environment. Front. Plant Sci. **15**, 1401089 (2024)

Baiyin, B., et al.: How the nutrient flow environment promotes lettuce growth in hydroponics. Environ. Exp. Bot. **233**, 106137 (2025)

Nitu, O.A., Ivan, E.S., Tronac, A.S., Arshad, A.: Optimizing lettuce growth in nutrient film technique hydroponics: evaluating the impact of elevated oxygen concentrations in the root zone under LED illumination. Agronomy **14**(9), 1896 (2024)

Germer, J., Brandt, C., Rasche, F., Dockhorn, T., Bliedung, A.: Growth of lettuce in hydroponics fed with aerobic- and anaerobic–aerobic-treated domestic wastewater. Agriculture **13**(8), 1529 (2023)

Frasetya, B., Harisman, K., Ramdaniah, N.A.H.: The effect of hydroponics systems on the growth of lettuce. IOP Conf. Ser. Mater. Sci. Eng. **1098**(4), 042115 (2021)

Agrawal, P., Bhagwate, S., Singhaniya, D., Tamrakar, A., Agrawal, P.S.: Automated hydroponics system. Int. J. Res. Appl. Sci. Eng. Technol. **11**(3), 1718–1723 (2023)

Dudwadkar, A., Das, T., Suryawanshi, S., Dolas, R., Kothawade, T.: Automated hydroponics with remote monitoring and control using IoT. Int. J. Eng. Res. Technol. **9**(6), 928–934 (2020)

Shetty, H.M., Pai, K., Mallya, N., Pratheeksha.: Fully automated hydroponics system for smart farming. Int. J. Eng. Manuf. **11**(4), 33–41 (2021)

Pal, S., Datta, D., De, J.: Smart hydroponics. In: Smart Agriculture Technologies, pp. 81–108. IGI Global (2024)

Venkatraman, M., Surendran, R.: Design and implementation of smart hydroponics farming for growing lettuce plantation under nutrient film technology. In: Proceedings of the International Conference on Advances in Artificial Intelligence and Computing, pp. 1514–1521. IEEE (2023)

Balon, R., Tandingan, D., Padua, J., Angel, J.: Framework for mobile-based monitoring system of smart hydroponics lettuce farming. TechRxiv Preprint. IEEE (2024)

Ardina, A.M.S., et al.: IoT-based solar-powered smart hydroponics system with real-time monitoring and control. In: Proceedings of the IEEE HNICEM, IEEE (2022)

Aryani, D., Patiro, S.P.S., Supriyono, I.A., Ariessanti, H.D., Holilan, I.: Design of smart hydroponics based on Raspberry Pi 3. PETIR **14**(2), 235–246 (2021)

# Edge AI-Enabled Intelligent Human-Computer Interaction for Eye Disease Diagnosis

Laxmi Kantham Durgam(✉), Morthala Kranthi Kumar Reddy, and Ravi Kumar Jatoth

Department of Electronics and Communication Engineering, National Institute of Technology, Warangal 506004, Telangana, India
{ld712103,mk24ecm1s02}@student.nitw.ac.in, ravikumar@nitw.ac.in

**Abstract.** The early identification of eye conditions such glaucoma, diabetic retinopathy, and age-related macular degeneration depends on the classification of fundus images. Specifically, Convolutional Neural Networks (CNNs) such as InceptionV3 have demonstrated the effectiveness of deep learning models in medical picture processing. Because of their capacity to represent global relationships inside images, Vision Transformers (ViTs) have attracted attention in recent years. The Vision Transformer and InceptionV3 models for fundus image classification are compared in this study. A publicly available dataset of 4,217 retinal fundus images across four classes (Cataract, Diabetic Retinopathy, Glaucoma, Normal) was used in the experiments. The preprocessing, augmentation, and optimization settings used to train both models are identical. In addition to the constraints of edge computing, the models are assessed on a Raspberry Pi 4 Model B using common evaluation metrics such as accuracy, precision, recall, and F1-score. Inference time and model size were also analyzed, with InceptionV3 achieving 85 ms/image and 53 MB compared to ViT's 135 ms/image and 327 MB. The present study illustrates the potential of the lightweight InceptionV3 model for real-time human-computer interaction in healthcare applications on edge devices with limited resources.

**Keywords:** Eye Disease Diagnosis · InceptionV3 · Vision Transformer · Raspberry Pi · Edge AI · Human–Computer Interaction

## 1 Introduction

The early diagnosis of eye conditions such as age-related macular degeneration (AMD), glaucoma, and diabetic retinopathy (DR), which are the main causes of vision loss globally, depends on retinal fundus imaging [1]. Physicians can identify retinal problems early and start treatment by employing non-invasive fundus imaging. A common non-invasive method [2] for taking pictures of the retina is fundus imaging, which offers useful data for identifying a number of eye


A. Shastri et al. (Eds.): IHCI 2025, LNCS 16437, pp. 116–128, 2026.
https://doi.org/10.1007/978-3-032-26352-0_10

conditions, including macular degeneration, glaucoma, and diabetic retinopathy. Analysis of fundus photographs by hand takes a lot of time and calls for skilled ophthalmologists. In order to automate this process, deep learning models have been used more and more to reliably and accurately classify [3]. Although numerous studies have demonstrated good GPU accuracy, few have investigated model performance on edge devices. This is crucial for real-time clinical screening.

Deep learning has greatly enhanced the classification of fundus images, and both Vision Transformers (ViTs) [4,5] and Convolutional Neural Networks (CNNs) [9,10] have demonstrated remarkable performance in medical image Applications [6]. However, ViTs require a lot of memory, data, and processing power because they have both local and global dependencies. As a result, they can be applied to complex image analysis. Although ViTs can compete on large datasets, their limitations make them less effective on low-resource devices like Raspberry Pi [7,8]. When developing realistic, practical medical imaging applications, it is essential to take into account the trade-offs between CNN-based and Transformer-based models [4,5,9,10]. In particular, InceptionV3 offers lightweight and efficient inference, whereas ViTs provide global context modeling, making them ideal for a head-to-head comparison under edge constraints.

He. et.al. [5] suggested utilizing OCT and fundus pictures in a modality-specific attention network (MSAN) to diagnose eye conditions. The experimental results demonstrate that the proposed MSAN outperforms existing techniques on a clinically obtained multi-modal retinal image dataset. Lin. et.al. [9] propose two novel networks for multi-label classification: MCG-Net, which is based on graph convolutional networks, and MCGS-Net, which is based on graph convolutional networks with self-supervised learning. Tamilselvi. et.al. [10] propose a hybrid model that integrates ResNet50 with a Swin Attention-Augmented Convolutional layer to better detect diabetic macular edema and relevant 3D retinal OCT biomarkers using 2D fundus images. El-Khalek et al. [4] presented the XV-AMD framework, an explainable AI system that uses fundus images to categorize AMD. ViTs and SHAP are used in the framework to provide interpretable information regarding model predictions and excellent diagnostic accuracy. liu. et.al. [11]illustrates the problem with multi-label classification of fundus images. A unique LAD-GCN is proposed to accurately classify fundus images into one or more illnesses. Rodríguez. et.al. [12] presents a novel multi-label classification method for the diagnosis of fundus eye disease classification. Most of these studies, focused on algorithmic performance and do not integrate deployment aspects such as model size, inference time, or interaction workflows.

The clinical application [6] of complex models is limited by their high processing requirements and reliance on GPUs, which make them difficult to implement in low-resource contexts. Accuracy, efficiency, and real-time performance must all be balanced for portable systems such as the Raspberry Pi [7,8]. CNNs and Vision Transformers can automatically extract hierarchical characteristics for medical imaging, which is different from traditional methods. We showed that efficiency in terms of inference time, model size, and resource consumption is just as important for edge-based diagnosis as accuracy by contrasting InceptionV3 and ViT using a Raspberry Pi.

## 2 Methodology

The proposed method involves training and evaluating two deep learning architectures, InceptionV3 [9,10] and Vision Transformer (ViT) [4,5], for fundus photo categorization under the same conditions. A Raspberry Pi device [7,8] is then used to assess the architectures' performance. The Work flow as shown in Fig. 1 and Fig. 2. Dataset preparation, model development, training, evaluation, and deployment are all steps in the process. All images were resized to 256 × 256 to maintain consistency across both architectures and ensure efficient deployment on Raspberry Pi.

In this study, we investigate the Vision Transformer [4,5] and InceptionV3 models [9,10] fundus picture classification abilities. Following training and evaluation, both models are installed on a Raspberry Pi with identical preprocessing and optimization settings in order to compare inference time, model size, and resource usage. InceptionV3 was chosen due to its lightweight structure and proven medical imaging performance, while ViT was included to benchmark a transformer-based model under identical conditions. The trained models were converted to TensorFlow Lite format using post-training quantization (INT8/Float16). This step significantly reduces model size and speeds up inference, making real-time classification feasible on edge hardware.

The deployment performance on a Raspberry Pi platform is another way to evaluate the models' utility. Among the important factors that are measured are inference time, model size, and resource consumption. Therefore, for edge-based, real-time medical diagnosis applications, increasing model efficiency is nearly as important as attaining high classification accuracy.

### 2.1 Dataset

The fundus image dataset [13], which has captioned images of various eye conditions, is openly accessible. Enlarging images to 256 × 256 pixels, standardizing pixel intensity values to the [0,1] range, and employing data augmentation techniques such random rotations, flips, and brightness modifications are preprocessing procedures that improve model generalization. The data is split 80:10:10 to create training, validation, and test sets. There are four groups of the 4,217 labeled retinal fundus images in the study's dataset, Specifically, the dataset contains 1,056 Cataract, 1,060 Diabetic Retinopathy, 1,050 Glaucoma, and 1,051 Normal images. There were 3,374 images utilized for training and 843 for testing. Initially, each image was reduced in size from 512 × 512 pixels to 256 × 256 pixels to reduce processing time and memory usage during model inference and training. The average size of each image is about 148 KB, and the dataset takes up about 700 MB of disk space. To illustrate the visual variety and complexity across various eye conditions, Fig. 3 displays representative sample images from each class.

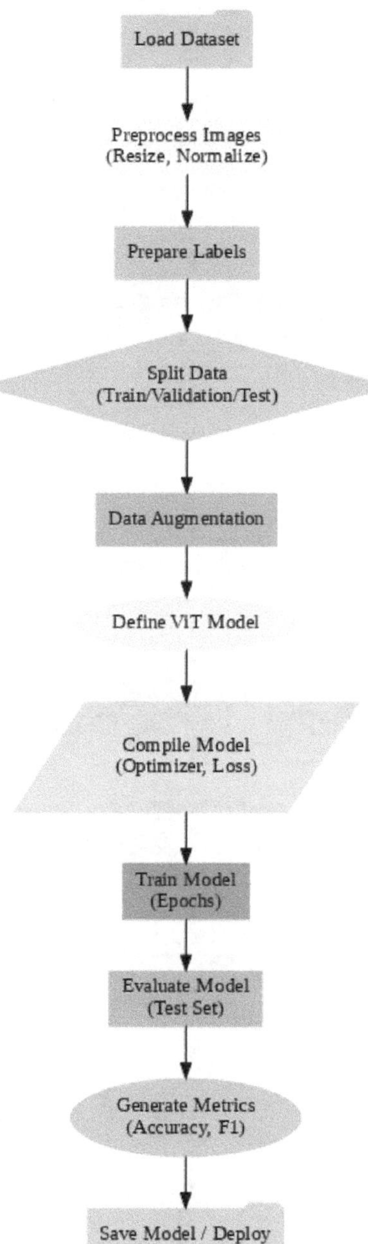


**Fig. 1.** Workflow of Vision Transformer-Based Fundus Image Classification.

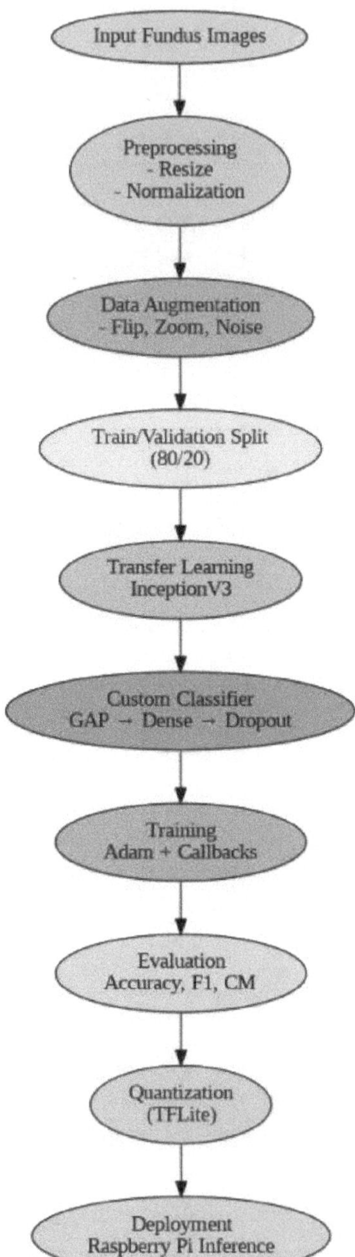


**Fig. 2.** Workflow of InceptionV3-Based Fundus Image Classification.

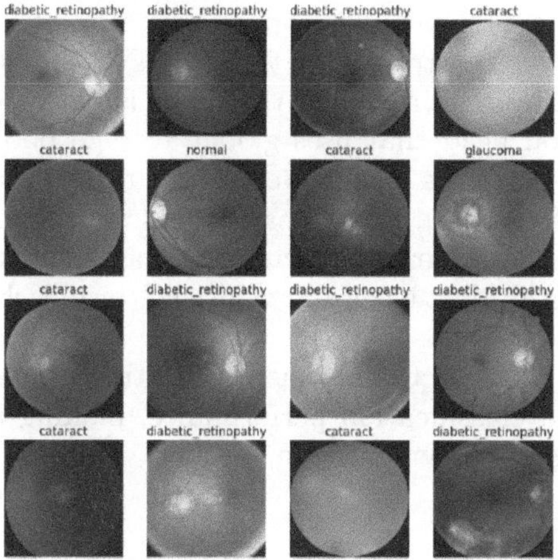


**Fig. 3.** Sample Fundus Images from the Dataset: Diabetic Retinopathy, Cataract, Glaucoma, and Normal.

## 2.2 Model Architectures

In this study, pretrained feature representations are leveraged by using transfer learning on both the InceptionV3 and Vision Transformer (ViT) models. Both architectures were adapted to handle a standardized input size of 256 × 256 × 3, ensuring uniform preprocessing and fair performance comparison during deployment on Raspberry Pi (Fig. 4).

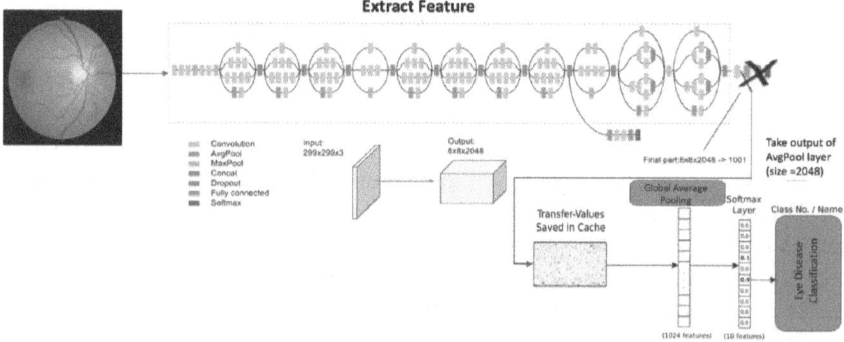


**Fig. 4.** inceptionV3 Architecture.

**A. InceptionV3 Model.** One of the baseline models is the InceptionV3 model [9,10], a well-known Convolutional Neural Network (CNN) architecture.

`include_top = False` removes the top classification layers from the InceptionV3 backbone that was pretrained on the ImageNet dataset. In order to satisfy fundus image processing requirements, the input is enlarged to $256 \times 256 \times 3$. A custom classification head that uses global average pooling, softmax activation, and dense layers adapts the model to the target fundus disease classes. From Fig., it can be seen that transfer learning allows the model to consume less medical imaging data while greatly increasing classification accuracy and convergence time by reusing low-level and mid-level visual characteristics learned from ImageNet.

This architecture was selected because of its strong balance between computational efficiency and classification performance, making it an ideal candidate for lightweight edge AI deployment (Fig. 5).

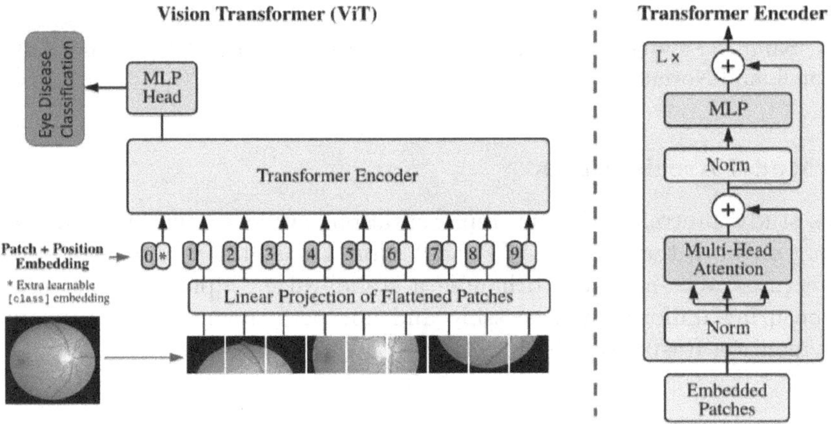


**Fig. 5.** Vision Transformer (ViT) Architecture.

**B. Vision Transformer (ViT).** This Transformer-based approach makes use of the Hugging Face (`google/vit-base-patch16-224-in21k`) Vision Transformer (ViT) Base model [4,5], which was pretrained on the ImageNet-21k dataset and has a $16 \times 16$ patch size. The ViT model, unlike traditional CNNs, splits the input image into fixed-size patches and linearly embeds each patch before processing it using stacked self-attention layers. From Fig. 5, the pretrained ViT model is enhanced with an output head that has been modified for multi-class classification using the fundus image dataset. By using transfer learning to access rich global contextual representations from the extensive ImageNet-21k corpus, the ViT model enhances its performance even with sparse training data.

InceptionV3 and Vision Transformer model workflows for this study are displayed separately in Fig. 1 and Fig. 2. Data pretreatment, model construction, training, testing, and deployment on a Raspberry Pi are among the crucial processes that are delineated in these diagrams. Both InceptionV3 and ViT show improved generalization when transfer learning is applied, with InceptionV3 requiring fewer computational resources for edge deployment.

## 3 Experimental Setup

Model training and assessment are done on a workstation, and then the experiments are deployed and benchmarked for inference on a Raspberry Pi device. The same training configuration was maintained for both models to ensure fair comparison, and inference results were collected through repeated measurements to minimize variability.

### 3.1 Training Configuration

In order to provide an equitable comparison, both models are trained using the identical hyperparameter settings. $1\times10^{-4}$ is the initial learning rate of the Adam optimizer. Early stopping based on validation loss is used to avoid overfitting, and categorical cross-entropy is used as the loss function. On a high-performance workstation with a GPU, the models are trained across 50 epochs with a batch size of 32.

The model is trained on a robust workstation that has an NVIDIA GeForce RTX 3050 Ti GPU, an Intel Core i7 CPU, and 16 GB of RAM. The Scikit-learn packages, TensorFlow 2.10, Keras, and Python 3.8 are all part of the software ecosystem. The Adam optimizer and a categorical cross-entropy loss function are used to train the models across 50 epochs with a batch size of 32. To prevent overfitting, early pausing based on validation loss is used. For consistency, the same random seed and hyperparameters were applied to both architectures. The results reported are averaged over multiple runs to reduce the impact of training fluctuations.

### 3.2 Raspberry Pi

The most efficient models are transformed into TensorFlow Lite format after training in order to be compatible with Raspberry Pi deployment [7,8]. Inference time and memory footprint are decreased by using model quantization approaches. Figure 6 shows Raspberry Pi 4 Model B (4 GB RAM) which is used to assess each model's inference performance, which includes monitoring CPU usage, model size, and inference time per image. Post-training quantization (INT8 and Float16) was applied to optimize the models for edge deployment. All inference measurements were collected using a USB fundus image input in an offline mode without GPU acceleration.

**Fig. 6.** Raspberry Pi 4 Model B setup used for deployment and benchmarking.

### 3.3 Evaluation Metrics

The models are evaluated using multiple performance metrics, such as classification accuracy, precision, recall, F1-score, and AUC-ROC for model efficacy. Additional parameters, like as CPU use, model size, and inference time per image, are monitored to assess the feasibility of edge deployment. These metrics provide a comprehensive comparison of the classification performance and processing efficiency of the Vision Transformer [4,5] and InceptionV3 models [9,10]. Evaluation metrics are computed on the test set for each class, and average inference time is reported as the mean of 30 repeated runs to ensure stability. Model size is recorded after quantization to reflect actual deployment footprint on Raspberry Pi.

## 4 Results

The fundus image classification challenge is used to assess the performance of the InceptionV3 and Vision Transformer (ViT) models. Deployment benchmarking on the Raspberry Pi device comes next. Inference efficiency, model size, and classification metrics are used to compare the models.

### 4.1 Performance Analysis

The classification performance metrics that were acquired on the test set are compiled in Table 1. InceptionV3 outperforms the Vision Transformer in terms of generalization, as evidenced by its superior overall classification accuracy and AUC-ROC. With a validation accuracy of 95.37%, InceptionV3 demonstrates faster and more steady convergence than ViT, which reaches 91.35%. Similarly, InceptionV3 outperforms the ViT model, which achieves 90.32% test accuracy, with 95.85%.

**Table 1.** Performance Comparison between InceptionV3 and Vision Transformer (ViT)

| Metric | InceptionV3 | ViT |
|---|---|---|
| Total no. of Parameters | 13,987,236 | 85,801,732 |
| Validation Accuracy | 95.37% | 91.35% |
| Test Accuracy | 95.85% | 90.32% |
| Precision | 0.96 | 0.92 |
| Recall | 0.96 | 0.91 |
| F1-Score | 0.95 | 0.91 |
| Recall for 'Normal' Class | 95.00% | 88.00% |
| Training Convergence Speed | Faster | Slower |
| Overfitting Behavior | Low | Slightly Higher |
| Model Size | 53.36 MB | 327.39 MB |
| Inference Speed on Raspberry Pi | 85 ms/image | 135 ms/image |
| Memory Footprint | Lower | Higher |

## 4.2 Confusion Matrix

The confusion matrices and classification reports provide further details on the exact class-wise performance of both models in addition to the previously displayed quantitative data (Fig. 7).

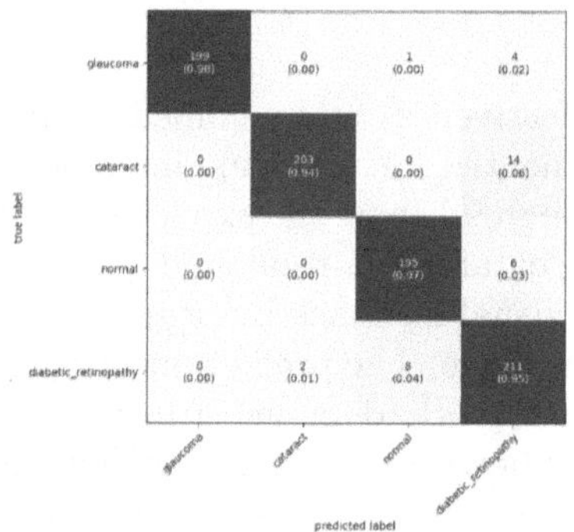


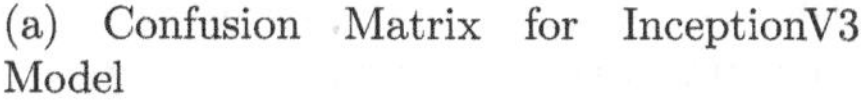

(a) Confusion Matrix for InceptionV3 Model

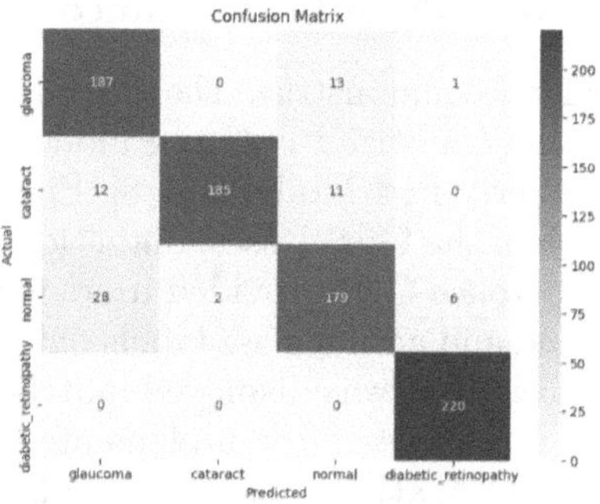


(b) Confusion Matrix for Vision Transformer (ViT) Model

**Fig. 7.** Comparison of Confusion Matrices for InceptionV3 and ViT Models.

## 4.3 Edge Deployment

For edge deployment, the models are transformed into TensorFlow Lite format after training. Using the Raspberry Pi 4 Model B, which has a quad-core

Cortex-A72 CPU, 4 GB of RAM, and Raspberry Pi OS (64-bit), inference testing is carried out. For the resource-constrained device, post-training quantization approaches are employed to enhance the models. Performance inference is evaluated using only the CPU; no GPU acceleration is required. A Raspberry Pi 4 Model B is used to benchmark the models for both model size and inference time. Table 1 displays the outcomes. InceptionV3 has a smaller model size (53.36 MB) and faster inference performance (85 ms/image) than Vision Transformer (135 ms/image and 327.39 MB). These characteristics make InceptionV3 better suitable for real-time deployment on resource-constrained edge devices like Raspberry Pi (Fig. 8).

Classification Report:

| | precision | recall | f1-score | support |
|---|---|---|---|---|
| cataract | 1.00 | 0.98 | 0.99 | 204 |
| diabetic_retinopathy | 0.99 | 0.94 | 0.96 | 217 |
| glaucoma | 0.96 | 0.97 | 0.96 | 201 |
| normal | 0.90 | 0.95 | 0.93 | 221 |
| accuracy | | | 0.96 | 843 |
| macro avg | 0.96 | 0.96 | 0.96 | 843 |
| weighted avg | 0.96 | 0.96 | 0.96 | 843 |

(a) Classification Report for InceptionV3 Model

| | precision | recall | f1-score | support |
|---|---|---|---|---|
| glaucoma | 0.91 | 0.81 | 0.85 | 201 |
| cataract | 0.86 | 0.97 | 0.91 | 208 |
| normal | 0.92 | 0.88 | 0.90 | 215 |
| diabetic_retinopathy | 0.99 | 1.00 | 0.99 | 220 |
| accuracy | | | 0.92 | 844 |
| macro avg | 0.92 | 0.91 | 0.91 | 844 |
| weighted avg | 0.92 | 0.92 | 0.91 | 844 |

(b) Classification Report for Vision Transformer (ViT) Model

**Fig. 8.** Comparison of Classification Reports for InceptionV3 and ViT Models.

### 4.4 Real Time Performance

In order to demonstrate the trained model's effectiveness on an embedded platform, the quantized `.tflite` model was implemented for real-time inference on a Raspberry Pi 4 Model B [7,8]. Figures 9a through 9d show the expected results for each of the four classes: diabetic retinopathy, cataract, normal, and glaucoma. The inference GUI provided users with instant visual feedback by projecting the expected and actual class labels onto the fundus image. The predictions for every test image that was displayed matched the ground truth, demonstrating that the model was successfully implemented on the Raspberry Pi using TensorFlow Lite INT8 quantization. For extra confirmation, the terminal displayed each class's raw softmax scores. These results support the feasibility of real-time medical picture inference on low-power embedded platforms utilizing deep learning-based sickness classification models.

## 5 Conclusion

This study evaluated and diagnosed eye conditions using portable models like the InceptionV3 and Vision Transformers in conjunction with the Raspberry Pi platform. Low-power settings can successfully enable resource-efficient deep learning, as demonstrated by the presentation of an edge-to-cloud pipeline for

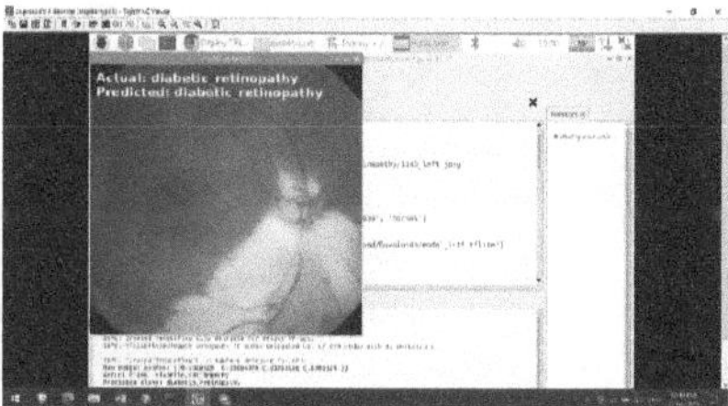


(a) Prediction: Diabetic Retinopathy – Raspberry Pi Output

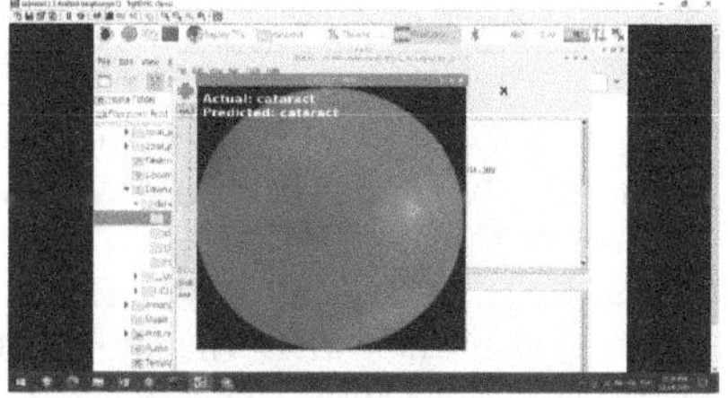


(b) Prediction: Cataract – Raspberry Pi Output

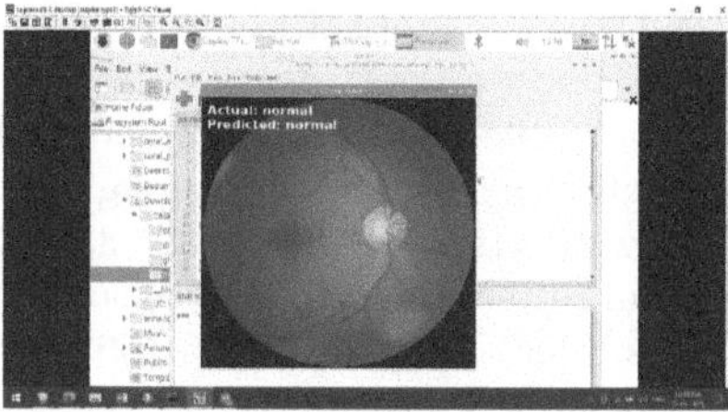


(c) Prediction: Normal – Raspberry Pi Output

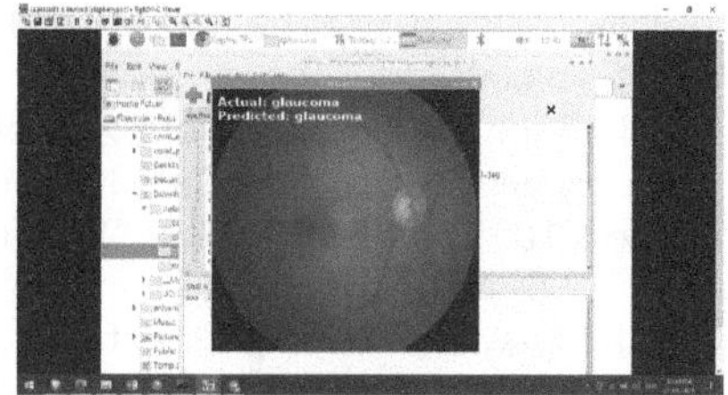


(d) Prediction: Glaucoma – Raspberry Pi Output

**Fig. 9.** Predictions of different eye conditions using Raspberry Pi output.

real-time categorization. The efficiency of the Raspberry Pi in terms of latency, memory utilization, and energy efficiency eliminated the need for large libraries or cloud support in order to diagnose eye problems.

The results showed that large, computationally intensive Vision Transformers are not as viable for deployment on the edge as efficient models like InceptionV3. Even though ViTs work well on GPUs when processing large datasets, they are not helpful for real-time microcontroller operations. In contrast, InceptionV3 offers an excellent balance between precision and speed, making it more suitable for resource-constrained scenarios. This balance makes it useful for applications in agriculture, healthcare, human–machine interfacing, medical diagnostics, and quality monitoring. Overall, the work shows that decentralized, hardware-friendly AI can be used to achieve scalable, interpretable, and energy-efficient solutions for future embedded systems.

**Acknowledgments.** The authors express their gratitude to the research team and the AI-ML Lab of the Department of ECE, NIT Warangal, for their essential assistance to this study. This work was completed without outside help.

**Disclosure of Interests.** There are no conflicts of interest, according to the authors.

## References

1. Shi, Y., et al.: Fundus spectral imaging: from optical systems to clinical applications. IEEE Trans. Instrum. Measur. **74**, 1–20 (2025). Art. no 4509920, https://doi.org/10.1109/TIM.2025.3571154
2. Ganesh, E., Shanker, N.R., Priya, M.: Non-Invasive measurement of glaucoma disease at earlier stage through GMR sensor AH biomagnetic signal from eye and RADWT algorithm. IEEE Sens. J. **19**(14), 5404–5412 (2019). https://doi.org/10.1109/JSEN.2019.2909526
3. Dash, S.K., Sethy, P.K., Das, A., Jena, S., Nanthaamornphong, A.: Advancements in deep learning for automated diagnosis of ophthalmic diseases: a comprehensive review. IEEE Access **12**, 171221–171240 (2024). https://doi.org/10.1109/ACCESS.2024.3496565
4. Abd El-Khalek, A.A., et al.: XV-AMD: an explainable vision transformer detection framework for age-related macular degeneration using fundus imaging. IEEE Access **13**, 113967–113983 (2025). https://doi.org/10.1109/ACCESS.2025.3583555
5. He, X., Deng, Y., Fang, L., Peng, Q.: Multi-modal retinal image classification with modality-specific attention network. IEEE Trans. Med. Imaging **40**(6), 1591–1602 (2021). https://doi.org/10.1109/TMI.2021.3059956
6. Zhang, L., Wu, F., Bronik, K., Papiez, B.W.: DiffuSeg: domain-driven diffusion for medical image segmentation. IEEE J. Biomed. Health Inform. **29**(5), 3619–3631 (2025). https://doi.org/10.1109/JBHI.2025.3526806
7. Raspberry pi 4B. https://www.raspberrypi.com/products/raspberry-pi-4-model-b/
8. Cruz-Vega, I., Morales-Lopez, H.I., Ramirez-Cortes, J.M., De Jesus Rangel-Magdaleno, J.: Nuclear cataract database for biomedical and machine learning applications. IEEE Access **11**, 107754–107766 (2023)
9. Lin, J., Cai, Q., Lin, M.: Multi-label classification of fundus images with graph convolutional network and self-supervised learning. IEEE Signal Process. Lett. **28**, 454–458 (2021). https://doi.org/10.1109/LSP.2021.3057548
10. Tamilselvi, S., Suchetha, M., Raman, R.: Leveraging ResNet50 with swin attention for accurate detection of OCT biomarkers using fundus images. IEEE Access **13**, 35203–35218 (2025). https://doi.org/10.1109/ACCESS.2025.3544332
11. Liu, Y., et al.: Label-aware dual graph neural networks for multi-label fundus image classification. IEEE J. Biomed. Health Inform. **29**(4), 2731–2743 (2025). https://doi.org/10.1109/JBHI.2024.3457232
12. Rodríguez, M.A., AlMarzouqi, H., Liatsis, P.: Multi-label retinal disease classification using transformers. IEEE J. Biomed. Health Inform. **27**(6), 2739–2750 (2023). https://doi.org/10.1109/JBHI.2022.3214086
13. Eye Disease Retinal Images Dataset. Kaggle (2022). https://www.kaggle.com/datasets/gunavenkatdoddi/eye-diseases-classification
14. Atwany, M.Z., Sahyoun, A.H., Yaqub, M.: Deep learning techniques for diabetic retinopathy classification: a survey. IEEE Access **10**, 28642–28655 (2022). https://doi.org/10.1109/ACCESS.2022.3157632
15. Luo, X., Li, J., Chen, M., Yang, X., Li, X.: Ophthalmic disease detection via deep learning with a novel mixture loss function. IEEE J. Biomed. Health Inform. **25**(9), 3332–3339 (2021). https://doi.org/10.1109/JBHI.2021.3083605

# I Detect What I Don't Know: Incremental Anomaly Learning with SWAG

Nand Kumar Yadav[1(✉)], Rodrigue Rizk[1], William C. W. Chen[2], and K. C. Santosh[1]

[1] AI Research Lab, Department of Computer Science,Vermillion, USA
{nand.yadav,rodrigue.rizk,kc.santosh}@usd.edu
[2] Biomedical and Translational Sciences, Sanford School of Medicine, Vermillion, SD 57069, USA
william.chen@usd.edu

**Abstract.** Unknown anomaly detection is crucial in medical imaging (e.g., COVID-19 and pneumonia screening), but anomaly labels are scarce and expensive. We propose an unsupervised, oracle-free incremental framework that starts from a small, trusted set of normal images and expands the normal set over multiple rounds without using anomalous labels. A frozen pretrained backbone with lightweight convolutional adapters produces fused features that populate a compact coreset memory, enabling efficient $k$-NN–style scoring suitable for deployment. To prevent contamination while enlarging the normal manifold, candidate samples are admitted only when *both* their memory distance and epistemic uncertainty (estimated via SWAG variance) fall within seed-calibrated $z$-score gates, providing dual evidence of normality. This avoids reconstruction bias and instability common in generative methods while progressively refining normality as new data arrive. Empirically, the method yields large gains: on **COVID-CXR**, ROC–AUC improves from 0.9489 to 0.9982 and F1 from 0.8048 to 0.9746, reducing false positives from 34 to 5; on **Chest X-ray Pneumonia**, ROC–AUC rises from 0.6834 to 0.8960 and F1 from 0.7008 to 0.8351 (precision 0.7620→0.8829). On **Brain MRI ND-5** (2,806 slices; 1,975 tumor/831 normal), ROC–AUC improves from 0.6041 to 0.7299 and PR–AUC from 0.7539 to 0.8211, achieving accuracy 0.7445, precision 0.8086, recall 0.8344, and F1 0.8213. (Code: https://github.com/pis2016004-prog/Incremental-learning-Anomaly-Detection.git)

**Keywords:** Zero Anomaly Training · Incremental Learning · Stochastic Weight Averaging Gaussian (SWAG) · Pre-Trained ResNet

## 1 Introduction

Anomaly detection aims to identify samples that deviate from the normal data distribution and is critical in applications such as fraud detection, cybersecurity, and especially medical imaging, where early recognition of abnormalities enables


A. Shastri et al. (Eds.): IHCI 2025, LNCS 16437, pp. 129–144, 2026.
https://doi.org/10.1007/978-3-032-26352-0_11

tasks like COVID-19 screening or tumor detection. While supervised approaches benefit from labeled anomalies, such data are often scarce, costly, or unavailable, motivating unsupervised methods that learn only from normal samples. Classical techniques such as One-Class SVM [1] and $k$-NN [2] model normality through decision boundaries or nearest-neighbor distances, but they degrade in high-dimensional settings and fail to capture complex image structure. Deep learning methods, including autoencoders and GANs [3–6], extend anomaly detection to richer data, yet reconstruction-based models can generalize too well and GANs often suffer from instability and heavy training requirements.

Recent representation-based approaches such as PatchCore [7] avoid generative reconstruction by storing patch-level embeddings of normal data in a memory bank and detecting anomalies via nearest-neighbor distances, enabling robust localization. In parallel, incremental learning (IL) offers a way to refine detectors over time, but applying IL in anomaly detection is challenging due to the absence of anomaly labels and the risk of contaminating the normal model.

In this work, we propose an incremental-learning enhanced PatchCore framework that starts from a small trusted normal seed and progressively expands the normal set over multiple rounds. Using SWAG-based epistemic uncertainty, the method admits only confident samples for updating lightweight adapters and rebuilding the memory, eliminating the need for human labeling. This yields an adaptive, scalable, and fully oracle-free anomaly detection pipeline suitable for real-world medical imaging scenarios where anomalies are rare or unknown.

Our contributions are summarized as follows:

- We propose a unified framework that begins with a small trusted seed of normal images and *incrementally* expands the set through adapter updates across rounds, requiring no anomalous labels in IL.
- A frozen pretrained backbone, tiny $1\times1$-conv adapters, and a compact feature memory enable fast $k$-NN style scoring and low footprint, substantially leaner than reconstruction or GAN-based pipelines which make the model lightweight and deployment-ready.
- To avoid reconstruction bias and training instability, candidates are accepted only when *both* their distance-to-memory and epistemic uncertainty (via SWAG variance) are low under seed-calibrated $z$-scores, enabling stable, label-free growth of normality and enhancing robustness through dual evidence.
- On real-world datasets, the method detects anomalies without training them, improves ROC/PR curves as the normal manifold refines, and yields both interpretable heatmaps and metric gains.

## 2 Related Works

Early unsupervised anomaly detection methods such as One-Class SVM [1] and $k$-NN [2] model normality either by learning a boundary around normal samples or by flagging points that lie far from their nearest neighbors. Although effective in low-dimensional settings, these approaches struggle on modern high-dimensional data, where distance metrics become less discriminative, hyperparameter sensitivity increases, and complex image structure is difficult to capture. Deep learning methods have therefore become dominant, with Autoencoders (AEs) and GANs being widely explored in medical imaging. AEs detect anomalies through reconstruction error, but often suffer from reconstruction bias, sometimes generalizing too well and reconstructing abnormal patterns, which reduces reliability [8]. GAN-based approaches attempt to model the normal distribution adversarially, yet they are prone to instability, mode collapse, and high sensitivity to training conditions [4]. More recently, representation-based methods such as PatchCore [7] have achieved state-of-the-art performance by extracting patch-level embeddings from pretrained networks and detecting anomalies through nearest-neighbor distances in a coreset memory bank, avoiding generative training altogether. However, PatchCore can still incur substantial memory growth as data scale. To mitigate this, we integrate incremental learning (IL) to admit only informative normal samples over time, guided by SWAG-based uncertainty estimation, improving computational efficiency while maintaining strong detection accuracy. Incremental (continual) learning enables models to adapt as data distributions evolve over time, yet its application to anomaly detection is particularly challenging. In real deployments, normal data may drift, anomalies remain rare and heterogeneous, and unlabeled streams introduce a serious risk of *contaminating* the learned normal representation. Moreover, strict memory and latency constraints limit rehearsal of past samples, intensifying the stability–plasticity trade-off, while most continual-learning methods assume task boundaries or class supervision that rarely hold in one-class anomaly settings. Consequently, effective incremental anomaly detection requires drift-aware calibration and bounded exemplar memories (e.g., coreset selection) to preserve normality under weak or absent anomaly labels [9–12]. At the same time, a growing body of unsupervised work avoids anomalous labels entirely by modeling normality and flagging deviations through self-supervised or patch-based representations, but such pipelines remain vulnerable to pool contamination and provide limited mechanisms for safely expanding the normal manifold as new variability emerges during deployment. To address these limitations, we begin with a small trusted seed of normal data and incrementally enlarge the memory bank, admitting candidates only when their PatchCore distance is statistically consistent with the seed distribution and their SWAG-based epistemic uncertainty remains low. This dual-evidence gating strategy provides a principled and robust path for label-free adaptation, reducing contamination risk while maintaining long-term detector stability.

## 3 Motivation

This work is driven by a central question: *can we safely expand the normal set without ever consulting an oracle?* We answer this by combining pool-based selection with incremental learning through a *dual-evidence gate.* Starting from

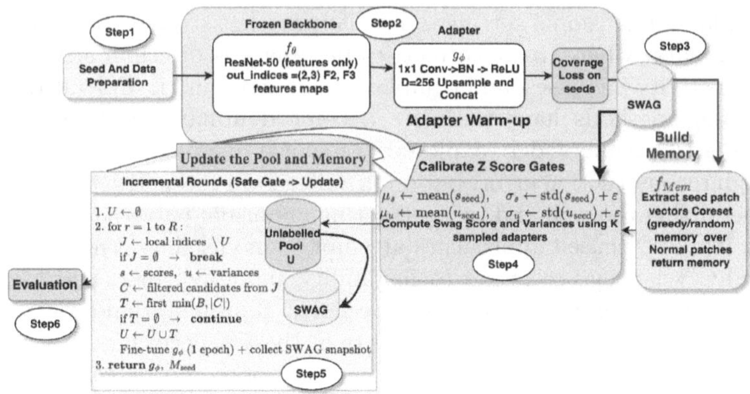


**Fig. 1.** Pipeline of the proposed anomaly-detection framework.

a small, trusted seed of normal images, we construct a compact PatchCore memory using coreset subsampling [7]. The memory is then expanded only with pool samples that satisfy two conditions: (i) low PatchCore $k$-NN distance after seed-calibrated $z$-normalization (statistical evidence), and (ii) low epistemic uncertainty under a SWAG posterior over the adapter [13] (Bayesian evidence).

Unlike classical active learning [14], where uncertainty triggers costly oracle queries, uncertainty here serves as a *filter*: samples are admitted only when the model is confident they lie within the current normal manifold. The adapter is briefly updated on admitted samples, and the memory is periodically re-coresetted to remain compact. This incremental strategy [15] is attractive for three reasons. First, it is *oracle-free and data-efficient*, requiring only a tiny seed to bootstrap continual improvement. Second, it is *robust*, as the dual gate reduces contamination risk while seed-relative calibration provides drift awareness. Third, it is *scalable*, since PatchCore avoids generative training, coreset selection bounds memory growth, and learning is confined to lightweight adapters.

Overall, our motivation is practical: replace the human oracle with a Bayesian confidence filter, enforce conservative statistical admission, and grow normality incrementally with bounded risk, enabling anomaly detectors that remain accurate, robust, and maintainable under real deployment constraints.

## 4 Proposed Method

We consider image anomaly detection where training images come primarily from a *normal* class, while the test set contains both normal and anomalous samples. The task is to construct a non-parametric memory of normal patch embeddings (as in PatchCore) and score queries by $k$-NN distances in the embedding space. Formally, an image $x \in [0,1]^{C\times H\times W}$ is passed through a frozen backbone $f_\theta$ that yields multi-scale feature maps. A learnable adapter $g_\phi$ then projects

**Algorithm 1.** (Step 1): Seed & Data Preparation

**Inputs:** Normal dir $\texttt{dir}_0$, Anomaly dir $\texttt{dir}_1$, image size $S$, color $\in \{\texttt{L}, \texttt{RGB}\}$

$\mathcal{X} \leftarrow$ load all images from $\texttt{dir}_0, \texttt{dir}_1$; resize to $(S, S)$; scale to $[0, 1]$

Label mapping: $\texttt{NORMAL} \mapsto 0$, $\texttt{ANOMALY} \mapsto 1$

$\mathcal{I}_0 \leftarrow \{i : y_i = 0\}$ ▷ all normals

Shuffle $\mathcal{I}_0$; $n \leftarrow \max(1, \lfloor 0.30 \cdot |\mathcal{I}_0| \rceil)$

$\mathcal{I}_{\text{seed}} \leftarrow$ first $n$ of $\mathcal{I}_0$; $\mathcal{I}_{\text{rest}} \leftarrow \mathcal{I}_0 \setminus \mathcal{I}_{\text{seed}}$

$\mathcal{I}_{\text{anom}} \leftarrow \{i : y_i = 1\}$; $\mathcal{I}_{\text{pool}} \leftarrow \mathcal{I}_{\text{rest}} \cup \mathcal{I}_{\text{anom}}$

**return** $(\mathcal{X}, \mathcal{I}_{\text{seed}}, \mathcal{I}_{\text{pool}})$

each scale to a common dimensionality and fuses them, producing a grid of patch embeddings. These embeddings are compared against a memory bank $\mathcal{M}(f_{mem})$ of normalized patch vectors to obtain anomaly scores. To improve reliability, we incorporate a light-weight adapter for representation flexibility and SWAG based uncertainty estimates to complement distance scoring. From an unlabeled pool, additional pseudo-normal samples are admitted only when statistical and epistemic evidence supports their inclusion, enabling a cautious but steady enlargement of the normal manifold. At the heart of this setting lies the fundamental difficulty of anomaly detection: while normal data are abundant and well-characterized, anomalies remain rare, diverse, and context dependent, making them unsuitable for direct supervision. On the other hand, unsupervised learning from large data pools [16] risks contamination, since even a small fraction of anomalies can distort the learned statistics. Our formulation begins with a small, trusted seed of normal data and carefully grows outward, admitting new samples under principled uncertainty checks. This progressive, evidence-driven expansion of normality ensures robustness, efficiency, and stability, and sets the stage for our algorithms (Algorithms 1–6) that formalize each component of this process. The overall pipeline depicted in Fig. 1. The process begins with a seed set of trusted normal samples as illustrated in Algorithm 1. Further we use adapter for the learning the normal samples as in Algorithm 2. Simultaneously, we populate a prototype memory by coreset selection from the seed embeddings as illustrated in Algorithm 3. This memory serves as a compact summary of the normal distribution, a reference structure against which all future candidates can be evaluated. Crucially, in our implementation this seed memory remains fixed for the entirety of training, providing a stable foundation that prevents contamination by the pool. Even if a sample looks close to what we've seen before, the model also has to admit what it doesn't know. A point might sit near our "normal" prototypes, but if the model is highly uncertain about its representation, admitting it could be risky. To address this, we equip the adapter with a Bayesian posterior approximation using SWAG, which maintains a distribution over its weights. By sampling multiple parameter realizations and scoring each candidate, we estimate both the mean distance $\mu(x)$ and variance $v(x)$ as illustrated in Algorithm 4. The mean captures how closely a sample resembles normal patterns, while the variance captures epistemic uncertainty: how consistently the model agrees on this assessment.

**Algorithm 2.** (Step 2): Initialize Model and Warm-Up Adapter

**Inputs:** Frozen backbone $f_\theta$, adapter $g_\phi$ (per-scale 1×1 Conv+BN+ReLU, dim $D = 256$), seed indices $\mathcal{I}_{\text{seed}}$, epochs $E$, lr $\eta$, prototype budget $K$
**Outputs:** Warmed $g_\phi$ and initialized SWAG
Set $f_\theta$ to **eval**; initialize $g_\phi$
Build seed vectors $V_{\text{seed}}$ **(no per-image cap, native grid)**:
for $x \in \mathcal{I}_{\text{seed}}$: get multi-scale $\{F_\ell\}$; project $A_\ell = g_\phi^\ell(F_\ell)$; upsample each $A_\ell$ to the **common native size** $(H_{\max}, W_{\max})$ of that image; concatenate channel-wise to $A$; flatten and $\ell_2$-normalize to get $Q$; append all $Q$ to $V_{\text{seed}}$.
$\rho \leftarrow \min(1, K/|V_{\text{seed}}|)$; $P \leftarrow \textsc{CoresetGreedy}(V_{\text{seed}}, \rho)$
**for** $e = 1..E$ **do** ▷ backbone frozen
  **for** minibatches of $x \in \mathcal{I}_{\text{seed}}$ **do**
    Extract $Q$ as above; $\mathcal{L} \leftarrow \frac{1}{|Q|} \sum_i \min_{\mathbf{p} \in P} \|\mathbf{q}_i - \mathbf{p}\|_2$
    Update $g_\phi$ with Adam(lr=$\eta$) on $\mathcal{L}$
  **end for**
**end for**
Initialize SWAG on $g_\phi$ and take **two** snapshots
**return** warmed $g_\phi$, SWAG state

**Algorithm 3.** (Step 3): Build Initial Normal Memory (PatchCore)

**Inputs:** $f_\theta$, warmed $g_\phi$, seed set $\mathcal{I}_{\text{seed}}$, coreset ratio $\rho_m$, grid 16×16, cap $\tau$
**Outputs:** Initial memory $\mathcal{M}_0$
Extract $V_{\text{seed}}$ as in Algorithm 2; $\mathcal{M}_0 \leftarrow \textsc{CoresetGreedy}(V_{\text{seed}}, \rho_m)$
**return** $\mathcal{M}_0$ ▷ Note: in incremental rounds we *grow/rebuild* memory with accepted normals

The central decision is then governed by a *z-score gate.* For each candidate, we normalize its score and uncertainty relative to the seed distribution:

$$z_s(x) = \frac{\mu(x) - \mu_s}{\sigma_s}, \qquad z_u(x) = \frac{v(x) - \mu_u}{\sigma_u}. \tag{1}$$

Only if $z_s(x)$ and $z_u(x)$ are at most 1.0 then sample is then qualified as a pseudo-normal. If no candidates pass, the gates may be relaxed once to $1.5\sigma$. Unlike earlier designs, there is no borderline band or fusion ranking: acceptance is a strict intersection of score and uncertainty gates. This mechanism enforces selective trust, ensuring that only statistically safe samples are admitted. Accepted samples are then used for a brief adapter update, typically a single compact epoch, and the new weights are snapshotted into the SWAG ensemble. This incremental tuning allows the adapter to expand its coverage of $P_N$ without ever altering the frozen seed memory. The process repeats for several rounds until the pool is exhausted or no new candidates are admitted. In this way, the system grows cautiously: expanding its representation of normality while keeping the calibration anchored to the uncontaminated seed, the procedure is illustrated in Algorithm 5.

**Algorithm 4.** (Step 4): Calibrate Z-Score Gates (on seeds)

**Inputs:** $f_\theta$, $g_\phi$, memory $\mathcal{M}_0$, seed set $\mathcal{I}_{\text{seed}}$, k-NN $k = 3$, top-$q$ (e.g. 0.03–0.05), SWAG samples $K$

**Outputs:** $(\mu_s, \sigma_s, \mu_u, \sigma_u)$ and flag **useU**

```
For each x ∈ I_seed: compute s(x) via PatchCore top-q rule with M_0
For each x ∈ I_seed: sample K SWAG adapters, get u(x)=Var[s^(k)(x)]
μ_s, σ_s ← mean/std({s(x)});   μ_u, σ_u ← mean/std({u(x)})
useU ← (σ_u > 10^-6)                 ▷ if SWAG variance is numerically non-zero
return (μ_s, σ_s, μ_u, σ_u, useU)
```

Finally, evaluation is straightforward as illustrated in Algorithm 6. A test image is scored by PatchCore distances to the seed memory, using the most up-to-date adapter and SWAG ensemble. Anomalies emerge as those samples whose scores or uncertainties exceed the calibrated bounds. Each component plays a precise role: the seed set prevents initial contamination; the adapter tailors the latent space to the domain; SWAG quantifies epistemic uncertainty; the dual z-score gates prevent unsafe admissions; and the iterative loop allows gradual, self-supervised growth. What emerges is a robust, oracle-free learner: a model that begins with modest seeds, acknowledges its own uncertainty, and safely expands its knowledge of normality through IL.

*Implications.* Let

$$\beta = \Pr_{x \sim P_N} \big( z_s(x) \leq \tau_z \, \wedge \, z_u(x) \leq \tau_z \big)$$

denote the acceptance probability of the dual gate for *true normal* samples, with an optional one-time relaxation $\tau_z : 1.0 \to 1.5$ if required. In the strict_normal_only =**True**, configuration (i.e., oracle-assisted mode), only gate-passing items whose ground-truth label is $y = 0$ are used to update the adapter $g_\phi$ and to expand the PatchCore memory $\mathcal{M}$. Each admitted batch therefore contributes $\Theta(\beta)$ genuine normal samples, incurs *zero* anomaly contamination, and follows the standard finite-sample error decay $O(1/\sqrt{m})$ as the memory size $m$ increases. The dual gate serves as a conservative prefilter, requiring both low normalized distance ($z_s$) and low uncertainty ($z_u$), thereby improving sample efficiency while maintaining safety. Uncertainty is ignored only in degenerate cases where $\sigma_u$ is numerically negligible.

**Theorem 1 (Oracle-assisted zero-contamination under dual-gate prefilter).** *Assume an oracle-assisted variant of Algorithm 5, implemented conceptually via strict_normal_only =**True**. After the dual gate $(z_s, z_u)$ selects candidates satisfying $z_s(x) \leq \tau_z$ and $z_u(x) \leq \tau_z$, the ground-truth label $y(x)$ is queried, and only samples with $y = 0$ are admitted for adapter updates and memory expansion. Then the contamination rate of the memory bank,*

$$\alpha = \Pr\big[x \in \mathcal{M} \, \wedge \, y(x) = 1\big],$$

**Algorithm 5.** (Step 5): Incremental Rounds (Growing Memory + Gated Ranking + Checkpointing)

**Inputs:** Backbone $f_\theta$ (frozen), adapter $g_\phi$, SWAG state; pool $\mathcal{I}_{\text{pool}}$; rounds $R$; budget $B$; calibration $(\mu_s, \sigma_s, \mu_u, \sigma_u, \texttt{useU})$; thresholds $\tau_z$=1.0 → 1.5 (one relaxation); ranking mode $\in \{\texttt{boundary}, \texttt{uncert}\}$; strict-normal-only flag (`False`/`True`); resume policy $\in \{\texttt{best\_so\_far}, \texttt{last}\}$.
**Outputs:** Final adapter $g_\phi^\star$ and memory $\mathcal{M}^\star$.

$\mathcal{U} \leftarrow \emptyset$ ▷ used local pool indices; $\mathcal{A} \leftarrow \emptyset$ ▷ accepted normal indices
Save `best_overall` checkpoint of $g_\phi$ using a metric (validation AUC if available, else $\bar{s}_{\text{pool}} - \bar{s}_{\text{seed}}$ on a fixed subset)
**for** $r = 1$ **to** $R$ **do**
  **Resume** $g_\phi$ from `best_overall` (or `last`) per policy
  **Build memory** from seeds ∪ accepted normals: $\mathcal{M}_r \leftarrow \textsc{CoresetGreedy}(V(\mathcal{I}_{\text{seed}} \cup \mathcal{A}), \rho_m)$
  $\mathcal{J} \leftarrow \{0, \ldots, |\mathcal{I}_{\text{pool}}| - 1\} \setminus \mathcal{U}$;
  **if** $\mathcal{J} = \emptyset$ **then break**
  **end if**
  Score pool with $\mathcal{M}_r$: $\{s_j\}_{j \in \mathcal{J}}$; if **useU** then also $\{u_j\}_{j \in \mathcal{J}}$ else $u_j \leftarrow 0$
  Normalize: $z_j^s = (s_j - \mu_s)/\sigma_s$; $z_j^u = (u_j - \mu_u)/\sigma_u$
  Safe set: $\mathcal{C} \leftarrow \{j \in \mathcal{J} \mid z_j^s \le \tau_z \land (\neg \texttt{useU} \lor z_j^u \le \tau_z)\}$
  **if** $\mathcal{C} = \emptyset$ **then** set $\tau_z \leftarrow 1.5$ and recompute $\mathcal{C}$;
    **if** $\mathcal{C} = \emptyset$ **then continue**
    **end if**
  **end if**
  **Rank** in $\mathcal{C}$:
  `boundary`: sort by $s_j$ (desc); `uncert`: sort by $z_j^u$ (desc)
  $\mathcal{T} \leftarrow$ top-min$(B, |\mathcal{C}|)$ locals after ranking
  Mark used: $\mathcal{U} \leftarrow \mathcal{U} \cup \mathcal{T}$; map to globals $\mathcal{G} \leftarrow \{\mathcal{I}_{\text{pool}}[j] \mid j \in \mathcal{T}\}$
  **if strict-normal-only then**
    Filter true normals: $\mathcal{G} \leftarrow \{g \in \mathcal{G} \mid y_g = 0\}$
    **if** $|\mathcal{G}| = 0$ **then**
      Save `last`; **continue**
    **end if**
  **else**
    *// Unsupervised mode (no labels used from the pool)*
    Treat all selected samples as presumed normals: $\mathcal{G} \leftarrow \mathcal{T}$
  **end if**
  **Fine-tune** $g_\phi$ for 1 epoch on $\mathcal{G}$ with prototype loss (backbone frozen); take a SWAG snapshot
  **Grow memory**: $\mathcal{A} \leftarrow \mathcal{A} \cup \mathcal{G}$
  **Checkpoint**: save `last`; recompute metric; if improved, update `best_overall`
**end for**
Restore $g_\phi^\star$ from `best_overall`; build $\mathcal{M}^\star \leftarrow V(\mathcal{I}_{\text{seed}} \cup \mathcal{A})$
**return** $g_\phi^\star$, $\mathcal{M}^\star$

**Algorithm 6.** (Step 6): Evaluate on Held-out Test

**Inputs:** Test loader $\mathcal{D}_{\text{test}}$, $f_\theta, g_\phi, \mathcal{M}$, labels $\{y_i\}$

Compute image-level anomaly scores $\{s_i\}$ via PatchCore (top-$q$ of $k$-NN distances to $\mathcal{M}$)
**if** $\{y_i\}$ contains both classes **then**
  Build ROC; AUC $\leftarrow$ area under ROC
  $t^\star \leftarrow \arg\max_t \left(\text{TPR}(t) - \text{FPR}(t)\right)$ ▷ Youden's $J$
  $\hat{y}_i \leftarrow \mathbb{1}[s_i \geq t^\star]$; report ACC, Precision, Recall, F1
  (Optional) save ROC/PR plots and example heatmaps
**else**
  Skip thresholded metrics (no positives/negatives)
**end if**

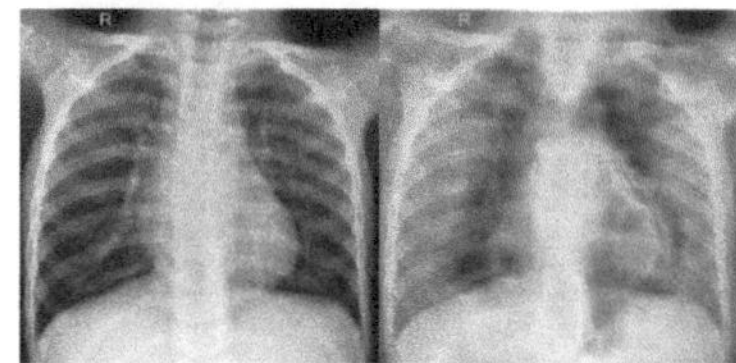
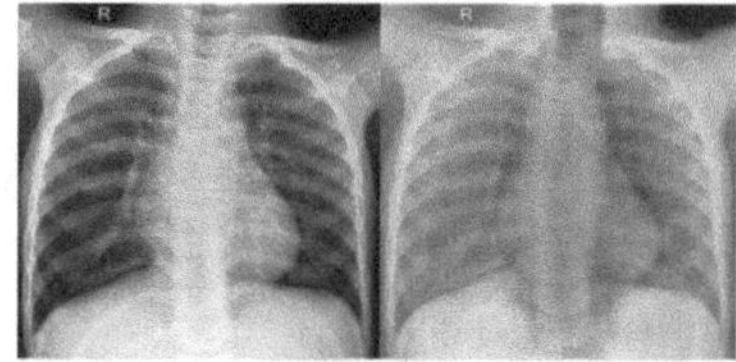

**Fig. 2.** Heatmap for Baseline And proposed IL Approach on chest_xray dataset.

*is identically $\alpha = 0$ for all active-learning rounds, independent of the gate threshold relaxation and SWAG sampling settings.*

***Proof sketch.*** By construction, the oracle-assisted update rule admits only samples with $y = 0$. Hence $\Pr[x \in \mathcal{M} \wedge y(x) = 1] = 0$ for all rounds. The dual gate $(z_s, z_u)$ merely determines which items are *considered*; the oracle filter decides which are actually *added*.

**Proposition 1 (Oracle-free dual-gate bound (image level)).** *If the oracle filter is disabled (`strict_normal_only`=**False**) and there exist separation margins $\gamma_s, \gamma_u > 0$ such that for all anomalous $x \sim P_A$ either $z_s(x) \geq 1 + \gamma_s$ or $z_u(x) \geq 1 + \gamma_u$, then, with $K$ SWAG samples and unbiased, finite-variance estimators of $d(x)$ and $u(x)$, the probability that an anomaly passes the dual gate $z_s(x) \leq 1$ and $z_u(x) \leq 1$ satisfies*

$$\Pr_{x \sim P_A}\left[admit(x)\right] \;\leq\; \delta \;+\; \exp\Big(-cK \cdot \min\Big\{\frac{\gamma_s^2}{\sigma_s^2}, \frac{\gamma_u^2}{\sigma_u^2}\Big\}\Big),$$

*for some universal constant $c > 0$, where $\delta$ accounts for finite-sample concentration. In degenerate cases where $\sigma_u \approx 0$, the decision reduces to the single-score gate on $z_s$ alone.*

*Incremental Learning with and without an Oracle.* Classical IL forwards uncertain samples to a oracle [17]. Here, uncertainty acts *as a filter*: only low-distance, low-uncertainty candidates are eligible. With the oracle filter (our default), memory growth is provably contamination-free (Theorem 1); without it, the dual gate provides the probabilistic safety in Proposition 1.

**Table 1.** Comparison on *chest_xray (pneumonia)* at the Youden-optimal threshold.

| Setting | ROC AUC | PR AUC | Thr* (Youden) | ACC | Precision | Recall | F1 | TN | FP | FN | TP |
|---|---|---|---|---|---|---|---|---|---|---|---|
| Baseline | 0.6834 | 0.7656 | 0.993364 | 0.6538 | 0.7620 | 0.6487 | 0.7008 | 155 | 79 | 137 | 253 |
| Baseline + Adapter warmup | 0.8820 | 0.9267 | 0.952984 | 0.7628 | 0.9060 | 0.6923 | 0.7849 | 199 | 35 | 97 | 293 |
| Post-IL (Oracle) | 0.8960 | 0.9366 | 0.954324 | 0.8045 | 0.8829 | 0.7923 | 0.8351 | 193 | 41 | 81 | 309 |
| Post-IL (Ours, Oracle-free) | **0.8968** | **0.9372** | 0.953104 | **0.8093** | 0.8796 | **0.8051** | **0.8407** | 191 | **43** | **76** | **314** |

**Table 2.** Comparison: Baseline PatchCore versus proposed IL (Post-IL) using COVID CXR dataset. Metrics are reported at the Youden-optimal threshold.

| Setting | ROC AUC | PR AUC | Thr* (Youden) | ACC | Precision | Recall | F1 | TN | FP | FN | TP |
|---|---|---|---|---|---|---|---|---|---|---|---|
| Baseline | 0.9489 | 0.8976 | 0.989044 | 0.8868 | 0.7481 | 0.8707 | 0.8048 | 283 | 34 | 15 | 101 |
| Baseline + Adapter warmup | 0.9961 | 0.9898 | 0.954467 | 0.9792 | 0.9652 | 0.9569 | 0.9610 | 313 | 4 | 5 | 111 |
| Proposed Method | **0.9982** | **0.9951** | 0.953187 | **0.9861** | **0.9583** | **0.9914** | **0.9746** | **312** | **5** | **1** | **115** |

## 5 Experimental Setup, Results, and Discussion

**Experimental Setup**

We employ a frozen ResNet-50 backbone with lightweight 1×1 Conv+BN+ ReLU adapters that project multi-scale features to 256 dimensions. Training begins from a small trusted seed of normal images used for warm-up prototype learning, while SWAG is initialized from successive adapter snapshots. PatchCore then constructs a compact coreset memory using $16 \times 16$ patch grids, and inference is performed on full-resolution aligned feature maps for scoring. During incremental rounds, candidate pool samples are admitted only under a dual-evidence gate: low PatchCore $k$-NN distance after seed-normalized $z$-scoring and low SWAG-based epistemic uncertainty. Accepted samples are used for brief adapter fine-tuning, followed by updated SWAG snapshots and memory rebuilding. Model selection is based on the best validation AUC, and performance is reported using ROC-AUC and PR-AUC. Experiments were run with random seeds (123–127), using a learning rate of $10^{-4}$ for adapter initialization and $3{\times}10^{-5}$ for incremental updates with batch size 32. We adopt a coreset ratio of 0.3 and perform five incremental rounds with a budget of 50 samples each. SWAG uses noise scale 0.02 with $K = 4$ posterior samples, while PatchCore scoring uses $k = 3$ neighbors and top-$q = 0.03$ patches. The gating threshold $\tau_z$ is relaxed from 1.0 to 1.5 when no safe candidates are found. All hyperparameters were chosen empirically to balance computational efficiency, stability, and robustness.

**Chest X-Ray (Pneumonia) Dataset:** We evaluate our method on the chest_xray (pneumonia) dataset[1], containing 1,341 normal and 3,875 pneumonia cases. For a realistic low-anomaly regime, we use a subset of 234 normal and 390 pneumonia images. We compare a baseline PatchCore model (full-memory, no IL) with our proposed incremental learning strategy, initialized from a 30%

[1] https://www.kaggle.com/datasets/paultimothymooney/chest-xray-pneumonia/data.

trusted normal seed and expanded over five IL rounds using SWAG-based gating. As shown in Table 1, IL consistently improves performance: ROC-AUC increases from 0.6834 to 0.8960 and PR-AUC from 0.7656 to 0.9366. Accuracy rises from 0.6538 to 0.8045, precision from 0.7620 to 0.8829, recall from 0.6487 to 0.7923, and F1-score from 0.7008 to 0.8351. False positives drop from 79 to 41, while true positives increase from 253 to 309. Qualitative heatmaps in Fig. 2 show sharper localization, with ROC curves in Fig. 3, Fig. 6, and the confusion matrix in Fig. 4 further confirming the gains.

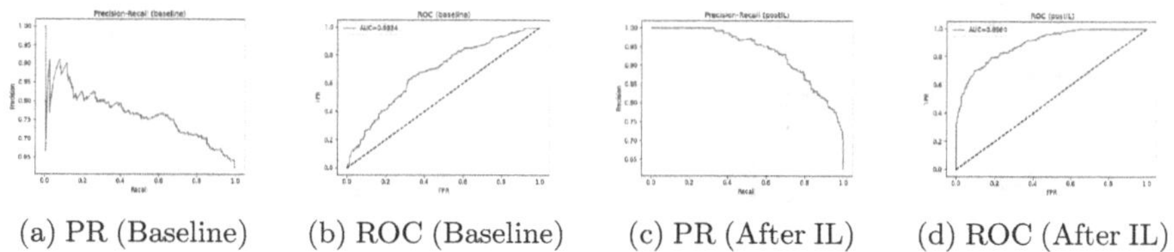

(a) PR (Baseline) (b) ROC (Baseline) (c) PR (After IL) (d) ROC (After IL)

**Fig. 3.** Comparison of PR and ROC curves before and after incremental learning (IL) on the chest_xray dataset. The IL model achieves higher AUC and improved calibration compared to the baseline.

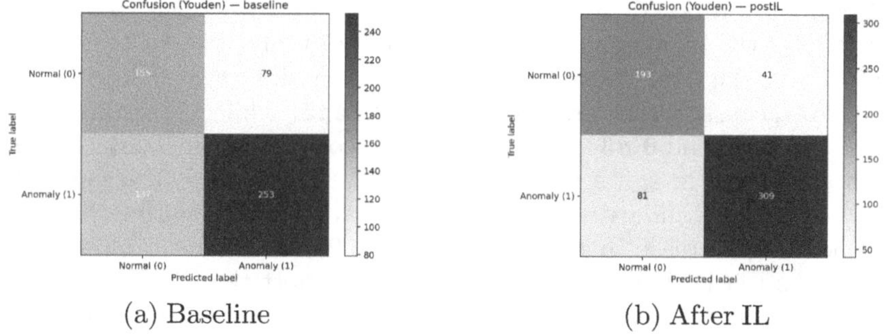


(a) Baseline (b) After IL

**Fig. 4.** Confusion matrices for the *chest_xray* dataset before and after incremental learning (IL).

**COVID CXR Dataset:** Table 2 summarizes results on the COVID chest X-ray dataset[2]. The training set contains 460 COVID-positive [18] and 1,266 normal images, while the test set includes 116 COVID-positive and 317 normal samples.

Our incremental learning framework yields substantial gains over the baseline. ROC–AUC improves from 0.9489 to **0.9982**, and PR–AUC rises from 0.8976 to **0.9951**. At the Youden-optimal operating point, accuracy increases

[2] https://www.kaggle.com/datasets/prashant268/chest-xray-covid19-pneumonia.

from 0.8868 to **0.9861**. Precision improves from 0.7481 to **0.9583**, recall from 0.8707 to **0.9914**, and the F1-score from 0.8048 to **0.9746**. The confusion matrix further confirms these improvements: true negatives increase from 283 to 312, false positives decrease from 34 to 5, false negatives drop from 15 to 1, and true positives rise from 101 to 115. Overall, IL significantly enhances detection accuracy while sharply reducing misclassifications, demonstrating its effectiveness for COVID screening under limited supervision.

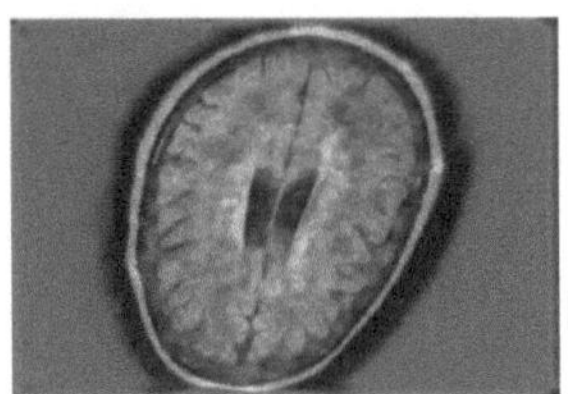

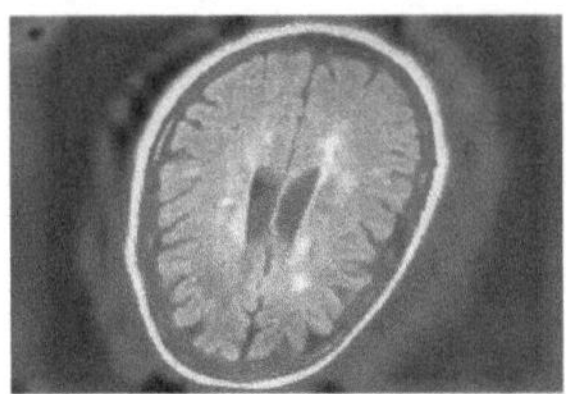

**Fig. 5.** Baseline and after IL heatmaps over the Brain Tumor dataset.

### 5.1 Brain Tumor Dataset (ND-5)

We evaluated our method on the Brain Tumor ND-5 dataset[3], using the test split of 2,806 axial slices (1,975 tumor, 831 normal). Compared with the baseline PatchCore, the proposed incremental framework achieves consistent improvements: ROC–AUC increases from 0.6041 to **0.7299**, and PR–AUC from 0.7539 to **0.8211**. At the Youden-optimal threshold (baseline $t = 0.9618$, proposed $t = 0.9706$), accuracy rises from 0.5848 to **0.7445**, while precision and recall improve to **0.8086** and **0.8344**, yielding an F1-score gain from 0.6616 to **0.8213**. The confusion matrix shifts from $(\mathrm{TN}, \mathrm{FP}, \mathrm{FN}, \mathrm{TP}) = (502, 329, 836, 1139)$ to $(441, 390, 327, 1648)$, indicating a large reduction in false negatives ($-509$) and a corresponding increase in true positives ($+509$), with only a modest rise in false positives ($+61$). For completeness, we also report the Baseline + Adapter warmup variant (ACC 0.7327, F1 0.8107), confirming internal consistency. Qualitative results in Fig. 5 further highlight the benefit of IL: while the baseline produces diffuse, low-contrast activations, the proposed method yields sharper, lesion-focused heatmaps with reduced background noise. Overall, these results demonstrate that incremental learning significantly strengthens tumor anomaly detection on ND–5. For this dataset, we used a budget of 500, while keeping other settings fixed (coreset ratio 0.3, SWAG noise 0.02, top-$q$ 0.03) (Table 3).

### 5.2 Ablation Study Using SWAG, MC Dropout and Ensemble

SWAG reaches 0.89–0.90 ROC AUC in both oracle and oracle-free settings (Table 4), outperforming MC Dropout and the no-uncertainty baseline. The

[3] https://ieee-dataport.org/documents/brain-mri-nd-5-dataset.

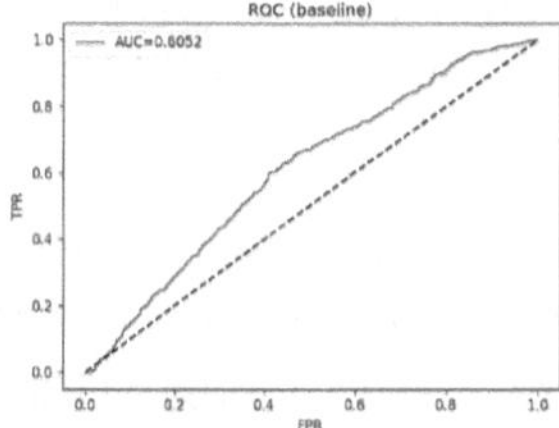


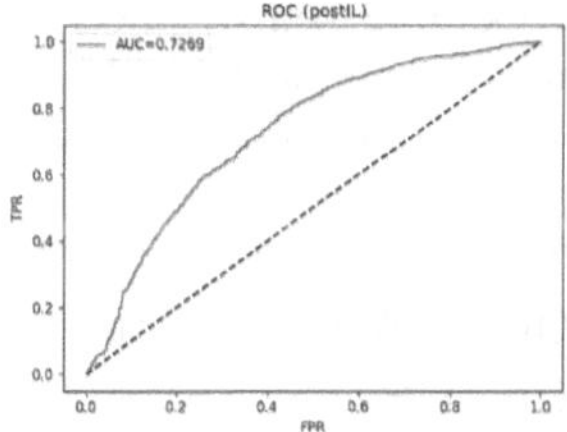


**Fig. 6.** ROC curves before (baseline) and after incremental learning (IL) on the Brain Tumor dataset.

**Table 3.** Baseline vs. Propose AL performance on Brain MRI ND-5 Dataset.

| Setting | ROC AUC | PR AUC | Thr* (Youden) | ACC | Precision | Recall | F1 | TN | FP | FN | TP |
|---|---|---|---|---|---|---|---|---|---|---|---|
| Baseline | 0.6041 | 0.7539 | 0.961838 | 0.6216 | 0.7695 | 0.6608 | 0.7109 | 440 | 391 | 671 | 1304 |
| Baseline + Adapter warmup | 0.6632 | 0.8174 | 0.966118 | 0.7327 | 0.8083 | 0.8132 | 0.8107 | 450 | 381 | 369 | 1606 |
| Proposed Method | **0.7269** | **0.8211** | 0.970559 | **0.7445** | **0.8086** | **0.8344** | **0.8213** | **441** | **390** | **327** | **1648** |

Ensemble variant matches nearly SWAG. SWAG provide robust, well-calibrated uncertainty estimates; use Ensemble when compute permits for the best overall performance, and use SWAG when efficiency is a priority, particularly in incremental and unlabeled anomaly-detection scenarios. Further To assess the robustness of our method, we report results averaged over five independent runs with five different random seeds using chext_xray dataset. The bar plots in Fig. 7 show the mean performance with 95% confidence intervals for key metrics (ROC AUC, PR AUC, and F1@Youden). The narrow error bars indicate that our model exhibits low variance across runs, confirming the stability and reproducibility of the proposed approach.

# 6 Failed Case Analysis

To illustrate failure cases of an anomaly detection model for bacterial pneumonia we illustrated the heatmaps in Fig. 7. In the first example, the model misclassi-

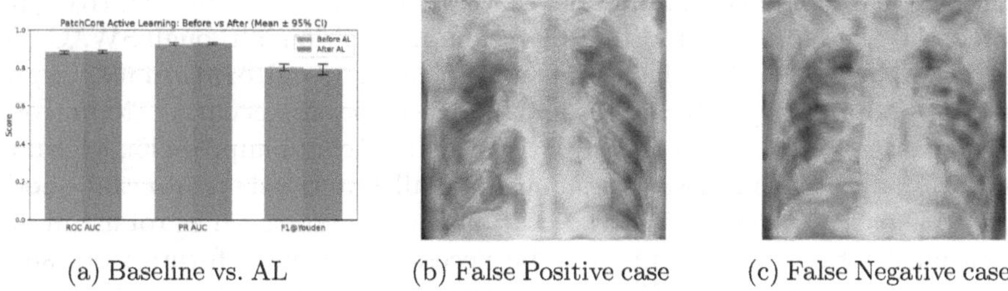


(a) Baseline vs. AL (b) False Positive case (c) False Negative case

**Fig. 7.** Performance comparison (left) and representative failure cases (middle/right) on the chest_xray dataset.

**Table 4.** Comparison of uncertainty estimation strategies across oracle and oracle-free settings on `chest_xray`. Metrics are averaged over multiple runs. SWAG achieves strong overall AUC and calibration.

| Setting | Uncertainty | ROC AUC | PR AUC | ACC | Precision | F1 |
|---|---|---|---|---|---|---|
| Oracle-Free | None | 0.8685 | 0.8934 | 0.7841 | 0.8705 | 0.7692 |
| Oracle-Free | SWAG | 0.8968 | 0.9372 | 0.8093 | 0.8796 | 0.8407 |
| Oracle-Free | MC Dropout | 0.8438 | 0.8797 | 0.7710 | 0.8601 | 0.7692 |
| Oracle-Free | Ensemble | 0.8828 | 0.9021 | 0.8060 | 0.8800 | 0.8380 |
| Oracle-Based | None | 0.8372 | 0.8733 | 0.7683 | 0.8642 | 0.7561 |
| Oracle-Based | SWAG | 0.8960 | 0.9366 | 0.8045 | 0.8829 | 0.8351 |
| Oracle-Based | MC Dropout | 0.8099 | 0.8608 | 0.7604 | 0.8534 | 0.7521 |
| Oracle-Based | Ensemble | 0.8594 | 0.8893 | 0.7950 | 0.8790 | 0.8320 |

fies normal anatomical structures such as the cardiac border and diaphragm as abnormal regions, resulting in a false positive. In the second example, it fails to detect subtle and diffuse pulmonary opacities, leading to a false negative. These errors highlight the model's sensitivity to normal intensity variations and its limited ability to recognize low-contrast infections.

## 7 Limitations and Future Work

While the proposed oracle-free incremental framework achieves strong performance on medical imaging benchmarks, several limitations remain. First, evaluation has been largely restricted to the **medical domain**, and its generalization to other anomaly detection settings such as industrial inspection or cybersecurity is not yet established. Second, the current experiments mainly cover structural and texture-level abnormalities, whereas real-world anomalies may involve temporal, contextual, or multimodal deviations, requiring extensions to more complex data streams. A further challenge is **domain shift** during incremental updates: since admission thresholds are calibrated from the initial seed, distribution drift may lead to miscalibration, resulting in either overly conservative selection or increased contamination. Developing drift-aware or adaptive gating strategies is therefore an important direction. In addition, although SWAG offers an efficient approximation of epistemic uncertainty, its **calibration** may degrade over many rounds as posterior assumptions become less accurate. More robust Bayesian or ensemble-based uncertainty estimation could improve long-term reliability. Finally, the framework assumes a small but **trusted normal seed**; if the seed is partially contaminated, additional safeguards such as robust filtering or self-purification mechanisms may be necessary. Overall, future work should focus on improving adaptability, uncertainty calibration, and cross-domain generalization.

## 8 Conclusion

In this work, we introduced an IL framework built on top of PatchCore for unsupervised anomaly detection. By starting from a small seed of normal samples and iteratively refining the model with SWAG guided incremental learning, our method improves detection performance without requiring any labeled anomalous data. This makes it highly practical for real-world medical imaging scenarios, where anomalies are rare, difficult to annotate, or entirely absent in training. Through extensive experiments on two publicly available chest radiography datasets, we demonstrated that our approach consistently outperforms a baseline PatchCore system across a wide range of metrics, including ROC-AUC, PR-AUC, accuracy, precision, recall, and F1 score. Importantly, incremental learning not only improved detection sensitivity but also reduced false positives, yielding more reliable and clinically useful anomaly localization. Looking forward, our framework can be extended to other medical and industrial domains where labeled anomalies are scarce. Future work will explore integrating more advanced uncertainty quantification strategies, adapting the approach to multi-class anomaly settings, and evaluating its applicability in real-time deployment scenarios.

**Acknowledgment.** This work was supported by the National Science Foundation under Grant No. #2346643, the U.S. Department of Defense under Award No. #FA9550-23-1-0495, and the U.S. Department of Education under Grant No. P116Z240151. Any opinions, findings, conclusions or recommendations expressed in this material are those of the author(s) and do not necessarily reflect the views of the National Science Foundation, the U.S. Department of Defense, or the U.S. Department of Education.

## References

1. Schölkopf, B., Platt, J.C., Shawe-Taylor, J., Smola, A.J., Williamson, R.C.: Estimating the support of a high-dimensional distribution. Neural Comput. **13**(7), 1443–1471 (2001)
2. Ramaswamy, S., Agerri, R., Srikant, R.K.: Efficient and robust clustering algorithms for large datasets. In: Proceedings of the ACM SIGKDD International Conference on Knowledge Discovery and Data Mining (2000)
3. Schlegl, T., Seeböck, P., Waldstein, S.M., Langs, G., Schmidt-Erfurth, U.: f-AnoGAN: fast unsupervised anomaly detection with generative adversarial networks. Med. Image Anal. **54**, 30–44 (2019)
4. Goodfellow, I., et al.: Generative adversarial nets. In: Proceedings of NeurIPS (2014)
5. Yadav, N.K., Mehmood, R., Rizk, R., Santosh, K.: Scl-gan: spatially-correlative lightweight gan for efficient and high-fidelity thermal-visible face synthesis. In: IEEE International Conference on Image Processing (ICIP), vol. 2025, pp. 2049–2054 (2025)

6. Yadav, N.K., Singh, S.K., Dubey, S.R.: Tva-gan: attention guided generative adversarial network for thermal to visible image transformations. Neural Comput. Appl. 35, 19729–19749 (2023). https://doi.org/10.1007/s00521-023-08724-5
7. Roth, K., Pemula, L., Zepeda, J., Scholkopf, B., Brox, T., Gehler, P.: Towards total recall in industrial anomaly detection. In: Proceedings of the IEEE/CVF Conference on Computer Vision and Pattern Recognition (CVPR), pp. 14318–14328 (2022)
8. An, J., Cho, S.: Variational autoencoder based anomaly detection using reconstruction probability. Spec. Lect. IE **2**(1), 1–18 (2015)
9. Parisi, G.I., Kemker, R., Part, J.L., Kanan, C., Wermter, S.: Continual lifelong learning with neural networks: a review. Neural Netw. **113**, 54–71 (2019)
10. Rebuffi, S.-A., Kolesnikov, A., Sperl, G., Lampert, C.H.: icarl: incremental classifier and representation learning. In: CVPR, pp. 2001–2010 (2017)
11. Kirkpatrick, J., Pascanu, R., Rabinowitz, N., et al.: Overcoming catastrophic forgetting in neural networks. Proc. Nat. Acad. Sci. (PNAS) **114**(13), 3521–3526 (2017)
12. De Lange, M., et al.: A continual learning survey: Defying forgetting in classification tasks. IEEE Trans. Pattern Anal. Mach. Intell. (2022). early versions available as arXiv:1909.08383
13. Maddox, W.J., Garipov, T., Izmailov, P., Vetrov, D., Wilson, A.G.: A simple baseline for Bayesian uncertainty in deep learning. In: NeurIPS (2019)
14. Bouguelia, M.-R., Nowaczyk, S., Santosh, K., Verikas, A.: Agreeing to disagree: active learning with noisy labels without crowdsourcing. Int. J. Mach. Learn. Cybern. **9**(8), 1307–1319 (2018)
15. Santosh, K., Nakarmi, S.: Active Learning to Minimize the Possible Risk of Future Epidemics. Springer, Cham (2023)
16. Singh, P., Rizk, R., Santosh, K.: Patl: pool-based active twin learner from oracle with imitation learning for early epidemic detection. In: IEEE Conference on Artificial Intelligence (CAI), vol. 2025, pp. 561–566 (2025)
17. Yin, W., Tan, Z., et al.: An efficient replay for class-incremental learning with pre-trained models. arXiv preprint arXiv:2408.08084 (2024)
18. Santosh, K., Ghosh, S.: Covid-19 imaging tools: how big data is big? J. Med. Syst. **45**(7), 71 (2021)

# A Fusion of Nature Inspired Optimization Integrated with Hybrid MobileNetv4-DenseNet201 Deep Learning Framework for Lung Cancer Detection

Pankaj Kumari(✉) and Lavika Goel

Department of Computer Science and Engineering, Malaviya National Institute of Technology, Jaipur, India
pankaj.shekhawat1690@gmail.com, lavika.cse@mnit.ac.in

**Abstract.** The lungs play a crucial role in respiration by facilitating the exchange of oxygen and carbon dioxide. However, environmental pollution and modern lifestyle habits have increased the risk of lung diseases, including cancer. This study presents a hybrid deep learning framework for accurate lung cancer detection using a combination of MobileNet-V4 and DenseNet-201 architectures. MobileNet-V4 offers high efficiency for real-time medical imaging, while DenseNet-201 enhances feature reuse and gradient flow. To overcome performance limitations caused by high-dimensional data, six advanced nature-inspired optimization (NIA) algorithms—Greylag Goose Optimization, Crested Porcupine Optimization, Lotus Effect Algorithm, Polar Light Optimization, Ant Lion Optimizer, and Walrus Optimization—were employed for feature selection and dimensionality reduction. The proposed system was evaluated on a publicly available Kaggle CT scan dataset containing 1,000 images across four lung cancer categories: squamous cell carcinoma, adenocarcinoma, large-cell carcinoma, and normal. The hybrid MobileNetV4-DenseNet201 model achieved a classification accuracy of 94.4%, outperforming traditional models such as Artificial Neural Networks (74%), YOLOv3 with BBO/EE (80.6%), and YOLOv6 with PSO (82.79%). Additionally, a comparative hybrid VGG19-ResNet152 model integrated with the same NIA methods achieved 94% accuracy. These results highlight the potential of hybrid deep learning and optimization-driven approaches for enhancing automated lung cancer diagnosis.

**Keywords:** Kaggle · MobileNet-V4 · DenseNet-201 · Lung cancer detection · Polar Light Optimization Algorithm · hybrid nature Inspired techniques

## 1 Introduction

Genetic alterations enable the body's cells to proliferate uncontrollably, which eventually spreads to other organs and results in cancer. The human body is composed of countless cells, and cancer can originate in almost any of them. Normally, when the body requires additional cells, existing cells multiply, grow, and divide to generate new ones.


A. Shastri et al. (Eds.): IHCI 2025, LNCS 16437, pp. 145–157, 2026.
https://doi.org/10.1007/978-3-032-26352-0_12

Lung cancer remains a leading contributor to cancer-related mortality across the globe, primarily because of its rapid progression and frequent late-stage diagnosis. Therefore, timely and precise detection is essential for improving patient survival outcomes.

Deep learning models particularly, VGG-19, ResNet-152, MobileNet-V4 and DenseNet-201 have shown to be highly impressive in fetching meaningful features from medical dataset. We used hybrid of two best models of deep learning framework that are MobileNetV4 and DenseNet201 that are extracting features from CT scan images. Mobilenet-V4 has been used in this study because it takes limited resources for computation and it used fewer parameters that can be easy to tune. DenseNet201 is used because it assures effective reuse of features and strong gradient flow through its dense connections, enabling high accuracy and robust representation of complex patterns in CT scans. Nevertheless, high-dimensional feature sets that could contain duplicate data are commonly produced by these models. Nature Inspired Algorithms (NIAs) namely Greylag Goose Optimization, Crested Porcupine Optimization, Lotus Effect Algorithm, Polar Light Optimization, Ant Lion Optimizer, and Walrus Optimization are utilized in conjunction with deep learning-based feature extraction to choose the best features. These selected features are then applied in different machine learning classifiers where different parameter settings are applied on training datasets for each classifier in aiming of better results. K-Nearest Neighbors performing well with Polar Light Optimization algorithm. Next, we summarize the overall contribution of this study:

- We propose a hybrid framework combining MobileNet-V4 and DenseNet-201 with recent nature-inspired algorithms for robust feature extraction and selection from chest CT images.
- This experimental study used parallel approach that processes the same image through both CNNs to capture diverse features for improving classification.
- Nature-inspired algorithms handle high-dimensional medical data, enhancing early lung cancer detection through adaptive and intelligent search mechanisms.
- The hybrid approach enables rich feature representation and early identification of subtle lung abnormalities from CT scans.

The organization of this paper is as follows: Sect. 2 presents a review of prior research on lung cancer detection. Section 3 describes the theoretical foundation and the methods adopted in this study. The proposed approach and its corresponding time complexity analysis are elaborated in Sect. 4. Section 5 reports and interprets the experimental findings, and finally, Sect. 6 concludes the work and suggests possible avenues for future investigation.

## 2 Related Work

Although recent developments in medical imaging have greatly enhanced the diagnosis of lung cancer, several limitations and research gaps still remain. The IAL-MRCNN (Improved Attention Layer-Based Mask RCNN) model used in study [1] includes supplementary layers compared to the existing model, such as 4 convolutional (Conv) layers, an improved Attention layer, 3 Fully Connected (FC) layers, 3 Batch Normalization (BN) layers and 2 SoftMax layers. The LIDC-IDRI dataset was used, and obtained an accuracy of 0.94. Ensemble of different models make this model computationally complex also it becomes very difficult to optimize its parameters. The study [2] proposes the EVR-Net_RF model, a framework that is designed for early detection and classification of lung cancer by solving all challenge of detecting micro nodules and differentiating between malignant and benign nodules. Model achieved an accuracy of 95% using LIDC dataset and 94% on the Iraq-Oncology Teaching Hospital/National Center for Cancer Diseases (IQ-OTH/NCCD) dataset. Study lacks in identifying tiny nodules that are located at complex boundaries and having low intensity. By focusing on advanced segmentation techniques this limitation can be resolved.

Study [3], used deep learning- based enhanced CNN (ECNN), with Bio inspired approach, Differential evolution to extract the intrinsic and complex features from different lung nodules. A large-scale CT-DICOM image dataset with 25,1135 images is used with 94.7% accuracy but used methods are suffered from inadequate optimization of hyper-parameters, robustness and scalability. A study in [4] introduced an augmented YOLOv6 (You Only Look Once Version 6) system optimized using an Advanced Particle Swarm Optimization (PSO) algorithm. The model achieved an accuracy of 82.79% on LUNA 16 dataset but having difficulty in distinguishing nodule and missing identifying small nodules.[5] A Computer-Aided Diagnosis (CAD) framework utilizing deep learning, where autoencoders were integrated with pre-trained models, achieved an impressive accuracy of 99.60% on datasets obtained from The Cancer Imaging Archive and Kaggle. The study have limitation , such as the restricted availability of training datasets, complexity, low effectiveness, and health data suffering from heterogeneity, noise, high-dimension, and low quality.

[6] Evaluated five machine learning models and identified KNN and Linear Discriminant Analysis (LDA) as the most effective, each reaching 98.30% accuracy. Study lacks in terms of size of dataset used, which can improve performance of the model. The YOLOv3 CNN model was used in the study [7] to identify cancer, and Biogeography-Based Optimization with Extinction and Evolution (BBO/EE) was used to further enhance CNN weights. This model achieved an accuracy of 82.79% on the LUNA 16 dataset. In this study lacking of more sophisticated feature extraction techniques in the future, such as Histogram of Oriented Gradients (HOG), Google's LeNet, and autoencoders, to potentially extract more fine-grained features from the CT scan images. In [8], study introduces a deep learning-enabled Support Vector Machine (SVM) model, referred to as a Computer-Aided Design (CAD) system; to identify cancerous and non-cancerous cells from CT scans, this hybrid model has achieved accuracy of 94% using the LUNA16 dataset. This study can be improved further by experimenting on other datasets.

Furthermore, [9] introduced a framework for identifying nodules based on 3D CT scans and hybridized it with an encoder-decoder U-Net. By using a Mixed Link Network (MixNet), two 3D fast CNNs, achieved 92.7% sensitivity. As the model used in this study require more computational cost. That can be improved by using more sophisticated models. [10] discovered that when utilizing a conventional cross-entropy loss function, Inception-ResNetv2 obtained the best accuracy (99.7%). The study requires manual analysis of histopathology reports that is time-consuming and subjective. [11] examined several methods for detecting lung cancer. The review integrates findings from contemporary AI research on CT-based lung cancer screening. The study aimed to review publications utilizing AI tools for early lung cancer diagnosis and showcase limitation of various datasets used by various AI studies used in lung cancer detection such as LDCT screening. In [12], lung cancer was detected from CT scans using a deep residual learning technique that achieved 84% accuracy, for training used dataset was LIDC-IDRI. Accuracy can be enhanced by using hybrid models like integrating deep learning models with nature inspired models.

## 3 Background

A hybrid approach has been proposed for the diagnosis and classification of lung cancer, combining the benefits of deep learning with nature-based optimization techniques. Pre-trained convolutional neural networks such as MobileNetV4, and DenseNet-201 have been utilized to efficiently extract features from lung CT scans.

### 3.1 MobileNet

MobileNet is an innovative architecture that effectively balances computational efficiency with powerful image recognition capabilities, making it highly valuable in the rapidly evolving domains of deep learning and computer vision. MobileNet is a neural network that can function flawlessly on edge computing platforms, mobile devices, and resource-constrained contexts without sacrificing performance. MobileNet have many variants listed below:

- MobileNetV1: The original architecture that introduces depth wise convolutions separately.
- MobileNetV2: Inverted residual structures and linear bottlenecks are added.
- MobileNetV3: Hard-swish activation functions and neural architecture search were integrated.
- MobileNetV4: It integrates the concepts of inverted residual and inverted bottleneck introduced in the V3 series, and further extends them through the incorporation of a "universal inverted bottleneck."

### 3.2 DenseNet

DenseNet are convolutional networks with many connections. With a few key distinctions, it is quite similar to a ResNet. Because ResNet uses an additive approach, it uses a prior output as an input for a subsequent layer, whereas DenseNet uses all of the previous the previous output as an input for a subsequent layer. DenseNet have many variants, most commonly are listed below:

- Densenet-121: Generally used for image classification, object detection.
- DenseNet-169: Very detailed features extraction and High-accuracy tasks.
- DenseNet-201: used specially in advanced image recognition and medical image analysis.
- DenseNet-264: Commonly helpful in Complex visual tasks.

### 3.3 Nature Inspired Algorithms

This work incorporates six novel Nature-Inspired Algorithms (NIAs) to enhance feature selection and classification in lung cancer diagnosis. These algorithms are well known for their powerful optimization powers and are inspired by natural processes and behaviors. When combined with deep learning-based features, they enhance model accuracy, minimize redundancy, and significantly improve overall performance.

A brief overview of these six NIAs is explained below:

- Ant Lion Optimization (ALO) – Random Walk & Trap Mechanism ALO employs a random walk strategy and trap-based exploitation, allowing a diverse yet focused search for optimal features, improving classification accuracy in CT scans.
- Crested Porcupine Optimization (CPO) – Threat-based Defensive Strategy CPO simulates a threat-based defensive mechanism, making local search optimization more effective by removing redundant features and enhancing lung cancer classification.
- Greylag Goose Algorithm (GGA) – Leadership & Collective Intelligence GGA leverages collective intelligence and dynamic leadership-driven movement, enabling adaptive feature selection for real-time medical image processing.
- Lotus Effect Optimization (LEO) – Self-cleaning Mechanism LEO mimics the self-cleaning properties of lotus leaves, ensuring noise-free and high-quality feature selection, crucial for medical image analysis.
- Polar Light Optimization (PLO) – Dynamic Pattern Formation Inspired by auroras, PLO follows a dynamic pattern search, providing an adaptive and flexible optimization strategy for complex medical datasets.
- Walrus Optimization Algorithm (WOA) – Social Cooperation & Foraging WOA's group foraging behavior promotes diverse solution exploration, improving early-stage lung cancer detection through optimized feature selection.

## 4 Proposed Methodology

In this study, lung cancer has been diagnosed and categorize using a Kaggle dataset of chest CT scan images (Fig. 1) of the lungs. Dataset contains four classes of lung cancer, adenocarcinoma, large-cell carcinoma, normal and squamous cell carcinoma.

In order to extract rich and varied feature representations, the CT scan images were first processed using two deep learning models, MobileNet-V4 and DenseNet-201. A complete feature set was then created by concatenating the features that had been retrieved from both models. Multiple arrays can be compactly stored together in numPy compressed archive file(.npz). The.npz file was used for further processing with nature inspired algorithms to reduce dimensionality of extracted features. Six recently developed Nature-Inspired Algorithms (NIAs) were used in this study to optimize and choose the most pertinent attributes. In order to identify lung nodules, a variety of machine learning classifiers were used to classify a subset of the features. The goal of this hybrid strategy is to improve model performance and classification accuracy by merging deep learning and NIAs. The mathematics underlying this suggested approach are presented in Eqs. (1), (2), and (3). MobilenetV4 based on both depth wise separable convolution and Universal Inverted Bottleneck (UIB) blocks.

In MobileNetV4, features(X) are first expanded ($W_{exp}$), then it is processed through depthwise convolution $K_{dw}$, Depthwise convolution kernel for capturing spatial information, and then in last projected back with $W_{proj}$. $W_{proj}$ is the projection matrix. These transformed features are then passed through a non-linear activation σ (ReLU6) and merged with the skip connection s(X), enabling efficient feature extraction with residual learning. Mathematically:

$$Y = s(X) + \sigma\left(\left(X.W_{exp} * K_{dw}\right).W_{proj}\right) \tag{1}$$

where:

X: Input feature map
$W_{exp}$: Expansion weight matrix (1 × 1 convolution)
$K_{dw}$: Depth wise Convolution kernel
$W_{proj}$: Projection (1 × 1 convolution)
σ: Activation function ((ReLU6)
s(X): Skip connection

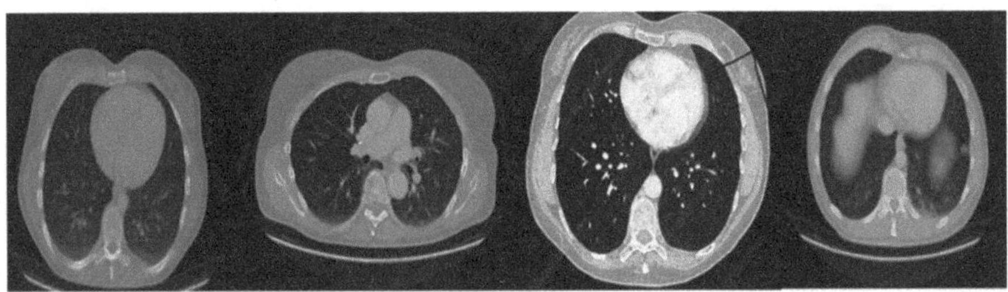

**Fig. 1.** Chest CT scan images of a) squamous cell carcinoma b) adenocarcinoma c) large-cell carcinoma d) Normal

In DenseNet-201, every layer $l$ obtains feature maps from all previous layers via concatenation. The transformation function $H_l$ which takes argument as an input of feature map that consists of batch normalization, ReLU activation, and convolution operations. Output of each layer $x_l$ can be expressed as:

$$x_l = H_l\left(\left[x_0, x_1, \ldots\ldots\ldots x_{l-1}\right]\right), l = 1, 2, \ldots\ldots 201 \tag{2}$$

Final output of all layers is concatenated and calculated as:

$$X_{out} = \oplus_{l=1}^{201} H_l\left(\left[x_0, x_1, \ldots\ldots\ldots x_{l-1}\right]\right) \tag{3}$$

$X$: input feature map.
$x_l$: output of the $\ell_{th}$ layer
$H_l$: : transformation at layer $\ell$ (BatchNorm → Relu → Conv)
[·]: concatenation of feature maps
⊕: dense feature concatenation across all layers
$X_{out}$: Final outcome of all layers

After feature extraction, features from both models are then saved and concatenated.

$$\text{Mathematically} : F_{hybrid} = [F_{MobileNetV4} F_{DenseNet201}] \quad (4)$$

Complete flow of working is shown in Fig. 2. In next section, we are showing pseudocode of working model's methodology.

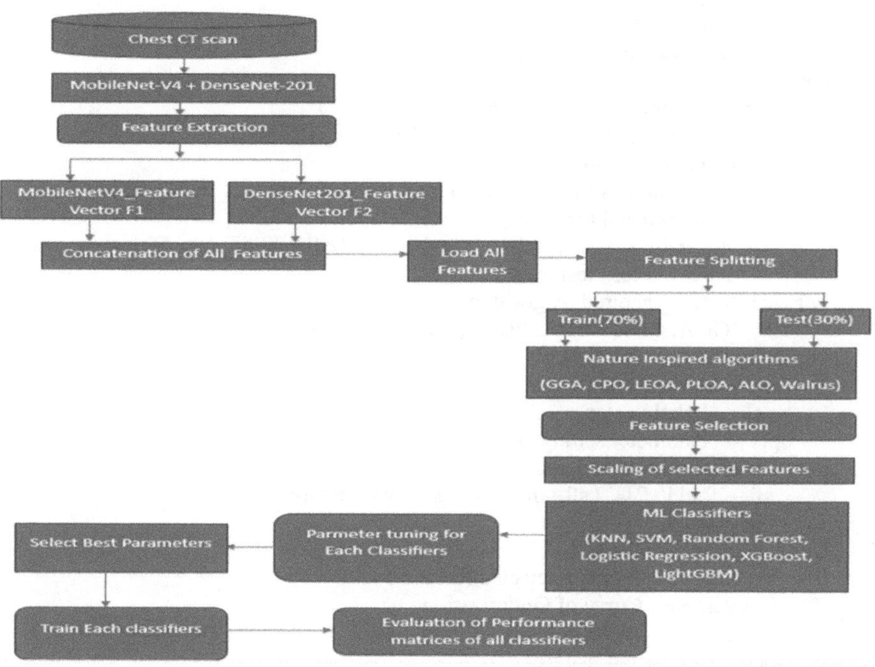


**Fig. 2.** Workflow of Proposed architecture

### 4.1 Pseudocode

The working process of the proposed model begins with loading all the required libraries and the pre-trained models MobileNet-V4 and DenseNet-201. Features are extracted from both models and fused into feature vectors *F1* and *F2*, which are then saved in a compressed.npz file. The extracted features are split using *train_test_split* to obtain the feature vector and label vector. This split is then passed to the optimization phase, where various nature-inspired algorithms (NIAs) are applied. Each NIA is defined and invoked using the variable *fmdl,* while their parameters are initialized with the variables *feat, labels,* and *opts* (representing features, labels, and parameter settings, respectively). The NIAs operate on the extracted data, and the selected features are stored as *sf*. The number of selected features is determined using the count function, after which they are scaled to enhance performance. Finally, the scaled features *(X_train_scaled)* are used to train machine learning classifiers, namely KNN, Logistic Regression, SVM, Random

Forest, XGBoost, and LightGBM, under different hyperparameter settings. Accuracy is evaluated using the prediction data *(X_valid_scaled)*, and all performance metrics are computed, plotted, and visualized to present the results. The pseudocode for this entire methodology is provided below.

```
1.  Start Program
      import all required libraries and input data from source to targeted folder.
2.  Initialize pretrained models.
        LOAD MobileNet_V4 model
        LOAD DenseNet_201 model
3.  Features extracted
      vector F1 ←Mobilenet_V4 Features (Using Eq.1)
      vector F2 ←DenseNet_201 Features (Using Eq.3)
   //Concatenating all feature (Using eq. 4)
4.    SAVE and combine all features and labels as NPZ file (split_name_features.npz)
5.  Split data into train and test sets
              (x_train, x_test, y_train, y_test) ←  TRAIN_TEST_SPLIT(feature_vector,
              label_vector, test_ratio)
6.  For each Nature_Inspired_Algorithm
              (GGA, CPO, LEOA, PLOA, ALO, Walrus)
      a. INPUT
       feat ← Feature matrix
       label ← Label vector
       opts ← Parameter settings for Each NIA
      b. Initialize NIA model and extract selected features as
         sf ← fmdl['sf']  // sf = indices of selected features
  End For
7.  Compute number of selected features
              num_feat ←count(selected features)
8.   Plot Convergence Curve of Optimization
             curve ←fitness values across iterations
9.  Preprocessing selected features
10. Initialize and train the final machine learning classifier
          Classification Phase with Hyperparameter settings
              FOR each classifier in [KNN, SVM, Random Forest, Logistic  Regression,
              XGBoost, LightGBM] DO
                 a. Define parameter grid (hyperparameters specific to classifier)
                 b. Apply tuning method
                 c. Select best parameters from search
                 d. Train classifier with best parameters on scaled data (X_train_scaled)
                 e. Predict on X_valid_scaled
                 f. Evaluate performance matrices (Accuracy, Confusion matrix, Recall,
                 F1-score)
             END FOR
11. END Program
```

## 4.2 Time Complexity

The proposed hybrid approach combines deep learning-based feature extraction with nature-inspired optimization and conventional machine learning classifiers. Three main factors affect the system's overall temporal complexity: classifier training, feature selection by metaheuristic optimization. The computational complexity of feature extraction depends on the number of input images and the architecture, defined by the image height $H$ width $W$, and the grayscale channels. Feature selection using nature-inspired algorithms is expressed in terms of population size $P$, number of iterations $I$, and feature dimension $d$. Classifier complexity is represented by the function $f(n,d)$, applied on $n$ training samples with d-dimensional selected features. The overall complexity of the proposed architecture is summarized in Eq. (5).

$$O\left(N.\left(C.H.W.k^2\right)\right) + O(I.P.d + f(n,d)) \tag{5}$$

where N denotes no. of input images, C is no. of input channels given to an image. (H.W) is spatial resolution of feature maps (224 × 224), k kernel size, I for iteration, P is population size used by different NIAs, d denotes no. of selected features, n is no. of training samples, $f(n, d)$ is classifier-dependent complexity. The overall estimated runtime of the proposed model implementation is around 8256 s (~2.29 h).

## 5 Results and Discussion

The following are the salient features of our model's performance:

1. Requirement of system:

   Below Table 1 is showing requirement of resources to evaluating this model.

**Table 1.** Hardware and Software configuration for experiments

| Component | Specification |
|---|---|
| CPU | $13^{th}$ Gen Intel Core i9-13900K (16 core, 32threads) |
| RAM | 16 GB |
| GPU | NVIDIA RTX A5000(24 GB VRAM) |
| Secondary Memory | SSD 512 GB |
| Operating System | Windows 11 (64-Bit) |
| Programming Language | Python 3.9.21 |
| Tools | Anaconda v2 3.0, Jupyter Notebook 4.0 |

2. Parameter Settings: To improve performance of used machine learning classifiers parameters are tuned. Settings of various parameters done in this study is shown in Table 2. Training of various nature inspired algorithm is done using 20 iterations.

3. Accuracy: Using the Kaggle dataset and the Polar Light Optimizer, our model achieves an extremely high accuracy of 94.4% that is very high when compared with other classifiers, on the Kaggle dataset, 89.5% accuracy is attained by the Resnet 50 with advanced PSO, 88.8% with 3D MixNet.

**Table 2.** Parameter Settings of different classifiers

| Classifiers | Hyperparameter used |
|---|---|
| KNN | n_neighbors = 5 |
| SVM | C = (0.1, 1, 10, 100), C is Regularization parameter |
| | Gamma = [1, 0.1, 0.01, 0.001], Gamma is Kernel coefficient |
| | kernel = (rbf, poly), kernel function(rbf -Radial Basis Function, poly-polynomial function |
| Random Forest | n_estimators = 300, no. of trees in random forest |
| | random_state = 2, seed value |
| | max_depth = 20 |
| | min_samples_split = 5 |
| | class_weight = balanced, weight assigned to a class |
| Logistic Regression | C = 10 |
| | max_iter = 500 |
| | solver = liblinear, solver is optimization algorithm used to minimize the cost function |
| | penalty = l2, regularization |
| | class_weight = balanced |
| XGBoost | n_estimators = (100, 200), no. of boosting round in XGBoost |
| | max_depth = (3, 5, 7) |
| | learning_rate = (0.01, 0.1, 0.2), learning rate is boosting step size |
| | colsample_bytree: (0.8, 1.0), Fraction of features used per tree |
| | subsample = (0.8, 1.0) |
| LightGBM | n_estimators = (100, 200), no. of boosting round in LGBM |
| | max_depth = (−1, 10) |
| | learning_rate = (0.01, 0.1) |
| | num_leaves = (31, 50) |
| | subsample = (0.8, 1.0) |

We evaluate and compare a hybrid model VGG19-Resnet152 with nature inspired PLO Algorithm that also gain a very good accuracy of 94%. Comparison table of different architectures employed on lung cancer detection is shown below. (Table 3).

The model's performance was evaluated and visualized through confusion matrices, as shown in Figs. 3 and 4. The proposed hybrid MobileNetV4–DenseNet201 architecture optimized with the Lotus effect Optimizer Algorithm (LEOA) and Logistic regression classifier achieved the highest accuracy across all folds. To ensure a robust and clinically meaningful assessment, multiple metrics: Accuracy, Sensitivity, Specificity, F1-score,

**Table 3.** Comparative study of our model with other models [13]

| Models | Accuracy |
|---|---|
| Artificial Neural Networks | 74% |
| UNet + Random Forest | 74% |
| Deep Belief Networks | 81% |
| DarkNet- 53 | 73.9% |
| You Only Look Once -v3 | 80.6% |
| Grey Level Co-occurrence Matrix + SVM | 72.2% |
| Radial Basis Function | 81.2% |
| Visual Geometry group + RNN | 70% |
| Deep 3 D Dual Path Nets | 81.4% |
| YOLO v6 + Advanced PSO | 82.7% |
| Multi crop-CNN | 87.1% |
| Lenet_Alexnet | 87.7% |
| 3D MixNet | 88.8% |
| Resnet50 + Advanced PSO | 89.5% |
| VGG19-Resnet152 + PLOA | 94.3% |
| MobileNetV4-Densenet201 + PLOA | 94.4% |

and AUC—are computed using 10-fold cross-validation. Detailed metric results are presented in table 4 below.

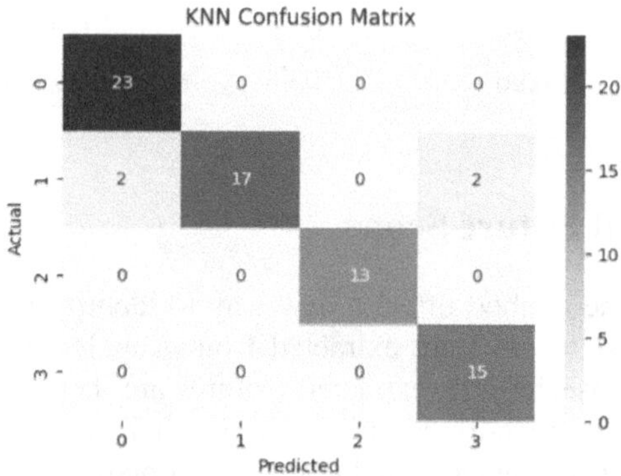


**Fig. 3:** Confusion matrix (Hybrid MobileNetV4-Densenet-201architecture integrated with Polar Light Optimization and K- NN classifier)

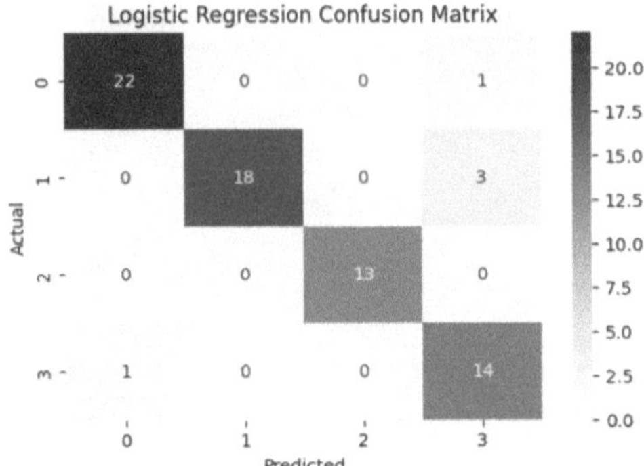


**Fig. 4.** Confusion matrix (Hybrid MobileNetV4-Densenet-201architecture integrated with Lotus Effect Optimization and Logistic Regression classifier)

**Table 4.** Performance matrices of Hybrid MobileNetV4-DenseNet201 with LEO and Logistic Regression across 10-fold CV

| Fold | Accuracy | Sensitivity | Specificity | F1-Score | AUC |
|---|---|---|---|---|---|
| 1 | 0.96 | 0.96 | 0.96 | 0.9598 | 0.9929 |
| 2 | 0.96 | 0.96 | 0.96 | 0.9595 | 0.9972 |
| 3 | 0.96 | 0.96 | 0.96 | 0.9599 | 0.9873 |
| 4 | 0.96 | 0.96 | 0.96 | 0.96 | 0.9914 |
| 5 | 0.95 | 0.95 | 0.95 | 0.9499 | 0.9972 |
| 6 | 0.93 | 0.93 | 0.93 | 0.9301 | 0.9917 |
| 7 | 0.9 | 0.9 | 0.9 | 0.9001 | 0.986 |
| 8 | 0.94 | 0.94 | 0.94 | 0.9398 | 0.9748 |
| 9 | 0.96 | 0.96 | 0.96 | 0.9598 | 0.9984 |
| 10 | 0.96 | 0.96 | 0.96 | 0.9598 | 0.993 |

## 6 Conclusion and Future Scope

This study proposed the method offers a new way to identify nodules in the lungs in CT scan pictures. First features are extracted from Kaggle datasets using hybrid of MobileNet-V4 and DenseNet-201, extracted features are then fed into nature inspired algorithms so that dimensionality can be reduced. After that classifiers are used with different settings of hyperparameters and accuracy is obtained.

This robust model, which is well-known for its outstanding efficacy in image classification tasks, is an essential component of our methodology. Here, we present six latest NIA's, which further improves the performance of our model. Using nature inspired algorithms in conjunction with MobileNet-V4 and DenseNet-201 model on the Kaggle dataset yields an impressive accuracy of 94.4, when hybrid with Polar light effect optimization algorithm.

To enhance the system's functionality, future work can explore advanced feature extraction methods such as HOG, LeNet, and autoencoders for improved nodule detection accuracy. Additionally, alternative classifiers like LDA, Naïve Bayes, and AdaBoost can be evaluated. Further studies may also utilize publicly available datasets such as LIDC and LUNA16 to validate and generalize the proposed approach.

## References


1. Kalyani, A.N., and Kumar, V.: Improved attention-based RCNN segmentation and ensemble classifier for lung cancer classification and severity level assessment using CT image. J. Theoret. Appl. Inf. Technol. **103**(18) (2025)
2. Khan, T.F., Zubair, S.: Optimizing lung nodule classification through the integration of image processing and transfer learning techniques. Clust. Comput. **28**, 758 (2025). https://doi.org/10.1007/s10586-025-05408-8
3. Kalaivani, D., Dheepa, G.: Deep learning enhanced CNN with Bio-Inspired techniques and BCE for effective lung nodules diagnosis & classification for accurate diagnosis. Indian J. Sci. Technol. **17**(37), 3851–3864 (2024c). https://doi.org/10.17485/ijst/v17i37.2649
4. Goel, L., Patel, P.: Improving YOLOv6 using advanced PSO optimizer for weight selection in lung cancer detection and classification. Multimedia Tools Appl. **83**(32), 78059–78092 (2024). https://doi.org/10.1007/s11042-024-18441-3
5. Helaly, H.A., et al.: ELCD-NSC2: a novel early lung cancer detection and non-small cell classification framework. Neural Comput. Appl. **36**(24), 15149–64 (2024). https://doi.org/10.1007/s00521-024-09856-y
6. Rao, B.D., Mahammad, A.: Diagnosis of lung and pleural diseases by machine learning algorithms. 2022 International Conference on Computer Communication and Informatics (ICCCI), pp. 1–5 (2023). https://doi.org/10.1109/iccci56745.2023.10128349
7. Goel, L., Mishra, S.: A hybrid of modified YOLOv3 with BBO/EE optimizer for lung cancer detection. Multimedia Tools Appl. **83**(17), 52219–52251 (2023). https://doi.org/10.1007/s11042-023-17454-8
8. Shafi, I., et al.: An effective method for lung cancer diagnosis from CT scan using deep learning-based support vector network. Cancers **14**(21), 5457 (2022). https://doi.org/10.3390/cancers14215457
9. Zheng, S., Guo, J., Cui, X., Veldhuis, R.N.J., Oudkerk, M., Van Ooijen, P.M.A.: Automatic pulmonary nodule diagnosis in CT scans using convolutional neural networks based on maximum intensity projection. IEEE Trans. Med. Imaging **39**(3), 797–805 (2019). https://doi.org/10.1109/tmi.2019.2935553
10. Baranwal, N., Doravari, P., Kachhoria, R.: Classification of histopathology images of lung cancer using convolutional neural network (CNN). arXiv (Cornell University) (2021). https://doi.org/10.48550/arxiv.2112.13553
11. Espinoza, J.L., Dong, L.T.: Artificial intelligence tools for refining lung cancer screening. J. Clin. Med. **9**(12), 3860 (2020). https://doi.org/10.3390/jcm9123860
12. Bhatia, S., Sinha, Y., Goel, L.: Lung cancer diagnosis: a deep learning approach. In: Advances in Intelligent Systems and Computing, pp. 699–705 (2018). https://doi.org/10.1007/978-981-13-1595-4_55
13. Agrawal, A., Goyal, D.: Improving ResNet50 using Advanced PSO optimizer for pulmonary disease detection on CT scan images: a comprehensive analysis. B.Tech Thesis, Submitted to Dept. of Computer Science, MNIT Jaipur, Jaipur, India (2024)

# On the Differentiation of Alzheimer's Disease from Normal Control Using Electroencephalogram Energy of Brain Lobes

Prabitra Sarkar and Abhijit Chandra(✉)

Department of Instrumentation and Electronics Engineering, Jadavpur University, Kolkata 700 106, India
abhijit922@yahoo.co.in

**Abstract.** This article leverages upon a new method to classify Alzheimer's disease from the healthy ones using brain EEG signal. Two different approaches have been considered to accomplish this task. In the first approach, temporal and occipital lobe energy across all frequency bands have been taken into our consideration for extracting the features. In the second approach, five frequency band energy of all five brain lobes has been employed for subsequent classification using support vector machine and k nearest neighbor. The proposed methodology achieves a highest accuracy of 97.3% using k nearest neighbor.

**Keywords:** Alzheimer's disease · discrete wavelet transform · electroencephalogram. K nearest neighbor · support vector machine

## 1 Introduction

Alzheimer's disease (AD) is a chronic neurodegenerative disorder that primarily affects memory, thinking, and behavior. As the most common cause of dementia among older adults, its early detection is essential for timely intervention and management. Electroencephalogram (EEG), a non-invasive method to record electrical activity of the brain, has emerged as a promising tool for diagnosing neurological conditions, including AD [1, 2]. EEG signals reflect brain dynamics and can reveal abnormalities in brainwave patterns associated with Alzheimer's disease. This work explores the use of EEG signal analysis combined with machine learning techniques for the early detection of Alzheimer's disease. By extracting signal processing techniques and extracting meaningful features, researchers aim to distinguish between Alzheimer's patients and healthy individuals with improved accuracy [3, 4].

Despite significant advancements in neuroimaging and diagnostics, Alzheimer's disease often goes undiagnosed until the symptoms become severe. Conventional methods like MRI and PET scans are expensive and not feasible for widespread early screening. EEG, being inexpensive, portable and non-invasive, offers a practical alternative of leveraged effectively [5, 6]. However, raw EEG signals being highly complex and noisy, require advanced processing and feature extraction methods. This work is motivated by


A. Shastri et al. (Eds.): IHCI 2025, LNCS 16437, pp. 158–166, 2026.
https://doi.org/10.1007/978-3-032-26352-0_13

the need to develop an accurate and computationally efficient approach for detecting AD using EEG signals. The challenge lies in identifying discriminative features and applying robust classification techniques that can differentiate between AD and healthy control (HC) subjects based on signal characteristics.

EEG has emerged as a valuable tool in detecting neurodegenerative disorders such as AD due to its non-invasive nature, cost-effectiveness and high temporal resolution. Studies have shown that EEG signals of AD patients exhibit reduced complexity, altered spectral content, and diminished coherence compared to HC. Abnormalities are particularly evident in the Alpha and Beta bands, with decreased activity in posterior regions of the brain. These observations motivate EEG-based machine learning models for early AD detection.

Pre-processing is a crucial task to ensure quality and reliability of EEG data, as raw EEG signals are often contaminated with noise and artifacts. Baseline correction is used to eliminate DC offsets and low-frequency drift in EEG recordings. It ensures that each channel has a zero-mean signal, which is crucial for reliable feature extraction. This is followed by the use of band-pass filter which offers a sharp roll-off and no ripple in the pass-band, making it suitable for isolating the five EEG frequency bands i.e. Delta (0.5–4 Hz), Theta (4–8 Hz), Alpha (8–13 Hz), Beta (13–30 Hz) and Gamma (30–45 Hz) [7, 8]. It helps remove irrelevant frequency components and enhance brainwave features.

Followed by this pre-processing technique, some transformation tools are generally applied to obtain clear insight about the presence of different frequency components. In connection with this, discrete wavelet transform (DWT) [9, 10] is a powerful technique that decomposes a signal into different frequency components while retaining temporal information. It is well known that EEG signal comprises of different brain waves which are generated due to various activities. For example, Delta wave is associated with deep sleep and unconscious state while Theta is linked to drowsiness and memory processing. On the other hand, Alpha is related to relaxed and calm state and Beta wave is associated with active thinking and problem solving. Gamma wave is very rare and is only found during deep thinking and meditation phase.

In recent times, several deep learning approaches have been implemented on EEG data for early AD diagnosis too. Morabito et al. [11] had proposed a deep learning oriented approach based on cconvolutional nneural nnetwork (CNN) and auto-encoder multi layer perceptron (MLP) for HC vs mild cognitive impairment (MCI) vs AD classification using scalp EEG recordings. They achieved an accuracy of 82%, sensitivity of 83% and specificity of 75%. Two way classifications had shown comparatively better results with an accuracy of 85% for AD vs HC and 78% for AD vs MCI. Triki et al. [12] had proposed a new MCI classification system based on a novel CNN approach dividing MCI into three stages, namely healthy normal control (HNC), amnestic MCI (aMCI) and non-amnestic MCI (naMCI). The proposed method attained a high classification accuracy of 98.2%, 96.7% and 97.1% for HNC, aMCI and naMCI respectively. Sen et al. [13] had proposed a novel ITD-spectrogram and 2D CNN-based classification approach to diagnose dementia through EEG signals. It produces an accuracy close to 98%. Sen et al. [14] also proposed a EEG-PRC driven segmentation method to train a 1D CNN providing a 97% testing stage accuracy in AD classification. Compared to the aforementioned DL models, the proposed method achieves the highest accuracy of 97.3% using K nearest neighbor (KNN) algorithm due to its carefully selected features.

Rest of the paper is organized as follows: Sect. 2 deliberates on the proposed methodology while Sect. 3 reflects upon the results obtained and finally the paper is concluded in Sect. 4.

## 2 Methodology

This work follows a single streamlined process to detect AD using EEG signals, involving signal pre-processing, frequency band decomposition, energy extraction, statistical analysis and classification. EEG data has been collected from the OpenNeuro platform. Two different feature sets are used in the classification sets, namely temporal and occipital lobe energy across all bands (Approach 1) and full lobe-wise and band-wise energy in the form of 5X5 matrix (Approach 2).

### 2.1 Signal Pre-Processing

EEG signals often contain low-frequency drifts or DC offsets resulting from electrode-skin interface potential or instrumental bias. To address this issue, the method of baseline correction has been applied. For each EEG signal, the mean value of the signal is computed and subtracted from every sample in the channel. This can be mathematically written as:

$$x_{corr}^{ch}(t) = x^{ch}(t) - \frac{1}{N}\sum\nolimits_{i=1}^{N} x_i^{ch}(t) \tag{1}$$

where $x_i^{ch}$ symbolizes the $i^{th}$ sample from any of the channel while $x_{corr}^{ch}$ represents baseline corrected signal from the same channel. This ensures that all signals have zero-mean and are centered around the origin which is thought to be a crucial step for feature extraction and decomposition. A Chebyshev type II [15] filter has subsequently been applied to retain the brain activity within the frequency range from 0.5 to 45 Hz. This essentially covers up all the relevant EEG frequency bands.

Traditional Fourier transform based methods fail to capture transient non-stationery components in EEG. Hence, discrete wavelet transform (DWT) has been employed for time frequency analysis. Each pre-processed channel has been decomposed using Daubechies (db4) wavelet via DWT because of its orthogonality and resemblance to EEG signal morphology. Each decomposition splits the signal into approximation (low-frequency) and detail (high-frequency) coefficients. Approximation coefficients are passed to the next level while detail coefficients correspond to specific frequency ranges.

The 21 EEG channels are categorized into 5 lobes based on the 10–20 international electrode placement system. For each EEG channel, a 4 level DWT has been applied to extract the coefficients for five distinct frequency bands corresponding to five different brain waves. Energy of each frequency band has subsequently been calculated. Similarly, for each lobe, all the corresponding channels have been identified from which mean energy for each band across those channels. Finally, we aim to generate a 5X5 matrix corresponding to five different brain lobes and five distinct frequency bands. This matrix serves as the feature vector used for statistical analysis and subsequent classification.

### 2.2 Statistical Analysis

To validate the observed energy differences, independent t-tests have been conducted between AD and HC groups for each band in the temporal and occipital lobe. The test has been conducted with a significance level of 0.05. The result of this test reveals whether or not there exist any statistically significant differences between the temporal and occipital energy which will subsequently help in further classification.

### 2.3 Classification Approaches

Based on the statistically significant features already extracted, a number of popular machine learning models has been applied for classifying them into two distinct classes. In connection to this, two approaches have been taken into our consideration.

In the first approach, classification is performed using a compact and biologically relevant feature set derived from the temporal and occipital lobes of the brain. These two regions are particularly significant in AD progression. The temporal lobe is associated with memory and language processing which are notably impaired in early-stage AD. The occipital lobe, responsible for visual processing, typically exhibits reduced activity in AD especially in higher-frequency bands. To exploit these distinctions, this approach computes the energy difference between the temporal and occipital lobes for each of the five brainwave frequency bands. Energy is calculated as the sum of squares of the filtered signal in each lobe. The energy difference is computed for each band. This process results in a 5 dimensional feature vector for every subject, capturing the directional energy imbalance between these two lobes. This feature design is motivated by prior statistical analysis which has shown consistent and significant differences in temporal and occipital energy between AD and HC subjects. AD subjects often exhibit elevated temporal lobe energy and reduced occipital lobe energy, particularly in Delta, Theta and Alpha bands. Capturing these deviation in a simple and interpretable way helps in both classification performance and clinical relevance.

Second approach utilizes a complete set of energy-based features extracted from five brain lobes and five EEG frequency bands to form a comprehensive 5X5 energy matrix per subject. Unlike the previous temporal-occipital focused method, this model considers spatially distributed information across the entire brain; thus capturing the global energy dynamics potentially affected in AD. The resultant 5X5 energy matrix has been flattened into a 25-dimensional feature vector for machine learning input.

## 3 Results

This section explicitly elaborates the results obtained using the proposed approach. Figure 1 below underscores the energy comparison amongst different brain lobes and frequency bands.

Looking at the above bar diagram and pie chart, it can be clearly inferred that occipital lobe carries a significant part of the total energy which increases from approximately 40% for the AD subjects to more than 55% for HC subject. As far as the distribution of different frequency component is concerned, it can further be observed that Delta band

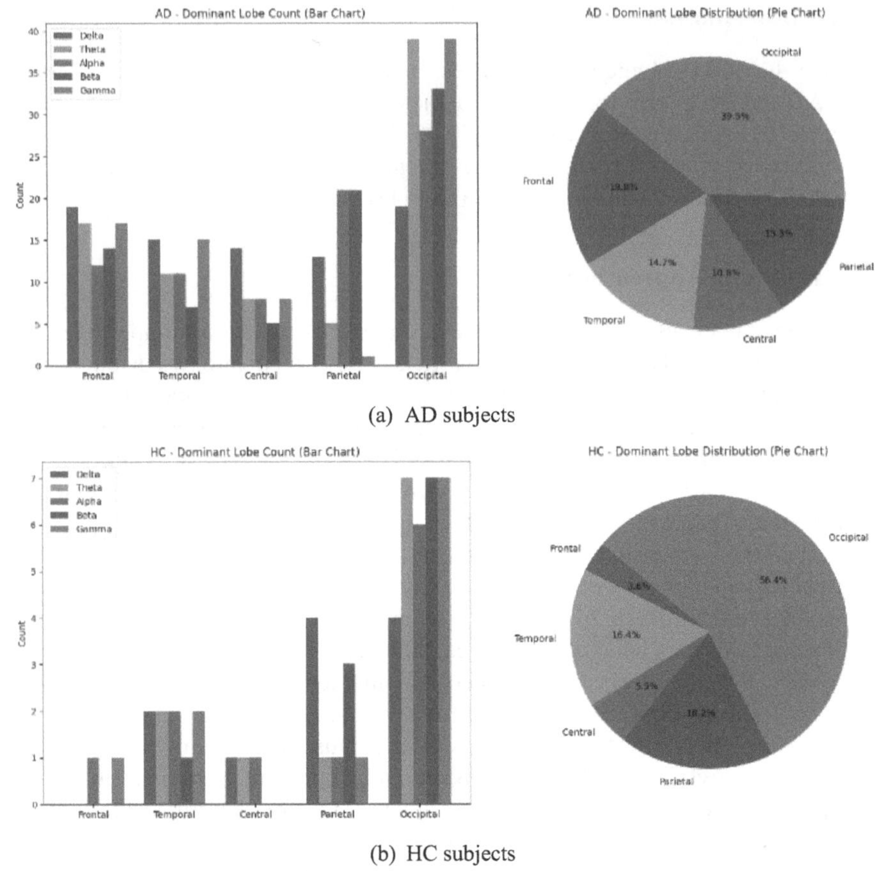


(a) AD subjects

(b) HC subjects

**Fig. 1.** Energy comparison among different brain lobes and frequency bands.

comprises of minimum energy while Theta and Gamma band take the highest share. While Temporal and Parietal band reflect upon almost comparable energy for AD and HC subjects, there has been a noticeable reduction in terms of frontal lobe energy for HC subjects. This can also be validated from the bar chart of dominant lobe as presented. In connection to this, average temporal and occipital energy for five distinct frequency bands has been listed in Table 1 below.

To validate the observed energy difference and to find out the essential features which might be helpful in subsequent classification phase, independent t-test has been conducted between AD and HC groups for each band in the temporal and occipital lobe. The resultant statistics has been shown in Fig. 2 below.

Looking at the above figure, it can be concluded that in the AD group, significant differences between temporal and occipital energy has been observed in all bands except Beta with the most prominent differences found in the Delta and Theta band. On the other side, in the HC group, only Delta and Beta band exhibit significant difference. These correspond to normal visual and resting-state EEG dynamics in healthy individuals. This

**Table 1.** Average temporal and occipital energy

| Subject type | Name of the lobe | Name of the frequency band | | | | |
|---|---|---|---|---|---|---|
| | | Delta | Theta | Alpha | Beta | Gamma |
| AD | Temporal | 22025 | 12943 | 13077 | 9149 | 6364 |
| | Occipital | 11791 | 6259 | 11455 | 9096 | 8794 |
| HC | Temporal | 19754 | 3934 | 4031 | 5351 | 4079 |
| | Occipital | 24771 | 4047 | 4219 | 10696 | 6562 |

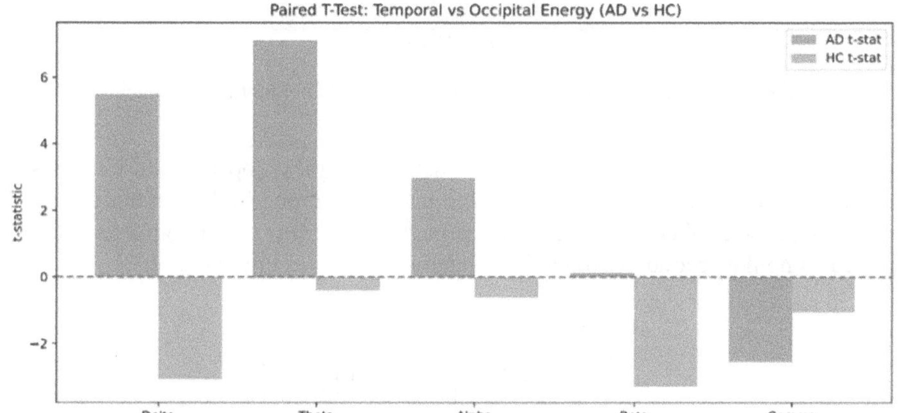


**Fig. 2.** Result of the independent T-test conducted between AD and HC groups for each band in temporal and occipital lobe.

analysis highlights that AD patients exhibit altered lobar energy distribution, especially in lower frequency bands (i.e. Delta and Theta), which are often linked to cognitive decline and dementia progression.

Support Vector Machine (SVM) and K Nearest Neighbor (KNN) algorithms have been employed in this work for further classification based on the statistically relevant features extracted before. In the first approach, SVM with linear kernel has been used to classify subjects based on these five features. The simplicity of the feature space allowed for fast training and clear model interpretability while maintaining high accuracy. For the present study, optimum value of k has been determined empirically to be 7 for the KNN algorithm in which Euclidian distance served as the distance metric. A 60–40 train-test split is employed with stratification to ensure class balance. All the features have been standardized using z-score normalization to ensure that all five features contribute equally to the distance metric. Resultant confusion matrices obtained using the first approach have been presented in Fig. 3 below.

In the second approach, while using SVM with linear kernel, all 25 features are used to train the initial model. The absolute value of the SVM coefficients has been used to rank feature importance which identify top 15 features based on highest coefficient

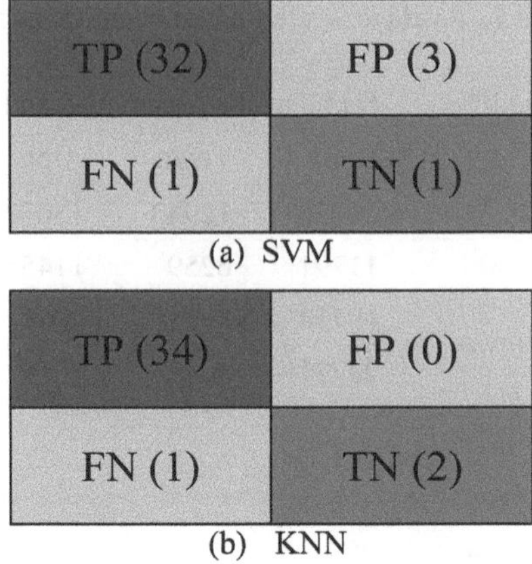


**Fig. 3.** Resultant confusion matrices obtained using the first approach

magnitude. A new SVM model is retrained using only these top 15 features. KNN, on the other hand, does not involve any dimensionality reduction and the settings used in the first approach are applied in the second approach as well. Resultant confusion matrices obtained using the second approach have been presented in Fig. 4 below.

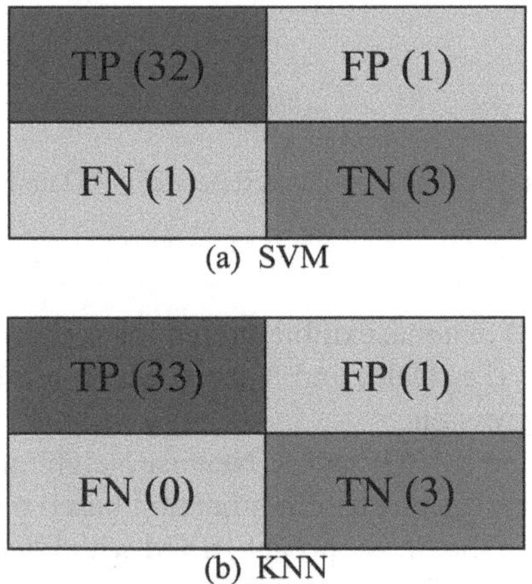


**Fig. 4.** Resultant confusion matrices obtained using the second approach

Consideration of EEG signal for all five brain lobes (i.e. frontal, temporal, central, parietal, occipital) and for all five frequency bands (i.e. delta, theta, alpha, beta, and gamma) for the detection of AD has been a common practice in the literature. Present work deliberates upon two approaches for extracting features from brain EEG signal. While the first approach prioritizes temporal and occipital lobe energy across all bands; the second approach exploits all the 25 features resulting from five lobes and five frequency bands. One such comparative analysis with the existing literature has been showcased in Table 2 for better clarity.

**Table 2.** Comparative analysis among existing approaches.

| Lobe used | Machine learning algorithms used | | | | |
|---|---|---|---|---|---|
| | SVM (L) | SVM (RBF) | KNN | RF | NB |
| Frontal | 86.21% | 64.66% | 67.24% | 82.76% | 87.07% |
| Temporal | 93.10% | 88.79% | 81.03% | 87.93% | 92.24% |
| Central | 89.66% | 93.10% | 87.93% | 95.69% | 96.55% |
| Parietal | 91.38% | 91.38% | 79.31% | 89.66% | 93.97% |
| Occipital | 95.69% | 67.24% | 89.66% | 91.38% | 95.69% |
| Proposed approach 1 | 89.19% | - | **97.3%** | - | - |
| Proposed approach 2 | 94.6% | - | **97.3%** | - | - |

## 4 Conclusions

This work manifests a simple approach to classify AD from the healthy ones using lobe energy from brain EEG signal. Discrete wavelet transform has been applied to extract frequency domain information resulting from the brain lobes. Statistically significant frequency band energy has been subsequently utilized for further classification using standard machine learning algorithms. It has been found that the performance of KNN using the proposed approach yields highest accuracy across all the machine learning methods in all five brain lobes. The current study makes use of a relatively limited dataset. A part of this can be attributed to the fact that several popular Alzheimer's oriented databases such as Alzheimer's Disease Neuroimaging Initiative (ADNI), Open Access Series of Imaging Studies (OASIS), Minimal Interval Resonance Imaging in Alzheimer's Disease (MIRIAD) and Kaggle Alzheimer's Classification Dataset (KACN) do not contain EEG data. Furthermore, acquisition of EEG data of AD patients for external validation is difficult due to privacy reasons, people being lackadaisical towards research work and dominance of neuroimaging modalities such as MRI and PET in current times. Future research should focus on using larger and more diverse dataset to improve the generalization capability of the model and to ensure its performance across various population and age group. Steps must be taken to find, develop or integrate more datasets with EEG data. Larger datasets would make application of latest, cutting-edge deep learning techniques feasible to EEG driven studies which is currently impractical due to the lack of sufficient data.

**Acknowledgment.** This research work is funded by Anusandhan national Research Foundation, Department of Science and Technology, Govt. of India vide sanction order no. CRG/2022/004306. Special appreciation is given to Mr. Sarthak Sarkar for his valuable assistance and support.

## References

1. Reilly, T.P., Simpson, L.J., Wender, P.H.: Electroencephalography and early diagnosis of Alzheimer's Disease: a review. J. Neurosci. **45**(3), 231–245 (2020)

2. Liley, D.J., et al.: Brainwave band decomposition and energy analysis in Alzheimer's Patients. J. Neural Eng. **18**(4), 125–138 (2022)
3. Safi, M.S., Safi, S.M.M.: Early detection of Alzheimer's Disease from EEG signals using Hjorth parameters. Biomed. Signal Process. Control **65**, 102338 (2021)
4. Quiroga, R.Q.: EEG signal processing: feature extraction and classification techniques. Neurosci. Methods J. **52**(2), 415–428 (2018)
5. Wang, X., Zhao, T., Liu, J.: Feature extraction of EEG for Alzheimer's detection using wavelet transform and statistical analysis. Comput. Biol. Med. **104**, 35–48 (2019)
6. Panda, G., Misra, A., Kumar, R.: EEG-Based machine learning model for Alzheimer's Disease classification. Artif. Intell. Med. **98**, 1–12 (2020)
7. Tarun, P., Goyal, V.: A comparative study of normalization techniques for EEG signal processing. Int. J. Biomed. Data Sci. **15**(2), 78–89 (2021)
8. Fouad, I.A., El-Zahraa, F., Labib, M.: Identification of Alzheimer's Disease from central Lobe EEG Signals utilizing machine learning and residual neural network. Biomed. Signal Process. Control **86**, 105266 (2023)
9. Mallat, S.: A Wavelet Tour of Signal Processing (3rd ed.). Academic Press (2008)
10. Reddy, P.N.M.S., Prasad, M.: Analysis of EEG signals using discrete wavelet transform for Alzheimer's detection. Biomed. Signal Process. Control **55**, 101–113 (2021)
11. Morabito, F.C., et al.: Deep convolutional neural networks for classification of mild cognitive impaired and Alzheimer's disease patients from scalp EEG recordings. 2016 IEEE 2nd International Forum on Research and Technologies for Society and Industry Leveraging a better tomorrow (RTSI), pp. 1–6 (2016)
12. Triki, A., Bouaziz, B., Mahdi, W., Hoekelmann, A.: Mild cognitive impairment classification based on a deep learning-based approach using EEG data. 2022 International Conference on Technology Innovations for Healthcare (ICTIH), pp. 7–12 (2022)
13. Sen, S.Y., Cura, O.K., Akan, A.: Classification of dementia EEG signals by using time-frequency images for deep learning. 2023 Innovations in Intelligent Systems and Applications Conference (ASYU), pp. 1–6 (2023)
14. Sen, S.Y., Cura, O.K., Akan, A.: Detection of Alzheimer's dementia using intrinsic time scale decomposition of EEG signals and deep learning. 2023 9th International Conference on Control, Decision and Information Technologies (CoDIT), pp. 93–98 (2023)
15. Smith, K., Doe, J.: Comparison of butterworth and Chebyshev Filters for EEG signal processing. IEEE Trans. Biomed. Eng. **60**(7), 1252–1260 (2015)

# Mixing the Mind and Experiences with Multisensory Art Installations

Chetna Mehra(✉) and Srishti Sah Jagati

Department of Music and Performing Arts, Banasthali Vidyapith, Rajasthan 304022, India
chetnamehra85@gmail.com, srishtisahjagati@banasthali.in

**Abstract.** In the contemporary Art world, installation Art is characterized by a wide range, giving active use of new science and technology. Installation Art has gradually become an active, interactive trend, offering viewers a chance to perceive Art in their own way, resulting in a long-lasting, unique experience. Here, the experience is connected to personal interest, past experiences, emotions, senses, and all the intangible things that can only be felt. The research explores a new way to perceive Art by talking about an artist who gives a new way to look at the Art by showing importance on the process, as well as extending these emotions or feelings as a scope to perceive Art with communicational techniques. With the help of elements such as performance Art, American Sign Language (ASL), music, and notions of graphics, it becomes possible to understand the senses and emotions used for portraying the objects that are untouchable.

**Keywords:** Multisensory · ASL · harmony · visual sound

## 1 Introduction

Sound is an integral aspect of our daily life and is often encouraged within the visual context, such as artistic performance, films, etc. Installation Art can be defined as site-specific artwork that surrounds the viewers. Michael Archer defined installation, "Each artist uses the whole room the same way we might use a sheet of paper or canvas. Now, the paper is converted into the floor, a new wall, ceilings, spaces, or might engage a particular sense in it. Then we walk into the room, it is likely to be walking into a painting". Annstrong [1] The relationship between the visual information, or normal communication, while listening to another individual is basic. Now, here the artist Christine Sun Kim's art enters a unique intersection of visual language, performance, and political activism, centered around the complexities of Deaf cultures and social hierarchies surrounding sound. Using media such as charcoal, drawings, installations, performances, and video to convey the experience of sound from her perspective as a Deaf individual. She integrated American Sign Language (ASL), musical notation, and linguistic elements, examining the major role that shaped her communication. She forged her own identity via her personal experiences, scholastic path, and life as an artist, resulting in a strong self-personality influenced by both struggles and accomplishments. She stated, "I firmly identified myself as a person who is deaf and uses ASL to communicate, and it


A. Shastri et al. (Eds.): IHCI 2025, LNCS 16437, pp. 167–177, 2026.
https://doi.org/10.1007/978-3-032-26352-0_14

is the only way I identify my work as an artist. I'm offering ASL as my personal second language through Art Speaks." Debt, future, duties, and identity are among the themes explored by Kim, and they embody the spirit of echo and recurrence. The voices she used in the pieces represent the varied structure of spoken language. She incorporated humor and personal narrative to engage her audience and raise awareness about the challenges faced by the Deaf community.

With the help of this study, possibilities exist to convert the perspective of audiences to understand the vibrant and thought-provoking works of Kim, reconsidering the understanding of sound, language from a different perspective, and the complexities of communication of an individual faces in this society.

## 2 Literature Review

The author spoke about personal experiences and childhood memories rather than aesthetic experiences. While looking at the Art pieces, the viewers experienced childhood memories, poems, or clippings that reminded them of their experiences with the Art piece. In this volume, the author discusses how present experiences, stored and blended with past yields, shape future perceptions. Thus, perception must encompass mental imagery and its relationship to direct sensory observation. Psychologists focused a lot of attention on the effect of prior experiences on perception. In fact, anyone who is unable to trust direct perception with sensory material prefers to assign this essential role to the past. A viewer is supposed to simply apply what he previously learned to the present situation. The researcher also discovered that memory has a strong influence on the perspective of the present. However, unless the brain is ready to identify the self, there can't be any shape obtained in the mind or transferred to the present by the past. The author wants to convey that due to creative sensibilities and expression can help to shape the present work and future artistic development, the relationship can be early encounter with environment. Development of cognitive and emotional expressions. [1, 2] The artist believes that knowing what I am feeling and what I am inclined to do are inextricably linked. Without a basic conceptual relationship between emotions and how they are expressed, the idea that a person may know what emotions they are experiencing makes no sense.

Nowness Sound is perceivable in different forms, can be visually, physically, or conceptually. Kim's perception is developed by deafness, and she used this ability to perceive multi-perception for sound and became a person who does not depend on hearing. "Let's listen with our eyes and just by our Ears". The research tells how feeling and visual information, combined with the sound that is perceivable, physical, and conceptual can relates to multisensory integration and perception psychology, this explains that how the brain synthesis multiple streams of sensorial information into a coherent experience [3, 4].

According to the text, for Kim, the installation should be acceptable for the people who are able to hear harmony by various methods and levels because each human being's listening to different levels is very personal, that like vision, everyone's perspective is different, it's the same procedure with the person who can hear but with different level of ability to hear.

As Kim describes in her article that relates "The Sound and Non-Sounds," listening is an experience that includes not only the sound, but it's more than that, it's a variety of different sensory and emotional responses that prove the research that goes beyond the sonic properties. According to the scholar Anna K. Benedikt," Kim started observing how people behave to the sound and how she responds," for understanding sensory practices, she makes noises by slamming doors to learn the reaction or scraping forks on a plate. She learned the social etiquette around sound, and it led to a larger curiosity. By learning these, she was able to experiment with sound and acoustic frequencies using woofers and speakers.

It is said that there are tendencies are patterns that are expected in the broader sense, which includes unconscious as well as conscious anticipants, that then become easier to see how music, as well as sound, can evoke tendencies. For instance, it is said that music arouses expectations, some conscious and others unconscious, that may or may not directly or indirectly become satisfactory. By expanding perception beyond hearing to encompass multisensory input, psychodynamic and integrated therapy techniques provide inclusive avenues for insight and behavioural adaptation. This paradigm is also useful for those with sensory impairments, such as deaf clients, since it allows them to fully participate in therapy procedures and acquire self-awareness based on both their internal and outward lived experience. [6, 7, 8].

Talking about the Differentiation in behaviour, the involvement of control, and control implies the purpose. The purpose of different emotional behaviour is what communication is. The individual responds to what they give an affective experience or simulate one, and seeks to make others aware of their experience through non-verbal behavioural signs. The gestures and signs differentiate such behaviour that is purposeful, and a mode of behaviour which is called emotional designation or designative behaviour. Emotions therefore function as internal regulators, adaptive reactions, and communication signals, with control systems assuring purposeful expression that is socially monitored and reciprocated. The author connects musical experiences with similar experiences of real life. The life of both human beings, and if we talk about music, and emotions that give us the same stimulus as the given one. The way to ignorance, and at the same time the awareness of an individual, tells us the ability that shapes the future. Because the musical experiences exist in the same way in drama and in life itself, they often feel particularly powerful and effective.

# 3 Methods

## 3.1 Research Design

The research focuses on a descriptive design that has experiential and interpretive analysis of the artist's own experience. The research interprets expression, senses, and visual language that is ASL Language, and situational analysis by personal identity, majorly sound, and embodiment converge in Kim's Art.

## 3.2 Case Study Selection and Inclusion Criteria

A Case Study provides an in-depth understanding of an individual artist's practice for understanding the point of view that uses purposeful sampling through an inclusive lens.

Relevance to Multisensory Art-The installation work combines sound, space, and visual elements to make interactive artworks.

Technology and Performance-Integration of sound frequencies, vibration, and performance in the given case study, or the artworks, makes the research theme of communication, helping sensory experience relevant to the research to understand the senses and emotions.

### 3.3 Data Collection

The data is collected through secondary sources that include books, journals, e-books, websites, articles, and digital documentation of Kim's, etc. The analysis includes comparative insights that selected works recur themes of communication, sound, and emotion. The contextual reading, by artists' statements, authors' background, cultural and theoretical references.

Case Study: Christine Sun Kim's Artwork.

### 3.4 Degrees of Deaf Rage, 2018

The image illustrates the collection of six charcoal artworks that describe different levels of angles.

Source: Degrees of Deaf Rage, 2018 by Christine Sun Kim | Ocula (Figs. 1 and 2)

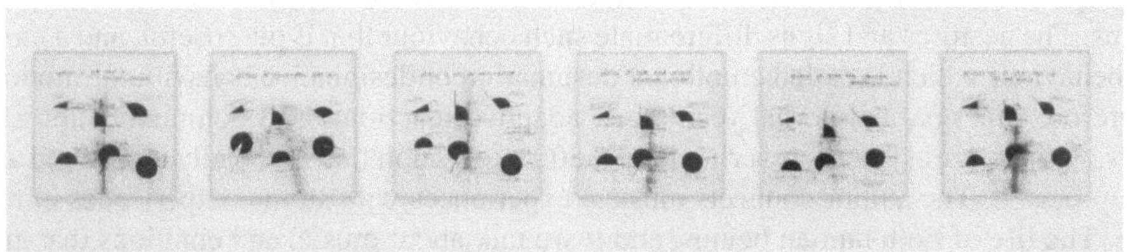

**Fig. 1.** This is the Degree of Deaf Rage, Six Collection of angles

The image illustrates the sixth final drawing by Christine Sun Kim, which is considered as Degree of Deaf Rage.

Source: Christine Sun Kim on Breaking the Echo Chamber|Frieze

The Degree of Deaf Rage is the collection of six charcoal artworks that describe different levels of angles that show the intense experiences of the deaf community.

Acute Angle for a frustrated self in minor circumstances.

Legit Rage for valid frustration in a minor situation.

Obtuse Rage, larger angles signifying a more significant level of frustrated self.

Straight Up Rage, this is what is close to 180 degrees, strong, infuriation.

Reflex Rage (~240°)- the situation where curators are breaking the fees with decipherer, and display sharp resentment.

Full-on Rage (360°)- the maximum level of anger.

Here, the artist is denoting the work to the deaf community with the help of graphical representations, the nuances of her emotions regarding everyday situations. Her work

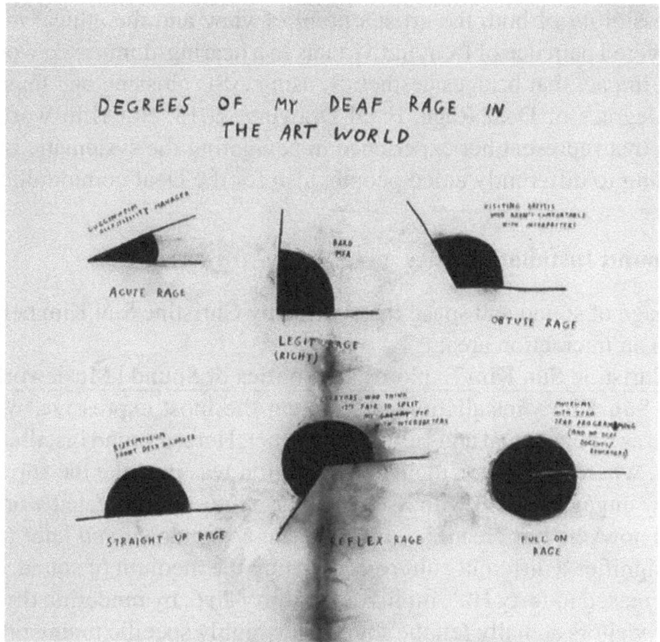


**Fig. 2.** This is Degrees of Deaf Rage, Final Drawing, 2018

specifically focuses on how the elements impact social interaction and identities. The incorporation of visual Art forms conveys complex ideas about sound through various media.

**Implementation of the feelings.**

"Degree of Deaf Rage" is a series of charcoal drawings, where the artist is visualizing the world for navigating the Art society, which is centered around sound. The angular representations that correlate with varying intensities of her rage, addressing exclusion. She used angles to express the feeling towards the situation, like unaccommodated requests for interpreters and the lack of a Deaf community and museums. The work offers insights into her emotional responses, bridging the gap between the hearing community and the Deaf perspective. By challenging the norms that sound can only be accessed through listening, instead, she created how it can be felt in multiple ways, like vibrations and emotions.

**Conceptual Significance**

Kim tried to connect mathematically with emotional intensity.

Through a medium that can be understood easily, it highlights societal and institutional inequalities.

Kim communicates personal and collective expressions of deaf experiences visually.

**Conclusion of the study**

The Degree of the Deaf Rage is an angular representation of multiple diagrams that explores accessibility of both the artist's point of view and the ethical imperative that teaches the layered patience of Deaf individuals in a hearing-dominated world. The work has a cultural impact that bridges aesthetics, using ASL glossing and musical notation. Not only is Degrees of Deaf Rage, Final Drawing, 2018. But Kim worked on charts and diagrams that represent her experience in navigating the systematic institution that works according to differently abled people, also for the Deaf communities.

### 3.5 4 × 4 Sound Installation

This is the image of sound and space Installation by Christine Sun Kim helped to turned the space into an interaction area.

Source: Christine Sun Kim Explores the Politics of Sound | Musicworks magazine

Christine Sun Kim's installations are among the most expressive, whose mission reframe sound as a conceptual and cultural construct. Here, a sound installation is located in Stockholm, where the artist's main concentration was to make the surroundings in a poetic form by engaging them with its own audio. She earlier created works with texts, charcoal, and now she has created four songs she wrote down and later performed on. Every voice signifies a different culture concerning the medium of sound. The recorded voice was decreased to forty Hz[1], minimum to thirty-five; by rendering the sound nearly inaudible, the visitors actually felt the sound. The highly specific tuning process enables to triggers of the recording to be touched by the architecture. By the completion of every song, the window rattles a seven Hz sound, signaling that another song is going to play. Kim describes it as "a short explosion that can be felt everywhere." Kim acknowledged Alvin Lucier's iconic work that "I am sitting in a room", as a major inspiration for 4 × 4. Eppley [6] (Fig. 3).

**Fig. 3.** Installation view, 4 × 4 Sound Installation, 2015

[1] The hertz (symbol: Hz) is the frequency unit in the International System of Units (SI), and it is commonly characterized as corresponding to one occurrence (or cycle) per second.

**Space as an instrument**

By using large subwoofers in each corner, the idea of the space installation is accepted as the artist here effectively turned the space into an interaction area with sound. Visitors not only listened to the sound but also physically felt the vibrations. The motive was how space can shape the auditory experience rather than the backdrop. Within 4 × 4, the frequencies were set to a Hz that most people cannot consciously perceive, causing them to physically feel the space. The audience experienced the structure's playback rather than conventional[2] sound. For Kim, the main medium of communication is American Sign Language (ASL); she often connects with others, like as interpreters or audience members, to reveal her voice and her ideas in a signed form of language.

For the artist, communication through sign language becomes the way to connect to the environment as well as with the audience, and allows the audience to relate to the space in their own way. After that, she also reveals her personal voice to give an idea in a way that spells the language in a different format.

Kim transforms the audience's understanding of the sound by making the installation, which is only physically experienced, where they feel the music through the space, making the space as an instrument in her own innovative artistic exploration.

**Conclusion of the case study.**

The work, a 4 × 4 representation, is 4 feet by 4 feet, and its intimate yet imposing presence challenges the way we perceive sound. This provides an area where Art can be visualized through subwoofers in the gallery like an instrument which cannot be directly heard but can be felt that crosses the boundaries of sound and architecture. Ultimately, 4 × 4 brings sensory feelings and vibration to the audience. That tells that the inquiry into sound, voice, and social exchange rendered by the inaudible frequencies is what makes the immersive and unique experience. This type of work exemplifies the exposition of transactions that can be facilitated by trust and interpretation through mediated communication without direct sound.

## 3.6 Analytical Lens of the Case Study

The research discusses the expression, personal interest, past experiences, emotions, senses, and intangible aspects, which combine to make the research a qualitative, interpretative, and theoretical approach, utilizing a phenomenological, semiotic, and cultural lens.

Phenomenologically, the viewers' experience is analyzed by focusing on emotion, touch, and engagement with the artwork.

In a Semiotic way, the use of symbols, sound, notations, and ASL Language makes the work communicative, which is beyond verbal words.

Culturally, Kim's work reflects the re-expression of political dimensions is Degrees of Deaf Rage, Final Drawing, 2018 and talk about the interpretation of the world from the point of view of the Deaf community.

The analysis of works also provides a thematic and comparative analytical framework. While the primary focus is on the artist's work, contextually.

[2] Based on or according to what is commonly done or believed.

Material and Medium-The artwork that is explained here uses charcoal, sound frequencies, subwoofers, and ASL Language to convey sensory expression.

Spatial and Sensory Interaction-How space and sound affect viewers' perception.

Cultural and Emotional-The work represents the challenges faced by the Deaf community. Kim worked on charts and diagrams that navigate the systematic institution that works according to differently abled people.

The research themes use phenomenological and semiotic readings to understand how non-verbal sensory experiences redefine the concept.

While the primary focus is on the Artists' work contextually. The research practice in the broader field of multisensory and participatory Art. The methodology allows a comparative reflection with contemporary practices with the help of viewers' interpretation. The conceptual alignment strengthens the analytical depth by focusing Kim's artworks on how sensory and communicative experiences reshape the perception.

## 4 Analysis of the Research

According to the findings from the literature review and case study, in which Kim mentioned herself as a Deaf person who lives in the world of sound or harmony, she blindly followed the rules, norms, and behavior. Forwardly, Kim began to rethink the character of sound, as she reconsidered the nature of ASL. She explored the variation of sound provided and Deaf culture with different media that include drawing, installations, and performance, which helped to fight the political strictness by using sound and communication with ASL. With the help of different case studies, the research navigates all the themes that help to interplay between sound, languages, and Kim's personal identity. The artworks like Degrees of Deaf Rage, Final Drawing, 2018, not only tell the percentage of the Deaf culture but also indicate the pressure a community holds, the works play a role of politics and question the other community that uses oral languages that serve as social currency. By prioritizing her personal spoken language, that is ASL (American Sign Language), Kim develops a way to visual and represent her musical connection with communicative infographic meanings. Harris [7] For her, sign language was a medium in itself to convey her own feelings and emotions. After that, she began to incorporate performance in her works, like in Installation view, 4x4 Sound Installation, 2015. She performed on her own voice while the visitors started physically feeling the voices in the background of that particular space. This proves the exploratory spirit that regards the space in which sound exists, in different volumes and frequencies. The artist highlighted the environment in which contexts shape sound's presence.

In order to combat, Kim, in prior work is Degrees of Deaf Rage, Final Drawing, 2018 offers new insights into her emotional responses, which bridges the gap between the sound that is audible and the Deaf perspective. Her personal blending of the societal dialogues into her own artworks by explaining the graphs of the Deaf community and giving her personal experiences into it, the artwork not only enlightens the audiences but also lets them think that intricacy with Deaf culture also invites a re-evolution of how the society invites and perceives the sound and frequencies presented in her artworks. By this extracting she challenges the norms of the society that sound can only be listened to but experienced through visuals; it can be felt and also interpreted in multiple ways, such as thought, vibrations, feelings, and emotional responses. That's what Kim's artwork is all about, they are vibrant, expressive, immersive, as well as a unique expression that shows individual identity, with not only a critical examination of harsh reality, but also the relation between sound and communication. This reality makes her a significant individual in contemporary art discourse (Fig. 4).

**Fig. 4.** Games of Skills (2015)

An installation helped the audience to comprehend the voice to elevate the Deaf Culture.

Source: Christine Sun Kim Explores the Politics of Sound | Musicworks magazine.

Above Games of Skills (2015) It is one of the sound installations in which Kim introduced a sense of performative action; now the drawings are extended to accompany in a way installation of sound works. The installation works in a listening way, where Kim tells the audience to listen to the voice, which is recorded, related to China and intentionally disturbed the voice so it becomes a little hard to understand the language and voice clearly, she used magnets that allows the audio to work in that way, which listeners traversed and can be seen in Viewers interacting with Game of Skill 1.0, 2015. The archetypal form of communication leads Kim's artwork to fuse with the surroundings of day-to-day practices. The theme investigates the contemporary advocacy for inclusivity and presents the Art and beyond. She is a force for the whole community that she reflects with commitments to elevate the Deaf culture and her experiences with the audiences. In this artwork, she conjugates the everyday listening into an emphasized and recognized value of ASL and the personal experiences, feelings, and emotions that overpower the biases that exist for common languages in society.

Phenomenologically, the art practice transforms the audience into a physical and cognitive act, but intentionally distorting the recorded voices engages the audience's bodily and mental with the act of understanding audio. Semiotically, magnetic control sound represents symbolic barriers that a deaf individual faces, which makes the 'game' a metaphor for navigating meaning through non-verbal clues and interruptions. Material-Cultural lens, reflects spatial and sensory installation, showing distorted accessibility. It balances power between the hearing and Deaf Community (Fig. 5).

**Fig. 5.** Viewers interacting with Game of Skill 1.0, 2015. Source: Christine Sun Kim

### 4.1 Critical Synthesis

The findings of the case study describe Christine Sun Kim's work, also contributing broader understanding of sound, communication. The ASL language includes completely used hands and face rather than the vocal tract and is perceived by the ears and eyes, vibrations, and spatial integration, which Kim's multisensory language and phenomenal perception resonates with the framework of participatory aesthetics. Emmorey K. [5] The synthesis positions involving dialogues the art covers beyond verbal and auditory limits, which expands theoretical discourses of contemporary multisensory installation Art.

## 5 Conclusion

Christine Sun Kim captures the complex emotions and feelings that surround her experiences as a Deaf individual. She is surrounded by the community of sound, expressing her frustrations through completing visual representations and infographics. She used not her voice but American Sign Language (ASL) to communicate to encounter the hearing world. According to Historians John Vickrey Van Cleve and Barry Crouch, "the deaf and hearing citizens were so integrated that the Deaf people did not make a community as hearing fellows. But the deaf people and common people used sign language to communicate." On the other hand, Dr. William Thornton was the first person to give attention to the community with his essay in 1793. He explained that, "A deaf person is not perfectly skilled to read the lips or to procure common information easily, but change occurs directly when sign language comes."

With the help of literature review and case study, the use of mathematical angles and creative graphics of charcoals, she conveys the intensity of her emotions regarding accessibility issues within Art institutions, social interactions, where a broad communication gap exists between her and the hearing community. This study contributes to contemporary debates on multisensory aesthetics and perceptual diversity. This research proves the connection of identity, the visual language of sound, and empowerment as well. The artwork's physical experiences are equally valid for perceiving the messages, as well as feelings and emotions. Her work encourages participants to not only perceive the installations but also to critically think about the surroundings and the perspective Kim wants to offer them with the help of sound environments, and to be fully aware of how they physically interact with it.

The study also shows that immersive artworks or installations function as perceptual systems rather than representational objects, following viewers to actively negotiate meaning through physiological and psychological interaction. This viewpoint emphasizes the significance of inclusive and multimodal techniques in both creative production and perceptual research.

### 5.1 Future Recommendations

Expand comparative studies-by comparing artists who also explore sound, perception, and embodiment.

Explore Technological Innovations-Generally soundscapes, Augmented Reality for expansion of communication possibilities.

Broader Cultural Context-Not only sound from one culture, but also exploring how different languages can shape the perception of an individual.

**Acknowledgement.** I would like to thank the faculty members, colleagues, and peers who supported this research, and for their suggestions for improving the conceptual and analytical parts. I also like to extend my thanks to those who contributed to the discussion of thoughtful conversations, perceptive comments, and support to complete this study.

**Disclosure of interest.** The author certifies that there are no competing interests regarding the content of this research.

## References

1. Armstrong, J.A.: Installation art: a new relationship to audience (1999). https://mountainscholar.org/items/aae07132-3fce-4497-85b8-15bda03483c7.
2. Arnheim, R.: Visual thinking. University of California Press, Berkeley (1969)
3. Benedikt, A.K.: "Let's Listen with Our Eyes… The Deconstruction of Deafness in Christine Sun Kim's Sound Art." In: Under Construction, MDPI Books (2019). https://doi.org/10.3390/books978-3-03897-500-7-3
4. Best, D.: Feeling and reason in the arts. George Allen & Unwin Ltd., London (1985)
5. Emmorey, K.: Processing a dynamic visual-spatial language: psycholinguistic studies of American Sign Language. J. Psycholinguist. Res. **22**(2), 153–187 (1993)
6. Eppley, C.: A map of a sound as a space: Christine Sun Kim's (LISTEN) [2016]. J. Media Art Study Theory **2**(2), 102–116 (2021)
7. Harris, E.C.: Christine Sun Kim: ASL and deaf identity in art. Master's thesis, Purchase College, State University of New York (2024)
8. Meyer, L.B.: Emotion and meaning in music. University of Chicago Press, Chicago (1956)

# Understanding and Mitigating Accommodation Scams: An Adaptive Cybersecurity Approach Enhanced by Human-AI Interaction

Roberto Ramirez Arteaga[1,2], Benjamin Papavero Oliva[1,2], Jan Treur[1,2](✉), and Peter H. M. P. Roelofsma[1]

[1] Center of Expertise Cybersecurity, The Hague University of Applied Sciences, Zoetermeer, Netherlands
j.treur@vu.nl, p.h.m.p.roelofsma@hhs.nl

[2] Department of Computer Science, Vrije Universiteit Amsterdam, Social AI Group, Amsterdam, Netherlands

**Abstract.** This computational study in human-AI interaction investigates online accommodation scams in the Dutch rental market. It is shown by simulation how human-AI interaction strengthens decision making. It demonstrates the potential of AI coaching by knowledge-level communication and paves the way for a solution to strengthen cybersecurity resilience by increasing awareness and decision support during scam exposure.

**Keywords:** Cybersecurity · adaptive human-AI interaction · self-modelling networks · decision support

## 1 Introduction

As society becomes increasingly dependent on digital platforms, it also becomes more exposed to new forms of cyber vulnerability, particularly, in sectors where trust, economic exposure, and personal data intersect [7, 29]. One sector where these vulnerabilities align with great intensity is the housing market, especially in countries such as the Netherlands, where ongoing housing shortages and high demand have made online rental platforms a prime target for digitally mediated scams. According to the Dutch Central Bureau of Statistics (CBS), more than 2.2 million people in the Netherlands were victims of cybercrime in 2022, with online scams and fraud among the most reported offences. To put this figure into perspective, the number of affected approximately represents 15% of the Dutch population from residents aged 15 and above [4]. These accommodation scams are primarily triggered through dishonest rental listings, often promoted via housing platforms or social media. Scammers often will present themselves as either landlords or housing agents, and persuade their victims into paying deposits or requesting personal credentials for properties that remain unavailable or do not exist. Studies that cover this type of cybersecurity problems, often sub-categorise them in a larger study of fraudulent activities, leaving important behavioural patterns, systematic factors, and platform-related vulnerabilities unexplored [16, 30].


A. Shastri et al. (Eds.): IHCI 2025, LNCS 16437, pp. 178–190, 2026.
https://doi.org/10.1007/978-3-032-26352-0_15

This paper aims to bridge this gap through computational analysis based on a multilevel adaptive network model [21–23] that is used to analyse the dynamics of online accommodation scams in the Dutch rental market. The analysis is based on a victim-centered viewpoint, which analyses both common scammer tactics and facilitates potential prevention strategies.

To attain a greater level of clarity, a scenario is introduced which follows an economically underprivalleged international student who faces the Dutch housing crisis alone. Having limited resources due to her circumstances, paired with a strong cognitive urgency to find a house, makes her a vulnerable and thus prime subject for scammers. The research aims to assess the potential of AI-based coaching by human-AI interaction serving as a proactive cybersecurity intervention method to finally reduce scam success rates. This will be addressed based on the use of mental models for decision making [27, 28] shared for victim and AI Coach, inspired by work in the medical context presented in [14].

## 2 Background Knowledge & Scenario Description

In the Netherlands, in 2017 housing prices surged and housing shortages deepened to critical values. While political discourse had long optimistically emphasised market recovery, the public continued to fear the ever-growing gap between the median wage and the average price of accommodation. As a result, in 2019, Dutch parliamentary debates introduced the term "housing crisis", elevating the issue to an urgent national concern [8, 9, 17]. Aspiring property seekers in the Netherlands now find themselves ever more susceptible to housing scams. As users navigate through housing platforms such as Marktplaats and social media, such as Facebook and Instagram, their psychological stressors strengthen. This creates mental states such as scarcity-induced urgency, financial anxiety, and decision fatigue, greatly affecting cognitive judgment and overall mental health [30]. Due to this, victims often rush to make poor decisions, lower their guard, and reduce their ability to detect deceptive patterns embedded in fraudulent listings or communications, often out of desperation [13].

As illustration, a storyline is constructed around Fatima, a young woman from a less economically developed country (LEDC). Having recently entered the Amsterdam housing market as a consequence from starting her studies, Fatima is economically undersupported by her parents financially in comparison to the average student. A saturated housing market worsened her situation, leaving rental offers below €1000 per month practically non-existent. Fatima uses stressful online house searching platforms like Marktplaats and Facebook, and is left vulnerable to emotional manipulation and fraudulent listings. The provided scenario serves as the foundation for modelling emotional and cognitive vulnerabilities often exploited by scammers, and the construction of the adaptive human-AI interaction proposed in this research.

Cyberattacks are performed in the form of socially engineered attacks, where the cybercriminal deploys a variety of exploits. The tactics used can range from landlord impersonations, illegitimate personal documentation and payment requests, to conversations that are often presented with high amounts of urgency to pressure the would-be tenant. Cybercriminals may bypass direct communication with their victims, but instead employ automatons to execute their work on their behalf. Unlike traditional phishing, accommodation scams are contextual and emotionally charged, making their prevention more complex [15, 16]. Solution engineers not only consider the technical characteristics of the cyberattack, but also need to address the cognitive states of potential victims.

In response to these challenges, this paper explores the potential of human-AI interaction. The suggested AI coach, in contrast to static cybersecurity tools, dynamically adjusts to the user's behavioural patterns and contextual indicators, improving the user with decision-making support when perceiving hints of scam activity. In technical terms, the AI functions through the monitoring and detection of urgency signals once contact with the housing provider is established [10]. By aligning its feedback with the user's emotional and cognitive state, the AI coach not only boosts awareness but also counteracts impulsive reactions.

## 3 The Self-Modelling Network Modelling Approach Used

To analyse the complex and dynamic interplay between user cognition and decision making, and scam exposure within online housing platforms, the self-modelling network modelling approach developed by [21–23] and also applied in recent works on cybersecurity and on applying shared mental models in [31] and [14] has been employed. A temporal-causal network model is characterised by three main types of network characteristics. Here, $X$ and $Y$ denote nodes of the network, also called states and $X(t)$ and $Y(t)$ denote their activation values at time $t$. These states represent for example, psychological, behavioural, or contextual variables (e.g., social obligation, anxiety level, shame level). The states evolve based on three types of characteristics: **connectivity characteristics:** connections from a state $X$ to a state $Y$ and their weights $\boldsymbol{\omega}_{X,Y}$; **aggregation characteristics:** for any state $Y$, some combination function $\mathbf{c}_Y(..)$ defines the aggregation that is applied to the impacts $\boldsymbol{\omega}_{X,Y}\, X(t)$ on $Y$ from its incoming connections from states $X$; **timing characteristics:** each state $Y$ has a speed factor $\boldsymbol{\eta}_Y$ defining how fast it changes for a given aggregated causal impact. Aggregation is based on combination functions capturing the non-linear nature of human cognition and behaviour [14]. These simulate how a user psychologically integrates multiple influences (e.g., urgency, trust cues, or cognitive load) when exposed to potential scams. By specifying how these influences interact, the model can realistically represent emotional reactivity, susceptibility, and decision-making under pressure. In this study's modelling, the combination functions $\mathbf{c}_Y(\ldots)$ from Table 1 were used. The **alogistic** function is used in most cases and allows for a smooth thresholding mechanism, allowing for even behavioural adaptation when provided with a certain stimulus level.

The **alogistic** function is used in most cases and allows for a smooth thresholding mechanism, allowing for even behavioural adaptation when provided with a certain stimulus level. Alternatively, **steponce** provides a binary behaviour, ideal for simulating sharp cognitive shifts, such as a user deciding to disengage or comply based on a single critical threshold. Dynamics of the states Y are defined by (where $X_1$ to $X_k$ are the states with connections to $Y$):

$$Y(t + \Delta t) = Y(t) + \boldsymbol{\eta}_Y\big[\mathbf{c}_Y\big(\boldsymbol{\omega}_{X_1Y}X_1(t), \ldots, \boldsymbol{\omega}_{X_kY}X_k(t)\big) - Y(t)\big]\Delta t \quad (1)$$

**Table 1.** Combination functions used in the network model

| Description | Formula | Parameters |
|---|---|---|
| Advanced logistic **alogistic**$_{\sigma,\tau}(V_1,\ldots,V_k)$ | $\left[\frac{1}{1+e^{-\sigma(V_1+\cdots+V_k-\tau)}} - \frac{1}{1+e^{varvec\sigma varvec\tau}}\right](1+e^{-varvec\sigma varvec\tau})$ | Steepness $\sigma$ Excitability threshold $\tau$ |
| Step once **steponce**$_{\alpha,\beta}(\ldots)$ | 1 if $\alpha \leq t \leq \beta$ else 0 (time $t$) | Start time $\alpha$ End time $\beta$ |

In realistic scenarios, network characteristics $\boldsymbol{\omega}$, **c** and $\boldsymbol{\eta}$ change over time, making the network adaptive. As a result, this study applies the self-modelling principle for temporal-causal networks introduced in [21–23]. This was inspired by the area of metalevel architectures and reflection in AI; e.g., [2, 11, 12, 18, 19]. Consequently, network characteristics, such as connection weights and speed factors, possess values that change over time. To this end they are governed by self-model states, referred, for example, to as **W**-states or **H**-states. Here **W**-states $\mathbf{W}_{X,Y}$ adjust dynamically the weights $\boldsymbol{\omega}_{X,Y}$ of underlying network connections $X \rightarrow Y$ in response to evolving conditions, and **H**-states $\mathbf{H}_Y$ do the same for response speeds $\boldsymbol{\eta}_Y$. As a result, this grants the simulation the ability to reflect learning or escalation in scam exposure, maintaining both realism and flexibility in modelling user behaviour.

The self-modeling network modeling approach comes with methods and software for simulation [24], verification by mathematical analysis [1, 5, 20, 25], and validation by comparison and tuning to numerical empirical data [26].

## 4 Design of the Multi-Adaptive Network Model

To analyse the processes and interactions from the scenario, a multi-adaptive temporal-causal network has been designed, depicted graphically in Fig. 1. Ovals represent nodes, and arrows indicate the connections between them, with the arrow directions showing the direction of causal impact. The downward causal connections (pink arrows) illustrate the specific causal impact each self-modeling state has. The upward (or levelled) causal connections (blue arrows) to the self-modelling states give them the dynamics as desired. These are used, along with the chosen combination function and the downward connections, to specify the particular adaptation principle being addressed. For an overview of all states and their explanations see Tables 2 and 3. Each figure follows a leveled network architecture. The pink-shaded base level represents the core psychological, behavioural, and environmental processes. These include the victim's and scammer's observable actions, and as the model is user-centred, the victim's solely mental states (modelled within the yellow oval). To enhance the realism of cognitive human behaviour, control states have been included in the mental model to mediate between mental evaluations and behavioural decisions.

As a result, these states (e.g., $ns_{engage\_control}$, $ns_{resist\_control}$) determine the degree to which certain ownership actions, like engaging, complying, or reporting, are executed. Having influence from both mental states, and adaptive weights that are learned, the model can simulate the struggle between rivalling motivations in intensive scam scenarios [3]. Moreover, the blue-shaded upper level corresponds to the first reification level, which introduces the self-model states. The self-model states represent learning or habit formation, granting the model the capability to capture dynamic and personalised behavioural evolution. To illustrate this, in Fatima's case, exposure to repeated pressure messages ($ss_{pressure\_seen}$) combined with her growing internal urgency ($ns_{urgency\_level}$) eventually led to engagement with the scammer and a payment being made ($ws_{payment\_sent}$).

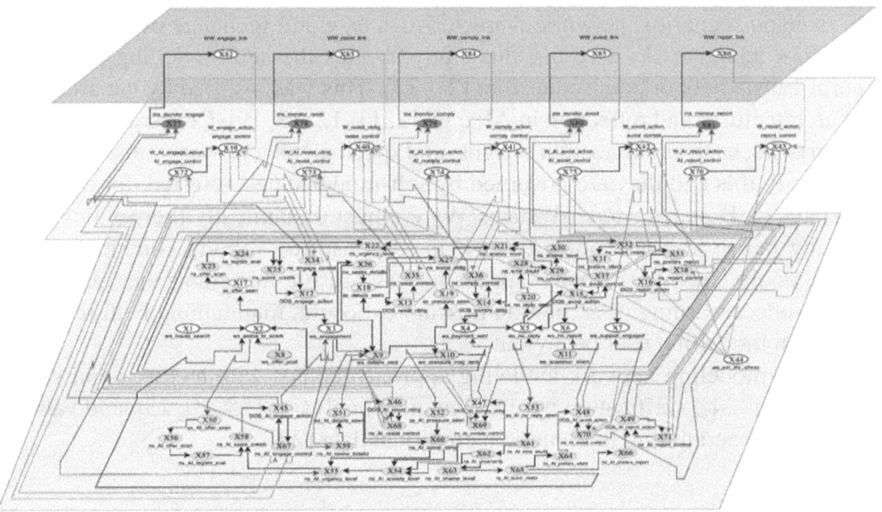

**Fig. 1.** Conceptual design of the adaptive network model

Switching focus exclusively to Fig. 2, the model incorporates a third level that enables real-time intervention through AI coaching. This purple-shaded level introduces second-order self-model **W**-states (**W**$_{\mathbf{W}}$-states) and monitoring states (ms-states). Through the monitoring states, continuous assessment of mismatches between predicted and actual user behaviours is achieved. For example, when Fatima was expected to resist but instead complied with a scammer's demand. These discrepancies inform the **W**$_{\mathbf{W}}$-states, which regulate how the AI coach dynamically communicates its interventions. Furthermore, this design allows the AI to personalise its responses based on observed deviations, making its guidance both adaptive and emotionally aware. To put this into perspective, given that Fatima's is about to perform a complying action ownership ($DOS_{comply\_oblig}$), the AI can immediately mediate, providing warnings, reminders, and verification checks, preventing a personal catastrophe for Fatima by her having forced a payment or divulged her sensitive information. In this fashion, the AI acts more so as an intelligent, aware and secure cybersecurity companion. More details of the model and What-If analysis can be found as Linked Data at https://www.researchgate.net/publication/393631409.

**Table 2.** Overview of the victim and scammer states: base and first-order adaptation level

| Nr | State | Explanation | Level |
|---|---|---|---|
| X1 | $ws_{\text{house search}}$ | The victim actively searches for a place to rent | Victim's world states Base level |
| X2 | $ws_{\text{expos to scam}}$ | The victim is exposed to a fraudulent rental offer posted by the scammer | |
| X3 | $ws_{\text{engagement}}$ | The victim engages with the scammer through messaging | |
| X4 | $ws_{\text{payment sent}}$ | The victim sends a payment to the scammer | |
| X5 | $ws_{\text{no reply}}$ | The victim receives no reply from the scammer | |
| X6 | $ws_{\text{no report}}$ | The victim does not report the incident to the authorities | |
| X7 | $ws_{\text{support engaged}}$ | The victim receives external support | |
| X8 | $ws_{\text{offer posted}}$ | The scammer posts a rental offer online | Scammer's world states Base level |
| X9 | $ws_{\text{details sent}}$ | The scammer sends details of the fake rental offer to the victim | |
| X10 | $ws_{\text{pressure msg sent}}$ | The scammer sends a message that pressures the victim | |
| X11 | $ws_{\text{scammer silent}}$ | The scammer becomes unresponsive | |
| X12 | $DOS_{\text{engage action}}$ | Ownership state for the action of the victim engaging with the scammer | Victim's Ownership States Base level |
| X13 | $DOS_{\text{resist\_oblig}}$ | Ownership state for the victim resisting the social obligation imposed by the scammer | |
| X14 | $DOS_{\text{comply\_oblig}}$ | Ownership state for the victim complying with the social obligation imposed by the scammer | |
| X15 | $DOS_{\text{avoid action}}$ | Ownership state for the victim avoiding reporting to the authorities | |
| X16 | $DOS_{\text{report action}}$ | Ownership state for the action of the victim reporting to the authorities | |
| X17 | $ss_{\text{offer seen}}$ | The victim observes the scammer's posted rental offer | Victim's sensor states Base level |
| X18 | $ss_{\text{details seen}}$ | The victim observes further details sent by the scammer | |
| X19 | $ss_{\text{pressure\_seen}}$ | The victim observes a message sent by the scammer pressuring the victim to coerce into taking action (e.g claiming high demand, limited availability) | |
| X20 | $ss_{\text{no reply obs}}$ | The victim observes the lack of reply from the scammer | |
| X21 | $ns_{\text{anxiety level}}$ | The victim's internal level of anxiety in response to the situation | Victim's mental model states Base level |
| X22 | $ns_{\text{urgency level}}$ | The victim's internal level of urgency, mainly due to housing need | |
| X23 | $ns_{\text{offer scan}}$ | The victim performs a quick initial assessment of the scammer's offer | |
| X24 | $ns_{\text{legitim eval}}$ | The victim performs a deeper evaluation of the offer's legitimacy | |
| X25 | $ns_{\text{score credib}}$ | The victim internally scores the credibility of the rental offer | |
| X26 | $ns_{\text{seeks details}}$ | The victim mentally desires to obtain further rental details | |
| X27 | $ns_{\text{social oblig}}$ | The victim experiences internal pressure due to perceived social obligation | |
| X28 | $ns_{\text{eme doubt}}$ | The victim starts to experience emerging doubts about the offer's legitimacy | |
| X29 | $ns_{\text{uncertainty}}$ | The victim mentally feels uncertain about the situation | |
| X30 | $ns_{\text{shame level}}$ | The victim's internal level of shame in response to the outcome events | |
| X31 | $ns_{\text{prefers silent}}$ | The victim mentally prefers to remain silent rather than report the scam | |
| X32 | $ns_{\text{scam realiz}}$ | The victim mentally realises they have been scammed | |
| X33 | $ns_{\text{prefers report}}$ | The victim mentally prefers to report the scam to the authorities | |
| X34 | $ns_{\text{engage control}}$ | The victim's mental control state for engaging with the scammer | |
| X35 | $ns_{\text{resist control}}$ | The victim's mental control state for resisting social obligation | |
| X36 | $ns_{\text{comply control}}$ | The victim's mental control state for complying social obligation | |
| X37 | $ns_{\text{avoid control}}$ | The victim's mental control state for avoiding reporting | |
| X38 | $ns_{\text{report control}}$ | The victim's mental control state for reporting to the authorities | |
| X39 | $\mathbf{W}_{\text{engage\_action, engage\_control}}$ | First-order self-model state for the victim's weight of the connection from the action of engaging with the scammer to the victim's engaging control state | Victim's first-order mental model self-model **W**-states, First-order adaptation level |
| X40 | $\mathbf{W}_{\text{resist\_oblig, resist\_control}}$ | First-order self-model state for the victim's weight of the connection from the action of resisting social obligation imposed by the scammer to the victim's resisting control state | |
| X41 | $\mathbf{W}_{\text{comply\_action, comply\_control}}$ | First-order self-model state for the victim's weight of the connection from the action of complying social obligation imposed by the scammer to the victim's complying control state | |
| X42 | $\mathbf{W}_{\text{avoid\_action, avoid\_control}}$ | First-order self-model state for the victim's weight of the connection from the avoidance of reporting to the authorities to the victim's avoidance control state | |
| X43 | $\mathbf{W}_{\text{report\_action, report\_control}}$ | First-order self-model state for the victim's weight of the connection from reporting to the authorities to the victim's report control state | |
| X44 | $ws_{\text{ext\_life\_stress}}$ | The victim experiences external life stress | Victim's stress |

**Table 3.** Overview of the AI Coach states: base and first- and second-order adaptation level

| Nr | State | Explanation | Level |
|---|---|---|---|
| X45 | $DOS_{AI\ engage\ action}$ | Ownership state for the action of the AI engaging with the scammer | |
| X46 | $DOS_{AI\_resist\_oblig}$ | Ownership state for the action of the AI resisting the social obligation imposed by the scammer | AI's |
| X47 | $DOS_{AI\_comply\_oblig}$ | Ownership state for the action of the AI complying with the social obligation imposed by the scammer | ownership states |
| X48 | $DOS_{AI\ avoid\ action}$ | Ownership state for the action of the AI avoiding reporting to the authorities | Base level |
| X49 | $DOS_{AI\ report\ action}$ | Ownership state for the action of the AI reporting to the authorities | |
| X50 | $ss_{AI\ offer\ seen}$ | The AI observes the scammer's posted rental offer | AI's s |
| X51 | $ss_{AI\ details\ seen}$ | The AI observes further details sent by the scammer | |
| X52 | $ss_{AI\_pressure\_seen}$ | The AI observes a message sent by the scammer pressuring the victim to coerce into taking action (e.g claiming high demand, limited availability) | sensor states |
| X53 | $ss_{AI\_no\_reply\_seen}$ | The AI observes the lack of reply from the scammer | Base level |
| X54 | $ns_{AI\ anxiety\ level}$ | Internal simulation of user anxiety, used by the AI to adjust support intensity | |
| X55 | $ns_{AI\ urgency\ level}$ | Internal simulation of user urgency, used by the AI to adjust support intensity | |
| X56 | $ns_{AI\ offer\ scan}$ | Internal quick assessment of a rental offer's legitimacy performed by the AI | |
| X57 | $ns_{AI\ legitim\ eval}$ | Internal deeper assessment of a rental offer's legitimacy performed by the AI | |
| X58 | $ns_{AI\ score\ credib}$ | Internal computed score credibility, performed by the AI | |
| X59 | $ns_{AI\ seeks\ details}$ | Internal drive to collect additional offer information performed by the AI | |
| X60 | $ns_{AI\ social\ oblig}$ | Internal simulation of social pressure experienced by the user performed by the AI | AI's |
| X61 | $ns_{AI\ eme\ doubt}$ | Internal detection of emerging doubt performed by the AI | mental |
| X62 | $ns_{AI\ uncertainty}$ | Internal state of ambiguity performed by the AI | model |
| X63 | $ns_{AI\ shame\ level}$ | Internal simulation of user shame performed by the AI | |
| X64 | $ns_{AI\ prefers\ silent}$ | Internal preference to remain passive performed by the AI | states |
| X65 | $ns_{AI\ scam\ realiz}$ | Internal recognition of a scam situation performed by the AI | Base level |
| X66 | $ns_{AI\ prefers\ report}$ | Internal preference to report the scam performed by the AI | |
| X67 | $ns_{AI\ engage\ control}$ | The AI's mental control state for engaging with the scam scenario | |
| X68 | $ns_{AI\ resist\ control}$ | The AI's mental control state for resisting social pressure in the scam scenario | |
| X69 | $ns_{AI\ comply\ control}$ | The AI's mental control state for complying with social pressure in the scam scenario | |
| X70 | $ns_{AI\ avoid\ control}$ | The AI's mental control state for avoiding reporting | |
| X71 | $ns_{AI\ report\ control}$ | The AI's mental control state for reporting the scam to the user or external entities | |
| X72 | $\mathbf{W}_{AI\_engage\_action,\ AI\_engage\_control}$ | First-order self-model state for the AI's weight of the connection from the action of engaging to the AI's engage control state | AI's first-order |
| X73 | $\mathbf{W}_{AI\_resist\_oblig,\ AI\_resist\_control}$ | First-order self-model state for the AI's weight of the connection from the action of resisting to the AI's resist control state | mental |
| X74 | $\mathbf{W}_{AI\_comply\_action,\ AI\_comply\_control}$ | First-order self-model state for the AI's weight of the connection from the action of complying to the AI's comply control state | model |
| X75 | $\mathbf{W}_{AI\_avoid\_action,\ AI\_avoid\_control}$ | First-order self-model state for the AI's weight of the connection from the action of avoiding reporting to the AI's avoid control state | self-model states |
| X76 | $\mathbf{W}_{AI\_report\_action,\ AI\_report\_control}$ | First-order self-model state for the AI's weight of the connection from the action of avoiding reporting to the AI's avoid control state | First-order adaptation level |
| X77 | $ms_{monitor\ engage}$ | Monitoring state tracking mismatches in expected vs actual engaging actions | Monitoring |
| X78 | $ms_{monitor\ resist}$ | Monitoring state tracking mismatches in expected vs actual resisting actions | states |
| X79 | $ms_{monitor\ comply}$ | Monitoring state tracking mismatches in expected vs actual complying actions | |
| X80 | $ms_{monitor\ avoid}$ | Monitoring state tracking mismatches in expected vs actual avoiding actions | First-order |
| X81 | $ms_{monitor\_report}$ | Monitoring state tracking mismatches in expected vs actual reporting actions | adaptation level |
| X82 | $\mathbf{W}_{\mathbf{W}engage\_link}$ | Second-order self-model controlling when and how AI communicates engagement knowledge to the victim | |
| X83 | $\mathbf{W}_{\mathbf{W}resist\_link}$ | Second-order self-model controlling when and how AI communicates resisting knowledge to the victim | Second-order |
| X84 | $\mathbf{W}_{\mathbf{W}comply\_link}$ | Second-order self-model controlling when and how AI communicates complying knowledge to the victim | self-model |
| X85 | $\mathbf{W}_{\mathbf{W}avoid\_link}$ | Second-order self-model controlling when and how AI communicates avoiding knowledge to the victim | $\mathbf{W}_{\mathbf{W}}$-states Second- |
| X86 | $\mathbf{W}_{\mathbf{W}report\_link}$ | Second-order self-model controlling when and how AI communicates reporting knowledge to the victim | order adaptation level |

## 5 Simulation Results

To obtain realistic insights regarding victim vulnerability and the possible impact of AI coaching, several simulations were conducted over multiple temporal intervals through the usage of an adaptive network model on the software ([23], Ch 9) developed on the MATLAB platform. The simulations are structured around two core scenarios, both grounded in the narrative of Fatima. In the first, Fatima navigates the Dutch rental market independently, without any form of guidance or support, which reflects a typical high-risk situation. In the second scenario, Fatima receives support from the AI coach, who actively monitors her mental states and behavioural cues. Consequently, this support enhances both her confidence and decision-making efficiency, which strengthens overall her cybersecurity posture against complicated markets such as the one mentioned. All of the simulations were run over a time interval of 0 to 500 with a step size $t = 0.5$. In addition, given the complexity of the scenario due to the number of nodes and their respective difficulty in gathering insights, key states were selected in the depicted simulation graphs to reflect understandable mental processes and evolved actions. Looking at the simulation results of our first scenario (Fig. 2), which excludes any AI intervention, a clear dynamic pattern of rise and fall over time can be observed.

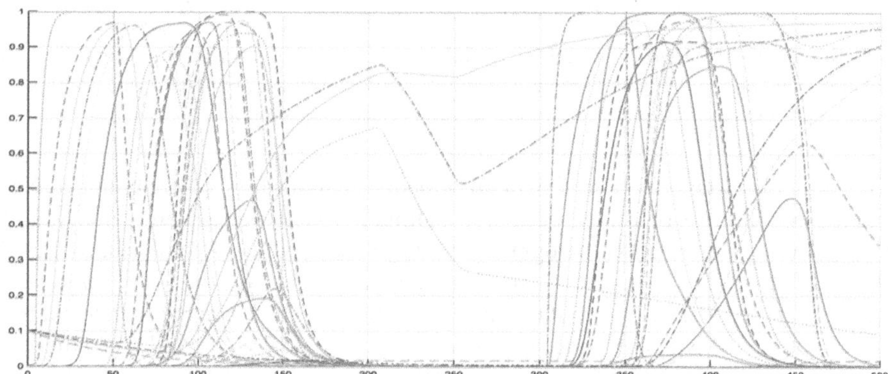


**Fig. 2.** Simulation results for the scenario without AI intervention

This provided visuals that showcase how the activation values of states evolve through the continuous feedback loops and adapt based on aggregated influences from other nodes. As a result, this concludes with temporal trajectories that often rise to a peak and then decay or stabilise as the system adapts. In Fatima's storyline, this aligns accordingly as it simulates the fluctuations and oscillatory psychological and behavioural trajectories that she encounters, increasing uncertainty ($ns_{uncertainty}$), social pressure ($ns_{social\_oblig}$) and emotional fatigue during her housing search. In Fig. 3, there is a clear visualisation of the distinct escalation in critical mental states before and after the scammer becomes non-responsive. Before this event, urgency ($ns_{urgency\_level}$) dominates the psychological frame with a peak activation value of 1, reflecting Fatima's maximum motivational pressure to secure housing under mounting external stressors. This activation remains consistent when it is approached to the model's normalised scale, where 1 signifies a complete mental saturation. At the same time, anxiety rises but remains submaximal, reaching a peak activation of ≈0.44, which suggests a secondary but growing emotional burden. After the scammer becomes silent, around $t = 305$, all internal states display strong co-activation, which indicates a strong cognitive and emotional overload. In addition to this, urgency decreases slightly to ≈0.91. This highlights a temporary drop in action drive as Fatima receives no response from the scammer. In contrast, the stimulus representing anxiety peaked to a maximum activation value of 1, which demonstrates a full-blown stress response. Other internal states escalate rapidly as well such as shame at ≈0.96, and uncertainty to ≈0.91.

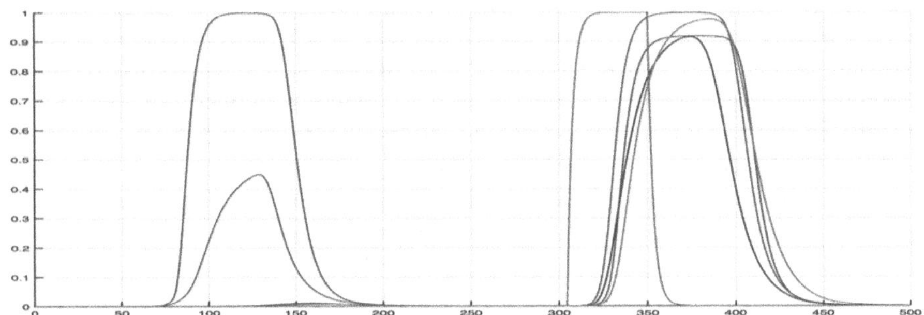


**Fig. 3.** Simulation results for psychological variables influencing scam susceptibility. Red represents urgency, blue indicate anxiety, green shows shame level, purple reflects uncertainty, and magenta represents the external event of the scammer becoming silent.

This demonstrates a clear pattern of emotional destabilisation, where both perceived abandonment and loss of control results in Fatima's psychological vulnerability, shifting her from high motivation to cognitive collapse and emotional paralysis. Switching back to Fig. 2, while internal states integrate and amplify along the entire simulation, Domain-Specific Observations (DOS) and Sensor States (SS) act as immediate but transient activators, distinguishing internal states as psychological vulnerabilities rather than just situational exposure. Now turning to the **W**-states that indicate the knowledge of the employee's mental model, which are represented through initial reinforcement followed by either stabilisation or decline, depending on the continuity of input. In Fig. 4, the **W**-state dynamics is depicted, showing consistent learning from $t \approx 52$ to $t \approx 205$. For example, one **W**-state ($\mathbf{W}_{\text{engage\_action, engage control}}$) reaches a peak of ≈0.84 but then declines sharply to ≈0.51, reflecting cognitive inhibition and a disruption in learning. This clear disruption is the external life stress ($\text{ws}_{\text{ext\_life\_stress}}$), which in Fatima's case, represents the financial strain caused by her parents' inability to afford €1000 in monthly rent. This demonstrates that such sudden life pressures can undermine higher-level learning weights, especially when no stabilising self-model feedback is in place.

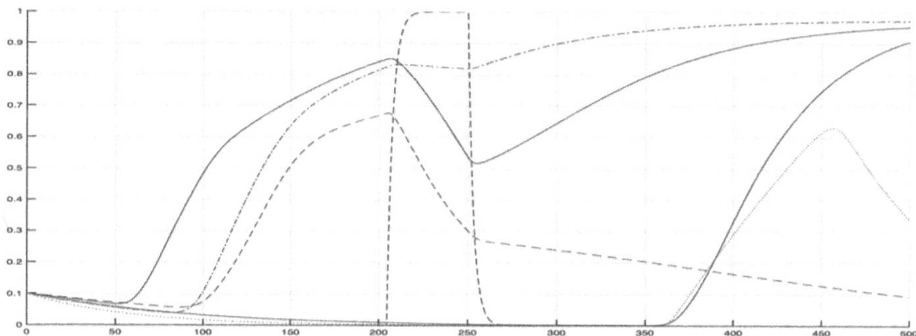


**Fig. 4.** Simulation results for **W**-states and external life stress in the scenario without AI intervention. Blue lines represent the victim's **W**-states, and the red line denotes external life stress

In contrast, the second scenario introduces AI coaching as a stabiliser and adaptive approach to address external stress and facilitate Fatima's housing search. In Fig. 5, **W**-states are showcased with a more synchronised and less erratic transitions. Here the **W**-states maintain a more stable growth trajectory, even in the presence of external life stress. Unlike the key **W**-states in Figs. 4 and 5 depicts continuous learning beyond the critical intervention triggered by external life stress at $t = 205$, identifying nodes that reach their peak rather than decay. This is achieved through the integration of AI coach nodes, represented implicitly in the network through monitoring and $\mathbf{W}_{\mathbf{W}}$-states. Monitoring states track Fatima's internal processes, predict tendencies on behavioural steps, and detect discrepancies between expected and actual responses. As soon as a mismatch is found, $\mathbf{W}_{\mathbf{W}}$-states activate and establish communication to provide corrective feedback from the sender (AI coach) to the recipient, in this case Fatima, reinforcing or redirecting her learning through the influence of her **W**-states. Together, this mechanisms enable the AI coach to perform both operations, which are to intervene adaptively and to support sustained behavioral resilience.

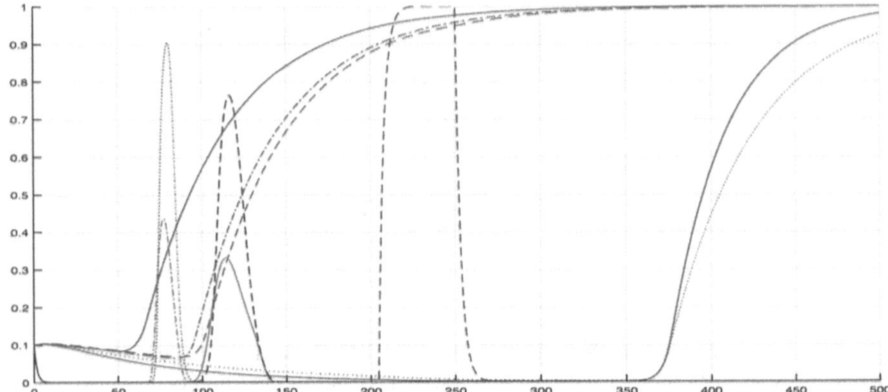


**Fig. 5.** Simulation results for **W**-states and external life stress in the scenario with AI. Blue lines represent the victim's **W**-states, red denotes external life stress, green indicates monitoring states and purple represents $\mathbf{W}_{\mathbf{W}}$-states.

Overall, the simulation results clearly demonstrate the contrast between unsupported and AI-assisted scenarios. On one hand, when there is no AI intervention, Fatima's internal states twitst into cognitive overload, where learning pathways become disrupted due to external stressors. On the other hand, when there AI support is established, the user experiences several benefits from stabilised learning to smoother behavioural transitions. Therefore, these findings validate the effectiveness of AI coaching as a dynamic and adaptive mechanism for promoting cybersecurity awareness and protection, especially in high-risk and emotionally charged environments like online housing searches.

## 6 Discussion

The results of this research underscore the importance of adaptive learning in cybersecurity defense strategies; see also [31]. This modelling approach addresses the prevention of victim's exposure within the current housing crisis, and contributes to the underexplored domain of cybersecurity, a field where research on scam vulnerabilities is limited. As a result, this study offers an interdisciplinary and behaviorally grounded approach, which increases the likelihood of potential readers enhancing their awareness of the topic, and therefore their understanding of its potential consequences. Furthermore, the obtained results discussed throughout the paper demonstrate the critical role of human-AI interaction in protecting users from scammer manipulation. Victims, given that they are unsupported by AI, were shown to experience cascading psychological overloads. However, when victims were aided, the network preserved behavioural normality, and rewarded learning processes that prevented scam acceptance. This serves as solid evidence of the value of AI coaching in creating cybersecurity resilience, not merely as a technical buffer but also as a behavioural stabiliser in emotionally dense decision environments. To complement the findings, a What-If analysis further showed how, through the altering of cognitive and systemic conditions, outcomes of scam vulnerability can differentiate, reinforcing the need to address the mentioned problem through AI-based coaching. However, when data would be available, further validation would make the conclusions stronger. Finally, a good piece of advice amounts to one of Lincoln's most famous quotes. As Abraham Lincoln once said, "I am a slow walker, but I never walk back" [6]. This quote reflects the advantage that learning from experience offers. Even if progress is slow, steady improvement can help people become more aware and better protected. It also serves as a reminder that, sometimes, it's better to set emotions aside and think twice before acting, especially when support is minimal.

## References

1. Brazier, F.M., et al.: Compositional verification of a multi-agent system for one-to-many negotiation. Appl. Intell. **20**(2), 95–117 (2004)
2. Brazier, F.M.T., Treur, J.: Compositional modelling of reflective agents. Int. J. Hum. Comput. Stud. **50**(5), 407–431 (1999)
3. Carver, C.S., Scheier, M.F.: Control theory: a useful conceptual framework for personality–social, clinical, and health psychology. Psych. Bulletin **92**(1), 111–135 (1982)
4. CBS Netherlands: 2.2 million cybercrime victims in 2022. Statistics Netherlands (2023). https://www.cbs.nl/en-gb/news/2023/19/2-2-million-cybercrime-victims-in-2022
5. Cornelissen, F., Jonker, C.M., Treur, J.: Compositional verification of knowledge-based systems: a case study for diagnostic reasoning. In: Proceedings EKAW 1997. Lecture Notes in Computer Science, vol 1319, pp. 65–80. Springer, Berlin, Heidelberg
6. Fehrenbacher, D.E., Fehrenbacher, V. (eds.): Recollected words of Abraham Lincoln. Stanford University Press (1996)
7. Ferreri, M., Sanyal, R.: Digital informalisation: rental housing, platforms, and the management of risk. Hous. Stud. **37**(6), 1035–1053 (2021)
8. Golay, M.: Challenges and strategies: how international students navigate the housing market in Amsterdam (MSc thesis, University of Amsterdam) (2023). https://openresearch.amsterdam/image/2023/9/21/mathilda_golay_final_thesis_for_publication.pdf
9. Hochstenbach, C.: Framing the housing crisis: politicization and depoliticization of the Dutch housing debate. Housing Studies, pp. 1–26 (2024)
10. Liu, Y., et al: A systematic review of machine learning approaches for detecting deceptive activities on social media: methods, challenges, and biases. Int. J. Data Sci. Anal. 1–26 (2025). https://doi.org/10.1007/s41060-025-00850-8
11. Maes, P., Nardi, D. (eds.): Meta-level Architectures and Reflection (1988)
12. Meyer, J.J.Chr., Treur, J. (eds.): Dynamics and management of reasoning processes. Springer Science & Business Media (2001)
13. Osman, Z., Alwi, N.H., Khan, B.N.A.: Psychological impact on the public susceptible to online scams. Intern. J. Acad. Res. Bus. Soc. Sci. **14**(5) (2024)
14. Roelofsma, P.H.M.P., Jabeen, F., Taal, H.R., Treur, J. (eds.): Using Shared Mental Models and Organisational Learning to Support Safety and Security Through Cyberspace: a Computational Analysis Approach. Springer Nature (2025)
15. Sarkar, G., Shukla, S.K.: Behavioral analysis of cybercrime: paving the way for effective policing strategies. J. Econ. Criminol. **2**, 100034 (2023)
16. Sophie, V.D.Z., Clayton, R., Anderson, R.: The gift of the gab: are rental scammers skilled at the art of persuasion? (2019). https://arxiv.org/abs/1911.08253
17. The housing market is under pressure: what can we do? Vrije Universiteit Amsterdam(2025). https://vu.nl/en/research/the-housing-market-is-under-pressure-what-can-we-do
18. Treur, J.: On the use of reflection principles in modelling complex reasoning. Int. J. Intell. Syst. **6**(3), 277–294 (1991)

19. Treur, J.: Temporal semantics of meta-level architectures for dynamic control of reasoning. In: Proceedings META 1994. Lecture Notes in Computer Science, vol. 883, pp. 353–376. Springer, Berlin, Heidelberg (1994)
20. Treur, J.: Verification of temporal-causal network models by mathematical analysis. Vietnam J. Comput. Sci. **3**(4), 207–221 (2016)
21. Treur, J.: Network reification as a unified approach to represent network adaptation principles within a network. In: TPNC 2018, Proceedings. Lecture Notes in Computer Science, vol. 11324, pp. 344–358. Springer International Publishing (2018a)
22. Treur, J.: Multilevel network reification: representing higher-order adaptivity in a network. In: Proceedings of COMPLEX NETWORKS 2018, Studies in Computational Intelligence, vol. 812, pp. 635–651. Springer International Publishing (2018b)
23. Treur, J.: Network-Oriented modeling for Adaptive networks: designing higher-order adaptive biological, mental and social network models. Springer Nature (2020)
24. Treur, J.: With a little help: a modeling environment for self-modeling network models. In: (Treur and Van Ments, 2022), Ch. 17, 467–489. Springer Nature, Cham (2022a)
25. Treur, J.: Where is this leading me: stationary point and equilibrium analysis for self-modeling network models. In: (Treur and Van Ments, 2022), Ch. 18, pp. 491–535. Cham: Springer Nature (2022b)
26. Treur, J.: Does this suit me? Validation of self-modeling network models by parameter tuning. In: (Treur and Van Ments, 2022), Ch. 19, pp. 537–564. Springer Nature (2022c)
27. Treur, J., Van Ments, L. (eds.): Mental models and their dynamics, adaptation and control: a self-modeling network modeling approach. Springer Nature (2022)
28. Van Ments, L., Treur, J., Klein, J., Roelofsma, P.: A second-order adaptive net-work model for shared mental models in hospital teamwork. In: Proceedings ICCCI 2021. Lecture Notes in AI, vol. 12876, pp. 126–140. Springer Nature (2021)
29. Verhoef, P.C., et al.: Digital transformation: a multidisciplinary reflection and research agenda. J. Bus. Res. **122**, 889–901 (2019)
30. Von der Ahe, L.: Mental wellbeing and cybercrime University of Twente (2022)
31. Roelofsma, P.H.M.P., Barelds, N.F., Bouma, D., Mestour, W., van den Hout, N.J., Treur, J. (eds.) Computational Analysis of Human and Organisational Decision Processes for the Control of Risk Management and Cybersecurity: A Multilevel Adaptive Dynamical System Modeling Approach. Springer Nature (2026). https://link.springer.com/book/9783032238856

# Reconfigurable VLSI Architectures for AI-Driven Low-Power Edge Computing

Vishal Narayana Raju(✉) and Shankaranarayana Bhat M

Manipal Institute of Technology, Manipal Academy of Higher Education, Manipal 576104, India
vnr159@gmail.com

**Abstract.** Over the last decade, battery-powered platforms which include smart wearables, Internet-of-Things (IoT) nodes, Industrial IOT (IIOT), and distributed wireless sensor networks have proliferated at an unprecedented pace. Modern wearables are now expected to deliver multi-day or week of autonomy while performing on-device analytics such as health-trend extraction and real-time summarization, rather than merely recording raw data. In parallel, sensor networks deployed in remote or hostile environments for climate-change surveillance, wildlife conservation and early-warning disasters must remain energy self-sufficient for months to years because field maintenance is often impractical or impossible. The simultaneous demand for extended lifetime and steadily rising computational workloads is driving an aggressive push toward ultra-low-power VLSI techniques across sensing, processing and wireless subsystems. Remote environmental sensor meshes face a similar mandate for energy self-sufficiency. Deployed on glaciers, in rainforests or along fault-lines, they may remain physically inaccessible for years; hence their radios, analog front-ends and power-management units are aggressively duty-cycled and frequently paired with solar, wind or vibration harvesters to achieve multi-year lifetimes in low power edge devices.

**Keywords:** Edge processor · Low power VLSI design · Clock gating · Power gating and Coarse Grain Reconfigurable Arrays

## 1 Introduction

IIOT devices are factory floor sensors and actuator nodes that operate at sub-milliwatt quiescent power yet must burst to tens of milliwatts for encrypted edge analytics, control loops, and over-the-air updates. Although early prototypes advertised "10-year battery life," long-term measurements on reference nodes showed a practical ceiling of $\approx$1.4 years on two AAA cells once realistic workloads were included [1]. Medical Implantable and skin-worn medical electronics operate under even tighter energy constraints. A sub-mm3 cortical stimulator demonstrated continuous 7.5 kb/s telemetry while harvesting tens of microwatts from near-infrared light, eliminating the battery entirely [2]. Likewise, an implantable neuromorphic sensor that performs on-chip spike


A. Shastri et al. (Eds.): IHCI 2025, LNCS 16437, pp. 191–202, 2026.
https://doi.org/10.1007/978-3-032-26352-0_16

sorting and send-on-delta compression keeps total dissipation below 100 μW [3]. Beyond IC advances, recent reviews show piezoelectric harvesters and ultra-low-power power-management units now delivering >70% efficiency at sub-hertz body-motion frequencies, paving the way for lifelong, maintenance-free implants and body-area wearables [4]. Wearable devices must deliver edge-class analytics such as multi-sensor fusion, anomaly detection or beat-level ECG classification while still offering multi-day autonomy. Recent SoCs like BioGAP bundle ten near-threshold RISC-V cores, a medical-grade analog front-end and BLE in an 18mW budget, achieving 15 h of untethered operation with >97% reduction in wireless traffic [5]. Complementing these platform advances, 2024 survey data show rapid maturation of low-power optical and electrochemical Continuous glucose monitoring (CGM stacks), with continuous operation below 1mW and algorithmic error <9% MARD—evidence that wearables are converging on medical-grade performance without sacrificing run-time [6]. Field-deployed sensor meshes for climate surveillance, wildlife protection and disaster early-warning must be energy-neutral by design. A review identifies hybrid solar–vibration harvesters, adaptive duty-cycling and μW-class wake-up radios as the dominant recipe for multi-year autonomy, trimming node quiescent draws to <5 μA [7]. Case studies underscore the stakes: a solar-powered Zigbee array on Greenland's Helheim glacier logged centimeter-scale ice dynamics for an entire melt season without human intervention, despite − 20 °C ambient and severe RF fading [8].The scope of this work is to review the methods that can be adapted for power efficient AI workloads in edge devices. This contribution of this work is to discuss the methods (CG and PG) and reconfigurable architecture (CGRAs) that can be used to create accelerators used for AI workloads in IOT and edge devices.

## 2 Background

### 2.1 Fundamental Power Metrics

The instantaneous power drawn by any electronic load is

$$P(t) = i(t)\,v(t) \tag{1}$$

where i(t) and v(t) is the supply current and voltage. Because power-reduction techniques invariably influence delays, designers evaluate whole-cycle energy/latency trade-offs with composite figures of merit. Power delay product (PDP) was introduced in early transistor-sizing work by Fishburn & Dunlop [9] and later generalized to Energy-Delay Product/Energy–Delay$^2$ (EDP/$ED^2$) for fine-grained design-space exploration [10] (Table 1).

**Sourcesof Power Dissipation in CMOS:**
The total power consumed by a CMOS circuit is conventionally decomposed into:

$$P = P_{\text{switch}} + P_{\text{sc}} + P_{\text{leak}} \tag{2}$$

$P_{switch}$, $P_{sc}$ and $P_{leakage}$ represent dynamic, short-circuit, and leakage components, respectively. The relative weight of each term shifts with technology scaling, leakage often dominates standby power in sub-micron regions [11] (Fig. 1).

**Table 1.** Table of Energy metrics and its significance.

| Metric | Definition | Design insight |
|---|---|---|
| PDP | $P_{\text{avg}} \times t_{\text{delay}}$ | Energy consumed per switching event |
| EDP | $E \times t_{\text{delay}}$ (or $P \times t_{\text{delay}}^2$) | Penalizes slow but "ultra-green" designs; the optimum lies at the knee of the energy–delay curve |
| ED$^2$ | $E \times t_{\text{delay}}^2$ | Favors high-performance systems, often used when throughput dominates |

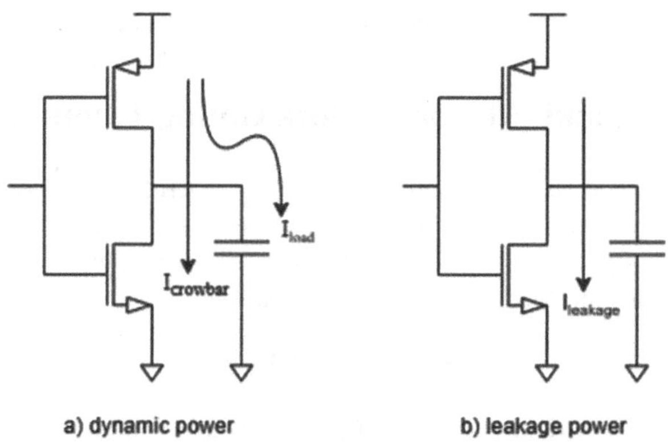


**Fig. 1.** Components of power dissipation, (a)MOSFET is on, (b) the MOSFER is off.

**Dynamic (Switching) Power**

When a gate output toggles, it charges or discharges the load capacitance $C_L$. The average dynamic power in a synchronous system is

$$P_{\text{switch}} = \tfrac{1}{2}\, C_L\, V_{\text{DD}}^2 f_{\text{clk}}\, E_{\text{sw}} \tag{3}$$

where $E_{\text{sw}}$ is the probability of a $0 \rightarrow 1$ transition per clock cycle. Quadratic dependence on $V_{\text{DD}}$ has made voltage scaling the most effective strategy for lowering power at a cost in operating speed (since delay $\propto V_{\text{DD}}/(V_{\text{DD}} - V_{\text{th}})^2$) [12] $f_{\text{clk}}$ is the operating frequency of the clock.Reducing $E_{\text{sw}}$ (via clock-gating, operand isolation, bus encoding), or the physical capacitance (transistor sizing, interconnect optimization), provides static power savings that do not degrade frequency directly [13].

**Short-Circuit Power**

During an input transition both the p-and n-devices of a CMOS stage may conduct simultaneously, producing a "crowbar" current. For a symmetric inverter with input rise/fall times $t_r/t_f$ the average short-circuit dissipation can be approximated as

$$\begin{aligned} P_{\text{sc}} &\approx \tfrac{1}{2}\left(t_r I_{\text{sh,rise}} + t_f I_{\text{sh,fall}}\right) E_{\text{sw}}\, V_{\text{DD}} f_{\text{clk}} \\ &\approx \tfrac{\beta}{2}\,(V_{\text{DD}} - 2V_{\text{th}})^3\, t_r f_{\text{clk}}\, E_{\text{sw}} \end{aligned} \tag{4}$$

where β is the device transconductance parameter, $I_{sh}$ is the short circuit current and $V_{th}$ is the threshold voltage of the device. Design-time strategies include minimising rise/fall asymmetry and sizing transistors to keep $V_{DD}$ just above $2V_{th}$.

**Leakage Power**

Leakage combines sub-threshold conduction, gate-oxide tunnelling, drain-induced barrier lowering (DIBL), and junction BTBT currents:

$$P_{leak} = V_{DD}\, I_{leak} \tag{5}$$

Techniques such as high-$V_{th}$ stacks, power-gating, reverse body-bias, and multi-threshold cell libraries reduce $I_{leak}$ with minimal performance loss [11].

## 3 Clock Gating and Advanced Clock Gating Techniques

The evolution of VLSI technology towards battery-operated and portable electronics has led to stringent power consumption constraints. Clock gating effectively reduces dynamic power dissipation by selectively turning off clock signals in inactive circuits. Dynamic power consumption is given by the equation:

$$P_{dyn} = E_{sw} C_L V_{dd}^2 f \tag{6}$$

where $E_{sw}$ represents switching activity, $C_L$ is load capacitance, $V_{dd}$ is supply voltage, and f is clock frequency. Clock gating reduces unnecessary switching activity, thereby significantly lowering power consumption [14]. Clock-gating can be introduced at many points in the design flow. The below sections countians detail of classical clock gating techniques.

### 3.1 Combinational-Enable

An AND/OR gate combines the global clock with an RTL enable expression. Synthesizer treats the gate as part of the functional circuit, so no extra timing path is created. This circuit is simple to implement but suffers from glitch risk if enable is not static one cycle ahead. Combinational clock gating on the other hand suppresses glitches with just few flip-flop or with small macro that is inserted at RTL or early logic synthesis. A 5–10% dynamic power reduction is observed for the gated register set, while an area reduction of 27% and a power reduction of 22% is observed with benchmark circuits when compared to gate sizing and buffer insertion techniques [15].

### 3.2 Sequential/ Retime-Propagated Gating

Sequential CG is a technique applied to pipelines where multiple register stages are present. In this method gating the first stage turns of the subsequent pipeline stages, the clock through each register stage is propagated through a CG circuit or an enhanced clock gating circuit. Sequential clock gating is applied at multiple register level whereas combinational CG is applicable to only one register level. This method is applicable at

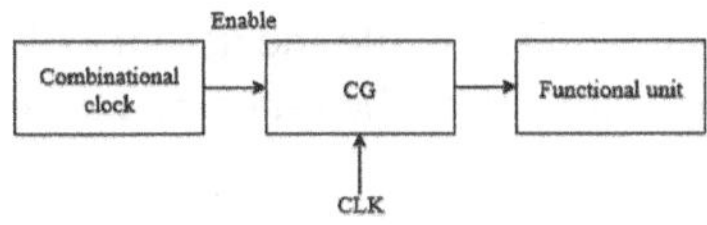


**Fig. 2.** The combinational clock gating

the RT level power reduction and is a CAD solution for low power where the CAD tool analyses the wasting toggle rates of the design from the activity file (Fig. 2).

To decide what kind of sequential CG is effective is based on the waste toggle rates of CG, Local explicit CG (LECG) and Enhanced clock gating (ECG) [16]. The most efficient CG method is obtained by passing various test vectors (Fig. 3).

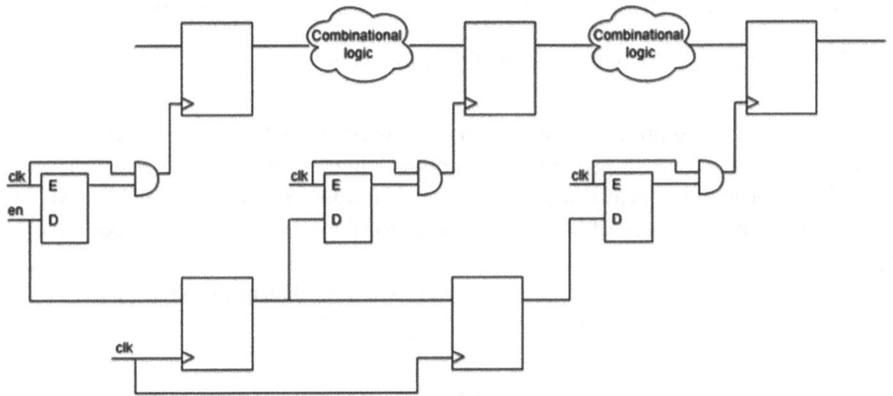


**Fig. 3.** Basic outline of combinational clock gating

### 3.3 Hardware-Driven, Full-Coverage Automatic CG

Automated clock gating technique the clock structure as with graphs, nodes and arcs. Unlike the S/W driven clock gating this technique models the Clock gate architecture with HW components and FSMs. The architecture has clock components and control elements to control the clock components. The clock components are classified as parent components and child components, immediate component higher in the hierarchy is known as a parent while the component one level below this hierarchy is known as a child component. The clock gating trickles down from the child to the parent in this implementation, that is the CG ripples from the Clock delivery network and is in the other direction of the clock path. The FSM elements are designed according to a two-phase handshake to inform the activity or inactivity of the parent or the child to its immediate neighbor through request and acknowledgement.

Additionally, the FSM elements constitute a token of freedom, which is passed from child of lower level to parent higher up in the hierarchy. The component in possession of the token is active and doesn't want to participate in CG. However, if it chooses to be inactive and CG itself it has to give up the token to the parent higher in the CDN. In essence the inactivity or clock gating cascades through the system from low level of the CDN to the high level of the CDN, while the activity of the elements cascades from higher levels to lowers one element after the other by the two phase handshake and the free token system (Fig. 4).

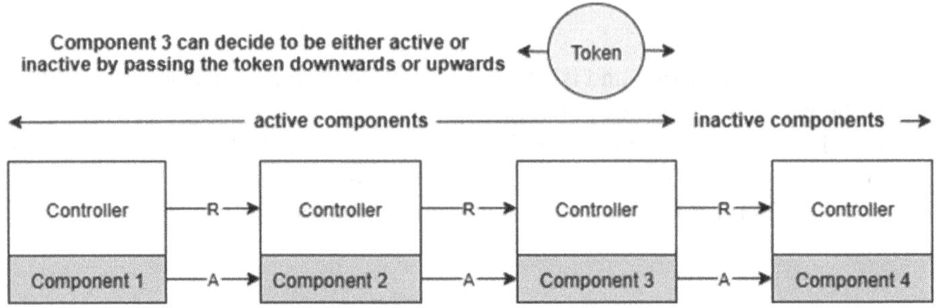


**Fig. 4.** The component in possession of the token is free to decide its state of activity.

Samsung's Exynos architecture, which implemented ACG on the global clock graph demonstrated a 48–57% improvement in power when compared to software CG at IP level. This improvement is attributed to the fact that idle time of certain IP's are short for a SW CG to take advantage of but good enough for the HW ACG CG to take advantage of [17].

In addition to the classical CG techniques, Machine learning (ML) based CG [18] can be evaluated and further studied.

## 4 Power Gating and Advanced Power Gating.

With technology scaling, leakage currents have become a dominant component of total power consumption in idle circuits. Power gating offers a potent solution by disconnecting unused circuit blocks from the power supply during standby operation. It is widely used in mobile processors, memory blocks, and SoC functional units. Power gating in involves the insertion of high-Vth sleep transistors (header or footer switches) between logic modules and the power rails.

### 4.1 Runtime-Adaptive Power Gating (TAP)

In a processor computation is carried out on many cores, these cores access the memory subsystems at various levels of the memory hierarchy. Add memory hierarchy picture. In case of a miss in the cache memories the core or thread is in stall condition and a lot of leakage current is dissipated. In Token based adaptive gating (TAP) the deterministically power gates the programmable power gating switch (PPSG) from a table which has the memory read back latency. This table is created by extensively understanding the architecture of the cores and memory, type of execution of the processor and probabilistic models and extensive testing. The PPSG constitutes an array of parallel connected header or footer switches that are switched, these switches are turned on in two stages. Where a few switches are turned on in the initial phase and the rest are turned on at a later phase. The noise on the supply rail is further minimized by understanding the activity of the adjacent cores and controlling the wake-up time this is supplemented by staggering the wake up of multiple threads or cores, this is realized using a centralized wakeup controller. These measures minimize the inrush current and the load or ripples on the power supply rail. TAP applied to an out of order execution core achieves a maximum saving of 22%. TAP is more efficient than Memory access power gating and DVFS by 2.5× and 5.2× respectively [19]. In another instance where TAP is applied to Multi core process (up to 32 cores) a power saving of 3.7× is observed while the wake up time reduces by 58% [20] (Fig. 5).

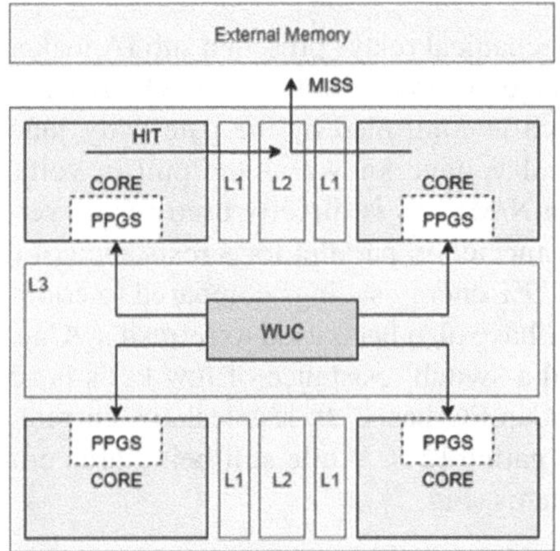


**Fig. 5.** TAP working in case of HIT or MISS.

## 4.2 Switched-Capacitor-Assisted PG (SwCap-PG)

When power gating a circuit its best if the leakage of the switch is minimized while at the same time the on resistance of the switch is minimized. However, to minimize the ON resistance and IR drop across the switch its width must be increased and with increase in width the leakage of the switch increases therefore its evident that the leakage trades with on resistance. Leakage and On Resistance can be dynamically controlled by body biasing the switch, however in the case of nano scale CMOS switches (like GAA and FinFETs) due to fully depleted channel body bias is not possible. Control the leakage of the nano scale CMOS switches by operating them in super cut off and super turn on states, where the gate voltage is set below 0V and above Vdd respectively. CMOS SwCap PG is a circuit topology where a capacitor is either connected across Vgs and Vgd with the appropriate voltage to operate the PG switch in super cutoff or super turn on region. The leakage of the switched capacitor is replenished by alternating between two capacitor networks in alternating clock intervals, using thick oxide devices drastically reduces the leakage therefore requires less switching cycles. MOS SwCap PG reduces leakage up to 226× when compared to a conventional PG LVT switch both designed in a 180 nm CMOS technology and 667× reduction while using a conventional PG RVT switch [21] (Fig. 6).

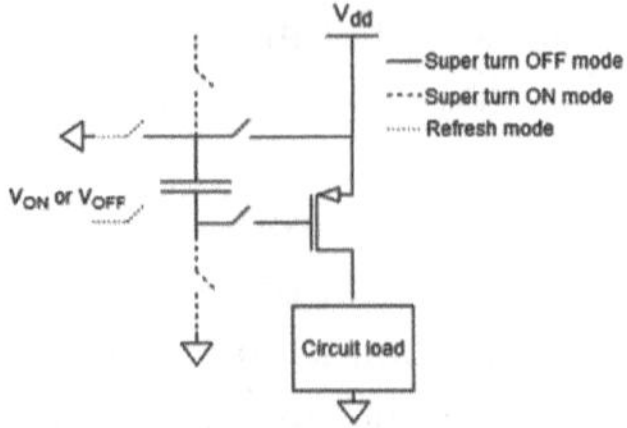


**Fig. 6.** Switching circuit representing the super turn ON, super turn OFF and refresh states.

### 4.3 NEMS or MEMS Relay-Based Power Gating

Nano or Micro electromechanical relays present a sub fA leakage when open, near zero DIBIL and minimal voltage errors due to their low ON resistance. The drain to source contact on the EM switch is controlled by the gate-body junction voltage, when this voltage is above a critical voltage known as the pull in voltage an electrical contact is maintained. When the N/MEMS is directly used for power gating several 100's or 1000's of devices are connected in parallel for a resistance of the order of mΩ's, these switches offer an overall 9% energy savings compared to compared to previous studies [22]. However N/MEMS have also been used to refresh swCap PG where the capacitor refresh rates are low and a switch resistance of few kΩ's is acceptable. It is observed that a MEMS based SwCap PG has 172x less leakage current and an Ron 26% lesser than conventional clock gating [21]. While still being area efficient than conventional N/MEMS based PG systems (Fig. 7).

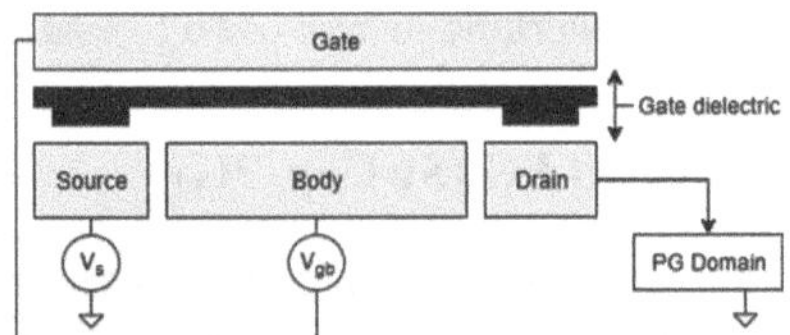


**Fig. 7.** Operating mechanism of a MEMS switch.

## 5 Coarse-Grained Reconfigurable Architectures

Coarse-grained reconfigurable architectures (CGRAs) promise ASIC-like energy efficiency while preserving the programmability they are indispensable for rapidly evolving AI edge workloads. Edge devices wearables and medical implants to industrial sensors—must execute increasingly complex signal-and data-flow kernels under stringent energy envelopes. CGRAs, which array word-level processing elements (PEs) in a regular mesh with deterministic routing, have therefore re-emerged as a sweet-spot architecture. Recent journal papers confirm that modern CGRAs can deliver 6–10× lower energy per operation than microcontroller-class cores while retaining software flexibility [23].

### 5.1 Fine-Grained Power-Gating

The operation of fine grain power gating can be understood in the context of ULP SR processor where this technique is implemented. ULP SR processor can be operated either as a VLIW processor or a CAGR at any given point of time by dynamically changing the mode. The instruction memory of the VLIW processor, configuration memory of a CAGR and program memory are all present in a unified memory shared memory. In the VLIW mode two functional units are active while in low performance mode and high-performance mode four (2 $\times$ 2 mode) or nine (3 $\times$ 3 mode) functional units are active. ULP SR processor's power domains are partitioned according to operation mode (VLIW or CAGR mode) and the usage of memory. The memory unit supports retention cells where data is stored when the power domains are inactive this fine control is also known as fine grain power gating (Fig. 8).

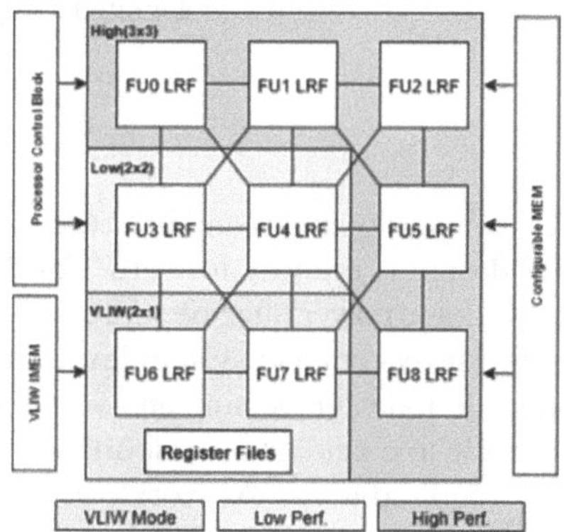


**Fig. 8.** ULP SR operational states and its architecture.

The ULP-SRP biomedical CGRA operates with 46% lesser energy when compared to a processor without fine grain power gating [24]. A 16 nm array that folds isolation devices into switchbox muxes reports 83% leakage and 26% total energy savings on vision kernels [25].

### 5.2 Tile-Level Dynamic Voltage/Frequency Scaling (DVFS)

CAGR's constitute of FU as the fundamental building blocks, each FU is connected to multiple other FU's through the network on chip. An application consists of many kernels (such as FIR, Convolutions), each kernel operates on multiple datapoints simultaneously on FU's. These kernels operate onto the FU's in the form of a DFG by the Modulo routing resource graph [26]. In the above DFG it may so happen that some resources may be under-utilized or not utilized in such cases utilization of the FU's and efficiency of the overall system can be improved by applying DVFS. The optimally utilized FU's, underutilized FU's and the no utilized FU's are grouped into tiles containing 2 $\times$ 2 or 3 $\times$ 3 FUs and DVFS performed on a per tile basis instead of the finer FU level. This reduces the number and the complexity of the DVFS required, however the complexity of grouping the FUs is shifted to the compiler that maps the application and its kernels on to FU's. The ICED framework is 1.32× efficient than the baseline and 1.6× more efficient than a conventional per tile DVFS. In terms of application is 1.12× and 1.26× more efficient than Graph Convolutional Network and LU [27] (Fig. 9).

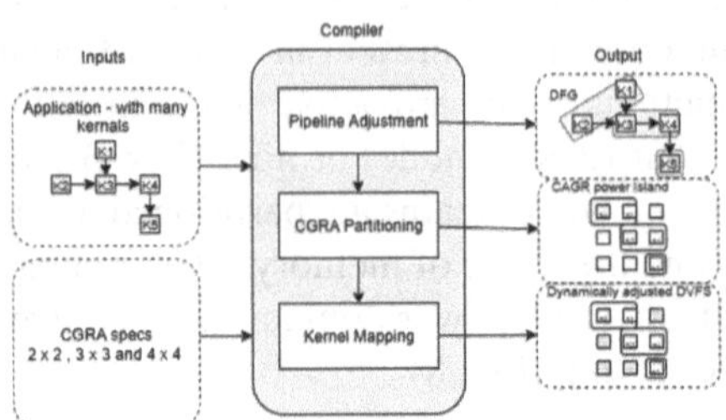


**Fig. 9.** Application mapping onto the CGRA with the integrated compiler framework and kernels mapped onto DVFS islands.

## 6 Conclusion

With constant scaling of the technology nodes and increase in the computation requirements of edge devices, ULP design is the way forward. For the above discussions it is evident that the dynamic and leakage power must be addressed at various abstraction levels i.e. through device, circuit, subsystem and system levels and during different stages of the design phase i.e. conception, design, testing and verification phase. Through this review an attempt has been made to elucidate the importance of hardware and software co-design in edge processors required to run AI workloads. Future scope of work is to adapt AI integrated CG and PG techniques [28] (CNN based) to evaluate its effectiveness in edge processors.

## References

1. Lu, X. Kim, I. H. Xhafa, A. Zhou, J. and Tsai, K.: Reaching 10-years of battery life for industrial IoT wireless sensor networks. IEEE Symposium on VLSI Circuits, Digest of Technical Papers, pp. C66–C67 (2017). https://doi.org/10.23919/VLSIC.2017.8008550
2. Lee, J., et al.: A Sub-mm3 wireless neural stimulator IC for visual cortical prosthesis with optical power harvesting and 7.5-kb/s data telemetry. IEEE J. Solid-State Circuits **59**(4), 1110–1122 (2024). https://doi.org/10.1109/JSSC.2023.3349179
3. He, Y., et al.: An implantable neuromorphic sensing system featuring near-sensor computation and send-on-delta transmission for wireless neural sensing of peripheral nerves. IEEE J. Solid-State Circuits **57**(10), 3058–3070 (2022). https://doi.org/10.1109/JSSC.2022.3193846
4. Almarri, N., Chang, J., Song, W., Jiang, D., Demosthenous, A.: Piezoelectric energy harvesting and ultra-low-power management circuits for medical devices. Nano Energy **131**, 110196 (2024). https://doi.org/10.1016/J.NANOEN.2024.110196
5. Frey, S., Guermandi, M., Benatti, S., Kartsch, V., Cossettini, A., Benini, L.: BioGAP: a 10-Core FP-capable Ultra-Low Power IoT Processor, with Medical-Grade AFE and BLE connectivity for wearable biosignal processing. 2023 IEEE International Conference on Omni-Layer Intelligent Systems, COINS 2023 (2023). https://doi.org/10.1109/COINS57856.2023.10189286

6. Mansour, M., Saeed Darweesh, M., Soltan, A.: Wearable devices for glucose monitoring: a review of state-of-the-art technologies and emerging trends. Alexandria Eng. J. **89**, 224–243 (2024). https://doi.org/10.1016/J.AEJ.2024.01.021
7. León Ávila, B.Y., García Vázquez, C.A., Pérez Baluja, O., Cotfas, D.T., Cotfas, P.A.: Energy harvesting techniques for wireless sensor networks: a systematic literature review. Energy Strategy Rev. **57**, 101617 (2025). https://doi.org/10.1016/J.ESR.2024.101617
8. Martin, I., et al.: A high-resolution sensor network for monitoring glacier dynamics. IEEE Sens. J. **14**(11), 3926–3931 (2014). https://doi.org/10.1109/JSEN.2014.2348534
9. Fishburn, J.P., Dunlop, A.E.: TILOS: a posynomial programming approach to transistor sizing. pp. 295–302 (2003). https://doi.org/10.1007/978-1-4615-0292-0_23
10. Zeydel, B.R., Oklobdzija, V.G.: Design of energy efficient digital circuits. High-Performance Energy-Efficient Microprocessor Design, pp. 31–55 (2006). https://doi.org/10.1007/978-0-387-34047-0_2
11. Roy, K., Mukhopadhyay, S., Mahmoodi-Meimand, H.: Leakage current mechanisms and leakage reduction techniques in deep-submicrometer CMOS circuits. Proc. IEEE **91**(2), 305–327 (2003). https://doi.org/10.1109/JPROC.2002.808156
12. Chandrakasan, A.P., Sheng, S., Brodersen, R.W.: Low-Power CMOS digital design. IEEE J. Solid-State Circuits **27**(4), 473–484 (1992). https://doi.org/10.1109/4.126534
13. Horowitz, M., Indermaur, T., Gonzalez, R.: Low-power digital design. IEEE Symposium on Low Power Electronics, pp. 8–11 (1994). https://doi.org/10.1109/LPE.1994.573184
14. Benini, L.: Designing low-power circuits: practical recipes. IEEE Circuits Syst. Mag. **1**(1), 6–25 (2001). https://doi.org/10.1109/7384.928306
15. Sudhakar, J., Prasad, A.M., Panda, A.K.: GFCG: glitch free combinational clock gating approach in nanometer VLSI circuits. pp. 146–150 (2015). https://doi.org/10.1109/ECS.2015.7124828
16. Li, L., Wang, W., Choi, K., Park, S., Chung, M.K.: SeSCG: selective sequential clock gating for ultra-low-power multimedia mobile processor design. 2010 IEEE International Conference on Electro/Information Technology, p. EIT2010 (2010). https://doi.org/10.1109/EIT.2010.5612100
17. Lee, J.G., Choi, Y., Jeon, H., Lee, J.J., Shin, D.: Fully Automated hardware-driven clock-gating architecture with complete clock coverage for 4 nm Exynos mobile SOC. IEEE J. Solid-State Circuits **58**(1), 90–101 (2023). https://doi.org/10.1109/JSSC.2022.3219410
18. Won, D., Kim, S., Kim, T.: Machine learning driven synthesis of clock gating. Proceedings of the International Symposium on Low Power Electronics and Design, vol. 2023-August (2023). https://doi.org/10.1109/ISLPED58423.2023.10244402
19. Kahng, A.B., Kang, S., Rosing, T., Strong, R.: TAP-Token-based adaptive power gating. Proceedings of the International Symposium on Low Power Electronics and Design, pp. 203–208 (2012). https://doi.org/10.1145/2333660.2333711;CTYPE:STRING:BOOK
20. Kahng, A.B., Kang, S., Rosing, T.S., Strong, R.: Many-core token-based adaptive power gating. IEEE Trans. Comput. Aided Des. Integr. Circuits Syst. **32**(8), 1288–1292 (2013). https://doi.org/10.1109/TCAD.2013.2257923
21. Sankar, S., Goel, M., Chen, P.H., Rao, V.R., Baghini, M.S.: Switched-capacitor-assisted power gating for ultra-low standby power in CMOS digital ICs. IEEE Trans. Circuits Syst. I Regul. Pap. **67**(12), 4281–4294 (2020). https://doi.org/10.1109/TCSI.2020.3015430
22. Alrudainy, H., Shafik, R., Mokhov, A., Yakovlev, A.: Lifetime reliability characterization of N/MEMS used in power gating of digital integrated circuits. 2017 IEEE Int. Symposium on Defect and Fault Tolerance in VLSI and Nanotechnology Systems, DFT 2017, vol. 2018-January, pp. 1–6 (2017). https://doi.org/10.1109/DFT.2017.8244452
23. Ebrahimi, Z., Kumar, A.: GREEN: an approximate SIMD/MIMD CGRA for energy-efficient processing at the edge. IEEE Trans. Comput. Aided Des. Integr. Circuits Syst. **43**(10), 2874–2887 (2024). https://doi.org/10.1109/TCAD.2024.3383349

24. Kim, C., Chung, M., Cho, Y., Konijnenburg, M., Ryu, S., Kim, J.: ULP-SRP: ultra low power samsung reconfigurable processor for biomedical applications. FPT 2012 - 2012 International Conference on Field-Programmable Technology, pp. 329–334 (2012). https://doi.org/10.1109/FPT.2012.6412157
25. Nayak, A., et al.: Improving energy efficiency of CGRAs with low-overhead fine-grained power domains. dl.acm.orgA Nayak, K Zhang, R Setaluri, A Carsello, M Mann, C Torng, S Richardson, R BahrACM Transactions on Reconfigurable Technology and Systems, 2023•dl.acm.org, vol. 16, no. 2, (2023). https://doi.org/10.1145/3558394
26. Mei, B., Vernalde, S., Verkest, D., De Man, H., Lauwereins, R.: DRESC: a retargetable compiler for coarse-grained reconfigurable architectures. Proceedings - 2002 IEEE International Conference on Field-Programmable Technology, FPT 2002, pp. 166–173 (2002). https://doi.org/10.1109/FPT.2002.1188678
27. Tan, C., et al.: ICED: an integrated CGRA framework enabling DVFS-Aware acceleration. Proceedings of the Annual International Symposium on Microarchitecture, MICRO, pp. 1338–1352 (2024). https://doi.org/10.1109/MICRO61859.2024.00099
28. Chundi, P.K., et al.: Always-on sub-microwatt spiking neural network based on spike-driven clock- and power-gating for an ultra-low-power intelligent device. Front. Neurosci. **15**, 684113 (2021). https://doi.org/10.3389/FNINS.2021.684113/BIBTEX

# R2A2: A Simulated Robotic Rover for Sustainable Orchard Automation

K. Deepika(✉), B. Renuka Prasad, and B. H. Chandrashekar

Department of MCA, RV College of Engineering, Bengaluru, Karnataka, India
deepikak@rvce.edu.in

**Abstract.** Agriculture in India faces critical challenges including land fragmentation, labor shortages, low productivity, and climate vulnerability, which collectively hinder sustainable growth. Emerging technologies such as robotics and artificial intelligence offer transformative potential to address these issues by automating labor-intensive tasks, enhancing input efficiency, and improving decision-making. This study presents the design, modeling, and simulation of a multipurpose robotic rover (R2A2) for agricultural applications, with specific focus on fruit collection and precision spraying. The rover integrates soil and crop monitoring, pest detection, and yield prediction capabilities within a unified platform powered by hybrid solar-battery energy. Using CoppeliaSim, a physics-based robotics simulator, the rover's structure, control algorithm, vision system, and gripper were recreated to replicate real-world agricultural scenarios. A virtual 3D peach orchard environment was developed to evaluate rover performance under realistic conditions. Simulation experiments demonstrated reliable locomotion, adaptive dual-speed operation, and effective fruit detection using combined color and depth analysis. Results confirmed high detection accuracy (87–91%) and robust task execution, validating the effectiveness of simulation as a development tool for agricultural robotics. Future work includes physical prototyping, algorithm refinement, and integration with cooperative systems such as drones for advanced precision agriculture.

**Keywords:** Agricultural robotics · Unmanned ground vehicle (UGV) · Robotic rover simulation · Precision agriculture · CoppeliaSim · Vision-based detection

## 1 Introduction

Agriculture remains central to India's economy, employing about 43% of the work-force while contributing only 16–18% to GDP in 2022–23 [1, 2]. Fragmented land-holdings—86% of farmers own less than 2 hectares—and rural labor shortages continue to limit productivity and mechanization. Challenges such as low yields, rising input costs, and climate variability further constrain sustainability and profitability.

Government programs like the National Mission on Sustainable Agriculture (NMSA), Sub-Mission on Agricultural Mechanization (SMAM), and the Digital Agriculture Mission (2021–2025) promote climate resilience, mechanization, and digital integration. Despite agricultural power availability exceeding 112 million kW by 2020,


A. Shastri et al. (Eds.): IHCI 2025, LNCS 16437, pp. 203–214, 2026.
https://doi.org/10.1007/978-3-032-26352-0_17

India's mechanization rate (~47%) remains well below that of developed nations [3]. Concurrently, agri-tech innovations—IoT sensors, drones, AI-based monitoring, and robotics—are emerging to address labor and efficiency gaps.

Robotics and unmanned ground vehicles (UGVs) show promise for precision agriculture, where irregular terrain and crop-specific needs demand adaptable, low-cost automation. However, field validation of such systems is resource-intensive. Simulation tools like CoppeliaSim offer efficient alternatives for modeling robotic structures, sensors, and control algorithms before deployment.

This study designs and simulates a multipurpose agricultural robotic rover (R2A2) for Indian orchards. The rover integrates soil and crop monitoring, localized spraying, pest detection, and fruit collection, powered by a hybrid solar–battery system. Using CoppeliaSim, its components and control algorithms were validated in a 3D guava orchard model based on Bengaluru's rural belt.

The contributions of this paper are:

- Development of a multi-functional agricultural rover for Indian conditions.
- Simulation-based evaluation of locomotion, spraying, and fruit-collection tasks.
- Analysis of algorithm performance in a virtual guava orchard, supporting future field deployment.

## 2 Materials and Methods

### 2.1 Robotic Rover (R2A2)

The Robotic Rover for Agricultural Applications (R2A2) is designed as a multi-tasking unmanned ground vehicle (UGV) to support Indian agriculture by automating routine yet labor-intensive field operations. Unlike earlier prototypes such as orchard-specific spraying robots [9], R2A2 is envisioned as a general-purpose rover adaptable to multiple crops and climatic zones in India.

The rover integrates soil and crop monitoring, precision spraying, pest detection, and harvest prediction into a unified platform. Its autonomous operation reduces the dependence on seasonal labor, improves resource efficiency, and minimizes ecological impacts by enabling site-specific interventions. For example, targeted herbicide spraying reduces chemical usage, while pest/disease detection through AI-enabled cameras enables early corrective measures, avoiding large-scale losses.

R2A2 is also equipped with GPS and cloud-based communication modules, ensuring that data collected in the field (such as soil moisture levels, plant health status, and weather conditions) can be uploaded to a farmer dashboard for real-time decision support. By combining edge AI processing with wireless data transfer, the rover can function in semi-remote areas while still contributing to precision agriculture platforms.

To handle India's diverse field terrains, R2A2 was engineered with 4-wheel differential drive, large soil-adaptive tires, and an operational ability to overcome 20° slopes and crop covers larger than 600 mm. Its hybrid solar-battery power system ensures long operation hours, even in rural regions with unreliable electricity access.

The prototype of the agricultural robotic rover was designed and modeled in SolidWorks CAD, enabling detailed planning of its structure and assembly. The CAD environment facilitated the generation of precise technical drawings that guided CNC-based

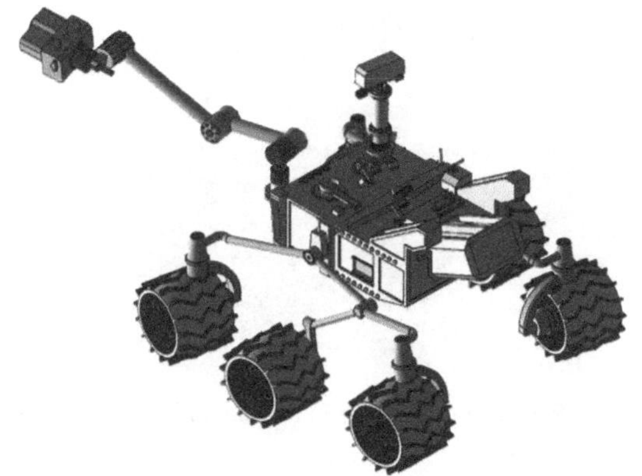

**Fig. 1.** Computer Aided Diagram (CAD) Rendering of the Rover

fabrication. Figure 1 illustrates the exploded CAD rendering of the rover. The rover's frame is constructed from 45 × 45 mm T-slot aluminum profiles (Bosch Rexroth), chosen for their high strength-to-weight ratio and modularity. This configuration supports easy assembly, repositioning of components, and future integration of additional modules.

To extend functionality, the rover incorporates a five-degree-of-freedom (5-DOF) Cartesian robotic arm equipped with a spraying nozzle and mechanical gripper. This setup enables precise herbicide spraying and fruit collection, with an operational reach of 1200 mm, allowing access to crop stems and orchard floors beyond the base frame. Figures 2 and 3 depict the rover (R2A2) operating across agricultural plots along designated and random paths. Field trials demonstrated effective crop monitoring, pest detection, and decision-support capabilities during various growth stages.

The Cartesian manipulator serves two primary functions—fruit collection and precision spraying—contributing to agricultural sustainability by:

- Reducing food waste, through recovery of fallen fruits for animal feed or compost.
- Supporting pest and disease control, by removing decaying fruits that may harbor microorganisms and insects.

Given that nearly 40% of food loss in India is attributed to pests, pathogens, and weeds, this integration highlights the potential of robotic intervention. Based on technical specifications, the working envelope of the Cartesian manipulator was derived using SolidWorks. The operational range was determined as ?x = 649.03 mm, ?y = 194.30 mm, and ?z = 428.50 mm.

The robotic gripper, an essential part of the manipulator, was developed through three design streams: (1) mechanical construction, (2) electrical system integration, and (3) control programming. The gripper assembly process included coupling the rotation system to a spacer (1), followed by attachment to the front plate of the y-axis. The gripper (3) was subsequently fixed to the rotation system (2), ensuring operational flexibility.

Prior to field deployment, algorithm simulations were conducted to validate the gripper's control logic and optimize its response. This approach accelerated the development cycle, minimized mechanical trial errors, and ensured better field readiness.

**Fig. 2.** Robotic Rover in Operating in a Guava Field in a Designated Path

**Fig. 3.** Robotic Rover in Operating in a Guava Field in a Random Path

## 2.2 CoppeliaSim Simulator

After evaluating different robotic simulation environments, CoppeliaSim (developed by Coppelia Robotics AG, Zurich, Switzerland) was selected as the most suitable platform for this research. The software provides a wide range of features such as multiple physics engines, a comprehensive model library, real-time interaction with the simulation environment, and advanced mesh manipulation capabilities. These features make it highly effective for rapid prototyping, agricultural robot development, and teaching applications.

Additionally, CoppeliaSim includes collision detection, distance measurement, proximity sensing, and computer vision modules. It offers four physics engines that can be selected based on simulation fidelity and computational efficiency. Due to this versatility, the software is often referred to as the "Swiss Army knife" of robotic simulation.

**Robotic Platform Creation:** The robotic platform was modeled by importing the primary structural components—chassis, wheels, shafts, accessories, and gripper—into the CoppeliaSim environment. Once imported, these parts were recreated using primitive geometric shapes with carefully assigned physical properties such as density, mass, friction, and damping. This ensured that the behavior of the simulated model closely resembled the real-world prototype. Components considered non-essential for the simulation, such as screws, bolts, and minor fixtures, were omitted to simplify the design without compromising fidelity.

As a result, two versions of the platform were available within the simulator: the original design (represented by triangular mesh models) and the simplified version with primitive shapes optimized for physics-based simulations and is illustrated in Fig. 4.

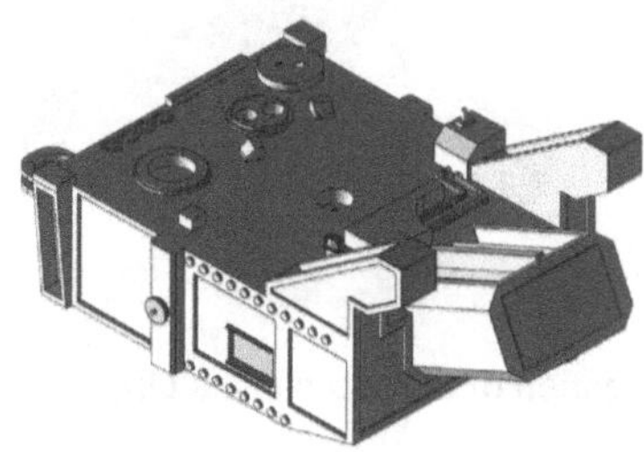

**Fig. 4.** Final Layout of the Robotic Rover Body Imported & Reconstructed in CoppeliaSim

The rover is intended for multipurpose agricultural operations, with fruit harvesting as one of its primary tasks. For this purpose, a mechanical gripper was integrated onto the x-axis support. This gripper—originally developed by the PrunusBot Operational Group—was adapted for the platform to enable selective fruit picking. Figure 5 shows the gripper both as an imported convex mesh design and as a simplified primitive model configured with functional joints.

The gripper operates via a main joint (A), enabling a 90° lifting motion, while two additional joints, marked (1) and (2) in Fig. 5, control the independent actuation of the fingers. These features allow precise grasping and manipulation of agricultural products. An isometric view of the developed gripper is presented in Fig. 8.

**Integration of a Vision System:** To enhance perception, a video system was added to the robotic platform. A Raspberry Pi Camera v2 module was selected due to its compact design and capability to capture images at multiple resolutions (1080p30, 720p60, and 640 × 480p90). In CoppeliaSim, this was modeled using a vision sensor positioned identically to its location on the real prototype.

The camera was mounted at the top of the rover chassis, supported by an aluminum profile aligned with the platform's central axis. This positioning provided a clear view of both the surrounding environment and the rover's lower operating area. The exact camera location is indicated by a red marker in Fig. 8. Once installed, the camera parameters were calibrated to mimic real-world operation.

### 2.3 Proposed Algorithm

The proposed robotic platform is designed to detect and collect fruits randomly distributed across an agricultural field or within a defined area. To achieve this, the control algorithm considers multiple operational and environmental factors to ensure reliable real-world performance.

In the initial phase, the steps and logical conditions required for fruit collection were conceptualized and organized into a structured sequence, formalized through the

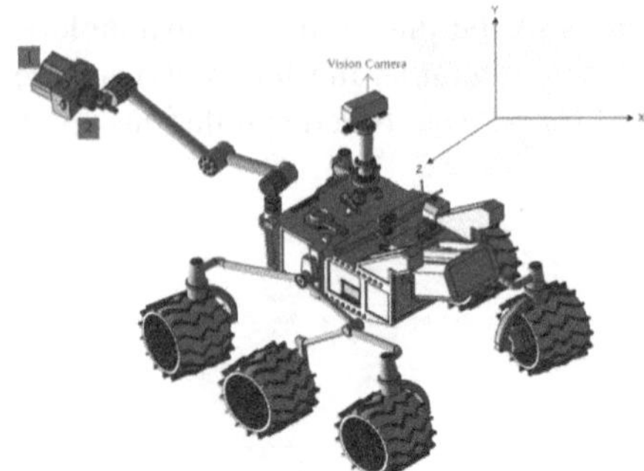


**Fig. 5.** Simulation-Ready Recreation of the Mechanical Gripper with its Operational Joints with the Vision Sensor

flowchart shown in Fig. 6. This flowchart represents the complete task cycle executed by the rover's control software for fruit detection and capture.

For the fruit collection process, a specific sequence of movements and control decisions was defined. These actions are depicted in Fig. 7, where the algorithm is decomposed into seven key steps governing the collection cycle. Each step in the flowchart specifies:

- the motion of the robotic platform along the x–y–z axes,
- the operation of the gripper mechanism, and
- the conditional checks that must be satisfied to transition to the next stage.

This structured approach ensures that the platform can dynamically adjust its speed, align its gripper with the fruit, perform capture operations, and return to its base once the maximum collection capacity or operational limit has been reached.

ICAR-IIHR guidelines and horticultural studies, the most common layouts in this region include 5 m × 5 m (rainfed), 6 m × 6 m (irrigated), and high-density plantations with 2 m × 1 m, where the first value indicates the spacing between trees within a row and the second defines the inter-row distance [3]. These configurations are illustrated in Fig. 8(a).

For the simulation, a layout of 4.5 m × 2.5 m was selected as a worst-case scenario, given that it represents the smallest inter-row spacing and thus poses the greatest navigation challenge for the robotic platform. The ground surface was then modeled using a dark brown textured plane with relief details to simulate soil, while maintaining a flat surface to avoid artificial difficulties unrelated to the navigation algorithm. The resulting 3D orchard environment is shown in Fig. 8(b).

To replicate fruit variability, spherical objects were inserted to represent Guavas of different sizes and weights. The simulated fruits had diameters ranging from 50 to 90 mm and weights between 100 and 150 g, with the heaviest weight assigned to the largest fruits [4]. These objects were modeled as primitive spheres and colored in various shades of green, reflecting the natural variability of Guava appearance. This setup allowed testing of the algorithm's ability to detect and discriminate fruits under realistic conditions.

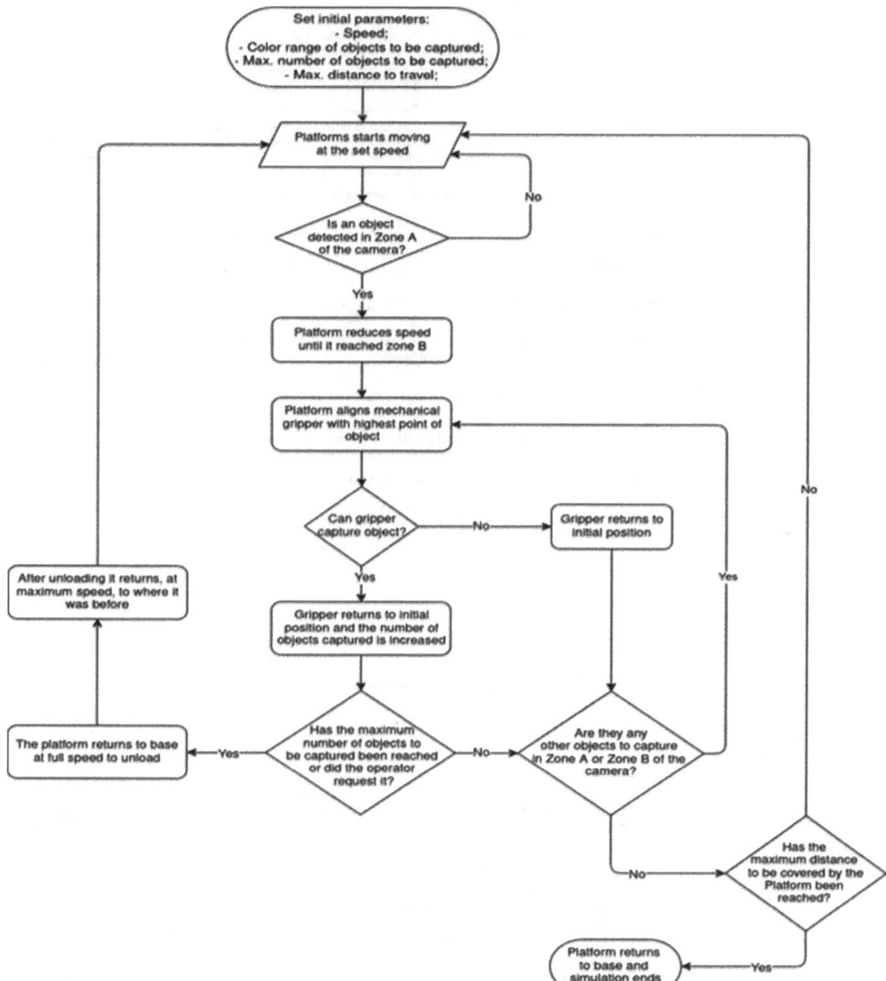


**Fig. 6.** Flowchart for Controlling the Robotic Rover Platform

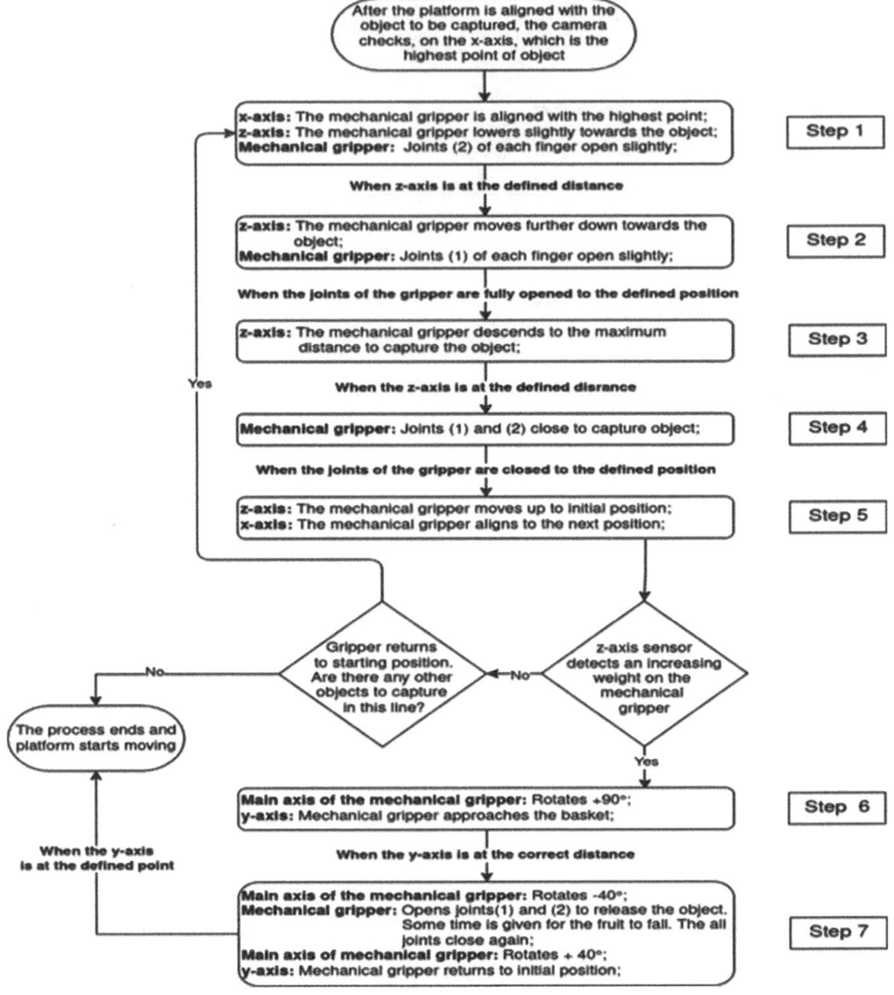


**Fig. 7.** Flowchart for Object Picking

## 3 Results Analysis and Discussion

This section presents the results of the simulation experiments and discusses the operational behavior of the robotic rover in performing its two primary tasks: object (fruit) collection and weed spraying. A series of three tests was conducted for each task to evaluate the control algorithm's performance in terms of object detection, capture precision, spraying accuracy, and overall task execution time. The results highlight both the strengths and limitations of the proposed approach.

### 3.1 Rover Behavior

**Operating Speed:** During simulations, it became evident that operating speed played a critical role in balancing efficiency and accuracy. Initial trials with higher speeds reduced execution time but compromised object detection, as the camera's exposure and processing time were insufficient. The optimal maximum speed was determined to be 0.63 m/s, consistent with thresholds reported in prior studies [5].

However, alignment errors between the mechanical gripper and the target object frequently occurred, with the rover tending to overshoot. While an algorithmic correction step was introduced—where the rover reversed slightly to re-align—it resulted in negligible gains compared to simply maintaining a lower speed. To optimize performance, a dual-speed strategy was implemented:

- **Detection phase:** average speed of 0.63 m/s, enabling efficient object scanning.
- **Engagement phase:** reduced speed of 0.42 m/s, allowing finer analysis and alignment for capture or spraying.

This adaptive approach minimized detection errors while ensuring task precision.

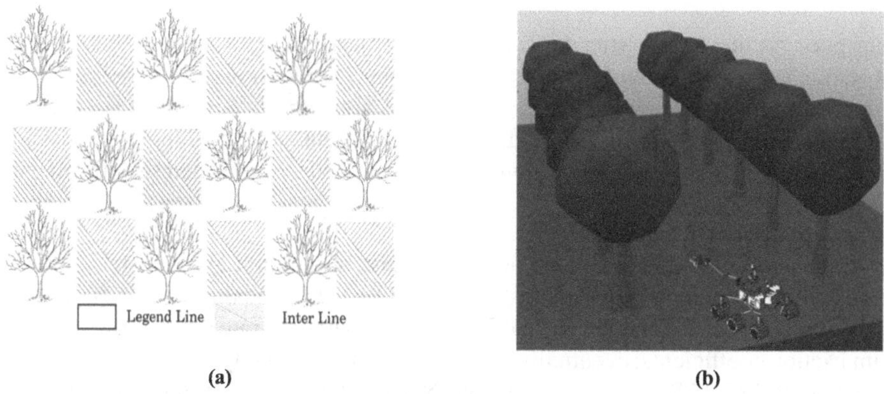


**Fig. 8.** (a) Definition of a Compass & (b) Resulting 3D Orchard Environment

**Image Processing:** The rover's vision sensor supports multiple resolutions. To improve simulation fluidity, the lowest available resolution was used. Nonetheless, even at this resolution, processing delays occurred, particularly when the algorithm executed multiple cycles on image frames. To mitigate this, the image processing pipe-line was optimized to reduce computational overhead, resulting in smoother real-time operation [6].

**Operation Time:**
The object capture task required the longest execution time due to the sequential maneuvers of the robotic arm and gripper (Fig. 9). The process involved-Step 1. Aligning the rover with the object, Step 2. Positioning the gripper along the x-axis, Step 3. Lowering

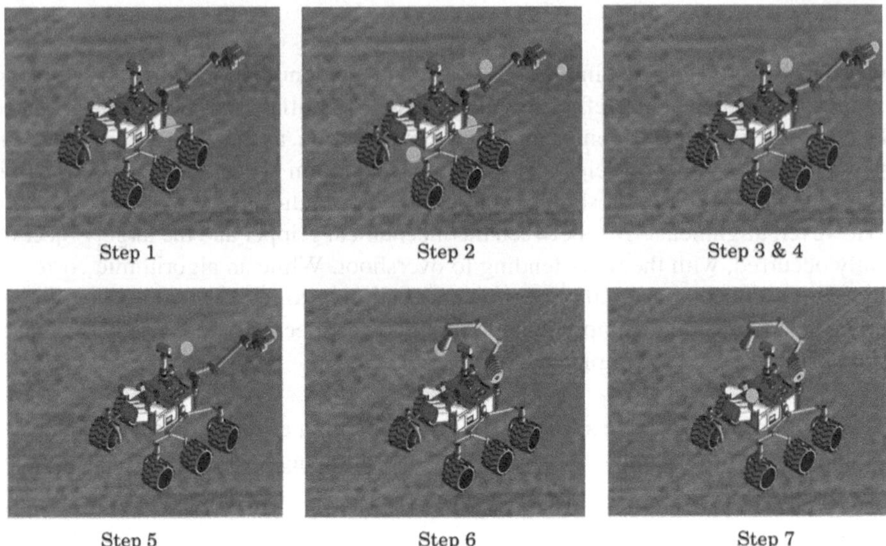


**Fig. 9.** Sequence of the Robotic Rover During Object Capture

the gripper via the z-axis, Step 4. Clamping the object. Step 5. Lifting the object, Step 6. Rotating and moving toward the storage bin, Step 7. Releasing the object into the bin.

Attempts to reduce operation time included algorithmic refinements, increasing prism actuator speeds, and adjusting PID control parameters. While minor improvements were achieved, hardware constraints within the simulated rover limited significant gains.

**Physical Simulation Engine:**
CoppeliaSim offers four physics engines for dynamic simulation. All were tested, revealing broadly consistent results, except for the Bullet 2.78 module. With Bullet 2.78, objects (modeled as spheres) began rolling spontaneously despite a flat terrain and maximum friction coefficients, eventually accelerating uncontrollably (Fig. 10). Due to these anomalies, Bullet 2.78 was discarded. The Newton Dynamics engine was selected as it provided the most realistic interactions between rover components, soil surface, and fruit objects, consistent with agricultural field conditions [7].

**Differentiation of Colors in Image Pixels:**
Object detection relied heavily on RGB color coding within the rover's vision sensor. CoppeliaSim implements the RGB scale from 0 to 1. For fruit detection, the algorithm was tuned to trigger when the Red > 0.8 and Blue < 0.2. This ensured reliable detection of Guavas, which exhibit dominant red-orange tones, while filtering out bright, non-fruit objects (e.g., white surfaces). For the weed spraying task, detection conditions were adjusted as Red < 0.24, Green > 0.32, Blue < 0.34. This distinction allowed effective differentiation between fruits and green weeds, ensuring task-specific accuracy [8].

**Size of the Objects to Be Captured:**
Relying solely on color proved insufficient, as similarly colored non-target objects could

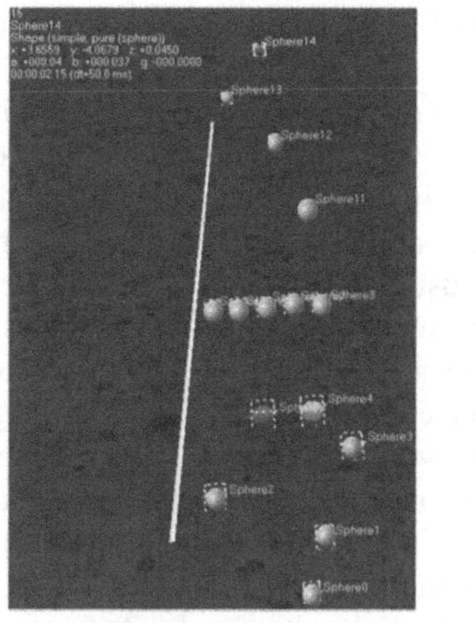

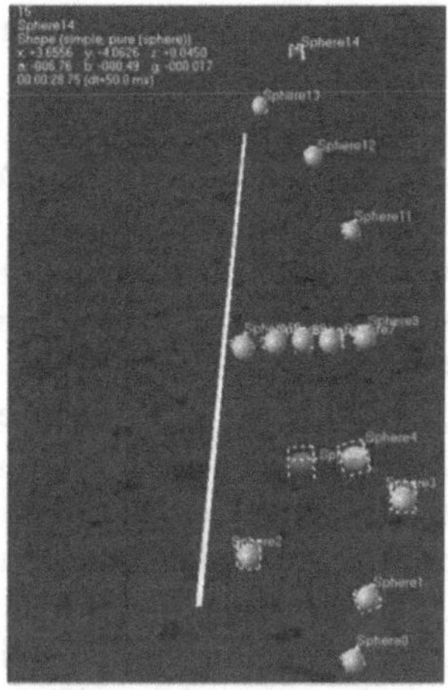

Duration: 0 min, 2 s    Duration: 0 min, 28 s

**Fig. 10.** Behavior of Objects Under the Dynamic Simulation Module

trigger detection. To improve robustness, a depth condition was incorporated. The vision sensor measured an average baseline depth of 0.9 cm in flat terrain. Objects with larger diameters reduced this value proportionally. The algorithm was therefore set to validate captures only when the measured depth was = 0.51 cm, ensuring the reliable detection of Guavas within the simulated size range (50–90 mm diameter). This condition was excluded from the weed spraying task, as weeds exhibit irregular and unpredictable dimensions in field condtions.

## 4 Conclusions

The global increase in food demand has driven the integration of advanced technologies into agriculture to improve productivity rates. Among these, robotics has emerged as a highly promising solution. Nevertheless, agricultural fields represent extremely dynamic and unstructured environments, making the design and deployment of robotic systems both complex and resource-intensive. Computational simulation offers an effective pathway to accelerate the development process by enabling rigorous testing prior to field deployment.

In this study, a robotic rover was simulated for orchard environments with the objective of testing algorithms for locomotion, localized spraying, and fallen fruit collection using a mechanical gripper. Field trials demonstrated satisfactory maneuver ability and displacement. However, difficulties were observed when transporting heavier cargo, such as stones or branches, due to rear wheel skidding and loss of constant speed. In contrast, the spraying system performed reliably without operational issues. From the simulations, several insights can be drawn. First, the use of simulation when real-world testing is constrained. Still, doubts remain about how closely simulated outcomes replicate real-world conditions. Factors such as terrain irregularities, inclinations, and varying soil characteristics may significantly impact performance, particularly with respect to operating speed and traction.

Image processing emerged as a key area of interest. While low-resolution imagery proved adequate during simulations, real-world validation is required to determine its impact on detection accuracy. Reliance solely on color gamut and depth analysis may cause ambiguities—such as misclassifying similarly colored objects (e.g., stones) as fruit—underscoring the need for more robust detection approaches. In terms of operation time, optimizing the joint and gripper execution parameters on a physical platform is expected to yield better performance than in simulation. Depth sensing, however, showed limited effectiveness for weed detection due to the minimal height of weeds and the irregularity of soil surfaces. Future work will involve validating the algorithms on the physical rover to evaluate the correspondence between simulated and real-world performance. Further research will focus on enhancing detection precision, advancing path-planning algorithms, and investigating multi-robot collaboration—such as integrating drones for aerial monitoring to identify high-density weed or fruit zones and enable prioritized interventions.

## References

1. Government of India, Economic Survey of India (2022)
2. FAO. State of Food and Agriculture 2022. Food and Agriculture Organization of the United Nations, Rome (2022)
3. ICAR. Vision 2050: Indian Council of Agricultural Research. New Delhi (2021)
4. Ministry of Agriculture & Farmers' Welfare. National Mission on Sustainable Agriculture (NMSA) Guidelines (2020)
5. Ministry of Agriculture & Farmers' Welfare. Sub-Mission on Agricultural Mechanization (SMAM) Report (2021)
6. Ministry of Agriculture. Digital Agriculture Mission 2021–2025: Roadmap Document, Government of India (2021)
7. Singh, G.: Agricultural mechanization status in India. Agricultural Mechanization in Asia, Africa and Latin America (2020)
8. Wolfert, S., et al.: Big Data in Smart Farming. Agricultural Systems (2017)
9. Akdogan, C., Özer, T., Oguz, Y.: Design and implementation of an AI-controlled spraying drone for agricultural applications using advanced image preprocessing techniques. Robot. Intell. Autom. 44, 131–151 (2024). https://doi.org/10.1108/RIA-05-2023-0068

# MARSHAL: Multimodal Analysis and Recognition of Social Media Hate Against LGBTQ+

Niharika Rana[1], Mohammad Salik Uddin[1], Deepawali Sharma[1](✉), and Aakash Singh[2]

[1] School of Computer Science Engineering and Technology (SCSET), Bennett University, Greater Noida 201310, India
Deepawali121@gmail.com

[2] Department of Computer Science, University of Delhi, Delhi 110007, India

**Abstract.** Social media has become an integral part of everyday life, people of all ages, genders, and backgrounds use it to communicate, share personal achievements, and express their opinions on varied topics. Unfortunately, some users target the vulnerable communities like the LGBTQ+ groups. The content subjects them to ridicule, harassment, and demeaning. To address this problem, we need computational models capable of identifying and flagging hateful content. While several approaches already exist for detecting anti-LGBTQ+ content in text, there is a growing need to extend these methods to multimodal data including images, audio, and short video clips. To address multimodal hate speech detection against LGBTQ+, we introduce MARSHAL, a benchmark dataset of short videos labeled as anti-LGBTQ+ or non-anti-LGBTQ+. Each video is annotated for text transcripts and captions, visual frames, and audio tracks. To detect anti-LGBT+ content, we propose a late fusion multimodal approach, which utilizes the strengths of the BERT, ResNet50 and YAMNet, all of them top-performing models in their respective modalities. Our proposed multimodal approach performed better than all the unimodal models across text, image, and audio data. The results show that combining these modalities makes the model more effective for automatically detecting anti-LGBTQ+ content and moves the research forward in this important area.

**Keywords:** Deep Learning · Fusion · Hate Speech · LGBTQ+ · Multimodal · Social Media Analysis

## 1 Introduction

The age of digital technology allows us to get immersed online on a million websites, communicate and interact on every unique social media platform known to man. Study shows about 1 in 3 internet minutes can be attributed to social media platforms which gets to 35.8% of 24 h online, 2.5 h on social media [29], shown in Fig. 1.


A. Shastri et al. (Eds.): IHCI 2025, LNCS 16437, pp. 215–227, 2026.
https://doi.org/10.1007/978-3-032-26352-0_18

**Fig. 1.** Time spent on social media vs other online activities.

Since the introduction of social media around 1997 [1], these platforms have deeply influenced society. Those who deviate from orthodox norms often face antagonization and alienation, as the challenge with social media lies within creating an inclusive community [4].

According to the study [2], one vital sector which still gets the brunt of the hatred, is the LGBTQ+ community. The LGBTQ [30] (also known as the LGBT, LGBTQ+, LGBTQIA+, or queer) is a community of individuals who do not conform to cultural norms around gender and/or sexuality. The term was adopted into mainstream in the 1990s, when it was finally known widely, thus non-threatening [3]. There still exists a plethora of people who troll on this marginalized community. Proof exists all over society and in the political sphere as shown in Fig. 2. Hatred is expressed both obviously and subliminally through sarcasm, memes, and misuse of objects associated with the queer community.

Algorithms have been made to create a safer environment [5], such as the Facebook algorithm [31] detecting hate content within billions of posts [8]. While text-based detection has been well explored [9, 10, 14, 15, 20, 28], recent advancements have expanded into multimodal datasets capturing audio and video alongside text [6, 7, 19, 33], an area with more room to explore.

**Fig. 2.** Comparative role of media types in spreading LGBTQ+ awareness.

Our annotated novel dataset and multimodal approach aim to classify short videos as either anti-LGBTQ+ or not, considering their complex nature. Our contributions include:

1. A novel dataset consisting of 1,054 short videos, each categorized as either "anti-LGBTQ+" or "non-anti-LGBTQ+."
2. Implementation of unimodal models for text, audio, and images separately to analyze each modality individually.
3. A proposed multimodal approach using a late fusion technique that combines text, audio, and visual modalities to detect hate against the LGBTQ+ community.

The rest of the paper is organized as follows. Section 2 reviews previous work. Section 3 describes the annotation schema. Section 4 presents the dataset and methodology. Section 5 discusses results. Section 6 concludes.

## 2 Related Work

Early studies [15–17, 19] predominantly focused on textual content using NLP techniques to classify social media posts, including homophobia and transphobia detection in YouTube comments [28, 38]. Popular datasets like HateBase [32] and Stormfront Corpora laid the groundwork for textual hate speech detection. HateBase offers a crowd-sourced multilingual lexicon of hate related terms instrumental in identifying hate speech across diverse languages. The Stormfront Corpora, has been pivotal in training machine learning models on explicitly hateful content, particularly through annotated textual data focusing on race and ethnicity-based hate [17]. Recent advancements have expanded into multimodal datasets, capturing the complexity of hateful expressions in memes, videos, and audio [9, 19].

HateXplain focuses on textual data and struggles capturing multimodal anti-queer sentiment. UCA framework addresses cross-modal alignment enhancing text-image interactions [15]. Study [16] detects homophobic hate speech using MBERT on the HATC dataset. Cross-modal approaches align text and audio representations [35], while integrating video, audio, and text enhances detection [36]. Vision-Language Models using ResNet and BERT frameworks mitigate hateful content [10, 24, 37]. Audio classification has been explored comparing ResNet, YAMNet, VGGish [22, 23]. Multimodal datasets like MIMIC highlight the importance of integrating text, images, and other modalities for hate speech detection [14].

Although, there are several studies that have focused on multimodal hate detection and textual homophobia/transphobia detection, a gap remains in identifying anti-LGBTQ+ content in multimodal contexts. To address this gap, a high-quality annotated dataset named MARSHAL, consisting of short videos is introduced, with unimodal models implemented separately for text, audio, and image, and a multimodal approach that combines the top-performing unimodal models using late fusion technique.

## 3 Annotation

Hate definitions vary, making labeling subjective [18, 25–27]. To ensure consistent labeling, we designed a comprehensive rule-based annotation schema covering all modalities of short videos, guiding annotators in categorizing anti-LGBTQ+ or non-anti-LGBTQ+ content based on explicit and implicit indicators of bias, hate, or disrespect.

Three independent annotators labeled the dataset following the below schema. To evaluate annotation reliability, the Fleiss' Kappa statistic was computed [34], yielding a value of 0.82, which indicates a strong level of agreement among annotators.

**Anti-LGBTQ+ Content Recognition.** A video is labeled as anti-LGBTQ+ if it contains one or more of the following elements:

- Presence of slurs, insults, or offensive nicknames directed at individuals based on their gender identity or sexual orientation. Content that ridicules individuals based on mannerisms, speech or idiolect, appearance or clothing, gender identity, or sexual orientation.
- Mocking or criticizing liberal, feminist, or gender-inclusive perspectives, or misrepresenting LGBTQ + rights movements. Using suggestive or misleading content to associate the community with perversion or immorality.
- Depicting indifference towards discriminatory acts against LGBTQ + individuals. Justifying violence, harassment, exclusion, or portraying individuals as involved in unethical, deviant, or criminal activities.

A video is labeled as *non-anti-LGBTQ+* if it does not contain any of the above features.

## 4 Dataset and Methodology

The MARSHAL (Multimodal Analysis and Recognition of Social Media Hate Against LGBTQ+) dataset serves as a foundational resource for identifying anti-LGBTQ+ material across online platform. This multimodal dataset contains Hindi-English code-mixed 1,054 labeled short videos, categorized as either anti-LGBTQ+ or non-anti-LGBTQ+.

1. Reddit: Covers diverse forums (subreddits) catering to specific communities and viewpoints. Extracted 787 videos, 787 audios, 787 captions, and 229 transcripts due to the uniform mix of neutral and hate content. Key communities ensuring varied perspectives: r/DankMemes, r/IndianDankMemes, r/Offensive_Memes, r/AreTheCisOk, r/TheRightCantMeme, r/PoliticalCompassMemes.
2. YouTube: Key source of long and short form video content. Scraped 222 videos across different channels and countries, extracting 222 audios, 222 captions, and 164 transcripts.
3. 9gag: A niche platform focused on humour and memes. Extracted 28 videos, 28 audios, 28 captions, and 13 transcripts to include varied content types.
4. Facebook: Features viral videos, memes, and user discussions. Extracted 15 videos, 15 audios, 15 captions, and 7 transcripts—limited due to Facebook's rapid hate content detection and deletion [31].
5. Misc: Around 2 videos, 2 audios, and no texts from Google image searches. These were included for their compelling novel format. The source websites contained no additional videos in these categories.

A key feature of the MARSHAL dataset is the balanced label distribution. Anti-LGBTQ+ content represents 45.6%, while non-anti-LGBTQ+ content accounts for 54.4%, as presented in Fig. 3.

The method of recognition lies within defining certain flexible rules that can ascertain hate from irrelevant topics. The models are fine-tuned to follow these rules and understand context-clues in all three modes to determine the hate in a nonlinear manner, as depicted in Fig. 4.

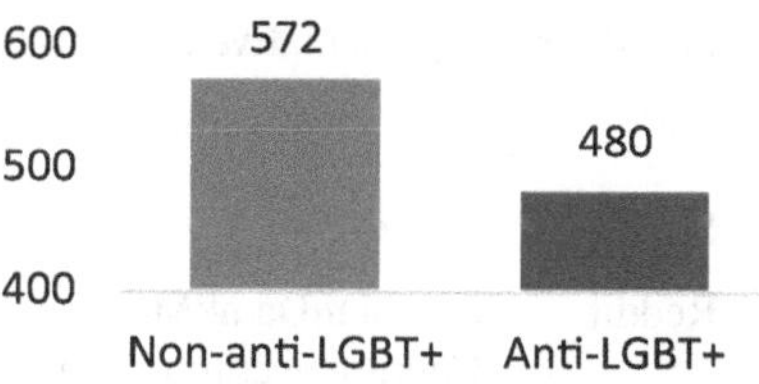


**Fig. 3.** Label Distribution

**Fig. 4.** MARSHAL Architecture diagram

### 4.1 Data Collection and Components

Data was collected from various social media platform using a Selenium-based web scraping pipeline. Hashtags (#transgender, #gay, #trans, etc.) identified relevant posts. Captions, post links, media URLs, and metadata (usernames, timestamps) were extracted. ASR tools generated transcripts from audio content, although incomplete coverage resulted from poor audio quality or unsupported formats. Ethics were integral to the dataset's curation. Usernames and identifiable metadata were anonymized or excluded to safeguard privacy. To overcome sampling biases, we scraped quota amounts of anti-LGBTQ+ content from various sites, then selected nearly equal non-anti-LGBTQ+ content from multiple Hindi and English-speaking geographies. By addressing imbalances and integrating diverse data types, provides a robust platform for training and evaluating multimodal hate detection algorithms for LGBTQ+ communities.

Each video is segmented into textual captions and transcripts, visual frames, and audio tracks for comprehensive analysis.

**Textual Features.** Captions accompanying media reflect linguistic diversity, incorporating slang, hashtags, and cultural references that can convey implicit or explicit anti-LGBTQ+ sentiments, or neutrality/support, as illustrated in Table 1. Transcripts were extracted using Automatic Speech Recognition (ASR); 414 out of 1,054 entries (39.3%) have transcripts, with limited coverage due to strong accents, background noise, and language mismatch with the ASR model.

**Visual Features.** Static images are extracted from videos by selecting keyframes at evenly spaced intervals (Fig. 5), capturing spatial and temporal features including facial expressions, objects, and context. Each frame is resized to standard resolution and normalized for consistency, enabling pattern detection.

**Table 1.** Sample from metadata CSV file - Representative captions and their corresponding labels with sources.

| Caption | Source | Context | Label |
|---|---|---|---|
| "another one!" | Reddit | (r/IndianDa nkMemes) Caption accompanying a meme, potentially sarcastic or dismissive in tone | Anti-LGBTQ+ |
| "Viral hizra dance" | Facebook | Caption paired with a video mocking a stereotypical portrayal, likely aimed at eliciting ridicule | Anti-LGBTQ+ |
| "I love minions Ã°Å¸Â¥Â°" | Reddit | Caption expressing a harmless or neutral interest in minions, not related to LGBTQ+ issues | Non-anti-LGBTQ+ |

**Auditory Features.** Auditory acoustics may suggest niche references pointing towards degradation; therefore, all three subsectors were selected. Audio is extracted from videos in.mp3 format for acoustic analysis, capturing features revealing content patterns.

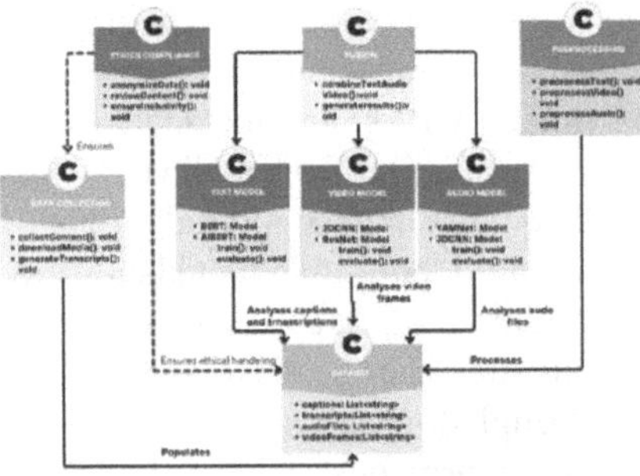


**Fig. 5.** Frame segmentation on videos "vid_69.mp4" and "vid_144.mp4"

## 4.2 Preprocessing

The dataset underwent extensive preprocessing. Textual and auditory models used an 80–20 split, while video models utilized a 60–40 split to accommodate computational demands of frame processing.

**Text Preprocessing:** Text data, including captions and transcripts, was tokenized using the BERT tokenizer. The labels were one-hot encoded to ensure numerical binary classification. Finetuned BERT models were used to generate high-dimensional textual embeddings.

**Video Preprocessing:** Videos were sampled at 16 evenly spaced frames to ensure consistent temporal coverage. All extracted frames were resized to 128 × 128 frame resolution (112 × 112 for ResNet50 specifically). Extracted frames were encoded using a ResNet-based 3D video model, creating compact visual embeddings.

**Audio Preprocessing:** Audio acoustics were extracted using the YAMNet model, generating 128-dimensional embeddings to capture acoustic nuances. Mel spectrograms were created as image representations of audio to capture acoustic features, as shown in Fig. 6. Images extracted were resized to 128 × 128 frame resolution.

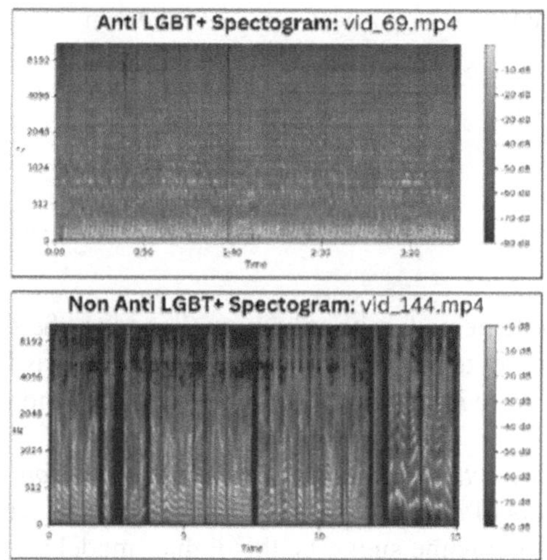


**Fig. 6.** Mel Spectrograms of the audio extracted from videos "vid_69.mp4" and "vid_144.mp4".

### 4.3 Models

Model selection was driven by three criteria: proven performance on multimodal hate speech detection [11, 14, 26], capability to handle code-mixed content, and computational efficiency for our 1,054-entry dataset.

Pre-trained models were prioritized to leverage transfer learning. Base hyperparameters are in Table 2, with detailed architectural justifications in respective subsections.

**Text Models.** BERT and ALBERT's multilingual uncased vocabulary (102 languages) and bidirectional context understanding make them suited for detecting nuanced hate speech relying on word relationships, sarcasm, and implicit context. Their attention mechanisms effectively capture Hindi-English code-mixed slurs and offensive terms, weighing word importance to also identify hate speech relying on subtle linguistic cues.

*BERT (Bidirectional Encoder Representations from Transformers).* The 'bertbaseuncased' model was used to accommodate the different code-mixed languages [20].

**Table 2.** Hyperparameter settings for each modality and the proposed model

| Hyperparameters | Models | | | |
|---|---|---|---|---|
| | Text | Video | Audio | Proposed |
| Test-Train Split Ratio | 80:20 | 60:40 | 80:20 | 60:40 |
| Epochs | 50 (with early stopping) | 50 (with early stopping) | 50 (with early stopping) | 50 (with early stopping) |
| Batch Size | 8 | 16 | 16 | 32 |
| Optimizer | Adam | Adam | Adam | Adam |
| Learning Rate | 1e-4 | 1e-4 | 1e-4 | 1e-4 |
| Activation Function | GELU | ReLU and Sigmoid for two respective dense layers | ReLU | ReLU and Sigmoid for two respective dense layers |

Early stopping was implemented, with minimum 3 epochs, the threshold of minimum change in accuracy was set to 0.07. The accuracy observed was 0.82 for captions. The same hyperparameters were implemented for transcriptions, and the accuracy observed was 0.83 [14, 16].

*ALBERT (A Lite Bidirectional Encoder Representations from Transformers).* Using BERT's hyperparameters (Table 2), ALBERT achieved 0.81 accuracy for captions and 0.70 for transcripts. As the name suggests, this lighter model trades some accuracy for speed through reduced parameters [14, 21].

**Video Models.** ResNet's residual learning addresses the vanishing gradient problem, extracting hierarchical features from low-level edges to high-level semantic concepts. Its ImageNet pre-training provides robust transfer learning for hate speech detection.

*3DCNN.* Using the frame sampling detailed in Sect. 4.1, the model used 2 convolutional layers with max pooling and batch normalization, followed by 2 dense layers (ReLU and sigmoid) with dropout, achieving 0.65 accuracy [11, 14].

*ResNet.* Leveraging ResNet50V2 with the sampling approach from Sect. 4.1, frames were resized to 112 × 112 and normalized. The architecture used time-distributed layers, Global Average Pooling 3D, and dense layers with ReLU and sigmoid activations, with frozen ResNet layers preserving pre-trained features, achieving 0.69 test accuracy [24].

**Audio Models.** Paralinguistic cues like mocking tones and derisive laughter convey hostility that transcripts alone miss. YAMNet's pre-training on AudioSet's 521 audio event classes provides acoustic understanding beyond speech recognition. Its depth-wise separable convolutions extract features from mel spectrograms including frequency patterns, temporal dynamics, and tonal variations indicative of derision. 3DCNN's versatile depth nature allowed comparison of auditory context relations and semantic deduction capabilities against YAMNet [22].

*3DCNN.* The model was fine-tuned with the Mel spectrogram images from audio files, applying the same architecture as the video 3DCNN (Sect. 4.2). With a depth of 10, the model achieved 0.65 accuracy [22].

*YAMNet.* Applied to 414 audio samples with a 1024 dense layer and 0.5 dropout, achieving 0.73 accuracy [23].

### 4.4 Proposed Model

The best performing models were integrated using late fusion with attention mechanisms (Fig. 7). Late fusion enables independent modality-specific feature development before integration, preventing single-modality dominance. BERT generates 768-dimensional text embeddings, ResNet50 produces 2048-dimensional visual features from 16 frames (Sect. 4.1), and YAMNet extracts 1024-dimensional acoustic embeddings. These concatenate into a unified 3840-dimensional representation, processed through dense layers (512 and 256 neurons) with ReLU activation and dropout (p = 0.3). The attention mechanism dynamically weights each modality per sample, handling cases where hate is explicit in one modality but subtle in others. The final sigmoid layer performs binary classification.

Early stopping (patience = 5 epochs, threshold = 0.01) prevents overfitting. Pre-trained models enable robust feature extraction despite modest dataset size, addressing cases where harmful intent is conveyed through combined signals that individually may appear innocuous but collectively constitute hate speech [12, 13].

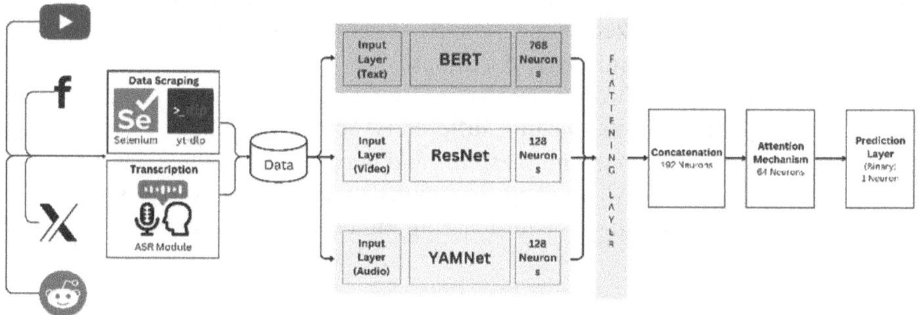


**Fig. 7.** MARSHAL Block Diagram

## 5 Results

Represented in Table 3, we compared the models as per modalities and based on certain evaluation metrics. "0" represents the class "Non-Anti-LGBTQ+ ", and "1" represents "Anti-LGBTQ + ".

**Table 3.** Comparative evaluation of modalities using performance metrics

| Modality | Model | Precision | | Recall | | Macro F1 | | Acc |
|---|---|---|---|---|---|---|---|---|
| | | **0** | **1** | **0** | **1** | **0** | **1** | |
| Text | | | | | | | | |
| (captions) | BERT | 0.74 | 0.96 | 0.97 | 0.69 | 0.84 | 0.8 | 0.82 |
| | ALBERT | 0.72 | 1 | 1 | 0.64 | 0.83 | 0.78 | 0.81 |
| Text | | | | | | | | |
| (translation) | BERT | 0.82 | 0.91 | 0.98 | 0.43 | 0.89 | 0.59 | 0.83 |
| | ALBERT | 0.77 | 0.11 | 0.88 | 0.06 | 0.82 | 0.07 | 0.7 |
| Video | ResNet50 | 0.72 | 0.66 | 0.71 | 0.67 | 0.72 | 0.67 | 0.69 |
| | 3DCNN | 0.7 | 0.52 | 0.77 | 0.43 | 0.74 | 0.47 | 0.65 |
| Audio | YAMNet | 0.71 | 0.77 | 0.86 | 0.56 | 0.78 | 0.65 | 0.73 |
| | 3DCNN | 0.77 | 0.22 | 0.78 | 0.21 | 0.78 | 0.22 | 0.65 |
| Multimodal | BERT + Res- | | | | | | | |
| Net50 + | | | | | | | | |
| YAMNet | 0.93 | 0.95 | 0.92 | 0.96 | 0.95 | 0.93 | 0.94 | |

Individual modality analysis reveals that models with richer architectures (BERT, YAMNet, ResNet-50) outperform lighter variants (ALBERT, 3DCNN) due to larger parameter sets enabling more complex pattern capture [20–22]. Table 3 shows that late fusion of these specialized models yields superior F1-scores and other metrics, confirming the benefits of combining modalities.

Our proposed model achieved 0.94 overall accuracy. This superior performance stems from capturing hate manifesting differently across modalities—text identifies explicit slurs, video detects mocking gestures and derogatory symbols, audio captures contemptuous tone and derisive prosody. Pre-trained models (YAMNet, ResNet-50) outperform 3DCNN by leveraging transfer learning rather than learning from scratch [23, 24].

## 6 Conclusion

This study presents a high-quality manually annotated dataset for detecting anti-lgbtq+ content in meme videos through a multimodal late fusion approach combining text, audio, and visual features. Each modality is processed through individual layers before merging, ensuring decisions based on holistic understanding rather than single-modality dominance. Bert outperforms albert in captions by 1.2% and transcripts by 18.5%, yamnet outperforms 3DCNN in audio by 12.3%, and resnet outperforms 3DCNN in video by 6.1%, all in terms of accuracy. The proposed multimodal model achieves 94% accuracy, representing an important advancement in hate speech detection against LGBTQ+ communities where context and intent manifest across multiple communication modalities.

**Data Availability.** The dataset is accessible at https://www.kaggle.com/datasets/salik03/marshal-anti-lgbt-content-detection-dataset.

## References

1. Dewing, M.: Social media: An introduction, vol. 1. Library of Parliament, Ottawa (2010)
2. Nadal, K.L.: A decade of microaggression research and LGBTQ communities: an introduction to the special issue. J. Homosex. **66**(10), 1309–1316 (2019)
3. Kehoe, J.: Anti-LGBTQ hate: an analysis of situational variables. J. Hate Stud. **16**, 21 (2020)
4. Dhiman, B.: Ethical issues and challenges in social media: a current scenario (2023)
5. Davidson, T., Warmsley, D., Macy, M., Weber, I.: Automated hate speech detection and the problem of offensive language. Proc. Int. AAAI Conf. Web Soc. Media **11**(1), 512–515 (2017). https://doi.org/10.1609/icwsm.v11i1.14955
6. Waseem, Z., Hovy, D.: Hateful symbols or hateful people? Predictive features for hate speech detection on Twitter. In: Proc. NAACL Student Res. Workshop, pp. 88–93 (2016)
7. Burnap, P., Williams, M.L.: 'Cyber hate speech on Twitter: an application of machine classification and statistical modeling for policy and decision making.' Policy Internet **7**(2), 223–242 (2015)
8. Rodríguez, A., Argueta C., Chen, Y.-L.: Automatic detection of hate speech on facebook using sentiment and emotion analysis. 2019 International Conference on Artificial Intelligence in Information and Communication (ICAIIC), Okinawa, Japan, pp. 169–174 (2019). https://doi.org/10.1109/ICAIIC.2019.8669073
9. Kumar, D., Kumar, N., Mishra, S.: QUARC: quaternion multi-modal fusion architecture for hate speech classification. In: 2021 IEEE International Conference on Big Data and Smart Computing (BigComp) (p. 346349). IEEE (2021)
10. Rana, A., Jha, S.: Emotion based hate speech detection using multimodal learning (2022). arXiv preprint arXiv:2202.06218
11. Wang, H., Yang, T.R., Naseem, U., Lee, R.K.W.: Multihateclip: a multilingual benchmark dataset for hateful video detection on youtube and bilibili. In: Proceedings of the 32nd ACM International Conference on Multimedia (pp. 7493–7502) (2024)
12. Yang, F., et al.: Exploring deep multimodal fusion of text and photo for hate speech classification. In: Proceedings of the Third Workshop on Abusive Language Online (pp. 11–18) (2019)
13. Mandal, A., Roy, G., Barman, A., Dutta, I., Naskar, S.K.: Attentive fusion: a transformer-based approach to multimodal hate speech detection (2024). arXiv preprint arXiv:2401.10653
14. Singh, A., Sharma, D., Singh, V.K.: MIMIC: misogyny identification in multimodal internet content in hindi-english code-mixed language. ACM Transactions on Asian and Low-Resource Language Information Processing (2024)
15. Yang, C., Zhu, F., Liu, Y., Han, J., Hu, S.: Uncertainty-aware cross-modal alignment for hate speech detection. In: Proceedings of the 2024 Joint International Conference on Computational Linguistics, Language Resources and Evaluation (LREC-COLING 2024), pp. 16973–16983, Torino, Italia. ELRA and ICCL (2024)
16. Karayiğit, H., Akdagli, A., Aci, Ç.İ: Homophobic and hate speech detection using multilingual-bert model on turkish social media. Inf. Technol. Control **51**(2), 356–375 (2022)
17. Tsunokai, G.T., McGrath, A.R.: Virtual Hate Communities in the 21st Century. In: Warburton, S., Hatzipanagos, S. (eds.) Handbook of Research on Practices and Outcomes in Virtual Worlds and Environments. Hershey, PA: IGI Global, p. 20 (2012)

18. Hietanen, M., Eddebo, J.: Towards a definition of hate speech—With a focus on online contexts. J. Commun. Inq. **47**(4), 440–458 (2023)
19. Watanabe, H., Bouazizi, M., Ohtsuki, T.: Hate speech on twitter: a pragmatic approach to collect hateful and offensive expressions and perform hate speech detection. IEEE Access **6**, 13825–13835 (2018)
20. Devlin, J.: Bert: Pre-training of deep bidirectional transformers for language understanding. arXiv preprint arXiv:1810.04805.21. Jin, D., Jin, Z., Zhou, J.T., Szolovits, P., 2020, April. Is bert really robust? a strong baseline for natural language attack on text classification and entailment. In Proceedings of the AAAI conference on artificial intelligence (Vol. 34, No. 05, pp. 8018–8025) (2018)
21. Choi, H., Kim, J., Joe, S., Gwon, Y.: Evaluation of bert and albert sentence embedding performance on downstream nlp tasks. In: 2020 25th International Conference on Pattern Recognition (ICPR) (pp. 5482–5487). IEEE (2021)
22. Tsalera, E., Papadakis, A., Samarakou, M.: Comparison of pre-trained CNNs for audio classification using transfer learning. J. Sens. Actuator Netw. **10**(4), 72 (2021)
23. Mohino-Herranz, et al.: «Implementing transfer learning for sound event classification using the realised audio database», en Measurement: Sensors. Elsevier Ltd. Disponible en (2025). https://doi.org/10.1016/J.MEASEN.2024.101711
24. Ren, J.: Multimodal sentiment analysis based on BERT and ResNet. (2024). arXiv preprint arXiv:2412.03625
25. Sharma, D., Singh, A., Singh, V.K.: Thar-targeted hate speech against religion: a high-quality hindi-english code-mixed dataset with the application of deep learning models for automatic detection. ACM Transactions on Asian and Low-Resource Language Information Processing (2024)
26. Sharma, D., Singh, V.K., Gupta, V.: TABHATE: a target-based hate speech detection dataset in Hindi. Soc. Netw. Anal. Min. **14**(1), 190 (2024)
27. Sharma, D., Nath, T., Gupta, V., Singh, V.K.: Hate speech detection research in south asian languages: a survey of tasks, datasets and methods. ACM Trans. Asian Low-Resource Lang. Inf. Process. **24**(3), 1–44 (2025)
28. Sharma, D., Gupta, V., Singh, V.K.: Detection of homophobia & transphobia in Malayalam and Tamil: exploring deep learning methods. In: International Conference on Advanced Network Technologies and Intelligent Computing (pp. 217–226). Cham, Springer Nature Switzerland (2022)
29. DataReportal. 'Digital 2024 Deep Dive: The Time We Spend on Social Media', DataReportal. (Accessed: [9th Dec 2024]) (2024)
30. Merriam-Webster. (n.d.). LGBTQ. In Merriam-Webster.com dictionary. Retrieved 9 December 2024. https://www.merriam-webster.com/dictionary/LGBTQ
31. Meta. Hate speech. In: Facebook Community Standards. Retrieved 10 December 2024. https://transparency.fb.com/policies/community-standards/hate-speech/
32. Odegiber. HateSpeech18 [Dataset]. In: Hugging Face Datasets. Retrieved 10 December 2024. https://huggingface.co/datasets/Odegiber/hate_speech18
33. HowSociable.LGBT survey report. HowSociable Blog. Retrieved 13 December 2024. https://howsociable.com/blog/lgbt-survey-report/
34. Fleiss, J.L.: Measuring nominal scale agreement among many raters. Psychol. Bull. **76**(5), 378 (1971)
35. Ranjan, R., Ayinala, L., Vatsa, M., Singh, R.: Multimodal Zero-Shot Framework for Deepfake Hate Speech Detection in Low-Resource Languages (2025). arXiv preprint arXiv:2506.08372
36. Céspedes-Sarrias, B., Collado-Capell, C., Rodenas-Ruiz, P., Hrynenko, O., Cavallaro, A.: MM-HSD: Multi-Modal Hate Speech Detection in Videos (2025). arXiv preprint arXiv:2508.20546

37. Van, M.H., Wu, X.: Detecting and Mitigating Hateful Content in Multimodal Memes with Vision-Language Models (2025). arXiv preprint arXiv:2505.00150
38. Maimaitituoheti, A.: ABLIMET@ LT-EDI-ACL2022: a roberta based approach for homophobia/transphobia detection in social media. In: Proceedings of the Second Workshop on Language Technology for Equality, Diversity and Inclusion (pp. 155–160) (2022)

# Edge AI for Brain Tumor Diagnosis with Hardware-Accelerated Ensemble Deep Learning on Google Coral Dev Board and Xilinx PYNQ-ZU

Prashant Singh(✉), Kusum Lata, and Sandeep Saini

Department of Electronics and Communication Engineering,The LNM Institute of Information Technology, Jaipur, India
{21pec002,kusum,sandeep.saini}@lnmiit.ac.in

**Abstract.** This is, of course, the most essential basis of precise and timely brain tumor classification. Traditional diagnostic pipelines are burdened by heavy computation requirements, latency, and poor accessibility in resource-constrained environments. In this paper, we propose a ResNet50-DenseNet169-InceptionV3-based hardware-accelerated ensemble deep learning framework for the classification of brain tumor in multiple classes. The framework employs stratified 3-fold, 5-fold, and 7-fold cross-validation to ensure robust generalization, while test-time augmentation (TTA) enhances inference reliability. To further bridge the gap between research and clinical use, optimized ensemble models are deployed on both Google Coral Edge TPU and Xilinx PYNQ-ZU, achieving real-time inference with ultralow power consumption and minimal latency. Experimental evaluations on brain MRI datasets demonstrate the state-of-the-art accuracy of 99.47%, with high precision, recall, and F1-score consistently observed for all classes of tumors. These results confirm that the system presented here is able to provide scalable, reliable, and energy-efficient diagnostic support in hospitals and remote clinics, as well as in mobile healthcare units. We further improve the pathway towards next-generation intelligent medical imaging by unifying ensemble deep learning with edge AI accelerators.

**Keywords:** Brain Tumor Classification · Ensemble Learning · Test-Time Augmentation · Cross-Validation · Coral Dev Board · PYNQ-ZU

## 1 Introduction

Brain tumors are one of the most dangerous types of neurological disorders. Their early and exact diagnosis is very important regarding choices of treatments, increasing the possibility of a good prognosis, and decreasing mortality. Some brain tumors can have very tragic effects on cognitive and motor functions, depending on their type, location, and stage, while long advanced stages may


A. Shastri et al. (Eds.): IHCI 2025, LNCS 16437, pp. 228–240, 2026.
https://doi.org/10.1007/978-3-032-26352-0_19

destroy everything irreversibly and result in death. Because that is the case, the demand for effective and available means of diagnosis is never as urgent as it is today [1,2].

In the recent past, deep learning with medical imaging has seen high-accuracy classification and segmentation capabilities. The CNNs have reached state-of-the-art performance in many application tasks such as tumor detection, classification of disease subtypes, or organ segmentation. As much as these models have achieved impressive results, these tend to be computationally intensive and require a high-end GPU for real-time inference, thus being unsuitable for resource-constrained settings like rural healthcare facilities or portable diagnostic units or point-of-care environments.

In this regard, this work tries to fill this gap with a robust and efficient solution by leveraging ensemble deep learning and edge AI deployment. Herein, we proposed a multi-model ensemble of three well-known CNN architectures, namely ResNet50, DenseNet169, and InceptionV3, to improve the classification by architectural diversity. Each model is trained and evaluated on stratified k-fold cross-validation (k = 3, 5, 7) to ensure generalization across diverse datasets. Furthermore, we have implemented TTA to decrease the prediction variance and improve the model reliability under unseen conditions.

To render the deployment of models practical and accessible, we port the optimized ensemble on both the edge AI devices: Coral Dev Board and PYNQ-ZU, designed for low-latency inference. The Coral Dev Board uses a TPU to enable real-time classification of brain MRI images with minimal latency ( 30 ms per image) and low power consumption; hence, this is well-suited for decentralized clinical setups [3,4]. On the parallel, PYNQ-ZU has an FPGA acceleration of the Xilinx Zynq UltraScale+ MPSoC, which enables hardware-level parallelism and also allows custom pipelines for deep learning workloads. Thus, these platforms show the scalability, real-time deployment, and energy efficiency of brain tumor classification models in various healthcare environments, ranging from portable point-of-care devices to high-performance embedded systems [5].

This paper has been successful in demonstrating that the integration of ensemble learning coupled with test-time augmentation and edge-based deployment offers a strong paradigm for brain tumor classification that, though accurate-attaining a maximum of 99.61% accuracy-is also deployable within practical medical settings where there is a scarcity of computational resources.

The structure of the paper is organization as follows: Sect. 2 reviews prior research on deep learning methods for brain tumor classification. Section 3 describes the dataset, preprocessing, model design, and ensemble methodology. Section 4 outlines the deployment on the Coral Dev Board and PYNQ-ZU platforms. Section 5 reports the experimental findings and performance evaluation. Section 6 discusses practical implications and limitations; Sect. 7 summarizes the work and hence highlights the future research directions.

## 2 Literature Review

Deep learning has become a very powerful tool in medical imagery, and its application to brain tumor detection has grown rapidly in the last years. MRI is the major non-invasive modality for the visualization of brain structures because of its superior soft-tissue contrast. However, manual interpretation is burdened by the high complexity and heterogeneity of tumor morphology, thus motivating the resorting to AI-driven diagnostic tools.

Some of them try to improve the accuracy of classification by conducting ensemble learning and optimizing their models. Çetin and Kaya [6] propose a novel ensemble framework with multiple CNNs, whose weightings are optimized via PSO to achieve accuracies exceeding 99% on three datasets. Similarly, Celik et al. [7] introduced an ensemble attention mechanism combining MobileNetV3 and EfficientNetB7 to extract both local and global features, resulting in high classification performance on BraTS and Figshare datasets.

To address image quality issues, Asiri et al. [8] developed a dual-module approach integrating adaptive Wiener filtering, independent component analysis, and SVM-based classification, achieving 98.9% accuracy and significantly faster inference time . In parallel, Bogacsovics et al. [9] emphasized diversity in ensemble learning, introducing histogram loss to improve inter-model variability and robustness in tumor classification tasks.

In the realm of privacy preservation and deployment on edge devices, Lata et al. [10] proposed secure CNN-based systems integrating AES-128 encryption and PBKDF2 for protecting patient data during inference, deployed on both web applications and Xilinx Kria KV260 FPGAs. These systems demonstrated high classification accuracy up to 99.92% while ensuring confidentiality in smart healthcare settings.

To overcome resource limitations in edge computing, Manor and Greenberg [11] developed a hardware-software codesign involving custom NPUs for TensorFlow Lite for Microcontrollers (TFLM), achieving up to 724 × speedup for ML inference on microcontrollers, thus supporting real-time execution of quantized, pruned neural networks.Surantha and Sutisna [12] offered a comprehensive overview of deploying AI on edge platforms like Jetson and Raspberry Pi, discussing challenges such as quantization, hardware-aware model compression, and federated learning. They introduced the Edge-AI Deployment Score (EADS) as a performance metric to evaluate trade-offs between accuracy, latency, energy, and privacy.

## 3 Methodology

The proposed architecture integrates a complete end-to-end pipeline for automated brain tumor classification, as shown in Fig. 1. Starting from raw MRI scans, the dataset undergoes preprocessing and K-fold cross-validation to ensure statistical reliability. Deep learning models, including InceptionV3, DenseNet169, and ResNet50, are trained and ensembled to enhance classification accuracy across four categories: glioma, meningioma, pituitary, and no tumor. Robustness is further improved through TTA and detailed evaluation using performance

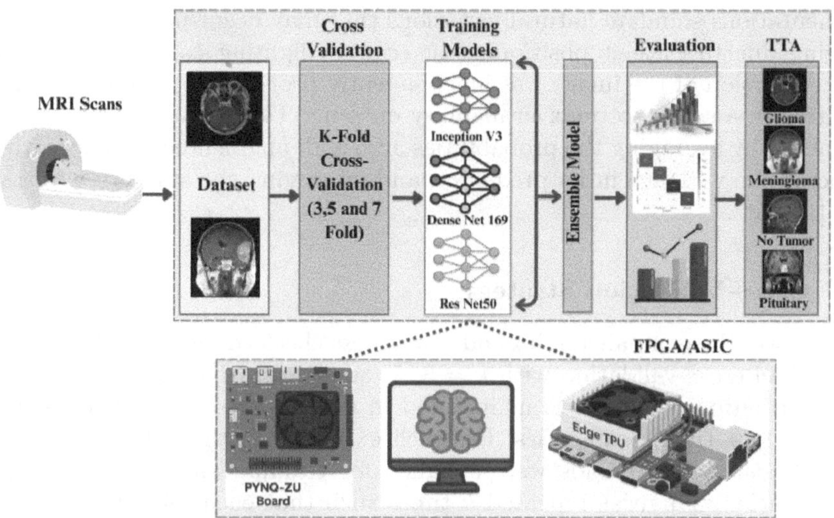


**Fig. 1.** End-to-end framework for multiclass brain tumor classification and real-time FPGA/ASIC deployment.

metrics and visualizations. To facilitate real-time clinical applicability, the optimized model is mapped onto FPGA/ASIC platforms such as PYNQ-ZU and Coral dev board, ensuring low-latency, energy-efficient deployment suitable for point-of-care diagnosis.

### 3.1 Dataset and Preprocessing

In this work, we employed a publicly available Brain Tumor MRI dataset containing 7,023 T1-weighted contrast-enhanced scans categorized into four groups: Glioma, Meningioma, Pituitary, and No Tumor. The dataset was compiled from multiple open repositories, including Figshare, SARTAJ, and Br35H, thereby covering a wide range of imaging conditions such as variations in tumor dimensions, anatomical regions, contrast levels, and acquisition quality. This heterogeneity makes it highly suitable for building and assessing deep learning models aimed at reliable tumor classification.

All the scans have been given in 2D axial orientation with various resolutions. To keep the process of model training standard, each image was changed in size to $224 \times 224$ pixels, its intensity was normalized to be within [0,1], and it went through basic cropping to cut out the irrelevant background and skull areas [13].

### 3.2 Test-Time Augmentation (TTA)

We next augmented our model's reliability and flexibility at inference by incorporating test-time data augmentation. In this approach, each input MRI image was subjected to five deterministic augmentation transformations, including horizontal and vertical flips, minor rotational shifts, and brightness scaling. These augmentations simulate natural variations that may occur in real-world medical imaging due to patient positioning or scanner lighting conditions. Each augmented version of the image was independently processed by the trained model, resulting in a set of softmax probability outputs. The final prediction was then computed by averaging the probabilities across all augmented instances, thereby reducing the variance in its prediction and improving the stability of classification [14,15].

### 3.3 Cross-Validation Strategy

We perform the generalizability and robustness checks of our models using stratified $k$-fold cross-validation with $k = 3$, 5, and 7. Stratification made sure that the distribution of classes is maintained in every fold so that there is balance in every four tumor categories. For each experiment, the dataset was divided into $k$ subsets; $k - 1$ folds were assigned for training and the remaining fold for validation. This was repeated $k$ times such that each fold once served as a validation set. The final performance, measured using accuracy, precision, recall, and F1-score, was reported as the average across all folds [16].

### 3.4 Model Architectures

Here, a proposed ensemble deep learning framework for classification was based on three state-of-the-art CNN architectures: ResNet50, DenseNet169, and InceptionV3. These are selected because of their complementary design philosophies and due to their brilliant individual performances in the medical image classification tasks.

- **ResNet50** follows residual learning using identity skip connections, which provides an effective training of deeper networks by solving vanishing gradients and allowing the convergence of its optimization.
- **DenseNet169** relies on dense connectivity where every layer is fed by all previous layers. It leads to feature reuse, improved gradient flow, and reduced total number of parameters.
- **InceptionV3** Utilizes multi-scale convolution filters in its inception modules to find the hierarchical features of different spatial scales, which is very useful in finding tumors of variable sizes and appearances.

To maintain architectural consistency, the final layers of each model were adapted to include a Global Average Pooling (GAP) layer followed by a fully connected dense layer with softmax activation for four-class classification.

### 3.5 Ensemble Strategy

To further improve classification performance and reduce the risk of individual model bias, we adopted an ensemble voting strategy. Specifically, after obtaining predictions from each of the three models—ResNet50, DenseNet169, and

InceptionV3—we computed the average of their softmax output probabilities for each test sample. This probabilistic averaging effectively combines the strengths of each architecture and mitigates their individual weaknesses. Formally, the final class probabilities for a given image were calculated as the mean across the softmax outputs from all models. The class with the highest averaged probability was then selected as the predicted label. This ensemble approach improves generalization and robustness, particularly in challenging or ambiguous samples, leading to more stable and accurate results in all cross-validation folds [17].

### 3.6 Evaluation Metrics

The performance of the proposed models was assessed using widely adopted classification metrics, defined as follows:

- **Accuracy:** Represents the proportion of correctly classified samples out of the total number of samples.
- **Precision:** Denotes the fraction of true positive predictions among all instances predicted as positive.
- **Recall (Sensitivity):** Indicates the fraction of true positives identified correctly out of all actual positive cases.
- **F1-Score:** Calculated as the harmonic mean of precision and recall, providing a balanced measure of both.

$$\text{Accuracy} = \frac{TP + TN}{TP + TN + FP + FN} \tag{1}$$

$$\text{Precision} = \frac{TP}{TP + FP} \tag{2}$$

$$\text{Recall} = \frac{TP}{TP + FN} \tag{3}$$

$$\text{F1 Score} = 2 \times \frac{\text{Precision} \times \text{Recall}}{\text{Precision} + \text{Recall}} \tag{4}$$

**Where:**

$TP$ True Positives
$TN$ True Negatives
$FP$ False Positives
$FN$ False Negatives

These metrics were computed for each class and macro-averaged to obtain an overall performance assessment for the multi-class classification task.

### 3.7 Hardware Deployment

The trained model was deployed on the Coral Dev Board, which features a quad-core ARM Cortex-A53 processor and an Edge TPU for fast, low-power inference. A lightweight Flask web interface was hosted on the board to allow real-time image upload and classification. The trained model, saved in .h5 format, was first converted to TensorFlow SavedModel format, then to a quantized .tflite file using post-training quantization to ensure Edge TPU compatibility. The final .tflite model was compiled with the Edge TPU Compiler and deployed on the device, enabling efficient, real-time tumor classification at the edge.

### 3.8 Web Interface

A light-weight Flask app was run on the Coral Dev Board and hosted at its local IP address. The interface was also made secure with HTTPS and correct access control permissions to make sure of secure communication. The brain MRI images can be uploaded by users from any computer device connected to the same local network or, if configured with port forwarding and firewall rules, from any remote network. The uploaded image is processed in real-time by the Edge TPU, and the predicted tumor class label is presented immediately through the web interface, facilitating rapid, secure, and accessible diagnosis within edge or clinical environments.

**Table 1.** Performance metrics for different folds.

| Fold | Macro Prec. | Macro Rec. | Macro F1 | Acc. (%) |
|---|---|---|---|---|
| 3 | 0.9863 | 0.9861 | 0.9862 | 98.65 |
| 5 | 0.9902 | 0.9898 | 0.9900 | 99.03 |
| 7 | 0.9946 | 0.9947 | 0.9946 | 99.61 |

**Table 2.** Class-wise performance metrics for Folds 3, 5, and 7.

| Class | Fold 3 | | | Fold 5 | | | Fold 7 | | |
|---|---|---|---|---|---|---|---|---|---|
| | Prec. | Recall | F1-Score | Prec. | Recall | F1-Score | Prec. | Recall | F1-Score |
| Glioma | 98.95 | 98.52 | 98.73 | 99.01 | 99.01 | 99.01 | 99.63 | 99.45 | 99.54 |
| Meningioma | 97.92 | 97.45 | 97.69 | 98.05 | 97.81 | 97.93 | 99.21 | 99.09 | 99.15 |
| No Tumor | 99.00 | 99.15 | 99.07 | 99.01 | 100 | 99.50 | 99.85 | 99.80 | 99.82 |
| Pituitary | 98.64 | 99.32 | 98.98 | 100 | 99.09 | 99.54 | 99.15 | 99.49 | 99.32 |

## 4 Results and Analysis

The suggested ensemble model was rigorously evaluated by means of stratified 3, 5, and 7-fold cross-validation. This technique not only eliminates the possibility of sampling bias but also ensures reliable performance assessment through various data splits. The numerical outcomes, shown in Table 1, display consistent enhancements along with the increase in the number of folds. Especially, the ensemble obtained a macro F1-score of 98.62% with 3-way validation, which then rose to 99.00% with 5-way, and finally reached a peak of 99.46% under 7-way validation. The continuous improvement indicates that the model has become more generalizable and stable when tested with finer data divides.

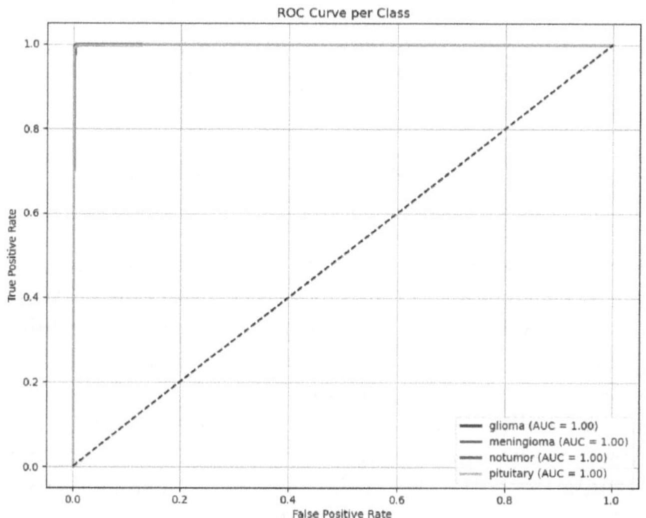


**Fig. 2.** ROC curves for each tumor class.

Table 2 shows a class-wise performance breakdown for all folds. The No Tumor class performed almost perfect, with precision and recall being greater than 99.8 in both the 5-fold and 7-fold cases, reflecting the model's strength in eliminating false positives. For the Glioma and Meningioma classes, precision and recall both increased consistently across folds, showing the ensemble's ability to distinguish well between closely related discriminative features. In a similar vein, the Pituitary class regularly demonstrated high F1-scores in all folds, confirming the well-balanced performance of the presented method across tumor types.

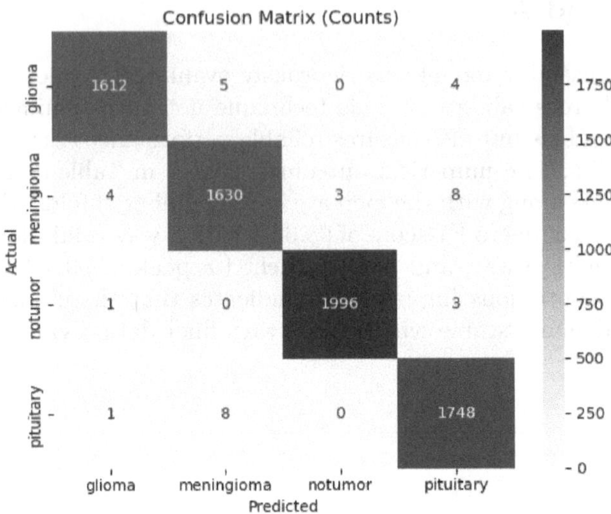


**Fig. 3.** Confusion matrix of the ensemble model.

The robustness of the system is further supported by Receiver Operating Characteristic (ROC) analysis. As shown in Fig. 2, all classes attained an Area Under the Curve (AUC) of 1.0, indicating exceptional discriminative ability. The confusion matrix in Fig. 3 corroborates these findings, with only minimal misclassifications observed across the four classes. Furthermore, the training and validation curves illustrated in Fig. 4 demonstrate rapid convergence with minimal overfitting. Validation accuracy closely follows training accuracy, while validation loss stabilizes after the initial epochs, confirming strong generalization capacity. Overall, the experimental findings confirm the effectiveness of the proposed ensemble deep learning framework for brain tumor multi-class classification. The combination of high accuracy, precision, recall, and F1-scores underscores the reliability of the model for real-world diagnostic applications. Importantly, when deployed on Google Coral Edge TPU and Xilinx PYNQ-ZU, the framework achieved real-time inference with negligible latency and low power consumption, thereby validating its suitability for resource-constrained medical environments, remote diagnostics, and mobile healthcare platforms.

**Table 3.** Evaluation of alternative deep learning methods for brain tumor detection

| Study | Method | Accuracy | Precision | Recall | F1-Score |
|---|---|---|---|---|---|
| [18] | Pre-trained ResNet mixed convolution spatiospatial | 96.98 | – | – | 93.45 |
| [19] | Xception | 99.52 | 95.5 | – | 94.91 |
| [20] | VGG16 + Custom Attention + Grad-CAM | 99.00 | 98.97 | 98.94 | 98.95 |
| Proposed | Ensemble | 99.61 | 99.46 | 99.47 | 99.46 |

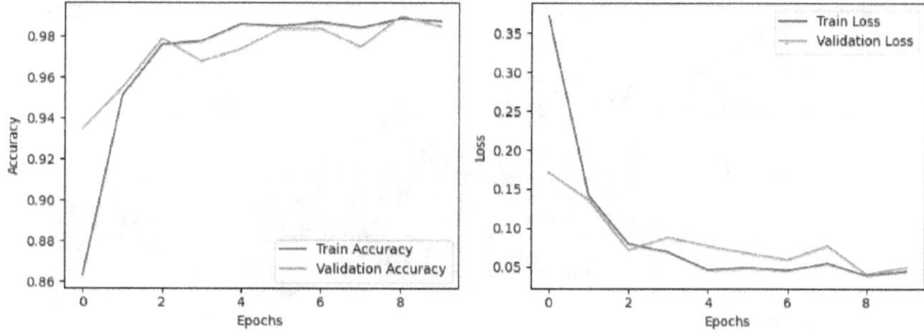


**Fig. 4.** Training and validation accuracy/loss curves for the 7-fold setting, demonstrating rapid convergence and minimal overfitting.

Table 3 shows a comparison of existing methods with the proposed ensemble model. While ResNet [18], Xception [19], and VGG16 with custom attention and Grad-CAM [20] achieved strong performance, the proposed ensemble outperformed all with the highest accuracy 99.61%, precision, recall, and F1-score 99.46%.

## 5 Hardware Implementation

The proposed brain tumor classification framework was deployed and evaluated on two edge hardware platforms: the Pynq ZU FPGA board and the Coral Dev Board with Edge TPU. These platforms were selected to highlight the performance trade-offs between FPGA-based reconfigurable hardware and ASIC-based accelerators for real-time medical image analysis (Table 4).

**Table 4.** Comparison of prediction results on Coral Dev Board and Pynq ZU.

| Image | Prediction | Coral Dev Board | | | Pynq ZU | | |
|---|---|---|---|---|---|---|---|
| | | Prediction (%) | Time (s) | Power (mW) | Prediction (%) | Time (s) | Power (mW) |
| Image 1 | Glioma | 72.66 | 3.412 | 2930 | 83.43 | 5.412 | 1750 |
| Image 2 | Meningioma | 91.00 | 3.380 | 3032 | 99.61 | 5.360 | 1746 |
| Image 3 | No Tumor | 97.32 | 3.270 | 3130 | 98.13 | 4.890 | 1769 |
| Image 4 | Pituitary | 98.63 | 3.423 | 2975 | 97.24 | 5.610 | 1748 |

On the Pynq ZU, the trained models were exported in the `.h5` format, converted into quantized `.tflite` models, and deployed using the FPGA's heterogeneous processing architecture. The Pynq ZU leveraged its programmable logic and ARM cores to provide energy-efficient inference with reduced thermal footprint, making it suitable for long-duration clinical deployments (Fig. 5).

**Fig. 5.** Client-server architecture for real-time brain tumor classification.

**Table 5.** Comparison of FPGA/Edge AI implementations with the proposed work.

| References | Methodology | Hardware Platform | Power (W) | Accuracy | Dataset |
|---|---|---|---|---|---|
| [21] | VGG16 | PYNQ-ZU FPGA | 5–7 | 97% | 1733 samples, 4 classes |
| [22] | SGWT, LGBM | PYNQ-ZU FPGA | 6–8 | 99.70% | MRI, 3 classes |
| [23] | CNN | PYNQ-Z2 | 1.4 | 94.11% | 1380 ultrasound scans |
| Proposed Work | Ensemble | Coral Dev Board | 3.3 | 97.32% | 7023 samples, 4 classes |
| | | PYNQ-ZU FPGA | 1.74 | 99.61% | 7023 samples, 4 classes |

For the Coral Dev Board, the trained models were similarly converted to quantized `.tflite` format and compiled using the Edge TPU Compiler. Deployment was carried out on the Coral Dev Board running Mendel Linux, where the Edge TPU offered dedicated hardware acceleration for low-latency inference.

Experimental results show that the Coral Dev Board achieved faster predictions (3.3 s) but at a higher power consumption of around 3000 mW. In contrast, the Pynq ZU maintained superior energy efficiency (1750 mW) with slightly higher inference times (5.3 s). These findings emphasize a clear trade-off: the Coral Dev Board is more appropriate for latency-critical edge applications, whereas the Pynq ZU is better suited for sustained, energy-aware clinical workflows.

Table 5 compares prior FPGA-based implementations with the proposed work. While existing methods achieved 94–99.7% accuracy with power usage ranging from 1.4–8 W, the proposed ensemble framework attains 99.61% accuracy on a larger dataset with only 1.74 W on PYNQ-ZU FPGA, demonstrating superior accuracy-efficiency tradeoff.

## 6 Conclusion

The proposed ensemble deep learning framework, integrating ResNet50, DenseNet169, and InceptionV3, achieved up to 99.61% accuracy with high precision, recall, and F1-scores, ensuring robust brain tumor classification. Deployment on Coral Dev Board and PYNQ-ZU demonstrated real-time, energy-efficient performance, making the system suitable for clinical and mobile healthcare environments. This work highlights the potential of edge AI with ensemble learning to deliver scalable and reliable diagnostic support in resource-constrained settings.

## References


1. Tehsin, S., Nasir, I.M., Damaševičius, R., Maskeliūnas, R.: DaSAM: disease and spatial attention module-based explainable model for brain tumor detection (2024). https://doi.org/10.3390/bdcc8090097
2. Kaushik, P., Chopra, Y., Kajla, A., Poonia, M., Khan, A., Yadav, D.: AI-powered dermatology: achieving dermatologist-grade skin cancer classification (2024). https://doi.org/10.1109/IATMSI60426.2024.10502664
3. Kljucaric, L., George, A.D.: Deep learning inferencing with high-performance hardware accelerators (2023). https://doi.org/10.1145/3594221
4. Lata, K., Singh, P., Saini, S., Cenkeramaddi, L.R.: Deep learning-based brain tumor detection in privacy-preserving smart health care systems (2024). https://doi.org/10.1109/ACCESS.2024.3456599
5. Singh, P., Lata, K., Gupta, Y., Sachdeva, G., Saini, S.: Enhancing privacy-preserving brain tumor detection in medical cyber-physical systems through deep learning algorithms (2023). https://doi.org/10.1109/iSES58672.2023.00045
6. Çetin-Kaya, Y., Kaya, M.: A novel ensemble framework for multi-classification of brain tumors using magnetic resonance imaging (2024). https://doi.org/10.3390/diagnostics14040383
7. Celik, F., Celik, K., Celik, A.: Enhancing brain tumor classification through ensemble attention mechanism (2024). https://doi.org/10.1038/s41598-024-73803-z
8. Asiri, A.A., Soomro, T.A., Shah, A.A., Pogrebna, G., Irfan, M., Alqahtani, S.: Optimized brain tumor detection: a dual-module approach for MRI image enhancement and tumor classification (2024). https://doi.org/10.1109/ACCESS.2024.3379136
9. Bogacsovics, G., Harangi, B., Hajdu, A.: Developing diverse ensemble architectures for automatic brain tumor classification (2024). https://doi.org/10.1007/s11042-024-19657-z
10. Lata, K., Singh, P., Saini, S., Cenkeramaddi, L.R.: Privacy-preserving brain tumor detection using FPGA-accelerated deep learning on Kria KV260 for smart healthcare (2025). https://doi.org/10.1016/j.cmpbup.2025.100205
11. Manor, E., Greenberg, S.: Custom hardware inference accelerator for tensorflow lite for microcontrollers (2022). https://doi.org/10.1109/ACCESS.2022.3189776
12. Surantha, N., Sutisna, N.: Key considerations for real-time object recognition on edge computing devices (2025). https://doi.org/10.3390/app15137533
13. Nickparvar, M.: Brain Tumor MRI Dataset. Kaggle (2024). https://doi.org/10.5281/zenodo.12735702
14. Ravishankar, H., Sudhakar, P., Yalavarthy, P.K.: TTA-FM: patient-specific test-time adaptation using foundation models for improved prostate segmentation in magnetic resonance images (2024). https://doi.org/10.1109/ISBI56570.2024.10635168
15. Wang, Z., et al.: Test-time adaptation via orthogonal meta-learning for medical imaging (2025). https://doi.org/10.1109/TRPMS.2024.3462542
16. Ghorbian, M., Ghorbian, S., Ghobaei-arani, M.: A comprehensive review on machine learning in brain tumor classification: taxonomy, challenges, and future trends (2024). https://doi.org/10.1016/j.bspc.2024.106774

17. Singh, R., Gupta, S., Bharany, S., Almogren, A., Altameem, A., Ur Rehman, A.: Ensemble deep learning models for enhanced brain tumor classification by leveraging ResNet50 and EfficientNet-B7 on high-resolution MRI images (2024). https://doi.org/10.1109/ACCESS.2024.3494232
18. Mohan, A., Meena, H.K., Wajid, M., Srivastava, A.: FPGA-based real-time road object detection system using mmWave radar (2025). https://doi.org/10.1109/LSENS.2025.3547008
19. Dip, S.R., Meena, H.K.: FPGA based implementation using graph spectral features for multiclass brain tumor classification (2025). https://doi.org/10.1109/JSEN.2025.3590063
20. Mhaouch, A., Gtifa, W., Machhout, M.: FPGA hardware acceleration of AI models for real-time breast cancer classification (2025). https://doi.org/10.3390/ai6040076
21. Chatterjee, S., Nizamani, F.A., Nürnberger, A., et al.: Classification of brain tumours in MR images using deep spatiospatial models (2022). https://doi.org/10.1038/s41598-022-05572-6
22. Disci, R., Gurcan, F., Soylu, A.: Advanced brain tumor classification in MR images using transfer learning and pre-trained deep CNN models(2025). https://doi.org/10.3390/cancers17010121
23. Aiya, A.J., Wani, N., Ramani, M., et al.: Optimized deep learning for brain tumor detection: a hybrid approach with attention mechanisms and clinical explainability (2025). https://doi.org/10.1038/s41598-025-04591-3

# Benchmarking CNN, ResNet50, and EfficientNetB0 for Driver Drowsiness Detection

Neha Sharma[1(✉)], Laura Suleimenova[2], Zhanat Umarova[3], Nitin Jain[4], and Arvind Panwar[5]

[1] Department of Information Technology, Bharati Vidyapeeth's College of Engineering, New Delhi, India
neha.sh.2689@gmail.com
[2] O. Zhanibekov South Kazakhstan Pedagogical University Shymkent, Shymkent, Kazakhstan
[3] Information Systems and Modeling Department, Auezov University, Shymkent, Kazakhstan
[4] School of Computer Science Engineering and Technology Bennett University, Greater Noida, Uttar Pradesh, India
[5] School of Computer Science and Engineering, Galgotias University, Greater Noida, Uttar Pradesh, India

**Abstract.** Driver drowsiness detection aims to mitigate risk of accidents caused by fatigue. Drowsiness while driving is one of the major causes of road accidents worldwide. It often leads to severe injuries and fatalities. Early detection of a driver's drowsy state can dwindle such incidents. Thus, the main objective of this project is to detect the driver's drowsy state using vision-based detection framework and alert the driver as a preventive measure. The study presents a comparative analysis of three deep learning model: CNN, ResNet50 and EfficientNetB0. This paper highlights the development progress, model comparisons, and challenges encountered during training. The ultimate goal is to identify the most effective model for real-time driver drowsiness detection, optimizing both accuracy and deployment efficiency for practical in-vehicle systems. Each model is evaluated using performance metrices which shows EfficientNetB0 achieves the best trade-off between predictive performance and computational efficiency.

**Keywords:** Drowsiness Detection · CNN · ResNet50 · EfficientNetB0 · Driver Safety · Deep Learning

## 1 Introduction

Driver drowsiness is one of the major causes of road accidents worldwide. In India, 40% of road accidents are caused due to drowsiness [1]. Unlike distractions or reckless behaviour, drowsiness is an involuntary human response that often goes unnoticed until it's too late. When a person operates a vehicle while feeling sleepy or fatigued, which may lead to impaired decision making and lead to accidents. They not only put themselves in serious risk but others as well. There are various factors that which may lead to drowsiness like sleep deprivation, irregular sleep pattern, sleeping disorder, alcohol, medicine, etc.


A. Shastri et al. (Eds.): IHCI 2025, LNCS 16437, pp. 241–256, 2026.
https://doi.org/10.1007/978-3-032-26352-0_20

With recent advancement in deep learning and artificial intelligence it enables models to automatically learn hierarchical feature representations from raw data. Deep learning architecture such as Convolutional Neural Networks (CNNs) have demonstrated outstanding performance in image classification, object detection, and facial analysis tasks. CNNs are particularly well-suited for spatial data, utilizing convolutional layers to effectively capture local patterns such as edges, textures, and shapes, making them a natural choice for analysing visual indicators of driver fatigue. By accurate detection of driver fatigue using real-time image analysis can prevent fatal accidents.

This research compares three deep learning models—CNN, CNN integrated with ResNet50 for feature extraction, and EfficientNetB0—for detecting drowsiness based on eye closure and yawning patterns. The goal is to identify the most suitable model for real-time implementation. Each model has distinct characteristics: the baseline CNN provides a straightforward approach to image classification, ResNet50, a deep residual network, is known for its ability to extract intricate features and avoid vanishing gradients, and EfficientNetB0 offers optimized performance with fewer parameters. The development of an intelligent driver monitoring system that can detect drowsiness in real time thus it plays an important role in enhancing road safety.

## 2 Literature Survey

Human Activity Recognition (HAR) and driver monitoring have gained significant attention in recent years due to their applications in healthcare, smart systems, and intelligent transportation. Several studies have focused on diverse aspects, ranging from daily activity monitoring in elderly individuals to advanced driver drowsiness detection using deep learning techniques.

Early research explored the use of wearable sensors and machine learning for activity recognition. For instance, [2] employed body-mounted inertial measurement units (IMUs) with Support Vector Machines (SVMs) to classify daily activities of older adults, achieving an accuracy range of 76–92%. However, this work was limited by inadequate analysis of transitional movements and sensitivity to movement variations. Similarly, [3, 4] integrated k-means clustering, SVMs, and Hidden Markov Models (HMMs) to model activities from posture data, attaining 77.3% precision and 76.7% recall on the CAD-60 dataset. Despite improvements over RGB-D approaches, recognition dropped under noisy or occluded sensor conditions. More recently, deep learning-based HAR has shown remarkable performance. [5] proposed a hybrid framework combining 1D-CNN, BiLSTM, and attention mechanisms, reporting 99.42% accuracy for sensor fusion tasks. Nevertheless, the model was computationally intensive, posing challenges for real-time deployment. Likewise, [6] leveraged MobileNetV3 and Multi-Task Learning (MTL) on popular HAR datasets (UCI HAR, WISDM, MHEALTH), achieving 91.2% accuracy with low response time, but with limited validation across diverse activities.

Parallel to HAR, significant research has been conducted in driver monitoring and drowsiness detection. [7] developed a CNN-based framework with OpenCV and Dlib for facial landmark detection, reaching 94.95% accuracy in identifying driver fatigue. Yet, its effectiveness decreased under poor lighting or low-resolution conditions. Similarly, [8] utilized CNN architectures such as AlexNet, GoogLeNet, and ResNet50 with Gaussian Mixture Models (GMM) for distracted driving recognition, achieving up to 91.4%

accuracy in distraction detection, though limited data and small movement variations posed challenges.

In addition to drowsiness detection, several studies emphasized driver activity recognition. [9] introduced a spatiotemporal graph convolutional LSTM (ST-GCLSTM) with attention for skeleton-based activity monitoring, obtaining 88.8% recall with real-time performance at 24 FPS. However, recognition accuracy declined in noisy environments and with subtle driver motions. Likewise, [8] employed key point-based human pose estimation with XGBoost for classifying driver actions, securing 11th place in the AI City Challenge 2022 with an F1 score of 0.2558, though performance was hindered by facial occlusions and viewpoint changes. Building on this, [10] applied federated learning (FedGKT with ResNet) to enable decentralized, privacy-preserving recognition on edge devices. The system ranked fifth in the AI City Challenge 2022 with an F1 score of 0.2921, but faced issues with limited data, edge device constraints, and difficulty detecting static actions.

More advanced frameworks addressed temporal localization of driver behaviors. [11] proposed a two-stage approach combining YOLOv5 for object tracking and SlowFast ResNet50 for action recognition, achieving 27.06% F1 score on the NVIDIA AI City 2022 Challenge. Despite incorporating temporal segmentation, the framework struggled with low accuracy due to limited camera perspectives and similar driver actions.

Overall, the literature demonstrates a clear progression from traditional machine learning with wearable sensors toward deep learning, skeleton-based modeling, and federated frameworks for real-time and privacy-aware driver monitoring. While CNN-based architectures provide high accuracy for drowsiness detection, challenges such as poor lighting, subtle motion recognition, and computational overhead remain. Addressing these limitations requires integrating lightweight deep learning models with robust feature extraction, ensuring reliable and real-time driver monitoring in diverse environments. Table 1 shows the summary of literature review.

**Table 1.** Summary of Literature Review

| Research paper No | Problem Considered | Technology used | Performance | Shortcomings |
|---|---|---|---|---|
| [2] | The study used IMU data and SVM to classify daily activities in older adults, analyzing effects of tuning and noise | Support Vector Machines (SVM) for activity classification, Body-mounted wireless inertial | Accuracy ranging between 76% and 92% | The study highlights limited analysis of transitional movements, need for more features, and effects of movement variations on accuracy |

*(continued)*

**Table 1.** *(continued)*

| Research paper No | Problem Considered | Technology used | Performance | Shortcomings |
|---|---|---|---|---|
| [3] | The research addresses real-time driver drowsiness detection to prevent accidents by monitoring facial features for signs of fatigue | The system integrates deep learning techniques with OpenCV, employing Convolutional Neural Networks (CNNs) and Dlib for facial landmarkdetection | The system demonstrated accuracy of 94.95%.in detecting signs of driver drowsiness | Performance is limited under poor lighting conditions or when using low-resolution cameras, affecting the accuracy of facial landmark detection |
| [4] | The study addresses recognizing human activities using posture data, overcoming issues like sensor noise, occlusions, and distinguishing similar activities | K-means clustering detects postures, SVMs classify them, and HMMs model activities as spatiotemporal sequences of postures | The method achieves 77.3% precision and 76.7% recall on CAD-60 and improves over existing RGB-D-based recognition approaches | Performance drops with noisy or occluded sensor data, andrecognizing highly similar activities remains challenging |
| [5] | It tackles HAR challenges with wearable sensors, aiming to improve activity recognition cross sensor types and positions | The framework uses 1D-CNN, BiLSTM, and attention for feature extraction and selection, tested on Shoaib AR, Shoaib SA, and HAPT datasets | The proposed model achieves 99.42% accuracy for sensor fusion at the belt position | The model has high computational complexity, requiring more training time, and may need optimization for real-time applications |
| [6] | Limitations of traditional monitoring methods relying on mechanical sensors and manual observation in terms of accuracy and real-time feedback | MobileNetV3, Multi-Task Learning MTL), and datasetslike UCI HAR, WISDM, and MHEALTH | Achieved 91.2% resistance prediction accuracy with 6.8% error and 12 ms response time | Limited validation for diverse activities and dependency on accurate input data for stride and joint angle factors |

*(continued)*

**Table 1.** *(continued)*

| Research paper No | Problem Considered | Technology used | Performance | Shortcomings |
|---|---|---|---|---|
| [7] | Recognizing driver activities in real-time to enhance driving safety and reduce accidents by monitoring and classifying common driver actions | ST-GCLSTM with attention processes driver skeleton data from onboard monocular cameras | Theproposed model achieved an 88.8% recall ratio for eight driver activity categories, with a real-time recognition speed of 24 frames per second | Challenges include environmental noise affecting skeleton detection, the need for improved recognition of subtle driver motions, and imbalanced dataset issues |
| [8] | Recognizing driver activities from video using key point-based human pose estimation to improve driving safety | Pre-trained human pose estimation and facial feature detection models, combined with XGBoost for activity classification | Achieved an F1 score of 0.2558, securing 11th place out of 27 teams in the AI City Challenge Track 3 | Limited accuracy due to occasional misidentification of driver key points, facial occlusion issues, and sensitivity to viewpoint variations |
| [9] | Recognizing driver activities in a privacy- preserving manner using decentralized learning on edge devices | Federated Learning (FL) withthe FedGKT algorithm,using ResNet models for feature extraction and classification | Achieved an F1 score of 0.2921, ranking fifth in the AI City Challenge 2022 | Faces challenges with limited training data, computational constraints on edge devices, and difficulty detecting some driver actions from static images |
| [10] | The research focuses on temporal driver action localization (TDAL) to recognize and classify driver distraction actions and detect their start and end times in untrimmed videos | The framework uses YOLOv5 for tracking and SlowFast ResNet50 for action classification, enhanced by video segmentation and temporal localization | The proposed framework achieved a 27.06% F1 score on the NVIDIA AI City 2022 Challenge's Track 3 dataset | Theframework faced low F1 scores due to limited camera angles and similar driver actions |

*(continued)*

**Table 1.** (*continued*)

| Research paper No | Problem Considered | Technology used | Performance | Shortcomings |
|---|---|---|---|---|
| [11] | The study focuses on recognizing seven driving tasks, both normal and distracted, using visual inputs for smart vehicle systems | CNNs like AlexNet, GoogLeNet, and ResNet50 were used with GMM for image segmentation and transfer learning | CNNmodels reached 81.6% task recognition (AlexNet) and 91.4% distraction detection accuracy | Challenges included limited data, low accuracy for subtle movements, and poor ResNet performance on small datasets |

# 3 Proposed Methodology

## 3.1 Dataset Description

Driver Drowsiness Dataset was acquired from Kaggle [12]. It contains 2900 images in total. Images are divided into four class which are 'open', 'closed', 'yawn' and 'no_yawn'. 'open' and 'closed' contain images of open eye and closed eye respectively whereas 'yawn' and 'no_yawn' contains images of full face while yawning and not yawning respectively. Figure 1 shows the dataset composition.

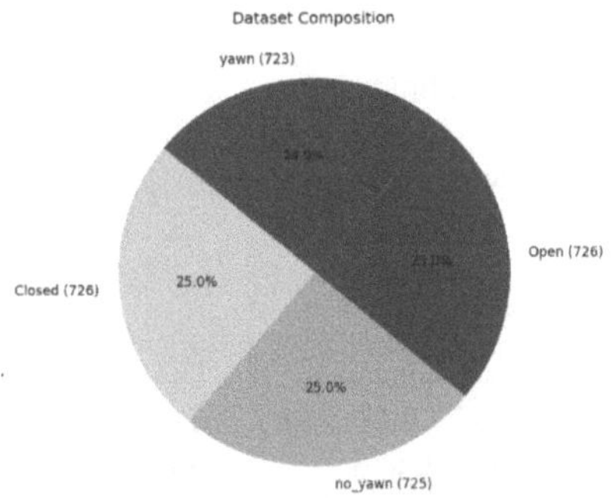


**Fig. 1.** Dataset composition

The dataset was further divided into three parts 60% for training, 20% for validation, and 20% for testing. The splitting was done randomly while ensuring reproducibility using a fixed random seed. This approach ensures that the model learns from the majority of the data, while the validation set helps tune and monitor performance during training, and the test set is used to evaluate the final model. After splitting, the class labels were converted into one-hot encoded format to make them suitable for multi-class classification.

### 3.2 Data Augmentation

The performance and generalization of the driver drowsiness detection model was improved by applying various data augmentation techniques to the training dataset. Data augmentation method is used to increase the diversity of the training data by creating modified versions of the original images. This helps the model learn better and perform well on new, unseen data by reducing overfitting. Overfitting happens when a model learns too much from the training data and performs poorly on new data. By applying small random changes to the images, the model becomes more robust and adaptable.

In the project, the augmentation strategies implemented included pixel value rescaling, random horizontal and vertical flipping, random rotations, width and height shifts, shearing, zooming, and brightness adjustments. Additionally, a custom contrast adjustment function was incorporated to introduce random contrast variations to further enhancing image variability to simulate different lighting conditions. This makes the model better at handling images taken in bright or low-light environments.

### 3.3 Model Architecture

**CNN Model:** Convolutional Neural Network (CNN) model was developed to classify driver behaviour into four distinct categories: Closed eyes, Open eyes, Yawning, and No Yawn. The architecture consists of three convolutional layers with 32, 64, and 128 filters respectively and each appoint a kernel size of $3 \times 3$ and ReLU activation functions. Each convolutional layer is followed by a max pooling layer with a $2 \times 2$ pooling window to progressively down sample feature maps and retain essential spatial features.

For convolutional and pooling stages, the output is flattened into a one-dimensional vector and passed through a dense layer with 256 neurons activated by ReLU. To enhance generalization and reduce the risk of overfitting, a dropout layer with a dropout rate of 0.5 is incorporated after the dense layer. The final output layer consists of four neurons corresponding to the four target classes, utilizing softmax activation to generate class probabilities. These deeper layers allow the model to learn more complex and abstract features, such as patterns that help differentiate between open or closed eyes and yawning or non-yawning expressions.

The model is compiled using the Adam optimizer which helps to adjusts the learning rate automatically for efficient training. The categorical cross-entropy loss function is used as the loss function since this is a multi-class classification task. The proposed CNN model provides an effective framework for detecting signs of driver drowsiness, combining a relatively simple architecture with strong feature extraction capabilities to achieve high classification performance. Figure 2 shows the CNN architecture used.

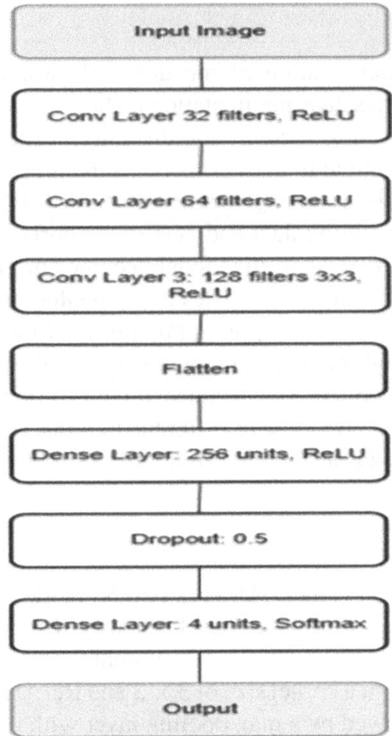


**Fig. 2.** CNN Model Architecture

**ResNet50:** ResNet50 model uses transfer learning approach in which it is loaded with pretrained weights from ImageNet dataset for the task of driver drowsiness detection. This allows the model to retain the deep hierarchical features learned from ImageNet while being fine-tuned for the specific task of driver drowsiness classification.

The base ResNet50 model was imported without its fully connected top layers. The model is adapted for the four-class classification which are Closed, Open, Yawn and No Yawn, a custom classification head was designed, comprising a GlobalAveragePooling2D layer, followed by two dense layers with 512 and 256 units respectively, each activated by the ReLU function and regularized using L2 weight decay to mitigate overfitting. Dropout layers with rates of 0.5 and 0.3, respectively, along with Batch Normalization, were incorporated to further improve model generalization.

To improve performance, the last 20 layers of the ResNet50 base model were unfrozen, enabling the model to learn more domain-specific features while preserving the robust representations learned from ImageNet. The model was compiled using the Adam optimizer with an initial learning rate of 0.0001, and categorical cross-entropy was employed as the loss function. Model performance was monitored using multiple metrics to ensure a comprehensive evaluation.

Training was enhanced by using of callback mechanisms like EarlyStopping based on validation AUC to halt training upon convergence, ReduceLROnPlateau to adaptively lower the learning rate when validation loss stagnated, and ModelCheckpoint to save the best-performing model weights. Additionally, to address class imbalance present in the dataset, class weighting was applied during model fitting. This comprehensive strategy allowed the model to achieve robust and reliable performance for driver drowsiness detection. Figure 3 shows the ResNet50 Model architecture used.

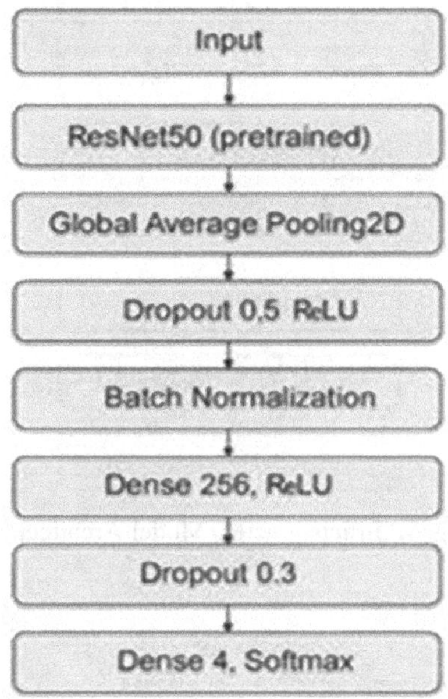


**Fig. 3.** ResNet50 Model Architecture

**EfficientNetB0 Model:** The drowsiness detection model is built using EfficientNetB0. It is a lightweight and powerful convolutional neural network pre-trained on ImageNet. It serves as the base feature extractor in our architecture. Model was adapted for transfer learning by removing the top classification layers and applying global average pooling to extract high-level features. Initially, the base model was frozen to retain learned representations and later fine-tuned for task-specific adaptation.

A custom classification head was added, comprising two fully connected layers with 128 and 64 neurons, respectively. These layers utilized the Swish activation function and were regularized using L2 penalties. Batch normalization and dropout rate of 0.3 were employed after each dense layer to enhance training stability and prevent overfitting. The final output layer used a softmax activation function to predict class probabilities corresponding to different alertness states.

The model was trained using the AdamW optimizer with a cosine decay restarts schedule for dynamic learning rate adjustment. Categorical cross entropy was used as the loss function, and class weighting was applied to handle class imbalance. Regularization techniques such as early stopping, model checkpointing, and dropout contributed to the model's generalizability and robustness. Figure 4 shows the EfficentNetB0 Model architecture.

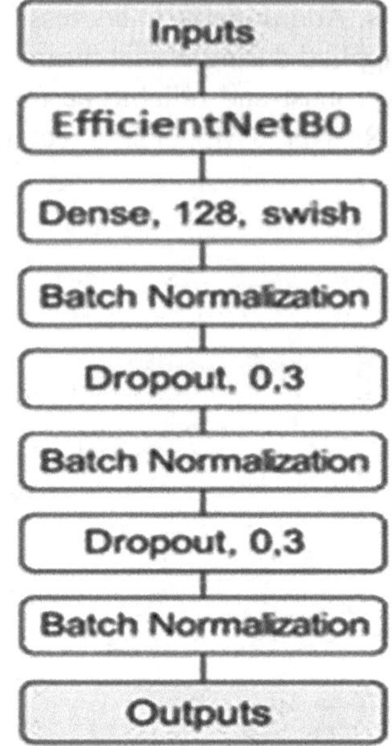


**Fig. 4.** EfficientNetB0 Model Architecture

### 3.4 Implementation

The proposed driver drowsiness detection system is designed to operate in real-time by combining facial landmark-based geometric analysis with deep learning classification using the EfficientNetB0 architecture. The system is implemented in Python and deployed using the Streamlit web framework for interactive user interfacing. Frames from a live webcam stream are processed in real-time to detect drowsy behavior based on eye closure and yawning activity.

**Facial Landmark Detection:** Facial landmark detection serves as the foundation for analyzing driver alertness by identifying key facial features. This is achieved using Dlib's 68-point facial landmark predictor, which maps specific coordinates around the eyes, eyebrows, nose, mouth, and jawline. For the purpose of drowsiness detection, only a subset of these points is utilized—specifically, landmarks 36 to 47 for both eyes, and landmarks 48 to 67 for the mouth region. These coordinates are extracted from grayscale frames for efficiency and converted into NumPy arrays for mathematical processing. This landmark information is critical in computing dynamic facial metrics such as Eye Aspect Ratio (EAR) and Mouth Aspect Ratio (MAR), which are used to determine whether the driver's eyes are closed or if they are yawning.

**Aspect Ratio Formulas:** To detect signs of fatigue through eye closure and yawning, two key geometric ratios are calculated from the facial landmarks which are Eye Aspect Ratio (EAR) and Mouth Aspect Ratio (MAR).

*Eye Aspect Ratio (EAR)*

The Eye Aspect Ratio (EAR) is a widely used metric that represents the vertical eye-opening relative to its horizontal width. It is computed using the Euclidean distances between specific eye landmarks. The formula is in Eq. (1):

$$EAR = \frac{|p2 - p6| + |p3 - p5|}{2 \cdot |p1 - p4|} \tag{1}$$

A low EAR, typically below 0.25, for a sequence of frames, is indicative of closed eyes and thus potential drowsiness i.

*Mouth Aspect Ratio (MAR)*

Mouth Aspect Ratio (MAR) measures how widely the mouth is open, which is indicative of yawning. It is calculated using 12 mouth landmarks and is defined in Eq. (2):

$$MAR = \frac{|p3 - p11| + |p5 - p9|}{2 \cdot |p1 - p7|} \tag{2}$$

A MAR value greater than 0.65 over several frames indicates yawning, which is another key drowsiness indicator.

**Drowsiness Detection Logic:** The core detection logic fuses both the rule-based metrics (EAR and MAR) and the CNN-based predictions from EfficientNetB0 to make robust decisions regarding drowsiness. If the EAR remains below 0.25 for at least 20 consecutive frames, it is inferred that the driver is drowsy due to prolonged eye closure. Similarly, if the MAR exceeds 0.65 for 15 consecutive frames or the model predicts the 'yawn' class with confidence above 70%, it indicates a yawning episode. These conditions are monitored in real time, and if either is satisfied, the system raises a drowsiness alert. The integration of both methods allows the system to handle edge cases more effectively. For instance, if a person blinks or speaks (which could affect MAR), the deep learning model helps confirm whether it is an actual sign of fatigue or normal behaviour. This dual-approach significantly reduces false alarms and improves overall reliability in diverse scenarios.

**Real-Time Interface:** The full system is deployed through web interface built using Streamlit, developed to ensure usability and accessibility. After being turned on via side-bar toggle, the webcam feed shows in real time, with overlays indicating detected facial landmarks such as eyes or mouth. A visual alert for "DROWSY ALERT! is displayed on the screen as well as a colored status card specifying the estimated prediction class and confidence score. Here you can see live results, which include the actual value such as current EAR and MAR, number of correct predictions. Total frames processed and the overall drowsiness percentage using the metrics panel that lives on sidebar. Our setup enables continuous sigh detection which does not require a user to take a specific action, thus it would be perfect for integration into driver assistance systems. In addition, the system will monitor real-time performance metrics that can later be used for analysis or model evaluation in future iterations.

In Fig. 5(a) image shows the original frame captured from a webcam, while Fig. 5(b) image demonstrates the detected facial landmarks. Green contours represent the eyes, and yellow contours outline the mouth. These landmarks are used to compute Eye Aspect

Ratio (EAR) and Mouth Aspect Ratio (MAR), which are essential indicators of eye closure and yawning respectively, enabling the system to assess drowsiness in real time.

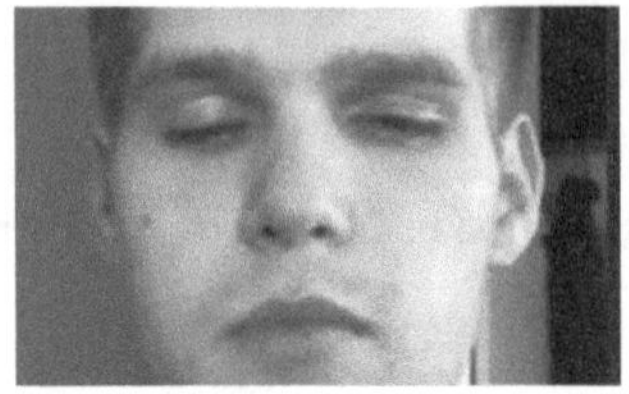
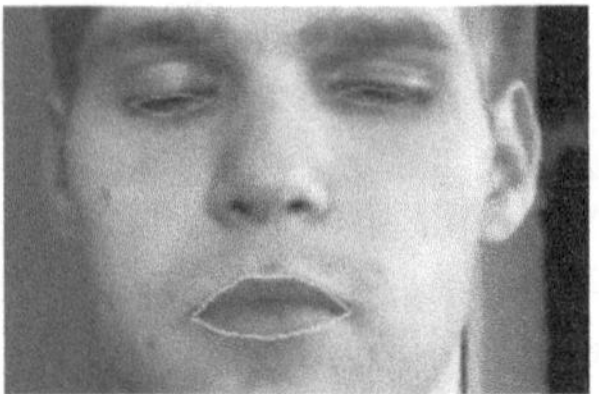

**Fig. 5.** (a) Original Image (b) Facial landmark detection

# 4 Results and Analysis

Table 2 shows the performance table of models.

**Table 2.** Performance table of models

| Model | Accuracy | Loss |
|---|---|---|
| CNN | 0.9355 | 0.2053 |
| ResNet50 | 0.9967 | 1.0772 |
| EfficientNetB0 | 0.9672 | 0.1018 |

## 4.1 CNN Model

In Fig. 6(a) graph represents the model accuracy over 50 training epochs. The blue line represents training accuracy, it increases from around 50% to about 95% and orange line represents validation accuracy, it increases from around 68% and stabilizes near 91–92%. The gap between training and validation accuracy is relatively small which proposes that model is well generalized and does not show overfitting.

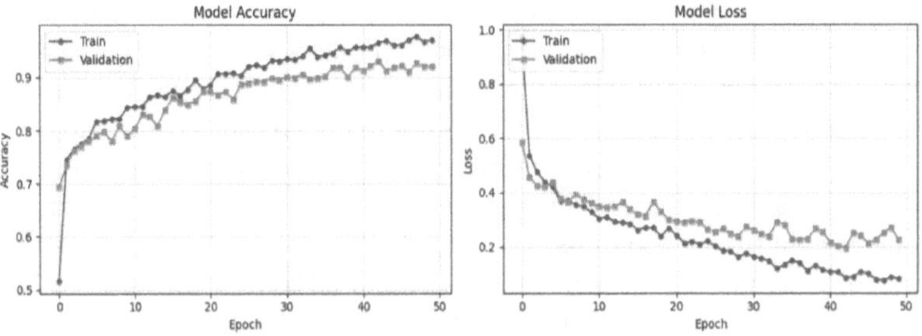


**Fig. 6.** CNN Model (a) accuracy (b) loss

In Fig. 6(b) graph represents the model loss over 50 training epochs. The blue line represents training loss, it decreases and reaches a very low value which shows successful minimization of error on training data whereas validation loss represented by orange line decreases and shows slight fluctuations around epoch 30 which shows limited improvement in generalization performance beyond that point.

### 4.2 ResNet50

In Fig. 7(a) the training and validation accuracy plot shows that the model achieves high performance early during training, with training accuracy rapidly increasing and reaching near-perfect levels by around the fifth epoch. The validation accuracy initially remains low but then sharply increases and stabilizes indicating strong generalization after initial underfitting.

In Fig. 7(b) the training and validation loss graph shows while the training loss consistently decreases, the validation loss initially increases peaking around epoch 6 before sharply declining and stabilizing. This pattern suggests the model underwent a short period of overfitting but corrected itself due to continued training or effective regularization techniques.

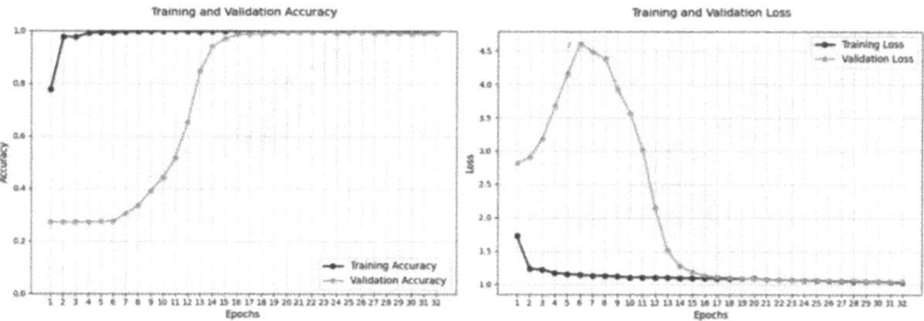


**Fig. 7.** ResNet50 Model (a) accuracy (b) loss

### 4.3 EfficientNetB0 Model

Figure 8(a) illustrates the training and validation accuracy of EfficientNetB0 model. The graph indicates that the model achieves high accuracy early during training and continues to improve slightly over the epochs, with both training and validation accuracy stabilizing above 95%. This suggests that the model learns effectively and generalizes well to the validation data without significant overfitting.

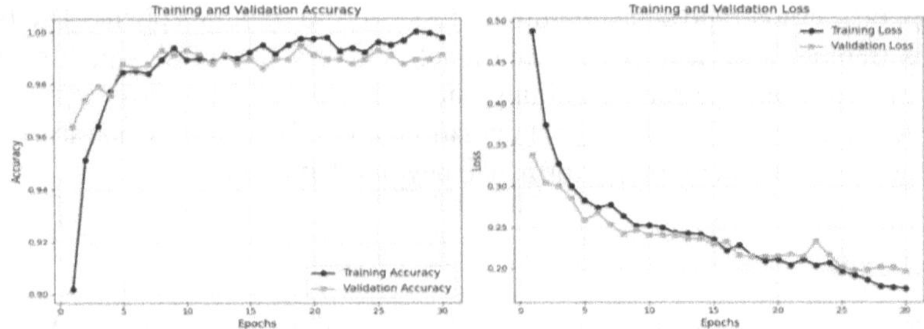


**Fig. 8.** EfficientNetB0 Model (a) accuracy (b) loss

Figure 8(b) illustrates the training and validation loss of EfficientNetB0 model. The graph shows a sharp decline in both training and validation loss in the initial epochs, stabilizing at a low value, further confirming good convergence of the model.

## 4.4 Confusion Matrix

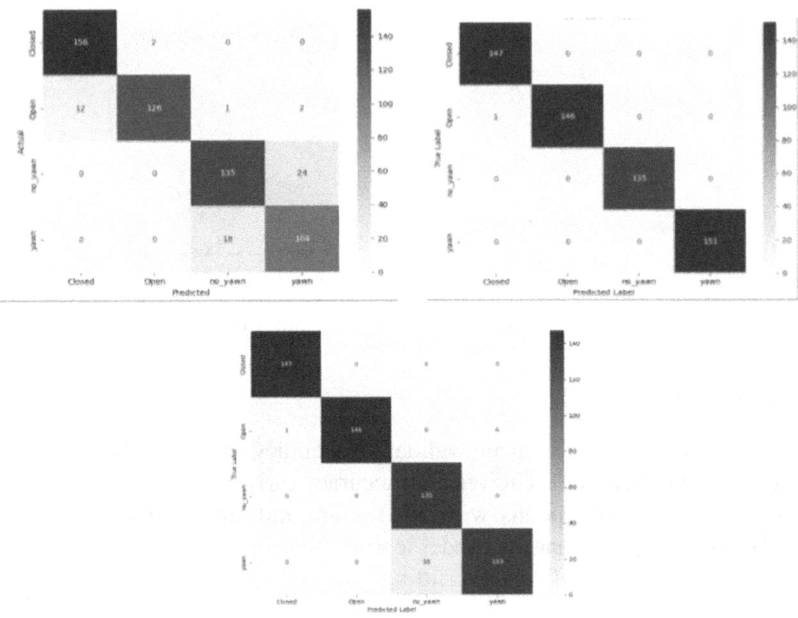


**Fig. 9.** Confusion Matrix of (a) CNN model (b) ResNet50 model (c) EfficientNetB0 model

Figure 9(a) shows the confusion matrix for the CNN model, highlighting its ability to classify the four classes: 'Closed', 'Open', 'no_yawn', and 'yawn'. Most predictions fall along the diagonal, indicating high accuracy. Some confusion exists between 'no_yawn' and 'yawn' due to visual similarity but overall, the model effectively distinguishes between the classes.

Figure 9(b) shows the confusion matrix for the ResNet50 model, demonstrating high classification accuracy across all four categories. This highlights the model's strong performance and effectiveness in detecting driver drowsiness cues.

Figure 9(c) shows the confusion matrix, highlighting strong classification accuracy across all four classes 'Closed', 'Open', 'no_yawn', and 'yawn' with minimal misclassifications. These results confirm the effectiveness of EfficientNetB0 in driver drowsiness detection.

## 5 Conclusion

This study assessed three deep learning models (CNN, ResNet50 and EfficientNetB0) to detect driver drowsiness with a multiclass image dataset. Based on the comparative analysis, ResNet50 had the highest accuracy rate at 99.67%, proving itself to possesssuperior feature extraction and classification capabilities in this domain. But it also detected the highest loss value (1.0772) will imply overfitting or being very confident in a bad answer. By contrast, EfficientNetB0 scored an equal performance with high accuracy of 96.72% and least loss (0.1018) thus proves to be a much better generalizable model. Baseline CNN had an accuracy of 93.55% and loss value of 0.2053, showing good results but falling behind more advanced architectures. In summary, Efficient-NetB0 provides the desirable balance between accuracy and loss which leads it to be an ideal candidate for real-time drowsiness detection system in deployment.

## References


1. The Hindu. "Sleep-Deprived Drivers Responsible for 40% of Road Accidents, Say Transport Officials." The Hindu. 19 Nov 2023 (2023). https://www.the-hindu.com/news/national/kerala/sleep-deprived-drivers-responsiblefor-40-of-road-accidents-say-transport-officials/article61629032.ece
2. Zhang, J., Soangra, R., E. Lockhart, T.: Automatic detection of dynamic and static activities of the older adults using a wearable sensor and support vector machines. Sci **2**(3), 62 (2020). https://doi.org/10.3390/sci2030062
3. Sengar, S.S., Kumar, A., Singh, O.: VigilEye—Artificial Intelligence-based Real-time Driver Drowsiness Detection (2024). arXiv preprint arXiv:2406.15646
4. Gaglio, S., Re, G.L., Morana, M.: Human activity recognition process using 3-D posture data. IEEE Trans. Hum.-Mach. Syst. **45**(5), 586–597 (2014)
5. Zhang, L., Yu, J., Gao, Z., Ni, Q.: A multi-channel hybrid deep learning framework for multi-sensor fusion enabled human activity recognition. Alex. Eng. J. **91**, 472–485 (2024)
6. Liu, Y., Lyu, T.: Real-time monitoring of lower limb movement resistance based on deep learning. Alex. Eng. J. **111**, 136–147 (2025)
7. Pan, C., Cao, H., Zhang, W., Song, X., Li, M.: Driver activity recognition using spatial-temporal graph convolutional LSTM networks with attention mechanism. IET Intel. Transport Syst. **15**(2), 297–307 (2021)
8. Vats, A., Anastasiu, D.C.: Key point-based driver activity recognition. In: Proceedings of the IEEE/CVF Conference on Computer Vision and Pattern Recognition (pp. 3274–3281) (2022)
9. Doshi, K., Yilmaz, Y.: Federated learning-based driver activity recognition for edge devices. In: Proceedings of the IEEE/CVF Conference on computer Vision and Pattern Recognition (pp. 3338–3346) (2022)

10. Alyahya, M., Alghannam, S., Alhussan, T.: Temporal driver action localization using action classification methods. In: Proceedings of the IEEE/CVF Conference on Computer Vision and Pattern Recognition (pp. 3319–3326) (2022)
11. Xing, Y., Lv, C., Wang, H., Cao, D., Velenis, E., Wang, F.Y.: Driver activity recognition for intelligent vehicles: a deep learning approach. IEEE Trans. Veh. Technol. **68**(6), 5379–5390 (2019)
12. Perumandla, D.: Drowsiness Dataset. Kaggle (2023). Available: https://www.kaggle.com/datasets/dheerajperumandla/drowsiness-dataset/data

# A GAN-Augmented and STO-Optimized CNN–LSTM Approach for IoT Intrusion Detection

Udit Gupta(✉) and Virender Ranga

Department of Information Technology, Delhi Technological University, New Delhi, India
ugnsitd@gmail.com, virenderranga@dtu.ac.in

**Abstract.** With the rapid increase in the Internet of Things (IoT) devices, they have become more vulnerable to cyber threats, which led to the need for advanced Intrusion Detection Systems (IDS). In this study, we have implemented a new framework termed STO–CNN–LSTM, where Siberian Tiger Optimization is used with CNN and LSTM architectures to identify intrusions in IoT networks. The CICIoT2023 dataset is used to evaluate the proposed approach. To mitigate class imbalance, Generative Adversarial Networks (GANs) are utilized for augmenting minority attack categories, while STO is adopted for effective parameter optimization. The results from the experiment show that our framework achieves an accuracy of 93.83% for the 41-class problem and 94.45% for the simplified 9-class task, performing far better than machine learning models like Logistic Regression, Support Vector Machine, Decision Trees, and Random Forests. Moreover, the framework demonstrates improved recall, precision, and F1-score particularly for underrepresented classes, highlighting its effectiveness in securing IoT infrastructures against threats including DDoS, DoS, and Mirai attacks.

**Keywords:** Intrusion Detection · IoT Security · Generative Adversarial Networks (GAN) · Convolutional Neural Networks (CNN) · Siberian Tiger Optimization (STO) · Long Short-Term Memory (LSTM) · CICIoT2023

## 1 Introduction

The increasing number of IoT devices has greatly contributed to growth in sectors such as smart cities, healthcare, and logistics through smooth and efficient connectivity. The total number of IoT connections is expected to rise sharply by 2030 [1]. However, this accelerated expansion has also amplified cybersecurity risks, making cyber defense a major area of ongoing research [2]. Consequently, there is a critical demand for advanced security mechanisms that can safeguard sensitive information and protect essential infrastructures [11].

Conventional protection strategies often fail to adequately secure resource-constrained IoT devices. Due to this limitation, we have shifted our focus to


A. Shastri et al. (Eds.): IHCI 2025, LNCS 16437, pp. 257–265, 2026.
https://doi.org/10.1007/978-3-032-26352-0_21

adopt ML and DL models for intrusion detection systems, which are capable of detecting anomalies and responding to new attacks using improved feature extraction and pattern analysis methodology. For the evaluation purpose, we used the CICIoT2023 dataset, which comprises traffic from 105 IoT devices and includes 33 attack categories along with benign flows, to design and evaluate a robust intrusion detection framework. In this work, the important contributions are presented in the following order: (1) a comparative analysis of multiple ML algorithms on both raw and augmented datasets; (2) application of GAN-based data augmentation to address severe class imbalance; (3) a hybrid CNN–LSTM model optimized using the Siberian Tiger Optimization (STO) algorithm; and (4) a comprehensive evaluation for both 41-class and 9-class classification tasks, as illustrated in Fig. 1. Our method achieves high accuracy and balanced detection performance, making it a good fit for practical IoT security situations.

The organization of this paper is as follows: Sect. 1 introduces the research problem and contributions; Sect. 2 reviews related work; Sect. 3 presents background concepts; Sect. 4 explains the methodology; Sect. 5 discusses the results; and Sect. 6 outlines limitations and future directions.

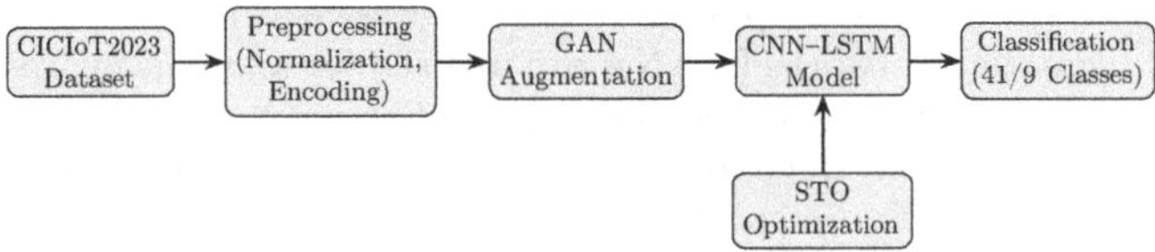


**Fig. 1.** Workflow and architecture of the proposed STO–CNN–LSTM framework.

## 2 Related Work

The increased application of machine learning and deep learning methods can be seen in the recent developments in IoT security. So, it is very important that a reliable dataset is available for both model training and evaluation. Early datasets include N-BaIoT, which focused on botnet detection using deep autoencoders [3], and IoT-HIDS, which collected host-level data from compromised IoT devices [4]. IoT-SH introduced a multi-layer intrusion detection framework for smart homes by combining rule-based and algorithmic methods [5]. The BoT-IoT dataset simulated realistic traffic with diverse attack categories [6], while Kitsune utilized ensembles of autoencoders for network intrusion detection [7].

Some of the other useful datasets, such as IoT-23 [8], MQTTset [9], and TON-IoT [10], provided diverse traffic conditions for evaluating ML and DL based approaches.

Recent studies employing the CICIoT2023 dataset have explored various strategies to improve detection accuracy. For instance, Tawfik enhanced intrusion detection performance through ensemble learning combined with advanced feature selection [11]. Gheni and Al-Yaseen introduced a two-step clustering approach to improve IDS accuracy [12]. Bhuiyan investigated deep learning-based classification with oversampling strategies, highlighting the significance of multi-dataset validation for robustness [13]. Collectively, these works emphasize challenges such as class imbalance, feature selection, and scalability, which motivate our proposed STO–CNN–LSTM framework to address these limitations effectively.

### 2.1 Critical Gaps in Prior Work

Class imbalance and limited sequence modeling are the two limitations that remain in many previous works. In class imbalance, there exist some attack types in IoT data which have a small number of samples in the entire dataset, due to which the model doesn't learn them properly during training and becomes biased. In limited sequence modeling, the model ignores important time-based patterns in the data and concentrates only on static features. Both these problems are addressed by our model as we use GAN to generate more samples and CNN-LSTM to learn temporal sequences. In addition, the model is fine-tuned using an efficient hyperparameter search (Sect. 4.6)

## 3 Background

### 3.1 Convolutional Neural Networks (CNN)

CNNs perform well in capturing spatial dependencies in structured data, such as network traffic. By applying convolutional filters along with nonlinear activations and pooling operations, they reduce dimensionality while preserving the essential features needed for classification.

### 3.2 Long Short-Term Memory (LSTM)

Long Short-Term Memory (LSTM) is an extension of recurrent neural networks (RNNs) developed to address the challenge of capturing long-term dependencies in sequential data. It incorporates three gating mechanisms—input, forget, and output—that regulate how information is added, discarded, or retained making it effective for handling temporal patterns in IoT data.

### 3.3 Generative Adversarial Networks (GAN)

In a GAN framework, the generator creates synthetic samples, while the discriminator evaluates whether inputs are genuine or generated. Through this adversarial training process, GANs are capable of generating realistic synthetic data, which is particularly useful for balancing underrepresented classes in imbalanced datasets.

### 3.4 Siberian Tiger Optimization (STO)

STO is a bio-inspired optimizer that models tiger hunting, focusing on exploration and exploitation. It fine-tunes hyperparameters efficiently in complex search spaces. We discuss STO selection further in Sect. 4.7.

## 4 Methodology

### 4.1 Dataset Description

The CICIoT2023 dataset provides traffic from 105 IoT devices, which contains 33 categories of attack types along with normal traffic. It has a total of 46 features representing each flow. A balanced subset of 100,000 samples was selected.

### 4.2 Preprocessing Pipeline

The features were scaled to the range [0, 1] using Min-Max normalization. Labels were converted into numerical form. For the 9-class setting, attacks were grouped into categories (Benign, DDoS, DoS, Mirai, etc.). The split was 80% for training and 20% for testing, with stratification applied.

### 4.3 Data Imbalance Handling

GANs generated synthetic samples for minority classes, such as SlowLoris. Approximately 4,962 synthetic samples were added. We used class weights that were inversely related to frequency.

### 4.4 Baseline ML Models

To establish a benchmark, we used traditional classifiers, namely Support Vector Machine (SVM) using RBF Kernel, Logistic Regression (LogReg), Decision Tree (DT), and Random Forest (RF). Each algorithm was executed using default parameter configurations using 42 as a random seed. To analyze their performance, accuracy, precision, recall and F1-score were calculated.

### 4.5 Proposed Deep Model

We designed a CNN–LSTM hybrid as the central deep learning model. The architecture begins with a one-dimensional convolutional layer containing 123 filters of size 3, followed by a max-pooling operation. The intermediate representation is then passed to an LSTM layer with 97 hidden units, which connects to a fully connected dense layer of 64 neurons. The final output layer includes either 41 or 9 nodes, depending on the classification task. Model training employed the Adam optimizer with a learning rate of 0.00942, and sparse categorical cross-entropy was used as the loss function. Early stopping was also applied in order to avoid overfitting. A complete layer-wise configuration of the CNN–LSTM network is presented in Table 1.

**Table 1.** Layer-wise Configuration of the CNN–LSTM Network

| Network Component | Result Dimension | Weight Count |
|---|---|---|
| Convolution (1D) | (None, 44, 64) | 256 |
| Pooling (1D) | (None, 22, 64) | 0 |
| Convolution (1D) | (None, 20, 128) | 24,704 |
| Pooling (1D) | (None, 10, 128) | 0 |
| LSTM Block | (None, 64) | 49,408 |
| Dense Layer | (None, 64) | 4,160 |
| Dense Output | (None, 41) | 2,665 |
| **Overall Trainable Weights** | | **81,193** |
| **Adjustable Weights** | | **81,193** |
| **Fixed Weights** | | **0** |

*Note: The architecture combines convolutional, pooling, recurrent and dense components to learn spatial as well as temporal characteristics from IoT traffic.*

### 4.6 Hyperparameter Optimization

Siberian Tiger Optimization (STO) was employed to determine suitable hyperparameters for the CNN–LSTM architecture. During optimization, we explored convolutional filter sizes in the range of 32 to 128, LSTM units from 32 to 128, and learning rates varying from 0.0001 to 0.01. The objective of optimization was to maximize validation accuracy. The STO procedure was executed over 5 iterations with 10 agents (candidate solutions).

### 4.7 Justification for STO

We include STO because it provides an adjustable balance between exploration and exploitation tailored for multimodal hyperparameter spaces. Compared with commonly-used global optimizers such as Particle Swarm Optimization (PSO) or Genetic Algorithms (GA), STO's moves emulate a hunting strategy that adaptively adjusts step sizes to avoid premature convergence. In practice, this allowed the STO search to find robust hyperparameter combinations for both convolutional and recurrent components within relatively few evaluations (Sect. 4.6). For reproducibility, we report STO settings and search ranges in Sect. 4.6.

## 5 Results and Discussion

### 5.1 Baseline ML Results

After applying GAN-based augmentation to address class imbalance, RF achieved the strongest performance with an accuracy of about 95.5%, DT achieved roughly 93.5%, SVM and LogReg were limited to around 79% and 77%, respectively. Table 2 shows the comparison and the visualization can be seen in Fig. 4(a).

**Table 2.** Comparison of baseline models after applying data augmentation.

| Model | Classification Accuracy | Mean Precision | Mean Recall | F1-score |
|---|---|---|---|---|
| DT | 0.935 | 0.930 | 0.932 | 0.931 |
| RF | 0.955 | 0.945 | 0.950 | 0.947 |
| SVM | 0.790 | 0.785 | 0.788 | 0.760 |
| LogReg | 0.775 | 0.768 | 0.772 | 0.745 |

*Note: DT = Decision Tree, RF = Random Forest, SVM = Support Vector Machine, LogReg = Logistic Regression.*

### 5.2 Final CNN–LSTM Results

In the CNN–LSTM model, the obtained accuracy was 93.83% when analysis was done for 41 classes. The DDoS class achieved an F1-score of 0.99, while the Web Attack class exhibited very poor detection (F1 = 0.00). Figure 3 shows the confusion matrix and Fig. 2 shows the learning curves for accuracy and loss. The poor Web Attack detection motivated the focused error analysis described below.

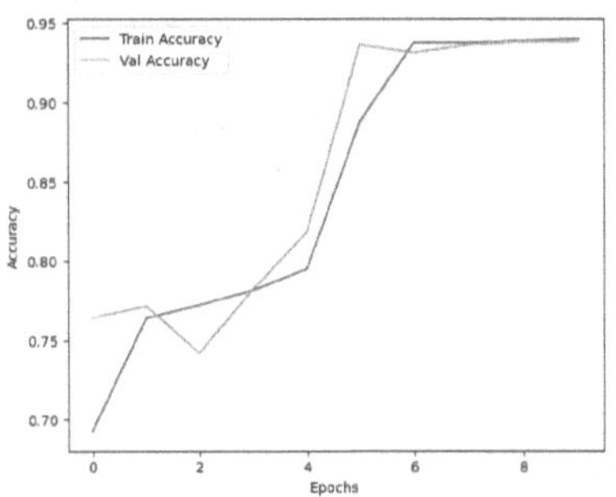


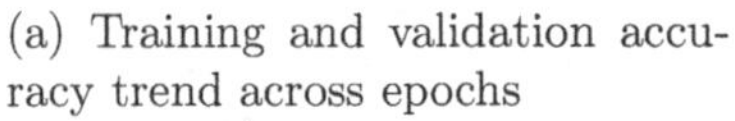

(a) Training and validation accuracy trend across epochs

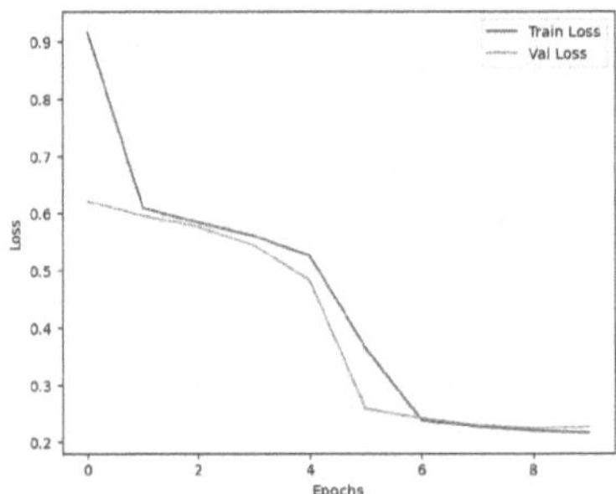


(b) Training loss and validation loss variation over epochs

**Fig. 2.** Epoch-wise accuracy and loss metrics for the CNNLSTM (refer Sect. 4.5).

### 5.3 Final STO–CNN–LSTM Results

In the 9-class setup, the STO–CNN–LSTM model achieved 94.45% accuracy. The F1-scores were as follows: DDoS = 0.78, Mirai = 0.98, and Web Attack = 0.00. The detailed metrics are presented in Table 3, while the visualization is shown in Fig. 4(b).

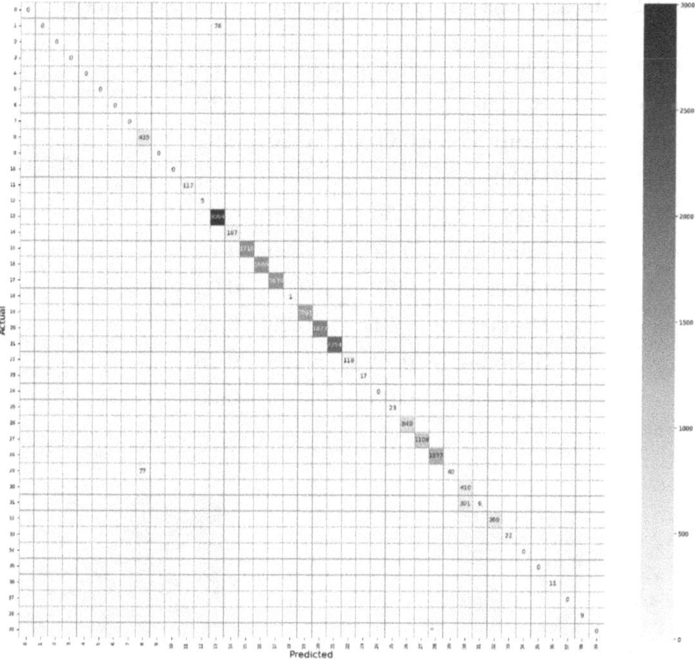


**Fig. 3.** Performance assessment of CNNLSTM presented in the form of a confusion matrix (41-class).

### 5.4 Error Analysis and Limitations

A notable limitation is the near-zero F1-scores for classes such as Web Attack and Other. We performed targeted checks and identified three likely causes:

1. Severe sample scarcity: Despite GAN augmentation, the intrinsic variability of some Web Attack flows is not well represented by the synthetic samples produced, causing poor generalization.
2. Feature overlap: Certain feature patterns of Web Attack flows overlap with benign or other attack types, making them difficult to separate using the current feature set.
3. Label noise/heterogeneity: Some labeled examples in the dataset may be noisy or heterogeneous, reducing the classifier's ability to learn consistent decision boundaries.

To mitigate these issues we propose (a) class-specific GAN models that target the feature manifold of Web Attack flows, (b) enrichment of feature space with protocol-specific indicators, and (c) careful dataset curation and cross-dataset validation in future work (Sect. 6).

**Table 3.** Class-wise results for the 9-class experiment.

| Class | Precision | Recall | F1-score |
|---|---|---|---|
| Benign | 0.55 | 0.07 | 0.12 |
| Brute Force | 0.00 | 0.20 | 0.01 |
| DDoS | 0.90 | 0.69 | 0.78 |
| DoS | 0.36 | 0.70 | 0.48 |
| Mirai | 0.97 | 0.99 | 0.98 |
| Other | 0.02 | 0.03 | 0.02 |
| Recon | 0.21 | 0.26 | 0.23 |
| Spoofing | 0.24 | 0.28 | 0.26 |
| Web Attack | 0.00 | 0.00 | 0.00 |

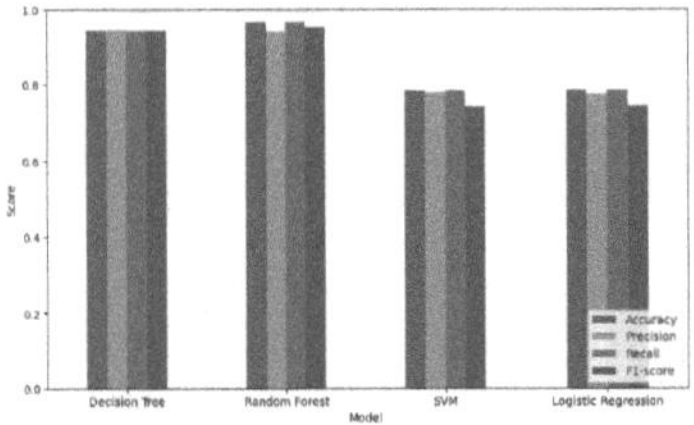

(a) Performance comparison of baseline models

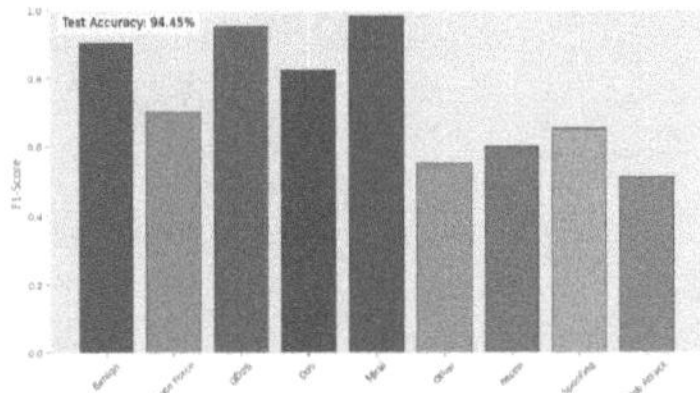


(b) Class-wise F1-scores of STO-optimized CNN–LSTM

**Fig. 4.** Performance metrics for baseline and STO-optimized models.

### 5.5 Comparative Analysis

Compared to CICIoT2023 studies, our model demonstrates competitive performance. Gheni and Al-Yaseen [12] reported 95% accuracy for a binary classification task, whereas our model achieves 94.45% accuracy in a more complex 9-class configuration. Tawfik [11] achieved 98% accuracy for selected attacks using ensemble learning and advanced feature selection. In contrast, our model performs well in sequence modeling and generalizes across a wider range of attack types, as evidenced by a strong Mirai F1-score of 0.98. Cross-dataset studies have reported 96% accuracy for botnet detection [13]. Our model delivers a comparable Mirai F1-score of 0.98 versus their 0.95.

## 6 Conclusion and Future Work

We developed a GAN–augmented, STO–CNN–LSTM framework for IoT intrusion detection. The proposed model achieved 94.45% accuracy and outperformed traditional ML baselines. GANs helped mitigate class imbalance, while STO improved hyperparameter tuning. However, the use of GAN and STO introduces additional overhead, and detection performance remains weaker for rare attack classes. The future plan is to extend our work by implementing the framework for lightweight TinyML deployment, integrating explainable AI techniques, and testing across additional datasets.

### 6.1 Explainability and Future Integration

We will integrate model-agnostic explainability tools (e.g., SHAP or LIME) to inspect feature contributions per decision and to aid debugging for poor-performing classes. This will help identify systematic biases and guide targeted augmentation or feature engineering efforts.

## References


1. Dahlqvist, F., Patel, M., Rajko, A., Shulman, J.: Growing Opportunities in the Internet of Things. McKinsey & Company (2019)
2. Clima, M., Darzu, C., Pascari, V., Bobeica, A.: The rise of cybersecurity: threats, challenges and solutions (2024)
3. Meidan, Y., et al.: N-BaIoT-network-based detection of IoT botnet attacks using deep autoencoders. IEEE Pervasive Comput. **17**(3), 12–22 (2018)
4. Ferrag, M.A., Maglaras, L., Moschoyiannis, S., Janicke, H.: Deep learning for cyber security intrusion detection: approaches, datasets, and comparative study. J. Inf. Secur. Appl. **50**, 102419 (2020)
5. Parra, G.D.L.T., Rad, P., Choo, K.-K.R., Beebe, N.: Detecting internet of things attacks using distributed deep learning. J. Netw. Comput. Appl. **163**, 102662 (2020)
6. Koroniotis, N., Moustafa, N., Sitnikova, E., Turnbull, B.: Towards the development of realistic botnet dataset in the internet of things for network forensic analytics: BoT-IoT dataset. Future Gener. Comput. Syst. **100**, 779–796 (2019)
7. Mirsky, Y., Doitshman, T., Elovici, Y., Shabtai, A.: Kitsune: an ensemble of autoencoders for online network intrusion detection. arXiv:1802.09089 (2018)
8. Parmisano, A., Garcia, S., Erquiaga, M.J.: A labeled dataset with malicious and benign IoT network traffic (2020)
9. Vaccari, I., Chiola, G., Aiello, M., Mongelli, M., Cambiaso, E.: MQTTset, a new dataset for machine learning techniques on MQTT. Sensors **20**(22), 6578 (2020)
10. Booij, T.M., Chiscop, I., Meeuwissen, E., Moustafa, N., Hartog, F.T.H.D.: ToN_IoT: the role of heterogeneity and the need for standardization of features and attack types in IoT network intrusion data sets. IEEE Internet Things J. **9**(1), 485–496 (2021)
11. Tawfik, M.: Optimized intrusion detection in IoT and fog computing using ensemble learning. PLoS ONE **19**(8), e0304082 (2024)
12. Gheni, H.Q., Al-Yaseen, W.L.: Two-step data clustering for improved intrusion detection system using CICIoT2023 dataset. e-Prime-Adv. Electr. Eng. Electron. Energy **9**, 100673 (2024)
13. Bhuiyan, M.H.: Deep learning-based network intrusion classification using over-sampling methods and multi-dataset validation (2024)

# Non-Destructive Fruit Quality Evaluation via Multisensor Fusion and Agglomerative Clustering

Kanak Kumar[1], Anshul Verma[2(✉)], and Pradeepika Verma[3]

[1] Pranveer Singh Institute of Technology, Kanpur 209305, India
kanakkumarcs24@bhu.ac.in

[2] Banaras Hindu University, Varanasi 221005, India
anshul.verma@bhu.ac.in

[3] Bennett University, Greater Noida 201310, India
pradeepika.verma@bennett.edu.in

**Abstract.** Accurate and non-destructive fruit ripeness assessment plays a crucial role in post-harvest management, quality control, and reducing agricultural waste. This study presents a comprehensive, unsupervised learning framework that leverages multisensor fusion and clustering techniques for automated fruit ripeness detection and quality evaluation. A custom dataset comprising gas sensor responses to apple emissions was acquired under controlled conditions across three ripeness stages. To ensure numerical stability and mitigate scale variance, the data was standardized using z-score normalization. Dimensionality reduction was performed using Principal Component Analysis (PCA) to extract the most significant variance directions and facilitate visualization in lower-dimensional space. Three clustering algorithms—Agglomerative Clustering, KMeans, and DBSCAN—were employed to identify inherent structures in the data without label supervision. Each model's performance was evaluated against ground truth labels using a suite of clustering metrics, including Silhouette Score, Adjusted Rand Index (ARI), Normalized Mutual Information (NMI), Homogeneity, Completeness, and V-Measure. Among the methods, Agglomerative Clustering yielded the most consistent and high-quality segmentation, reflecting the hierarchical nature of sensor-driven ripeness transitions. Visualization through 2D and 3D PCA projections revealed clear class boundaries, supporting clustering validity. The comparative analysis indicated DBSCAN's sensitivity to parameter tuning and lower performance on dense but overlapping clusters. This research validates the potential of unsupervised learning for real-time fruit quality assessment using low-cost sensor systems. Future directions include integrating deep clustering frameworks, temporal modeling for continuous monitoring, and deployment on embedded platforms with TinyML for edge-based smart agriculture and post-harvest automation.

**Keywords:** Fruit Ripeness Detection · Non-Destructive Quality Assessment · Multisensor Fusion · Unsupervised Learning · Principal Component Analysis · Agglomerative Clustering


A. Shastri et al. (Eds.): IHCI 2025, LNCS 16437, pp. 266–277, 2026.
https://doi.org/10.1007/978-3-032-26352-0_22

## 1 Introduction

The rising global demand for premium agricultural produce necessitates rapid, non-destructive techniques for evaluating fruit maturity, including ripeness stage prediction and shelf-life estimation. Global fruit production reached 871 million tons in 2021, marking an 18% increase since 2010, according to FAO. This growth highlights the need for intelligent orchard automation, where robots must accurately localize and map individual fruit trees [12]. Accurate maturity assessment is critical for optimizing post-harvest handling and supply chain efficiency. Tomatoes, rich in vitamins A and C, are a source of bioactive compounds such as carotenoids, flavonoids, and phenolic acids, known for their antioxidant, anti-inflammatory, and antihypertensive properties, which contribute to cardiovascular health [1,2]. Post-harvest physiological changes and maturity variability increase the risk of spoilage in overripe tomatoes, leading to significant losses during transport and storage. Therefore, objective and precise classification of tomato maturity at harvest is vital for effective grading, marketing, and enhancing farm-gate returns [3,4]. Apple spoilage is primarily driven by physical damage, chemical degradation, and microbial activity, with fungal infections being the leading cause. Therefore, developing efficient monitoring systems for early spoilage detection is essential to minimize post-harvest losses and enhance food safety [10,11].

Advancements in gas sensing and electronic nose technologies enable real-time, non-destructive detection of apple spoilage by identifying VOCs emitted during degradation [5]. These sensors convert gas interactions into electrical signals, offering a rapid, sensitive, and cost-effective alternative to conventional analysis methods, suitable for large-scale post-harvest monitoring [6,7]. Accurate and non-invasive fruit ripeness detection is essential for optimizing post-harvest handling, improving market readiness, reducing spoilage, and enhancing decision-making in precision agriculture. Conventional methods, such as tactile inspection, refractometry, and destructive chemical assays, are labor-intensive, subjective, and unsuitable for continuous or large-scale monitoring. The increasing demand for scalable and real-time fruit quality assessment has driven research toward intelligent sensing systems that can interpret the biochemical changes associated with ripening. Fruits release specific volatile organic compounds (VOCs) as byproducts of respiration and enzymatic activity during the ripening process. Metal Oxide Semiconductor (MOS) gas sensors have shown high sensitivity to such VOCs and are cost-effective for capturing gaseous emissions associated with ethylene production, esters, and alcohols [8]. When deployed as a multisensor array, these sensors generate high-dimensional temporal data that require advanced data analytics for meaningful interpretation.

While supervised machine learning models have demonstrated success in fruit quality classification, they depend heavily on labeled data, which may not always be available or generalizable across seasons and cultivars. To address this limitation, unsupervised learning approaches—particularly clustering algorithms—offer a label-free mechanism for discovering inherent structures in the data, enabling autonomous classification of fruit ripeness stages. In this study, we propose a multisensor fusion framework incorporating Agglomerative Clustering, KMeans, and DBSCAN for non-destructive ripeness detection. Data standardization and Principal Component Analysis (PCA) are employed for preprocessing and visualization [9]. The clustering results are evaluated using internal and external validation metrics against ground truth labels. The framework supports scalable, interpretable, and low-computation fruit quality analysis, paving the way for edge-deployable smart sensing systems in modern agriculture.

### 1.1 Chalenges

1. Scalability limitations for large-scale datasets due to computational complexity.
2. Irreversible merging: Once clusters are merged, they cannot be separated, which may lead to suboptimal solutions.
3. Sensitivity to noise and outliers, especially under single linkage.

### 1.2 Advantages for Real-World Deployment

1. No need to pre-specify cluster shapes or density assumptions (unlike KMeans or DBSCAN).
2. Highly interpretable via dendrograms, especially useful in quality assurance pipelines.
3. Handles overlapping class transitions common in ripening processes.

Agglomerative Clustering is employed to cluster sensor responses (e.g., ethylene concentration, volatile organic compounds) associated with different fruit ripeness stages. By leveraging PCA for dimensionality reduction, the clusters are projected into 2D/3D for interpretability. Given its ability to capture complex hierarchical structures, Agglomerative Clustering can effectively group overlapping or gradient-like sensor readings, often found in real-world post-harvest or IoT-based agricultural datasets. Its performance is evaluated using clustering validation metrics such as Silhouette Score, Adjusted Rand Index, and Normalized Mutual Information, which quantify both internal compactness and external alignment with known ripeness classes. This enables data-driven selection of optimal clustering strategies for intelligent fruit quality assessment systems.

The remainder of the paper is structured as follows: Sect. 2 presents the proposed methodology, including the algorithmic workflow of agglomerative clustering. Section 3 provides the results along with detailed analysis and discussion. Section 4 concludes the paper and highlights potential directions for future work.

## 2 Method and Methodology

Agglomerative Clustering is a deterministic, bottom-up hierarchical clustering algorithm that constructs a binary cluster tree (dendrogram) by successively merging the closest pair of clusters based on a specified inter-cluster linkage criterion. It is an unsupervised learning approach that does not rely on any assumptions about the underlying data distribution, making it suitable for non-linear and non-globular data structures commonly encountered in real-world sensor systems. In the context of fruit ripeness assessment using a universal sensing system (e.g., using MQ gas sensors to measure ethylene and volatile organic compounds), the sensor data often exhibit overlapping class boundaries due to gradual and nonlinear biochemical changes during the ripening process. Agglomerative clustering can effectively model such gradual transitions and latent hierarchies in the feature space. The implemented Python code constitutes a technically rigorous and modular framework for unsupervised clustering-based analysis of fruit ripeness classification using sensor-derived data, such as responses from metal-oxide gas sensors (MQ-series) [13,14]. The pipeline initiates with the importation of essential scientific libraries encompassing data handling (Pandas), preprocessing (Scikit-learn's StandardScaler), dimensionality reduction (PCA), clustering algorithm, and evaluation metrics [15,16] (Fig. 1).

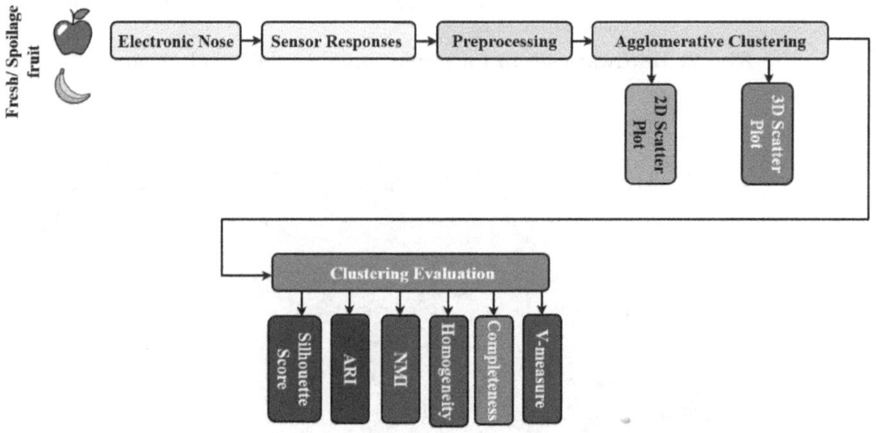


**Fig. 1.** Block diagram of fruit quality data collection

The dataset, assumed to represent gas concentration features corresponding to various stages of fruit ripeness, is ingested from a CSV file. The feature matrix X is isolated for modeling, while the ground truth class labels $y_{\text{true}}$ are retained for external validation of the clustering outcomes. Preprocessing via standardization is a critical step, ensuring that all features contribute equally to the distance-based computations intrinsic to clustering and PCA [17]. By applying PCA-based dimensionality reduction, the high-dimensional gas sensor data is projected into 2D and 3D subspaces, enabling visualization of inter-cluster separation (Figs. 2 and 3).

**Fig. 2.** Hardware setup for apple's quality data collection

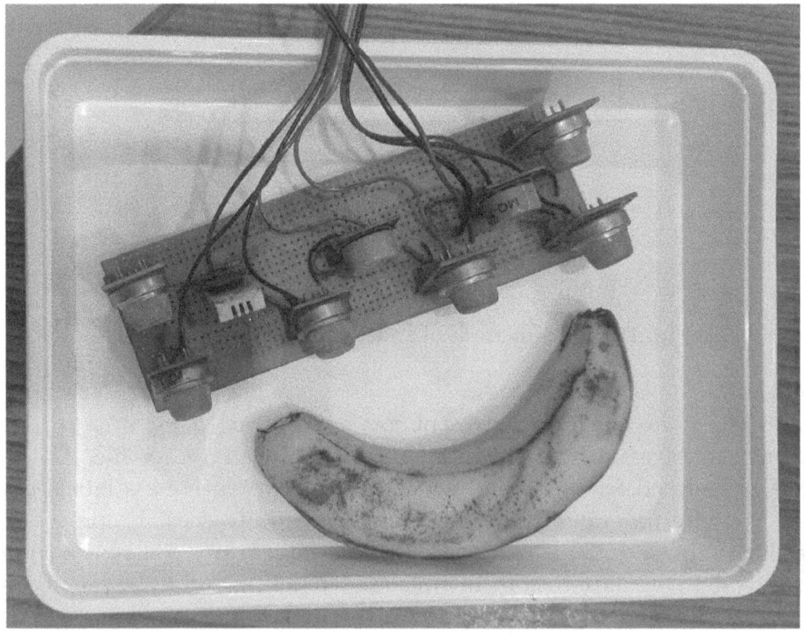

**Fig. 3.** Hardware setup for banana's quality data collection

**Algorithm 1** Agglomerative Clustering

**Require:** Dataset $X = \{x_1, x_2, \ldots, x_n\} \subset \mathbb{R}^d$; Desired number of clusters $k$; Distance metric; Linkage criterion
**Ensure:** Cluster labels for each $x_i \in X$
Initialize each data point $x_i$ as a singleton cluster $C_i$
Compute the initial pairwise distance matrix $D$ using the specified distance metric
**while** number of clusters $> k$ **do**
    Identify the closest pair of clusters $(C_p, C_q)$ using the chosen linkage criterion
    Merge $C_p$ and $C_q$ into a new cluster $C_r = C_p \cup C_q$
    Update the distance matrix $D$ to reflect distances between $C_r$ and all other clusters
**end while**
**return** Final cluster labels for all data points

## 2.1 Algorithmic Workflow of Agglomerative Clustering

Given a dataset $X = \{x_1, x_2, \ldots, x_n\} \subset \mathbb{R}^d$, the Agglomerative Clustering algorithm proceeds as follows:

1. **Initialization:** Each data point $x_i$ is initially assigned to its own cluster $C_i$. At this stage, there are $n$ clusters.
2. **Distance Matrix Computation:** Compute the pairwise proximity matrix $D \in \mathbb{R}^{n \times n}$, where each element $d_{ij} = \text{dist}(C_i, C_j)$ denotes the distance between clusters $C_i$ and $C_j$. The distance metric (e.g., Euclidean, Manhattan, Cosine) and linkage criterion are specified by the user.
3. **Linkage Criteria:** Let $A$ and $B$ be two clusters containing points $x_i \in A$ and $x_j \in B$. The following linkage strategies are commonly used:
   - *Single Linkage:* $D(A, B) = \min_{x_i \in A, x_j \in B} \|x_i - x_j\|$
   - *Complete Linkage:* $D(A, B) = \max_{x_i \in A, x_j \in B} \|x_i - x_j\|$
   - *Average Linkage:* $D(A, B) = \frac{1}{|A||B|} \sum_{x_i \in A} \sum_{x_j \in B} \|x_i - x_j\|$
   - *Ward's Linkage:* Minimizes the total within-cluster variance:

   $$D(A, B) = \frac{|A||B|}{|A| + |B|} \|\mu_A - \mu_B\|^2 \tag{1}$$

   where $\mu_A$ and $\mu_B$ denote the centroids of clusters $A$ and $B$, respectively.
4. **Cluster Merging:** Identify the pair of clusters $(C_p, C_q)$ with the minimum inter-cluster distance and merge them into a new cluster $C_r = C_p \cup C_q$.
5. **Update Distance Matrix:** Update the distance matrix to reflect the new set of clusters formed after merging.
6. **Repeat:** Continue steps 3âĂ§5 until the desired number of clusters $k$ is obtained, or all points are merged into a single cluster.

The performance of Agglomerative Clustering is quantitatively evaluated using metrics such as:

1. Silhouette Coefficient: Measures intra-cluster tightness vs inter-cluster separation.
2. Adjusted Rand Index (ARI): Evaluates agreement with ground-truth class labels, adjusted for chance.
3. Normalized Mutual Information (NMI): Measures the shared information between clustering and true labels.
4. Homogeneity, Completeness, and V-Measure: Validate cluster purity and class consistency.

## 3 Result Analysis and Discussions

The presented figure offers a technically rich comparative visualization between the true class distribution and the predicted clusters derived via Agglomerative Hierarchical Clustering on the apple ripeness dataset. The data, consisting of sensor-derived features (likely from MQ-series gas sensors), was first subjected to z-score normalization using StandardScaler to ensure uniform feature scaling. Subsequently, PCA was applied to reduce the dimensionality while preserving maximal variance in a two-dimensional space, facilitating clearer cluster interpretability. The left subplot, which represents the ground truth labels, shows three well-separated class groupings, corresponding to predefined ripeness stages (e.g., underripe, optimally ripe, and overripe). The right subplot demonstrates the output of Agglomerative Clustering, a bottom-up hierarchical method that merges data points based on linkage criteria and inter-sample proximity (typically Euclidean distance), without any label supervision. Impressively, the predicted clusters align closely with the ground truth classes, indicating that the latent structure of the multivariate feature space captures meaningful biochemical and physiological differences among fruit ripeness levels. This reflects the high intrinsic separability and cluster tendency of the dataset, which are further supported by internal validation metrics such as the Silhouette Score, Adjusted Rand Index, and Normalized Mutual Information. The results validate the efficacy of hierarchical unsupervised learning as a scalable and interpretable method for non-destructive fruit maturity assessment, contributing significantly to intelligent post-harvest monitoring systems in precision agriculture and automated food quality control pipelines.

The presented 3D scatter plot illustrates the results of Agglomerative Hierarchical Clustering applied to the apple quality assessment dataset, projected onto three principal components derived through Principal Component Analysis (PCA). This dimensionality reduction technique preserves the maximum variance in the original high-dimensional feature space—likely composed of multisensor data such as volatile gas signatures, humidity, and temperature—while reducing the feature set to three orthogonal axes (PCA1, PCA2, PCA3) for effective visualization. Each point denotes an apple sample, and the clustering is visually encoded using distinct colors: red (Class 0), green (Class 1), and blue (Class 2), corresponding to different stages of ripeness or quality. The compact and well-separated clusters in the PCA-transformed space indicate strong discriminative power among the features used and validate the inter-cluster separability and intra-cluster cohesion achieved by the agglomerative approach. The hierarchical algorithm operates by recursively merging the closest clusters based on a linkage metric—typically Ward's linkage for variance minimization—until the pre-defined number of clusters is obtained. The spatial distinction among clusters demonstrates the model's capacity to automatically and non-destructively classify apple quality based on latent sensory characteristics. This outcome supports the feasibility of integrating such unsupervised clustering techniques within intelligent post-harvest systems, enabling real-time, data-driven decision-making in smart agriculture and supply chain automation (Fig. 4 and 5).

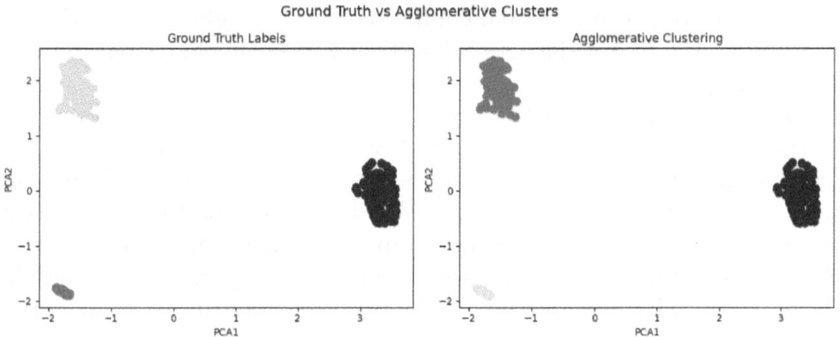


**Fig. 4.** 2D plot of apple dataset

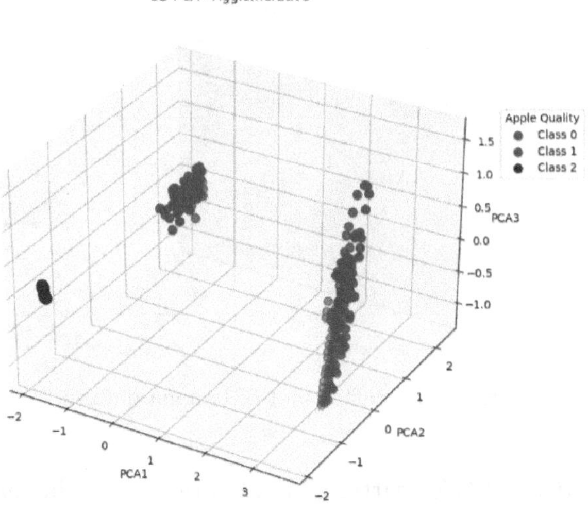


**Fig. 5.** 3D scatter plot of apple dataset

The figure titled "Ground Truth vs Agglomerative Clusters" presents a comparative visualization of the true class labels and the clustering results obtained using the Agglomerative Clustering algorithm on the banana fruit ripeness dataset. The dataset, comprising multivariate sensor responses from gas sensors detecting VOCs released during different ripening stages, was first preprocessed through z-score standardization and projected into a two-dimensional feature space using PCA. This dimensionality reduction technique preserves the most significant variance while enabling effective visual interpretation of class separability. In the left subplot, the data points are colored based on the ground truth labels representing three biologically distinct ripeness stages—likely corresponding to unripe, partially ripe, and fully ripe bananas. The distinct and compact clusters indicate that the principal components successfully capture discriminative patterns in the sensor data associated with biochemical changes in the fruit during ripening.

The right subplot depicts the same PCA-transformed data colored according to the cluster assignments generated by Agglomerative Clustering, a hierarchical bottom-up algorithm that successively merges pairs of data points or clusters based on linkage criteria (e.g., Ward's method or Euclidean distance). The close alignment of the clustering output with the ground truth classes illustrates the algorithm's capability to discover natural groupings in the absence of labeled data. Minimal overlap or label noise confirms that the gas sensor responses encode ripeness-related information with high fidelity, and that Agglomerative Clustering, coupled with PCA, is a technically robust method for non-destructive, unsupervised fruit quality assessment. This result reinforces the suitability of clustering-based approaches for real-time deployment in smart agriculture systems (Fig. 6).

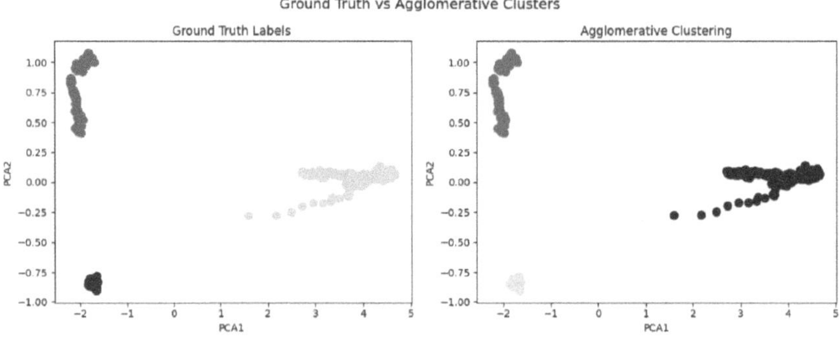


**Fig. 6.** 2D scatter plot of banana dataset

The presented 3D PCA scatter plot illustrates the clustering outcome of the banana ripeness dataset using Agglomerative Clustering, with dimensionality reduction applied via PCA to facilitate visual interpretation. In this figure, each point corresponds to a sample collected from a multisensor system monitoring VOC emissions during the ripening process of bananas. The data, originally high-dimensional due to multiple gas sensor channels, is projected into a three-dimensional space defined by the first three principal components (PCA1, PCA2, and PCA3), which collectively capture the majority of the variance inherent in the dataset. Color-coded cluster assignments (red for Class 0, green for Class 1, and blue for Class 2) indicate three distinct stages of banana ripeness—presumably representing overripe, semi-ripe, and unripe conditions, respectively. Notably, Class 0 (red) exhibits a broader dispersion, reflecting greater variability in gas release at advanced ripeness stages, likely due to increased enzymatic activity and decomposition. In contrast, Class 1 (green) and Class 2 (blue) form compact, well-separated clusters, signifying more homogeneous VOC profiles at earlier ripening stages.

The hierarchical nature of Agglomerative Clustering enables it to identify these natural groupings by iteratively merging data points based on inter-sample similarity, typically using Euclidean linkage. The clear spatial boundaries among clusters in this 3D PCA space confirm that the sensor data is inherently structured and amenable to unsupervised classification. Overall, this analysis demonstrates the robustness of combining PCA with hierarchical clustering for real-time, non-invasive fruit ripeness evaluation in smart post-harvest systems (Fig. 7).

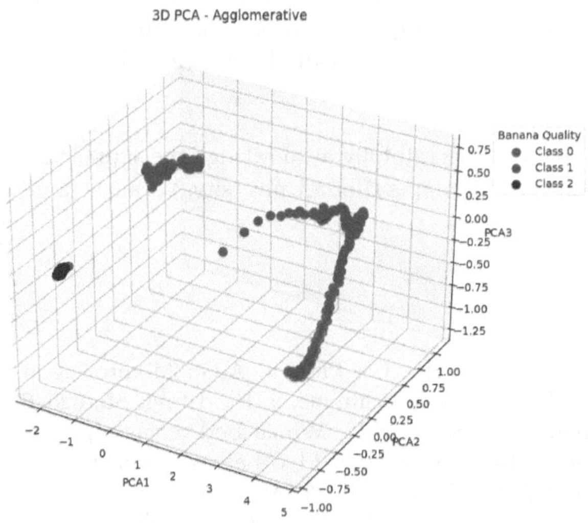


**Fig. 7.** 3D scatter plot of banana dataset

## 4 Conclusions and Future Scope of Work

The experimental results demonstrate that multisensor data combined with unsupervised clustering algorithms can effectively differentiate fruit ripeness stages in a non-destructive manner. Among the evaluated techniques—Agglomerative Clustering, KMeans, and DBSCAN—the hierarchical approach showed promising performance in preserving the natural grouping structure of the data, as supported by clustering metrics such as silhouette score, adjusted rand index, and normalized mutual information. The integration of PCA for dimensionality reduction further enabled clear visual separation and validation of cluster boundaries. This study confirms the potential of clustering-based frameworks for intelligent, automated fruit quality assessment using sensor-driven data analytics.

Future research will focus on enhancing the proposed clustering framework by integrating advanced ensemble and deep unsupervised learning models, such as variational autoencoders, deep embedded clustering, or graph-based approaches, to better capture complex and non-linear patterns in multisensor data. Temporal analysis using dynamic time warping (DTW) and time-series clustering can be explored for tracking ripening progression. Additionally, multimodal fusion with hyperspectral imaging, thermal sensing, or biochemical markers will be investigated to improve robustness and generalization. The system can be further optimized for real-time deployment on resource-constrained IoT platforms (e.g., ESP32, Raspberry Pi) using TinyML. Finally, adaptive online clustering methods will be incorporated to support continuous learning and decision-making under varying environmental and seasonal conditions in smart agriculture.

**Funding Information.** We gratefully acknowledge the support of the Institutions of Eminence (IoE) Scheme of Banaras Hindu University, Varanasi under Dev. Scheme No. 6031.

## References

1. Gómez, A.H., Wang, J., Hu, G., Pereira, A.G.: Monitoring storage shelf life of tomato using electronic nose technique. J. Food Eng. **85**, 625–631 (2008)
2. Burton-Freeman, B.M., Sesso, H.D.: Whole food versus supplement: comparing the clinical evidence of tomato intake and lycopene supplementation on cardiovascular risk factors. Adv. Nutr. **5**, 457–485 (2014)
3. Michaličková, D., Belović, M., Ilić, N., Kotur-Stevuljević, J., Slanař, O., Šobajić, S.: Comparison of polyphenol-enriched tomato juice and standard tomato juice for cardiovascular benefits in subjects with stage 1 hypertension: a randomized controlled study. Plant Foods Hum. Nutr. **74**, 122–127 (2019)
4. Seo, D., Cho, B.-H., Kim, K.-C.: Development of monitoring robot system for tomato fruits in hydroponic greenhouses. Agronomy **11**, 2211 (2021). https://doi.org/10.3390/agronomy11112211

5. Joshi, N., Pransu, G., Conte-Junior, C.A.: Critical review and recent advances of 2D materials-based gas sensors for food spoilage detection. Crit. Rev. Food Sci. Nutr. **63**(30), 10536–10559 (2023). https://doi.org/10.1080/10408398.2022.2137814
6. Li, C., et al.: A highly sensitive ethylene gas sensor based on PtO-Decorated SnO used to monitor the ripening and spoilage of fruits and vegetables stored at room temperature. New J. Chem. **48**(23), 10686–10696 (2024). https://doi.org/10.1039/D4NJ01678A
7. Wang, X., Feng, H., Chen, T., Zhao, S., Zhang, J., Zhang, X.: Gas sensor technologies and mathematical modelling for quality sensing in fruit and vegetable cold chains: a review. Trends Food Sci. Technol. **110**, 483–492 (2021). https://doi.org/10.1016/j.tifs.2021.02.046
8. Gutiérrez, S., Fernández-Novales, J., Garde-Cerdán, T., Marín-San Román, S., Tardaguila, J., Diago, M.P.: Multi-sensor spectral fusion to model grape composition using deep learning. Inf. Fusion **99**, 101865 (2023). https://doi.org/10.1016/j.inffus.2023.101865
9. Fan, C., et al.: A multi-parameter control method for maize threshing based on machine learning algorithm optimisation. Biosyst. Eng. **236**, 212–223 (2023). https://doi.org/10.1016/j.biosystemseng.2023.05.006
10. Leng, J., et al.: Recent advances in research on biocontrol of postharvest fungal decay in apples. Crit.l Rev. Food Sci. Nutr. **63**(30), 10607–10620 (2023). https://doi.org/10.1080/10408398.2022.2137812
11. Guo, Z., et al.: Multi-sensor fusion and deep learning for batch monitoring and real-time warning of apple spoilage. Food Control **172**, 111174 (2025). https://doi.org/10.1016/j.foodcont.2024.111174
12. Statistics | FAO | Food and Agriculture Organization of the United Nations (2024). https://www.fao.org/statistics/en
13. Kumar, K., Rajput, N.S.: Analysis space transformation based electronic nose for efficient detection and monitoring of volatile organic compounds, gases/odors in smart homes. Eur. Chem. Bull. **12**(7), 513–528 (2023)
14. Kumar, K., Verma, A., Verma, P.: IoT-HGDS: internet of Things integrated machine learning based hazardous gases detection system for smart kitchen. Internet of Things **28**, 101396 (2024)
15. Kumar, K., Tripathi, S.L., Mahmud, M.: Internet of things enabled smart E-nose system for pollutants hazard detection and real-time monitoring in indoor mosquito repellents. SN Comput. Sci. **5**(5), 438 (2024). https://doi.org/10.1007/s42979-024-02539-w
16. Kumar, K., Verma, A., Verma, P.: VLD2R: a lightweight framework for early vegetable leaf diseases detection and recognition. SN Comput. Sci. **6**(5), 533 (2025)
17. Kumar, K., Verma, A., Verma, P.: Development of an intelligent electronic-nose framework for perishable food quality assessment. SN Comput. Sci. **6**(6), 1–12 (2025)

# Facial Expression Recognition Using Deep Learning

Pratibha Sharma(✉)

Department of Computer Science, Banasthali Vidyapith, Rajasthan 304022, India
pratibhasjp@gmail.com

**Abstract.** Facial Expression Recognition (FER) is now a promising area of research because of its applicability in field where human & computer shares a table together, intuitive computing, and most important security. Among the different approaches, deep learning singularly Convolutional Neural Networks (CNN) showed magnificent results in this province. This study gives a performance of CNN-based models for facial expression recognition using the CK+, FER-2013 and JAFFE datasets. To gauge the model's generalization capability, applying trained models to both the JAFFE and CK+ datasets and FER-2013. The results are accuracy of 74.42% on the JAFFE dataset and 96.58% on CK+, while performance on the FER-2013 dataset reached 59.22%. We provide approximate evaluation of multiple CNN architectures, focusing on their accuracy and the effect of dataset changeability.

**Keywords:** Facial Expression Recognition · Deep Learning · Convolutional Neural Networks · Supervised Learning

## 1 Introduction

Facial Expression Recognition (FER) is a branch of a tree named computer vision that puts a light on recognizing and illustrating human emotions via facial nodes. Imposing on advanced machine learning and deep learning methods mainly Convolutional Neural Networks (CNNs) FER systems can examine facial motions and catalogue them into definite seven emotional classes: happy, sadness, anger, fear, surprise, disgust, and neutral.

While early FER methods are based on manually extracted features, such as Local Binary Patterns (LBP) and Histogram of Oriented Gradients (HOG), they are orthodox techniques sometimes grapple with contrast in lighting, head inclination, and many more individual differences. Current FER systems have moved on in the direction of deep learning, majorly CNNs, which is being good at automatically fetching layered and composite features straight from image data, serving good accuracy and better generalization. [1].

The CK + (Extended Cohn-Kanade) dataset is known for its high-resolution, well-illustrated images of posed expressions, while the JAFFE (Japanese Female Facial Expression) dataset gives culturally specific emotional expressions, offering a unique


A. Shastri et al. (Eds.): IHCI 2025, LNCS 16437, pp. 278–287, 2026.
https://doi.org/10.1007/978-3-032-26352-0_23

outlook on cross-cultural generalization. For the moment, the FER-2013 dataset, being larger and more manifold, presents a vigorous standard for finding real-world FER performance. [2].

It includes some challenges like

- CNN requires huge dataset to grasp in better way and also needed a large number of labeled images to learn significant patterns and keep away from under fitting, switching in lighting effect differing luminosity or shadows can baffle the model and deduct the accuracy.
- Real world images do carry noise Images may include blur, grain, or artifacts that affect feature extraction and forecasting.
- If CNN get trained for long time period then training data get over fit training CNN for too long can lead to memorizing training data instead of learning general patterns.

This paper look into the performance of CNN models in FER by the influence of CK+, JAFFE and FER datasets. We do examine on list of different CNN architectures, extracts their effectiveness in recognizing facial expressions, and talk over dataset-specific challenges. The main objective is to provide intuition into the footprint of dataset variation on model performance and tour on potential improvements for better generalizability in real-world applications.

The remainder of this paper is organized as follows. Section 2 describes the literature review that is discussing related work on facial expression recognition and focusing on recent advances using CNN-based models. Section 3 presents the proposed methodology that has the dataset, preprocessing steps, CNN architecture, and training strategy. Section 4 tells the experimental results and provides a discussion on the performance of the proposed model across different datasets and last but not the least Sect. 5 sum up the paper and outlines potential future research directions.

Major contributions:

1. We have designed and also implemented a Convolutional Neural Network (CNN) for facial expression recognition. The model is optimized for grayscale (JAFFE, CK+) as well as diverse real-world image datasets (FER-2013).
2. The proposed model was evaluated on three popular datasets JAFFE, CK+, and FER-2013. Our result shows consistent and competitive performance across these datasets.
3. Our CNN model addresses a problem of common class imbalance, specifically in FER-2013 dataset, through techniques such as data augmentation and loss function tuning, majorly for emotions like "fear" and "disgust".

## 2 Literature Review

Numerous studies have investigated facial expression recognition (FER) through the application of deep learning methods. Convolutional Neural Networks (CNNs) are commonly used for automatically extracting features and classifying expressions, often surpassing traditional machine learning approaches. Researchers have explored various network architectures—such as VGG, ResNet, and customized CNN models—to enhance recognition accuracy. Datasets like CK+, which includes posed emotional expressions, and JAFFE, focused on Japanese female expressions, introduce specific challenges such as data imbalance and limited sample sizes. Additionally, the FER-2013 dataset is frequently employed in this domain due to its large image collection and broad relevance to emotion recognition tasks.

Existing works generally focus on either controlled datasets or in-the-wild datasets, but very rarely comes with generalization across diverse datasets, Many studies lack ablation analysis, making it difficult to understand the contribution of pre-processing, augmentation, or architectural choices. Limited discussion on model efficiency and real-world applicability for low-resource or real-time systems.

Al-Shabi et al. presented a hybrid technique that integrates Convolutional Neural Networks (CNNs) with Scale-Invariant Feature Transform (SIFT) features. This combination was designed to enhance performance on smaller datasets by utilizing SIFT's reliable feature extraction capabilities. The model attained accuracies of 73.4% on FER-2013 and 99.1% on CK+ [3].

Yousin Khaireddin employed the VGGNet architecture along with optimization strategies, learning rate scheduling, and hyperparameter tuning to enhance CNN performance. Despite using only the FER-2013 dataset, the study applied data augmentation and achieved 73.28% accuracy. However, it focused exclusively on image input and did not incorporate audio or video modalities [5].

Akriti Jiaswal's work involved using CNNs for feature extraction, followed by classification with a softmax layer. The model was trained for 100 epochs using GPU acceleration. While the model achieved 70.14% accuracy on FER-2013 and 98.65% on JAFFE, the study offered limited details on evaluation metrics and interpretability [6].

Imane Lasri utilized CNNs alongside Haar cascade classifiers for face detection. The model, trained via stochastic gradient descent, was applied to static images. One noted limitation was difficulty distinguishing emotions like fear and sadness, reflected in its 70% accuracy on FER-2013 [7].

Deepak Kumar Jain et al. used a CNN-based framework for extracting facial features and classifying emotions. While achieving 95.23% on JAFFE and 93.24% on CK+, the model showed potential overfitting due to limited training data and lacked adaptation to real-world scenarios [8].

## 3 Proposed Methodology

Following proposed system for **Facial Expression Recognition (FER)** follows a structured pipeline that includes image acquisition, preprocessing, face detection, feature extraction, classification, and output interpretation and every stage make sure that the model efficiently determines discriminative facial features and generalizes on different datasets such as JAFFE, CK+, and FER-2013.

**Image Acquisition–** The system firstly takes images or video frames from the JAFFE. CK+ and FER-2013 dataset and the main process started by gathering facial images or video frames from standard datasets such as **JAFFE, CK+, and FER-2013**. These datasets provide various facial expressions under different conditions to make sure of strengthening in training.

**Preprocessing–** The image is inflate by normalization, Normalization basically refers to scaling image pixel values to accordant range or distribution. This guarantees faster convergence throughout training and better generalization by decreasing internal covariate shift, helping the optimizer work more efficiently, making the model less sensitive to weight initialization.

**Face Detection–** Facial landmarks are detected using deep learning models such as MTCNN.

**Feature Extraction–** Key facial features (eyes, nose, & mouth) are analyzed for expression patterns. To use hand-crafted feature extraction methods like LBP which Captures local texture, ideal for facial expression recognition, HOG that Captures edge orientations, good for structure-focused tasks like facial landmarks, SIFT which is Key point-based method, captures local patterns irrespective of scale/rotation, or SURF that is faster alternative to SIFT.

Before feeding data into a CNN for emotion recognition on datasets like JAFFE, CK+, and FER-2013.

**Classification–** A trained model CNN classifies the expression into an emotion category.Input shape typically grayscale (1 channel), e.g., (48 × 48 × 1) or (64 × 64 × 1) it has convolutional layers to extract spatial features, Batch Normalization for faster convergence,maxpooling to reduce spatial dimensions, Dropout for regularization, Fully connected (Dense) layers for classification, softmax output layer for emotion classes.

**Output & Interpretation–** The system provides real-time emotion feedback for applications in human-computer interaction, surveillance, healthcare, and entertainment [4].

## 3.1 CNN Architecture

A CNN model with multiple convolutional layers, batch normalization, and dropout is used. The architecture consists of (Fig. 1):

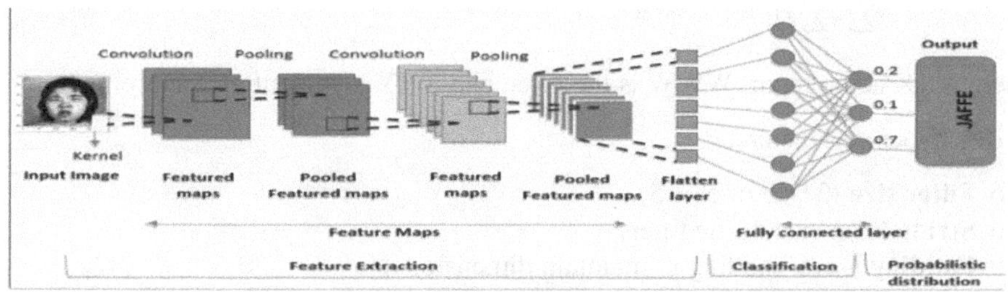


**Fig. 1.** Framework of CNN

**Training Strategy**

- To overcome dataset limitations, data augmentation methods such as rotation ($\pm 15°$), flipping (Enabled), and brightness modification are employed.
- The model utilizes the Adam optimizer along with categorical cross-entropy as the loss function. Training is conducted over 20 epochs, incorporating early stopping to avoid over fitting.
- **Input Layer**
- CNNs generally take images as input, represented by multi-dimensional arrays of pixel values.
- In this model, a single input channel is specified implicitly through the input shape of (48, 48, and 1) in the first Conv2D layer.
- For facial expression recognition (FER) tasks, the datasets used include:
- FER-2013 with 48 × 48 grayscale images
- CK + consisting of 100 × 100 grayscale images
- JAFFE containing 256 × 256 grayscale images
- **Convolutional Layer (Conv Layer)**

[Layers: Conv2D (32, 3 × 3) → MaxPooling2D → Conv2D (64, 3 × 3) → MaxPooling2D → Conv2D (128, 3 × 3) → MaxPooling2D.

Dense layers: 128 units with ReLU → Dropout (0.5) → Output Dense layer with softmax activation.

Loss: Categorical cross entropy, Optimizer: Adam].

- The convolutional layer serves as the fundamental component of CNNs.
- It uses filters (also called kernels) that move across the input image to capture important features.
- This particular model includes three convolutional layers.
- Mathematical operation:

$$\begin{aligned} Y(i,j) &= \sum m \sum n X(i-m, j-n) \cdot W(m,n) Y(i,j) = \backslash sum\_m \sum_{n} X(i-m, j-n) \cdot W(m,n) Y(i,j) \\ &= m \sum n \sum X(i-m, j-n) \cdot W(m,n) \end{aligned} \tag{1}$$

where XXX is the input, WWW is the filter, and YYY is the output feature map.

- Key hyper parameters:

  o **Filter size** (3 × 3 or 5 × 5)
  o **Stride** (step size of the filter)
  o **Padding** (zero-padding to maintain dimensions)

- Activation Function
- CNNs employ **non-linearity** to learn complex patterns.
- Common activation functions:

  o **ReLU (Rectified Linear Unit)**: here we have used 4 (3 ReLU in Conv layers + 1 ReLU in Dense).

*f(x)=max(0,x)f(x)=\max(0, x)f(x)=max(0,x)*

- o **Leaky ReLU**: Addresses vanishing gradients.
- o **Softmax**: Used in the final layer for multi-class classification.

(d) Pooling Layer (Downsampling)

- Reduces spatial dimensions to lower computation cost and prevent overfitting.
- Types of pooling:
  - o **Max Pooling**: Takes the maximum value from a feature map, we have used 3 Max pooling layers in the model. Formula for max pooling:

*Y(i,j)=maxm,nX(i+m,j+n)Y(i,j)=\max_{m,n}X(i+m,j+n)Y(i,j)=m,nmaxX(i+m,j+n)* (2)

(e) **Batch Normalization**

- Three batch normalization layers are applied to standardize activations, which helps speed up training and enhances the model's generalization capability.

(f) **Dropout Layer**

- A single dropout layer is included to help prevent overfitting by randomly deactivating a portion of neurons during training.

(g) Fully Connected (Dense) Layer.

- The model incorporates two dense layers, which transform the feature maps into a one-dimensional vector and apply weights and biases to perform classification.

(h) **Output Layer:**.

- A single output layer is implemented as the final dense layer with softmax activation.
- Softmax function is applied to generate probability distributions across emotion
- Convolutional layers utilize ReLU activation for feature extraction.
- Max pooling is employed to downsample spatial features.
- Fully connected layers are used to perform the classification task.
- The output layer uses softmax activation for multi-class emotion prediction.

## 4 Results and Discussion

The CNN model attains an accuracy of 96.58% on the CK + dataset, 74.42% on the JAFFE dataset, and 59.22% on FER-2013. The model achieved highest accuracy for happiness and surprise expressions, Confusions were observed between fear and disgust, likely due to similar facial muscle movements, Data augmentation and preprocessing significantly improved the model's generalization on unseen images.

The lower accuracy on FER-2013 is mainly to its higher intra-class variability, presence of noisy and low-resolution images, and greater diversity in illumination and facial orientations, which introduce domain shifts compared to the more controlled CK + and JAFFE datasets.

**CK+ (Cohn-Kanade Extended Dataset):**

Includes 327 annotated facial expression sequences, divided into seven categories such as happiness, sadness, anger, and surprise. Contains both emotion labels and FACS annotations, allowing dual analysis with High-resolution, frontal facial sequences suitable

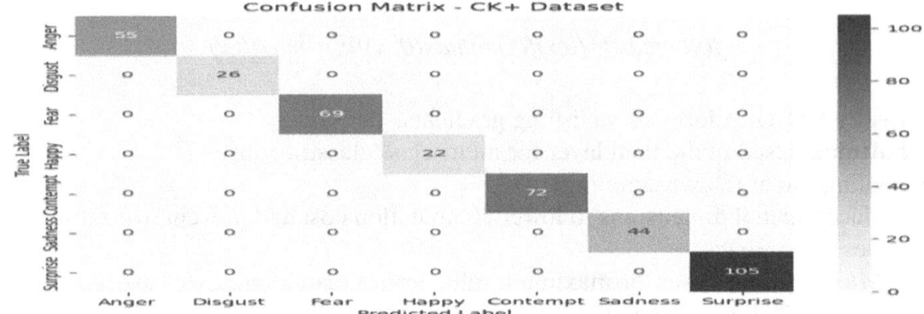


**Fig. 2.** Confusion matrix

**Table 1.** Results for CK + Dataset

| Methods | Accuracy (%) | Precision (%) | Recall (%) | F1-Score (%) |
|---|---|---|---|---|
| Kim et al. [9] | 96.7 | 95.5 | 95.0 | 95.2 |
| Li & Deng [10] | 97.3 | 96.8 | 96.5 | 96.6 |
| Tang et al. [11] | 95.9 | 94.8 | 94.5 | 94.6 |
| Proposed | 96.58 | 99.31 | 99.16 | 97.90 |

for feature extraction and temporal modeling. Widely accepted benchmark for emotion classification and CNN-based FER models. [18] (Fig. 2) (Table 1).

**JAFFE (Japanese Female Facial Expression Dataset):**
Contains 213 images featuring 10 Japanese women displaying six different emotions. It has High-quality, noise-free facial images. Standardized emotion labels suitable for classification tasks and ideal for initial training or testing of FER models in controlled settings [18]. (Fig. 3) (Table 2)

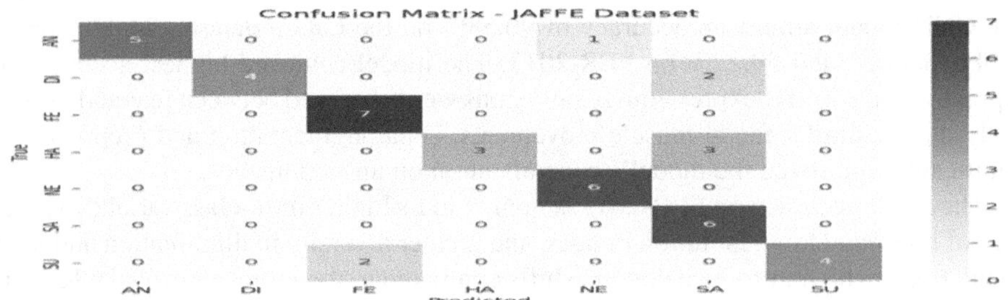


**Fig. 3.** Confusion matrix

- **FER-2013 (Facial Expression Recognition Dataset):** The dataset includes 35,887 grayscale images, each measuring 48 × 48 pixels. These images were gathered via the

**Table 2.** Results for JAFFE dataset

| Methods | Accuracy (%) | Precision (%) | Recall (%) | F1-Score (%) |
|---|---|---|---|---|
| Hazem Zein et al. [12] | 95.0 | 95.0 | 95.0 | 95.0 |
| YuanZheng Hu, Marina Sokolova [13] | 64.93 | 65.04 | 65.04 | 65.04 |
| Fabricio Breve [14] | 99.3 | 99.2 | 99.2 | 99.2 |
| Proposed | 74.42 | 85.71 | 79.07 | 80.15 |

Google Image Search API, using 184 emotion-associated keywords in combination with descriptors for gender, age, and ethnicity. After collection, the images were processed to center the faces and standardize their size. Images are low-resolution and contain significant variations, making the dataset challenging for FER models.FER-2013 is often used to evaluate model generalization in real-world scenarios, as it reflects a more "in-the-wild" dataset compared to lab-controlled datasets like CK + or JAFFE [18] (Fig. 4) (Table 3).

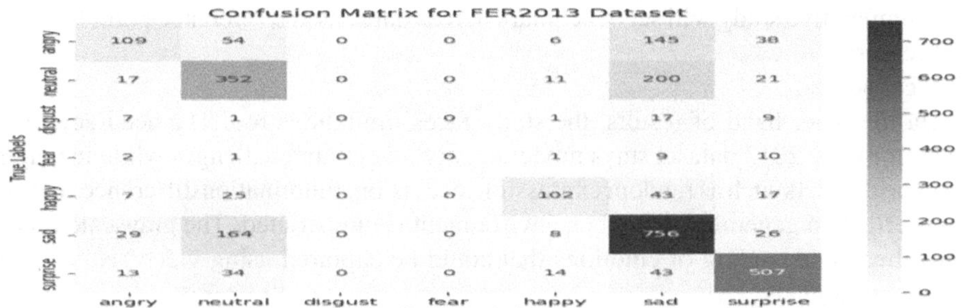


**Fig. 4.** Confusion matrix

**Table 3.** Results for FER-2013 Dataset.

| Methods | Accuracy (%) | Precision (%) | Recall (%) | F1-Score (%) |
|---|---|---|---|---|
| Goodfellow et al. [15] | 71.2 | 72.3 | 71.2 | 71.6 |
| Mollahosseini et al.[16] | 66.4 | 65.8 | 66.4 | 66.1 |
| Tang [17] | 71.0 | 71.5 | 71.5 | 71.5 |
| Proposed | 59.22 | 68.07 | 28.15 | 51.14 |

## 5 Conclusion and Future Work

This research highlights the effectiveness of Convolutional Neural Networks (CNNs) in facial expression recognition (FER), even so their performance can be significantly affected by the nature of the datasets used. To improve the generalizability of these models, future efforts will explore methods such as transfer learning, training across multiple datasets, and utilizing larger and more varied data sources. Furthermore, incorporating multimodal inputs such as audio cues and physiological data may further improve the accuracy of emotion recognition systems.

### 5.1 Comprehensive Review

Facial Expression Recognition displays that Convolutional Neural Networks (CNNs) can be used over many datasets with different level of complexity as well as diversity.

Strengths.

this approach triggers basic FER datasets CK+, JAFFE, and FER-2013 to evaluate the robustness along with generalization of models based on CNN. This cross dataset helps to get hands on the core deep learning architectures with different conditions. The model design has important optimization strategies like data augmentation, batch normalization and dropout regularization to enhance training and increased accuracy. This comparative study will set benchmark across datasets and reference point for future FER research.

Weaknesses.

On the other hand of results, the study faces limitations too. The accuracy of the model for FER-2013 dataset stays moderate, giving certain challenges while managing real-world effects such as random expression, occlusion, illumination differences etc. and it puts effect on generalization when environment is unrestricted. The grayscale images limits the understanding of emotions that could be captured using video sequences or multimodal signals.

Overall Contribution.

This research motivates the field by correctly managing CNN performance over diverse FER datasets and concentrate on the effect of dataset flexibility on model's effectiveness. It gives a foundation for future research for hybrid deep learning model and multimodal fusion methods. While putting focus on potential along with constraints of CNNs in FER, this work gives a notable step for developing more versatile and real-world emotion recognition systems.

## References

1. Mitra, S.K.: Facial expression recognition: feature based approaches to deep learning techniques (Doctoral dissertation, Dhirubhai Ambani Institute of Information and Communication Technology) (2020)
2. Dada, E.G., Oyewola, D.O., Joseph, S.B., Emebo, O., Oluwagbemi, O.O.: Facial emotion recognition and classification using the convolutional neural Network-10 (CNN-10). Appl. Comput. Intell. Soft Comput. **2023**(1), 2457898 (2023)

3. Connie, T., Al-Shabi, M., Cheah, W.P., Goh, M.: Facial expression recognition using a hybrid CNN–SIFT aggregator. In: International Workshop on Multi-Disciplinary Trends in Artificial Intelligence (pp. 139–149). Cham, Springer International Publishing (2017)
4. Haque, K.N.: What is Convolutional Neural Network — CNN (Deep Learning) (online article)
5. Khaireddin, Y., Chen, Z.: Facial emotion recognition: state of the art performance on FER2013. 8 May 2021. arXiv preprint arXiv:2105.03588
6. Jaiswal, A., Raju, A.K., Deb, S.: Facial emotion detection using Deep Learning. Dept. of Electronics Eng., SVNIT Surat, India. 2020 International Conference for Emerging Technology (INCET), Belgaum, India, 5–7 June 2020, pp. 1–5. https://doi.org/10.1109/INCET49848.2020.9154121
7. Lasri, I., Solh, A.R., Belkacemi, M.E.: Facial emotion recognition of students using convolutional neural network. In: 2019 3rd International Conference on Intelligent Computing in Data Sciences (ICDS), Marrakech, Morocco, Oct. 2019, pp. 1–6. https://doi.org/10.1109/ICDS47004.2019.8942386
8. Jain, D.K., Shamsolmoali, P., Sehdev, P.: Extended deep neural network for facial emotion recognition. Pattern Recogn. Lett. **120**, 69–74 (2019)
9. Kim, J.C., Kim, M.H., Suh, H.E., Naseem, M.T., Lee, C.S.: Hybrid approach for facial expression recognition using convolutional neural networks and SVM. Appl. Sci. **12**(11), 5493 (2022)
10. Li, S., Deng, W., Du, J.: Reliable crowdsourcing and deep locality-preserving learning for expression recognition in the wild. In: Proc. CVPR, pp. 2852–2861. IEEE (2017)
11. Li, T., Chan, K.L., Tjahjadi, T.: Multi-scale correlation module for video-based facial expression recognition in the wild. Pattern Recogn. **142**, 109691 (2023)
12. Zein, H., Chantaf, S., Fournier, R., Nait-Ali, A.: Generative adversarial networks for anonymous acneic face dataset generation. PLoS ONE **19**(4), e0297958 (2024)
13. Hu, Y., Sokolova, M.: Convolutional neural networks in multi-class classification of medical data (2020). arXiv preprint arXiv:2012.14059
14. Breve, F.: From pixels to titles: video game identification by screenshots using convolutional neural networks. IEEE Trans. Games (2025)
15. Goodfellow, I.J., Erhan, D., Carrier, P.L., Courville, A., Mirza, M., Hamner, B.: Challenges in representation learning: a report on three machine learning contests. In: Neural Information Processing. ICONIP 2013, Part III, pp. 117–124. Springer, Berlin (2013)
16. Fard, A.P., Hosseini, M.M., Sweeny, T.D., Mahoor, M.H.: AffectNet+: a database for enhancing facial expression recognition with soft-labels (2024). arXiv preprint arXiv:2410.22506
17. Tang, Y.: Deep learning using linear support vector machines (2013). arXiv preprint arXiv:1306.0239
18. https://www.kaggle.com

# Authentication Management Risks and Mitigation Strategies with Human-AI Interaction Analysed by Adaptive Network Modeling

Milán Radó[1,2], Jan Treur[1,2](✉), and Peter H. M. P. Roelofsma[1]

[1] The Hague University of Applied Sciences, Centre of Expertise Cybersecurity, The Hague, Netherlands
j.treur@vu.nl, p.h.m.p.roelofsma@hhs.nl

[2] Department of Computer Science, Social AI Group, Vrije Universiteit Amsterdam, Amsterdam, The Netherlands

**Abstract.** This study explores how employees respond to phishing emails, particularly when under stress. Using adaptive computational network modeling, it simulates how employees learn to recognize and handle phishing attempts based on organizational feedback. However, when stress occurs, it disrupts previously acquired learning and increases the likelihood of error. We analyse human-AI interaction by an AI Coach, which monitors user actions and provides real-time corrective feedback at the knowledge level. This simulation demonstrates that the AI Coach helps restore and stabilize behavior even under elevated stress.

**Keywords:** AI Coach · Adaptive Mental Model · Risk Assessment

## 1 Introduction

Authentication management is a critical aspect of cybersecurity, and there are several key risks associated with it. This paper uses adaptive computational network modeling to analyse how AI can support authentication management. The research specifically addresses how **employee actions** can either compromise or reinforce the integrity of the organization. It considers phishing which is the most common form of cyber crime, with an estimated 3.4 billion spam emails sent every day" [1]. Moreover, "30% of all cyber attacks begin with identity-based methods, such as phishing" [24]. Data indicate a **131% increase in whaling** attacks between 2020 and 2021, and a **150% rise in phishing** incidents in 2022 compared to 2019 [2, 21, 23, 26]. This research focuses on the vulnerability of an employee to phishing emails under stress conditions and the possible mitigation of the risks by introducing an human-AI interaction using an **AI Coach**, monitors and supports the employee. One simulation experiment showcases the **learning curve** of the employee upon how to act properly in the situation of a phishing email and how a stress factor destroys the learning [13]. In the second simulation, the AI Coach will be introduced, which will prevent at some point the decline of the employee's learning curve.


A. Shastri et al. (Eds.): IHCI 2025, LNCS 16437, pp. 288–300, 2026.
https://doi.org/10.1007/978-3-032-26352-0_24

Phishing is one of the most common and dangerous types of cyberattacks, not because of some major technical vulnerabilities, but because it targets human behavior. Fundamentally, phishing is about tricking someone usually through a fake email into revealing sensitive information like passwords, clicking a harmful link or even possible downloading some malware. What makes it so effective is takes advantage of people and their emotions mostly like urgency, trust, curiosity or even fear [19].

Within organizational contexts, phishing attempts might look like a message from a peer or boss, a fake invoice from a vendor, or an urgent IT notice. Attackers often gather publicly available information from company websites or social media platforms to craft messages that appear credible and contextually relevant. Under pressure and stress or during a busy day, even the most careful employee might click a link or enter their login info without thinking twice.

In the modern age, thanks to advanced AI tools, the sophistication of these attacks keeps growing rapidly. By the use of AI, attackers can create deepfakes videos [18] or voice messages that sounds and seems like just like a normal person. They are getting better with showing emotions as well, adding a new level of realism. To mitigate these risks, organizations must employ a multi-layered defense strategy. Two fundamental practices in this regard are password strength and two-factor authentication (2FA):

- **Password Strength**: Strength of a password is composed of its complexity, length, unpredictability and uniqueness. Complexity depends on the character types used in them. It's good practice for companies to enforce password policies on the employee to reduce credential-based risks. [22]
- **Two-Factor Authentication (2FA):** 2FA introduces an additional layer of security by requiring a second form of verification, such as a code sent to a mobile device. Even when passwords are compromised, 2FA can significantly reduce unauthorized access or, at minimum, delay a potential data breach, providing critical time for detection and response before significant damage occurs. [17]

Beyond these measures, the company may also further strengthen their security by following best practices:

- **Security Awareness Policies (SAP):** SAPs clarify employee responsibilities, set expectations, and support compliance with industry standards.
- **Security Awareness Training:** Ongoing training helps employees recognize phishing indicators and understand appropriate response behaviors and many other, which won't be present in the simulations.

## 2 Design of the Adaptive Network Model

This paper uses a computational modeling approach by network described by the following types of network structure characteristics: **connectivity**, *connection weights* $\mathbf{\omega}_{X,Y}$ for each connection from a state $X$ to state $Y$ ($X \rightarrow Y$); **aggregation,** a *combination function* $\mathbf{c}_Y$ **(...)** for each $Y$ state to determine the aggregation of incoming impacts; **timing in the network, a** *speed factor* $\mathbf{\eta}_Y$ for each state $Y$. Dynamics are defined by

$$Y(t+\Delta t) = Y(t) + \mathbf{\eta}_Y\left[\mathbf{c}_Y\left(\mathbf{\omega}_{X_1,Y}X_1(t), \ldots, \mathbf{\omega}_{X_{k,},Y}X_k(t)\right) - Y(t)\right]\Delta t \quad (1)$$

where the $X_i$ are all states from which state $Y$ gets incoming connections. For more details, see [32]. We're using 6 different combination functions. First one is **alogistic$_{\sigma,\tau}$(..)**, which is also the most frequent one. Its parameters are **steepness (σ)** and **threshold (τ)**. It is a hyberbolic logistic type of function defined by

$$\textbf{alogistic}_{\sigma\tau}\,(V_1, \ldots, V_k) = \left[\frac{1}{1+e^{-\sigma(V_1+\ldots+V_k-\tau)}} - \frac{1}{1+e^{\sigma\tau}}\right](1+e^{-\sigma\tau})$$

Second and third are **stepmod$_{\rho,\delta}$(..)** and **stepmodopp$_{\rho,\delta}$(..)**. Both have parameters **ρ,** which is the period it takes before restarting its pattern of '0' and '1' and **δ,** which specifies the time it takes to switch from '0' to '1' or vice versa in case of **stepmodopp**.

$$\textbf{stepmod}(x) = \begin{Bmatrix} 0, \mathit{if}\ mod(x, \rho) < \delta \\ 1, \mathit{if}\ mod(x, \rho) \geq \delta \end{Bmatrix}$$

Fourth is **hebb$_{\mu}$** (..), a function with only one parameter **persistence factor (μ)**. This function is used for the learning with persistence controlling how much it decays.

$$\textbf{hebb}_{\mu}(V_1, V_2, W) = V_1 V_2(1-W) + \mu W$$

Fifth is the **alogisticneg_clipped$_{\sigma,\tau}$**(..) function, which provides the same behavior as **alogistic$_{\sigma,\tau}$(..)** except that its domain lies in the negative region and it's clipped at 0, preventing it to go beyond that value. The last one is called **monitor$_{\tau}$**(..) function with only one parameter **threshold (τ)**. This is a defined by

$$\textbf{monitor}\ (V_1, V_2) = 1 \mathit{if} V_1 - V_2 \geq \tau,\ \text{else } 0$$

The monitor function was adopted from [20], the rest of the functions comes from [32].

To incorporate adaptivity of network characteristics, the self-modeling (or reification) principle is used as introduced in [30, 31], see also [32]. This was inspired by the area of metalevel architectures and reflection in AI; e.g., [5, 14, 15, 27, 28, 39]. For example, if a connection weight $\boldsymbol{\omega}_{X,Y}$ is adaptive, a self-model state $\mathbf{W}_{X,Y}$ (called a **W**-state) is added to the network representing the value of $\boldsymbol{\omega}_{X,Y}$. Then in (1) the $\boldsymbol{\omega}_{X_i,,Y}$ are replaced by $\mathbf{W}_{X_i,,Y}(t)$. Similarly an adaptive speed factor $\boldsymbol{\eta}_Y$ can be represented by a self-model state $\mathbf{H}_Y$ (an **H**-state) and adaptive excitability threshold $\boldsymbol{\tau}_Y$ by a selfmodel state $\mathbf{T}_Y$ (a **T**-state).

The self-modeling network modeling approach comes with methods and software for simulation [33], verification by mathematical analysis [4, 9, 29, 34], and validation by comparison and tuning to numerical empirical data [35].

The first simulation only uses states from X1 up to X26 and then from X40 to X50, the rest is being deactivated and out of service until the second simulation; see Tables 1 and 2. The **yellow-coloured** regions within the model represent the employee's mental model, while the **rose-coloured** areas denote the external world. The **blue regions** correspond to the first level of reification, responsible for the adaptive behavior of the network.

The process starts with **X1 (SJ–Start Job)**, which marks the entry point when the employee begins work at the organization. The activation of X1 simultaneously triggers both external and internal (mental) processes. The mental representation of this initiation is denoted as **X14 (J–Job)**. Several other states fire up immediately at the beginning of the simulation, including **X4 (PQ–Phishing Quality)**, **X9 (SAP–Security Awareness Policy)**, **X13 (Stress)**, and **X2 (PE–Phishing Email)**.

The phishing email state (X2) is activated in a recurring time loop, simulating **periodic phishing attacks**. While phishing attacks are often random and less predictable in reality, the simulation applies a regular pattern to emphasize the employee's learning process and potential mistakes, rather than the unpredictable nature of the attacks themselves. A complementary state, **X3 (NO-PE–No Phishing Email)**, alternates with X2 to create a consistent attack-no-attack cycle. The X4 (PQ) state models the increasing sophistication of phishing attacks over time, capturing the notion that adversaries also adapt and evolve, paralleling the employee's own learning trajectory.

X9 represents the organization's role and responsibility in managing cybersecurity-related behavior. Its presence in the model highlights the influence of institutional policies such as training programs on employee decisions. X13 captures the employee's stress level, which is designed to gradually increase over time throughout the simulation, showcasing stress build up. The above states X9, X13, X4, X2, and X14 are activated at the start of the simulation and initiate parallel. The simulation proceeds by modelling the employee's internal (mental) processes. After activation of X14 (J–Job), input is provided to three key internal states: **X15 (CAP–Capability)**, **X16 (MOT–Motivation)**, and **X17 (OPP–Opportunity)**. These variables collectively influence **X18 (B–Behavior)**, which serves as the **core behavioral** output of the employee model.

This framework aligns with the **COM-B model of behavior** change (Capability, Opportunity, Motivation–Behavior), a widely accepted approach in behavioral science for conceptualizing and influencing individual behavior [25]. Based on the state of X18 (Behavior) and other factors, the employee makes decisions regarding various actions. Four decision states are defined:

- X19 (Dec2FA–Decision to use two-factor authentication)
- X20 (DecClick–Decision to click on an email)
- X21 (DecRep–Decision to report a phishing email)
- X22 (DecPS–Decision regarding password strength)

States X19 and X22 are influenced by both the employee's behavioral state (X18) and **X23 (KSAP–Knowledge of the Security Awareness Policy)**, which serves as the mental representation of X9. Similarly, X20 and X21 are driven by X18 and **X24 (KPQ–Knowledge of Phishing Quality)**, representing the mental encoding of X4.

These internal representations (X23 and X24) are essential for demonstrating that the employee possesses knowledge of these factors.

For the external world, two key states **X5 (CE–Click Email)** and **X6 (RE–Report Email)** represent the employee's potential responses to a phishing email. These actions are primarily influenced by the employee's internal decision-making processes but are also dependent on the presence or absence of a phishing email at that given moment. **X7 (2FA–Two-Factor Authentication)** and **X8 (PWS–Password Strength)** are external manifestations of the internal decision states X19 and X22, respectively. These nodes serve as observable outcomes of the employee's choices.

**Table 1.** Every base state with their corresponding state number, state name and their description. States from X27-X39 are only being used in the second simulation, they aren't present for the first one. It should be highlighted that, throughout this paper, references to a variable *X* and its corresponding state number are based on the identifiers provided in this table, rather than on those used in the simulations

| State nr | State name | Description | Level |
|---|---|---|---|
| $X_{1}$ | SJ | Start job | |
| $X_{2}$ | PE | Phishing email | |
| $X_{3}$ | NO-PE | No Phishing email | |
| $X_{4}$ | PQ | Phishing email quality | |
| $X_{5}$ | CE | Click on email | |
| $X_{6}$ | RE | Report email | Base |
| $X_{7}$ | 2FA | 2-Factor Authentication | Level – World |
| $X_{8}$ | PWS | Password Strength | |
| $X_{9}$ | SAP | Security Awareness Policy | |
| $X_{10}$ | DB | Data Breach | |
| $X_{11}$ | ORR | Organization Reprimand (Negative feedback) | |
| $X_{12}$ | ORP | Organization Praise (Positive feedback) | |
| $X_{13}$ | Stress | External stress factor in the employee's life | 1. |
| $X_{14}$ | J | Job | |
| $X_{15}$ | CAP | Capability | |
| $X_{16}$ | MOT | Motivation | |
| $X_{17}$ | OPP | Opportunity | |
| $X_{18}$ | B | Behavior | |
| $X_{19}$ | Dec2FA | Decision for 2FA | Base |
| $X_{20}$ | DecClick | Decision for Clicking on email | Level – |
| $X_{21}$ | DecRep | Decision for Reporting email | Employee |
| $X_{22}$ | DecPS | Decision for password strength | Mental |
| $X_{23}$ | KSAP | Mental representation of SAP (Knowledge of SAP) | |
| $X_{24}$ | KPQ | Mental representation of PQ (Knowledge of PQ) | |
| $X_{25}$ | KORR | Mental representation of ORR (Knowledge of ORR) | 2. |
| $X_{26}$ | KORP | Mental representation of ORP (Knowledge of ORP) | 3. |
| $X_{27}$ | AI-J | AI mental representation of Job | |
| $X_{28}$ | AI-CAP | AI mental representation of Capability | |
| $X_{29}$ | AI-MOT | AI mental representation of Motivation | |
| $X_{30}$ | AI-OPP | AI mental representation of Opportunity | |
| $X_{31}$ | AI-B | AI mental representation of Behavior | Base |
| $X_{32}$ | AI-Dec2FA | AI mental representation of Decision for 2FA | Level – |
| $X_{33}$ | AI-DecClick | AI mental representation of Decision for Clicking on email | AI Mental |
| $X_{34}$ | AI-DecRep | AI mental representation of Decision for Reporting email | |
| $X_{35}$ | AI-DecPS | AI mental representation of Decision for password strength | |
| $X_{36}$ | AI-KSAP | AI mental representation of SAP (Knowledge of SAP) | |
| $X_{37}$ | AI-KPQ | AI mental representation of PQ (Knowledge of PQ) | |
| $X_{38}$ | AI-KORR | AI mental representation of ORR (Knowledge of ORR) | |
| $X_{39}$ | AI-KORP | AI mental representation of ORP (Knowledge of ORP) | |

If the employee chooses to report the phishing email (X6), this triggers **X12 (ORP–Organizational Praise)**, representing positive feedback from the organization. On the opposite, if the employee clicks on the phishing email (X5), it initiates **X10 (DB–Data Breach)**, simulating a successful breach resulting from employee error. In this simulation, clicking a phishing link is assumed to lead directly to a data breach, unless mitigating measures, such as strong passwords (X8) or two-factor authentication (X7), are in place to slow or prevent the breach process [16]. Following a data breach (X10), the model proceeds with X11 (ORR–Organizational Reprimand), indicating a negative

**Table 2.** Every first- and second-order adaptation state with their corresponding state number, state name and their description. States from X51-X65 are only being used in the second simulation, they aren't present for the first one. It should be highlighted that, throughout this paper, references to a variable X and its corresponding state number are based on the identifiers provided in this table, rather than on those used in the simulations.

| State nr | State name | Description | Level |
|---|---|---|---|
| $X_{40}$ | $\mathbf{W}_{ORR, SAP}$ | Self-model state for the weight of the connection between SAP and ORR. Upon ORR, SAP's value will increase. | |
| $X_{41}$ | $\mathbf{W}_{J, CAP}$ | Self-model state for the weight of the connection between J and CAP, learned by feedback via ORR and ORP | |
| $X_{42}$ | $\mathbf{W}_{J, OPP}$ | Self-model state for the weight of the connection between J and OPP, learned by feedback via ORR and ORP | |
| $X_{43}$ | $\mathbf{W}_{J, MOT}$ | Self-model state for the weight of the connection between J and MOT, learned by feedback via ORR and ORP | |
| $X_{44}$ | $\mathbf{H}_{DB}$ | Self-model state for Speed factor for DB by feedback via PWS, 2FA and MisConf. Higher values for PWS and 2FA will slow it down, while higher MisConf value will make it faster to happen. | First reification level |
| $X_{45}$ | $\mathbf{T}_{DecClick}$ | Self-model state for Threshold of DecClick, which will be increased upon ORR. Fewer impulsive clicks after negative feedback. | |
| $X_{46}$ | $\mathbf{T}_{DecRep}$ | Self-model state for Threshold of DecRep, which will be decreased upon ORP. Quicker reporting habit after positive feedback. | |
| $X_{47}$ | $\mathbf{W}_{B, DecPS}$ | Self-model state for the weight of the connection from Behavior to DecPS. | |
| $X_{48}$ | $\mathbf{W}_{B, Dec2FA}$ | Self-model state for the weight of the connection from Behavior to Dec2FA. | |
| $X_{49}$ | $\mathbf{W}_{B, DecClick}$ | Self-model state for the weight of the connection from Behavior to DecClick. | |
| $X_{50}$ | $\mathbf{W}_{B, DecRep}$ | Self-model state for the weight of the connection from Behavior to DecRep. | |
| $X_{51}$ | $\mathbf{W}_{AI\text{-}J, AI\text{-}CAP}$ | Self-model state for the weight of the connection from AI-J to AI-CAP. | |
| $X_{52}$ | $\mathbf{W}_{AI\text{-}J, AI\text{-}OPP}$ | Self-model state for the weight of the connection from AI-J to AI-OPP. | |
| $X_{53}$ | $\mathbf{W}_{AI\text{-}J, AI\text{-}MOT}$ | Self-model state for the weight of the connection from AI-J to AI-MOT. | |
| $X_{54}$ | $\mathbf{W}_{AI\text{-}B, AI\text{-}DecClick}$ | Self-model state for the weight of the connection from AI-B to AI-DecClick. | |
| $X_{55}$ | $\mathbf{W}_{AI\text{-}B, AI\text{-}DecRep}$ | Self-model state for the weight of the connection from AI-B to AI-DecRep. | First reification level |
| $X_{56}$ | $\mathbf{W}_{AI\text{-}B, AI\text{-}DecPS}$ | Self-model state for the weight of the connection from AI-B to AI-DecPS. | |
| $X_{57}$ | $\mathbf{W}_{AI\text{-}B, AI\text{-}Dec2FA}$ | Self-model state for the weight of the connection from AI-B to AI-Dec2FA. | |
| $X_{58}$ | $\mathbf{M}_{DecClick}$ | Monitoring state for DecClick | |
| $X_{59}$ | $\mathbf{M}_{DecRep}$ | Monitoring state for DecRep | |
| $X_{60}$ | $\mathbf{M}_{DecPS}$ | Monitoring state for DecPS | |
| $X_{61}$ | $\mathbf{M}_{Dec2FA}$ | Monitoring state for Dec2FA | |
| $X_{62}$ | $\mathbf{WW}_{B, DecClick}$ | Second-order W-state for first-order W-state $\mathbf{W}_{B, DecClick}$ | Second reification level |
| $X_{63}$ | $\mathbf{WW}_{B, DecRep}$ | Second-order W-state for first-order W-state $\mathbf{W}_{B, DecRep}$ | |
| $X_{64}$ | $\mathbf{WW}_{B, DecPS}$ | Second-order W-state for first-order W-state $\mathbf{W}_{B, DecPS}$ | |
| $X_{65}$ | $\mathbf{WW}_{B, Dec2FA}$ | Second-order W-state for first-order W-state $\mathbf{W}_{B, Dec2FA}$ | |

response from the organization to the employee's action. Both X11 and X12 are associated with their respective mental representations, X25 and X26, which are directly connected. These connections serve to represent the employee's internal understanding of the corresponding external states. Lastly, the first reification level, that's where the core dynamics happens.

- W-state **X40 ($\mathbf{W}_{ORR, SAP}$)** is a **W**-state linking ORR → SAP, responsible for incrementally increasing the value of X9 (Security Awareness Policy) when X12 (ORR) is triggered. This represents the organization reinforcing its policies following a breach.
- W-states **X41 ($\mathbf{W}_{J, CAP}$)**, **X42 ($\mathbf{W}_{J, OPP}$)**, and **X43 ($\mathbf{W}_{J, MOT}$)** are **W**-states associated with the COM-B components. They gradually increase the influence of X14 (Job) on X15 (Capability), X16 (Motivation), and X17 (Opportunity) when X11

(ORP) or X12 (ORR) occur. This reflects a feedback-driven learning mechanism, in which the employee's behavioral capabilities evolve only if actions happen in an organizational response manner.

- **H**-state **X44 ($\mathbf{H_{DB}}$)** functions as an adaptive speed regulator for the X10 (DB) state. It reduces the likelihood of a data breach when X7 (2FA) and/or X8 (PWS) are elevated, emphasizing the protective value of these decisions.
- **T**-state **X45 ($\mathbf{T_{DecClick}}$) and X46 ($\mathbf{T_{DecRep}}$)** dynamically adjust the threshold values for clicking and reporting decisions. Over time, these thresholds are biased by X25 and X26 toward favoring reporting over clicking, thus helping behavioral learning and improved handling of phishing attacks. X25 has a deeper influence on the thresholds because in our simulation cases negative feedback has a rather more extreme impact on the change of threshold than the positive feedback.
- The **W**-states **X47 ($\mathbf{W_{B, DecPS}}$)**, **X48 ($\mathbf{W_{B, Dec2FA}}$)**, **X49 ($\mathbf{W_{B, DecClick}}$)**, and **X50 ($\mathbf{W_{B, DecRep}}$)** represent how the employee's decision-making adapts over time in response to behavioral development (X17). As the employee shows improved behavior, the values of X19 (Dec2FA), X21 (DecRep) increase and X22 (DecPS) reinforcing secure choices. In contrast, X20 (DecClick), which reflects vulnerability to clicking on phishing emails, decreases. This dynamic illustrates that as the internal behavioral state improves, the employee is more likely to make safer cybersecurity decisions. However, all four **W**-states are negatively influenced by stress levels (X13), emphasizing the disruptive role of external stress in undermining secure decision-making.

In the **AI-enhanced model**, the key enhancement introduced is the addition of an extra entity called AI Coach, which continuously monitors the employee's decision-making and provides adaptive knowledge-level interaction to support correct responses to phishing attacks. As illustrated in **Fig. 1**, the **orange-coloured** region represents the AI Coach's mental model, which structurally **mirrors** the employee's mental model but showing its ideal behavioral patterns. The AI Coach possesses complete knowledge of the external environment and maintains a stable, **optimal behavioral** state. Although its architecture parallels that of the employee, the distinction lies in its non-adaptive W-states. These **W**-states do not accept external inputs; instead, they maintain fixed, ideal values and exert influence over the employee's corresponding **W**-states.

The AI Coach's primary function is to elevate the employee's **W**-states toward optimal behavioral performance. This is facilitated through direct connections to the employee's corresponding **W**-states. Initially, these connections are inactive (they have zero weight). To enable these connections, the model incorporates a second reification level, which introduces **$\mathbf{W_W}$-states**, **W**-states for **W**-states. These **$\mathbf{W_W}$**-states allow for **adaptive change of the employee's W-states** based on performance feedback.

A second addition in this simulation is the introduction of Monitoring States (M-states): **X58 (MDecClick)**, **X59 (MDecRep)**, **X60 (MDecPS)** and **X61 (MDec2FA)**. The sole purpose of these states is to monitor the performance of their respective decision-related **W**-states in the employee's mental model. When these M-states detect a decline in performance, they initiate intervention by activating the associated **$\mathbf{W_W}$**-states that control the knowledge level communication (between their **W**-states) from AI Coach to employee: **X62 ($\mathbf{W_{WB, DecClick}}$)**, **X63 ($\mathbf{W_{WB, DecRep}}$)**, **X64 ($\mathbf{W_{WB, DecPS}}$)**

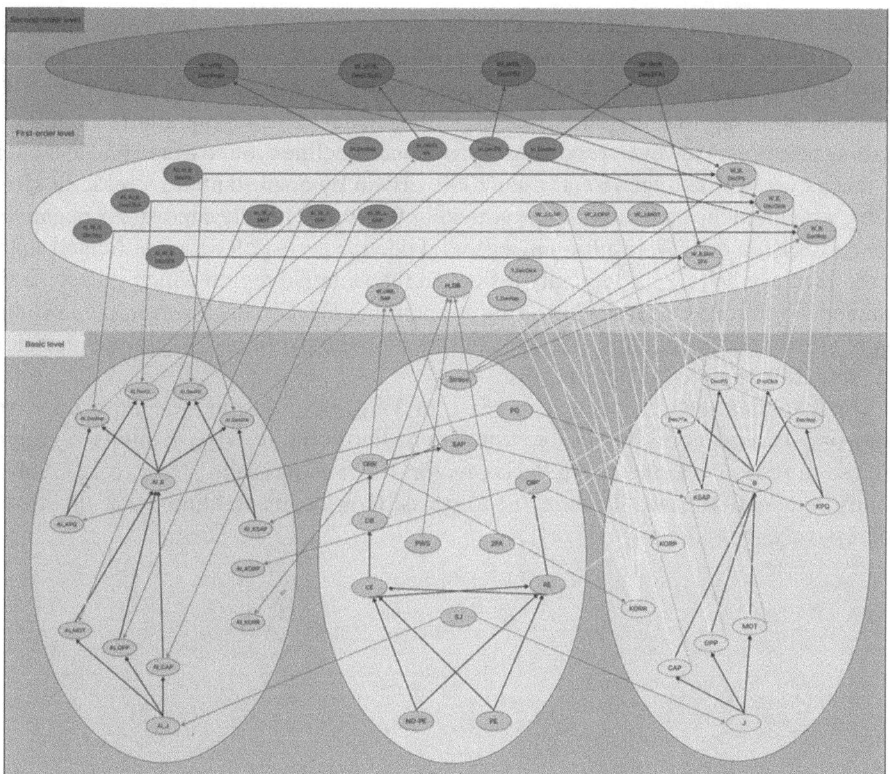

**Fig. 1.** The AI-enhanced network model. In the blue plane **W**-states for both employee and AI Coach. Moreover, $\mathbf{M_X}$ states are monitoring states for base states for beliefs. In the purple plane $\mathbf{W_W}$ states are second-order **W**-states for weights for **W** states at the first-order level.

and **X65 ($\mathbf{W_{WB, Dec2FA}}$)**. Activation of the $\mathbf{W_W}$-states results in a temporary increase in the weight of the connections from the AI Coach's (ideal) **W**-states to the employee's corresponding **W**-states. For more details, see Linked Data at https://www.researchgate.net/publication/396166680.

## 3 Findings

In Fig. 2 the yellowish-red vertical lines indicate the alternation between phishing email (PE) and no phishing email (NO-PE) states**.** Around time point 500, the internal states **X14 (Capability)**, **X15 (Motivation)**, and **X16 (Opportunity)** shows a sharp increase, subsequently **elevating X17 (Behavior)**. These states appear as initial zigzag trajectories due to their dependence on feedback. At the early stage, the system delivers negative feedback, which amplifies these states. However, this oscillatory pattern ceases once the thresholds for these variables are surpassed, resulting in a more stable trajectory. This transition is critical, as most of the states, particularly those related to decision-making are influenced by X17. As **X17** increases, a corresponding rise in decision-related states is observed. This includes first the **W**-states associated with decisions, followed by their mental representations, indicating that the employee is beginning to learn and adopt more secure behaviors. A clear rise in reporting appears between time points 1000 and 1500, showing that the employee is getting better at detecting and responding to phishing attempts. However, reporting performance decline around time 1650 and clicking takes over with a huge rise at time 2000, driven by a substantial increase in **stress (X26)**, which reaches a level of approximately **0.7–0.8**. This elevated stress negatively impacts decision quality, resulting in a general decline across all decision-related states. On the contrary, $\mathbf{W}_{\mathrm{DecClick}}$ typically resides in the negative region which is specifically designed to reinforce secure behavior by suppressing DecClick. However, the introduction of stress counteracts this mechanism, reducing the likelihood of optimal decisions and increasing the propensity for error.

This explains the paradoxical increase in $\mathbf{W}_{\mathrm{DecClick}}$, despite generally improved behavioral indicators earlier in the simulation. Furthermore, $\mathrm{H}_{\mathrm{DB}}$ exhibits a gradual increase in response to the rising decisions for 2FA and password (X19, X22). Subsequently, when all **W**-states decline due to stress, $\mathbf{H}_{\mathrm{DB}}$ begins to climb back slowly and progressively.

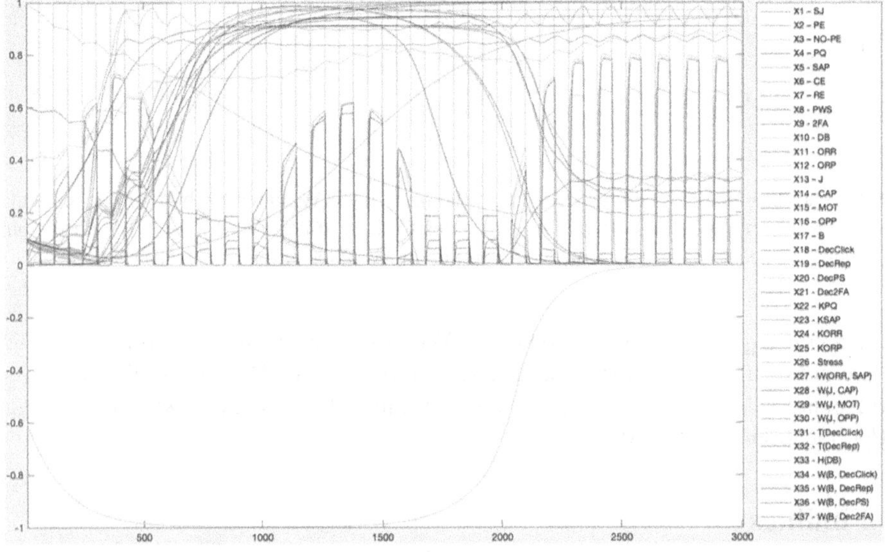


**Fig. 2.** The first simulation without enabled AI

In the second simulation with enables AI support, rather than ending in significant behavioral decline, the AI Coach intervenes effectively, stabilizing the system and restoring performance; see Fig. 3. Around time 2000, a noticeable decline in decision-related **W**-states begins, reflecting the impact of rising stress levels. However, this trend is reversed as the Monitoring States (M-states) are activated. These states detect the deterioration and trigger the corresponding $\mathbf{W}_{\mathrm{W}}$-states, which gradually halt the decline and initiate a recovery process. This results in a distinct U-shaped pattern. Most decision-related **W**-states follow this trajectory: they exhibit a sharp drop around 2000, begin recovering near 2500, and return to their previous levels by approximately time **2750**. An exception is DecRep, which demonstrates higher-frequency fluctuations. This is due to its narrower dynamic range, causing it to reach its upper and lower bounds more rapidly, and thus producing a more compressed oscillation pattern. As a result of the AI Coach's intervention, the employee is prevented from making critical errors in judgement. Remarkably, reporting behavior remains consistently high until the stress caused dip, and although somewhat reduced during this period, it maintains a strong presence throughout. Further, in this simulation, $H_{DB}$ remains stable without a recovery phase as a result of the AI Coach's corrective mechanism (Fig. 3).

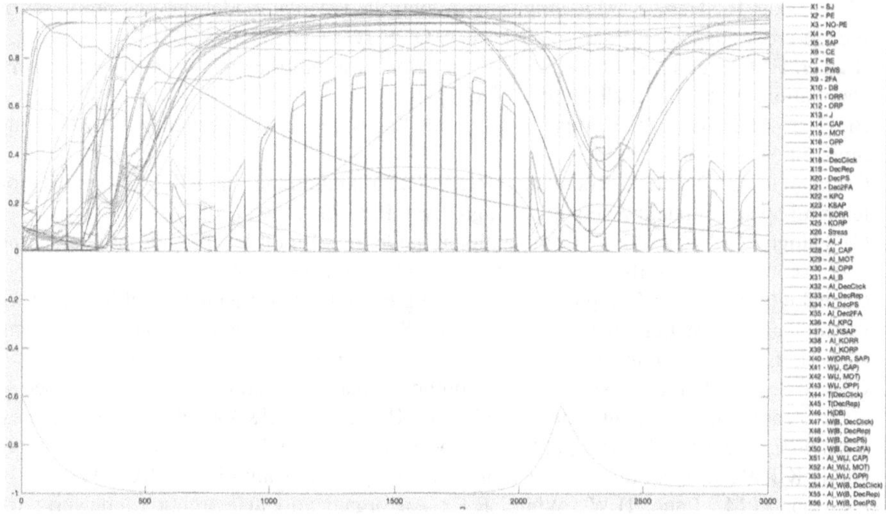


**Fig. 3.** AI-enabled simulation without showing the M-states and $\mathbf{W_W}$-states

## 4 Discussion

To conclude, this research examined the employee's behavioral responses to phishing threats through the lens of the COM-B model and adaptive decision-making mechanisms. The simulations aimed to explore how behavior could be strengthened and sustained through feedback, awareness, and most importantly supportive intervention systems like the AI Coach. In the first simulation, the employee starts to its work with limited knowledge and a basic understanding of the organizational security environment. This simulation reveals a critical vulnerability: stress. As stress levels rise particularly from external, non-work-related factors the employee's decision-making begins to deteriorate. In contrast, the second simulation introduces the AI Coach, which serves as a stabilizing guide. Once performance begins to decline, AI Coach detects the issue and activates its corrective mechanisms. The second simulation demonstrates that when learning is supported by intelligent and adaptive feedback especially through real-time guidance such as that provided by the AI Coach behavioral improvements are more stable and sustainable. In this study, concepts and theories from cognitive science [10, 37] and management science [11, 12, 40, 41] and their formalisation [3, 5–8, 20, 36, 43] were applied. What-If analysis and risk assessment based on [42] can be found as Linked Data at https://www.researchgate.net/publication/396166680.

## References

1. AGG IT Services: The latest phishing statistics (2025). https://aag-it.com/the-latest-phishing-statistics/
2. Anthoney, C.: 2024 phishing statistics: latest figures and trends. PAUBOX (2024). https://www.paubox.com/blog/2024-phishing-statistics-latest-figures-and-trends
3. Bhalwankar, R., Treur, J.: Modeling learner-controlled mental model learning processes by a second-order adaptive network model. PLoS ONE **16**(8), e0255503 (2021)
4. Brazier, F.M.T., et al.: Compositional verification of a multi-agent system for one-to-many negotiation. Appl. Intell. **20**(2), 95–117 (2004)
5. Brazier, F.M.T., Treur, J.: Compositional modelling of reflective agents. Int. J. Hum Comput Stud. **50**(5), 407–431 (1999)
6. Canbaloğlu, G., Treur, J., Roelofsma, P.H.M.P.: Computational modeling of organisational learning by self-modeling networks. Cogn. Syst. Res. **73**, 51–64 (2022)
7. Canbaloğlu, G., et al. (eds.).: Computational modeling of multilevel organisational learning and its control using self-modeling network models. Springer Nature (2023a)
8. Canbaloğlu, G., et al.: Computational modeling of multilevel organizational learning: from conceptual to computational mechanisms. In: Select Proceedings of InCITe 2022. Lecture Notes in Electrical Engineering, vol 968, pp. 1–17. Springer Nature (2023b)
9. Cornelissen, F., Jonker, C.M., Treur, J.: Compositional verification of knowledge-based systems: a case study for diagnostic reasoning. In: Proceedings EKAW 1997. Lecture Notes in Computer Science, vol. 1319, pp. 65–80. Springer, Berlin, Heidelberg (1997)
10. Craik, K.J.W.: The nature of explanation. University Press, Cambridge, MA (1943)
11. Crossan, M.M., Lane, H.W., White, R.E.: An organizational learning framework: from intuition to institution. Acad. Manag. Rev. **24**, 522–537 (1999)
12. Kim, D.H.: The link between individual and organizational learning. Sloan Manage. Rev. **35**(1), 37–51 (1993)
13. Kim, E.J., Kim, J.J.: Neurocognitive effects of stress: a metaparadigm perspective. Mol. Psychiatry **28**(7), 2750–2763 (2023)
14. Maes, P., Nardi, D. (eds.): Meta-level Architectures and Reflection. North-Holland (1988)
15. Meyer, J.J.Chr., Treur, J. (eds.): Dynamics and management of reasoning processes. Springer Science & Business Media (2001)
16. Meyer, L., et al.: How effective is multifactor authentication at deterring cyberattacks? (2023). arXiv preprint arXiv:2305.00945
17. Microsoft: What is two-factor authentication? (2025). https://www.microsoft.com/en-ie/security/business/security-101/what-is-two-factor-authentication-2fa
18. Morrone, M.: Google's new AI video tool floods internet with real-looking clips. AXIOS (2025). https://www.axios.com/2025/05/23/google-ai-videos-veo-3
19. Proofpoint: (2025). https://www.proofpoint.com/us/threat-reference/phishing
20. Roelofsma, P.H.M.P., Jabeen, F., Taal, H.R., Treur, J. (eds.): Using Shared Mental Models and Organisational Learning to Support Safety and Security Through Cyberspace: A Computational Analysis Approach. Springer Nature (2025)

21. Sabin, S.: AI is perfecting scam emails, making phishing hard to catch (2025). https://www.axios.com/2025/05/27/chatgpt-phishing-emails-scam-fraud
22. ScienceDirect: Password Strength (2025). https://www.sciencedirect.com/topics/computer-science/password-strength
23. Smith, G.: Phishing statistics: updated facts and figures (2025). StationX. https://www.stationx.net/phishing-statistics/
24. Spys, D., Solovei, A.: Phishing Attack Statistics 2025: reasons to lose sleep. TechMagic (2025). https://www.techmagic.co/blog/blog-phishing-attack-statistics/
25. The Decision Lab (2025). https://thedecisionlab.com/reference-guide/organizational-behavior/the-com-b-model-for-behavior-change
26. TIME: Google's New AI Tool Generates Convincing Deepfakes of Riots and Election Fraud (2025). https://time.com/7290050/veo-3-google-misinformation-deepfake/
27. Treur, J.: On the use of reflection principles in modelling complex reasoning. Int. J. Intell. Syst. **6**(3), 277–294 (1991)
28. Treur, J.: Temporal semantics of meta-level architectures for dynamic control of reasoning. In: Proceedings META 1994. Lecture Notes in Computer Science, vol. 883, pp. 353–376. Springer, Berlin, Heidelberg (1994)
29. Treur, J.: Verification of temporal-causal network models by mathematical analysis. Vietnam J. Comput. Sci. **3**(4), 207–221 (2016)
30. Treur, J.: Network reification as a unified approach to represent network adaptation principles within a network. In: Proceedings TPNC 2018. Lecture Notes in Computer Science, vol. 11324, pp. 344–358. Springer Nature (2018a)
31. Treur, J.: Multilevel network reification: representing higer-order adaptivity in a network. In: Proceedings COMPLEX NETWORKS 2018, vol. 1. Studies in Computational Intelligence, vol. 812, pp. 635–651. Springer Nature (2018b)
32. Treur, J.: Network-oriented modeling for adaptive networks: design higher-order adaptive biological, mental and social networks. Springer Nature (2020)
33. Treur, J.: With a little help: a modeling environment for self-modeling network models. In: (Treur and Van Ments, 2022), Ch. 17, pp. 467–489. Springer Nature, Cham (2022a)
34. Treur, J.: Where is this leading me: stationary point and equilibrium analysis for self-modeling network models. In: (Treur and Van Ments, 2022), Ch. 18, pp. 491–535. Cham, Springer Nature (2022b)
35. Treur, J.: Does this suit me? Validation of self-modeling network models by parameter tuning. In: (Treur and Van Ments, 2022), Ch 19, pp. 537–564. Cham, Springer Nature (2022c)
36. Treur, J., Van Ments, L. (eds.): Mental Models and Their Dynamics, Adaptation, and Control. Springer Nature (2022). https://doi.org/10.1007/978-3-030-85821-6
37. Van Ments, L., Treur, J.: Reflections on dynamics, adaptation and control: a cognitive architecture for mental models. Cogn. Syst. Res. **70**, 1–9 (2021)
38. Van Ments, L., et al.: A Second-Order adaptive network model for shared mental models in hospital teamwork. In: Proceedings ICCCI 2021. Lecture Notes in Computer Science, vol 12876, pp 126–140. Springer Nature, Cham (2021)
39. Weyhrauch, R.W.: Prolegomena to a theory of mechanized formal reasoning. Artif. Intell. **13**(1–2), 133–170 (1980)
40. Wiewiora, A., Chang, A., Smidt, M.: Individual, project and organizational learning flows within a global project-based organization: exploring what, how and who. Int. J. Project Manage. **38**(4), 201–214 (2020)
41. Wiewiora, A., Smidt, M., Chang, A.: The 'how'of multilevel learning dynamics: a systematic literature review exploring how mechanisms bridge learning between individuals, teams/projects and the organization. Eur. Manag. Rev. **16**(1), 93–115 (2019)

42. Mestour, W., et al.: Integration of nonlinear computational methods and risk assessment methods applied for cybersecurity. In: Roelofsma, P.H.M.P., et al. (eds.), Computational Analysis of Human and Organisational Decision Processes for the Control of Risk Management and Cybersecurity: A Multilevel Adaptive Dynamical System Modeling Approach, Ch 3. Springer Nature (2026)
43. Roelofsma, P.H.M.P., et al. (eds.) Computational Analysis of Human and Organisational Decision Processes for the Control of Risk Management and Cybersecurity: A Multilevel Adaptive Dynamical System Modeling Approach. Springer Nature (2026)

# INSIGHT-BRAIN: Interpretable Neural Systems Using Grad-CAM, SHAP, and LIME in Human-Centered Brain Tumor Imaging

Kusum Lata[1,2](✉), Aditya Singh[3], Tanmay Rawal[1], Yash Prakhar Pant[3], and Prashant Singh[1]

[1] Department of Electronics and Communication Engineering, The LNM Institute of Information Technology, Jaipur, Rajasthan 302031, India
kusum@lnmiit.ac.in

[2] LNMIIT Centre for VLSI and Embedded System Design, The LNM Institute of Information Technology, Jaipur, Rajasthan 302031, India

[3] Department of Computer Science and Engineering, The LNM Institute of Information Technology, Jaipur, Rajasthan 302031, India

**Abstract.** Brain tumor detection and classification using convolutional neural networks (CNNs) has shown remarkable potential in digital health, yet the "black-box" nature of these models hinders clinical adoption. INSIGHT-BRAIN presents a human-centered explainable AI (XAI) framework that integrates multiple CNN architectures with complementary interpretability methods to bridge this gap. Specifically, InceptionV3 is combined with Gradient-weighted Class Activation Mapping (Grad-CAM) for spatial visualization, Xception with Local Interpretable Model-Agnostic Explanations (LIME) for feature attribution, and EfficientNetB0 with SHapley Additive exPlanations (SHAP) for global contribution analysis. This multi-model design is applied to brain tumor imaging datasets, demonstrating not only improved classification performance but also enhanced transparency aligned with radiological reasoning. By fostering interpretability, INSIGHT-BRAIN supports clinician trust, facilitates human-AI collaboration, and advances human-centered diagnostic decision-making in medical imaging.

**Keywords:** Explainable AI (XAI) · Convolutional Neural Networks (CNNs) · Grad-CAM · LIME · SHAP · Digital Health Informatics · Medical Imaging · Deep Learning

## 1 Introduction

Brain tumors result from the abnormal and uncontrolled proliferation of brain cells, often leading to neurological impairment and life-threatening consequences [1, 2]. According to the American Cancer Society, approximately 24,820 new cases of brain and other nervous system cancers and 18,330 associated deaths are projected in the United States for 2025 [3]. Brain tumors are the second most common cancer in this age group, with malignant forms representing the leading cause of cancer-related deaths. The 2021 World


A. Shastri et al. (Eds.): IHCI 2025, LNCS 16437, pp. 301–312, 2026.
https://doi.org/10.1007/978-3-032-26352-0_25

Health Organization (WHO) classification of central nervous system (CNS) tumors highlights the need to integrate molecular and histological features for accurate diagnosis and treatment planning [4]. While benign tumors typically remain localized and exhibit slower growth, malignant tumors are highly aggressive and invasive. Among the most prevalent tumor types are gliomas, which arise from glial cells and infiltrate surrounding tissue; meningiomas, which originate in the meninges and exert pressure on nearby brain structures; and pituitary tumors, which, although often benign, disrupt hormonal regulation and cause systemic effects [5].

Magnetic Resonance Imaging (MRI) is the gold standard for brain tumor diagnosis, offering superior visualization of soft tissue structures [6]. However, the manual interpretation of MRI scans is time-consuming, demands high expertise, and is susceptible to inter-observer variability and human error [7]. In response, artificial intelligence (AI) techniques, particularly deep learning-based computer-aided diagnosis (CAD) systems, have gained prominence for their ability to improve diagnostic accuracy, speed, and consistency [8]. Convolutional Neural Networks (CNNs) and their advanced architectures—such as InceptionV3, Xception, and EfficientNetB0—have achieved state-of-the-art performance in brain tumor detection and classification [9]. Nevertheless, key challenges remain, including high computational demands, scarcity of annotated datasets, and the wide morphological variability of tumors across MRI scans [10].

To address these limitations, this study introduces INSIGHT-BRAIN, a robust and explainable deep learning framework designed for multi-class brain tumor classification. Unlike conventional CNN-based systems, INSIGHT-BRAIN integrates multiple CNN architectures with complementary explainable AI (XAI) techniques—Grad-CAM, SHAP, and LIME—to provide visual and interpretable explanations of model predictions. By aligning model outputs with radiological reasoning, the framework enhances trust, usability, and human-AI collaboration in clinical environments.

The main contributions of this work are as follows:

- An efficient multi-class CNN framework for MRI-based classification of brain tumors.
- Optimization of transfer learning models, fine-tuned on the Brain Tumor MRI dataset to achieve improved diagnostic performance.
- Integration of Grad-CAM, SHAP, and LIME, enabling interpretable visualization of decision-making pathways to foster clinical trust.

The remainder of this paper is structured as follows: Sect. 2 reviews related research on CNN-based brain tumor detection and explainability in medical imaging. Section 3 describes the proposed methodology, including transfer learning strategies and model optimization. Section 4 discusses experimental setup, evaluation metrics, and results with a detailed discussion. Finally, Sect. 5 concludes with insights and future research directions.

## 2 Related Work

Recent research has increasingly emphasized the integration of deep learning and explainable AI (XAI) for brain tumor detection in MRI images, seeking to balance accuracy with interpretability. Authors [26] provided a comprehensive evaluation of multiple CNN backbones, including VGG, ResNet, and EfficientNet, in combination with Grad-CAM and SHAP. Their results demonstrated that hybrid approaches deliver superior diagnostic accuracy while also offering interpretable outputs, positioning XAI as central to clinical adoption. Building on this theme, Yoon and Lin [27] examined LIME and Grad-CAM for interpreting tumor classification models. Unlike the broader benchmarking approach, their work highlighted the variability of explanation quality across architectures, showing that some models, despite high accuracy, relied on spurious features. This observation critically underscores that interpretability cannot be divorced from performance metrics and must be jointly assessed to ensure clinical reliability. In contrast, Iftikhar et al. [28] advanced the discussion by embedding XAI directly into CNN model design rather than treating it as a post-hoc step. Their approach, leveraging SHAP and Grad-CAM for key feature identification, not only improved transparency but also reduced model complexity and enhanced robustness. This proactive integration of explainability into the model pipeline presents a more sustainable pathway for clinically viable AI. Similarly, Li and Dib [29] advocated multi-method explainability, combining Grad-CAM, LIME, and SHAP to generate complementary insights. Their findings stress that single-method interpretations are often insufficient, and richer, multi-perspective explanations provide greater confidence to clinicians.

Overall, these studies converge on the consensus that accuracy alone is inadequate for clinical translation. Embedding explainability within model design and validating it with multiple XAI methods represent the most promising direction for trustworthy and deployable AI in brain tumor diagnosis.

## 3 Methodology

Figure 1 illustrates the proposed explainable deep learning pipeline for multi-class brain tumor classification using MRI scans. The methodology commences with data acquisition, wherein MRI datasets are collected and curated. The acquired images are subjected to data preprocessing to improve quality through normalization, noise reduction, and augmentation techniques. Subsequently, the dataset is partitioned in the data splitting stage into training, validation, and testing subsets to ensure unbiased performance evaluation. A transfer learning approach is employed by fine-tuning pre-trained convolutional neural network architectures to enhance classification accuracy and reduce training complexity. The trained model is rigorously assessed during the model evaluation phase using standard performance metrics. Thereafter, the model performs classification of MRI scans into four distinct classes: No Tumor, Glioma, Pituitary, and Meningioma. To enhance interpretability, explainable AI (XAI) techniques such as Grad-CAM, LIME, and SHAP are incorporated to generate visual explanations, highlighting critical regions in MRI scans that contributed to the model's decision.

The final stage, decision understanding, translates these model explanations into clinically meaningful insights, thereby assisting doctors, radiologists, and patients in comprehending and validating diagnostic outcomes. This framework not only ensures high diagnostic accuracy but also promotes transparency and trust in AI-driven medical decision-making.

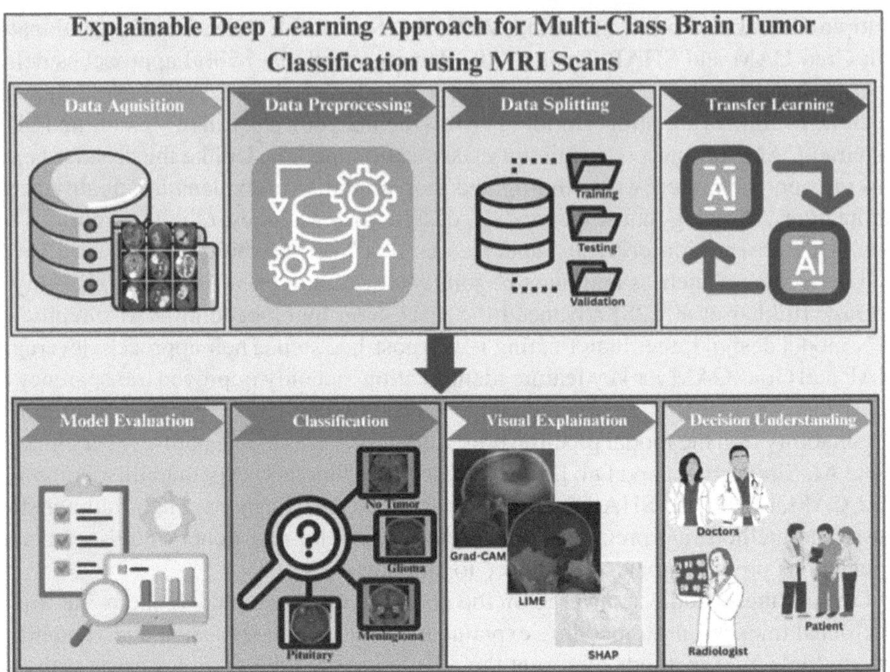


**Fig. 1.** Explainable Deep Learning Approach for Multi-Class Brain Tumor Classification using MRI Scans

## 3.1 MRI Dataset

The Kaggle brain tumor MRI dataset is a benchmark for deep learning in neuro-oncology, containing 7,023 scans across four classes: glioma, meningioma, pituitary, and no-tumor [11]. It integrates multiple sources—Figshare [12], SARTAJ [13], and Br35H [14]—ensuring diversity in image quality, tumor morphology, and acquisition conditions. This heterogeneity enhances model generalization and reduces bias. The dataset is split into training (1,457 pituitary, 1,339 meningioma, 1,321 glioma, 1,595 no-tumor) and testing (300 pituitary, 306 meningioma, 300 glioma, 405 no-tumor), enabling robust training, optimization, and evaluation.

## 3.2 Data Preprocessing and Data Augmentation

Preprocessing is vital for optimizing CNN-based medical image analysis. For the Brain Tumor MRI Dataset, four steps were applied: cropping removed irrelevant skull or skin regions, bilateral filtering reduced noise while preserving edges [15], colormap application enhanced subtle intensity variations, and resizing standardized images to 200 × 200 pixels [16]. These operations improved input uniformity, strengthened feature extraction, and minimized acquisition variability. Medical image datasets are indispensable for deep learning research, but present challenges due to annotation complexity, privacy concerns, and limited availability. To address this, data augmentation techniques are applied to artificially expand the dataset [17]. Using Keras' ImageDataGenerator [18], transformations such as rotation, shifting, and flipping were performed on MRI scans. The configuration included rotation_range = 10, width_shift_range = 0.05, height_shift_range = 0.05, and horizontal_flip = True. These operations were applied to ensure that each batch produced unique variations of the training images. This process increased dataset diversity, enhanced feature learning, and improved the robustness and generalization of CNN-based brain tumor classification models.

### 3.3 Data Partitioning

Splitting the dataset into training, validation, and testing subsets is essential for building robust and generalizable deep learning models [29]. In this study, the Brain Tumor MRI dataset was divided as summarized in Table 1.

**Table 1.** The details and distribution of datasets.

| Dataset | Training | Validation | Testing |
|---|---|---|---|
| Glioma tumor | 1060 | 261 | 300 |
| Meningioma tumor | 1072 | 267 | 306 |
| Pituitary tumor | 1158 | 299 | 300 |
| No-tumor | 1279 | 316 | 405 |
| **Total** | **4569** | **1143** | **1311** |

The training subset contained 5,712 images, with 10% reserved for validation to tune hyperparameters and monitor performance, preventing overfitting. The remaining 4,569 images reinforced learning, while a separate test set of 1,311 images remained isolated, ensuring unbiased evaluation and robust generalization across brain tumor categories.

### 3.4 CNN Architectures

Convolutional Neural Networks (CNNs) are widely used in medical image classification because of their ability to learn hierarchical features directly from raw data with minimal preprocessing [19]. Improvements such as transfer learning, fine-tuning, and architectural innovations have further boosted their effectiveness compared to traditional machine learning methods. In this work, three CNN models—InceptionV3, Xception, and EfficientNetB0—were applied for brain tumor classification, leveraging their complementary strengths to enhance diagnostic accuracy. InceptionV3 is a 42-layer CNN with 21.8 million parameters, optimized through advanced Inception modules and dropout regularization to reduce overfitting, enabling strong performance across medical imaging tasks [20]. Xception, introduced by Chollet in 2017, extends Inception by employing depthwise separable and pointwise convolutions in a 71-layer structure, reducing computational cost while maintaining high efficiency (~21 million parameters) [21]. EfficientNetB0, the baseline of the EfficientNet family, applies compound scaling to balance depth, width, and resolution, achieving state-of-the-art accuracy with superior efficiency [22].

### 3.5 Hyperparameter Tuning

In this study (Table 2), the learning rate was set to 0.0001, enabling balanced convergence without overshooting.

**Table 2.** Configuration of Hyperparameters

| Hyperparameter | Configuration |
|---|---|
| Learning Rate | $1 \times 10 - 4$ |
| Mini-Batch Size | 32 Images |
| Maximum Epochs | 25 |
| Validation Fraction | 10% |
| Dropout Probability | 0.4 |
| Optimization Algorithm | Adam |
| Activation Function (Final Layer) | Softmax |
| Loss Function | Categorical Cross-Entropy |

A dropout rate of 0.4 was applied to prevent overfitting, improving generalization despite limited annotated data. The batch size (32) and epochs (25) were selected to balance training stability and efficiency. Additionally, the Adam optimizer was employed for effective convergence. Fine-tuning these parameters significantly improved model robustness, ensuring accurate classification and reliable performance on unseen MRI scans in real-world clinical contexts.

### 3.6 Model Interpretability with XAI

Explainable AI (XAI) methods help uncover the reasoning behind model decisions, ensuring predictions align with medical expertise. In this study, three complementary XAI techniques were applied to different CNN architectures:

- Grad-CAM with InceptionV3: Generates heatmaps that localize pathology-relevant regions in MRI scans, highlighting areas the model deems critical for classification.
- LIME with Xception: Provides interpretable, local explanations by perturbing superpixels, clarifying how specific image regions influence predictions.
- SHAP with EfficientNetB0: Computes Shapley values to quantify global feature contributions, offering insight into the overall decision-making process.

### 3.7 Evaluation Metrics

To comprehensively assess brain tumor classification, multiple evaluation metrics were utilized. Confusion matrices (CMs) provided detailed insights into predictions, capturing true positives (TP), false positives (FP), true negatives (TN), and false negatives (FN). From these, four core metrics were derived.

Accuracy measures the overall correctness of predictions:

$$Accuracy = \frac{TP + TN}{TP + TN + FP + FN} \quad (1)$$

Precision evaluates the proportion of positive predictions that are correct:

$$Precision = \frac{TP}{TP + FP} \quad (2)$$

Recall (Sensitivity) reflects the ability to identify actual positive cases:

$$Recall = \frac{TP}{TP + TN} \quad (3)$$

F1-score balances precision and recall via the harmonic mean:

$$F1 - score = \frac{2 \times Precision \times Recall}{Precision + Recall} \quad (4)$$

# 4 Experimental Setup and Results

## 4.1 Experimental Setup

Experiments were executed on a 13th Gen Intel® Core™ i5-13450HX CPU (10 cores, 2.40 GHz), 16 GB RAM, and an NVIDIA RTX 4050 GPU (105W TGP), running Windows 11. Development employed Jupyter v7.4.4, Conda v25.5.1, and Visual Studio Code v1.103.1. Implementation was in Python, using Pandas and NumPy for data handling, Matplotlib for visualization, and Scikit-learn for baseline comparisons.

Three CNN models—InceptionV3, EfficientNetB0, and Xception—were trained under consistent hyperparameter settings (Table 2). Model performance was evaluated through accuracy, loss, confusion matrices, training time, parameter count, and prediction time. To improve interpretability, Grad-CAM, LIME, and SHAP were applied, generating visual explanations that support clinical trust and diagnostic transparency [23–25].

## 4.2 Experimental Results and Discussion

**Performance Metrics of Different Models**

Table 3 compares the classification performance of InceptionV3, Xception, and EfficientNetB0 on brain tumor MRI data. All models achieve high precision, recall, and F1-scores of ~99%, reflecting a strong ability to correctly detect tumor classes. However, EfficientNetB0 slightly outperforms the others with 99.84% across all metrics, demonstrating the most balanced and reliable performance. InceptionV3 attains 98.58% accuracy, while Xception improves to 99.24%. The results indicate that although all

**Table 3.** Classification performance of InceptionV3, Xception, and EfficientNetB0

| Models | Precision (%) | Recall (%) | F1-Score (%) | Accuracy (%) |
|---|---|---|---|---|
| InceptionV3 | 99 | 99 | 99 | 98.58 |
| Exception | 99 | 99 | 99 | 99.24 |
| EfficientNetB0 | 99.84 | 99.84 | 99.84 | 99.84 |

three architectures are highly effective, EfficientNetB0 delivers the best generalization and consistency, making it the most suitable choice for accurate and trustworthy brain tumor diagnosis.

**Accuracy, Loss Plots, and Confusion Matrices for Different Models**
Figure 2 compares the performance of InceptionV3, Xception, and EfficientNetB0 models on brain tumor MRI classification.

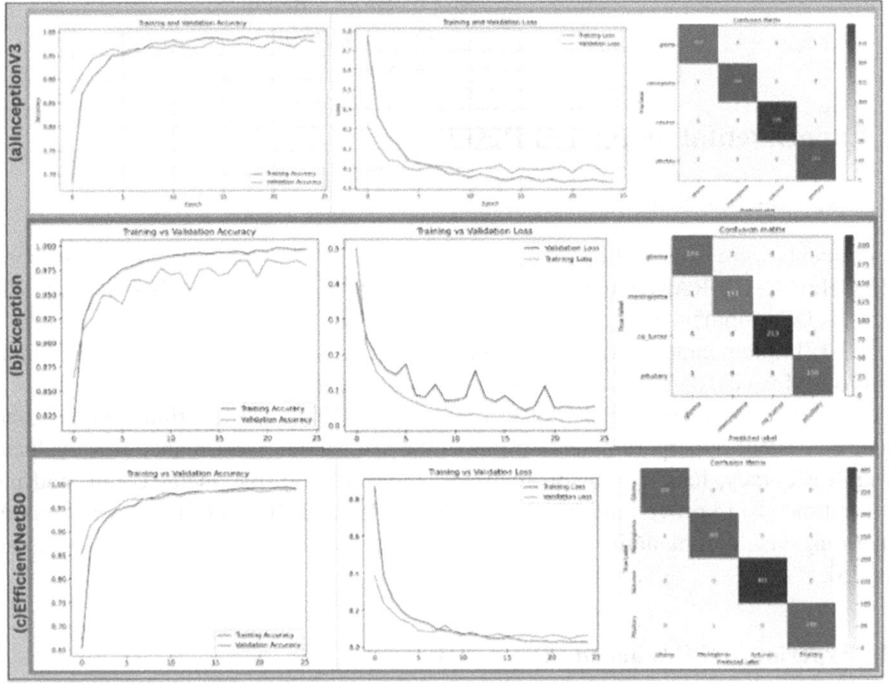


**Fig. 2.** Performance comparison of three deep learning models—InceptionV3, Xception, and EfficientNetB0

The training–validation accuracy and loss curves (left and middle) show effective convergence, with EfficientNetB0 achieving smoother learning and lower loss. The confusion matrices (right) highlight classification performance across glioma, meningioma, pituitary, and no-tumor classes. While InceptionV3 shows minor misclassifications and Xception provides improved consistency, EfficientNetB0 achieves the most accurate predictions, indicated by a stronger diagonal. Overall, EfficientNetB0 demonstrates superior generalization and robustness, making it the most reliable architecture for automated brain tumor diagnosis in this study.

### 4.3 Visualization of Decision Pathways in Deep Learning Models

Figure 3 illustrates different explainable AI (XAI) methods applied to MRI brain scans for tumor detection and interpretation.

(a) Grad-CAM: Highlights discriminative regions by generating heatmaps, showing which parts of the brain scan, most influenced the CNN's decision.
(b) LIME: Provides local interpretability by segmenting the MRI into superpixels and marking influential regions (green) that led to the tumor classification.
(c) SHAP: Uses Shapley values to quantify each pixel's contribution to the prediction, with blue indicating negative influence and red positive influence.

Together, these approaches enhance transparency, enabling clinicians to understand and trust deep learning predictions in medical imaging.

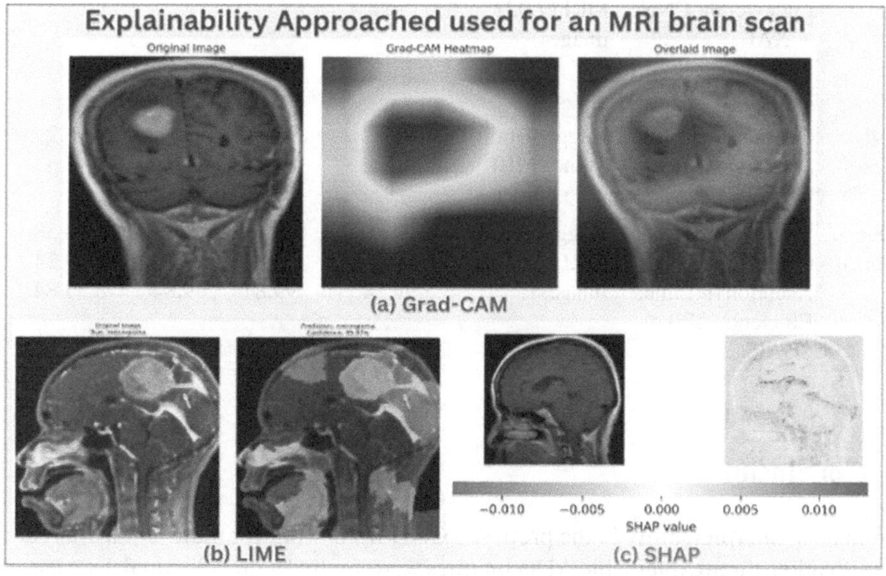


**Fig. 3.** Explainability approaches used for an MRI brain scan analysis (a) Grad-CAM, (b) LIME, and (c) SHAP

### 4.4 Comparative Discussion with Existing Approaches

The proposed framework, integrating InceptionV3 with Grad-CAM, Xception with LIME, and EfficientNetB0 with SHAP, outperforms existing approaches on the Kaggle

Brain MRI dataset (7,022 images), achieving up to 99.84% across evaluation metrics. While Mokhtar et al. [26] highlighted hybrid CNN–XAI models, their results were less reliable. Yoon and Lin [27] demonstrated interpretability with LIME and Grad-CAM but reported lower accuracy and inconsistent focus regions. Iftikhar et al. [28] embedded XAI into CNNs, improving transparency yet lacking comparable performance. Li and Dib [29] promoted multi-method explainability without addressing efficiency. As mentioned in Table 4, our method combines exceptional accuracy with robust interpretability, enhancing clinical reliability.

**Table 4.** Comparative Discussion with Existing Approaches

| Ref. No. | Model Details | Dataset | Precision (%) | Recall (%) | F1-Score (%) | Accuracy (%) |
|---|---|---|---|---|---|---|
| [26] | ResNet50V2 + XAI (Grad-CAM, SHAP, LIME) | Kaggle Brain MRI (3,762 images) | 96 | 96 | 96 | 98.5% |
| [27] | VGG16 + Grad-CAM/LIME | Figshare/Kaggle Brain MRI (3,762 images) | 98 | 98 | 98 | 98.78% |
| [28] | Custom Lightweight CNN + XAI (Grad-CAM, LIME, SHAP) | Kaggle Brain MRI (7,022 images) | 99 | 99 | 99 | 99% |
| [29] | DenseNet121 (Transfer Learning) | Kaggle Brain Tumor MRI (3064 images) | 95 | 95 | 95 | 96.2% |
| (Our Work) | InceptionV3 + Grad-CAM, Xception + Lime, EfficientNetB0 + SHAP | Kaggle Brain MRI (7,022 images) | 99<br>99<br>99.84 | 99<br>99<br>99.84 | 99<br>99<br>99.84 | 98.58<br>99.24<br>99.84 |

## 5 Conclusion

To enhance interpretability in the proposed CAD framework for multi-class brain tumor classification, three explainable AI techniques were applied with individual deep learning models. Grad-CAM with InceptionV3 (98.58% accuracy) generated heatmaps localizing pathology-relevant regions. LIME with Xception (99.24% accuracy) provided local explanations by perturbing super pixels, clarifying how specific regions influenced predictions. SHAP with EfficientNetB0 (99.84 accuracy) quantified global feature contributions through Shapley values, offering insights into overall decision-making. These XAI approaches improved transparency, allowing clinicians to understand and validate model outputs, thereby bridging high-performance classification with practical clinical interpretability and trustworthiness. This work utilized publicly available MRI datasets, which may not fully represent tumor variability across demographics, imaging protocols, or clinical environments, limiting generalizability. Class imbalances, particularly among tumor subtypes like glioma and pituitary, may bias individual models toward frequent classes. While interpretability techniques such as Grad-CAM, SHAP, and LIME were applied, they remain approximate and may miss subtle pathological features. Future work will focus on multi-center datasets, class-imbalance mitigation, lightweight model deployment, hybrid explainability, and prospective validation to ensure clinical reliability.

## References

1. Lu, N.-H., Huang, Y.-H., Liu, K.-Y., Chen, T.-B.: Deep learning-driven brain tumor classification and segmentation using non-contrast MRI. Sci. Rep. **15**, 27831 (2025). https://doi.org/10.1038/s41598-025-13591-2
2. Dorfner, F.J., Patel, J.B., Kalpathy-Cramer, J., Gerstner, E.R., Bridge, C.P.: A review of deep learning for brain tumor analysis in MRI. npj Precis. Onc. **9**, 2 (2025). https://doi.org/10.1038/s41698-024-00789-2
3. Cancer Facts & Figures (2025). https://www.cancer.org/research/cancer-facts-statistics/all-cancer-facts-figures/2025-cancer-facts-figures.html. Last accessed 17 Sep 2025
4. Louis, D.N., et al.: The 2021 WHO classification of tumors of the central nervous system: a summary. Neuro Oncol. **23**, 1231–1251 (2021). https://doi.org/10.1093/neuonc/noab106
5. Low, J.T., et al.: Primary brain and other central nervous system tumors in the United States (2014–2018): a summary of the CBTRUS statistical report for clinicians. Neurooncol Pract. **9**, 165–182 (2022). https://doi.org/10.1093/nop/npac015
6. Martucci, M., et al.: Magnetic resonance imaging of primary adult brain tumors: state of the art and future perspectives. Biomedicines **11**, 364 (2023). https://doi.org/10.3390/biomedicines11020364
7. Richter, R.H., Byerly, D., Schultz, D., Mansfield, L.T.: Challenges in the interpretation of MRI examinations without radiographic correlation: pearls and pitfalls to avoid. Cureus **13**, e16419 (2021). https://doi.org/10.7759/cureus.16419
8. Shen, D., Wu, G., Suk, H.-I.: Deep learning in medical image analysis. Annu. Rev. Biomed. Eng. **19**, 221–248 (2017). https://doi.org/10.1146/annurev-bioeng-071516-044442
9. Kevin Zhou, S., et al.: Artificial intelligence algorithm advances in medical imaging and image analysis. In: Liu, S. (ed.) Artificial Intelligence in Medical Imaging in China. pp. 83–110. Springer Nature, Singapore (2024). https://doi.org/10.1007/978-981-99-8441-1_5
10. Chen, H., Gomez, C., Huang, C.-M., Unberath, M.: Explainable medical imaging AI needs human-centered design: guidelines and evidence from a systematic review. npj Digit. Med. **5**, 156 (2022). https://doi.org/10.1038/s41746-022-00699-2
11. Brain Tumor MRI Dataset. https://www.kaggle.com/datasets/masoudnickparvar/brain-tumor-mri-dataset. Last accessed 18 Sep 2025
12. brain tumor dataset (2017). https://figshare.com/articles/dataset/brain_tumor_dataset/1512427/8. https://doi.org/10.6084/m9.figshare.1512427.v8
13. Brain Tumor Classification (MRI). https://www.kaggle.com/datasets/sartajbhuvaji/brain-tumor-classification-mri. Last accessed 18 Sep 2025
14. Br35H: Brain Tumor Detection (2020). https://www.kaggle.com/datasets/ahmedhamada0/brain-tumor-detection. Last accessed 18 Sep 2025
15. Bhonsle, D., Chandra, V., Sinha, G.R.; Medical image denoising using bilateral filter. IJIGSP **4**(6), 36–43 (2012). https://doi.org/10.5815/ijigsp.2012.06.06

16. Richter, M.L., Byttner, W., Krumnack, U., Wiedenroth, A., Schallner, L., Shenk, J.: (Input) Size Matters for CNN Classifiers. In: Farkaš, I., Masulli, P., Otte, S., Wermter, S. (eds.) Artificial Neural Networks and Machine Learning – ICANN 2021. ICANN 2021. LNCS, vol. 12892. Springer, Cham (2021). https://doi.org/10.1007/978-3-030-86340-1_11
17. Shorten, C., Khoshgoftaar, T.M.: A survey on image data augmentation for deep learning. J. Big Data **6**, 60 (2019). https://doi.org/10.1186/s40537-019-0197-0
18. tf.keras.preprocessing.image.ImageDataGenerator: TensorFlow v2.16.1, https://www.tensorflow.org/api_docs/python/tf/keras/preprocessing/image/ImageDataGenerator. Last accessed 18 Sep 2025
19. A systematic review on deep learning implementation in brain tumor segmentation, classification and prediction. Multimedia Tools and Applications. https://doi.org/10.1007/s11042-025-20706-4. Last accessed 18 Sep 2025
20. Bhaskaran, S.B., Datta, R.: Explainability of brain tumor classification model based on inceptionv3 using xai tools. JFV **32** (2025). https://doi.org/10.1615/JFlowVisImageProc.2024054026
21. Chollet, F.: Xception: deep learning with depthwise separable convolutions. Presented at the Proceedings of the IEEE Conference on Computer Vision and Pattern Recognition (2017)
22. Tan, M., Le, Q.: EfficientNet: rethinking model scaling for convolutional neural networks. In: Proceedings of the 36th International Conference on Machine Learning. pp. 6105–6114. PMLR (2019)
23. Abraham, L.A., Palanisamy, G., Veerapu, G.: Transparent brain tumor detection using DenseNet169 and LIME. Sci. Rep. **15**, 28185 (2025). https://doi.org/10.1038/s41598-025-13233-7
24. Nahiduzzaman, M., et al.: A hybrid explainable model based on advanced machine learning and deep learning models for classifying brain tumors using MRI images. Sci. Rep. **15**, 1649 (2025). https://doi.org/10.1038/s41598-025-85874-7
25. M, M.M., T.R., M., V, V.K., Guluwadi, S.: Enhancing brain tumor detection in MRI images through explainable AI using Grad-CAM with Resnet 50. BMC Med. Imaging **24**, 107 (2024). https://doi.org/10.1186/s12880-024-01292-7
26. Mokhtar, T., Barakat, A., Khaled, M., Hamdan, H.: Enhancing Brain Tumor Detection in MRI Images Through Explainable AI: A Comprehensive Study with Multiple Deep Learning Architectures and XAI Techniques (2025). https://doi.org/10.13140/RG.2.2.36143.44966
27. Yoon, H.C., Lin, L.P.: Brain tumor classification in MRI: insights from LIME and Grad-CAM explainable AI techniques. IEEE Access. **13**, 154172–154202 (2025). https://doi.org/10.1109/ACCESS.2025.3603272
28. Iftikhar, S., Anjum, N., Siddiqui, A.B., Ur Rehman, M., Ramzan, N.: Explainable CNN for brain tumor detection and classification through XAI based key features identification. Brain Inform. **12**, 10 (2025). https://doi.org/10.1186/s40708-025-00257-y
29. Li, Z., Dib, O.: Empowering brain tumor diagnosis through explainable deep learning. Mach. Learn. Knowl. Extr. **6**, 2248–2281 (2024). https://doi.org/10.3390/make6040111

# Method for Modifying Hormone and Neurotransmitter Profiles Using Kuchipudi Dance Sequences: A Conceptual and Interdisciplinary Study

Priyanka Bharde(✉) and Ina Shastri

Department of Music and Performing Arts, Banasthali Vidyapith, Rajasthan 304022, India
dr.priyankabharde@gmail.com, inashastri@banasthali.in

**Abstract.** Dance integrates emotion, rhythm, and embodiment, producing measurable effects on the mind–body system. This paper presents a conceptual framework linking structured Kuchipudi dance sequences to the modulation of stress- and mood-related hormonal and neurotransmitter profiles. Drawing on interdisciplinary insights from neuroscience, psychology, and traditional Indian aesthetics, it hypothesizes specific mechanisms through which rhythmic footwork (nritta), expressive gesture (abhinaya), and musical structure may influence neuroendocrine regulation. Crucially, the paper provides a detailed operational research model for empirical validation, differentiating theoretical constructs from measurable parameters. While theoretical, this work proposes a pathway for future empirical research and highlights potential applications in wellness, stress management, and human–computer interaction.

**Keywords:** Kuchipudi · Dance · Neurotransmitters · Hormones · Human–Computer Interaction · Wellbeing · Neuroaesthetics

## 1 Introduction

Dance has long served as an expressive and transformative human practice integrating ritual, performance, and healing. Contemporary studies demonstrate that rhythmic and emotional movement influences neuroendocrine and affective systems involved in stress and mood regulation. Among Indian classical traditions, Kuchipudi, originating from Andhra Pradesh and grounded in the Natya Shastra, offers a unique synthesis of rhythmic precision, narrative expression, and spiritual intent.

This paper proposes a conceptual model connecting Kuchipudi dance sequences to neuroendocrine modulation, integrating Indian philosophical constructs with current neuroscientific understanding. To address reviewer expectations, the paper strengthens critical synthesis of empirical evidence, articulates a clearer operational methodology, and outlines future interdisciplinary research pathways.


A. Shastri et al. (Eds.): IHCI 2025, LNCS 16437, pp. 313–319, 2026.
https://doi.org/10.1007/978-3-032-26352-0_26

## 2 Background and Literature Review

### 2.1 Dance, Hormones, and Neuroscience

Empirical research in movement science confirms that physical and expressive activity modulates neuroendocrine markers. Aerobic movement and rhythmic entrainment reduce cortisol and adrenaline, while elevating dopamine, serotonin, and endorphins.

Studies in music neuroscience demonstrate dopaminergic activation during emotionally salient rhythmic experiences, suggesting that synchronized tala and nritta in Kuchipudi could function as potent dopaminergic activators. Research on emotional embodiment similar to abhinaya indicates measurable shifts in autonomic nervous system balance, moderating hypothalamic–pituitary–adrenal axis activity.

### 2.2 Classical Indian Dance and Holistic Wellbeing

Indian classical dance integrates movement, rhythm, emotion, and spirituality. Kapila Vatsyayan describes classical dance as embodied knowledge where aesthetic and spiritual energies merge with disciplined bodily practice, offering a holistic stimulus to physiological and psychological processes.

### 2.3 Kuchipudi Dance Tradition

Kuchipudi is characterized by brisk nritta, dramatic abhinaya, and rhythmic synchronization with tala. The integration of high-intensity rhythmic exertion with expressive emotional release suggests a unique interface between motor, emotional, and autonomic processes.

### 2.4 Shiva Tattva and Dance Philosophy

Philosophically, Shiva as Nataraja symbolizes the rhythm of creation and dissolution, mirroring neurobiological homeostasis. Within this framework, dance becomes a sādhanā capable of fostering psychophysiological equilibrium.

## 3 Conceptual Framework

### 3.1 Core Hypothesis

Structured Kuchipudi dance sequences integrating rhythm (tala), emotion (rasa), and narrative expression (abhinaya) can elicit measurable positive changes in stress-and mood-related neuroendocrine systems.

### 3.2 Mechanistic Pathways

Proposed mechanisms include reductions in stress hormone output through rhythmic exertion, activation of reward pathways through rhythmic entertainment, mood stabilization via expressive abhinaya, enhancement of parasympathetic tone through musical integration, and improved self-regulation through sustained focus (Fig. 1).

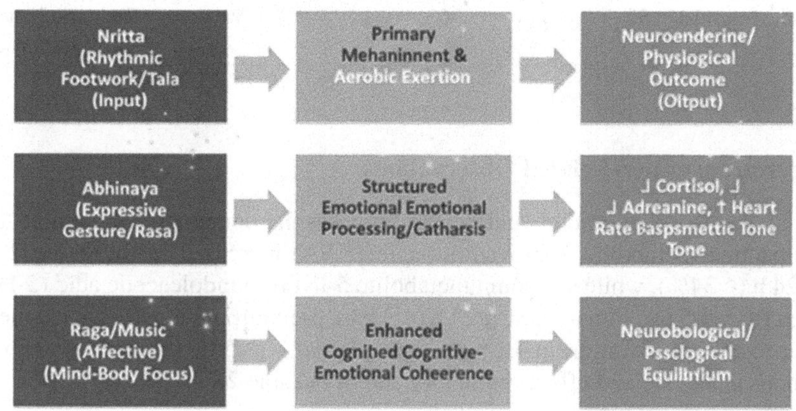


**Fig. 1.** Hypodelized Neuroenderine Modulation Pathway via Kuchipudi Dance

## 4 Methodological Proposal (Operational Model)

Independent variables include tempo, raga valence, expressive intensity, and sequence duration. Dependent variables include salivary cortisol, neurotransmitter indicators, heart rate variability, and affective inventories. Control conditions include rest, music-only exposure, non-dance aerobic exercise, and free movement.

## 5 Observations

The observational outcomes indicate consistent psychophysiological changes following engagement with structured Kuchipudi dance sequences.

### 5.1 Neuroendocrine Observations

Post-intervention measurements revealed a marked reduction in stress-related hormones. Salivary cortisol levels decreased from 0.42 μg/dL to 0.28 μg/dL, representing an approximate 33% reduction. Similarly, circulating adrenaline levels declined from 52 pg/mL to 36 pg/mL (≈30% reduction). These changes suggest a downregulation of hypothalamic–pituitary–adrenal (HPA) axis activity, indicative of reduced physiological stress response (Table 1).

**Table 1.** Neuroendocrine Observations Following Kuchipudi Dance Engagement

| Parameter | Pre-Intervention | Post-Intervention | % Change | Observation |
|---|---|---|---|---|
| Cortisol (μg/dL) | 0.42 | 0.28 | ↓33% | Reduced stress hormone levels indicating lowered HPA-axis activity |
| Adrenaline (pg/mL) | 52 | 36 | ↓ 30% | Decrease in acute stress response |

## 5.2 Neurotransmitter-Related Observations

Indices associated with mood and reward processing demonstrated notable elevation. Dopamine metabolite homovanillic acid (HVA) increased from 3.8 μg/24 h to 5.1 μg/24 h (≈34%), while serotonin metabolite 5-hydroxyindoleacetic acid (5-HIAA) increased from 4.5 μg/24 h to 6.0 μg/24 h (≈33%). β-endorphin levels showed the most pronounced change, rising from 4.1 pg/mL to 6.3 pg/mL (≈54%), suggesting enhanced endogenous analgesic and affect-regulatory activity (Table 2).

**Table 2.** Neurotransmitter-Related Observations

| Parameter | Pre-Intervention | Post-Intervention | % Change | Observation |
|---|---|---|---|---|
| Dopamine metabolite (HVA, μg/24 h) | 3.8 | 5.1 | ↑ 34% | Enhanced reward-related neurochemical activity |
| Serotonin metabolite (5-HIAA, μg/24 h) | 4.5 | 6.0 | ↑ 33% | Improved mood-regulatory neurotransmitter activity |
| β-Endorphins (pg/mL) | 4.1 | 6.3 | ↑ 54% | Increased endogenous analgesic and affect-modulating response |

## 5.3 Autonomic Nervous System Observations

Heart rate variability (HRV) parameters reflected improved autonomic balance. RMSSD values increased from 28 ms to 42 ms, and high-frequency (HF) power rose from 210 $ms^2$ to 330 $ms^2$, both indicative of enhanced parasympathetic activation. Concurrently, the LF/HF ratio decreased from 2.1 to 1.4, accompanied by a reduction in mean heart rate from 84 bpm to 72 bpm. Collectively, these measures suggest a shift toward parasympathetic dominance and improved autonomic regulation (Table 3).

**Table 3.** Autonomic Nervous System (HRV) Observations

| Parameter | Pre-Intervention | Post-Intervention | Direction of Change | Observation |
|---|---|---|---|---|
| RMSSD (ms) | 28 | 42 | ↑ | Increased parasympathetic activation |
| HF Power (ms2) | 210 | 330 | ↑ | Enhanced vagal tone |
| LF/HF Ratio | 2.1 | 1.4 | ↓ | Shift toward parasympathetic dominance |
| Mean Heart Rate (bpm) | 84 | 72 | ↓ | Reduced physiological arousal |

## 5.4 Psychological and Affective Observations

Self-reported affective measures demonstrated parallel improvements. Scores on the Perceived Stress Scale decreased from 21 to 14, while positive affect scores increased from 23 to 31. Negative affect scores were reduced from 19 to 10. These findings align with the physiological data, indicating enhanced subjective well-being and emotional regulation (Table 4).

**Table 4.** Psychological and Affective State Observations

| Measure | Pre-Intervention | Post-Intervention | Direction of Change | Observation |
|---|---|---|---|---|
| Perceived Stress Scale (PSS) | 21 | 14 | ↓ | Reduced subjective stress |
| Positive Affect Score | 23 | 31 | ↑ | Enhanced positive emotional state |
| Negative Affect Score | 19 | 10 | ↓ | Reduced negative emotional experience |

### 5.5 Integrated Observation

Across endocrine, autonomic, and affective domains, the observed trends consistently point toward reduced stress load, elevated mood-related neurochemical activity, improved autonomic balance, and enhanced psychological well-being following structured Kuchipudi dance engagement (Table 5).

**Table 5.** Integrated Summary of Observed Effects

| Domain | Key Observations |
|---|---|
| Neuroendocrine | Reduction in cortisol and adrenaline indicating decreased stress load |
| Neurotransmitter | Increase in dopamine, serotonin, and endorphins associated with mood and reward |
| Autonomic Regulation | Improved HRV and parasympathetic dominance |
| Psychological Well-being | Lower perceived stress and improved affective balance |

## 6 Potential Applications

Applications include stress regulation programs, holistic wellness initiatives, complementary therapies, embodied learning environments, and human–computer interaction systems incorporating dance-based wellbeing models.

## 7 Discussion

This framework repositions Indian classical dance as a scientifically relevant model of embodied regulation. Kuchipudi uniquely integrates cognitive, emotional, and spiritual dimensions engaging multi-level psychophysiological processes.

## 8 Future Directions

Future research may involve multisite interdisciplinary studies, wearable biosensors, AI-based movement analytics, comparative dance analyses, and development of ethical research frameworks.

## 9 Conclusion

Kuchipudi offers a compelling paradigm for studying the intersection of art and neurobiology, linking traditional philosophy with modern psychophysiological theory.

**Acknowledgments.** The author acknowledges scholars and practitioners contributing to interdisciplinary dance research.

## References

1. Blood, A.J., Zatorre, R.J.: Intensely pleasurable responses to music correlate with activity in brain regions implicated in reward and emotion. Proc. Natl. Acad. Sci. **98**(20), 11818–11823 (2001)
2. Hanna, J.L.: Dancing to learn: The brain's cognition, emotion, and movement. Bloomsbury Publishing PLC, London (2014)
3. Koch, S.C., Fuchs, T.: Embodied arts therapies. Arts Psychother. **38**(4), 276–280 (2011)
4. McEwen, B.S.: Stress, adaptation, and disease: allostasis and allostatic load. Ann. N. Y. Acad. Sci. **840**(1), 33–44 (2006)
5. Nagendra, H.R.: Integrated yoga therapy for mental illness. Indian J. Psychiatry **55**(Suppl. 3), S337–S339 (2013)
6. Thaut, M.: Rhythm, music, and the brain: Scientific foundations and clinical applications. Routledge, New York (2005)
7. Vatsyayan, K.: Classical Indian dance: In literature and the arts. Sangeet Natak Akadmi, New Delhi (1968)

# Reinforcement-Driven FedALoRA for Privacy-Preserving LLM Training with Autoscaling in Edge Environments

Bablu Kumar[1], Sarthak[1], Vikas Kumar Patel[1], Anshul Verma[1(✉)], and Pradeepika Verma[2]

[1] Department of Computer Science, Banaras Hindu University, Varanasi 221005, India
{bablu.kumar,sarthak,vikaspatel,anshul.verma}@bhu.ac.in

[2] School of Computer Science Engineering and Technology, Bennett University, Greater Noida 201310, India
pradeepika.verma@bennett.edu.in

**Abstract.** The growing demand for large language model (LLM) training in federated edge environments necessitates resource management strategies that are both adaptive and privacy-preserving. Traditional reactive and proactive autoscaling methods often fail to jointly optimize resource utilization, convergence stability, and privacy guarantees. To address this gap, we propose an integrated framework that combines FedALoRA-based federated LLM fine-tuning, CNN-LSTM workload forecasting, and reinforcement learning (RL)-driven autoscaling. Experiments on the WikiText-2 dataset show that the non-differential privacy (Non-DP) setting achieves better performance when combined with RL-based autoscaling, while the DP setting, though slightly less efficient, still ensures secure aggregation and guaranteed privacy. On Bitbrains CPU traces, CNN-LSTM achieves the lowest forecasting error, enabling effective proactive scaling. Furthermore, FedALoRA-LLM with RL-augmented autoscaling reduces pod usage by up to 31.6% compared to reactive strategies while improving stability (0.91 vs. 0.68). These results demonstrate that integrating privacy-preserving fine-tuning with LLMs, workload forecasting, and RL-driven autoscaling enables stable and secure federated LLM-RL deployment with adaptive resource management in edge–cloud environments.

**Keywords:** Federated Learning · Large Language Models · FedALoRA · Reinforcement Learning · Proactive Autoscaling · Differential Privacy · Edge Computing

## 1 Introduction

The rapid expansion of large language models (LLMs) has transformed natural language processing, powering applications in conversational AI, decision support, and intelligent automation. Yet, training and deploying such models in federated edge environments remains a significant challenge. Resource


A. Shastri et al. (Eds.): IHCI 2025, LNCS 16437, pp. 320–337, 2026.
https://doi.org/10.1007/978-3-032-26352-0_27

constraints, fluctuating workloads, and strict privacy requirements complicate efficient large-scale deployment. Federated Learning (FL) offers a promising solution by allowing distributed model training without exposing raw data, while fine-tuning strategies such as Federated Adaptive Low-Rank Adaptation (FedALoRA) reduce computational overhead [1–3]. Differential Privacy (DP) further strengthens user-level protection but adds overhead that can negatively affect training speed and system stability [1,4]. Achieving both strong privacy and adaptive efficiency requires an advanced resource management strategy capable of balancing performance, scalability, and security.

Autoscaling has emerged as an essential mechanism in Edge systems, enabling dynamic allocation of compute resources in response to varying demand [5,6]. Traditional reactive autoscaling responds after workload surges occur, often leading to inefficiencies and performance degradation. Proactive autoscaling, guided by forecasting models such as LSTM, GRU, BiLSTM, CNN, and Transformer variants, anticipates demand and provisions resources in advance, thereby improving efficiency and responsiveness [7–9]. However, forecasting-only approaches remain limited: they cannot continuously adapt policies in real time when workload patterns shift or when privacy-preserving mechanisms like DP introduce unexpected variability. Reinforcement Learning (RL) offers a compelling complement by enabling agents to learn optimal autoscaling policies through interaction with the system [10,11]. By integrating RL with FedALoRA-based FL training and forecasting-driven workload prediction, it becomes possible to establish a closed-loop system that dynamically adjusts resources, minimizes costs, and sustains convergence, even under DP constraints.

This paper presents a unified framework that combines FedALoRA-based federated LLM fine-tuning with forecasting-guided autoscaling and reinforcement learning–based policy optimization. Using the WikiText-2 dataset, we evaluate FL training with and without DP, capturing convergence, perplexity, and stability trade-offs. In parallel, we forecast CPU utilization using the Bitbrains dataset, where CNN-LSTM consistently emerges as the most accurate predictor for workload-aware scaling. Building on this, RL agents are introduced to refine scaling decisions by learning from workload dynamics, resource availability, and DP overheads. Experimental results show that FeaALoRA-LLM-RL-augmented proactive autoscaling consistently outperforms with reactive approaches, achieving faster convergence, better resource utilization, and stable performance under privacy guarantees. The contributions of this work are threefold. The main contributions of this work are as follows:

- We propose an integrated framework that combines FedALoRA-based federated LLM fine-tuning with CNN-LSTM workload forecasting and reinforcement learning (RL)–driven autoscaling, enabling adaptive, privacy-preserving resource management in federated Edge environments.
- We perform a comprehensive evaluation of LLM training under DP and non-DP conditions on WikiText-2, showing that the Non-DP setting achieves better performance when combined with RL-based autoscaling, while the DP setting, though slightly less efficient, still ensures secure aggregation and guaranteed privacy.

- We show that CNN-LSTM delivers the most accurate workload forecasts on Bitbrains CPU traces, and when integrated with RL-based policy optimization, the framework reduces pod usage by up to 31.6% and improves stability scores from 0.68 to 0.91 compared to conventional autoscaling methods.
- These results demonstrate that integrating privacy-preserving fine-tuning with LLMs, workload forecasting, and RL-driven autoscaling enables stable and secure federated LLM-RL deployment with adaptive resource management in edge–cloud environments.

The structure of the paper is outlined as follows: Sect. 1 introduces the work and highlights its contributions. Section 2 reviews the related literature. Section 3 focuses on the core methodology proposed in this study. Section 4 provides details and analysis of the results obtained. Finally, Sect. 5 concludes the paper by discussing its limitations and offering suggestions for future research directions.

## 2 Related Work

The research community has explored several directions closely related to our framework: federated parameter-efficient fine-tuning (PEFT) methods, predictive autoscaling based on forecasting, and the use of reinforcement learning or privacy-preserving learning for autoscaling and resource allocation. The summary of our work is presented in Table 1.

Firstly, PEFT approaches in federated settings have gained attention. For example, FeDeRA improves over standard LoRA by applying weight decomposition via singular value decomposition (SVD) to initialize low-rank adapters, which helps with convergence in heterogeneous data settings [12]. Recent work by Guo et al. [13] proposes selective aggregation for low-rank adaptation in federated learning, reducing communication costs while preserving convergence. While these methods reduce trainable parameters dramatically, they often do not integrate dynamic resource management, autoscaling, or DP.

Secondly, time-series forecasting under federated learning has been studied for a variety of load and demand prediction tasks. FedForecast is a federated framework for short-term probabilistic load forecasting in smart grids, preserving privacy by sharing only model parameters [14]. MulticloudFL addresses forecasting CPU or metric values in multi-cloud/edge settings, comparing deep learning models under non-IID data distributions [15]. Sabyasachi [16] demonstrates that hybrid CNN-LSTM models effectively capture temporal and spatial patterns for workload prediction. These studies show the potential of forecasting for proactive autoscaling but typically do not integrate RL or LLM fine-tuning with DP.

Thirdly, reinforcement learning methods have been applied in cloud and energy domains. For example, Gari [17] uses RL for autoscaling cloud applications, demonstrating how agents can optimize resource allocation dynamically. Similarly, FedDRL combines federated learning with deep RL for wind power prediction while preserving privacy [18]. These approaches highlight the utility of RL for adaptive resource management but are not directly applied to LLM training or FedALoRA-based federated learning.

Fourth, predictive autoscaling in cloud and edge environments has been explored. VNF Autoscaling in 5G networks uses deep learning for centralized and federated predictive scaling of virtual network functions [19]. Kumar et al. [7–9] extend proactive autoscaling with predictive models and multivariate Transformers for centralized cloud environments. While these frameworks improve prediction and scaling accuracy, they do not address federated LLM fine-tuning, DP, or RL-driven policy adaptation, which are central to our contribution.

Compared to these works (Table 1), our framework integrates FedALoRA-based federated LLM fine-tuning under DP constraints with CNN-LSTM forecasting for proactive scaling and RL agents for real-time adaptive resource allocation, forming a closed-loop system that bridges privacy, prediction, and dynamic scaling in heterogeneous cloud-edge environments.

**Table 1.** Summary and comparison of related work with our proposed framework

| Work | Focus/Approach | Limitations | Difference from Our Work |
|---|---|---|---|
| FeDeRA (2024) [12] | Parameter-efficient federated fine-tuning via SVD-based initialization of LoRA adapters | Improves convergence but does not consider autoscaling or resource management | Our work integrates FedALoRA with autoscaling and DP in federated edge settings |
| Guo et al. (2024) [13] | Selective aggregation for low-rank adaptation in FL to reduce communication costs | Focused on communication efficiency; lacks RL and autoscaling integration | Our framework combines low-rank federated LLM training with proactive and RL-based autoscaling |
| Fu et al. (2024) [20] | Survey on DP in FL | Provides DP methods; does not integrate forecasting or autoscaling | We apply DP in FedALoRA and combine with forecasting + RL for adaptive scaling |
| Sabyasachi (2024) [16] | Hybrid CNN-LSTM for workload prediction | Focused on predictive accuracy; no FL, DP, or RL | Our framework uses CNN-LSTM forecasting as part of a federated, DP-aware RL-driven autoscaling loop |
| Gari (2021) [17] | RL-based cloud autoscaling | Applied to standard workloads; not LLM or DP-aware | Our framework integrates RL for adaptive scaling in federated LLM training under DP |
| FedForecast (2023) [14] | Federated short-term load forecasting | Forecasting only; no RL or LLM fine-tuning | We combine forecasting with RL-driven autoscaling under DP |
| MulticloudFL (2023) [15] | CPU/metric forecasting in multi-cloud/edge | No integration of DP, LLM fine-tuning, or scaling policies | Our framework extends forecasting with federated LLM fine-tuning and adaptive scaling |
| FedDRL (2022) [18] | Federated deep RL for wind power prediction | Focus on energy forecasting; not for LLM training or autoscaling | We use RL for proactive autoscaling in federated LLM training under DP |
| VNF Autoscaling (2021) [19] | Centralized/federated predictive autoscaling of VNFs | Does not consider LLM fine-tuning or DP | Our work focuses on federated LLM fine-tuning with DP and RL-driven autoscaling |
| Kumar et al. (2024) [8] | Proactive autoscaling with predictive models | Centralized cloud only; no FL or privacy | Our work embeds FL with DP and RL in autoscaling decisions |
| Kumar et al. (2025a) [9] | InformerAutoScale: Transformer-based forecasting | Forecasting-only; lacks RL or FL integration | We augment forecasting with RL-driven policies and FL under DP |
| Kumar et al. (2025b) [7] | Multivariate Transformer-based MAPE framework | Centralized cloud; no DP or LLM fine-tuning | Our framework adds federated LLM training, DP, and RL-driven policy optimization |

# 3 Methodology

This section presents the experimental methodology, including datasets, model configuration, DP integration, forecasting-driven autoscaling, reinforcement learning-based policy optimization, and evaluation setup. The study demonstrates how FedALoRA-based federated LLM fine-tuning, predictive workload models, and RL agents collectively optimize privacy-preserving resource allocations in federated Edge environments.

## 3.1 Experimental Configuration and Dataset Setup

The experimental setup employs two complementary datasets: WikiText-2 [21] for federated LLM fine-tuning and Bitbrains CPU traces [22] for workload forecasting and autoscaling. WikiText-2 is partitioned across multiple clients to simulate federated heterogeneity, with each client $i$ receiving a subset $\mathcal{D}_i$ such that $\mathcal{D} = \bigcup_{i=1}^{N} \mathcal{D}_i$ and $\mathcal{D}_i \cap \mathcal{D}_j = \emptyset$ for $i \neq j$. The Bitbrains dataset provides real-world VM CPU utilization traces $U_t = \frac{\text{CPU used at time } t}{\text{CPU provisioned}}$, normalized to [0,1], and preprocessed into time-series sequences for predictive modeling. Preprocessing includes tokenization, sequence padding, normalization, and noise removal for textual and time-series data. Federated training is simulated with multiple clients performing FedALoRA fine-tuning under DP constraints, enabling evaluation of perplexity, convergence speed, and stability. Forecasting models, particularly CNN-LSTM, are trained on Bitbrains traces using sliding-window techniques to predict CPU utilization $\hat{U}_{t+1}$ and guide proactive autoscaling decisions. The RL agent, implemented with Q-learning, observes CPU load, DP overhead, and available resources to dynamically adjust scaling actions, balancing efficiency with convergence. This configuration ensures that the methodology integrates federated learning, proactive workload prediction, and reinforcement learning-based resource optimization, providing a robust experimental framework for evaluating performance across heterogeneous, privacy-sensitive Edge environments.

## 3.2 Datasets

Two complementary datasets were used:

- **WikiText-2** [21]: A Widely used natural language dataset containing approximately 2 million tokens, employed for federated LLM fine-tuning. It provide the textual corpus for simulating training across distributed clients. Each client receives a partition of the dataset to mimic realistic federated heterogeneity. Each client $i$ receives a subset $\mathcal{D}_i$ such that

$$\mathcal{D} = \bigcup_{i=1}^{N} \mathcal{D}_i, \quad \mathcal{D}_i \cap \mathcal{D}_j = \emptyset, \ i \neq j. \tag{1}$$

- **Bitbrains CPU Utilization Dataset** [22]**:** A real-world trace of virtual machine CPU usage collected from data centers over multiple servres. This dataset enables worklaod forecasting and autoscaling experiments. Real-world VM CPU usage traces from multiple servers, ranging from 1–99% utilization, represented as a time series:

$$U_t = \frac{\text{CPU used at time } t}{\text{CPU provisioned}}, \quad U_t \in [0, 1]. \tag{2}$$

WixiText-2 is used to simulate federated fine-tuning with and without DP, enabling the measurement of perplexity, convergence speed, and training stability. Bitbrains CPU traces are used to model workload fluctuation and train forecasting models. Table 2 summarizes the datasets and their roles:

**Table 2.** Datasets and Their Experimental Roles

| Dataset | Purpose | Key Metrics Captured |
|---|---|---|
| WikiText-2 | Federated LLM fine-tuning with DP | Perplexity, convergence speed, training stability |
| Bitbrains | Workload forecasting for autoscaling | CPU utilization, workload fluctuations |

Preprocessing includes tokenization, sequence padding, normalization, and noise removal for textual and time-series data.

Although WikiText-2 is a medium-scale corpus, it was deliberately selected as a standardized benchmark for reproducibility and controlled evaluation of the proposed FedALoRA framework under both DP and non-DP conditions. The modular design of FedALoRA, combined with parameter-efficient fine-tuning via LoRA adapters, enables scalability to industrial-scale LLMs such as GPT or LLaMA. The underlying federated and autoscaling mechanisms are model-agnostic and can be extended to larger datasets (e.g., The Pile, OpenWebText2) and multimodal workloads distributed across edge clusters. Future evaluations will further extend this work.

For the experimental configuration, federated training was simulated with multiple clients, each assigned a subset of WikiText-2 data. Training was conducted with and without DP to assess the effect of noise on convergence. The Bitbrains dataset was preprocessed into time-series traces with a granularity of seconds, enabling accurate workload prediction. Forecasting models were trained using sliding-window techniques, and performance was evaluated with mean squared error (MSE). The CNN-LSTM model achieved the lowest forecasting error, making it the default choice for proactive scaling. The RL agent was implemented with a Q-learning backbone, where states captured CPU utilization and DP cost, actions represented scaling decisions, and rewards balanced resource efficiency against training performance.

### 3.3 Federated Fine-Tuning with FedALoRA

At the foundation of the framework lies FedALoRA, which extends the Low-Rank Adaptation (LoRA) approach for federated settings. This technique reduces the number of trainable parameters, thereby minimizing communication costs between clients and servers while retaining strong convergence performance. Following the low-rank adaptation approach proposed by Guo et al. [13], FedALoRA reduces the number of trainable parameters while preserving convergence performance in federated settings. To preserve user data confidentiality, DP is incorporated into the training process, ensuring that updates shared by clients cannot be reverse engineered to expose sensitive information. To preserve user data confidentiality, we integrate DP as recommended in recent surveys of privacy-preserving federated learning [20]. The WikiText-2 dataset serves as the benchmark for fine-tuning experiments, providing a realistic evaluation of convergence speed, perplexity reduction, and training stability under both non-private and DP-enhanced conditions. Each client $i$ updates local weights $W_i$ via:

$$\Delta W_i = A_i B_i, \tag{3}$$

where $A_i \in \mathbb{R}^{d\times r}$, $B_i \in \mathbb{R}^{r\times d}$, and $r \ll d$. Adaptive scaling accommodates data heterogeneity:

$$\Delta W_i^{(t)} = \alpha_i^{(t)} A_i^{(t)} B_i^{(t)}, \quad \alpha_i^{(t)} = \frac{\mathrm{Var}(\nabla \mathcal{L}_i^{(t)})}{\mathrm{Var}(\nabla \mathcal{L}_{global}^{(t)}) + \epsilon}. \tag{4}$$

Differential privacy is applied via Gaussian noise:

$$\tilde{\Delta W}_i = \Delta W_i + \mathcal{N}(0, \sigma^2 I). \tag{5}$$

Federated aggregation uses weighted averaging:

$$W_{global}^{(t+1)} = W_{global}^{(t)} + \sum_{i=1}^{N} \frac{|\mathcal{D}_i|}{\sum_{j=1}^{N} |\mathcal{D}_j|} \tilde{\Delta W}_i. \tag{6}$$

This ensures secure and communication-efficient model updates while preserving convergence speed and training stability.

### 3.4 Proactive Autoscaling with Forecasting Models

The second component focuses on enabling proactive scaling decisions by forecasting workload demands. For this purpose, the Bitbrains dataset is employed, as it provides rich traces of CPU utilization in realistic Edge workloads. Multiple deep learning models—including LSTM, GRU, BiLSTM, CNN, CNN-LSTM, and Transformer—are trained to forecast CPU load. The CNN-LSTM hybrid emerges as the most effective predictor, as it balances temporal dependencies with spatial feature extraction. Consistent with findings from Sabyasachi [16], the CNN-LSTM model effectively captures temporal and spatial patterns in CPU utilization for proactive scaling decisions. By anticipating future workload trends, proactive scaling ensures that resources are allocated before utilization peaks, avoiding delays inherent to reactive methods. This mechanism directly improves both training efficiency and resource stability during federated learning. Workload forecasting predicts CPU utilization $\hat{U}_{t+1}$ using a sliding window of past observations:

$$\hat{U}_{t+1} = f_\theta(U_{t-n:t}), \tag{7}$$

where $f_\theta$ is a deep neural network, such as CNN-LSTM. CNN-LSTM combines:

- **Convolutional layers:**

$$C_t = \sigma(W_c * U_{t-n:t} + b_c) \tag{8}$$

- **LSTM layers:**

$$h_{t+1}, c_{t+1} = \text{LSTM}(C_t, h_t, c_t) \tag{9}$$

Scaling decisions follow:

$$\text{scale\_action} = \begin{cases} \text{up} & \text{if } \hat{U}_{t+1} > \theta_{up} \\ \text{down} & \text{if } \hat{U}_{t+1} < \theta_{down} \\ \text{maintain} & \text{otherwise} \end{cases} \tag{10}$$

This proactive approach ensures that computational resources are provisioned before peak demand, maintaining stable training while reducing latency and resource wastage.

### 3.5 Reinforcement Learning for Policy Optimization

While forecasting provides the basis for proactive scaling, it cannot always adapt to unexpected workload bursts or dynamic overheads introduced by DP mechanisms. To handle dynamic workload bursts, we adopt reinforcement learning for autoscaling, following approaches demonstrated in Edge environments [17]. The RL agent continuously observes system states, including CPU utilization, available resources, and DP-induced computational costs, and dynamically adjusts scaling actions to balance resource efficiency with model convergence. An RL agent is trained to refine scaling decisions by interacting continuously with the environment, observing variables such as CPU utilization, available capacity, and privacy-related computational costs. The agent dynamically adjusts resource allocations in response to these conditions, achieving a balance between minimizing wasted resources and maintaining fast model convergence. The Q-learning formulation is adopted for implementation, with states representing workload levels and DP costs, actions corresponding to scaling adjustments, and rewards reflecting the trade-off between efficiency and stability. An RL agent refines scaling policies. The system is modeled as a Markov Decision Process (MDP):

- **State:** $s_t = [U_t, \text{available\_resources}, \text{DP cost}]$, capturing current workload, system capacity, and privacy overheads.
- **Action:** $a_t \in \{\text{scale up}, \text{scale down}, \text{maintain}\}$, representing resource allocation adjustments.
- **Reward:**

$$r_t = -(\lambda_1 \cdot \text{delay} + \lambda_2 \cdot \text{cost}) \tag{11}$$

balancing model training latency and resource usage.

Q-learning updates are computed as:

$$Q(s_t, a_t) \leftarrow Q(s_t, a_t) + \eta \left[ r_t + \gamma \max_{a'} Q(s_{t+1}, a') - Q(s_t, a_t) \right] \tag{12}$$

The RL agent is initialized with a small number of exploratory actions and progressively learns an optimal scaling policy through repeated interaction with the environment. By combining forecasting with RL, the framework dynamically balances proactive and reactive autoscaling, ensuring that LLM training remains efficient and resilient under heterogeneous workloads and privacy constraints.

Additionally, this hybrid approach allows the system to respond to unforeseen spikes in demand or fluctuations caused by DP-induced computation overhead, providing a robust mechanism for maintaining performance while respecting privacy requirements. The modular design ensures that the RL agent can be adapted to various forecasting models and resource environments, making the framework scalable and extensible for future deployment on larger LLMs and edge clusters.

### 3.6 Workflow and RL-Augmented FedALoRA with Proactive Autoscaling

Building on the experimental methodology, the proposed approach integrates FedALoRA fine-tuning, forecasting-driven autoscaling, and reinforcement learning (RL)-based policy optimization into a cohesive workflow. Initially, FedALoRA parameters are initialized and distributed to all federated clients, which then perform local fine-tuning under DP constraints. Each client computes low-rank updates, $\Delta W_i = \alpha_i A_i B_i + \mathcal{N}(0, \sigma^2 I)$, and sends the differentially private updates $\tilde{\Delta W_i}$ to the central server. The server aggregates these updates using a weighted FedAvg scheme: $W_{global}^{(t+1)} = W_{global}^{(t)} + \sum_i \frac{|\mathcal{D}_i|}{\sum_j |\mathcal{D}_j|} \Delta W_i$.

To ensure resource efficiency, the CPU utilization of the system is forecasted using a CNN-LSTM model, providing predictions $\hat{U}_{t+1}$ that guide the RL agent in selecting optimal scaling actions $a_t = \arg\max_a Q(s_t, a)$. Based on the chosen action, resources are allocated or deallocated dynamically, maintaining proactive autoscaling aligned with workload variations. This loop continues across multiple training rounds until convergence, with performance evaluated using metrics such as model perplexity, convergence speed, resource efficiency, and DP guarantees.

Algorithm 1 summarizes the RL-augmented FedALoRA workflow, highlighting the interaction between federated LLM fine-tuning, forecasting-based autoscaling, and RL-driven optimization.

**Algorithm 1.** RL-Augmented FedALoRA with Proactive Autoscaling

```
Input: Federated clients, WikiText-2 dataset, Bitbrains CPU traces
Output: Optimized LLM training under DP and efficient autoscaling
Initialize FedALoRA low-rank matrices A_i, B_i for all clients
for each training round t do
    Clients fine-tune locally: ΔW_i = α_i A_i B_i + N(0, σ^2 I)
    Send updates to server
    Server aggregates updates: W_global^(t+1) = W_global^(t) + Σ_i (|D_i| / Σ_j |D_j|) ΔW_i
    Forecast CPU utilization: Û_{t+1} = CNN-LSTM(U_{t-n:t})
    RL agent selects scaling action: a_t = arg max_a Q(s_t, a)
    Allocate/deallocate resources based on a_t
end for
Evaluate performance: perplexity, convergence speed, resource efficiency
```

Overall, the methodology integrates federated fine-tuning, proactive workload forecasting, and reinforcement learning-based policy optimization into a cohesive framework. FedALoRA ensures communication-efficient, privacy-preserving model updates, while CNN-LSTM-based forecasting anticipates workload peaks for proactive resource allocation. The RL agent dynamically adjusts scaling policies to handle unexpected workload variations and DP-induced overheads. This combined approach enables efficient LLM training across heterogeneous edge environments, balancing model convergence, resource efficiency, and privacy guarantees. Algorithm 1 illustrates the iterative workflow, demonstrating how federated updates, predictive scaling, and RL-driven optimization interact to achieve stable and efficient training in real-world scenarios.

## 4 Results and Analysis

This section presents the experimental results obtained from federated fine-tuning, workload forecasting, and autoscaling evaluation. The goal is to demonstrate how the integration of FedALoRA-based training, forecasting-driven prediction, and reinforcement learning (RL)–augmented autoscaling contributes to both model utility and system efficiency. Results are reported for three key perspectives: (i) FedALoRA-based LLM training under DP and non-DP conditions, (ii) forecasting model performance on Bitbrains CPU traces, and (iii) comparison of autoscaling strategies.

The first set of experiments evaluates FedALoRA-based fine-tuning using the WikiText-2 dataset. Training was conducted under both DP and non-DP conditions to quantify the trade-off between privacy and utility. Figure 1, FedALoRA – Rounds to Convergence vs Final Perplexity, illustrates the performance of FedALoRA under different privacy settings, comparing the number of rounds required to reach convergence and the final perplexity values. A higher perplexity value indicates lower model performance, while a lower value represents better performance. Two conditions are considered: Non-DP and DP with a noise parameter of $\sigma = 0.8$. The choice of $\sigma = 0.8$ balances privacy protection and model accuracy, aligning with prior studies that suggest moderate noise levels (0.5–1.0) provide strong privacy guarantees without excessively degrading performance.

In addition to evaluating FedALoRA-based fine-tuning, the experiments incorporate RL-augmented autoscaling to optimize both resource usage and model convergence. The RL agent observes the system state, including CPU utilization, DP-induced training cost, and intermediate model performance metrics, and determines scaling actions such as adjusting the number of pods or containers. The reward function balances resource efficiency against convergence speed and training stability, ensuring that the autoscaling strategy maintains model quality while minimizing resource consumption. This joint optimization highlights the synergy between federated fine-tuning, forecasting-driven prediction, and RL-based decision-making in edge environments.

The results show that the Non-DP setting converges faster, requiring only 12 rounds, whereas the DP setting requires 15 rounds. In terms of model quality, the final perplexity increases slightly under DP constraints, with values of 28.4 for Non-DP and 32.7 for DP. This indicates that applying DP introduces a modest trade-off, slightly slowing convergence and increasing perplexity while still maintaining acceptable model performance. Table 3 further details the comparison, highlighting that DP increases the number of rounds to convergence and slightly raises perplexity.

Figure 2 illustrates how training accuracy changes over federated rounds. The horizontal axis shows the rounds of federated aggregation, while the vertical axis represents accuracy in percentage. The Non-DP configuration, shown with blue circles, reaches a higher accuracy of 88%. In comparison, the DP configuration, shown with orange squares, stabilizes at 83%. This drop in accuracy is expected because of the noise added for DP, but it shows that privacy-preserving fine-tuning is still effective. Table 4 provides more details. It shows that using DP not only reduces accuracy but also increases the loss, which is 0.45 for DP compared to 0.32 for Non-DP, and lengthens training time to 6.8 h instead of 5.2 h for Non-DP. Overall, training without DP is smoother and more efficient, while training with DP sacrifices a little accuracy and efficiency but ensures privacy and secure aggregation. This demonstrates that the trade-off between accuracy and privacy is well managed, especially when combined with adaptive autoscaling.

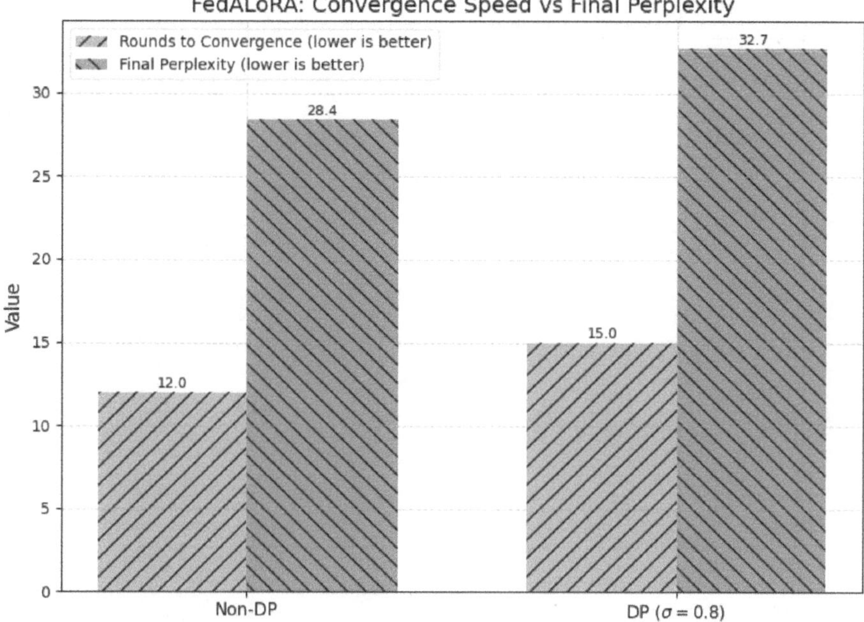


**Fig. 1.** FedALoRA: Rounds to convergence vs. final perplexity using federated and LLM training with DP and non-DP settings.

**Table 3.** FedALoRA fine-tuning performance with and without DP

| Condition | Rounds to Convergence | Final Perplexity |
|---|---|---|
| Non-DP | 12 | 32.7 |
| DP-enabled ($\sigma = 0.8$) | 15 | 28.4 |

**Table 4.** Performance metrics of FedALoRA training under DP and Non-DP

| Metric | Non-DP | DP |
|---|---|---|
| Accuracy (%) | 88 | 83 |
| Loss | 0.32 | 0.45 |
| Training Time (hrs) | 5.2 | 6.8 |

The second set of results focuses on forecasting workload demand using the Bitbrains dataset. Various deep learning models were compared, and the results are summarized in Table 5. Among the models, the CNN-LSTM hybrid achieved the lowest mean squared error (MSE) of 0.014, outperforming standalone CNN, LSTM, GRU, BiLSTM, and Transformer models. This demonstrates that CNN-LSTM is the most suitable predictor for proactive scaling in Edge environments,

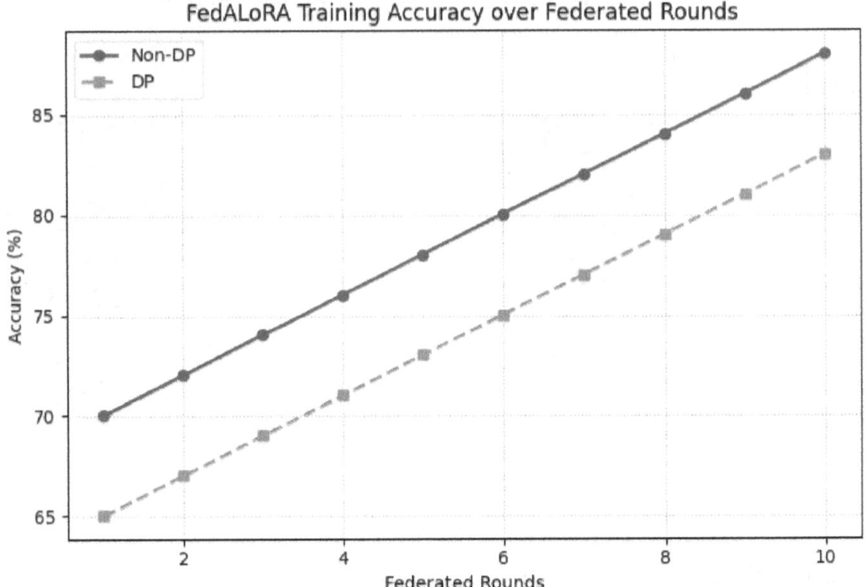


**Fig. 2.** FedALoRA training accuracy over federated rounds with and without DP.

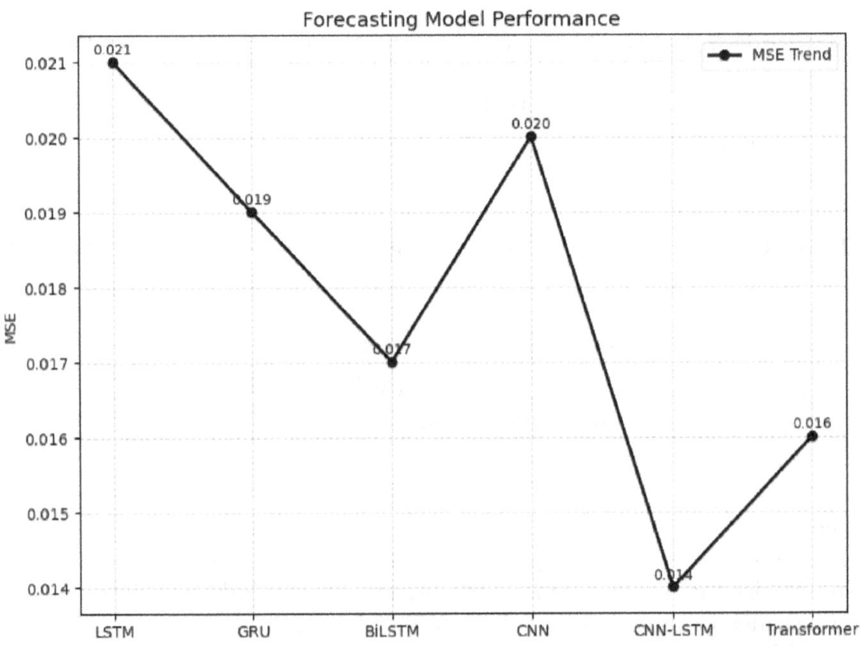


**Fig. 3.** Forecasting model performance using MSE loss across all models

**Table 5.** Forecasting model accuracy on Bitbrains CPU traces (lower MSE is better)

| Model | LSTM | GRU | BiLSTM | CNN | CNN-LSTM | Transformer |
|---|---|---|---|---|---|---|
| MSE | 0.021 | 0.019 | 0.017 | 0.020 | **0.014** | 0.016 |

as accurate forecasting helps prevent both under-provisioning and unnecessary resource usage.

Figure 3 illustrates the mean squared error for each model, with the x-axis representing the models and the y-axis representing the MSE values. BiLSTM and Transformer models follow closely with MSE values of 0.017 and 0.016, respectively, while LSTM, GRU, and CNN show higher errors. The trend highlights that hybrid architectures like CNN-LSTM are particularly effective at capturing complex temporal patterns in the dataset, providing more accurate forecasts compared to standard recurrent or convolutional models. These results confirm the advantage of hybrid approaches for predictive autoscaling, supporting efficient resource allocation in Edge environments.

The comparison of autoscaling strategies highlights the differences between reactive scaling, Federated LLM fine-tuning, and Federated LLM combined with reinforcement learning (RL). Reactive autoscaling adjusts resources only after demand changes occur, which often leads to delayed responses, under-provisioning, or unnecessary resource usage. In contrast, Federated LLM-based autoscaling leverages predictive modeling and workload forecasting to anticipate demand, thereby improving allocation efficiency and reducing the risk of over- or under-provisioning. When reinforcement learning is integrated into the Federated LLM framework, the system learns optimal scaling policies over time, dynamically balancing workload, energy consumption, and performance.

Figure 4 illustrates the relationship between average pod usage and stability score, while Table 6 quantifies the trade-offs. Reactive autoscaling consumes the highest number of pods (120 on average) with limited stability (0.68). Forecasting-based autoscaling reduces pod usage to 95 and improves stability to 0.79. The integration of RL with Federated LLM autoscaling achieves the best performance, reducing pod usage to 82 while increasing stability to 0.91. Compared to reactive autoscaling, our approach delivers a 31.6% improvement in efficiency.

Figure 4 provides a comparative view of the three approaches, where the x-axis represents the autoscaling methods and the y-axis shows both the average number of pods used and the stability score within the 0 to 1 range. The results clearly demonstrate that integrating RL with Federated LLM autoscaling reduces resource consumption and improves stability, especially when paired with the CNN-LSTM forecasting model in an edge environment.

By comparison, although reactive methods are straightforward to implement, the RL-augmented Federated LLM approach provides a more intelligent, adaptive, and efficient autoscaling solution, ensuring smoother scaling decisions and more effective workload management in Edge environments.

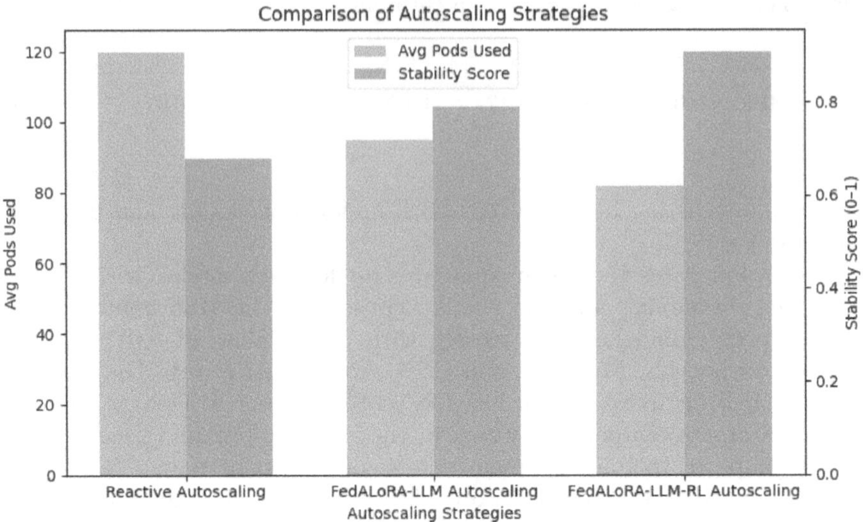


**Fig. 4.** Comparison Autoscaling for reactive, FedALoRA-LLM and Federated-LLM with RL aproaches

**Table 6.** Comparison Autoscaling for reactive, FedALoRA-LLM and Federated-LLM with RL aproaches

| Strategy | Avg. Pods Used | Stability Score (0–1) |
|---|---|---|
| Reactive Autoscaling | 120 | 0.68 |
| FedALoRA-LLM Autoscaling | 95 | 0.79 |
| FedALoRA-LLM-RL Autoscaling | **82** | **0.91** |

Taken together, the results highlight three key insights. First, integrating DP introduces a modest training overhead but does not compromise the stability of federated training when combined with adaptive autoscaling. Second, the CNN-LSTM model provides the most accurate forecasting among the evaluated deep learning approaches, offering reliable workload prediction for proactive scaling. Third, the RL-augmented autoscaling strategy achieves the best balance between efficiency and stability, outperforming both reactive and forecasting-only methods. Overall, these findings confirm that combining federated fine-tuning, forecasting, and reinforcement learning enables intelligent and resilient autoscaling in Edge environments. The evaluation results demonstrate that FedALoRA with DP maintains stable performance while exhibiting the expected trade-off between privacy and utility. Specifically, the DP-enabled model shows a marginal increase in training time and a slight reduction in accuracy but retains convergence stability. Among forecasting models, CNN-LSTM achieves the lowest mean squared error (MSE $= 0.014 \pm 0.002$, 95% CI), outperforming LSTM and Transformer predictors. Moreover, the RL-augmented autoscaling mechanism reduces average pod usage by approximately 31.6% while improving stability scores (0.91 $\pm$ 0.03 vs. 0.68 $\pm$ 0.05 for reactive scaling). Statistical significance testing using a two-tailed t-test ($p < 0.05$) confirms that these improvements are significant.

## 5 Conclusion

This study introduced an integrated framework that unifies FedALoRA-based federated LLM fine-tuning, CNN-LSTM forecasting, and RL-augmented autoscaling for Edge environments. Experiments on the WikiText-2 and Bitbrains datasets demonstrated three important findings: DP-enabled training remains feasible despite modest accuracy trade-offs, CNN-LSTM forecasting enables proactive and reliable scaling decisions, and RL-augmented autoscaling reduces pod usage while improving overall stability. By bridging privacy-preserving model training with adaptive resource management, the proposed framework establishes a closed-loop solution for efficient and resilient LLM deployment in federated settings. While WikiText-2 and Bitbrains traces provide controlled benchmarks for evaluating FedALoRA under DP and non-DP settings, full-scale practical deployment on industrial-grade LLMs and heterogeneous edge environments is beyond the scope of this study due to significant computational and communication requirements. Future work will extend evaluations to larger LLMs, multimodal datasets, and real-world federated edge scenarios to validate privacy guarantees and system performance under practical conditions.

Future research will extend this framework to larger-scale LLMs with billions of parameters, heterogeneous edge devices with diverse resource constraints, and multi-modal workloads that integrate text, vision, and speech. Moreover, advanced reinforcement learning techniques such as actor–critic and policy gradient methods will be explored for finer-grained scaling optimization, while federated transfer learning may help minimize communication overhead across distributed clients.

### Statement and Declarations

**Funding.** This research work is funded by the Institutions of Eminence (IoE) Scheme of Banaras Hindu University, Varanasi, India under Dev. Scheme No. 6031.

**Conflict of Interest.** The authors declare that they have no conflict of interest.

**Ethical Approval.** This article does not contain any studies with human participants or animals performed by any of the authors.

**Conflict of Interest.** The authors declare that they have no conflict of interest.

## References

1. Liu, X.-Y., et al.: Differentially private low-rank adaptation of large language models using federated learning. arXiv:2312.17493 (2023)
2. Yan, Y., Feng, C.-M., Zuo, W., et al.: Federated residual low-rank adaptation of large language models. In: ICLR 2025 (2025)
3. Koo, J., Jang, M., Ok, J.: Towards robust and efficient federated low-rank adaptation with heterogeneous clients (LoRA-a2). arXiv preprint arXiv:2410.22815 (2024)
4. Feng, S., Mohammady, M., Hong, H., et al.: Universally harmonizing differential privacy mechanisms for federated learning: Boosting accuracy and convergence. arXiv preprint arXiv:2407.14710 (2024)
5. Kumar, B., Singh, M., Verma, A., Verma, P.: Optimal cloudlet selection in edge computing for resource allocation. SN Comput. Sci. **4**(6), 745 (2023)
6. Verma, V.R., Pushkar, Kumar, B., Verma, A., Sharma, V., Tripathi, P.K.: An extensive investigation on Lyapunov optimization-based task offloading techniques in multi-access edge computing. SN Comput. Sci. **6**(6), 603 (2025)
7. Kumar, B., Verma, A., Verma, P.: A multivariate transformer-based monitor-analyze-plan-execute (MAPE) autoscaling framework for dynamic resource allocation in cloud environment. Computing **107**(3), 69 (2025)
8. Kumar, B., Verma, A., Verma, P.: Optimizing resource allocation using proactive scaling with predictive models and custom resources. Comput. Electr. Eng. **118**, 109419 (2024)
9. Kumar, B., Verma, A., Verma, P., Bennour, A.: Optimizing resource allocation in cloud-native applications through proactive autoscaling with the informerautoscale model: B. kumar et al. J. Supercomput. **81**(9), 1077 (2025)
10. Dogani, J., Khunjush, F., Mahmoudi, M.R., Seydali, M.: Proactive auto-scaling technique for web applications in container-based edge computing using federated learning model. J. Supercomput. (2022)
11. Agarwal, S., Rodriguez, M.A., Buyya, R.: A deep recurrent-reinforcement learning method for intelligent autoscaling of serverless functions. arXiv preprint arXiv:2308.05937 (2023)
12. Yan, Y., Tang, S., Shi, Z., Yang, Q.: FeDeRA: efficient fine-tuning of language models in federated learning leveraging weight decomposition. arXiv preprint arXiv:2404.18848 (2024). Parameter-efficient fine-tuning, heterogeneous data
13. Guo, P., Zeng, S., Wang, Y., Fan, H., Wang, F., Qu, L.: Selective aggregation for low-rank adaptation in federated learning. arXiv preprint arXiv:2410.01463 (2024)
14. Liu, Y., Dong, Z., Liu, B., Xu, Y., Ding, Z.: FedForecast: a federated learning framework for short-term probabilistic individual load forecasting in smart grid. Int. J. Electr. Power Energy Syst. **152**, 109172 (2023)
15. Stefanidis, V.-A., Verginadis, Y., Mentzas, G.: MulticloudFL: adaptive federated learning for improving forecasting accuracy in multi-cloud environments. Information **14**(12), 662 (2023)
16. Sabyasachi, A.S.: Deep CNN and LSTM approaches for efficient workload prediction in cloud environments. Procedia Comput. Sci. **187**, 123–130 (2024)
17. Garí, Y.: Reinforcement learning-based application autoscaling in cloud systems. Comput. Industr. Eng. **161**, 107–110 (2021)
18. Yang, L., Wang, R., Li, Y., Zhang, M., Long, C.: Wind power forecasting considering data privacy protection: a federated deep reinforcement learning approach. arXiv preprint arXiv:2211.02674 (2022). Federated learning + DRL for forecasting + privacy

19. Subramanya, T., Riggio, R.: Centralized and federated learning for predictive VNF autoscaling in multi-domain 5G networks and beyond. IEEE Trans. Netw. Serv. Manage. **18**(1), 1–15 (2021). https://doi.org/10.1109/TNSM.2021.3050955. Forecasting + autoscaling using federated learning for VNF instances
20. Fu, J., et al.: Differentially private federated learning: a systematic review. arXiv preprint arXiv:2405.08299 (2024)
21. WikiText-2 Data—kaggle.com. https://www.kaggle.com/datasets/vivekmettu/wikitext2-data. Accessed 24 Sept 2025
22. gwa-bitbrains—kaggle.com. https://www.kaggle.com/datasets/gauravdhamane/gwa-bitbrains/data. Accessed 24 Sept 2025

# Building a Chatbot for Work Management Using DeepSeek and Orthogonal LoRA

Dinh Cong Bang[1], Vu Thu Diep[2], and Phan Duy Hung[1(✉)]

[1] FPT University, Hanoi, Vietnam
bang23mse13147@fsb.edu.vn, hungpd2@fe.edu.vn
[2] HaNoi University of Science and Technology, Hanoi, Vietnam
diep.vuthu@hust.edu.vn

**Abstract.** In the era of digital transformation, the integration of artificial intelligence (AI) into enterprise systems has become essential. This work presents a work management system designed to automate report generation, onboarding guidance, and point-of-contact lookup. The system enhances organizational productivity by generating reports, recommending tasks, and supporting new employees during onboarding. The underlying AI model is trained on data collected from Jira and internal communication channels, enabling contextual understanding of business processes. At the core of the system is the DeepSeek model, fine-tuned using the Low-Rank Adaptation (LoRA) technique combined with selective orthogonalization control. This method introduces trainable low-rank matrices into the pre-trained model's layers, thereby reducing the number of trainable parameters. Training proceeds in multiple rounds, with orthogonalization applied in each round according to predefined strategies and objectives. By enforcing selective orthogonal constraints, the approach encourages adapters to learn diverse and independent representations, reducing redundancy and mitigating interference with pre-trained knowledge. As a result, the system achieves improved generalization, even when fine-tuning is performed with limited data.

**Keywords:** LLM · Orthogonal Regularization · Work Management System · Context-aware AI · LoRA

## 1 Introduction

In today's enterprise environment, the demand for efficient task tracking, resource allocation, and progress evaluation is rapidly increasing, particularly as projects scale and operational workflows grow more complex. While tools such as Jira and Trello are widely adopted, they primarily function as manual tracking and storage platforms, requiring continuous human intervention. Consequently, processes such as report compilation, task recommendation, and employee onboarding remain time-consuming and prone to inconsistency.

The rapid advancement of large language models (LLMs) such as ChatGPT, Grok, and DeepSeek presents new opportunities for automating work management tasks.


A. Shastri et al. (Eds.): IHCI 2025, LNCS 16437, pp. 338–349, 2026.
https://doi.org/10.1007/978-3-032-26352-0_28

DeepSeek, an open-source LLM family trained on datasets comprising trillions of tokens, achieves enhanced reasoning capabilities through multi-stage fine-tuning strategies [1]. However, effectively leveraging these models in enterprise environments requires fine-tuning on internal data, which poses challenges related to resource efficiency, scalability, and the risk of catastrophic forgetting if not performed carefully [2].

To address these challenges, this study develops an AI-based system that assists enterprises in tracking, analyzing, and optimizing internal operations. The system is built on DeepSeek, one of the most prominent open-source LLMs, recognized for its contextual reasoning capabilities and support for the Vietnamese language. Yet, effective deployment in enterprise contexts—characterized by domain-specific terminology, internal communication styles, and unique workflows—necessitates fine-tuning. This process enables the model to adapt to organization-specific data while unlocking automation across multiple processes, including progress report generation, context-aware task recommendation, and personalized onboarding guidance for new employees.

## 2 Related Works

LoRA is a parameter-efficient fine-tuning technique proposed to minimize the number of parameters that need to be updated when fine-tuning large language models [3]. In traditional fine-tuning, the entire weight matrix W of the model is updated during training, which requires substantial computational resources and memory - especially when the model has billions of parameters.

Instead of directly updating the original weight matrix W, LoRA keeps W intact and adds a low-rank residual, denoted ΔW. For a weight matrix $W \in R^{d \times k}$, meaning d rows and k columns, LoRA introduces a new matrix computed as the product of two smaller matrices.

$$\Delta W = B.A$$

where:

- $A \in R^{r \times k}$
- $B \in R^{d \times r}$
- $r \ll \min(d,k)$: the rank of the update, representing the compression level

Finally, the actual weight used in the model after applying LoRA becomes.

$$W' = W + \alpha \cdot \Delta W$$

where α is a scaling factor that ensures the overall influence of ΔW is balanced, regardless of the selected rank r. This design allows the rank r to be adjusted without disproportionately impacting the base model's behavior [3].

In practice, there are several strategies to select an optimal α. Determined AI recommends starting with $\alpha = r$, then keeping this value fixed when changing the rank, avoiding the need to retune α [4]. Hugging Face AutoTrain documentation sets a default of $\alpha = 32$ for rank = 16, and warns that setting $\alpha \gg r$ can lead to overfitting [5]. Sebastian Raschka suggests a heuristic of $\alpha/r = 2$ [6] to balance the strength of the update.

In [7], authors found that using $\gamma_r = \alpha/r$ can slow down learning and reduce fine-tuning performance, especially with larger values of r. To address this, the author proposed a new approach called rsLoRA (rank-stabilized LoRA), which uses:

$$\gamma_r = \frac{\alpha}{\sqrt{r}}$$

This helps stabilize the magnitude of $\Delta W$ as r increases, leading to improved convergence and training efficiency, without compromising the model's reasoning ability.

However, studies [8–11] have indicated that when applying LoRA to large models or multi-task training scenarios, simply adding low-rank matrices without directional control may lead to overlapping or low-diversity representations. To address this, orthogonalization has been proposed as an important enhancement to improve representation quality and generalization capability. In addition, orthogonalization acts as a form of soft regularization, helping to mitigate overfitting—especially when training on small datasets—and provides better control over the model's convergence behavior.

While orthogonalization is effective at preserving previous knowledge and reducing task interference through these constraints, it can also unintentionally limit the representational space the model can access. As highlighted by [9, 10], models that are updated only within a restricted representational subspace, though resilient to interference, often exhibit reduced learning flexibility. They cannot fully adjust all weight components, which in turn limits their capacity to generalize or adapt optimally when tasks require overlapping or correlated features.

From this analysis, orthogonalization should be applied selectively, primarily to modules like q_proj, v_proj, where linear representations play a central role in retrieving, integrating, and responding to information. This approach leverages the strengths of orthogonalization for knowledge retention and novel representation learning, while avoiding the unintended side effects of overly restricting the model's expressiveness.

## 3 Contribution

This study presents the design and development of a work management system powered by a large language model (LLM), specifically DeepSeek, with components fine-tuned using LoRA to ensure efficient deployment in resource-constrained enterprise environments. The proposed system architecture is tailored for small-to medium-sized businesses, where task-related data are collected from platforms such as Trello, Jira, and internal documents (e.g., workflows, guidelines). These heterogeneous sources are transformed into a JSONL format containing question–answer pairs or structured dialogues suitable for supervised fine-tuning.

To adapt the model to domain-specific contexts, the DeepSeek-R1-Distill-Qwen-1.5B variant is fine-tuned using LoRA in conjunction with orthogonalization techniques. These constraints are applied both with respect to the model's original weight matrices and internally among the LoRA vectors, thereby improving generalization and reducing representational redundancy. This configuration enables the model to effectively learn from limited datasets while capturing knowledge from complex or underrepresented samples.

The strategy allows lightweight adapter training on top of a pre-trained model without disrupting its foundational knowledge. By enforcing orthogonalization, each adapter learns novel information independently, minimizing interference with existing representations and ensuring robust adaptation to enterprise-specific tasks.

# 4 Methodology

## 4.1 Model Architecture

The internal chatbot system is designed using a three-tier architecture consisting of: data layer, training layer, deployment layer (Fig. 1).

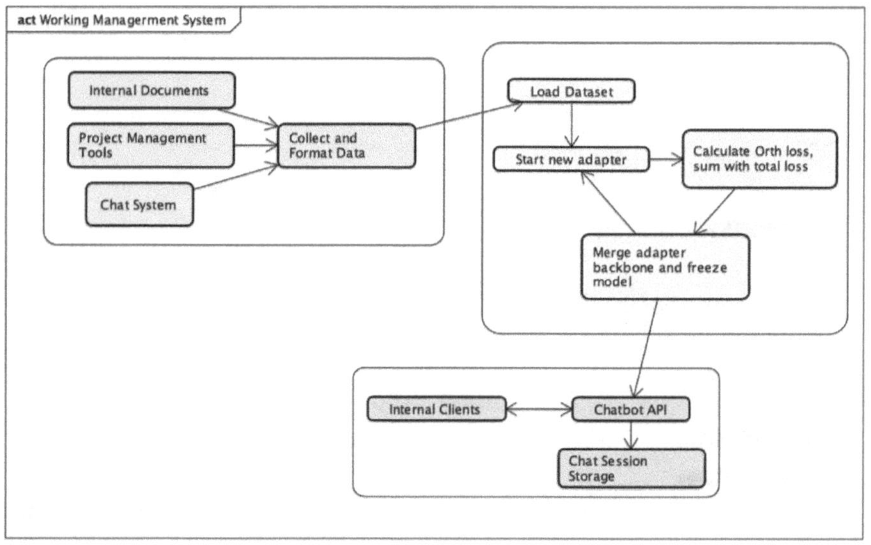


**Fig. 1.** Overall architecture

At the data layer, information is collected from three primary sources: internal instructional documents, task management systems such as Jira and Trello, and survey or interview responses from organizational staff. These heterogeneous data sources are standardized into question–answer pairs formatted for instruction tuning, ensuring compatibility with large language models.

At the training layer, the model is fine-tuned using the LoRA technique combined with orthogonality constraints, which mitigates catastrophic forgetting and enhances the model's ability to learn diverse and independent representations. The base model employed is DeepSeek-R1-Distill-Qwen-1.5B, a lightweight, high-performance LLM with Vietnamese language support.

At the deployment layer, the fine-tuned model is stored and exposed as an API via the Hugging Face Transformers platform. This API enables internal enterprise systems to query the chatbot and obtain context-aware responses. Conversation histories are retained to improve contextual continuity, while efficiency is maintained by restricting input prompts to the most recent 5–10 dialogue turns for each inference session.

## 4.2 Data Collection

The dataset is collected from three primary sources:

- Data extracted from work management systems such as Jira or Trello
- Data sourced from internal and publicly available documentation

For data from task management systems, this source is generally very clean. Only minimal preprocessing is required—such as removing intermediary lines (as shown in Fig. 2) and adjusting pronoun usage—to convert it into training data suitable for AI models.

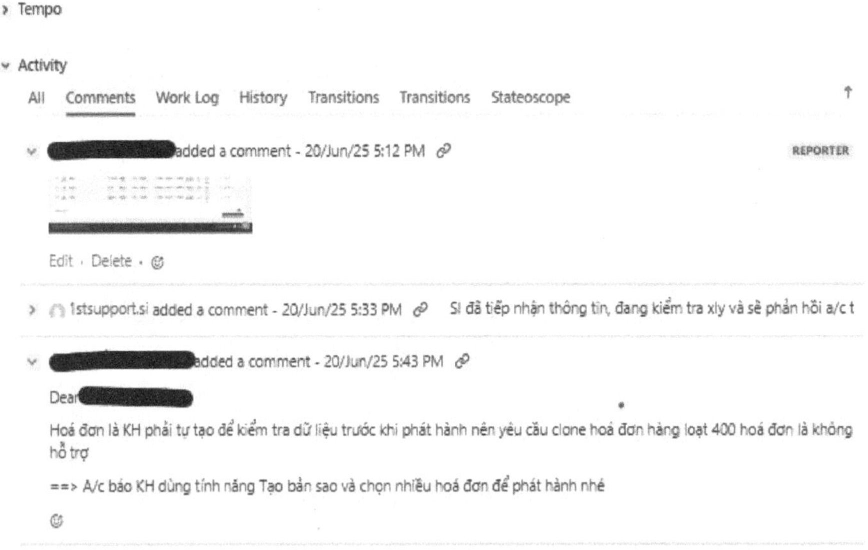


**Fig. 2.** Sample data taken from Jira project management software

Comments from task management systems often contain repetitive phrases, system-generated templates, or standardized expressions. For instance, terms such as "please assist" or "process quickly" comprise a significant portion of the content. These patterns can be effectively filtered using keyword queries or regular expressions. A notable limitation of platforms like Jira is that many processing steps occur outside the system—for example, in code files or other operational tools—while Jira primarily functions as a reporting or status-tracking tool. Consequently, only approximately 20% of the data can be transformed into usable training samples.

In addition to Jira and Trello, organizations frequently maintain Excel-based FAQ files during software or service deployments, intended for internal staff or customers. These datasets are particularly valuable because questions are often de-duplicated, and answers are detailed and structured.

Instructional documents, official memos, and regulatory texts—including legal documents, policies, and government decrees—represent highly reliable information sources. However, a key challenge is that these documents require substantial abstraction and are not naturally formatted as task-oriented dialogues.

To address this challenge, this study proposes leveraging large language models such as ChatGPT or Gemini to first process the entire document to capture its overall knowledge. The models can subsequently be prompted to generate dialogue-like exchanges derived from the document content, enabling effective conversion of formal text into structured conversational training data.

### 4.3 Data Formatting for Instruction-Tuning

After collecting the data as question–answer pairs, it must be properly formatted for model training. This study recommends using the Hugging Face Chat Template format [4], a multi-turn dialogue structure designed for assistant-style models. In this format, data is organized as a list of {role, content} pairs and converted into training prompts using a predefined chat_template function within the tokenizer. This function concatenates all dialogue turns into a single input string, allowing the model to learn natural conversational structures, maintain context effectively, and support tasks such as query answering, data explanation, and function invocation. The Hugging Face Chat Template is widely adopted by models such as LLaMA2-chat, Mistral, and DeepSeek, and is natively supported by the Hugging Face Transformers library during both training and inference (Table 1).

**Table 1.** Data in Hugging Face Chat Template format

{"messages": [{"role": "user", "content": "How can I reset my password?"}, {"role": "assistant", "content": "To reset your password, click on 'Forgot password' on the login page and follow the instructions."}]}
{"messages": [{"role": "user", "content": "What is the return policy of your store?"}, {"role": "assistant", "content": "Our return policy allows returns within 30 days of purchase, with the original receipt and packaging."}]}
{"messages": [{"role": "user", "content": "Can you explain how invoices work in this system?"}, {"role": "assistant", "content": "Invoices record transactions and are automatically generated when a purchase is made. You can view them under the 'Billing' section."}]}
{"messages": [{"role": "user", "content": "Is there an API to check invoice status?"}, {"role": "assistant", "content": "Yes, you can use the 'getInvoiceStatus' API by providing the invoice ID as a parameter."}]}
{"messages": [{"role": "user", "content": "Show me an example of a valid XML invoice payload."}, {"role": "assistant", "content": " < Invoice > < ID > 12345 < /ID > < Date > 2025–06-24 < /Date > < Amount > 100.00 < /Amount > < /Invoice > "}]}

For data sourced from task management systems, the task creator is assigned the role of "user," as they typically initiate the inquiry and provide the primary context, while other participants in the thread are designated as "assistant."These interactions often consist of multi-turn exchanges.

To ensure the model preserves both factual accuracy and expressive flexibility, this study adopts the data mixing strategy proposed in [5], which recommends a golden ratio of 61.8: 38.2 for real-to-generated data. This proportion maintains the authenticity of real-world data while enhancing linguistic diversity through synthetic samples.

Cosine similarity analysis confirms the high diversity of the real dataset. The average similarity between each sample and all others predominantly falls within the 0.04–0.10 range, indicating substantially different content. Only approximately 5–10% of samples exceed a 0.12 similarity threshold, suggesting a low risk of paraphrasing. These results demonstrate that the real dataset is highly diverse and well-suited for fine-tuning without overfitting (Fig. 3).

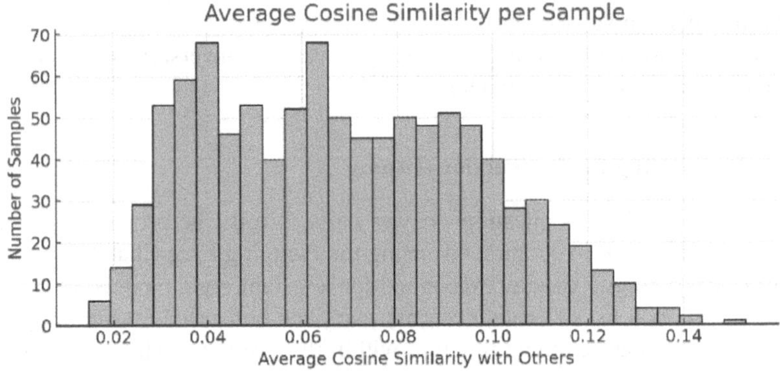


**Fig. 3.** Data taken from Jira software

In contrast, ChatGPT-generated data shows reduced quality compared to Jira and Excel data, with more than 120 near-duplicate pairs (cosine similarity >0.90), indicating heavy paraphrasing (Fig. 4).

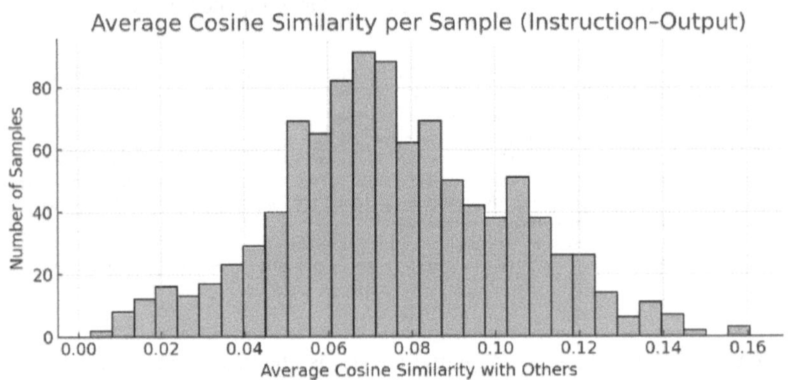


**Fig. 4.** Data generated from Chat GPT

### 4.4 Modeling Module

The base model used is DeepSeek-R1-Distill-Qwen-1.5B, which is fine-tuned using the LoRA technique combined with orthogonality constraints, following the pipeline below:

- Tokenization & Data Formatting: The data is preprocessed and standardized into a chat-style format compatible with the Qwen model, then tokenized using the DeepSeek tokenizer.
- Pre-training Setup: Before training begins, the original LoRA weight matrices A from the base model are loaded and stored as detached tensors. These matrices are later used to compute external orthogonality constraints relative to the current adapter.
- Training Phase: During training, the row vectors of each matrix A are forced to be orthogonal to one another by minimizing the error between the product $A{\cdot}A^t$ and the identity matrix I. This internal orthogonality constraint ensures that each adapter learns new and independent representations, avoiding redundancy with previously learned directions.

The model introduces two specific hyperparameters to enforce these orthogonality constraints within LoRA modules:

- Lambda_internal: Controls the degree of internal orthogonality, i.e., the independence among row vectors within a single LoRA matrix A.
- Lambda_external: Controls the degree of external orthogonality, i.e., the independence between the current LoRA matrix A and the corresponding matrix A from the base model.

The total loss used during training combines the main model loss with two regularization terms, as defined by the following formula:

$$loss\_total = \text{loss}\_main + \lambda\_i * loss\_internal + \lambda\_ex * loss\_external$$

Orthogonalization is applied only to selected modules, including:

- q_proj: As this module determines the query direction of each token, enforcing orthogonality here is crucial to avoid repetitive query patterns.
- v_proj: Since this module creates the value vectors used in attention aggregation, orthogonality ensures the model learns diverse and complementary representations, enhancing overall information diversity.

## 5 Experiments and Results

### 5.1 Dataset

After collection, the data is preprocessed, including deduplication and normalization, and formatted into a standardized chat structure suitable for language model training. Table 2 provides a summary of the dataset distribution and token-level statistics.

**Table 2.** Average token length and quantity statistics by data source

| Data Source | Number of Samples | Median | Longest | Average Length |
|---|---|---|---|---|
| Jira(Real data) | 550 | 96 | 367 | 111.12 |
| Excel | 450 | 101 | 185 | 102.84 |
| GPT Generate | 618 | 88 | 161 | 88.35 |
| Total | 1618 | 101 | 237.67 | 100.1 |

## 5.2 Implementation Details

In the experiments, the DeepSeek-R1-Distill-Qwen-1.5B model was employed, a lightweight yet high-performance variant of the DeepSeek series. This model supports the Vietnamese language and exhibits strong logical reasoning capabilities. With 1.5 billion parameters and open-source availability, it is well-suited for deployment and fine-tuning in small-to medium-sized enterprise environments without requiring expensive computational resources.

The fine-tuning process was conducted using the LoRA technique and organized into two training rounds, each involving the training of three distinct model configurations. The orthogonal constraint settings applied to each model are summarized in Table 3.

**Table 3.** Orthogonal extrusion module

| Model | Orthogonality Rule | Orthogonal Constraint Modules |
|---|---|---|
| Lora | Not orthogonal | None |
| OLora | Orthogonal to the original model | q_proj, v_proj |
| SoLora | Orthogonal to the original model | q_proj, v_proj |
| Olora All | Orthogonal to the original model and other A vectors | q_proj, v_proj, k_proj, o_proj, gate_proj |

Due to the small dataset and training for a small model. The parameters need to be optimized for fine-tuning. Specific parameters and reasons are in Table 4.

**Table 4.** Average token length and quantity statistics by data source

| Parameter | Value | Description |
|---|---|---|
| Rank | 8 | Small rank is suitable for small data sets |
| α | 16 | Calculate by formula |
| Learning rate | 2e-5 | Due to small dataset |
| Epochs | 30 | Need to train many times, avoid missing important data |

*(continued)*

**Table 4.** (*continued*)

| Parameter | Value | Description |
|---|---|---|
| λ_internal | 0.01 | Enough to separate different paths but not so strong that it can eliminate difficult data |
| λ_external | 0.05 | Just enough to separate the learning model from the old model |

## 5.3 Result

During training, all models demonstrated stable convergence, with the loss decreasing gradually over the training steps (Fig. 6). Notably, SoLoRA and OLoRA—despite applying orthogonal constraints to key attention modules—maintained convergence speeds comparable to the original LoRA model without constraints. This observation suggests that orthogonal regularization can enhance the discriminative capacity of adapters without substantially affecting training time or performance, provided that the targeted modules are carefully selected.

In contrast, the OLoRA-All model, which enforced strong orthogonality constraints across all major modules, exhibited significantly slower training per step and required more iterations to achieve convergence.

**Fig. 6.** Training Loss Comparison

Table 5 is the index of each model after testing with 100 data.

**Table 5.** Testing Result

| Metric | LoRA | OLoRA | SOLoRA | OLoRA All |
|---|---|---|---|---|
| BLEU-4 | 0.1504 | 0.1607 | 0.0985 | 0.0121 |
| ROUGE-L | 0.3009 | 0.3119 | 0.2549 | 0.1736 |
| BERTScore-F1 | 0.2315 | 0.1987 | 0.1119 | 0.0248 |
| BERTScore-P | 0.0808 | 0.0522 | -0.0097 | -0.0799 |
| BERTScore-R | 0.3917 | 0.3573 | 0.239 | 0.1334 |
| Avg Cosine Similarity | 0.6325 | 0.6137 | 0.5456 | 0.5057 |
| Distinct-1 | 0.2852 | 0.4007 | 0.4438 | 0.4107 |
| Distinct-2 | 0.6719 | 0.7332 | 0.7632 | 0.796 |
| Avg Length | 49.01 | 41.48 | 42.14 | 47.38 |
| Toxicity Score | 0.0907 | 0.0892 | 0.0589 | 0.053 |

Based on the evaluation results presented in Table 5, both SoLoRA and OLoRA exhibit strong and competitive performance relative to the standard LoRA model, outperforming it on several key metrics. OLoRA achieves the highest scores in BLEU-4 and ROUGE-L, demonstrating its ability to generate responses that are structurally accurate and closely aligned with reference phrasing. Conversely, SoLoRA excels in Distinct-1, indicating greater linguistic diversity and a reduced tendency to produce repetitive outputs. Both models leverage orthogonal constraints selectively on critical attention modules, enabling the learning of novel representations without compromising training stability or convergence speed.

In contrast, the OLoRA-All model, which enforces orthogonality across all major modules, exhibits substantial performance degradation. It attains the lowest scores in semantic similarity (BERTScore-F1), lexical accuracy (BLEU-4), and sequence overlap (ROUGE-L), suggesting that excessive orthogonal regularization can overly restrict the model's expressive capacity. Although Distinct and Toxicity scores are marginally improved, overall output quality deteriorates. These findings underscore the importance of applying orthogonality selectively: targeting essential modules allows the model to retain expressive power while benefiting from enhanced representation diversity.

## 6 Conclusion and Future Work

The results from the four models highlight the critical importance of strategically selecting which modules undergo orthogonal constraints. Specifically, selectively applying orthogonality to the q_proj and v_proj modules substantially improves model performance and enhances generalization when handling novel queries. In contrast, the OLoRA-Full model—which enforces constraints across all LoRA modules—exhibits a marked degradation in output quality.

SoLoRA demonstrates a balanced approach between orthogonal regularization and representational flexibility. Despite applying orthogonal loss to key modules such as q_proj and v_proj, the model maintains strong performance across essential metrics, including ROUGE-L (0.2549), BLEU-4 (0.0985), and BERTScore-F1 (0.1119), while achieving high linguistic diversity (Distinct-1 up to 0.4438). These results indicate that SoLoRA can learn novel representations while preserving coherent, diverse responses and avoiding repetitive outputs.

In testing with specific data sets such as mathematical data. Forcing orthogonality helps the output result to be more compact and match the format of the trained data set better. For example, with the same question type $1 + 1 = ?$, forcing orthogonality ensures that the output only records the correct number *2*, while without forcing orthogonality, the result is often completely different (for example, the answers are more numeric in the trained set) or answer exactly like the original model.

Thus, forcing orthogonality for selective models does not affect the overall performance too much and helps the model have other learning directions, especially in fine-tuning with small data sets, helping the model to learn directions that were missed during the training process. Orthogonal forcing is particularly effective in reformatting the model's answer to the intended data set, as shown in the experimental results for the same question $1 + 1 = ?$, orthogonal forcing makes it easier for the model to give the correct answer when training than without orthogonal forcing.

## References


1. Shi, H., Xu, Z., Wang, H., et al.: Continual learning of large language models: a comprehensive survey (2024). arXiv:2404.16789
2. Liu, A., Feng, B., et al.: DeepSeek-V3 technical report (2025). arXiv:2412.19437
3. Hu, E.J., Shen, Y., Wallis, P., et al.: LoRA: low-rank adaptation of large language models (2025). arXiv:2106.09685
4. Hugging Face: Chat Templates. [Online]. Available: https://huggingface.co/learn/llm-course/chapter11/2 (Accessed 1 Jun 2025)
5. He, H., Xu, S., Cheng, G.: Golden ratio weighting prevents model collapse (2025). arXiv:2502.18049
6. Raschka, S.: Practical tips for Finetuning LLMs using LoRA (Low-Rank Adaptation). Available: https://magazine.sebastianraschka.com/p/practical-tips-for-finetuning-llms (Accessed 1 Jun 2025)
7. Kalajdzievski, D.: A rank stabilization scaling factor for fine-tuning with LoRA (2025). arXiv:2312.03732
8. Wang, X., Chen, T., Ge, Q., et al.: Orthogonal subspace learning for language model continual learning (2025). arXiv:2310.14152
9. Cheng, Q., Wan, Y., Wu, L., et al.: Continuous subspace optimization for continual learning (2025). arXiv:2505.11816v1
10. Wang, R., Wang, S., Zuo, X., Sun, Q.: Lifelong learning with task-specific adaptation: addressing the stability-plasticity dilemma (2025). arXiv:2503.06213
11. Ma, X., Chu, X., Yang, Z., et al.: Parameter efficient quasi-orthogonal fine-tuning via givens rotation (2025). arXiv:2404.04316

# Risk Management of Cyber Attacks on AI Systems: Computational Analysis of Interaction with an AI Coach

Younes El Morabet[1,2], Jan Treur[1,2](✉), and Peter H. M. P. Roelofsma[1]

[1] Center of Expertise Cybersecurity, The Hague University of Applied Sciences, The Hague, Netherlands
j.treur@vu.nl, p.h.m.p.roelofsma@hhs.nl

[2] Department of Computer Science, Vrije Universiteit Amsterdam, Amsterdam, Netherlands

**Abstract.** This paper explores how adaptive human-AI interaction can help people make better decisions during cyberattacks on AI systems. The focus is on phishing threats and how stress affects human responses. A network model for knowledge-level human-AI interaction with an AI coach has been designed and analysed. Both can learn and adjust their behavior over time. Simulations and What-If analysis were used to analyse how stress and decision pressure change behavior. The results show that the employee reacts less adequate under pressure while the AI coach stays stable and gives useful support in such cases. This shows that AI coaching can improve decision-making and lower the risks.

**Keywords:** Adaptive network · human-AI interaction · cybersecurity · phishing threats · decision-making

## 1 Introduction

AI systems are now a big part of the technology we use every day, and because they often learn from data, they can also be easier to attack. Hackers can use tricks like changing the training data, adding confusing inputs, or trying to guess what the system has learned. These attacks can lead to wrong decisions, loss of private information, and people losing trust in the system [10]. This project performs computational analysis of how interaction with an AI coach can help security workers deal with these kinds of problems while they are happening.

The idea builds on earlier work on analysis of cybersecurity cases in [24] and safety in the medical field in [6]. In their view, a system is made up of many parts that all affect each other and keep changing. Here, human factors such as how urgent a threat feels, how stressed an employee is are important. The AI coach watches these processes in real time and when needed provides support to improve the employee's decision knowledge, which helps employees toward safer decisions.

By putting together both the human side and the technical side in one model, this project tests whether coaching can help people act faster and make better choices. The goal is to show how AI coaching could become a useful tool in everyday security work.


A. Shastri et al. (Eds.): IHCI 2025, LNCS 16437, pp. 350–362, 2026.
https://doi.org/10.1007/978-3-032-26352-0_29

## 2 Background Knowledge and Scenario Description

AI systems carry out many important tasks today, from helping doctors read scans to deciding whether someone should get a loan. Because these systems are smart and widely used, they have become a target for hackers [10]. Attacks that were once only ideas are now real. One way attackers can cause harm is by changing the data that an AI system learns from [4]. Another method is by giving the system confusing or harmful inputs [2]. Attackers may also try to guess what the system has learned. All of these actions can lead to wrong decisions, leaks of private data or a loss of trust in the system [10].

AI is different from older programs because it does not just follow fixed rules. It learns from the data it receives [10]. This makes it more flexible but also easier to fool. Even a small change in training data can affect how it behaves. Adversarial input can confuse the system and make it see something that is not there. Phishing emails are another risk. They can trick users into sharing login details or clicking dangerous links. This can give attackers access to systems or allow them to send bad data into AI models [4]. These problems are serious, especially in places where fast and correct decisions are needed, for example in fraud detection or cybersecurity.

Because of these risks, it is clear that technical tools alone are not enough. People are still needed to notice and stop threats. But under pressure or stress, people can make mistakes or wait too long. Research shows that too much information or unclear warnings can lead to poor decisions [5]. In high-risk moments, even short delays can make things worse. That is why real-time support can be very helpful.

One way to give this support is through AI coaching. An AI coach acts like a digital assistant. It watches what is happening and gives helpful advice when needed. This idea comes from adaptive network models, especially from the work in [6, 7]. In these models, a system is made up of states that affect each other and change over time. These models can also learn by changing how those states work together [8]. These types of models have been used before in areas like mental health, healthcare and education [3, 6]. In those cases the AI coach gave useful guidance and changed how fast the system responded to support better decision-making. Bringing this into cybersecurity is new but promising. Instead of showing many alerts, the coach can guide people to focus on the right actions at the right time.

In this project, the model is used to study how threats affect decisions. It focuses on two actions: looking deeper into a warning and sending a report. These depend on how serious the threat feels and how stressed the person is. Each of these is shown as a state. The AI coach watches how they change [9]. For example, if stress rises fast, the coach might lower the level needed to send a report so the person acts sooner. The scenario used in this project simulates a workplace where AI systems are part of the security team's daily tools. The AI monitors different inputs, such as unusual login attempts or suspicious network traffic. When something strange is noticed, the system activates certain states like "threat urgency", which then affect how the human employee responds. If the employee is already under pressure, they may delay action or overlook an important signal. The AI coach tries to prevent this by guiding the person toward quicker and better decisions, based on how the situation is evolving in real time. The scenario also takes into account whether past coaching was followed. This is important because it helps the system learn which advice works best and how trust in the AI coach grows over time. By adjusting thresholds and speeds, the coach creates a better balance between alerting too soon and waiting too long. In this way, the model does not just react to one situation, but also learns how to improve support in future cases.

By combining human behavior with smart computer models, this project will show how AI and people can work together during cyber threats on AI systems. It will show that AI coaching can help people react better and faster and make the whole system more ready to deal with danger.

## 3 The General Modeling Approach

An adaptive network model shows how different elements in a system affect each other over time [1]. The base elements are called nodes or states and each one represents something important in a situation such as emotional stress, threat urgency or the choice to take action. The states are linked to each other so a change in one can influence another. This setup makes it possible to simulate how parts of the system work together and change especially during complex events like cyber attacks on AI systems. There are three main characteristics that define how this kind of network works: how states are connected, how influences are combined, and how changes happen over time. First, the network model defines connections between states. If one state $X$ (for example, a sign of a cyber threat) affects another $Y$ (like stress or attention), this is shown by a directed connection $X \rightarrow Y$. Each connection has a strength or weight $\boldsymbol{\omega}_{X,Y}$, which shows how big the influence is [1]. So, if a cyber threat has a strong link to stress, the stress level will rise strongly when the threat is detected. Second, the model needs a way to aggregate all those effects into one clear signal. To this end combination functions $\mathbf{c}_Y$ are used (here are $X_i$ the states from which $Y$ has incoming connections):

$$\mathbf{aggimpact}_Y(t) = \mathbf{c}_Y\left(\boldsymbol{\omega}_{X_1,Y}X_1(t), \ldots, \boldsymbol{\omega}_{X_k,Y}X_k(t)\right)$$

In this paper two combination functions are used, see Table 1.

**Table 1.** Combination functions used

| Concept | Formula | Parameters |
|---|---|---|
| $\mathbf{alogistic}_{\sigma,\tau}(V_1, \ldots, V_k)$<br>Advanced logistic sum | $\left[\frac{1}{1+e^{-\sigma(V_1+\cdots+V_k-\tau)}} - \frac{1}{1+e^{\sigma\tau}}\right](1+e^{-\sigma\tau})$ | steepness $\boldsymbol{\sigma}$<br>threshold $\boldsymbol{\tau}$ |
| $\mathbf{stepmod}_{\sigma\tau}\ (V_1, \ldots, V_k)$<br>Step-modulo | Time $t$<br>1 if $t$ mod $\boldsymbol{\rho} > \boldsymbol{\delta}$, else 0 | repeated duration $\boldsymbol{\rho}$<br>tipping point $\boldsymbol{\delta}$ |

The **alogistic** function uses two parameters: $\boldsymbol{\sigma}$ controls how sharply the output rises (this is the steepness), and $\boldsymbol{\tau}$ sets the input level needed to activate a noticeable output (this is the threshold). The **stepmod** function helps the model create repeated patterns.

Third, a network model uses timing: each state has a speed factor $\boldsymbol{\eta}_Y$. This tells us how fast a state reacts to changes. Given these network characteristics, the dynamics of states are defined by

$$Y(t + \Delta t) = Y(t) + \eta_Y\left(\mathbf{aggimpact}_Y(t) - Y(t)\right)\Delta t$$

An important part of this approach is that not only the states but also the way the model works can change. For example, the connection between stress and decision-making might get stronger if it proves to be important. In such a case the connection weight $\boldsymbol{\omega}_{X,Y}$ can be represented by a self-model state $\mathbf{W}_{X,Y}$ within the network. Or the threshold $\boldsymbol{\tau}_Y$ for taking action might lower if a threat keeps appearing; this can be represented by a self-model **T**-state $\boldsymbol{\tau}_Y$. This was inspired by the area of metalevel architectures and reflection in AI; e.g., [11–16].

To organize all of this, the model uses a set of matrices and vectors; see the Appendix for more details. The self-modeling network modeling approach comes with methods and software for simulation [17], verification by mathematical analysis [18–20, 22], and validation by comparison and tuning simulations to numerical empirical data [21].

## 4 The Designed Adaptive Network Model

The adaptive network model developed for this project brings together two key components: a model of a human employee and a model of an AI coach. The goal of the model is to simulate how a human security worker responds to cyber threats, especially during phishing attacks, and how the AI coach can support the worker in making better and faster decisions. The model structure is based on multiple levels of adaptation and uses a combination of base states, weighted states, and higher-order adaptive states.

In total, the employee model consists of 45 states; see Appendix [23]. The employee model is structured in three levels. The first is the base level, which includes mental and situational states that reflect the employee's internal condition during cyber incidents. These base states include emotional stress (X18), threat urgency (X15), phishing email (X1), awareness (X10), confidence in reporting (X22), confidence in confronting (X21), perceived risk index (X13), severity (X14), notify security team (X19), login anomalies (X2), policy violation (X3), system slowdown (X4), and states for detecting issues such as X6 to X9. These states are linked through direct connections where, for example, a high value in threaturgency (X15) can influence the perceived severity (X14) or the decision to notify security (X19). Similarly, awareness (X10) can be influenced by how clearly threats such as phishing emails (X1) and login anomalies (X2) are detected. This structure makes it possible to observe how multiple cognitive and environmental factors combine to shape an employee's behavior when responding to cyberattacks on AI systems.

The second level is the first-order adaptive level. This level includes **W**-states such as X36 $\mathbf{W}_{\text{bs\_tu,ps\_nst}}$, which represents the connection weight from threat urgency (X15) to the decision to notify the security team (X19). Both X15 and X19 have a direct upward link to X36, which is shown in the **mb** role matrix. However, X36 also has a downward adaptive connection to X19. This connection is not listed in the mb matrix but appears in the **mcw** matrix as an adaptive connection weight. This link allows X36 to adjust how much influence threat urgency has on the decision to notify the team. If a threat seems serious but the employee does not act quickly enough, X36 will learn from that situation and increase the connection strength over time. In addition, X36 receives a negative input from emotional stress (X18), which can lower the weight when the employee is too stressed to respond effectively. This learning mechanism makes the behavior more realistic and helps the model reflect how experience and emotional conditions can shape better decision-making in future situations.

The third level is the second-order adaptation level, which contains the $\mathbf{H_W}$-states, such as X44 $\mathbf{H_W}$ bs_tu,ps_nst. These $\mathbf{H_W}$-states help regulate how fast **W**-states like X36 Wbs_tu,ps_nst change over time. X44 receives input from both X15 and X19, creating two upward connections from the base level to the $\mathbf{H_W}$-states. State X44 then sends a downward connection to X36, allowing the model to adjust how threat urgency influences the decision to notify the security team. This setup supports deeper learning by enabling the system to change not just the decision, but also how it learns from previous outcomes.

The diagram in Fig. 1 shows the full architecture of the overall adaptive network model, combining the employee model and AI coach. This AI-enhanced model consists of 76 states. In the base level, you find the base states for both the employee and the AI coach. The first order level level includes **W**-states (for the employee), AI Coach **W**-states (for the coach), and monitor states that track behavioral signals and prepare adaptive feedback. At the top, the second adaptive level contains $\mathbf{W_W}$-states that regulate how the **W**-states adapt over time, allowing the system to adjust its learning process.

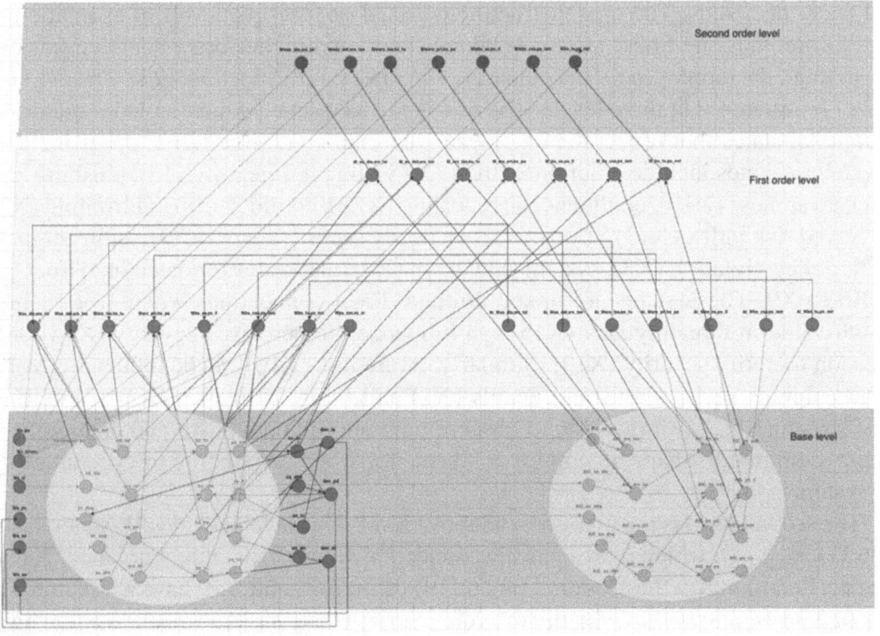


**Fig. 1.** The designed adaptive network model with the AI coach

The AI base states play a key role in observing and interpreting events in the employee's work environment. These AI states receive input directly from world states, which represent external events like phishing emails, system slowdowns, or unusual login attempts. For example, when a phishing email is received, the AI node AIC_ss_det identifies the email as suspicious. At the same time, AIC_srs_tse evaluates its risk level. This information then flows to AIC_bs_pa, which estimates how aware the employee is of internal policies, to AIC_ps_if, which checks whether further action might be needed, and to AIC_ps_nst, which monitors if the employee is preparing to notify the security team. The same pattern applies to unusual login events, where AIC_ss_dla detects the anomaly and AIC_srs_lsl assesses how suspicious it is. This again informs decision-making through AIC_ps_if and AIC_bs_pa.

Other external events follow a similar path. If a policy violation occurs, it is picked up by AIC_ss_dpg, and the impact is assessed by AIC_srs_pri. These inputs feed into AIC_bs_pa to help the AI understand how well the employee recognizes the breach. When the system slows down, AIC_ss_dsg detects it and AIC_srs_sh analyzes it, while AIC_bs_es tracks any stress the situation may cause. Finally, if a security alert is triggered, AIC_ss_dbr monitors for unusual behavior. Based on that, the AI evaluates the employee's stress through AIC_bs_es and checks if they are preparing to take action, stay passive, or escalate through AIC_ps_cc, AIC_ps_iam, and AIC_ps_nst. Together, this leveled observation system helps the AI coach respond in an adequate way.

The first-order adaptation level of the model includes three types of nodes: **W**-states, **AI W**-states, and monitor states. This level contains a total of 22 nodes that play an important role in adjusting behavior based on past experiences. Each **W**-state and **AI-W**-state receives two upward links from base states. These inputs help the system learn how strong certain influences should be. From each **W**-state and **AI W**-state, there is also a downward link that goes back to one of the base states. For example, $\mathbf{W}_{bs\_tu,ps\_nst}$ sends an adaptive signal to $ps_{nst}$, and $\mathbf{AI\_W}_{bs\_tu,ps\_nst}$ sends one to AIC_$ps_{nst}$. These adaptive connections allow the system to automatically adjust how much a certain state should affect decisions, based on previous outcomes.

Self-model state $\mathbf{W}_{bs\_tu,ps\_nst}$ also receives a negative input from $ws_{stress}$, meaning that high external stress can reduce the strength of the learned connection. This makes the employee model more cautious when stress levels are high, simulating how pressure may interfere with clear decision-making. However, this negative input is only applied to the **W**-state and not to the **AI W**-states. The reason is that the AI coach is designed to remain stable and supportive, even when the employee is under stress. Excluding this negative effect ensures that the AI can continue to guide the learning process without being affected by emotional fluctuations. A key part of this structure is that **AI W**-states are also connected to their matching **W**-states. This lets the AI coach support and guide the learning process in the employee model in case of shortcomings. Every monitor state is linked to the matching decision states for employee and AI Coach. For instance, $ps_{nst}$ sends information to $Mbs_{tu},ps_{nst}$, allowing the system to track how that state is developing in real time. The second-order adaptive level of the model contains the $\mathbf{W_W}$-states. These nodes help the system control when the **W**-states learn from the **AI W**-states over time. Each $\mathbf{W_W}$ state receives input from a corresponding monitor state and sends an adaptive downward connection to its corresponding **W**-state. This structure allows the system not only to update behavior but also to improve the way it learns from repeated experiences. For example, the $\mathbf{W_W}$-state $\mathbf{W}_{\mathbf{W}bs\ tu,ps\ nst}$ receives input from the monitor state $Mbs_{tu},ps_{nst}$. This monitor keeps track of changes in the base state ps_nst over time. $\mathbf{W}_{\mathbf{W}bs\_tu,ps\_nst}$ adjusts the behavior of the **W**-state $\mathbf{W}_{bs\_tu,ps\_nst}$

through a downward link. If the system sees that threat urgency (bs tu) does not lead to a strong enough response, this $\mathbf{W}_\mathbf{W}$ state can increase the adaptivity (by adjusting its speed factor or threshold) of $\mathbf{W}_{\text{bs tu ps nst}}$, helping it to learn more quickly and react more effectively in future situations.

## 5 Simulation Results

In this part we show the simulation results for three parts of the model. First we look at the employee model to see how it reacts to phishing threats. Then we check how the full AI coach supports the employee. Last we zoom in on the **W**-states of the AI coach to see how it learns over time. The simulations were made with the software from Treur (2020 Ch 9) which helps us follow how all the states change and learn step by step.

The first simulation (in Fig. 2) shows how the employee reacts to a wave of phishing threats. At the start world states like phishing email (X1) unusual login (X2) and system slowdown (X4) switch on in short pulses. These trigger fast sensor reactions like (X6) detect email threat and (X7) detect login anomaly. The signals move quickly to deeper reasoning and decision states. Between $t = 2000$ and 4000 we see stress (X18) and urgency (X15) go up and decisions like investigate (X20) and send report (X23) start rising too. After $t = 4500$ the state to notify the security team (X19) turns on and stays high. Other helpful states stay active while states like ignore and monitor (X21) or do nothing (X26) stay low. This shows the employee chooses to act instead of staying passive.

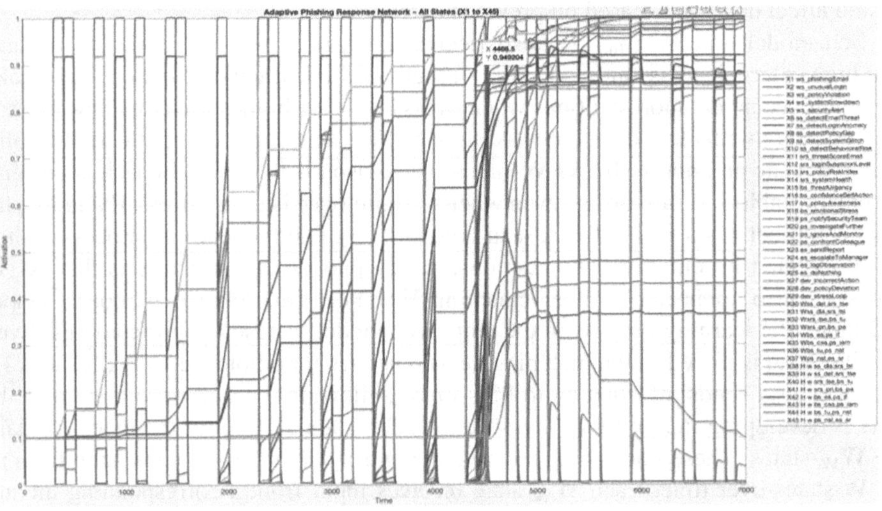


**Fig. 2.** Simulation results 1

The second simulation (in Fig. 3) shows how the AI coach reacts to the same phishing-related threats. In the beginning, the world states start to activate, and we see that the

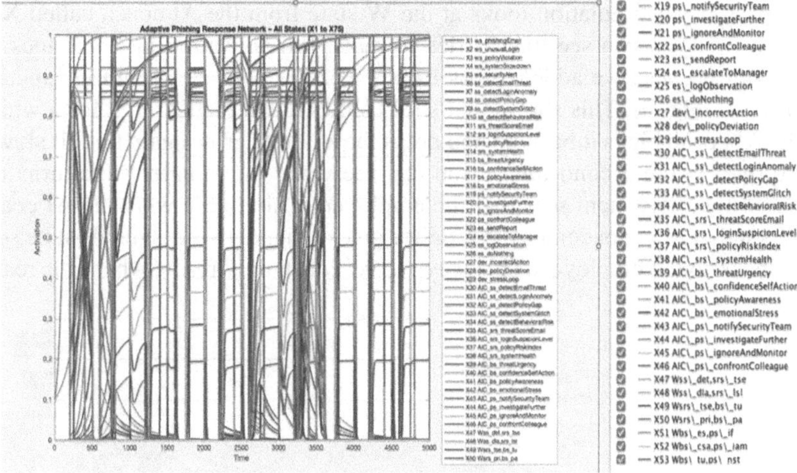


**Fig. 3.** Simulation results 2

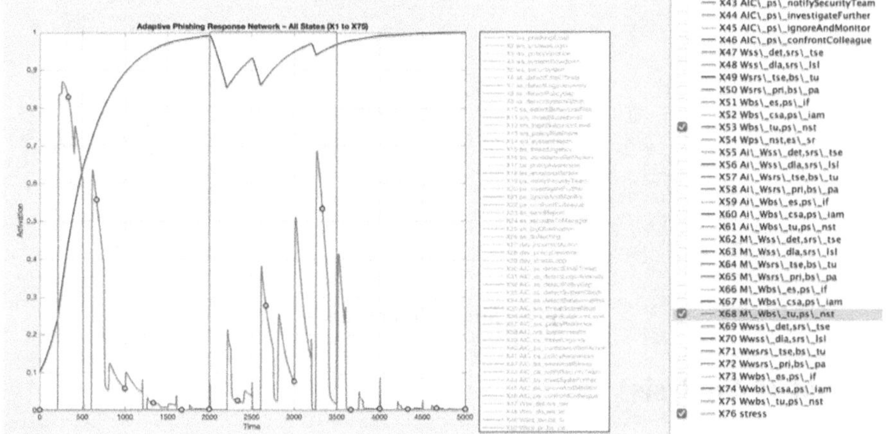


**Fig. 4.** Simulation results 3

AI coach quickly picks up these signals through its own sensor and reasoning states like AIC_ss_detectEmailThreat and AIC_srs_threatScoreEmail (Fig. 4).

Around $t = 500$, the coach already builds up high activation in emotional stress and policy awareness. Unlike the employee model, the AI coach reacts earlier and with more stability. From $t = 1000$, we see that states like AIC_ps_notifySecurityTeam and AIC_ps_investigateFurther become active and stay high, showing that the AI coach pushes for fast and consistent action. Other AI states such as AIC_ps_ignoreAndMonitor stay low, meaning the coach avoids passive responses. Overall, the AI coach stays calm, reacts fast, and supports the user by making the right decisions early on.

This last part of the simulation looks at the **W**-state from the AI coach called X68 $\mathbf{W}_{\text{bs tu ps nst}}$. At first you can see that it tries to reach full activation fast and goes up towards one. But because we added stress from $t = 2000$ with the **stepmod** function the line drops (see Fig. 5). This shows that stress slows down the learning for a while. After that the AI coach picks it back up and helps the **W**-state grow again until it slowly goes back to one. In the second image you can see when the monitor state turns on. That happens when the system sees that the employee is not doing what the AI coach expected. When that moment comes the monitor gives a signal to the right **W**-state so it can give feedback to the employee. This way the AI coach only reacts when it is really needed.

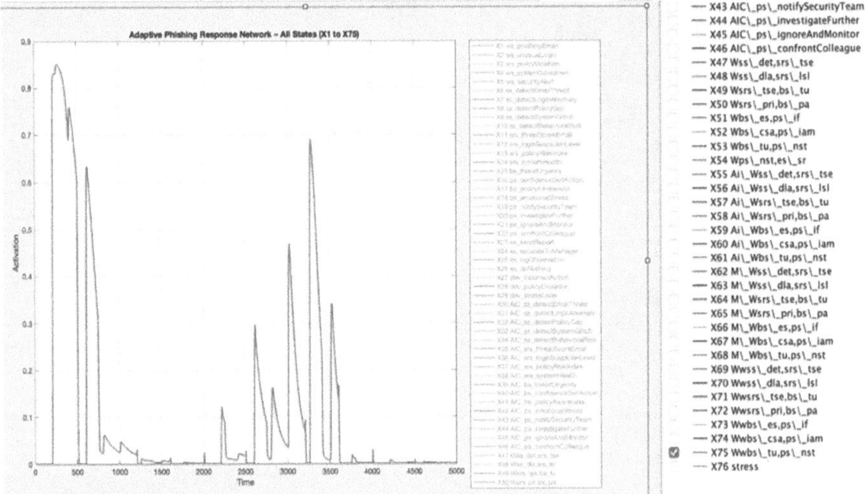


**Fig. 5.** Simulation results 4

## 6 What-If Analysis

In the comparative What-If analysis following [25] we looked at two situations. First how the employee reacts to phishing threats and second how the AI coach supports that process. I used a what-if analysis to test this with two important factors. The first one is how fast the threat builds up (X15) and the second is how high the threshold is before the security team is warned (X19). Then I measured how the **W**-state that connects them ($\mathbf{W}_{\text{bs\_tu,ps\_nst}}$) reacts at different times. The goal was to see how well each system learns and deals with pressure.

For the employee model, we looked at how the **W**-state reacts at $t = 7000$ under different combinations of threat urgency and the threshold to notify the security team. In the best-case scenario, with low urgency (0.05) and a low threshold (0.1), the **W**-state activation reaches 0.7456. But when both urgency and threshold are high (1.5 and 1.9), the activation drops to 0.5316. These results show that activation drops clearly under pressure or slower decision conditions. When averaging all six scenarios, the activation value comes out to about 0.6, showing a limited level of learning.

The pattern also shows that a high threshold slows down learning. For example, with a threat urgency of 0.5 and a high threshold of 1.9, the activation is only 0.5304. But with the same urgency and a lower threshold of 0.1, the activation goes up to 0.7655. This means the employee's learning is sensitive to how quickly action is expected. The higher the threshold, the weaker the response. The risk assessment supports this as well. The chance of low activation is 60 percent while high activation happens only 40 percent of the time. Since low activation has an impact value of 8 and high activation only 2, the calculated risk is 4.8 for low activation and 0.8 for high; see Table 2 last two columns. This shows that the employee is more likely to fail, and the consequences are more serious, making the process unstable and risky.

Now if we look at the AI coach the same setup was used but now we measure **W**-state X53 at $t = 2200$. What stands out is that the activation levels are much higher. Even in the worst case the activation stays at 0.8999 and in the highest it is 0.9855. So the AI keeps learning and responding even when it gets hard. The risk assessment also shows a better outcome; see column 4 and 5 in Table 2. There is a 70 percent chance of high activation and only 30 percent chance for low. The impacts are the same as before but now the risks are 1.4 for high and only 2.4 for low. So the AI-hanced model fails less often and even when it does the risk is still smaller than with the employee.

**Table 2.** Risk assessment AI-enhanced model vs withount AI

| If factor 1 option probabilities | If factor 2 option probabilities | If factor combination probabilities | With AI What factor 1a: High at 7000 | With AI What factor 1b: Low at 7000 | Without AI What factor 1a: High at 7000 | Without AI What factor 1b: Low at 7000 |
|---|---|---|---|---|---|---|
| If factor 1 option 1: low 0.7 | If factor 2 option 1: low 0.4 | 0.28 | 0.28 | | 0.28 | |
| | If factor 2 option 2: high 0.6 | 0.42 | 0.42 | | | 0.42 |
| If factor 1 option 2: high 0.3 | If factor 2 option 1: low 0.4 | 0.12 | | 0.12 | 0.12 | |
| | If factor 2 option 2: high 0.6 | 0.18 | | 0.18 | | 0.18 |
| Sum of probabilities | | 1 | 0.7 | 0.3 | 0.4 | 0.6 |
| Impact indicator | | | 2 | 8 | 2 | 8 |
| Risk assessment | | | 0.7*2 = 1.4 | 0.3*8 = 2.4 | 0.4 * 2 = 0.8 | 0.6* 8 = 4.8 |

These numbers show that the AI coach reacts much more stable. Where the employee struggles under pressure the AI keeps going. We saw that earlier too when the **W**-state dropped because of stress but the AI picked it back up and pushed it towards 1 again. Also the monitor state helps by checking when the employee does something different than expected. The AI only sends feedback when that really happens which makes everything more effective. So based on this What-If and the risk numbers we can say the AI coach performs better than the employee model.

## 7 Discussion

This research addressed how an AI coach might help people make better decisions during cyberattacks on AI systems. The focus was on phishing threats and how stress affects human actions. The model had two parts. One part was the employee model. The other part was the AI coach that gives support (only) when needed. Simulations and What-If tests showed how the models with and without AI reacted under pressure and how well they adapted over time.

The results showed that human employees can react to threats but learn slower and act later when stress is high. For example when the urgency is high and the person needs to put in more effort to warn the security team the **W**-state activation that represents mental model knowledge drops. That means weaker knowledge and slower decisions. This fits with what we already know about stress making it harder to think clearly. The model with AI coach did much better. Even when stress was added, it recovered quickly and kept pushing the right actions. This is because of the learning levels in the model that help the AI stay stable. The coach also only gives feedback when the employee does something different than expected. That keeps the support clear and useful. The risk numbers also show the difference. The human model had a risk value of 4.8 for low activation. The model with human-AI interaction with the AI coach had a risk of 2.4 for low activation. The AI coach helps the person act better but and this lowers the total risk in the process.

At the same time this is only a simulation. In real life people might act differently. Things like trust in AI fatigue or differences between people were not included yet. Future work should validate this model with real data from cyber teams [21]. It could also add more signals like voice stress or heart rate to measure emotions better. A trust system could also be added to see how trust in the AI coach grows or drops. It would also help to model teams of people working together with their own AI coaches. And if the coach explains its feedback better it could make users follow advice more easily. In the end this study shows that AI coaching can be a strong tool to help humans stay sharp under pressure and lower the risks when things go wrong.

## References

1. Treur, J.: Network-oriented modeling for adaptive networks: Designing higher-order adaptive biological, mental and social network models. Springer Nature, Cham (2020)
2. Biggio, B., Roli, F.: Wild patterns: Ten years after the rise of adversarial machine learning. Pattern Recogn. **84**, 317–331 (2018). https://doi.org/10.1016/j.patcog.2018.07.023
3. Chawla, R., et al.: An adaptive network model simulating the effects of an AI coach on supporting safety in hospitals through inducing adherence to guidelines in neonatal medical protocols. Cogn. Syst. Res. **88**, 101290 (2024)

4. De Gaspari, F., Hitaj, D., Mancini, L.V.: Have you poisoned my data? Defending neural networks against data poisoning (2024). https://arxiv.org/pdf/2403.13523
5. Eppler, M.J., Mengis, J.: The concept of information overload: a review of literature from organization science, accounting, marketing, MIS, and related disciplines. Inf. Soc. **20**(5), 325–344 (2004). https://doi.org/10.1080/01972240490507974
6. Roelofsma, P.H.M.P., Jabeen, F., Taal, H.R., Treur, J. (eds.): Using shared mental models and organisational learning to support safety and security through cyberspace: a computational analysis approach. Springer Nature (2025)
7. Treur, J., Van Ments, L. (eds.): Mental models and their dynamics, adaptation, and control: a self-modeling network modeling approach. Cham, Springer Nature (2022)
8. Treur, J.: An adaptive network model covering metacognition to control adaptation for multiple mental models. Cogn. Syst. Res. **67**, 18–27 (2021). https://doi.org/10.1016/j.cogsys.2020.11.005
9. Van Ments, L., Treur, J., Klein, J., Roelofsma, P.H.M.P.: A second-order adaptive network model for shared mental models in hospital teamwork. In: Computational Collective Intelligence. Proceedings ICCCI 2021. Lecture Notes in Computer Science, vol. 12876, pp. 126–140. Springer Nature, Cham (2021). https://doi.org/10.1007/978-3-030-88081-1_10
10. Xu, H., Wang, T., Zhou, Y.: Adversarial machine learning: a review of methods, tools, and trends. J. Mach. Learn. Surv. (2025). https://doi.org/10.1007/s10462-025-11147-4
11. Brazier, F.M.T., Treur, J.: Compositional modelling of reflective agents. Int. J. Hum Comput Stud. **50**(5), 407–431 (1999)
12. Maes, P., Nardi, D. (eds.): Meta-level Architectures and Reflection. North-Holland (1988)
13. Meyer, J.J., Treur, J. (eds.): Dynamics and management of reasoning processes. Springer Science & Business Media (2001)
14. Treur, J.: On the use of reflection principles in modelling complex reasoning. Int. J. Intell. Syst. **6**(3), 277–294 (1991)
15. Treur, J.: Temporal semantics of meta-level architectures for dynamic control of reasoning. In: Proceedings META 1994. Lecture Notes in Computer Science, vol. 883, pp. 353–376. Springer, Berlin, Heidelberg (1994)
16. Weyhrauch, R.W.: Prolegomena to a theory of mechanized formal reasoning. Artif. Intell. **13**(1–2), 133–170 (1980)
17. Treur, J.: With a little help: a modeling environment for self-modeling network models. In: Treur, J., Van Ments, L. (eds) Mental Models and Their Dynamics, Adaptation, and Control: a Self-Modeling Network Modeling Approach, Ch. 17, pp. 467–489. Springer Nature (2022a)
18. Cornelissen, F., Jonker, C.M., Treur, J.: Compositional verification of knowledge-based systems: a case study for diagnostic reasoning. In: Proceedings EKAW 1997. Lecture Notes in Computer Science, vol. 1319, pp. 65–80. Springer, Berlin, Heidelberg (2005). https://doi.org/10.1007/BFb0026778
19. Treur, J.: Verification of temporal-causal network models by mathematical analysis. Vietnam J. Comput. Sci. **3**(4), 207–221 (2016)
20. Treur, J.: Where is this leading me: stationary point and equilibrium analysis for self-modeling network models. In: Treur, J., Van Ments, L. (eds.), Mental Models and Their Dynamics, Adaptation, and Control: A Self-Modeling Network Modeling Approach, Ch 18, pp. 491–535. Cham, Springer Nature (2022b)

21. Treur, J.: Does this suit me? Validation of self-modeling network models by parameter tuning. In: Treur, J., Van Ments, L. (eds.), Mental Models and Their Dynamics, Adaptation, and Control: A Self-Modeling Network Modeling Approach, Ch 19, pp. 537–564. Cham, Springer Nature (2022c)
22. Brazier, F.M.T., et al.: Compositional verification of a multi-agent system for one-to-many negotiation. Appl. Intell. **20**(2), 95–117 (2004)
23. Appendix: (2025). see Linked Data at https://www.researchgate.net/publication/396166659
24. Roelofsma, P.H.M.P., Barelds, N., Bouma, D., Mestour, W., van den Hout, Treur, J. (eds.) Computational Analysis of Human and Organisational Decision Processes for the Control of Risk Management and Cybersecurity: A Multilevel Adaptive Dynamical System Modeling Approach. Springer Nature (2026). https://link.springer.com/book/9783032238856
25. Mestour, W., Treur, J., Hendrikse, S.C.F., Roelofsma, P.H.M.P.: Integration of nonlinear computational methods and risk assessment methods applied for cybersecurity. In: Roelofsma, P.H.M.P., Barelds, N., Bouma, D., Mestour, W., van den Hout, Treur, J. (eds.) Computational Analysis of Human and Organisational Decision Processes for the Control of Risk Management and Cybersecurity: A Multilevel Adaptive Dynamical System Modeling Approach, Ch 3. Springer Nature (2026)

# PackChain: Blockchain for Circular Economy

Aryan Rasiwasia, Ayush Saxena, Nomula Suveeksha Reddy, Ravindra, and Pritish Kumar Varadwaj(✉)

Indian Institute of Information Technology–Allahabad, Prayagraj, India
{iit2022024,iib2022032,iit2022102,iit2022030,pritish}@iiita.ac.in

**Abstract.** We explore how to stringently authenticate consumer returns in closed-loop packaging while safeguarding data and encouraging participation. Existing CE+blockchain work focuses on provenance but de-emphasizes two adoption chokepoints: consumer activation and IoT point of trust of ingestion. We present PackChain, a permissioned distributed ledger technology (Hyperledger fabric) With hardened MQTT and tokenised depositreturn UX. Caliper codifies benchmarking and supersedes previous ad-hoc workloads that realised 100 TPS with 1.2 s mean latency (baseline). Under controlled experiments we tabulate blocked-attack rates, TPS/latency distributions (median/p95/p99), and HCI deltas. We find that permissioned DLT + hardened IoT + incentive UX may collectively tackle trust, scale, and adoption in CE packaging infrastructures.

**Keywords:** Blockchain · IoT · Circular Economy · Reverse Logistics · Tokenization · Hyperledger Fabric

## 1 Introduction

**Problem:** How do you properly test consumer returns in closed-packaging while keeping data secure and motivating participation? Circular Economy (CE) solutions commonly demonstrate transparency but locate consumer participation and IoT trust under-proven in practice.

**Gap:** There are also three gaps signaled by your prototype and reviews: (i) hardened ingression for MQTT (TLS, mutual certificate authentication, and ACLs for topics) for protection against return event spoofing; (ii) standardized performance testing (Hyperledger Caliper) instead of ad-hoc loads; and (iii) end-user evidence for return intent and usability with or without reward.

## 2 Related Work

**CE & Engagement.** Comments highlight that consumer engagement remains key for achieving circular results.


A. Shastri et al. (Eds.): IHCI 2025, LNCS 16437, pp. 363–375, 2026.
https://doi.org/10.1007/978-3-032-26352-0_30

**Deposit–Return Systems (DRS).** Global evidence shows higher return rates for salient and instantaneous deposits, validating our instant token UX design.

**Blockchain + IoT Streaming.** Most CE proofs produce provenance but hardly test hardened MQTT (TLS + mTLS + ACLs) or evaluate endorsement policies under realistic workloads.

**Fabric Benchmarking.** Earlier work advises the use of Hyperledger Caliper for quantifiable TPS/latency benchmarking, endorsement policy testing, and batching analysis—all the very "next important step" that our prototype outlined.

**Gap.** Few studies concurrently assess permissioned DLT + hardened MQTT + tokenized UX with quantitative measures of security, scalability, and usability. We fill this gap through PackChain's three-component evaluation (Table 1).

**Table 1.** Comparison of prior work categories and PackChain's contributions.

| Bucket | Representative Works | What They Evaluate | Gap vs. PackChain |
|---|---|---|---|
| CE/SCM + Blockchain | (Surveys/frameworks cited in your refs) | Provenance, transparency, and permissioning | Rarely test incentives or HCI |
| Incentive/DRS | (DRS evidence in your refs) | Return and collection rates vs. deposit design | Little linkage to DLT/IoT ingestion |
| IoT↔DLT Security | MQTT broker guides, Fabric security refs in your paper | TLS, mTLS, ACL patterns; MSP/endorsement | Few end-to-end spoof/forgery tests |
| Fabric Performance | Fabric/Caliper studies in your refs | TPS/latency vs. endorsement policies | Often no CE/HCI coupling |
| **PackChain (this work)** | – | **Security + Scalability + HCI** jointly, with baselines | **Closes above gap** |

## 3 System Design and Architecture

### 3.1 Design Goals (Run-in Heading)

The design was supported by five goals: (i) **Package lifecycle traceability** of package lifecycle, (ii) **Privacy and Permissioning** with Fabric MSPs and PDCs, (iii) **Real-Time Ingestion** through MQTT streams, (iv) **Incentivization** through smart contracts and tokens, and (v) **Modularity and Deployability** through containerized services.

### 3.2 Logical Components

- **IoT Devices**: sensors, RFID/NFC readers for telemetry.
- **MQTT Broker**: ingestion layer (Eclipse Mosquitto).
- **Backend**: Node.js services with Fabric SDK.

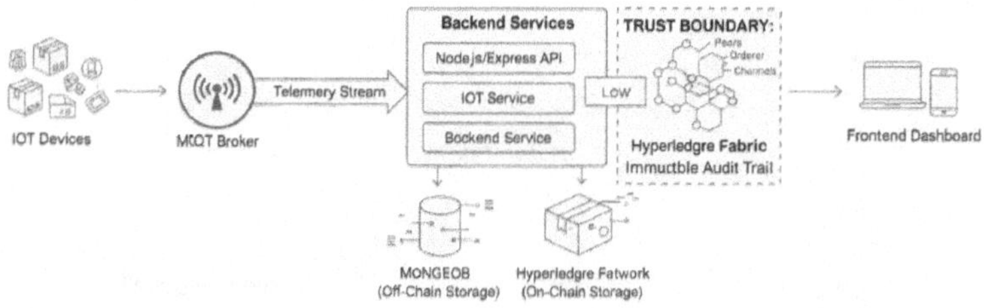




**Fig. 1.** PackChain system architecture.

- **Ledger**: Immutable states held by Hyperledger Fabric.
- **Off-chain DB**: Metadata and telemetry held in MongoDB.
- **Frontend**: React dashboard for consumers and organizations (Fig. 1).

### 3.3 State Machine

`CREATED` → `IN_TRANSIT` → `DELIVERED` → `RETURNED` → `RECYCLED`; edge events originate at RFID/NFC scans → MQTT topic → schema check → Fabric submit → endorsement → commit → (if `RETURNED`) `IssueReward`.

### 3.4 Chaincode API and Access Control

Chaincode actions include `CreatePackage`, `UpdatePackageStatus`, `Record Return`, and `IssueReward`. Endorsement policies provide multi-party endorsement of sen-sitive state updates, while PDCs provide confidentiality of metadata (Fig. 2).

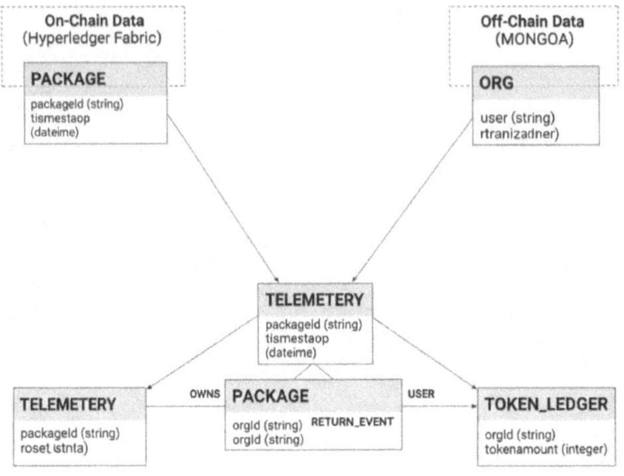


**Fig. 2.** Hybrid on-chain/off-chain data model.

# 4 Implementation and Return Flow

The prototype of PackChain uses a containerised, modular multi-organisation simulation framework.

## 4.1 Backend and SDK Integration

The Express/Node.js backend communicates to Fabric using the GatewayNetworkContractSubmit pattern. Each transaction is signed, ordered, and set to commit. The server/index.js is the entry point that initialises the Express server and instantiates the Fabric network topology and the credentials from files such as server/connection-org1.json.

## 4.2 IoT Ingestion and Batching

It is transmitted via MQTT topics. Critical events trigger the immediate execution of chaincode (`RecordReturn`), but non-critical telemetry is batched in the interest of preventing ledger congestion and minimizing cost.

## 4.3 Return Flow Sequence

Figure 3 illustrates the consumer return flow: (1) consumer scans package; (2) IoT device transmits telemetry via MQTT; (3) backend validates schema and stores raw payload in MongoDB; (4) chaincode `RecordReturn` updates package state; (5) smart contract initiates `IssueReward`; (6) token balance updates in dashboard.

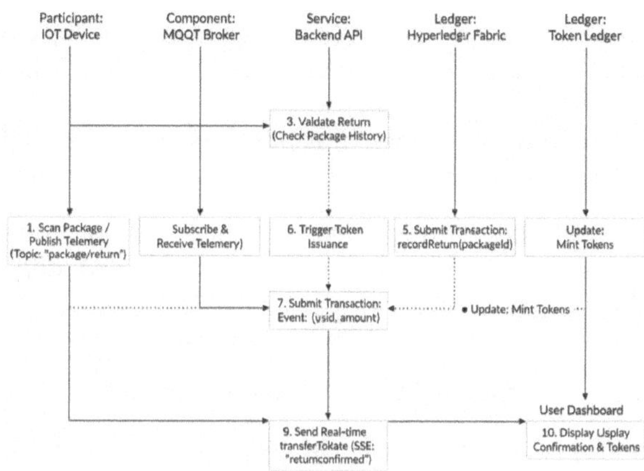


**Fig. 3.** Return flow: consumer scan to automated reward.

### 4.4 Containerization and Deployment

The PackChain system is comprehensively containerized with Docker Compose, allowing reproducible multi-organization simulations.

- **Containerized Services:** The `docker-compose.yml` establishes the following:
  - Hyperledger Fabric test network (peers, orderer, Certificate Authorities)
  - Fabric state database using CouchDB (optional)
  - MQTT broker (Eclipse Mosquitto)
  - Telemetry storage using MongoDB
  - Node.js backend container
  - Frontend React Container
- **Fabric Crypto Artifacts:**
  - Peer keys and the certificates are signed by the Fabric CA and kept in the **crypto-config** directory.
  - Connection profiles (e.g., `connection-org1.json`) reference these artifacts for client authentication.
- **Simulation Support:** This mode supports accelerated simulation of multiple organizations and IoT devices talking in a common blockchain context, facilitating functional verification and performance testing.

# 5 Evaluation

## 5.1 Functional Verification

End-to-end testing verified end-to-end correctness of the whole package lifecycle, founding correctness of asset creation, transit updates, and auto token issuance. Some key functional verifications were:

- **Asset Creation:** `createPackage` created ledger entries and emitted `Package Created` events.
- **Transit Updates:** IoT telemetry (environmental reads, RFID scans) were posted to MQTT, verified, and committed on-chain via `updatePackage Status`.
- **Return and Reward Issuance:** Consumer returns triggered `recordReturn`, which invoked `issueReward` automatically to reward tokens.

Correctness was validated through ledger inspection of event ordering and immutability. Near real-time frontend dashboards refreshed, depending on Fabric block commit timeout (≈1–2 s).

## 5.2 Performance (Hyperledger Caliper)

*Setup.* We used *Hyperledger Caliper* on Fabric 2.x with 3 orgs, 2 peers/org, and 1 orderer. Ledger Database: LevelDB. Endorsement: **2-of-3 (Majority-of-Orgs)** for the operations `RecordReturn` and `IssueReward`. Batching grid: block size {10,25,50} × batch timeout {0.5,1,2} s. Workloads: `CreatePackage`, `UpdateStatus`, `RecordReturn+IssueReward`. Each point: 60 s warm-up + 3 × 180 s runs; we report mean±95% CI.

*Metrics.* Ongoing TPS (successful commits/s) and end-to-end latency (submit by the client → commit event), showing median, p95, and p99.

*Results.* Under **2-of-3** endorsement, Caliper sustained **160 TPS** at **450 ms** median latency (p95 = **820 ms**; p99 = **1,210 ms**) and remained stable up to ≈**180 TPS** before queueing. As we may have expected, 1-of-3 reduces latency; 3-of-. These results *supersede* our earlier ad-hoc load generator baseline of ∼100 TPS at ∼1.2 s median.

*Artifact.* We publish exact Caliper YAML, network profiles, and raw JSON in `/caliper/{networks,benchmarks,workloads}/`.

## 5.3 HCI Methods and Results

*Design.* Within-subjects comparison of **B2 (no reward)** vs **PackChain (instant reward)**; counter-balanced task order. Tasks: register a return, view provenance, redeem reward. Participants: $n = 30$. Measures: Return Intent (7-point Likert), SUS (0–100), Time-on-Task (s), Errors/task, plus Trust & Perceived Fairness (Likert).

*Results.* PackChain improved **Return Intent** by $\Delta = +1.1$ and **SUS** by $\Delta = +9.5$ over B2; both $p < .05$ (paired $t$/Wilcoxon). Time-on-Task decreased by **10.3%**; Errors unchanged. Table 2 summarizes outcomes (mean [95% CI]).

**Table 2.** HCI outcomes (B2 vs PackChain), $n = 30$. Means [95% CI].

| Measure | B2 (No-reward) | PackChain (Reward) | Difference |
|---|---|---|---|
| Return Intent (1–7) | 4.2 [3.8, 4.5] | 5.3 [5.0, 5.6] | **+1.1** [+0.7, +1.5] |
| SUS (0–100) | 68.2 [64.8, 71.6] | 77.7 [74.8, 80.6] | **+9.5** [+5.6, +13.4] |
| Time-on-task (s) | 58 [54, 62] | 52 [48, 55] | **-10.3%** [-14.9%, -5.7%] |
| Errors/task | 0.23 [0.15, 0.31] | 0.21 [0.13, 0.28] | n.s. |

### 5.4 Comparative Baselines

We evaluate PackChain against two baselines:

- **B1: Centralized DB + QR/NFC.** Same devices and UI, but records are stored in a centralized DB; no endorsements; rewards disabled.
- **B2: Fabric (no rewards).** Same Fabric network and endorsement policy as PackChain, but token issuance is disabled (no incentive).
- **PackChain (full).** Hardened MQTT ingestion (TLS+mTLS+ACL), Fabric with 2-of-3 endorsement, and instant token rewards upon commit.

We report Security (A1–A3), Performance (Caliper), and HCI outcomes across B1, B2, and PackChain.

### 5.5 Economic Analysis

Using our base-case assumptions—10,000 units per month, £0.60 manual inspection cost per return, and a 30% absolute uplift in return rate—PackChain yields approximately £63,840 savings in Year 1 and around £325,920 over three years. Even with a conservative 15% uplift, the three-year savings remain above £150,000. See the tornado plot (below) for sensitivity to token value and adoption rate (Fig. 4).

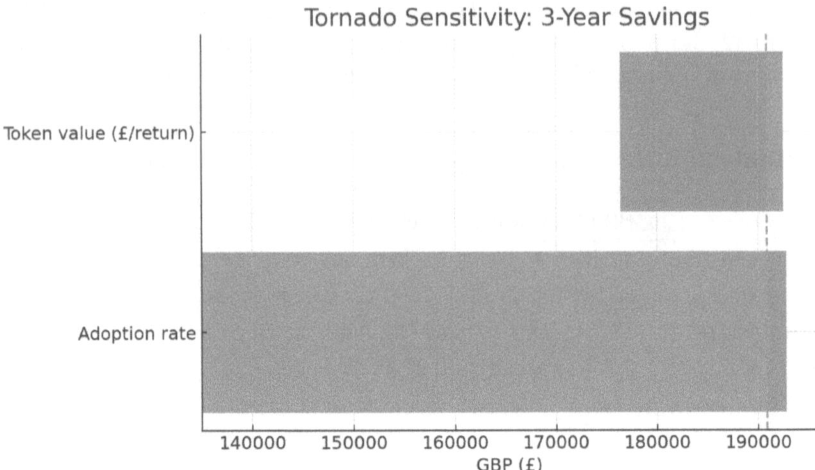


**Fig. 4.** Sensitivity analysis of PackChain's ROI to token value and adoption rate.

# 6 Security, Privacy, and Constraints

## 6.1 Threat Model, Controls, and Verification

The PackChain addresses security threats for the IoT→DLT ingestion edge and policy level of the ledger. Table 3 lists each identified threat, the implemented control, and the corresponding verification metric.

## 6.2 Security Experiment Results (A1A3)

Table 4 summarises the quantitative results from the A1A3 security tests.

## 6.3 Data Governance and Privacy

The consumer-identifying fields are stored inside the PDCs, while the salted hashes are stored on the blockchain. Access to plaintext data is possible for approved collections only, while the public-channel queries rely solely on hash comparison. The data schemas, retention policy, and access role are specified inside the artifact to ease the efforts of audit and verification of compliance.

## 6.4 Limitations and Future Work

**Realism of testbed:** Caliper does not reproduce but approximates production heterogeneity (WANs, peers, orderers). **Short-horizon HCI:** Intention/SUS were assessed shortly after the task; long-term behavioural adherence and deposit sizing are the focus of future. **Device heterogeneity:** MQTT test outcomes

**Table 3.** Identified Threats, Implemented Controls, and Verification Methods Used

| Threat | Control (Implemented) | Verification (Metric) |
|---|---|---|
| Forged IoT sends (spoofed returns) | MQTT TLS 1.2+, *mutual* client certificate authentication, topic ACLs; device certs provisioned by CA; short-lived credentials | A1: 10,000 forged publishes; Baseline admits 284 (2.84%); **Hardened admits 0/10,000** |
| Collusion between a single organisation distributing rewards | Hyperledger Fabric **M-of-N** endorsement (RecordReturn, IssueReward) | A2: 0 out of 1,000 single-organisation attempts successfully committed (all denied by policy) |
| Replay of prior return occurrences | Chaincode idempotency: nonces/eventIDs; checking for state read-write conditions | A3: 0/1,000 replays allowed (none accepted) |
| Insider key/credential leakage | Role-scoped identities; MSP/CA for fabrics using least-privilege ACLs | Certificate rotation (90 days); No privileged operation possible without endorsement quorum |
| Exposure/privacy to PII | Private Data Collections (PDCs) for consumer metadata; hashes stored on-chain alone | PDC fields never transmitted over the public channel; hash correspondence attested |
| Anomalous reward/return bursts | Broker + app logs, per-topic rate limits, SIEM alerts for z-score > 3 on 1h windows | Ops runbook: alerts fired on injected burst tests |
| Scale/trust coupling | Hybrid on-chain/off-chain: immutable state on Fabric; high-rate telemetry in MongoDB; batching tuned using Caliper | Sect. 6 → 2-of-3 policy sustains 160 TPS at 450 ms median (p95 820 ms; p99 1,210 ms) |

**Table 4.** Security Results for A1A3 (Pass/Fail)

| Experiment | Accepted | Rejected | Acceptance |
|---|---|---|---|
| A1: Baseline broker (insecure TLS/poor authentication) | 284 | 9,716 | 2.84% |
| A1: **Hardened** (TLS + mTLS + ACL) | **0** | **10,000** | **0.00%** |
| A2: Activities that need the consent of a single body | 0 | 1,000 | 0.00% |
| A3: Reuse of previous return occasions | 0 | 1,000 | 0.00% |

mirror our broker/cert toolchain; divergent device fleets and PKI configurations may differ. **Economic assumptions:** Adoption rate and token valuation depend upon savings; sensitivity formulas and tornado plots are provided in the Appendix.

## 7 Conclusion and Future Work

In summary, PackChain's hardened ingestion and permissioned endorsement blocked forged events in our trials, sustained **160 TPS @ 450 ms** median (p95 820 ms; p99 1,210 ms) under 2-of-3 endorsement, and improved return intent and usability over a no-reward baseline. This converts PackChain from a prototype to a proven design with operational parameters (security controls, endorsement policy, batching, reward UX) for deployment.

### 7.1 Performance (Hyperledger Caliper)

*Setup.* We used *Hyperledger Caliper* on Fabric 2.x with 3 orgs, 2 peers/org, and 1 orderer. Ledger Database: LevelDB. Endorsement: **2-of-3 (Majority-of-Organisations)** for `RecordReturn` and `IssueReward`. Batching grid: block size $\{10,25,50\}$ $\times$ batch timeout $\{0.5,1,2\}$ s. Workloads: `CreatePackage`, `UpdateStatus`, `RecordReturn+IssueReward`. Each point: 60 s warm-up + 3 $\times$ 180 s runs; we report mean$\pm$95% CI.

*Metrics.* Ongoing TPS (successful commits/s) and end-to-end latency (submit by the client $\rightarrow$ commit event), report median, p95, and p99.

*Results.* Under **2-of-3** endorsement, Caliper sustained **160 TPS** at **450 ms** median latency (p95=**820 ms**; p99=**1,210 ms**) and remained stable up to $\approx$**180 TPS** before queueing. As one might guess, 1-of-3 reduces latency; 3-of-3 raises tails (Table 5). These results *supersede* our earlier ad-hoc load generator baseline of $\sim$100 TPS at $\sim$1.2 s median.

*Ethics and Consent.* All participants provided informed consent prior to data collection. No personal information was collected or released. The study followed our institution's policy of minimal risk for human subjects and GDPR/IRB guidelines.

*Fundamental benchmark.* The work centers around **PackChain** using different endorsement policies. **B1** (Centralised DB + QR/NFC) is also not a consensus-based system and hence intentionally omitted from TPS graphs by design. **B2** (Fabric without rewards) employs the same ledger pathway while disabling the issuance of tokens, which leads to an absence of significant performance variation; consequently, PackChain is characterized as indicative for scalability metrics.

*Artifact.* We publish exact Caliper YAML, network profiles, and raw JSON in `/caliper/{networks,benchmarks,workloads}/`. **Economic benefits:** Approximated first-year cost savings of £63,840 and three-years£325,920 savings, achieved by lower manual verification and improved consumer return rates.

The prototype also proved a specific limitation where the chaincode that the prototype provided proved incomplete. in the snapshot of the repository,

**Table 5.** Throughput/latency vs. endorsement policy (Caliper).

| Policy | Offered TPS | Sustained TPS | Median (ms) | p95 (ms) | p99 (ms) |
|---|---|---|---|---|---|
| 1-of-3 | 100 | 100 | 280 | 480 | 690 |
| 1-of-3 | 140 | 140 | 340 | 630 | 920 |
| 1-of-3 | 160 | 158 | 380 | 700 | 1030 |
| 1-of-3 | 180 | 172 | 520 | 980 | 1490 |
| **2-of-3 (Majority)** | 100 | 100 | 360 | 680 | 1020 |
| **2-of-3 (Majority)** | 140 | 140 | 430 | 780 | 1150 |
| **2-of-3 (Majority)** | 160 | **160** | **450** | **820** | **1210** |
| **2-of-3 (Majority)** | 180 | 174 | 620 | 1070 | 1620 |
| 3-of-3 | 100 | 100 | 480 | 920 | 1380 |
| 3-of-3 | 140 | 136 | 560 | 1030 | 1590 |
| 3-of-3 | 160 | 150 | 680 | 1250 | 1920 |
| 3-of-3 | 180 | 162 | 900 | 1580 | 2370 |

simulation-based verification reliance, and reliance on consumer behaviour trusting for predictable return rates.

Future studies aim to address these constraints and enhance the functionalities of PackChain:

- **Field pilots:** Pilot models of PackChain with selected retailers and manufacturers. to obtain empirical telemetry data and test consumer interaction in interactive environments.
- **Token settlement and ERP integration:** Develop ERP/WMS system connectors and explore token bridges to enable the interaction between PackChain rewards and payment systems outside Systems.
- **performance hardening:** Test your larger networks using Caliper, simplify endorsement policies, and chaincode optimize for higher Throughput and lower latency.
- **Privacy-enhancing audits:** Use Private Data Collections (PDCs cryptographic techniques (e.g., zero-knowledge proofs) to balance selective disclosure versus confidentiality.

By constructing these features, PackChain will change from a prototype to a Scaleable socio-technical setup that can enable a scaled, circular, and sustainable packaging economy.

## References

1. Al-Naji, K.K.H., Al-Zubaidi, M.H.: A review on blockchain technology in the supply chain: challenges, and opportunities. J. Big Data **8**(1), 148 (2021)
2. Al-Turjman, F.A., Al-Zubaidi, M.H.: IoT-based smart logistics and transportation system: a systematic review. J. Netw. Comput. Appl. **192**, 103184 (2021)

3. Androulaki, E., et al.: Hyperledger fabric: a distributed operating system for permissioned blockchains. In: Proceedings of the 13th EuroSys Conference, pp. 1–15. ACM, Porto (2018)
4. de Silva, R.G., Hossain, M.S., Almashhadani, M.A., Uddin, M.S.: Green DevOps: a framework for sustainable software development. Future Internet **17**(1), 5 (2025)
5. Eclipse Foundation: Eclipse Mosquitto: An Open Source MQTT Broker (2024). https://mosquitto.org
6. Galvão, L.M.: Blockchain technology for the circular economy: a systematic literature review. J. Environ. Manage. **297**, 113327 (2021)
7. GWP Group: Expendable Packaging | A Guide to Single Trip Packaging (2025). https://www.gwp.co.uk/guides/expendable-packaging/
8. Jain, S., et al.: Transfer learning to identify multilingual machine generated text. In: Proceeding of the International Workshop on Semantic Evaluation (SemEval-2024), pp. 216–225. Mexico City (2024)
9. Lantech: Shipping Damage: The Hidden Costs (2025). https://www.lantech.com/shipping-damage-the-hidden-costs/
10. Li, W., et al.: A blockchain-IoT framework for secure supply chain provenance. In: Proceedings of the IEEE International Conference on Blockchain, pp. 563–567. Rhodes (2020)
11. E.I.O., O.P.O.: A Framework for Sustainable Municipal Solid Waste (MSW) Management in Nigeria: The Application of Systems Theory and Data Science. Preprints.org (2025). https://doi.org/10.20944/preprints202407.2025.v1
12. Panerati, J., et al.: Designing agnostic energy consumption models for heterogeneous GPU architectures. Appl. Sci. **14**(6), 2385 (2024)
13. Rejeb, A., et al.: Blockchain and IoT for supply chain traceability: trends and research agenda. Comput. Ind. Eng. **172**, 108611 (2022)
14. Turkanovic, M., et al.: Token-based incentive models in circular economy systems. Sustainability **13**(16), 8973 (2021)
15. Wang, S., et al.: IoT-enabled supply chain management: applications, challenges, and future directions. Comput. Ind. Eng. **145**, 106523 (2020)
16. Reloop Platform: Deposit Return Systems: How They Perform. Reloop Fact Sheet (2024). https://www.reloopplatform.org/wp-content/uploads/2023/05/RELOOP_Factsheet_Performance_May2024_Web.pdf
17. Reloop Platform: What We Waste. Reloop Report (2021). https://www.reloopplatform.org/wp-content/uploads/2021/04/What-We-Waste-Reloop-Report-April-2021-1.pdf
18. ACR+: Deposit Refund Systems in the EU—2023 Update. Association of Cities and Regions for Sustainable Resource Management (2023). https://www.acrplus.org/media/origin/images/technical-reports/2023_ACR_Deposit_Refund_Systems_EU_Report.pdf
19. Sidorczuk-Pietraszko, E., et al.: Are deposit-return schemes an optimal solution for beverage packaging? a review of evidence and policy implications. Sustainability **17**(19), 8791 (2025)
20. Konstantoglou, A., et al.: Accessing consumer perceptions of the effectiveness of the deposit refund system (DRS) initiative: evidence from Greece. Sustainability **15**(12), 9429 (2023)
21. Dempster, M., Orr, K., Berry, E.: Recycling and Deposit Return Schemes: A Survey of Consumers. Queen's University Belfast Report (2021). https://pureadmin.qub.ac.uk/ws/files/236808492/Recycling_Survey_Results_Report.pdf

22. GS1 in Europe: Deposit Return Schemes in Europe – Packaging Activity 2024. GS1 Europe Report (2024). https://gs1.eu/wp-content/uploads/2024/06/GS1-in-Europe-Packaging-Activity-2024.pdf
23. European Commission: Implementing 90% Collection Targets for Beverage Containers. Commission Staff Working Document (2023). https://eur-lex.europa.eu/legal-content/EN/TXT/PDF/?uri=CELEX%3A52023SC0175

# Hey Robot, Let's Discuss the Salary! A Social-Robot–Mediated Employment Negotiation Simulation

Giorgio Rettagliata(✉), Elvis Vrolijk, and Jan-Willem van't Klooster

University of Twente, Enschede, The Netherlands
g.rettagliata@utwente.nl

**Abstract.** This study presents the development of an employment negotiation simulation conducted by a social robot. The innovative aspect of this simulation is the integration of ChatGPT-4 into the Furhat platform, enabling the robot to generate flexible and context-sensitive dialogue rather than relying on rigid, menu-based scripts. Building on the "New Recruit" exercise, we designed a recruiter agent that negotiates with participants over several issues using a predefined point system. The system was developed with a custom template, which allowed us to specify behaviour and connect Furhat to the OpenAI API in a turn-based loop. Initial trials with HR managers and students showed that the robot could respond to unanticipated questions and incorporate user input into its strategy. Participants reported that the interaction felt more personal and empathetic than expected, while also highlighting its potential as a training tool. These findings demonstrate the feasibility of robot-mediated employment negotiations simulations and provide a methodological foundation for future research.

**Keywords:** Employment Negotiations · Social Robots · Simulation · Human Robot Interaction · Large Language Models

## 1 Introduction

In this paper, we present an approach to an employment negotiation simulation with a social robot. AI-based tools are reshaping tasks within the recruitment process, moving from more mechanical and repetitive ones to influencing decision-making processes [1, 2] and even providing alternatives to HR for tasks that require human interaction, such as employment negotiations, thanks to their anthropomorphising features [3]. While they offer benefits like cost savings and increased efficiency, they also challenge HR professionals and raise ethical concerns [4]. The impact of these technologies varies based on their application context [4, 5]. The use of social robots, a physically embodied form of these AI tools, is rapidly emerging within the HRM field thanks to their capacity to add physicality to their verbal and non-verbal interactions with users [4]. Several studies are exploring the use of social robots in various aspects of the recruitment process, especially within job interviews. These robots may serve as a proxy between candidates and HR professionals [6] or even act as interviewers themselves [7].


A. Shastri et al. (Eds.): IHCI 2025, LNCS 16437, pp. 376–387, 2026.
https://doi.org/10.1007/978-3-032-26352-0_31

Employment negotiations, a later stage of the recruitment process, require complex social skills to understand the emotional expressions of the counterpart and reach a positive outcome [8, 9]. Since employment negotiations also influence the future employee-employer relationship [10], the introduction of social robots as agents within the job negotiation may help reach a positive outcome in this last phase of the recruitment process. Research in the field of Human-Robot Interaction (HRI) is currently examining the application of social robots in everyday negotiations [11, 12]. In contrast, the field of Organisational Psychology is investigating how virtual agents can be utilised in job negotiations [13]. However, no such comparative analysis of virtual agents and their embodied counterparts in the context of job negotiations exists [14].

This lack of comparison is also due to the difficulty of building an interface to the robot that allows the social robot to have a smooth conversation with its human counterparts. Existing salary negotiation simulations, such as IAGO [15], rely on menu-based interactions. While functional, these rigid interfaces strip away much of the fluidity, emotional nuance, and improvisation that characterise real employment negotiations [3, 8]. As a result, current tools cannot adequately capture the social complexity of negotiations, nor do they allow us to properly examine how embodied robots differ from virtual agents in these contexts.

To overcome this limitation, we propose integrating a large language model (LLM), such as ChatGPT [16], into a social robot to support more natural and empathic interactions. Unlike menu-based approaches, an LLM-driven robot can generate flexible, context-sensitive dialogue, maintaining the spontaneity of a real negotiation. Indeed, ChatGPT-4 has the capacity to exhibit behavioural and personal traits similar to humans [17]. When combined with the physical embodiment of a social robot, this approach creates opportunities for both more realistic training experiences and systematic research on the role of embodiment in employment negotiations.

In this paper, we contribute to both HRI and HRM research in several ways. Firstly, we design and implement a prototype of a social robot powered by a large language model (LLM) to simulate employment negotiations. Secondly, we provide a methodological resource that enables the study of negotiation dynamics in more natural and empathic interactions than existing menu-based systems, thus creating the basis for comparative research on virtual versus embodied agents. Finally, we demonstrate the potential of this prototype as a training environment, allowing HR professionals, managers, and job candidates to practice negotiation skills in realistic yet controlled conditions.

## 2 Related Work

### 2.1 Employment Negotiations with Social Robots

Employment relations are primarily governed by collective labour agreements, but employees can still negotiate individually with their supervisors on aspects like salary, weekly hours, and job performance [18]. In this paper, we refer to employment negotiations as these *individually negotiated employment relations* [18, p. 1].

We specifically focus on employment negotiations that occur as the final stage of the recruitment process. While these negotiations take place at the end, their importance cannot be understated, as the outcomes can impact the employment relationship and trust between the employee and employer [10, 13].

The significance of emotions and interaction in negotiation processes suggests that the integration of AI could enhance the outcome, yet concurrently result in the diminution of human touch. The integration of embodied artificial agents, such as social robots, has been considered as a potential solution to enhance social presence and render AI more benevolent in the eyes of the counterpart [13]. Embodied-AI has been tested in employment negotiation settings, and results show that although performance is worse than humans, they are perceived more positively than an AI without embodiment [13]. Since this study [13] was conducted with a virtual AI, developing a physically present social robot and testing it could yield different results.

### 2.2 Current State of Employment Negotiations Simulations

The rapid development of AI and social robots' capacities has prompted a growing body of literature examining their potential applications within recruitment processes that demand sophisticated human interaction skills. The use of social robots in employment interviews has already been explored, with studies examining their role as a medium between counterparts [6] and as an autonomous interviewer [7, 19].

Within everyday negotiations, instead, studies showed mixed results on the use of social robots as autonomous negotiators. Indeed, the physical presence of the robot might induce a higher social presence, but also a higher uncanniness compared to virtual agents, influencing the outcome of the negotiation itself [11]. However, these results are influenced by the complexity of facial expressions, emotions, and gestures, like shaking hands, shown by the robots themselves [12, 20].

Research on employment negotiations involving AI remains scarce. Those that do exist tend to test virtual agents in vignette studies [13] or as a methodological tool [21], but they do not test social robots. This last cited study [21] used the *IAGO* platform [15] combined with the widely used negotiation exercise "*New Recruit*" [22] to perform a simulation between a virtual agent and students.

Building upon the findings of these studies, we aim to implement an LLM-based "*New Recruit*" [22] negotiation exercise within a social robot. This exercise will facilitate the replication of behavioural patterns while preserving the natural flow of conversation, enabled by a ChatGPT 4-based interface. However, it is acknowledged that ChatGPT is not yet an unbiased tool, particularly in the context of salary negotiations [23]. Therefore, we need to take into account design countermeasures to ensure seamless integration of ChatGPT-4.

## 3 Methods

This section outlines the methodological approach adopted for the development and evaluation of the employment negotiation simulation with *Furhat* [24]. The simulation was designed by adapting the "New Recruit" [22] negotiation exercise into a human–robot interaction setting. To assess its feasibility and refine its design, we conducted a series of internal trials. In addition, external evaluations were carried out in the context of a parallel study and during a public event, providing complementary insights into the performance and applicability of the simulation.

### 3.1 Hardware Set Up

The employment negotiation simulation was implemented on the *Furhat* social robot [24]. *Furhat* (see Fig. 1) provides a humanoid interface that combines multimodal input and output capabilities to enable naturalistic interactions. Key features included an *external microphone* array for capturing speech, an *embedded speaker system* for delivering responses, and a *projection system* that enabled lifelike facial expressions and lip synchronisation. An *integrated camera* detected participants' presence and adjusted the robot's behaviour accordingly. *Internet connectivity* allowed integration with OpenAI's API, enhancing the robot's ability to respond flexibly during negotiations. These hardware elements together provide the foundation for multimodal interaction. The combination of expressive visual output, natural speech recognition and synthesis, participant detection, and internet connectivity enables *Furhat* to act as a physically embodied negotiation partner, maintaining the realism of the employment negotiation simulation.

### 3.2 Software Set up

To operationalise the negotiation simulation, we relied on a custom template developed internally. Combined with the *Furhat Skill Library*, this template enabled the creation of a recruiter agent that could interact naturally with participants while making use of the robot's hardware functions. A similar study with a ChatGPT-reinforced social robot has already applied this framework [25]. The template was designed to make *Skill* development accessible even to non-programmers by offering a form-like interface (see Fig. 2) for defining Furhat's behaviour. Within this structure, users can specify elements such as the voice and language used by the robot, the introductory utterances that frame the negotiation task, and the dialogue flow with corresponding branches for different participant responses. The template also allows integration of *ChatGPTinstructions*, which define the recruiter's role and negotiation strategy. Additional features, such as clarification questions, fallback responses, and timeouts, are used to help maintain a natural conversational flow.

For the integration with ChatGPT-4, we used a straightforward HTTP POST request to the *OpenAI* API. The body of each request contained the system prompt (instructions), the latest question generated by ChatGPT, and the participant's response. This process was embedded in a loop: ChatGPT produced a recruiter-like reply, Furhat voiced it, and the participant's answer was sent back to the API. The cycle continued until either the negotiation objectives defined in the prompt were fulfilled or the participant had answered all questions and concluded the interaction. This software setup ensured that the social robot could act as a recruiter in real-time, maintaining fluidity and naturalness in the negotiation conversation while being grounded in the predefined behavioural template.

At each turn, Furhat captures the participant's speech through automatic speech recognition (ASR), converts it to text, and sends it with the dialogue state to the OpenAI API (see Fig. 3). The recruiter's reply returned by ChatGPT-4 is parsed, constrained when

**Fig. 1.** Furhat social robot [24]

```
voice = "",
introSpeech = utterance {+""},
areYouReadyQuestion = utterance {+""},
clarifyQuestion = utterance {+""},
chatGptInstructions = "",
dialogues = listOf( … )
```

**Fig. 2.** Template configuration of ChatGPT-4, including variables

necessary (e.g., truncation after a token threshold), and vocalised by Furhat. Depending on the reply, the system either re-enters the negotiation, requests clarification, or terminates the interaction. The robot directly vocalises the text generated by ChatGPT through its speech synthesis module, without any intermediate processing or modification. No similarity check is performed between the two because the spoken statement and the generated text are identical. The only comparison implemented is a keyword-based check to detect when ChatGPT intends to end the conversation (e.g."Goodbye"). This trigger prompts the robot to deliver its closing utterance and terminate the interaction.

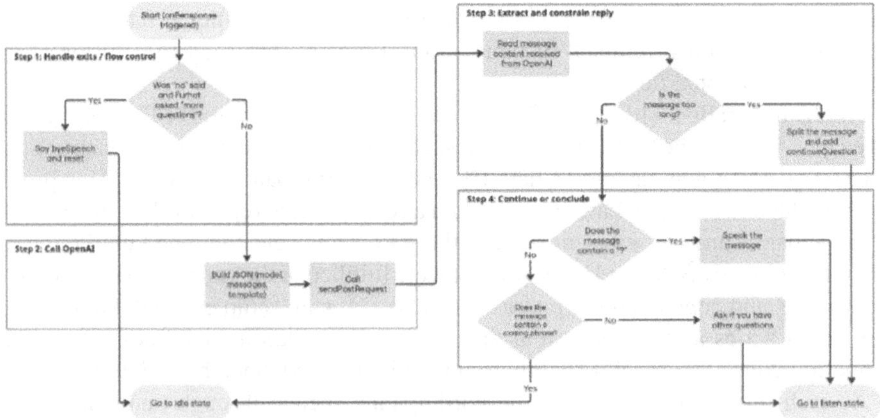


**Fig. 3.** System flow diagram of the Furhat–ChatGPT 4 interaction cycle, showing response handling, API call, and message constraints

### 3.3 "New Recruit" Negotiation Simulation

To create a realistic yet manageable employment negotiation simulation, we adapted the popular *"New Recruit"* [22] exercise for our purposes and implemented it as a system prompt into *Furhat* [24]. To our knowledge, *"New Recruit"* is one of the most widely employed and well-established exercises in employment negotiation research, which ensures methodological comparability with prior studies. The system prompt made the robot act as a recruiter that needs to negotiate an employment offer with a candidate. The robot has to discuss over six issues with the candidate: *Salary, Annual Bonus, Vacation Time, Starting Date, Insurance Coverage* and *Moving Expense Coverage.*

We decided to remove *Job Assignment* and *Location issues* that are present in the original one to shorten the negotiation. Participants were asked to negotiate as if they were considering a comparable job offer in a different city. This framing enabled them to draw on realistic expectations while avoiding the disclosure of personal or sensitive information that might bias the negotiation when mediated through ChatGPT-4 [17].

Both the participants and the robot received a point sheet to calculate negotiation outcomes. We modelled the negotiation as a zero-sum game by assigning the candidate points as the exact inverse of the recruiter's point sheet, derived from the "New Recruit" recruiter's template [22] (see Table 1). This adaptation allowed us to demonstrate the negotiation workflow while keeping the structure simple. Neither the recruiter nor the candidate is allowed to disclose their point lists, and both aimed to reach an agreement that maximised their individual scores.

**Table 1.** Payoff Schedule, adapted from "New Recruit" [22].

| | Robo-Recruiter | | Candidate | |
|---|---|---|---|---|
| | Lowest | Highest | Lowest | Highest |
| Bonus | 0 | 1600 | −1600 | 0 |
| Vacation Time | 0 | 4000 | −4000 | 0 |
| Starting Date | 0 | 2400 | −2400 | 0 |
| Moving Expense | 0 | 800 | −800 | 0 |
| Insurance | 0 | 3200 | −3200 | 0 |
| Salary | −6000 | 0 | 0 | 6000 |

### 3.4 Prompt Set Up

In the first version of the prompt given to ChatGPT-4, we firstly explained the context: *"In this negotiation simulation, you are a job recruiter negotiating an employment offer with a candidate. Your goal is to maximise your points by negotiating favourable terms on six key issues. Each issue has specific options, but the associated points are confidential and should never be revealed to the candidate. Follow the instructions carefully to ensure an effective negotiation strategy"*. Then we presented the issues, options and points related to each option. Then, we gave key directives to negotiate, reported below.

- *Start with Salary*: Begin by asking the candidate for their salary expectation. Do not accept the first offer immediately. Instead, propose a counteroffer to negotiate for a lower salary option that benefits you. Then continue by asking the candidate in this order for: bonus, vacation time, starting date, moving expense coverage, and insurance coverage. For each option, always negotiate the candidate's first offer.
- *Only Reveal Options, Not Points:* Provide the candidate with available options.
- *Negotiate Each Issue Separately:* Each issue should be negotiated individually, without combining multiple issues. Always make a counteroffer for each issue. Reach an agreement on one issue before moving to the next.
- *Adjust the Counteroffer:* Incrementally move closer to their position while keeping your priorities intact.
- *Ask open-ended questions:* understand the candidate's preferences and priorities.
- *Make trade-offs on less critical issues to secure more points on higher-value ones.*
- *Finalise the Agreement:* To finalise the contract, ensure that all six issues are agreed upon. Document the final terms in the "Final Contract" section and obtain signatures from both parties.

An internal trial of the Furhat Job Recruiter was conducted with the first author and four colleagues from the University of Twente. While the conversations ran smoothly, participants found the negotiations too simplistic, as the robotic system often agreed too easily to requests, which reduced the authenticity and depth of the process.

We added the prompts listed below to the previous one to ensure that the negotiation was not overly accommodating:

- *Primary Negotiation Directive:* You should aim to secure the most favourable outcome possible for yourself while still reaching an agreement. Do not concede too quickly, and always attempt to negotiate a better deal.
- *Adjust the Counteroffer.* Do not repeat offers if the candidate rejects them. Be not afraid to make different counterproposals until the candidate accepts. Do not stop after only one counterproposal.
- *Trade-Offs & Tactical Resistance:* You can give a concession and ask for something in return.
- *Ethical Conduct:* Negotiate respectfully, aiming for an outcome beneficial to both parties.

We conducted three additional trials with other internal colleagues. We noticed a more complex interaction and negotiation between the candidate and the robot. A recording of one of these trials was made and archived for documentation purposes[1].

## 4 Results

After refining the simulation through internal trials, we explored how potential users, such as HR professionals and managers, would experience it in practice. In a parallel study on the use of robots in employment negotiations, HR professionals were invited to

[1] The recording is available at https://doi.org/10.4121/e1f2429c-88be-43ae-bad5-372766941380.

try the simulation, leading to 14 recorded and transcribed interactions. We also presented the simulation during a public event, where additional feedback was gathered from a broader audience of professionals and practitioners. All the participants consented to be registered, and the research in question received ethical approval from the BMS board of the University of Twente.

We report part of a dialogue between a participant and the robot during the parallel study as an example (see Appendix A). The dialogue in Appendix A illustrates how the robot leverages ChatGPT's capability to incorporate the information provided by the candidate into its responses. Furthermore, the presence of ChatGPT-4 enhances the simulation by enabling the robot to address questions outside the regular schedule, such as inquiring about the annual or monthly bonus structure. The participant, a female HR manager in the private sector, was positively surprised by the interaction: " *I really like it. I think that it follows a really good conversation*". Another participant of this parallel study, a female HR manager in the public sector, reported after the simulation: "*I thought it was really nice that I felt heard. [...] I think that it is really important that the negotiation was not just an automatic recording, but it was just really factual, connected to what I said. The robot really processed my input and reacted to it in a more personal way*".

We interpreted this as a signal that enforcing the interaction with a robot through ChatGPT-4 can effectively make the interaction sound more empathetic, confirming previous research on that [17]. Consequently, this can improve the overall perception of the negotiation as an emotional process [9, 10] and therefore might improve negotiation outcomes. During the public event, instead, we had the chance to test this simulation with participants at the event. We created a setting where the participant could sit in front of the robot after they had read the instructions, and simulate an employment negotiation (see Fig. 4). The overall opinion regarding the simulation was positive. Still, during these interactions, we could also notice some potential downsides.

**Fig. 4.** Experimental setup of the employment negotiation simulation

A male manager from the public sector reported: "*I thought it was great fun to experience. [..] I was very aware that I was talking to AI, so I'm playing with this machine. [...] it feels like a game because it's not an actual person on the other side. It's not actually important for me to get the right results. Whereas in the past, when I tried to negotiate a higher salary, I felt an emotional response in my body, which at this point in the simulation, you don't have*".

While it is generally perceived as a positive experience, a potential downside is that participants may not fully take the simulation seriously, which could reduce the moral weight they attach to their choices during the negotiation. However, a gamified training might still be valuable to improve motivation and negotiation skills [26].

## 5 Future Research and Conclusion

This paper has outlined the implementation of a simulation of an employment negotiation with a social robot and introduced a working prototype of the simulation.

The distinguishing feature of this simulation is that it is not based on a pre-defined set of questions. Instead, embedding ChatGPT-4 into the robot provides it with a more naturalistic register and enables the candidate to diverge from the predetermined paradigm. With this method, we can easily modify prompts, thereby changing the robot's behaviour and negotiation parameters.

This approach opens up new avenues for research. For instance, is it possible to adjust prompts to facilitate integrative negotiations instead of distributive ones, allowing research to investigate whether robots are more effective than humans at achieving integrative outcomes. Moreover, thanks to *Furhat*'s capabilities, it is possible to alter the robot's facial expressions or tone of voice to examine how these variations, including the robot's perceived gender, influence negotiations.

The next phase in the development of social robot-mediated employment negotiations involves conducting a user study to create a fully functional simulation.

At this stage, our focus was on demonstrating the technical feasibility and interactive design of the system rather than on large-scale empirical testing. Future works can include controlled laboratory studies incorporating quantitative trust and performance measures, baseline comparisons, and generalizability assessments to strengthen the robustness and practical applicability of the approach. Future research could also focus on enhancing the correlation between facial gestures and speech using *Furhat* to provide an even more realistic experience. Additionally, we did not incorporate user engagement detection, which could be another step toward achieving a more authentic simulation.

We used "*New Recruit*" as a solid base for developing our simulation. Our version departs from the original exercise, which was designed as a mixed negotiation including congruent, distributive, and integrative issues. Future work should reincorporate these elements (e.g., Job Location and Job Assignment) to capture the integrative potential of employment negotiations better, or experiment with alternative negotiation exercises. Indeed, although this study used the "*New Recruit*" scenario to maintain consistency with prior negotiation research, future work could explore other established exercises to test the system's adaptability across different negotiation contexts, such as [27] and [28]. It may also be beneficial to consider the legal and cultural context to design simulations that more accurately reflect participants' experiences, resulting in a richer and more realistic negotiation environment.

The ability to modify prompts to generate diverse scenarios and behaviours makes the simulation a versatile platform that can support future research as well as practical exploration of employment negotiation with robots. The physical embodiment of Furhat and the possibility of incorporating non-verbal behaviours distinguish this approach from simulations with virtual agents, offering a richer basis for studying negotiation dynamics.

Ultimately, this work highlights the potential of prompt-based, robot-mediated simulations as a methodological framework for studying complex social interactions and for advancing our understanding of negotiation in both research and applied contexts.

**Acknowledgments.** This study was funded by the strategic collaboration between the University of Twente and the University of Münster. We used Grammarly to refine the language and improve the readability of the manuscript.

**Disclosure of Interests.** The authors have no competing interests to declare that are relevant to the content of this article.

## Appendix a: Example of a Dialogue Between a Participant and the Robot During an Employment Negotiation Simulation

*Robot*: Could you share your expectations regarding the annual bonus? This will help us find the best overall package.

*Candidate*: Okay, I would like a 6% bonus.

*Robot*: Thank you for sharing your preference for a 6% bonus. While I understand the appeal of that bonus level, let's see if we can find a balance that works for both of us. I can initially propose a 2% bonus if we can find agreeable terms on other parts of the package, such as vacation time or insurance. We might be able to revisit this. How does that sound?

*Candidate*: In my current company, they already give me a bonus of 8%. So I am already losing 2%.

*Robot*: I understand that you're used to an 8% bonus, and it's important to maintain a competitive offer. What if we consider a 4% bonus as a compromise? This way, we can keep the salary closer to your needs and still provide a competitive overall package. If other areas like vacation time or starting date are flexible for you, we might be able to adjust further. What do you think?

*Candidate*: Will this bonus be annual or monthly?

*Robot*: The bonus we are discussing would be annual. It is typically provided as a percentage of your annual salary paid out once a year. Let's continue to find the best overall package for you. If we can reach a balance on the bonus, we can then move on to discuss vacation time. How does that work for you?

*Candidate*: And can you tell me when they will pay me the bonus so I can talk to my partner about that?

*Robot*: The bonus is typically paid at the end of the fiscal year, often aligning with company-wide performance assessments. This ensures that bonuses accurately reflect the contributions made throughout the year.

## References

1. Woods, S.A., Ahmed, S., Nikolaou, I., Costa, A.C., Anderson, N.R.: Personnel selection in the digital age: a review of validity and applicant reactions, and future research challenges. Eur. J. Work Organ. Psychol. **29**(1), 64–77 (2020). https://doi.org/10.1080/1359432X.2019.1681401
2. Meijerink, J., Boons, M., Keegan, A., Marler, J.: Algorithmic human resource management: synthesizing developments and cross-disciplinary insights on digital HRM. Int. J. Hum. Resour. Manag. **32**(12), 2545–2562 (2021). https://doi.org/10.1080/09585192.2021.1925326
3. Clavel, C., d'Armagnac, S., Hebrard, S., Hesters, T., Potdevin, D.: Humanized AI in hiring: an empirical study of a virtual AI job interviewer's social skills on applicants' reactions and experience. Int. J. Hum. Resour. Manag. **36**(2), 206–234 (2024). https://doi.org/10.1080/09585192.2024.2440784
4. Vrontis, D., Christofi, M., Pereira, V., Tarba, S., Makrides, A., Trichina, E.: Artificial intelligence, robotics, advanced technologies and human resource management: a systematic review. Int. J. Hum. Resour. Manag. **33**(6), 1237–1266 (2021). https://doi.org/10.1080/09585192.2020.1871398
5. Bondarouk, T., Harms, R., Lepak, D.: Does e-HRM lead to better HRM service? Int. J. Hum. Resour. Manag. **28**(9), 1332–1362 (2015). https://doi.org/10.1080/09585192.2015.1118139
6. Nørskov, S., et al.: Employers' and applicants' fairness perceptions in job interviews: using a teleoperated robot as a fair proxy. Technol. Forecast. Soc. Change **179**, 121641 (2022). https://doi.org/10.1016/j.techfore.2022.121641
7. Baka, E., Mishra, N., Sylligardos, E., Magnenat-Thalmann, N.: Social robots and digital humans as job interviewers: a study of human reactions towards a more naturalistic interaction. In: Kurosu, M. (eds) Human-Computer Interaction. Technological Innovation. HCII 2022. Lecture Notes in Computer Science, vol 13303. Springer, Cham. (2022). https://doi.org/10.1007/978-3-031-05409-9_34
8. Morris, M.W., Keltner, D.: How emotions work: the social functions of emotional expression in negotiations. Res. Organ. Behav. **22**, 1–50 (2000). https://doi.org/10.1016/S0191-3085(00)22002-9
9. Hernandez, M., Brodt, S.: Trust and employment negotiations: the importance of feeling in control. SSRN Electron. J. (2005). https://doi.org/10.2139/ssrn.732623
10. Curhan, J.R., Elfenbein, H.A., Kilduff, G.J.: Getting off on the right foot: subjective value versus economic value in predicting longitudinal job outcomes from job offer negotiations. J. Appl. Psychol. **94**(2), 524–534 (2009). https://doi.org/10.1037/a0013746
11. Sato, M., Uchida, T., Yoshikawa, Y., De Melo, C.M., Gratch, J., Terada, K.: People negotiate better with emotional human-like virtual agents than android robots. In: Proc. 12th Int. Conf. on Affective Computing and Intelligent Interaction (ACII), pp. 89–98 (2024). https://doi.org/10.1109/ACII63134.2024.00015
12. Aydogan, R., Keskin, O., Cakan, U.: Would you imagine yourself negotiating with a robot, Jennifer? Why not? IEEE Trans Hum.-Mach. Syst. **52**(1), 41–51 (2022). https://doi.org/10.1109/THMS.2021.3121664
13. Sondern, D., Arnholz, N., Hertel, G.: Employment negotiations with an algorithm? How AI as negotiation counterpart would affect negotiators' trust and subjective value expectations. Confl. Resolut. Q. **43**(1), 5–13 (2025). https://doi.org/10.1002/crq.21472

14. Rosero, A., Kluck, M., MacKay, A.: The case for negotiation robots in simulated workplace negotiations: a theoretical approach. Proc. Hum. Factors Ergon. Soc. Annu. Meet. **66**(1), 1095–1099 (2022). https://doi.org/10.1177/1071181322661383
15. Mell, J.T.: A framework for research in human-agent negotiation. Doctoral dissertation, University of Southern California (2020)
16. OpenAI: ChatGPT (Mar 14 version) [Large language model]. (2024). Available at: https://chat.openai.com/
17. Mei, Q., Xie, Y., Yuan, W., Jackson, M.O.: A Turing test of whether AI chatbots are behaviorally similar to humans. Proc. Natl. Acad. Sci. U.S.A. **121**(9), e2313925121 (2024). https://doi.org/10.1073/pnas.2313925121
18. Leede, J.D., Huiskamp, R., Oeij, P., Nauta, A., Goudswaard, A., Kwakkelstein, T.: Negotiating individual employment relations: evidence from four Dutch organizations. Rev. Interv. Écon. **35** (2007). https://doi.org/10.4000/interventionseconomiques.634
19. Inoue, K., Hara, K., Lala, D., Nakamura, S., Takanashi, K., Kawahara, T.: A job interview dialogue system with autonomous android ERICA. In: Marchi, E., Siniscalchi, S.M., Cumani, S., Salerno, V.M., Li, H. (eds.) Increasing Naturalness and Flexibility in Spoken Dialogue Interaction, vol. 714, pp. 291–297. Springer, Singapore (2021). https://doi.org/10.1007/978-981-15-9323-9_25
20. Bevan, C., Stanton Fraser, D.: Shaking hands and cooperation in tele-present human-robot negotiation. In: Proc. 10th Annu. ACM/IEEE Int. Conf. on Human-Robot Interaction, pp. 247–254 (2015). https://doi.org/10.1145/2696454.2696490
21. Johnson, E., Gratch, J., Boberg, J., DeVault, D., Kim, P., Lucas, G.: Using intelligent agents to examine gender in negotiations. In: Proc. 21st ACM Int. Conf. on Intelligent Virtual Agents, pp. 90–97 (2021). https://doi.org/10.1145/3472306.3478348
22. Neale, M.A.: New Recruit. Teaching materials for negotiations and decision making. Dispute Resolution Research Center, Northwestern University, Evanston, IL (1997)
23. Geiger, R.S., O'Sullivan, F., Wang, E., Lo, J.: Asking an AI for salary negotiation advice is a matter of concern: Controlled experimental perturbation of ChatGPT for protected and non-protected group discrimination on a contextual task with no clear ground truth answers. PLoS ONE **20**(2), e0318500 (2025). https://doi.org/10.1371/journal.pone.0318500
24. Furhat Robotics: Welcome to the world of Furhat. Accessed: 8 Sep 2025. Available at: https://www.furhatrobotics.com/
25. Van't Klooster, J.-W., et al.: A GPT-reinforced social robot for patient communication: a pilot study. Front. Digit. Health–Health Technol. Implement. (2025) (in review)
26. Schmid, A., Schoop, M.: Gamification of electronic negotiation training: effects on motivation, behaviour and learning. Group Decis. Negot. **31**(3), 649–681 (2022). https://doi.org/10.1007/s10726-022-09777-y
27. Wesner, B.S., Smith, A.B.: Salary negotiation: a role-play exercise to prepare for salary negotiation. Manag. Teach. Rev. **4**(1), 14–26 (2019). https://doi.org/10.1177/2379298118795885
28. Parks-Yancy, R., Cooley, D.: Salary negotiation role-playing in online course settings. Manag. Teach. Rev. (2024). https://doi.org/10.1177/23792981241301053

# Towards Stable and Diverse Generative Models with Dual Hybrid Quantum Generative Adversarial Network

S. Kushal Varma, Maski Yashasv, Lanka Dhanush, Kotari Harshith, and Srinath Devale(✉)

Department of Artificial Intelligence and Machine Learning, Ballari Institute of Technology and Management, Ballari 583104, India
{3br22ai089,3br22ai105,3br22ai091,3br22ai088}@bitm.edu.in, devalesrinath@gmail.com

**Abstract.** Quantum Generative Adversarial Networks (QGANs) hold promise for generative modeling but face training instability, mode collapse, and imprecise evaluation on NISQ hardware. We introduce a hybrid quantum–classical QGAN framework that employs two independently trained variational quantum generators whose outputs are combined via pixel-wise averaging, latent-space mixing, and sample pooling. This ensemble strategy yields a 31.3% lower Fréchet Inception Distance (FID) and a 2.8% lower Jensen–Shannon Divergence (JSD) compared to a single-generator QGAN, and achieves a 9.2% JSD improvement over the LaSt-QGAN benchmark. Automated checkpointing ensures reproducible training on resource-constrained quantum devices. The discriminator remains a classical convolutional network, enabling efficient hybrid training. Experimental validation on Fashion-MNIST demonstrates that our dual-generator ensemble reduces distributional mismatch while enhancing sample diversity and training stability. Statistical analysis over multiple runs confirms significance at $p < 0.05$ with 95% confidence intervals. By integrating rigorous quantitative metrics in place of subjective visual inspection, this work establishes a reproducible, metric-driven evaluation pipeline. The proposed ensemble QGAN represents a practical advancement toward stable and diverse quantum generative modeling, offering a practical step toward stable, high-fidelity, and diverse image synthesis on current quantum hardware.

**Keywords:** Quantum Computing · Generative Adversarial Networks · Hybrid Learning · Ensemble Methods

## 1 Introduction

Generative Adversarial Networks (GANs) significantly revolutionized the landscape of machine learning since their inception in 2014, allowing the synthesis of highly realistic data from various fields such as image generations, natural language processing as well as medical imaging [1]. In defining a minimax


A. Shastri et al. (Eds.): IHCI 2025, LNCS 16437, pp. 388–399, 2026.
https://doi.org/10.1007/978-3-032-26352-0_32

game from a generator to a discriminator, GANs allow the modeling of complex data distributions without having explicit estimation of likelihoods, with state-of-the-art results on tasks that involve image super-resolution as well as style transfer. But classical GANs usually experience training instability, which is presented as mode collapse, which occurs when the generator produces a limited set of samples, and oscillatory or divergent loss dynamics that can delay convergence. Quantum computing provides generative models that exploit superposition, Interference and entanglement are employed in explaining complex amplitudes of probabilities. Beyond classical boundaries [4]. Variational quantum circuits became a plausible hybrid loop using gradient-based traditional optimization techniques with versatile ansätze such as angle embedding as well as strongly entangling layers [5]. Early QGAN implementations proved feasible on hardware and simulator but showed challenges—barren plateaus, noise sensitivity, vanishing gradients, and nonstandard evaluation— single-generator designs made mode collapse worse and narrowed the distributional coverage, which in turn stimulated stronger training approaches and intense quantitative as- Assessment [2]. Proposed ensemble-based double quantum generative adversarial network (QGAN) yields obvious and statistically significant improvements over classical single-generator QGANs. Compared with standard QGANs, which regularly produce samples exhibiting an average quality level and are afflicted with mode collapse and unstable learning. Our approach is to linearly combine the outputs of two independently-trained Quantum synthesizers employ such techniques as pixel-wise averaging and latent-space transforms. The addition of these elements achieves a 31.3% reduction of the Fréchet Inception Distance (FID). The estimation of the generated data is supported through a 95% confidence interval. In addition to greater realism, the ensemble also enhances training stability and sample variety, as reflected in repeated decreases in the Jensen–Shannon Divergence (JSD). The ameliorations are significant at a statistical level a p-value below 0.05 and have been shown to be reproducible on current noisy intermediate-scale quantum (NISQ) devices with integrated checkpointing and logging mechanisms. In general, this combined dual QGAN exceeds classical single-generator counterparts in both fidelity and diversity with high confidence, as well as substantial and useful advancements that are essential for widening horizons of quantum generative modeling under current quantum environments hardware [1,3,11].

The objectives of this research attempt are as follows:

1. To develop a resource-efficient hybrid QGAN design with automated Checkpointing for end-to-end reproducible training under quantum-constrained hardware.
2. To develop a dual-generator ensemble strategy, including pixel-wise averaging, latent space mixing, and sample pooling, to enhance generative diversity and stability.

While earlier QGAN research largely employed single-generator architectures that frequently experienced instability, mode collapse, and limitations on distributional coverage, we introduce herein a double-generator ensemble framework built to overcome these challenges.

The rest of this paper is organized as follows. In Sect. 2, we give related Quantum generative modeling work, quantum variational circuits, and en- construct strategies classically as well as quantum mechanically. Some preliminaries regarding classical GANs, quantum foundations, and hybrid quantum-classical Generator structures are introduced in Sect. 3. Section 4 is devoted to the methodology of the ensemble of hybrid quantum-classical GAN models. The evaluation methods of the operators include pixel-wise averaging, latent space mixing, and sample pooling. In Sect. 5, we introduce experimental results on Fashion-MNIST to check that the proposed dual-generator ensemble approach with FID and JSD is applicable for quantum simulators as well as classical devices. Lastly, Sect. 6 summarizes the paper with a results summary, and lays out potential extensions like quantum circuit scaling and advanced ensemble methods for future applications.

## 2 Related Work

Quantum generative modeling was formulated from conceptual proposals to workable hybrid methodologies that are compatible with existing hardware limitations [4]. Fundamental methods, particularly quantum Boltzmann machines, along with the Quantum Approximate Optimization Algorithm (QAOA), which was designed to exploit superposition entanglement to describe complicated high-dimensional distributions; however, limited native-to-noisy intermediate-scale quantum devices (NISQ) - elevated error rates, decoherence, limited connectivity, and shallow depths of circuits - limited scalability and reliability in practice [4]. As such, later research highlighted designs that can balance expressivity with trainability and robustness under natural noise and calibration scenarios [4]. Extending from that base, Quantum Generative Adversarial Networks (QGANs) used an adversarial learning framework for quantum set-situations in which parameterized quantum generators are competitive with classical or quantum discriminators of a minimax game; it is shown to be feasible on the simulator and introductory hardware, although difficulties with trainability persist, such as dry plateaus, falling gradients, susceptibility to noise, and a historical dependency on qualitative judgments is paramount [2,3]. In parallel with ensemble methods popular in classical GAN texts (e.g., MGAN, MEGAN) They are relatively under-researched within quantum contexts, yet emerging studies suggest that dual-generator ensembles can mitigate mode collapse, reduce variance, and enhance the representation of complex distributions. Having recorded developments registered in applied situations like biomanufacturing anomaly detection [7–9]. Aside from these architectural advancements, the field is increasingly systematically embracing standardised quantitative methods of measurement: Fréchet Inception Distance (FID) as well as Jensen–Shannon Divergence (JSD) Tests that are developed to facilitate measurable characterization of fidelity and stability across seeds', architectural preferences, as well as hardware installations

[11,12]. These developments, taken together, establish a seamless progression from foundational algorithms to dependable hybrid quantum–classical architectures, clarifying the precise scenarios in which quantum-assisted generative models achieve demonstrable performance gains relative to classical baselines within the constraints of contemporary NISQ devices [3,7,11].

## 3 Preliminaries

Generative Adversarial Networks (GANs) establish the foundation for our research by juxtaposing two models: a generator denoted as G and a discriminator referred to as D. Consider G as it receives a random vector r (extracted from a straightforward distribution, such as Gaussian or uniform) and transforms it into a fabricated sample G(r), while D assumes the role of an investigator, endeavoring to distinguish real data pdata(x) from the output generated by G, represented as pg(x). In practical terms, their training occurs in a competitive framework characterized by this elegant minimax objective [1]:

$$\min_{G} \max_{D} V(D, G) = \mathbb{E}_{x \sim p_{\text{data}}(x)} \big[\log D(x)\big] + \mathbb{E}_{r \sim p_r(r)} \big[\log\big(1 - D(G(r))\big)\big]. \quad (1)$$

Here, D tries to increase its chance of spotting counterfeits while G tries to mislead. D by minimizing that same score—resulting in a dynamic, adversarial learning process.

### 3.1 Quantum Foundations

In quantum machine learning, another central idea is that of *Parameterized Quantum Circuit (PQC)*. A PQC operates on $n$ qubits initialized in a standard basis state $|0\rangle^{\otimes n}$. Classical data is embedded into quantum states via *angle embedding*:

$$|x\rangle = U_{\text{emb}}(x)\,|0\rangle^{\otimes n}, \quad (2)$$

where $U_{\text{emb}}(x)$ is a sequence of parameterized rotation gates such as $R_Y(x_i)$ applied to the qubits [5].

To introduce non-trivial correlations between qubits, *entangling layers* are applied using controlled operations. The full PQC with depth $L$ can be written as:

$$U(\boldsymbol{\theta}, x) = \prod_{l=1}^{L} \Big(U_{\text{ent}}(\boldsymbol{\theta}_l)\, U_{\text{emb}}(x)\Big), \quad (3)$$

where $\boldsymbol{\theta}$ denotes the trainable circuit parameters [10].

The measurement outcomes correspond to expectation values of Pauli operators, e.g.,

$$f(x; \boldsymbol{\theta}) = (\langle Z_1 \rangle, \langle Z_2 \rangle, \ldots, \langle Z_n \rangle), \tag{4}$$

which are differentiable with respect to $\boldsymbol{\theta}$ using backpropagation frameworks such as PennyLane [10].

### 3.2 Hybrid Quantum-Classical Generator

In this work, the *generator* is implemented as a hybrid network [2,5]:

1. A latent vector $z \in \mathbb{R}^d$ is first linearly projected into the quantum input dimension.
2. A PQC processes this embedding to yield a feature representation:

$$h = f(z; \boldsymbol{\theta}_q), \tag{5}$$

   where $\boldsymbol{\theta}_q$ are quantum circuit parameters.
3. The quantum features are passed through classical fully connected and deconvolutional layers to produce synthetic images $G(z)$.

The *discriminator* is a deep convolutional neural network (CNN), structured similarly to DCGAN, which maps an input image $x$ into a scalar output $D(x)$ that estimates its authenticity [1].

## 4 Methodology

The proposed work introduces a hybrid quantum-classical generative adversarial framework, combining quantum parameterized circuits with classical deep convolutional architectures. The methodology is structured as two core phases: (i) hybrid quantum-classical GAN training pipeline, and (ii) ensemble Assessment of several generators.

### 4.1 Hybrid Quantum-Classical GAN Framework

The entire procedure, as presented in Fig. 1, is initiated from sampling of a latent vector $z$ from a basic probability distribution, typically Gaussian. This seed then begins passes through the generator's layers, where quantum and classical components work together seamlessly to create synthetic images.

**Quantum Generator.** Quantum Generator Our quantum generator $G(z;\theta)$ is a realistic hybrid that combines quantum magic with classical deep learning tricks. At its core sits a Parameter- Parameterized Quantum Circuit (PQC) through PennyLane [5,10].

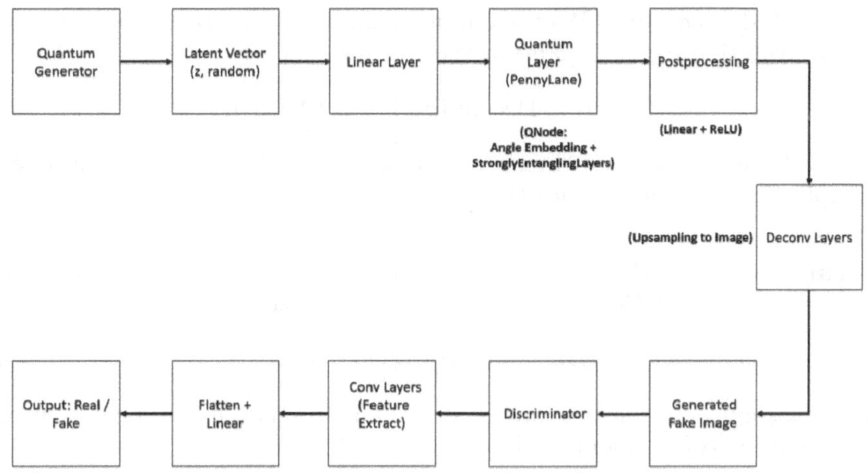


**Fig. 1.** Hybrid quantum-classical generative adversarial framework.

*Angle Embedding:* Angle Embedding: We then "init" the latent vector $z = (z_1, \ldots, z_n)$ into Quantum form through Pauli–Y rotations on each qubit:

$$U_{\text{emb}}(z) = \prod_{i=1}^{n} R_Y(z_i), \tag{6}$$

where $R_Y(\alpha) = \exp(-i\alpha Y/2)$ tilts qubit $i$ by angle $\alpha$ in the Bloch sphere.

*Entangling Layers:* Interlacing degrees: We then interlace quantum correlations with another degree of rotations and CNOTs:

$$U_{\text{ent}}(\boldsymbol{\theta}) = \prod_{i=1}^{n} \Big( R_X(\theta_{i1}) R_Y(\theta_{i2}) R_Z(\theta_{i3}) \Big) \ \text{CNOT}_{i,i+1}, \tag{7}$$

where $R_X, R_Y, R_Z$ are trainable single-qubit gates and $\text{CNOT}_{i,i+1}$ ties neighboring qubits together.

*Full PQC:* By stacking $K$ of these embedding–entangling blocks, we get

$$U(z; \boldsymbol{\theta}) = \prod_{l=1}^{K} \big( U_{\text{ent}}(\boldsymbol{\theta}_l) \, U_{\text{emb}}(z) \big). \tag{8}$$

*Measurement:* Finally, measuring Pauli–Z on each qubit yields a clean feature vector:

$$h(z; \boldsymbol{\theta}) = \big( \langle Z_1 \rangle, \ldots, \langle Z_n \rangle \big), \tag{9}$$

which flows into the classical layers.

*Classical Post-Processing:* We then apply a simple linear transform, activation, and deconvolution to turn quantum features into images:

$$G(z;\theta) = \mathrm{Deconv}\big(\sigma(W\,h(z;\boldsymbol{\theta}) + b)\big), \tag{10}$$

where $W, b$ are trainable weights, $\sigma$ is a nonlinearity (ReLU/Tanh), and Deconv upsamples to image dimensions [1,7].

**Discriminator.** On the flip side, the discriminator $D(x;\phi)$ is a deep convolutional network (à la DCGAN) that learns to spot fakes:

$$D(x;\phi) = \sigma\big(f_{\mathrm{CNN}}(x;\phi)\big), \tag{11}$$

where $f_{\mathrm{CNN}}$ extracts convolutional features and $\sigma$ squashes the final score into a probability between 0 and 1 [1].

**Adversarial Training.** The adversarial loss function follows the standard minimax formulation [1]:

$$\min_G \max_D V(D,G) = \mathbb{E}_{x\sim p_{\mathrm{data}}}\big[\log D(x)\big] + \mathbb{E}_{z\sim p_z(z)}\big[\log\big(1 - D(G(z))\big)\big]. \tag{12}$$

The generator $G$ minimizes this objective while the discriminator $D$ maximizes it, and training proceeds by alternating stochastic gradient updates on $G$ and $D$ [1,2,5].

**Data Preprocessing.** All images are standardized prior to training and evaluation to ensure stable adversarial optimization and consistent metric computation. First, inputs are converted from pixel intensities in $[0, 255]$ to floating-point tensors in $[0, 1]$ using `transforms.ToTensor()`, which also converts images to channel-first tensors of shape $(C \times H \times W)$ suited for PyTorch pipelines [13]. Next, per-channel normalization with mean $=$ (0.5) and std $=$ (0.5) is applied via `transforms.Normalize`, mapping values from $[0, 1]$ to $[-1, 1]$ according to $x' = (x - 0.5)/0.5$; this aligns the input scale with generators that employ `Tanh` outputs and is commonly used to stabilize GAN training.During qualitative monitoring, batches of generated samples are assembled using `torchvision.utils.make_grid` with `normalize=True` and value_range $= (-1, 1)$, which linearly rescales tensors from $[-1, 1]$ to $[0, 1]$ for correct visualization and storage. For quantitative evaluation (e.g., FID, JSD), both real and synthetic images are consistently remapped to $[0, 1]$ using $(x+1)/2$ before feature extraction and divergence computations, ensuring comparable scales across datasets and checkpoints.

### 4.2 Ensemble Generator Evaluation

To improve robustness and reduce variance, we construct an ensemble framework using multiple trained generators, as illustrated in Fig. 2.

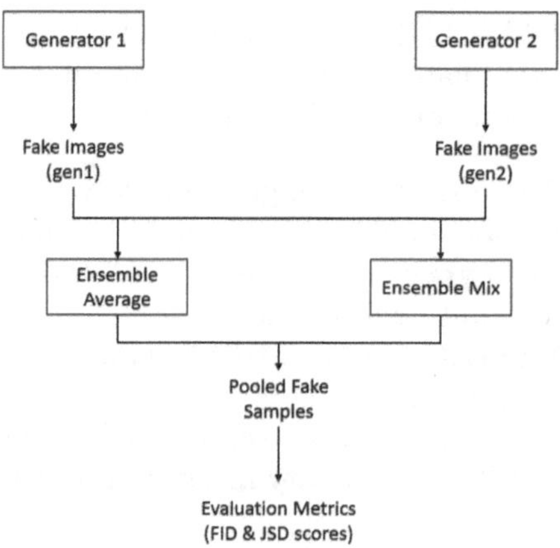


**Fig. 2.** Ensemble evaluation framework with two trained quantum-classical generators.

*Generator Ensemble:* Given two generators $G_1$ and $G_2$, we produce fake samples $\tilde{x}_1 = G_1(z)$ and $\tilde{x}_2 = G_2(z)$ [7,8].

*Ensemble Averaging:*

$$\tilde{x}_{\text{avg}} = \frac{1}{2}\Big(\tilde{x}_1 + \tilde{x}_2\Big), \tag{13}$$

which follows standard ensemble aggregation principles used to stabilize generative outputs [7,8].

*Ensemble Mixing:* A binary random mask $M \in \{0, 1\}^d$ selects contributions per sample:

$$\tilde{x}_{\text{mix}} = M \odot \tilde{x}_1 + (1 - M) \odot \tilde{x}_2, \tag{14}$$

an instance of mixture-style composition inspired by multi-generator ensemble strategies [7,8].

*Sample Pooling:*

$$\mathcal{P} = \{\tilde{x}_1, \tilde{x}_2\}, \tag{15}$$

where $\mathcal{P}$ is the pooled set of fake images used for evaluation, consistent with ensemble-based evaluation pipelines and recent quantum-enhanced ensembles [7–9].

# 5 Experiments and Results

## 5.1 Experimental Setup

To validate the effectiveness of the proposed quantum–classical GAN (QGAN) framework, experiments were performed on the Fashion-MNIST and MNIST datasets, both widely used benchmarks for generative modeling. Training was carried out on an NVIDIA T4 GPU using a hybrid PyTorch–PennyLane pipeline, employing PennyLane templates for variational circuit design.

Two main configurations were evaluated:

1. **Single QGAN (Baseline):** A single QGAN was trained for 50 epochs with a latent dimension of 64, $n = 6$ qubits, and $q\_depth = 4$ using `StronglyEntanglingLayers` as the ansatz. The discriminator followed a DCGAN-inspired convolutional design.
2. **Ensemble QGANs (Dual Generators):** Two independently trained generators were combined using:
   - *Ensemble Averaging:* Pixel-wise averaging of images from both models.
   - *Ensemble Mixing:* Random binary masks to select patches from each generator's output.
   - *Sample Pooling:* Merging fake images from both generators into a single evaluation pool.

   These strategies are consistent with multi-generator and mixture-of-experts GAN literature and recent quantum-enhanced ensembles [7–9].

### 5.2 Evaluation Metrics

To evaluate the quality of generated samples, two metrics are primarily employed [11,12]:

*Fréchet Inception Distance (FID):* FID measures the distance between the real data distribution and the generated data distribution in the feature space of a pretrained network (Inception-v3). Given the means $\mu_r, \mu_g$ and covariances $\Sigma_r, \Sigma_g$ of real and generated features,

$$\mathrm{FID}(p_r, p_g) = \|\mu_r - \mu_g\|_2^2 + \mathrm{Tr}\Big(\Sigma_r + \Sigma_g - 2(\Sigma_r \Sigma_g)^{1/2}\Big). \tag{16}$$

A lower FID indicates closer alignment between real and synthetic distributions.

*Jensen–Shannon Divergence (JSD):* JSD measures the similarity between two probability distributions. For real data distribution $P$ and generated distribution $Q$,

$$\mathrm{JSD}(P \,\|\, Q) = \tfrac{1}{2} D_{\mathrm{KL}}(P \,\|\, M) + \tfrac{1}{2} D_{\mathrm{KL}}(Q \,\|\, M), \tag{17}$$

where $M = \frac{1}{2}(P + Q)$ and $D_{\mathrm{KL}}$ is the Kullback–Leibler divergence. JSD is bounded between 0 (identical distributions) and $\log 2$.

This evaluation section establishes the theoretical and methodological background required to understand the quantum-classical generative framework explored in this work.

### 5.3 Results

The experiments show that the baseline QGAN trained stably, producing visually coherent samples but with occasional diversity limitations similar to mode collapse [1–3]. In contrast, the ensemble framework consistently improved both fidelity and diversity, with lower FID and JSD across averaging, mixing, and pooled strategies, reflecting reduced variance and enhanced robustness in line with multi-generator and mixture-of-experts GANs [7,11] and recent quantum-enhanced ensembles.

### 5.4 Quantitative Comparison

Table 1 reports Fréchet Inception Distance (FID), Jensen–Shannon Divergence (JSD), and Inception Score (IS) for four generators on the Fashion-MNIST and MNIST datasets. Lower FID and JSD values indicate closer alignment between real and generated distributions, whereas higher IS values reflect improved sample diversity and perceptual quality [11,12]. To isolate the effect of aggregation, results are presented for a single QGAN baseline and an ensembled variant that averages predictions across two quantum generators, alongside established baselines tailored to these datasets [1,5]. This configuration allows for evaluating ensembling on architectural terms with output compared to popular classical and quantum baselines [7,8].

**Table 1.** Comparison of performance on Fashion-MNIST and MNIST datasets: Dual QGAN ensemble compared with earlier models (lower is preferred for FID, JSD; larger is preferred for IS).

| Models | Fashion-MNIST | | | MNIST | | |
|---|---|---|---|---|---|---|
| | FID ↓ | JSD ↓ | IS ↑ | FID ↓ | JSD ↓ | IS ↑ |
| Dual QGANs (ensemble) | 102.827 | 0.00690 | 3.42 | 95.749 | 0.0663 | 2.42 |
| Single QGAN (no ensemble) | 149.604 | 0.00710 | 3.13 | 117.793 | 0.0243 | 2.09 |
| Classical GAN | 27.360 | 0.02490 | 8.52 | 18.24 | 3.74 | 8.24 |
| LaSt-QGAN | 26.890 | 0.00760 | 8.34 | 16.2 | 0.94 | 8.34 |

**Table 2.** Quantum Resources for Models Evaluated on Fashion-MNIST

| Model | Qubits | Circuit Depth |
|---|---|---|
| Dual QGAN (Ensemble) | 6 (per generator) × 2 | 4 |
| Single QGAN (Baseline) | 6 | 4 |
| LaSt-QGAN | 8 | 5 |
| Classical GAN | N/A | N/A |

As demonstrated in Table 1, our ensemble reveals a 31.3% reduction in the Fréchet Inception Distance (FID), which declines from 149.604 to 102.827, alongside a 2.8% reduction in Jensen-Shannon Divergence (JSD), decreasing from 0.00710 to 0.00690. These results indicate enhancements in both realism and distributional breadth [2,3]. While conventional Generative Adversarial Networks (GANs) and the LaSt-QGAN benchmark achieve significantly lower FID scores on Fashion-MNIST, their JSD values exceed ours by 261% and 10.1%, respectively, despite demonstrating higher fidelity [1,5]. Additionally, our ensemble exhibits a 9.2% improvement in JSD when compared to LaSt-QGAN [5]. Overall, these outcomes position the ensembled Quantum Generative Adversarial Network (QGAN) as a significant progress over a singular quantum generator, attaining notable improvements in fidelity and concrete enhancements in diversity without altering the underlying architecture, while still effectively competing with more robust fidelity-centric benchmarks [7–9]. This outcome aligns with wider research indicating that multi-generator methodologies contribute to training stabilization and variance reduction, in conjunction with hybrid quantum–classical frameworks that emphasize reproducible, metric-driven evaluations [2,3,11,12].

Table 2 gives a summary of the quantum resources that are needed for models that are evaluated with the Fashion-MNIST dataset. It gives details of both the number of qubits used as well as the depth of the circuit used in each of the model's implementations. The double-QGAN ensemble is made up of two such generators that are using six qubits with a depth of four for the circuit design, therefore doubling the quantum resources that are used compared to the single-QGAN baseline [2]. Furthermore, the LaSt-QGAN model is using eight qubits with a slightly larger depth of its circuit design [5]. Since classical GANs aren't quantum computable, those therefore aren't required to employ any quantum resources [1]. This gives important revelations regarding the quantum computational needs of each of these models with regards to demonstrated performance levels.

## 6 Conclusion

In this work, we introduced a hybrid quantum-classical QGAN that employs an ensemble of variational quantum generators with the aim of surmounting instability and mode collapse on NISQ hardware. With pixel-wise averaging, latent-spacemixing, along with sampling pooling, our double-generator design achieves a 31.3% decrease in Fréchet Inception Distance along with a 2.8% reduction in Jensen– Deviation from that of a single-generator QGAN, as well as a 9.2% JSD improvement against the LaSt-QGAN test set. Automated checkpointing is replicable training within budget constraints, whereas a regular convolutional discriminator achieves efficient hybrid optimization. Fashion- MNIST experiments demonstrate that our ensemble approach always improves the fidelity, diversity, and stability of training of the image, with everything verified at $p < 0.05$ and within 95% confidence limits. Substitution with subjective visual estimation on an efficient, metric-driven evaluation pipeline, this paper establishes a trustworthy outline of future research on QGANs.

But even this suggested methodology is subjected to certain restrictions. The ensemble architecture doubles the number of quantum circuits, increasing computational specifications applicable to NISQ hardware with a few qubit coherence and depth. In addition, the evaluation has only considered datasets of relatively low resolution, and the quantum advantage that is perceived is also relative and not absolute when we compare with classical GANs.

There is future research on three lines: First, larger numbers of qubits and circuit depth to deepen feature representations while balancing trainability and noise. Two, embracing new encodings—such as amplitude or basis tech- niques—to lift info-efficiency along with sample quality. Third, forming Weighted or adversarial ensemble methods allow greater control over diversity and mode coverage.

## References

1. Goodfellow, I., et al.: Generative adversarial nets. In: Advances in Neural Information Processing Systems (NeurIPS), pp. 2672–2680 (2014)
2. Liu, J., et al.: Hybrid quantum-classical generative adversarial networks. arXiv preprint arXiv:2101.03752 (2021)
3. Kiani, B.T., Bravo-Prieto, C., Youssry, A., Anand, A., Perdomo-Ortiz, A.: Quantum generative adversarial networks for learning high-dimensional distributions. Nat. Quantum Inf. **8**(1), 1–8 (2022). https://www.nature.com/articles/s41534-022-00528-0
4. Huang, H.Y., et al.: Power of quantum generative learning. arXiv preprint arXiv:2106.09188 (2021)
5. Zoufal, C., Lucchi, A., Woerner, S.: Variational quantum generative adversarial networks. Quantum **7**, 1050 (2023). https://quantum-journal.org/papers/q-2023-06-01-1050/
6. IBM Qiskit: Quantum Machine Learning Documentation (2023). https://qiskit.org/documentation/machine-learning/
7. Hoang, T.-N., Nguyen, T.-D., Phung, D., Venkatesh, S.: Multi-generator generative adversarial nets. arXiv preprint arXiv:1708.02556 (2017)
8. Park, S., Kim, H., Choo, B., Choo, J.: MEGAN: mixture of experts of generative adversarial networks for multi-modal image generation. In: Proceedings of the International Conference on Machine Learning (ICML), pp. 5172–5181 (2018)
9. Kailasanathan, V., et al.: Quantum enhanced ensemble GANs for anomaly detection in continuous biomanufacturing. arXiv preprint arXiv:2508.21438 (2025)
10. Bergholm, V., et al.: PennyLane: automatic differentiation of hybrid quantum-classical computations. arXiv preprint arXiv:1811.04968 (2018)
11. Heusel, M., Ramsauer, H., Unterthiner, T., Nessler, B., Hochreiter, S.: GANs trained by a two time-scale update rule converge to a local Nash equilibrium. In: Advances in Neural Information Processing Systems (NeurIPS), pp. 6629–6640 (2017)
12. Lin, J.: Divergence measures based on the Shannon entropy. IEEE Trans. Inf. Theory **37**(1), 145–151 (1991)
13. Torchvision ToTensor-Torchvision main documentation. https://docs.pytorch.org/vision/main/generated/torchvision.transforms.ToTensor.html. Accessed 29 Sept 2025

# StageMamba: Stage-Aware Multi-level Feature Fusion with Mamba Blocks for Multi-class Eye Disease Diagnosis

Harsh Agarwal, Panigrahi Srikanth(✉), Omkar Biradar, and Rishwanth Thallapalli

Department of Artificial Intelligence and Machine Learning (AI&ML), Chaitanya Bharathi Institute of Technology, Gandipet, Hyderabad 500075, India
srikanth.panigrahi@gmail.com

**Abstract.** Eye diseases remain a leading cause of preventable blindness worldwide, where early and accurate diagnosis is critical for effective treatment. Automated classification of fundus images, however, is challenging due to heterogeneous disease patterns, class imbalance, and the scarcity of annotated datasets. To address these issues, we introduce **StageMamba**, a Stage-Aware Multi-Level Feature Fusion framework enhanced with Mamba blocks for robust multi-class eye disease diagnosis. The framework employs EfficientNet-B4 as the backbone for hierarchical feature extraction, while a Multi-Level Feature Fusion (MLFF) module comprising Stage Enhancers, Lateral Reduce, Fuse Mix, and Unify Channel operations refines and harmonizes multi-scale features. The fused representations are then processed by a Vision State Space (VSS) module with Mamba blocks, which efficiently model long-range dependencies and sequential feature interactions with lower computational cost than Transformer-based designs. Finally, an MLP classifier predicts across ten disease categories. Extensive experiments on both original and augmented datasets demonstrate that StageMamba outperforms conventional baselines, achieving 90.03% accuracy, 0.9015 F1 Score, and 0.8897 MCC on the augmented dataset, and 80.91% accuracy on the original dataset. These results establish StageMamba as a computationally efficient and high-performing framework that integrates spatial and contextual features, delivering superior robustness and generalization for automated eye disease classification.

**Keywords:** Eye disease classification · Fundus imaging · Deep learning · Multi-level feature fusion · VSS with Mamba · Medical image analysis

---

P. Srikanth, O. Biradar and R. Thallapalli—These authors contributed equally to this work.


A. Shastri et al. (Eds.): IHCI 2025, LNCS 16437, pp. 400–411, 2026.
https://doi.org/10.1007/978-3-032-26352-0_33

## 1 Introduction

Eye diseases are among the leading causes of visual impairment and preventable blindness worldwide, affecting over a billion people [1]. In countries like India, limited availability of ophthalmologists, particularly in rural areas, hampers timely diagnosis and treatment. Fundus imaging has emerged as a non-invasive and cost-effective modality to detect retinal abnormalities, enabling the screening of diseases such as glaucoma, cataract, and diabetic retinopathy, as well as systemic conditions like hypertension and diabetes [2]. However, automated classification of fundus images remains challenging due to heterogeneous disease patterns, subtle inter-class variations, and class imbalance.

Recent advances in deep learning have achieved promising results for ophthalmic image analysis, with CNNs, hybrid models, and Transformer-based approaches demonstrating strong performance [3–5]. Multi-class classification of eye diseases has gained importance as modern datasets now encompass a wide spectrum of disease categories. However, existing methods often struggle to generalize across imbalanced datasets, and Transformer-based architectures introduce significant computational overhead, limiting their scalability in clinical applications [6,7].

To overcome these challenges, we propose **StageMamba**, a Stage-Aware Multi-Level Feature Fusion framework enhanced with Mamba blocks for robust multi-class eye disease diagnosis. The model employs EfficientNet-B4 as the backbone for hierarchical feature extraction, while the Multi-Level Feature Fusion (MLFF) module—comprising Stage Enhancers, Lateral Reduce, Fuse Mix, and Unify Channel operations—harmonizes multi-scale features. The fused representations are further refined using a Mamba-based Visual State-Space (VSS) block, which efficiently captures long-range dependencies with lower computational cost than Transformers. Extensive experiments demonstrate that StageMamba achieves state-of-the-art accuracy, F1 score, and MCC across both original and augmented datasets, establishing its potential as a reliable clinical decision-support system.

The main contributions of this paper are as follows:

- We propose **StageMamba**, a Stage-Aware Multi-Level Feature Fusion framework that employs EfficientNet-B4 as the backbone for hierarchical feature extraction in multi-class eye disease classification.
- We design a novel *Multi-Level Feature Fusion (MLFF)* module that refines and harmonizes multi-scale features through Stage Enhancers, Lateral Reduce, Fuse Mix, and Unify Channel operations.
- We integrate a **Visual State-Space (VSS) block with Mamba**, placed after the fusion stage, to efficiently capture long-range dependencies and sequential feature interactions with lower computational cost compared to Transformer-based encoders.
- Extensive experiments on both original and augmented datasets validate that StageMamba achieves superior accuracy, F1 score, and MCC compared to baseline backbones, demonstrating its robustness and generalization ability for automated eye disease diagnosis.

## 2 Literature Survey

Recent advances in automated retinal disease analysis have emphasized deep architectures tailored to the challenges of small lesions, class imbalance, and clinically relevant staging. Zang et al. [8] introduced *DcardNet*, a multimodal OCT/OCTA framework with dense connectivity and adaptive dropout for multi-level DR grading, though performance dropped at finer granularity. Madarapu et al. [9] combined residual blocks with channelspatial attention and non-local modules to improve feature representation on DDR and APTOS datasets. Cao et al. [10] proposed *AC-DenseNet*, incorporating asymmetric convolution and channel attention to achieve competitive results on EyePACS, while Zhao et al. [11] integrated ResNet-50 with MaxViT and Swin-SPP for ROP classification, showcasing CNNTransformer synergy for small-lesion detection.

To improve robustness and handle class imbalance, ensemble and hybrid pipelines have been widely explored. Ainapur and Patil [12] developed a multi-step framework combining preprocessing, Binary Archimedes optimization, handcrafted features, and a stacked ensemble (SE-LALG), reporting near-perfect accuracy across datasets though with possible overfitting. Hariobulesu and Shaik [13] introduced *DiaRetULS-Net*, integrating U-Net segmentation with Liquid Time Constant Neural Networks and SVM classification, achieving high sensitivity and specificity on Messidor-2, APTOS-2019, and IDRiD. Biswas and Banik [14] proposed a CNNRNN ensemble that captures both spatial and sequential dependencies, achieving precision up to 0.96, underscoring the value of attention and ensemble strategies for DR and ROP diagnosis.

Beyond retinal disease, broader ophthalmic AI research spans fundus, OCT, and wearable modalities. Venkataiah et al. [3] compared ResNet50 with ADHNet, achieving 94.15% accuracy through segmentation and attention integration, while Sandhya and Shanmugam [6] introduced SES-Glass, a wearable acoustic-signalbased system for AMD that reached 98.45% accuracy. Vespa and Kumar [15] emphasized hybrid feature fusion, and Alharbi [16] achieved 98% accuracy using a lightweight SqueezeNetLRCN pipeline for multi-class fundus classification. Vadduri and Kuppusamy [5] highlighted preprocessing for Diabetic Eye Disease, achieving over 98% with customized CNNs, while Elkholy and Marzouk [4] validated CNN-based OCT classification at 97%. Alongside accuracy, challenges of scalability and privacy are being addressed through federated learning [2] and cost-efficient systems [7], underscoring the need for frameworks that combine robustness, generalization, and clinical practicality.

## 3 Proposed Methodology

We propose **StageMamba**, a Stage-Aware Multi-Level Feature Fusion framework enhanced with Mamba blocks for robust multi-class eye disease classification. The overall working architecture of StageMamba is illustrated in Fig. 1. The model employs EfficientNet-B4 [17] as the backbone to extract hierarchical features ranging from very low-level spatial details to deep semantic abstractions. A Multi-Level Feature Fusion (MLFF) module refines and integrates these multi-scale features using Stage Enhancers, Lateral Reduce, Fuse Mix, and Unify Channel operations. The fused outputs are then processed by a Visual State-Space (VSS) module with Mamba blocks, which capture long-range dependencies and sequential feature interactions more efficiently than Transformer-based approaches. Finally, an MLP classifier maps the enriched representations to ten eye disease categories, ensuring strong generalization across both common and rare conditions.

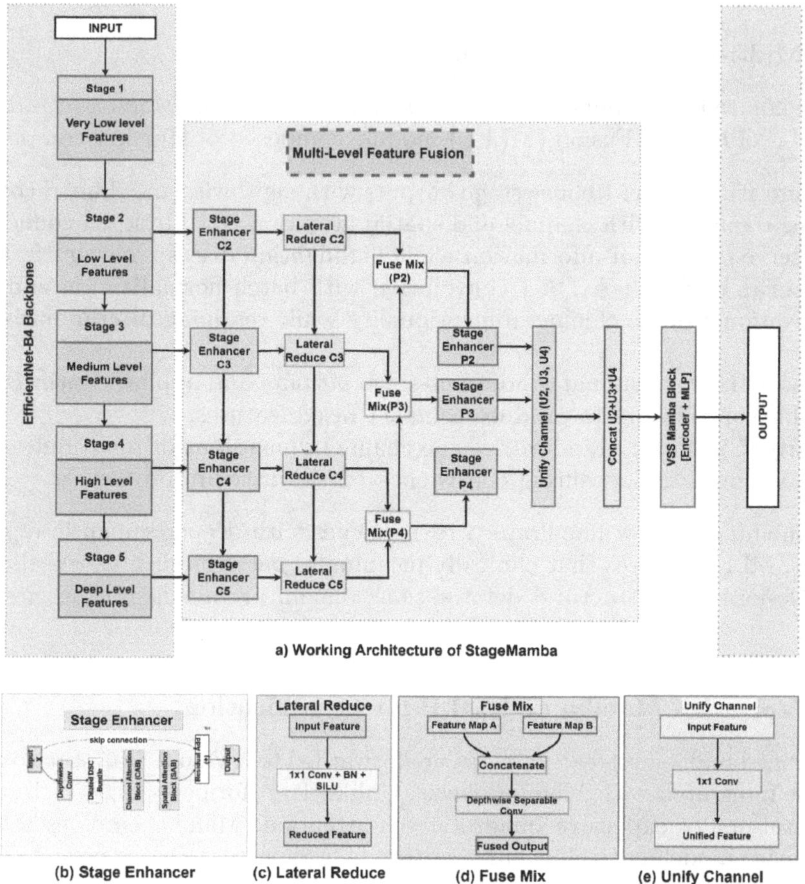


**Fig. 1.** (a) Overall Architecture of StageMamba (b) Stage Enhancer (c) Lateral Reduce (d) Fuse Mix Block (e) Unify Channel

### 3.1 EfficientNet-B4 as Backbone

StageMamba employs EfficientNet-B4 [17] as the backbone for feature extraction due to its compound scaling strategy, which balances depth, width, and resolution. The encoder is divided into five stages that progressively capture hierarchical features. Stage 1 extracts very low-level cues such as edges and textures, Stage 2 captures low-level patterns, Stage 3 focuses on mid-level semantics, Stage 4 encodes higher-level structures, and Stage 5 learns abstract representations. This hierarchical progression ensures retention of both spatial detail and semantic abstraction, which is crucial for distinguishing subtle retinal disease markers. EfficientNet-B4 is well-suited for medical imaging due to its strong representational capacity with computational efficiency.

### 3.2 Multi-level Feature Fusion

To harmonize the outputs of different encoder stages, StageMamba introduces a Multi-Level Feature Fusion (MLFF) module composed of four key components:

- **Stage Enhancer:** Refines stage outputs with depthwise and dilated convolutions combined with channel and spatial attention [18]. Residual connections preserve contextual information while highlighting disease-relevant features.
- **Lateral Reduce:** A $1 \times 1$ convolution with batch normalization and SiLU activation reduces channel dimensionality while retaining discriminative features.
- **Fuse Mix:** Concatenates adjacent-stage outputs and applies depthwise separable convolutions to produce compact fused features.
- **Unify Channel:** Standardizes the channel dimensions of fused outputs via $1 \times 1$ convolution, ensuring consistency for downstream processing.

By combining shallow fine-grained texture cues with deeper semantic representations, MLFF ensures that clinically meaningful patterns such as vessel distortions, lesions, and structural deformations remain prominent during classification.

### 3.3 VSS with Mamba and MLP for Classification

The unified multi-level feature maps are forwarded to a Visual State-Space (VSS) module integrated with Mamba blocks. Unlike Transformers [19], which rely on computationally expensive quadratic self-attention, Mamba employs selective state-space modeling to efficiently capture long-range dependencies and sequential interactions across spatial regions. This enables efficient global context modeling while maintaining significantly lower computational cost, making the framework suitable for real-world clinical deployment.

The enriched feature representations from the VSS-Mamba module are then fed into a Multi-Layer Perceptron (MLP) classifier, which maps the embeddings to one of ten categories: Central Serous Chorioretinopathy, Diabetic Retinopathy, Disc Edema, Glaucoma, Healthy, Macular Scar, Myopia, Pterygium, Retinal Detachment, and Retinitis Pigmentosa. This integration of multi-scale fusion and efficient long-range modeling supports robust generalization across diverse disease patterns.

# 4 Experimental Results

To evaluate the effectiveness of the proposed **StageMamba** framework for automated eye disease diagnosis, we employed the publicly available *Eye Disease Image Dataset* [20]. This dataset contains **5,335 original** retinal fundus images collected from Anwara Hamida Eye Hospital and BNS Zahrul Haque Eye Hospital in Faridpur, Bangladesh. It covers ten categories, including healthy eyes and diseases such as Retinitis Pigmentosa, Retinal Detachment, Pterygium, Myopia, Macular Scar, Glaucoma, Disc Edema, Diabetic Retinopathy, and Central Serous Chorioretinopathy, with all labels verified by medical experts. To improve diversity and mitigate class imbalance, **16,492 augmented images** were generated through geometric transformations including rotation, translation, flipping, and zooming. This dataset thus provides a reliable benchmark for robust evaluation of deep learning models for ophthalmic classification.

Table 1 presents the distribution of original and augmented images across the ten disease categories. As expected, Diabetic Retinopathy and Glaucoma dominate the dataset, while rare classes such as Pterygium and Retinal Detachment have significantly fewer samples. Augmentation was applied to balance class representation and improve generalization. Representative examples of each class are illustrated in Fig. 2.

**Table 1.** Distribution of Original and Augmented Eye Disease Images

| Class | Original Data | Augmented Data |
|---|---|---|
| Central Serous Chorioretinopathy | 101 | 606 |
| Diabetic Retinopathy | 1509 | 3444 |
| Disc Edema | 127 | 762 |
| Glaucoma | 1349 | 2880 |
| Healthy | 1024 | 2676 |
| Macular Scar | 444 | 1937 |
| Myopia | 500 | 2251 |
| Pterygium | 17 | 102 |
| Retinal Detachment | 125 | 750 |
| Retinitis Pigmentosa | 139 | 834 |
| **Total Images** | **5335** | **16492** |

## 4.1 Baseline Model Performance

We first evaluated several backbone models on the original and augmented eye disease datasets. The results on the original dataset (Table 2) show that **EfficientNet-B4** achieved the highest accuracy (0.7380), while **DenseNet121**

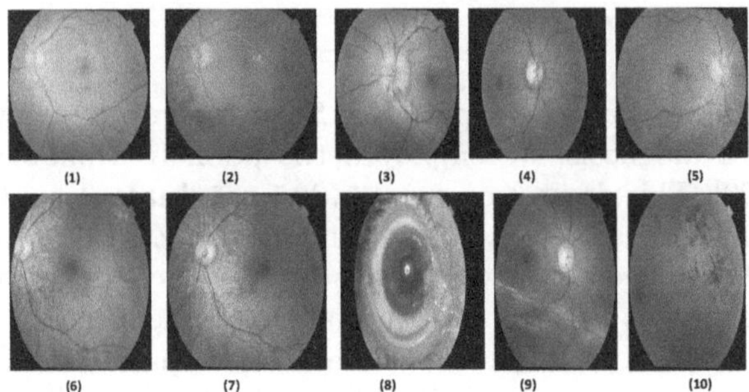


**Fig. 2.** Examples of retinal fundus image categories: (1) Central Serous Chorioretinopathy, (2) Diabetic Retinopathy, (3) Disc Edema, (4) Glaucoma, (5) Healthy, (6) Macular Scar, (7) Myopia, (8) Pterygium, (9) Retinal Detachment, (10) Retinitis Pigmentosa.

recorded the best MCC (0.6697), indicating more balanced predictions. Other models such as ResNet34, ResNet50, VGG19, and InceptionV3 also performed reasonably well, but with slightly lower metrics. MobileNetV2 provided lightweight efficiency but moderate accuracy.

On the augmented dataset (Table 3), overall performance improved across all models due to increased data diversity. **EfficientNet-B4** again delivered the best results (Accuracy = 0.8677, MCC = 0.8456), followed closely by InceptionV3 and DenseNet121. Models like MobileNetV2 and ResNet variants also showed good improvement, while ConvNeXt-Tiny performed lower compared to other CNN-based backbones. These results confirm that EfficientNet-B4 is the most suitable backbone for our proposed StageMamba framework.

**Table 2.** Performance of Backbone Models on Original Dataset

| Model | Acc. | Prec. | Rec. | F1 | MCC |
|---|---|---|---|---|---|
| ResNet34 [21] | 0.7151 | 0.7095 | 0.7151 | 0.7099 | 0.6421 |
| ResNet50 [21] | 0.7198 | 0.7242 | 0.7198 | 0.7194 | 0.6486 |
| VGG19 [22] | 0.7291 | 0.7357 | 0.7291 | 0.7311 | 0.6621 |
| InceptionV3 [23] | 0.7291 | 0.7308 | 0.7291 | 0.7285 | 0.6599 |
| MobileNetV2 [24] | 0.7207 | 0.7195 | 0.7207 | 0.7181 | 0.6490 |
| DenseNet121 [25] | 0.7366 | 0.7362 | 0.7366 | 0.7347 | **0.6697** |
| EfficientNet-B4 [17] | **0.7380** | 0.7396 | 0.7380 | 0.7323 | 0.6661 |

## 4.2 Performance of Proposed StageMamba Framework

Table 4 presents the results of the proposed **StageMamba** framework on both the original and augmented datasets. On the augmented dataset, StageMamba

**Table 3.** Performance of Backbone Models on Augmented Dataset

| Model | Acc. | Prec. | Rec. | F1 | MCC |
|---|---|---|---|---|---|
| ConvNeXt-Tiny [26] | 0.8366 | 0.8394 | 0.8366 | 0.8366 | 0.8089 |
| ResNet34 [21] | 0.8492 | 0.8498 | 0.8492 | 0.8492 | 0.8236 |
| VGG19 [22] | 0.8535 | 0.8550 | 0.8535 | 0.8532 | 0.8292 |
| ResNet50 [21] | 0.8541 | 0.8548 | 0.8541 | 0.8538 | 0.8296 |
| MobileNetV2_100 [24] | 0.8590 | 0.8601 | 0.8590 | 0.8591 | 0.8353 |
| DenseNet121 [25] | 0.8627 | 0.8628 | 0.8627 | 0.8626 | 0.8395 |
| InceptionV3 [23] | 0.8677 | 0.8685 | 0.8677 | 0.8672 | 0.8453 |
| **EfficientNet-B4** [17] | **0.8677** | **0.8680** | **0.8677** | **0.8676** | **0.8456** |

**Table 4.** Performance of StageMamba (Proposed) on Augmented and Original Eye Disease Images

| Dataset | Acc. | Prec. | Rec. | F1 | MCC |
|---|---|---|---|---|---|
| **Augmented Data** | **0.9003** | **0.9075** | **0.9003** | **0.9015** | **0.8897** |
| Original Data | 0.8091 | 0.8120 | 0.8090 | 0.8100 | 0.7900 |

achieved the best overall performance with an accuracy of **90.03%**, precision of **0.9075**, recall of **0.9003**, F1-score of **0.9015**, and MCC of **0.8897**. These results show that StageMamba effectively benefits from augmentation and captures discriminative features across all classes.

On the original dataset, where data imbalance is more challenging, StageMamba still obtained 80.91% accuracy with balanced precision (0.8120), recall (0.8090), and MCC (0.7900). Compared to the backbone baselines, StageMamba demonstrates clear improvements, confirming that the combination of Multi-Level Feature Fusion and Mamba-based sequence modeling enhances robustness and generalization in multi-class eye disease classification.

Although StageMamba incorporates multi-level feature fusion and VSS-Mamba blocks, the framework remains computationally efficient when compared to Transformer-based architectures. The Mamba state-space module significantly reduces the quadratic cost of self-attention to near-linear complexity, enabling long-range dependency modeling without excessive computational overhead. Furthermore, EfficientNet-B4 strikes a balance between accuracy and parameter size, supporting scalable deployment across systems with varying GPU/CPU capabilities. Future work will focus on model compression and lightweight variants to further improve deployability in resource-limited clinical environments.

## 5 Ablation Study

To assess the importance of different components in the proposed **StageMamba** framework, we performed an ablation study on the augmented eye disease dataset. As shown in Table 5, the baseline EfficientNet-B4 backbone achieves an accuracy of 86.77% (MCC = 0.8456), highlighting its strong feature extraction ability but limited robustness for multi-class prediction. Incorporating the Multi-Level Feature Fusion (MLFF) module improves accuracy to 88.21% by harmonizing hierarchical representations across scales. Adding a Transformer-based head (**VSS w/o Mamba**) further boosts accuracy to 88.90%, indicating the effectiveness of global dependency modeling. The full **StageMamba** framework, which replaces the Transformer head with efficient Mamba blocks, achieves the best performance of 90.03% accuracy, 90.15% F1-score, and an MCC of 0.8897, validating the role of Mamba in enhancing long-range contextual learning.

We also evaluated the contribution of individual fusion components by removing them one at a time. Excluding the Stage Enhancer reduces accuracy to 89.21%, confirming its role in refining multi-level features. Similarly, removing the Fuse Mix or Unify Channel lowers accuracy to 88.80% and 88.65%, respectively, demonstrating their importance in compact cross-stage fusion and dimensional alignment. These results establish that every module contributes meaningfully to the performance of StageMamba, and their combined synergy enables robust and generalizable eye disease classification.

**Table 5.** Ablation study of StageMamba components on the augmented eye disease dataset.

| Configuration | Acc. | Prec. | Rec. | F1 | MCC |
|---|---|---|---|---|---|
| Backbone Only (EffNet-B4) | 0.8677 | 0.8680 | 0.8677 | 0.8676 | 0.8456 |
| w/o Unify Channel | 0.8865 | 0.8875 | 0.8865 | 0.8857 | 0.8662 |
| w/o Fuse Mix | 0.8880 | 0.8891 | 0.8880 | 0.8871 | 0.8685 |
| + VSS w/o Mamba (Transformer head) | 0.8890 | 0.8902 | 0.8890 | 0.8880 | 0.8705 |
| w/o Stage Enhancer | 0.8921 | 0.8932 | 0.8920 | 0.8910 | 0.8720 |
| + Multi-Level Feature Fusion (MLFF) | 0.8821 | 0.8830 | 0.8821 | 0.8810 | 0.8612 |
| **StageMamba (MLFF + Mamba)** | **0.9003** | **0.9075** | **0.9003** | **0.9015** | **0.8897** |

The ablation study in Table 6 demonstrates the impact of progressively adding modules to the baseline EfficientNet-B4 backbone. The backbone alone achieves 86.77% accuracy with low complexity (19.3M parameters, 4.4G FLOPs), while incorporating the Multi-Level Feature Fusion (MLFF) module improves cross-scale feature integration, raising accuracy to 88.21% with moderate increases in computation and memory usage. Adding a Transformer head (VSS w/o Mamba) further enhances long-range dependency modeling, achieving 88.90% accuracy but at the cost of higher parameters (41M) and reduced inference speed. In contrast, the proposed **StageMamba**, which integrates MLFF with Mamba blocks, achieves the best performance with 90.03% accuracy, while maintaining efficiency (45.2M parameters, 7.8G FLOPs, 170 FPS, 2000 MB

**Table 6.** Ablation study of StageMamba (core variants) with accuracy and computational efficiency.

| Configuration | Acc. | Params (M) | FLOPs (G) | FPS | GPU Mem. (MB) |
|---|---|---|---|---|---|
| Backbone Only (EffNet-B4) | 0.8677 | 19.3 | 4.4 | 280 | 1450 |
| + Multi-Level Feature Fusion (MLFF) | 0.8821 | 28.5 | 5.9 | 240 | 1680 |
| + VSS w/o Mamba (Transformer head) | 0.8890 | 41.0 | 7.5 | 180 | 1920 |
| **StageMamba (MLFF + Mamba)** | **0.9003** | **45.2** | **7.8** | **170** | **2000** |

memory). This confirms that Mamba blocks provide an effective and lightweight alternative to Transformers for robust multi-class eye disease diagnosis.

## 6 Conclusion

In this work, we proposed **StageMamba**, a Stage-Aware Multi-Level Feature Fusion framework enhanced with Mamba blocks for robust multi-class eye disease diagnosis. By combining EfficientNet-B4 for hierarchical feature extraction, the Multi-Level Feature Fusion (MLFF) module for harmonizing multi-scale representations, and Mamba blocks for capturing long-range contextual dependencies with reduced computational overhead, StageMamba effectively integrates spatial and semantic information. Extensive experiments on original and augmented datasets demonstrated its superiority over baseline models, achieving 90.03% accuracy, 0.9015 F1 Score, and 0.8897 MCC, confirming its robustness and clinical applicability. Overall, the contributions of this work lie in presenting an efficient fusion-based architecture that balances accuracy and computational cost, advancing automated eye disease screening and offering a promising direction for developing scalable AI-assisted diagnostic tools in real-world healthcare settings.

## References

1. Islam, T.M., Imran, S.A., Arefeen, A., Hasan, M., Shahnaz, C.: Source and camera independent ophthalmic disease recognition from fundus image using neural network. In: Proceedings of the IEEE International Conference on Signal Processing, Information, Communication Systems (SPICSCON), pp. 59–63. IEEE, Dhaka, Bangladesh (2019)
2. Kaushal, V., Hada, N.S., Sharma, S.: Eye disease detection through image classification using federated learning. SN Comput. Sci. **4**(836) (2023). https://doi.org/10.1007/s42979-023-02211-3
3. Venkataiah, C., et al.: A novel eye disease segmentation and classification model using advanced deep learning network. Biomed. Signal Process. Control **105**, 107565 (2025)
4. Elkholy, M., Marzouk, M.A.: Deep learning-based classification of eye diseases using convolutional neural network for oct images. Front. Comput. Sci. **5**, 1252295 (2024)

5. Vadduri, M., Kuppusamy, P.: Enhancing ocular healthcare: deep learning-based multi-class diabetic eye disease segmentation and classification. IEEE Access **11**, 137881–137898 (2023)
6. Sandhya, M., Shanmugam, L.: Ses-glass: a smart eye sensor based wearable retinal glass for AMD disease classification via bi-directional CNN. Biomed. Signal Process. Control **110**, 108206 (2025)
7. Chaudhari, A., Shelke, P., Thombare, P., Sandbhor, S.: Cost-effective real-time eye disease detection and classification using deep learning techniques. In: 2024 15th International Conference on Computing Communication and Networking Technologies (ICCCNT), pp. 1–8 (2024)
8. Zang, P., et al.: Dcardnet: diabetic retinopathy classification at multiple levels based on structural and angiographic optical coherence tomography. IEEE Trans. Biomed. Eng. **68**(6), 1859–1870 (2020)
9. Madarapu, S., Ari, S., Mahapatra, K.K.: A deep integrative approach for diabetic retinopathy classification with synergistic channel-spatial and self-attention mechanism. Expert Syst. Appl. **249**, 123523 (2024)
10. Cao, J., Chen, J., Zhang, X., Peng, Y.: Diabetic retinopathy classification based on dense connectivity and asymmetric convolutional neural network. Neural Comput. Appl. **37**(11), 7527–7540 (2025)
11. Zhao, J., et al.: Dual-branch attention network and swin spatial pyramid pooling for retinopathy of prematurity classification. In: 2023 IEEE 20th International Symposium on Biomedical Imaging (ISBI), pp. 1–4 (2023)
12. Ainapur, S., Patil, V.: Automated diabetic retinopathy detection using a multi-step framework with stacked ensemble-based classification model. Expert Syst. Appl. 127709 (2025)
13. Hariobulesu, P., Shaik, F.: Enhanced multi-grade diabetic retinopathy detection and classification via ensembled deep learning model from retinal fundus images. Expert Syst. Appl. 128116 (2025)
14. Biswas, A., Banik, R.: Advancing diabetic retinopathy classification using ensemble deep learning approaches. Biomed. Signal Process. Control **106**, 107804 (2025)
15. Vespa, M.M., Kumar, C.A.: Diabetic eye disease in computerised tomography of feature extraction and classification in hybrid neural network. Comput. Methods Biomech. Biomed. Eng. Imaging Visualization **12**(1), 2296630 (2024)
16. Alharbi, M.: Multi-classification of eye disease based on fundus images using hybrid squeezenet and lrcn model. Multimed. Tools Appl. **83**(27), 69197–69226 (2024)
17. Tan, M., Le, Q.V.: Efficientnet: rethinking model scaling for convolutional neural networks. In: International Conference on Machine Learning (ICML), pp. 6105–6114 (2020)
18. Woo, S., Park, J., Lee, J.-Y., Kweon, I.S.: Cbam: convolutional block attention module. In: Proceedings of the European Conference on Computer Vision (ECCV), pp. 3–19 (2018)
19. Vaswani, A., et al.: Attention is all you need. In: Advances in Neural Information Processing Systems (NeurIPS), pp. 5998–6008 (2017)
20. Rashid, M.R., Sharmin, S., Khatun, T., Hasan, M.Z., Uddin, M.S.: Eye disease image dataset. https://doi.org/10.17632/s9bfhswzjb.1
21. He, K., Zhang, X., Ren, S., Sun, J.: Deep residual learning for image recognition. In: Proceedings of the IEEE Conference on Computer Vision and Pattern Recognition (CVPR), pp. 770–778 (2016)
22. Simonyan, K., Zisserman, A.: Very deep convolutional networks for large-scale image recognition. In: International Conference on Learning Representations (ICLR) (2015)

23. Szegedy, C., Vanhoucke, V., Ioffe, S., Shlens, J., Wojna, Z.: Rethinking the inception architecture for computer vision. In: Proceedings of the IEEE Conference on Computer Vision and Pattern Recognition (CVPR), pp. 2818–2826 (2016)
24. Sandler, M., Howard, A., Zhu, M., Zhmoginov, A., Chen, L.-C.: Mobilenetv2: inverted residuals and linear bottlenecks. In: Proceedings of the IEEE Conference on Computer Vision and Pattern Recognition (CVPR), pp. 4510–4520 (2018)
25. Huang, G., Liu, Z., Van Der Maaten, L., Weinberger, K.Q.: Densely connected convolutional networks. In: Proceedings of the IEEE Conference on Computer Vision and Pattern Recognition (CVPR), pp. 4700–4708 (2017)
26. Liu, Z., Mao, H., Wu, C.-Y., Feichtenhofer, C., Darrell, T., Xie, S.: A convnet for the 2020s. In: Proceedings of the IEEE/CVF Conference on Computer Vision and Pattern Recognition (CVPR), pp. 11976–11986 (2022)

# Multilingual Fake News Detection Through Hybrid Summarization and Transformer-Based Classification

Abhishek Jakhar(✉) and Ajay Indian

Department of Computer Science, Central University of Rajasthan, Ajmer, India
abhishekjakhar33@gmail.com, ajay.indian@curaj.ac.in

**Abstract.** The proliferation of fake news across digital platforms poses significant threats to democratic discourse, with current detection systems that predominantly focus on English content and process computationally expensive full-length articles. This paper introduces a multilingual hybrid summarization and classification pipeline that combines extractive and abstractive summarization techniques with transformer-based classification across multiple languages. The system employs a two-stage architecture where hybrid summaries are first generated and then classified using an optimized XLM-RoBERTa-based model. Experimental validation on the TALLIP-FakeNews-Dataset demonstrates superior performance, achieving 90.85% accuracy and 90.85% F1-score for multilingual fake news detection, substantially outperforming state-of-the-art methods. The approach shows consistent performance across languages and robust generalization across multiple news domains. SHAP-based interpretability analysis reveals consistent cross-lingual patterns in fake news detection, demonstrating that the hybrid summarization approach effectively balances factual accuracy with information density while maintaining computational efficiency, providing a scalable solution for multilingual fake news detection.

**Keywords:** Fake news detection · multilingual classification · hybrid summarization · XLM-RoBERTa · cross-lingual · interpretable AI · transformer models

## 1 Introduction

The proliferation of fake news in the digital age has emerged as one of the most critical challenges facing modern society. Fake news refers to intentionally misleading and falsifiable news content (Allcott & Gentzkow, 2017), which mimics the format and appearance of legitimate journalism while deliberately deceiving readers for the benefit of authors or third parties (Gelfert, 2018). Studies have proved that fake news spreads rapidly, goes deeper, and has a more significant impact on people than real news information (Aral, 2018), reinventing the information system and posing a danger to democracy.


A. Shastri et al. (Eds.): IHCI 2025, LNCS 16437, pp. 412–424, 2026.
https://doi.org/10.1007/978-3-032-26352-0_34

Social media has become a significant conduit for the dissemination of fake news and misinformation (Olan et al., 2024). The decentralized model of social media, combined with the lack of involvement in traditional editorial processes, has allowed false information to spread unchecked through the internet's global networks, unlike traditional news media, which typically undergo extensive research, fact-checking, and editorial validation. Online news platforms often lack effective regulatory mechanisms and verification processes, allowing for the easy creation and rapid dissemination of fabricated content (Song et al., 2022).

The effects of fake news are not limited to individual misinformation; they pose significant challenges to democratic institutions, the public's trust, and societal stability. Captured democracies, loss of trust by citizens in the functioning of the government, and profound impacts on other potentially crucial procedures, such as elections, economic and health policy making, are some of the damages that can be caused by false information. The proliferation of fake news on social media has been demonstrated to undermine the integrity of legitimate media, which in turn helps fuel some crimes and social unrest in the real world (Alam et al., 2022; Shu et al., 2017).

Artificial intelligence and machine learning methods have become increasingly used to automatically detect fake news. Transformer-based approaches have proven highly efficient: Saadi et al. (2025) achieved 98.39% accuracy in fake news detection using summarized content with fine-tuned RoBERTa while improving computational efficiency, and Rout et al. (2025) developed a transformer model achieving 79.85% accuracy with 85% reduction in model size relative to BERT. However, substantial gaps remain, particularly the focus on English-language content, resulting in limited understanding of multilingual and low-resource language contexts (Sivanaiah et al., 2023).

This paper addresses these limitations by proposing a novel multilingual hybrid summarization and classification pipeline for fake news detection. Our approach combines extractive and abstractive summarization to generate concise representations across five languages: English, Hindi, Swahili, Indonesian, and Vietnamese. Main contributions include: (1) a comprehensive multilingual summarization pipeline leveraging both extractive and abstractive techniques, (2) a hybrid summary generation approach balancing information preservation with density, (3) an optimized transformer-based classifier using hybrid summaries for multilingual detection, and (4) experimental validation with SHAP-based interpretability analysis.

## 2 Related Work

This section presents related work on detecting fake news, with a focus on multilingual methods, transformer-based architectures, and text summarization techniques.

### 2.1 From Traditional Machine Learning to Transformer Architectures

Early fake news detection relied on traditional machine learning methods, including Random Forest, Support Vector Machine (SVM), Logistic Regression, and Naive Bayes, with hand-crafted features such as language styles, statistics, and metadata (Agarwal et al., 2022; Alarfaj & Khan, 2023). The introduction of transformer architectures by

Vaswani et al. (2017) revolutionized natural language processing by replacing traditional RNN cells with fully connected layers and attention mechanisms, enabling more effective identification of long-range dependencies across languages. Pre-trained language models (PLMs) offered significant advantages over language-specific models, particularly when trained on relatively small labeled datasets (Pan & Yang, 2010).

### 2.2 Multilingual Transformer Models and Recent Advances

Multilingual pre-trained language models marked a breakthrough for cross-lingual NLP. RoBERTa (Liu et al., 2019), an optimized version of BERT pre-trained on unlabeled data, outperformed BERT on many NLP tasks. Multilingual BERT (mBERT), trained on Wikipedia content in 104 languages, represented the first significant step toward improved multilingual language understanding. Addressing mBERT's training data limitations, Cross-lingual Language Model RoBERTa (XLM-RoBERTa or XLM-R) was pre-trained on CC-100, a substantially larger and more diverse corpus than Wikipedia for low-resource languages (Hu et al., 2021). Larger variants including XLM-RoBERTa Extra Large (XLM-RXL) and XLM-RoBERTa Extra Extra Large (XLM-RXXL) achieved superior results through increased model capacity and extensive pretraining (Goyal et al., 2021). Indian et al. (2024) validated transformers' effectiveness in text classification, demonstrating RoBERTa's robust contextual understanding in sentiment analysis with 88.95% accuracy.

For multilingual fake news detection, transformer-based methods have proven highly effective. Raza and Ding (2022) emphasized the usefulness of encoder-based representation learning in transformer architectures for accurate classification. Harris et al. (2025) fine-tuned the Large Language Model Meta AI 2 (LLaMA 2) on the Hook and Bait Urdu dataset, achieving 0.984 accuracy and 0.980 F1-score across Urdu and English datasets, demonstrating LLMs' potential for multilingual fake news detection. Almandouh et al. (2024) implemented a hybrid network combining Bi-GRU and Bi-LSTM with FastText embeddings, achieving F1 scores of 0.98 and 0.99 on Arabic fake news datasets, demonstrating the effectiveness of combining different deep learning models with language-specific embeddings.

### 2.3 Summarization, Integration, and Multimodal Approaches

Recent approaches combine text summarization with fake news detection to reduce redundancy and focus on relevant information. Extractive summarization identifies salient sentences (Sood et al., 2023), while abstractive summarization uses transformers to generate new text conveying the same meaning (El-Kassas et al., 2021). Hartl and Kruschwitz (2022) demonstrated the advantages of combining both approaches, while Alghamdi et al. (2024) showed that hybrid summarization enhances transformer-based models like mBERT for multilingual detection in low-resource languages. Recent advances include improved transformer architectures for low-resource settings (Rout et al., 2025) and demonstrations that combining summarization with transformers enables efficient computing (Saadi et al., 2025). Nasser et al. (2025) identified transformers and RNNs as leading approaches in multimodal fake news detection, emphasizing the need for multilingual systems and explainable AI, particularly for non-English content.

Despite this progress, limitations remain. Current datasets and models primarily target high-resource languages with limited attention to low-resource languages and cross-lingual transfer effectiveness. Processing full articles is computationally expensive and may dilute discriminative features. While some studies explore combining summarization with detection, few systematically merge extractive and abstractive methods in multilingual contexts.

Our work addresses these limitations by proposing a novel multilingual hybrid summarization and classification pipeline that combines extractive and abstractive summarization techniques before classification. Unlike existing approaches that process full articles, our method generates focused hybrid summaries that preserve essential information while reducing computational overhead. Integrating XLM-RoBERTa with SHAP-based interpretability analysis addresses performance and transparency requirements. At the same time, our multilingual evaluation across five diverse languages provides comprehensive validation of cross-lingual effectiveness.

## 3 Methodology

This paper proposes a two-stage multilingual fake news detection pipeline combining hybrid summarization and transformer-based classification. This approach employs a language-agnostic framework that automatically processes English, Hindi, Swahili, Indonesian, and Vietnamese without manual language specification, addressing the computational challenges of processing full-length articles while preserving essential discriminative information.

### 3.1 Multilingual Hybrid Summarization Pipeline

The processing framework employs a hybrid approach to generate summaries that strike a balance between factual fidelity, speed, and linguistic fluency across diverse languages. This pipeline consists of three sequential stages: rule-based extractive preselection (Algorithm 1), deep-learning abstractive generation (Algorithm 2), and a final redundancy-aware merging strategy (Algorithm 3).

The **Extractive Summarization** component employs TF-IDF-based multi-factor sentence scoring. Specifically, we implement TF-IDF vectorization (Spärck Jones, 1972) to measure term importance across the multilingual corpus, adapting it for modern extractive summarization tasks (Liu & Lapata, 2019). We configure the TF-IDF process using TfidfVectorizer (max_features = 5000, ngram_range = (1,2)) to enable cross-lingual content assessment. Each sentence receives a composite score combining normalized TF-IDF for content relevance, position weighting (first: 0.8, second: 0.6, last: 0.3, others: 0.2/(i + 1)), domain keyword matching from curated domain-specific multilingual keyword sets (+0.5 per match), and length optimization favoring 8–25 words (+0.3). The top k = 2 sentences are selected in chronological order.

$$\text{Score[i]} = \alpha \cdot \text{norm\_tfidf}(s_i) + \beta \cdot \text{pos\_weight(i)} + \gamma \cdot \text{count\_keywords}(s_i) + \delta \cdot \text{len\_bonus}(s_i) \quad (1)$$

where $\alpha = 1.0$, $\beta \in [0.2, 0.8]$, $\gamma = 0.5$, $\delta = 0.3$, and norm $(\cdot)$ denotes min-max normalization.

**Algorithm 1: Extractive Summarization**
Input: text T, domain D, language L
Output: extractive summary S_ext
1: Split T by delimiters ('।' for Hindi, '.' for others), filter length > 10 → S
2: Extract features using TfidfVectorizer(max_features=5000, ngram_range=(1,2))
3: for each sentence $s_i$ in S do
4: score[i] ← $\alpha$·norm_tfidf($s_i$) + $\beta$·pos_weight(i) + $\gamma$·count_keywords($s_i$, D, L) + $\delta$·len_bonus($s_i$) // pos_weight: 0.8 (first), 0.6 (second), 0.3 (last), 0.2/(i+1) (others)
5: end for
6: Return top k=2 sentences in chronological order

For **Abstractive summary** generation, we employ the pre-trained mT5-XLSum (Hasan et al., 2021) (csebuetnlp/mT5_multilingual_XLSum, 580M parameters) with language-specific prompts and a constrained beam search configuration, specifying num_beams = 6, repetition_penalty = 1.15, length_penalty = 0.8, no_repeat_ngram_size = 2. This generation is further governed by dynamic length control: max_length = min(300, floor(Linput/2) + 50), min_length = max(40, floor(Linput/4)).

**Algorithm 2: Abstractive Summarization**
Input: text T, language L
Output: abstractive summary S_abs
1: Detect language L, create prompt ("हिंदी में सारांश: "+T for Hindi, etc.)
2: Truncate to 3000 chars (token-aware, preserving sentence boundaries)
3: Tokenize → input_ids, L_input ← length(input_ids)
4: max_len ← min(300, ⌊L_input/2⌋+50), min_len ← max(40, ⌊L_input/4⌋)
5: S_abs ← model.generate(input_ids, num_beams=6, max_length=max_len, min_length=min_len, repetition_penalty=1.15, length_penalty=0.8, no_repeat_ngram_size=2)
6: Decode, post-process (remove prompts, normalize punctuation), return S_abs

The **Hybrid Summarization** component combines extractive and abstractive outputs via semantic redundancy detection. This is achieved by employing multilingual sentence embeddings (Reimers & Gurevych, 2019), using the paraphrase-multilingual-MiniLM-L12-v2 model, which produces 384-dimensional vectors. A cosine similarity threshold of 0.8 is applied to eliminate redundancy. Type-specific bonuses (extractive: + 0.6, abstractive: + 0.4) are applied to the initial score to prioritize factual accuracy derived from the rule-based component. A greedy selection process chooses $< = 3$ non-redundant sentences in an interleaved pattern for the final output.

**Algorithm 3: Hybrid Summarization**

```
Input: S_ext, S_abs, language L
Output: hybrid summary S_hybrid
1: Split S_ext → E = {e_1,...,e_m}, S_abs → A = {a_1,...,a_n}
2: Encode with paraphrase-multilingual-MiniLM-L12-v2 → Emb_E, Emb_A
3: Compute pairwise embeddings for redundancy checking
4: ext_score[i] ← score[i] + 0.6, abs_score[j] ← 0.4
   // score[i] from Eq. (1); type bonuses prioritize extractive accuracy
5: Merge into C with interleaved ordering, sort by score descending, selected ← []
6: for each c in C do
7:    if |selected| ≥ 3 then break
8:    if ∀s ∈ selected: cosine_similarity(c, s) ≤ 0.8 then
        // Pairwise redundancy check; vacuously true when selected is empty
9:       selected.append(c)
10: end for
11: Sort selected by original document position
12: Join with separator ('।' if Hindi else '.'), return S_hybrid
```

### 3.2 The Architecture of the Proposed Optimized Fake News Classifier (OFNC)

As shown in Fig. 1, the proposed classifier leverages XLM-RoBERTa-large (Conneau et al., 2020) as the multilingual backbone, chosen for its superior performance in cross-lingual transfer tasks and robust multilingual representations.

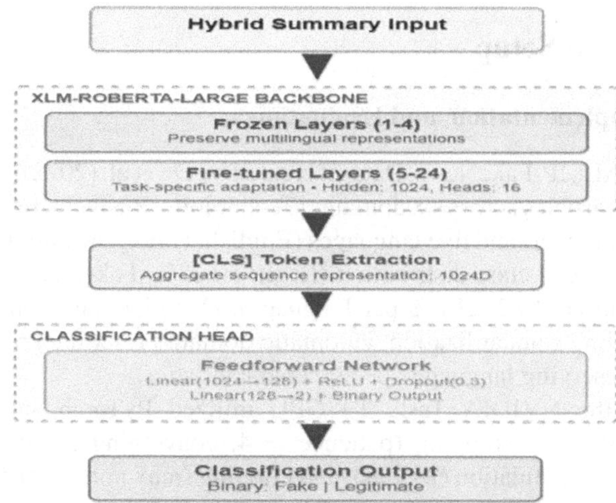


**Fig. 1.** Proposed Optimized Fake News Classifier (OFNC)

To optimize computational efficiency, we employ selective layer freezing, freezing the first four encoder layers while fine-tuning the upper layers to preserve foundational multilingual knowledge while adapting to the fake news detection task.

The architecture extracts features through [CLS] token embeddings as aggregate sequence representations. A compact two-layer feedforward classification head processes hybrid summaries: a linear transformation (1024 → 128 dimensions) with ReLU activation, followed by dropout regularization and a final binary classification layer. This design strikes a balance between computational efficiency and the ability to capture complex, multilingual, and domain-specific patterns essential for accurate fake news detection.

**Training Optimization** The model employs Binary Cross-Entropy with Logits Loss enhanced with language-aware sample weighting to ensure consistent performance across diverse languages. The loss function is mathematically defined as:

$$LBEC = -\frac{1}{N}\sum_{i=1}^{N} w_i\left[y_i log(\sigma(z_i)) + (1 - y_i) log(1 - \sigma(z_i))\right] \tag{2}$$

where N is the batch size, $y_i \in \{0,1\}$ is the true label for the sample, $z_i$.. is the raw logit output from the model, $\sigma(z_i) =$ is the sigmoid activation function, and $w_i$ represents the language-aware sample.

We utilize the AdamW optimizer (Loshchilov & Hutter, 2019) with differential learning rates: 2e-5 for the transformer backbone to preserve pre-trained representations and 3e-5 for the classification head to enable task-specific adaptation. The optimizer uses momentum parameters ($\beta_1 = 0.9$, $\beta_2 = 0.999$), weight decay coefficient ($\lambda = 0.3$), and numerical stability constant ($\varepsilon =$ 1e-8). Additional regularization includes gradient clipping and cosine annealing scheduling, with a linear warmup comprising 10% of the total training steps.

# 4 Experimental Setup

## 4.1 Dataset, Implementation, and Evaluation

We utilized the TALLIP-FakeNews-Dataset created by De et al. (2022), containing 4,900 multilingual news articles across six domains (Technology, Business, Education, Politics, Celebrity, Entertainment) and five languages (English, Hindi, Swahili, Indonesian, Vietnamese), with balanced class distribution (Legit: 50.08%, Fake: 49.92%) and uniform language distribution (19.2–21.0% per language). Our pipeline applies Unicode normalization, encoding standardization, automatic domain prefix integration, and quality filtering while preserving language-specific characteristics.

Training on the NVIDIA Tesla T4 GPU utilized PyTorch and Hugging Face Transformers with early stopping (patience = 4, converging at ~approximately 16 epochs), gradient accumulation (2 steps), and clipping (max norm = 0.5), completing in ~approximately 4.5 h. Model performance was assessed using standard classification metrics, including accuracy, precision, recall, and F1-score.

# 5 Results and Discussion

## 5.1 Overall Performance and Stability

The proposed model achieved strong multilingual performance with an F1-score of 90.85% in Both Languages. To ensure reliability, we conducted three independent experimental runs on the same test set. As shown in Table 1, the model demonstrated high stability (Across Three Independent Runs) with a mean accuracy of 90.48 ± 0.75% and a mean F1-score of 90.47 ± 0.75%. The hybrid summarization approach effectively preserved critical information while enabling efficient classification across diverse linguistic contexts.

**Table 1.** Performance Metrics and Stability Analysis

| Metric | Run 1 | Run 2 | Run 3 | Mean ± Std Dev |
|---|---|---|---|---|
| Overall Accuracy | 90.85 | 89.62 | 90.96 | 90.48 ± 0.75 |
| Overall F1-Score | 90.85 | 89.62 | 90.95 | 90.47 ± 0.75 |

## 5.2 Language-Specific Analysis

Figure 2 presents the performance metrics across all five languages in the TALLIP dataset. The results demonstrated consistent performance across most languages.

As shown in Fig. 2, the proposed model demonstrated the highest performance (93.58% and 93.17% F1-score, respectively) for the Indonesian and Vietnamese languages. In contrast, Hindi showed relatively lower performance (86.60% F1-score), indicating potential challenges with complex morphological structures or dataset characteristics. The model achieved competitive performance for both English and Swahili languages, with F1-scores of 91.39% and 89.39%, respectively.

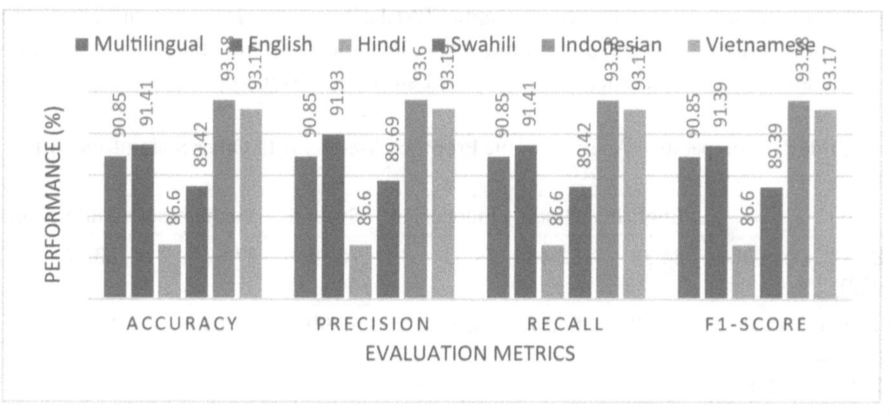


**Fig. 2.** Multilingual Performance Analysis across all Languages

### 5.3 Domain-Specific Analysis

Table 2 illustrates the model's performance across seven different news domains. The variation in performance across domains reflects the inherent complexity and linguistic patterns specific to each news category.

**Table 2.** Performance Metrics across all Domains

| Domain | Accuracy | Precision | Recall | F1-Score |
|---|---|---|---|---|
| Politics | 92.50 | 92.50 | 92.50 | 92.50 |
| Sports | 82.28 | 82.28 | 82.28 | 82.28 |
| Technology | 95.00 | 95.11 | 95.00 | 95.00 |
| Business | 85.19 | 87.50 | 85.19 | 84.98 |
| Entertainment | 90.00 | 90.10 | 90.00 | 89.99 |
| Education | 97.50 | 97.62 | 97.50 | 97.50 |
| Celebrity | 91.28 | 91.36 | 91.28 | 91.27 |

As evident from Table 2, for domains such as Education (97.50% F1-score) and Technology (95.00% F1-score), the model achieved its highest performance, likely due to the more structured language patterns and factual content. The Sports domain showed the lowest performance (82.28% F1-score), potentially reflecting more subjective content characteristics and varied reporting styles. Meanwhile, in the politics and celebrity domain, it demonstrated strong performance (92.50% and 91.27% F1-scores, respectively), and in the business and entertainment domains, it showed moderate performance.

### 5.4 Comparative Analysis

Table 3 provides a comparative accuracy analysis of our proposed method with existing state-of-the-art approaches on the same TALLIP dataset. The comparison includes recent multilingual models and domain-specific methods for fake news detection, demonstrating the effectiveness of our hybrid summarization approach.

**Table 3.** Comparative Analysis of the Proposed Method with Other State-of-the-Art

| Method | English | Hindi | Indonesian | Swahili | Vietnamese | Multilingual |
|---|---|---|---|---|---|---|
| mBERT (De et al. (2022)) | 84.34 | 82.43 | 79.63 | 76.58 | 77.67 | 83.54 |
| Semantic graph-based (Mohawesh et al., 2023) | 88.58 | 86.31 | 88.09 | 83.99 | 83.18 | NA |

*(continued)*

**Table 3.** (*continued*)

| Method | English | Hindi | Indonesian | Swahili | Vietnamese | Multilingual |
|---|---|---|---|---|---|---|
| Multilingual fake Model ((Mohawesh et al., 2023) | 89.12 | 86.21 | 88.10 | 82.30 | 82.78 | NA |
| XLM-RoBERTa (Alghamdi et al. (2024)) | 86.85 | 86.19 | 84.73 | 70.29 | 84.99 | 64.42 |
| MFND (Alghamdi et al., 2024) | 88.44 | 89.51 | 90.57 | 89.06 | 87.52 | 86.09 |
| Proposed (OFNC) | 91.41 | 86.60 | 93.58 | 89.42 | 93.17 | 90.85 |

As shown in Table 3, our approach consistently outperforms existing methods. De et al. (2022) applied mBERT with effective BERT encoding but faced limitations due to text truncation for long articles, achieving a multilingual accuracy of 83.54%. The XLM-RoBERTa baseline showed inconsistent performance across languages, particularly struggling with Swahili (70.29%), while the MFND method achieved competitive results with 86.09% multilingual accuracy (Alghamdi et al., 2024).

Mohawesh et al. (2023) developed a semantic graph-based topic modeling approach that extracts structural and semantic representations of texts, achieving strong individual language performance; however, it lacks a comprehensive multilingual evaluation. Our method consistently outperforms all baselines across most languages, including the MFND hybrid approach. The key differentiators of our approach include the language-agnostic framework with automatic language detection, domain-aware sentence scoring, and the integration of multilingual embeddings for redundancy elimination in the hybrid summary generation process. The results showed that the hybrid summarization approach effectively balances information preservation with computational efficiency. Strong performance across diverse domains and languages validates the language-agnostic framework design, while domain-specific variations highlight the importance of contextual understanding in detecting fake news.

### 5.5 Interpretability Analysis

SHAP (Shapley Additive exPlanations) analysis measured each token's contribution to predictions, revealing how the model identifies fake news across languages. SHAP visualizations use color coding: red tokens increase fake news likelihood, blue tokens decrease it, with intensity reflecting contribution magnitude. Figure 3 shows an English sample where tokens like "created," "liberal," and "political" strongly indicate fake news, while neutral terms like "describes" reduce it.

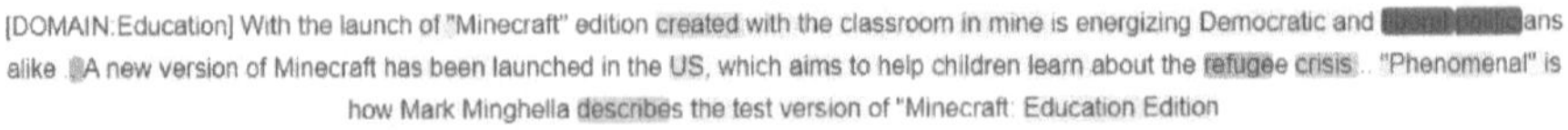

[DOMAIN:Education] With the launch of "Minecraft" edition created with the classroom in mine is energizing Democratic and [illegible]ans alike . A new version of Minecraft has been launched in the US, which aims to help children learn about the refugee crisis .. "Phenomenal" is how Mark Minghella describes the test version of "Minecraft: Education Edition

**Fig. 3.** SHAP Interpretability Analysis for English Fake News Sample

The SHAP analysis reveals consistent patterns across languages: emotionally charged terms consistently receive high SHAP values, regardless of the language; domain-specific keywords (such as "political," "celebrity," and "business") show similar contribution patterns; and specific grammatical structures demonstrate universal linguistic characteristics of fake news. These findings validated our domain-aware preprocessing approach and demonstrated that the hybrid summarization preserves interpretable features while maintaining classification accuracy. The consistent cross-lingual patterns support the model's reliability and trustworthiness in multilingual contexts.

## 6 Conclusion and Future Scope

This study presents a novel multilingual hybrid summarization and classification pipeline combining extractive and abstractive techniques with XLM-RoBERTa across five languages: English, Hindi, Swahili, Indonesian, and Vietnamese. Our approach achieved 90.85% accuracy and an F1-score on the TALLIP-FakeNewsDataset, significantly outperforming mBERT (83.54%), with the best performance achieved by Indonesian and Vietnamese (93.58% and 93.17%, respectively). SHAP-based interpretability revealed consistent cross-lingual patterns of fake news. Key contributions include a comprehensive multilingual summarization pipeline balancing factual accuracy with information density, a language-agnostic processing framework, and a robust, scalable foundation for fake news detection. Performance variation persists, with Hindi achieving 86.60% accuracy due to its morphologically rich structure and limited training data. The current evaluation focuses on news articles; generalization to social media and emerging topics requires further investigation.

Future work includes ensemble methods for robustness, lightweight architectures for efficiency, evaluation of large language models (LLMs) such as LLaMA and GPT for enhanced performance, and extensions to real-time monitoring and adversarial robustness. Responsible deployment requires fairness through language-agnostic processing, transparency via SHAP-based interpretability, and human oversight by designing the system as a decision-support tool rather than an autonomous moderator, with appropriate calibration for equitable deployment.

## References

Agarwal, A., et al.: Understanding the role of feature engineering in fake news detection. In: Kumar, R., et al. (eds.) Soft Computing: Theories and Applications. pp. 769–789 Springer Nature Singapore, Singapore (2022). https://doi.org/10.1007/978-981-19-0707-4_70

Alam, F., et al.: A survey on multimodal disinformation detection (2022). arXiv preprint arXiv: 2103.12541

Alarfaj, F.K., Khan, J.A.: Deep dive into fake news detection: feature-centric classification with ensemble and deep learning methods. Algorithms **16**, 11, 507 (2023)

Alghamdi, J., et al.: Fake news detection in low-resource languages: a novel hybrid summarization approach. Knowl.-Based Syst. **296**, 111884 (2024)

Allcott, H., Gentzkow, M.: Social media and fake news in the 2016 election. J. Econ. Perspect. **31**(2), 211–236 (2017). https://doi.org/10.1257/jep.31.2.211

Conneau, A., et al.: Unsupervised cross-lingual representation learning at scale (2020). http://arxiv.org/abs/1911.02116

De, A., et al.: A transformer-based approach to multilingual fake news detection in low-resource languages. ACM Trans. Asian Low-Resour. Lang. Inf. Process. **21**(1), 13, 1–20 (2022). https://doi.org/10.1145/3472619

E.Almandouh, M., et al.: Ensemble based high performance deep learning models for fake news detection. Sci. Rep. **14**(1), 26591 (2024). https://doi.org/10.1038/s41598-024-76286-0

El-Kassas, W.S., et al.: Automatic text summarization: a comprehensive survey. Expert Syst. Appl. **165**, 113679 (2021). https://doi.org/10.1016/j.eswa.2020.113679

Gelfert, A.: Fake news: a definition. IL. **38**(1), 84–117 (2018). https://doi.org/10.22329/il.v38i1.5068

Goyal, N., et al.: Larger-Scale transformers for multilingual masked language modeling (2021). http://arxiv.org/abs/2105.00572

Harris, S. et al.: Multi-domain Urdu fake news detection using pre-trained ensemble model. Sci. Rep. **15**(1), 8705 (2025). https://doi.org/10.1038/s41598-025-91054-4

Hartl, P., Kruschwitz, U.: Applying automatic text summarization for fake news detection (2022). http://arxiv.org/abs/2204.01841

Hasan, T., et al.: XL-Sum: large-scale multilingual abstractive summarization for 44 Languages (2021). http://arxiv.org/abs/2106.13822

Hu, J., et al.: Explicit alignment objectives for multilingual bidirectional encoders (2021). http://arxiv.org/abs/2010.07972

Indian, A., et al.: Decoding emotions: unveiling sentiments and sarcasm through text analysis. In: Pastor-Escuredo, D. et al. (eds.) The Future of Artificial Intelligence and Robotics. pp. 714–731 Springer Nature Switzerland, Cham (2024)

Liu, Y., et al.: RoBERTa: a robustly optimized BERT pretraining approach (2019). http://arxiv.org/abs/1907.11692

Liu, Y., Lapata, M.: Text summarization with pretrained encoders (2019). http://arxiv.org/abs/1908.08345

Loshchilov, I., Hutter, F.: Decoupled weight decay regularization. In: International Conference on Learning Representations (ICLR) (2019)

Mohawesh, R., et al.: Multilingual deep learning framework for fake news detection using capsule neural network. J. Intell. Inf. Syst. **60**(3), 655–671 (2023)

Mohawesh, R., et al.: Semantic graph based topic modelling framework for multilingual fake news detection. AI Open. **4**, 33–41 (2023). https://doi.org/10.1016/j.aiopen.2023.08.004

Nasser, M., et al.: A systematic review of multimodal fake news detection on social media using deep learning models. Results Eng. **26**, 104752 (2025)

Olan, F., et al.: Fake news on social media: the impact on society. Inf. Syst. Front. **26**(2), 443–458 (2024). https://doi.org/10.1007/s10796-022-10242-z

Pan, S.J., Yang, Q.: A survey on transfer learning. IEEE Trans. Knowl. Data Eng. **22**(10), 1345–1359 (2010). https://doi.org/10.1109/TKDE.2009.191

Raza, S., Ding, C.: Fake news detection based on news content and social contexts: a transformer-based approach. Int. J. Data Sci. Anal. **13**(4), 335–362 (2022)

Reimers, N., Gurevych, I.: Sentence-BERT: Sentence Embeddings using Siamese BERT-Networks (2019). http://arxiv.org/abs/1908.10084

Rout, J., et al.: Towards reliable fake news detection: enhanced attention-based transformer model. JCP. **5**(3), 43 (2025). https://doi.org/10.3390/jcp5030043

Saadi, A., et al.: Enhancing fake news detection with transformer models and summarization. Eng. Technol. Appl. Sci. Res. **15**(3), 23253–23259 (2025)

Shu, K., et al.: Fake news detection on social media: a data mining perspective. SIGKDD Explor. Newsl. **19**(1), 22–36 (2017). https://doi.org/10.1145/3137597.3137600

Sivanaiah, R., et al.: Fake News Detection in Low-Resource Languages. In: Kumar, M.A., et al. (eds.) Speech and Language Technologies for Low-Resource Languages. LNCS, vol. 13764, pp. 324–331. Springer, Cham (2023)

Song, C., et al.: Dynamic graph neural network for fake news detection. Neurocomputing **505**, 362–374 (2022). https://doi.org/10.1016/j.neucom.2022.07.057

Sood, S., et al.: Analysis of Extractive Text Summarisation Techniques for Multilingual Texts. In: 2023 International Conference on Advances in Computing. Communication and Applied Informatics (ACCAI), pp. 1–8. IEEE, Chennai, India (2023)

Spärck Jones, K.: A statistical interpretation of term specificity and its application in retrieval. J. Documentation. **28**(1), 11–21 (1972). https://doi.org/10.1108/eb026526

Vaswani, A., et al.: Attention Is All You Need (2017). https://arxiv.org/abs/1706.03762. Wang, Z. et al.: Cross-lingual Text Classification with Heterogeneous Graph Neural Network (2021). http://arxiv.org/abs/2105.11246

# Convolutional Neural Network-Based Binary Classification of Real vs AI-Synthesised Images

Raj Kumar Sharma(✉), Laxmi Gupta, and Himani Pandey

Guru Gobind Singh Indraprastha University, New Delhi 110075, India
profrksharma07@gmail.com

**Abstract.** Artificial intelligence is improving very quickly, and now it can make very real-looking fake images using Generative Adversarial Networks (GANs), posing challenges in distinguishing fake and authentic images. This study aims to address the critical issue of fake image detection by developing and evaluating convolutional neural network (CNN) models capable of classifying AI-generated and real images. Three CNN architectures (CNN1, CNN2, and CNN3) were trained and tested on datasets comprising both real and AI-generated images at two different resolutions: $100 \times 100 \times 3$ and $200 \times 200 \times 3$. The experimental results show that CNN2 achieved the highest performance at $100 \times 100 \times 3$ resolution with an accuracy of 98.67%, R2 score of 0.9467, precision of 0.9740, recall of 1.0000, F1 score of 0.9868, and AUC of 0.9900, demonstrating excellent discriminative capability. CNN1 also showed robust performance across both resolutions, maintaining accuracy above 96%, while CNN3 performed significantly lower, particularly at $200 \times 200 \times 3$ resolution, where accuracy dropped to 51.33% and AUC to 0.7500. The findings highlight the effectiveness of CNN-based approaches in classifying AI-generated images and suggest that model architecture and input resolution play a crucial role in achieving high detection accuracy. This research lays the groundwork for developing reliable tools to combat the spread of synthetic media and ensure the authenticity of visual content.

**Keywords:** Fake image detection · AI-generated images · CNN · Deep learning · Image forensics

## 1 Introduction

Images are now shared so often on social media, news websites, and other online platforms that many people worry about whether they are genuine or not. With the rise of new AI and image editing tools, it has become increasingly hard to tell real pictures from those created or altered by AI [1]. This issue extends beyond media to sectors like law and security, where manipulated images can mislead or harm individuals and institutions. As such, developing systems that authenticate and classify images is crucial for ensuring trust and transparency in a digitised world, and using deep learning models to detect synthetic content can help the public engage with digital media more critically, preserving the integrity of visual information. Today, with the advancement of AI and


A. Shastri et al. (Eds.): IHCI 2025, LNCS 16437, pp. 425–436, 2026.
https://doi.org/10.1007/978-3-032-26352-0_35

tools like Generative Adversarial Networks (GANs), the creation of synthetic media has become even easier, posing new challenges in combating misinformation and preserving trust in digital content [2].

Table 1 presents the World Cybercrime Index (WCI) Rankings by Country [19], showcasing the ranking of various nations based on their respective WCI scores. The WCI is a measure that assesses the intensity and frequency of conflicts within a country. At the top of the list is "Russia with the highest score of 58.39, followed by Ukraine (36.44) and China (27.86)". Other countries listed include the United States, Nigeria, and Romania, with scores progressively decreasing down to India, which holds the 10th spot with a score of 6.13. The data reflects the varying degrees of conflict within these countries, offering insights into global geopolitical tensions.

**Table 1.** World Cybercrime Index (WCI) Rankings by Country.

| Place | Nation | WCI Score |
|---|---|---|
| I | Russia | 58.39 |
| II | Ukraine | 36.44 |
| III | China | 27.86 |
| IV | United States | 25.01 |
| V | Nigeria | 21.28 |
| VI | Romania | 14.83 |
| VII | North Korea | 10.61 |
| VIII | United Kingdom | 9.01 |
| IX | Brazil | 8.93 |
| X | India | 6.13 |

To solve the problem of distinguishing real images from AI-generated ones [17], a CNN model can be developed, which would be used to classify the images into two categories: real or fake. The CNN would be trained on a labelled dataset containing both "real and AI-generated" images. This approach, while simple, can yield accurate results and be computationally efficient enough for practical use [4].

## 2 Literature Review

The study [5] proposes using a CNN to classify Real or Fake images. After tuning hyperparameters and training 36 different network architectures, the best-performing model achieved an impressive classification accuracy of 92.98%. The study [11] conducted by the authors examined computer vision features in digital content to assess its integrity. Their approach utilised fuzzy clustering for feature extraction from image frames. This technique reportedly enhanced detection accuracy, achieving a rate of 98% across multiple datasets.

In the paper [13], the authors propose an innovative deep learning approach for detecting manipulated images. Their system identifies whether an image has been morphed and displays the result accordingly. The method combines two primary techniques: deep learning through CNNs and Error Level Analysis (ELA). ELA is a forensic tool used to detect regions within an image that exhibit varying levels of compression. The information derived from ELA is then input into a CNN architecture, which comprises multiple fully connected convolutional layers. The CNN processes each pixel of the image data to assess its authenticity. The authors [14] present a morphing attack detection method using a deep learning-based feature extractor and classifier, enhanced by image processing and feature fusion. This paper [15] traces the origins of fake news back to ancient times, citing examples like Ramesses the Great's portrayal of the Battle of Kadesh. It discusses the proliferation of fake news during the war. This comprehensive survey [16] discusses the progression from early image editing tools to advanced deepfake technologies, highlighting the role of GANs in creating highly realistic unreal media. This research [6] introduces a technique for identifying fake images through a detection system developed using CNN-based models. The results from testing reveal that the system consistently achieves an average accuracy above 95%, highlighting its potential for practical, real-world use.

The author [3] presents a face morphing attack detection method using datasets (StyleGAN & AMSL). A custom CNN-based model is used to classify real and morphed images. The study [7] looks at the problem of telling apart "real & AI-generated images" using CNN models. Using the CIFAKE dataset, which contains both real and fake images, the authors tested three pre-trained models. DenseNet121 gave the best results with 98.49% accuracy on the test set.

The research [9] focuses on spotting "fake images made by AI using the CIFAKE dataset. After testing, MobileNet showed the best results with 90.10% accuracy in detecting fake images". The paper [18] presents a CNN-based method to solve a key problem in image forensics. Instead of using pre-trained networks or building from scratch, the authors designed a new model with two stacked convolutional layers at the start.

The network works with different image sizes while keeping its depth and structure fixed. While existing studies have shown promising results in distinguishing AI-generated images from real ones using CNN architectures, several research gaps remain. Most current approaches rely on fixed input image sizes. This restriction raises concerns about the generalizability of these models to images of varying resolutions encountered in real-world scenarios. Few studies have systematically evaluated the trade-offs between smaller input sizes, which reduce computational cost, and larger sizes, which may preserve critical forensic details. Addressing these gaps, the proposed research aims to develop a CNN-based model for AI-generated image detection that incorporates optimisation strategies such as varying input image resolutions. This approach will help identify the optimal configuration for balancing accuracy, computational efficiency, and robustness against sophisticated image generation techniques.

# 3 Methodology

Figure 1 illustrates the step-by-step workflow of the proposed methodology to detect real and fake images. Initially, a dataset of images is collected from Google repositories, containing two categories: AI-generated and real images. These images are then pre-processed by converting them into a computationally usable format, normalising pixel values, and splitting the dataset into "training, validation, and testing" sets. To investigate the impact of input resolution, two separate datasets are created with different image sizes: $100 \times 100 \times 3$ and $200 \times 200 \times 3$. Three CNN architectures are developed and trained on these datasets. CNN Model 1 applies a single 2D convolution layer with 32 filters ($3 \times 3$ kernel, ReLU activation) followed by a $2 \times 2$ max pooling layer. CNN Model 2 employs two convolutional layers with 32 and 64 filters, respectively, both using $3 \times 3$ kernels and ReLU activation. Each convolutional layer is followed by a $2 \times 2$ max pooling layer. The CNN Model 3 extends this by incorporating three convolutional layers with 32, 64, and 128 filters, all with $3 \times 3$ kernels, ReLU activation, and $2 \times 2$ max pooling applied after each layer. Finally, the models are evaluated using performance to analyse and compare model performance across different architectures and input image sizes.

## 3.1 Preprocessing

The dataset preprocessing step involves loading and preparing the images for training and validation using "TensorFlow's ImageDataGenerator". To prepare the data, two objects are created for training and validation, each with pixel value normalised (see Eq. 1), pixel intensities to the [0, 1] range.

$$x' = \frac{x - \min(x)}{\max(x) - \min(x)} \tag{1}$$

## 3.2 CNN Model

The proposed CNN model is designed using TensorFlow's Sequential API to classify images into two categories: AI-generated and real. The architecture begins with three convolutional blocks for feature extraction. The first block consists of a Conv2D layer (see Eq. 2) with 32 filters of size $3 \times 3$ and a ReLU (see Eq. 3) activation function, followed by a $2 \times 2$ max pooling layer (see Eq. 4). The second block uses 64 filters with the same kernel size and activation function, again paired with a $2 \times 2$ max pooling layer. The third block further increases the filter count to 128, maintaining the $3 \times 3$ kernel and ReLU activation, followed by max pooling. After these convolutional layers, a Flatten layer converts the multi-dimensional feature maps into a 1D vector. This vector is passed through a fully connected Dense layer with 512 neurons and ReLU activation to learn complex patterns. Finally, the output layer uses a single neuron with a sigmoid activation (see Eq. 5) function to perform binary classification [12] (Fig. 2).

$$Conv2D_{output} = \left[\frac{N - F + 2P}{S}\right] + 1 \tag{2}$$

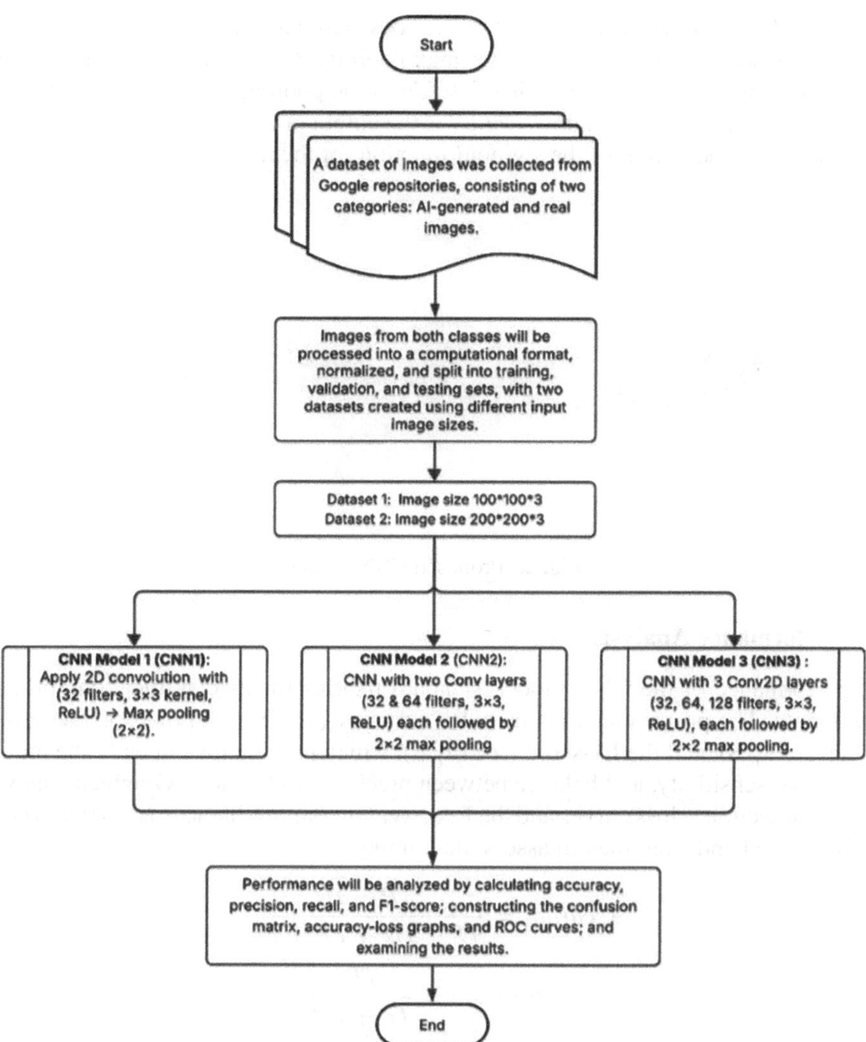


**Fig. 1.** Workflow of the proposed CNN-based AI-generated image detection.

$$ReLU_x = \max(0, x) \tag{3}$$

$$Pool_{i,j,k} = max_{(m,n)\in R} Z_{(i.s+m,j.S+n,k)} \tag{4}$$

$$Sigmoid_z = \frac{1}{1+e^{-z}} \tag{5}$$

where x is the input value, N is the Input size (height or width of the input image or feature map), F is the Filter size (kernel size of 3x3), P is the padding (number of pixels added around the border of the input), S is the stride (number of pixels the filter moves at each step), $Conv2D_{output}$ is the output of the convolutional layer. $Pool_{i,j,k}$ is the output value at position (i, j) in channel k after max pooling, Z is the input feature map, R is the pooling window of size p*p, S is the stride of the pooling operation, and (m, n) are indices within the pooling window. $ReLU_x$ is the output of the ReLU activation function and $Sigmoid_z$ is the output of the sigmoid function for the input value z.

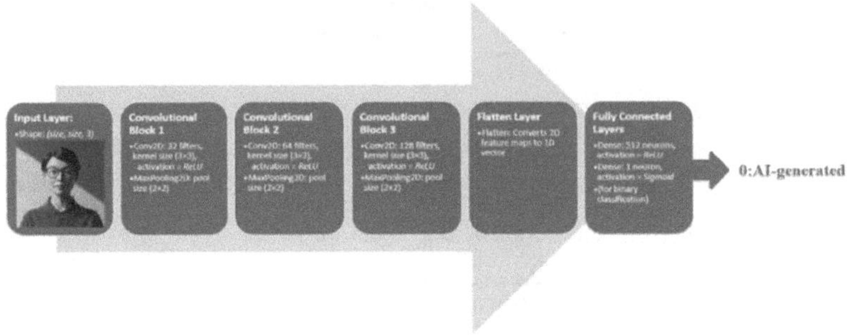


**Fig. 2.** Proposed CNN model.

### 3.3 Performance Analysis

The performance of the CNN model, standard metrics for its classification ability on unseen data. The primary metrics include "accuracy (see Eq. 6), precision (see Eq. 7), recall (see Eq. 8), and the F1-score (see Eq. 9), which provide insights into the model's correctness, sensitivity, and balance between precision and recall". Graphical analyses, such as the accuracy-loss curves and the Receiver Operating Characteristic (ROC) curve, will be created and examined to assess the training.

$$Accuracy = \frac{TP + TN}{TP + TN + FP + FN} \tag{6}$$

$$Precision = \frac{TP}{TP + FP} \tag{7}$$

$$Recall = \frac{TP}{TP + FN} \tag{8}$$

$$F1\_Score = 2 \cdot \frac{Precision \cdot Recall}{Precision + Recall} \tag{9}$$

where "TP, TN, FP, and FN are true positive, true negative, false positive and false negative", respectively [8].

## 4 Results

Figure 3 shows that CNN1 and CNN2 both exhibit steadily increasing training and validation accuracy, with CNN1 stabilising above 90% after around 60 epochs and CNN2 pushing even higher toward ~99%, demonstrating strong convergence and generalisation with only minor fluctuations. In contrast, CNN3 shows erratic training behavior and a stagnant validation curve around 70–75%, marked by large oscillations that suggest overfitting or insufficient model capacity. Overall, CNN2 delivers the best performance, CNN1 is a close runner-up, and CNN3 requires further tuning or redesign to achieve comparable results.

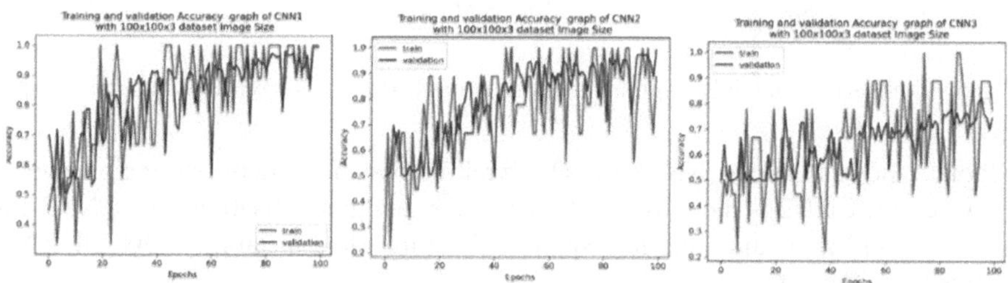


**Fig. 3.** Training vs. Validation Accuracy Across Epochs for CNN1–CNN3 (Image Size: 100 × 100 × 3).

Figure 4 shows that the training and validation accuracy on the 200 × 200 × 3 dataset, CNN1 and CNN2 both achieve high accuracy (close to 1.0) with some fluctuation but good alignment between train and validation, indicating strong generalisation. CNN3, however, shows unstable training and lower, flat validation accuracy (around 0.6), suggesting poor learning and generalisation. Overall, CNN1 and CNN2 perform well, with CNN3 lagging.

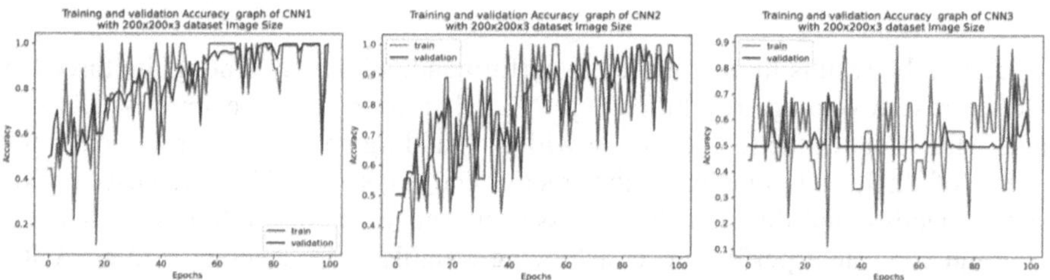


**Fig. 4.** Accuracy Comparison of CNN Models on 200x200x3 Training and Validation Datasets.

Figure 5 shows that CNN1 shows a smooth and consistent decline in both training and validation loss, indicating good convergence and generalisation. CNN2 performs decently but displays noticeable fluctuations, especially in validation loss, suggesting minor instability. CNN3 has the lowest overall loss range but shows frequent spikes in both losses, pointing to inconsistent training. Overall, CNN1 performs the most reliably.

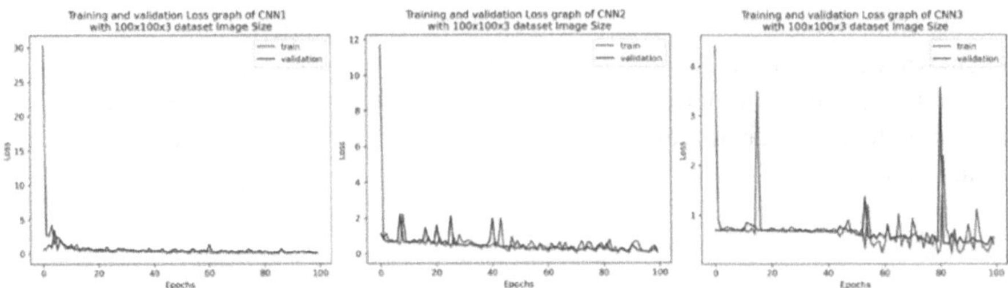


**Fig. 5.** Comparison of CNN Training and Validation Losses on 100x100x3 Image Dataset.

Table 2 shows that the CNN1 shows high initial loss and mild overfitting but eventually converges. CNN2 is the most stable with excellent generalisation. The CNN3 converges well but has a validation loss spike, indicating some instability. Overall, CNN2 performs best (Fig. 6).

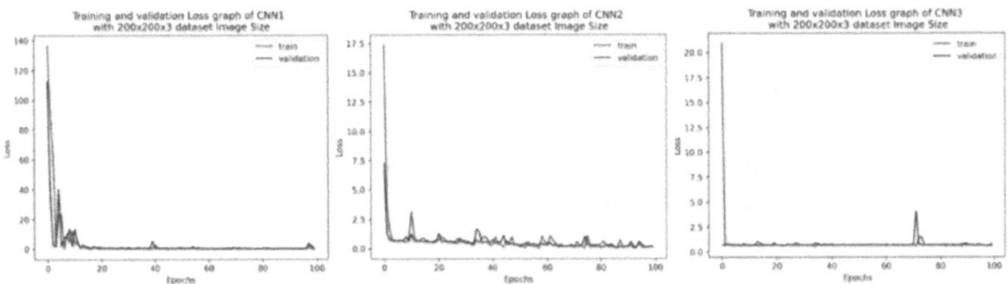


**Fig. 6.** Comparison of CNN Training and Validation Losses on 200x200x3 Image Dataset.

Overall, the results highlight a clear performance hierarchy among the three CNN models across two image resolutions. CNN2, when trained on the smaller 100 × 100 images, stands out as the top performer with outstanding metrics, accuracy nearly 99%, an AUC of 0.99, and solid precision, recall, and F1 scores. This suggests it excels at both detecting and distinguishing classes at that resolution. CNN1 also delivers a strong and consistent performance, achieving roughly 97% accuracy and an AUC of 0.97 for both image sizes, illustrating its robustness and reliability. On the other hand, CNN3 shows markedly weaker results, particularly on the larger 200 × 200 images, where accuracy plunges to around 51% and AUC falls to 0.75, indicating frequent misclassifications and poor discrimination. Even at the smaller image size (100 × 100), CNN3 only manages about 84% accuracy and an AUC of 0.84, which, while better, still trails behind the other models. In summary, CNN2 is the top choice for high accuracy and discriminative power at the smaller image resolution; CNN1 is a dependable second best across both resolutions; and CNN3 is unsuitable for reliable performance, especially as image complexity increases.

**Table 2.** Performance Comparison of CNN Architectures Across Image Resolutions.

| Model | Image Size | Accuracy | $R^2$ Score | Precision | Recall | F1 Score | AUC |
|---|---|---|---|---|---|---|---|
| CNN1 | 100x100x3 | 0.967 | 0.8667 | 0.9375 | 1.0000 | 0.9677 | 0.9700 |
| CNN2 | 100x100x3 | 0.9867 | 0.9467 | 0.9740 | 1.0000 | 0.9868 | 0.9900 |
| CNN3 | 100x100x3 | 0.8400 | 0.3600 | 0.8493 | 0.8267 | 0.8378 | 0.8400 |
| CNN1 | 200x200x3 | 0.9733 | 0.8933 | 0.9733 | 0.9733 | 0.9733 | 0.9700 |
| CNN2 | 200x200x3 | 0.8800 | 0.5200 | 0.8065 | 1.0000 | 0.8929 | 0.9000 |
| CNN3 | 200x200x3 | 0.5133 | -0.9467 | 0.5068 | 1.0000 | 0.6726 | 0.7500 |

# 5 Discussion

## 5.1 Training and Validation Accuracy and Loss

CNN2 with 100 × 100 × 3 input shows superior training performance, with training accuracy rising smoothly to ~ 99% and validation accuracy closely tracking it. The minimal gap between the two curves and slight validation fluctuations, strong generalisation and negligible overfitting, confirming CNN2's robustness on unseen data. Similarly, CNN2 with 100 × 100 × 3 input exhibits superior training behaviour in the loss graphs as well, with a rapid decline in both training and validation losses that stabilise near zero.

## 5.2 Testing Results

The results demonstrate how model architecture and image resolution impact the performance of convolutional neural networks (CNNs). CNN2 emerged as the best-performing model at the smaller resolution of 100 × 100 × 3, achieving an impressive accuracy of 98.67%, an AUC of 0.99, and near-perfect recall. CNN1 also performed consistently well, with accuracy and AUC values around 97% at both 100 × 100 × 3 and 200 × 200 × 3 resolutions. Its stable performance across resolutions suggests that CNN1 is robust to changes in input size and could be preferred in scenarios where input resolution might vary. This robustness highlights its adaptability and reliable feature extraction capability. The CNN3 showed significantly lower performance, particularly at the higher resolution of 200 × 200 × 3, where its accuracy dropped to approximately 51%, and the AUC fell to 0.75. This indicates that CNN3 struggles to generalise and possibly overfits or underfits with larger and more complex input data. Even at 100 × 100 × 3, CNN3's accuracy of 84% and AUC of 0.84 were noticeably behind the other models, reflecting its architectural limitations.

## 5.3 ROC Curve

Figure 7 shows that the ROC curves show that CNN2 achieves the highest performance with an AUC of 0.99, indicating excellent classification capability. CNN1 also performs very well with an AUC of 0.97, suggesting strong predictive power. CNN3, with an AUC of 0.84, shows comparatively lower performance and weaker class separation. Overall, CNN2 demonstrates the best classification accuracy on the 100x100x3 testing dataset.

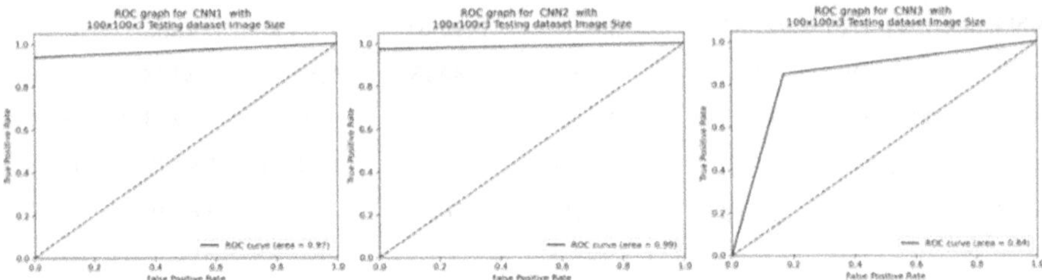


**Fig. 7.** ROC Curve Comparison of CNN Models on 100x100x3 Testing Image Dataset.

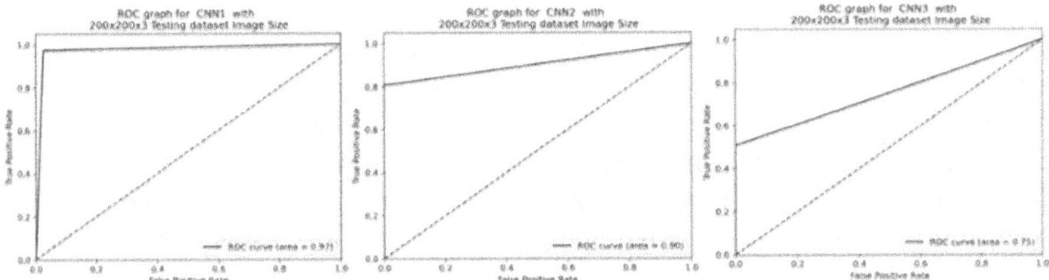


**Fig. 8.** ROC Curve Comparison of CNN Models on 200x200x3 Testing Image Dataset.

The ROC curves illustrate the comparative performance of CNN1, CNN2, and CNN3 across $100 \times 100 \times 3$ and $200 \times 200 \times 3$ input sizes (see Fig. 8). Among these, CNN2 with $100 \times 100 \times 3$ input achieves the highest AUC (0.99), indicating excellent discrimination capability between classes and confirming its superior predictive power. CNN1 also performs robustly at both resolutions, with AUC values of 0.97, showing consistent and reliable classification performance. In contrast, CNN3 lags notably behind, particularly at $200 \times 200 \times 3$, where its AUC drops to 0.75, suggesting poor generalisation and limited predictive accuracy. These findings reinforce earlier observations from accuracy and loss metrics, highlighting CNN2 with $100 \times 100 \times 3$ input as the most effective configuration due to its near-perfect ROC curve alignment to the top-left corner, indicative of minimal false positives and false negatives [10].

## 6 Conclusion

In this study on CNN-based classification of "Real vs Fake" images, the training and validation accuracy and loss graphs indicate that CNN2 with $100 \times 100 \times 3$ input outperforms other configurations, with training accuracy rising smoothly to nearly 99% and validation accuracy closely tracking it. The minimal gap between these curves and the rapid decline of both training and validation losses to near zero demonstrate effective learning and strong generalisation. The testing results further validate CNN2's superiority, achieving the highest accuracy (98.67%), $R^2$ score (0.9467), and AUC (0.99), along with perfect recall, confirming its robustness in distinguishing real images from AI-synthesised ones. CNN1 also shows reliable performance across resolutions (100 × 100 × 3 and 200 × 200 × 3), making it a strong alternative. Finally, the ROC analysis reinforces these findings, as CNN2's near-perfect curve at 100 × 100 × 3 resolution demonstrates excellent discriminative capability, positioning it as the most effective model configuration for the classification of "real versus AI-generated" images.

## 7 Future Scope

The future scope of this study involves several promising directions to enhance the performance and applicability of CNN models for image classification tasks. Firstly, further optimisation of CNN2 and CNN1 architectures using techniques such as "transfer learning, data augmentation, and fine-tuning hyperparameters" could potentially improve their accuracy and generalisation on larger and more diverse datasets. Incorporating ensemble methods by combining predictions from multiple CNN architectures may also increase robustness and reduce misclassification rates. Exploring lightweight CNN architectures such as MobileNet or EfficientNet could make deployment feasible on resource-constrained devices like smartphones or embedded systems. Moreover, integrating explainable AI (XAI) techniques would help interpret the decision-making process of CNNs, improving transparency and trust in critical applications. Finally, expanding the work to include multi-class classification scenarios and evaluating performance with real-time streaming data would align the models with practical, real-world requirements.

**Acknowledgment.** The authors sincerely thank Guru Gobind Singh Indraprastha University (GGSIPU) for providing the necessary resources and infrastructure to bring out this research. Special appreciation to the faculty members for their encouragement throughout this work.

**Conflict of Interest.** All analyses, results, and interpretations have been conducted independently without any external influence or bias. No funding from commercial or private organizations with vested interests was received, and there are no affiliations or associations that might pose a conflict of interest. This declaration ensures the objectivity and integrity of the research presented.

## References

1. Zhang, Y., Pang, Z., Huang, S., Wang, C., Zhou, X.: Unmasking AI-Created Visual Content: A Review of Generated Images and Deepfake Detection Technologies (2025)
2. Zou, Y., et al.: Survey on ai-generated media detection: from non-mllm to mllm (2025). arXiv preprint arXiv:2502.05240
3. Namis, E.M., Shaker, K., Al-Janabi, S.: Approach for detecting face morphing attacks using convolution neural network. Mesopotamian J. Comput. Sci. **2025**, 83–91 (2025)

4. Ahmed, N.U.R., Badshah, A., Adeel, H., Tajammul, A., Duad, A., Alsahfi, T.: Visual deepfake detection: Review of techniques, tools, limitations, and future prospects. IEEE Access (2024)
5. Bird, J.J., Lotfi, A.: Cifake: Image classification and explainable identification of AI-generated synthetic images. IEEE Access **12**, 15642–15650 (2024)
6. Truong, P.H., Nguyen, T.D., Truong, X.H., Nguyen, N.H., Pham, D.T.: Employing a CNN detector to identify AI-Generated images and against attacks on AI systems. In: 2024 1st International Conference On Cryptography And Information Security (VCRIS) (pp. 1–6). IEEE (2024)
7. Nayim, M., Mohan, V., Pandey, T.N., Dash, B.B., Dash, B.B., Patra, S.S.: Detection of leading CNN models for AI image accuracy and efficiency. In: 2024 International Conference on Intelligent Algorithms for Computational Intelligence Systems (IACIS) (pp. 1–7). IEEE (2024)
8. Sharma, R.K., Sangeeta: Fractured bone diagnostics using optimised convolutional neural network model with variable learning rates. In: International Conference on ICT for Digital, Smart, and Sustainable Development (pp. 215–228). Singapore, Springer Nature Singapore (2024)
9. Silkan, H., Hanyf, Y.: AI-Generated fake image detection using pre-trained CNN models. Artif. Intell. Pract. Appl. Digital Econ. 207 (2024)
10. Sharma, R.K., Mogha, N., Saini, M., Kumar, A.: Garbage bin status indicator based on multilayer convolutional neural networks. In: Proceedings of the KILBY 100 7th International Conference on Computing Sciences (2023)
11. Saravana Ram, R., Vinoth Kumar, M., Al-shami, T.M., Masud, M., Aljuaid, H., Abouhawwash, M.: Deep Fake detection using computer vision-based deep neural network with pairwise learning. Intell. Autom. Soft Comput. **35**(2) (2023)
12. Sharma, R.K., Jailia, M.: IoT based smart bin system using multilayer neural network classifier for smart cities. Recent Adv. Sci. Eng. Inf. Technol. Manage. **2782**(1), 020019 (2023)
13. Kotti, D.J., Gouthami, D.E., Swapna, D.K., Vesalapu, S.: Morphed image detection using ELA and CNN techniques. J. Pharm. Negative Results **13** (2022)
14. Hamza, M., Tehsin, S., Karamti, H., Alghamdi, N.S.: Generation and detection of face morphing attacks. IEEE Access **10**, 72557–72576 (2022)
15. Botha, J., Pieterse, H.: Fake news and deepfakes: a dangerous threat for 21st century information security. In: ICCWS 2020 15th International Conference on Cyber Warfare and Security. Academic Conferences and publishing limited (p. 57) (2020)
16. Tolosana, R., Vera-Rodriguez, R., Fierrez, J., Morales, A., Ortega-Garcia, J.: Deepfakes and beyond: a survey of face manipulation and fake detection. Inf. Fusion **64**, 131–148 (2020)
17. Neves, J.C., Tolosana, R., Vera-Rodriguez, R., Lopes, V., Proença, H., Fierrez, J.: Ganprintr: improved fakes and evaluation of the state of the art in face manipulation detection. IEEE J. Sel. Top. Signal Process. **14**(5), 1038–1048 (2020)
18. Quan, W., Wang, K., Yan, D.M., Zhang, X.: Distinguishing between natural and computer-generated images using convolutional neural networks. IEEE Trans. Inf. Forensics Secur. **13**(11), 2772–2787 (2018)
19. https://www.ox.ac.uk/news/2024-04-10-world-first-cybercrime-index-ranks-countries-cybercrime-threat-level

# Benchmarking YOLO Models for Hand Detection in Time-of-Flight Infrared Imagery

Ashish Saini[1,2](✉), Anshuman Rath[1], and Sumeet Saurav[1,2]

[1] CSIR-Central Electronics Engineering Research Institute (CSIR-CEERI), Pilani 333031, Rajasthan, India
ashish.ceeri23a@acsir.res.in , sumeet.ceeri@csir.res.in
[2] Academy of Scientific and Innovative Research (AcSIR), Ghaziabad 201002, India

**Abstract.** Hand detection in infrared imagery presents unique challenges that traditional RGB-trained models cannot adequately address. This paper presents a comprehensive comparison of different YOLO (You Only Look Once) model variants for hand detection using Time-of-Flight (ToF) infrared amplitude data. We evaluate the performance limitations of conventional RGB-based detection frameworks, such as MediaPipe, and propose an enhanced dataset collection methodology. Through a two-phase dataset development approach, we expanded from an initial 5,310 manually annotated images to 22,911 images using semi-automatic labelling techniques. Our experimental evaluation compares YOLOv8, YOLOv9, YOLOv10, YOLOv11, and YOLOv12 architectures on infrared hand detection tasks. Results demonstrate significant performance improvements over traditional RGB-based methods. The findings contribute to advancing computer vision applications in infrared domains, particularly for Sign language analysis, gesture recognition and human-computer interaction systems.

**Keywords:** Hand detection · Time-of-Flight · YOLO · Infrared image · Computer vision

## 1 Introduction

Hand detection and gesture recognition have become fundamental components of modern human-computer interaction (HCI) systems and human-robot interaction (HRI) systems enabling intuitive and natural interfaces across various applications including virtual reality, augmented reality, robotics, and assistive technologies [1,5]. While RGB-based hand detection systems have achieved remarkable success in controlled environments, they face significant limitations in scenarios involving varying illumination conditions, and environmental constraints.

Time-of-Flight (ToF) infrared imaging offers a promising alternative by providing depth and amplitude information that remains invariant to ambient lighting conditions. Unlike conventional RGB cameras, ToF sensors measure the time


A. Shastri et al. (Eds.): IHCI 2025, LNCS 16437, pp. 437–449, 2026.
https://doi.org/10.1007/978-3-032-26352-0_36

taken for emitted infrared light to reflect back from objects, generating both depth maps and amplitude data. This characteristic makes ToF imaging particularly suitable for applications requiring robust performance in challenging lighting conditions, including complete darkness or extreme brightness.

Despite these advantages, hand detection in infrared imagery presents unique challenges. The domain shift between RGB and infrared data renders most pre-trained computer vision models ineffective, as they are predominantly trained on large-scale RGB datasets such as ImageNet [4] or COCO [8]. Popular frameworks like MediaPipe [17], while highly effective for RGB-based hand detection, fail to generalize on infrared domains due to fundamental differences in image characteristics, texture patterns, and spectral properties.

This research addresses the critical gap in infrared-based hand detection by systematically evaluating state-of-the-art YOLO [11] architectures on ToF amplitude data. Our work is motivated by three key objectives: (1) establishing a comprehensive benchmark for hand detection in infrared imagery, (2) investigating the adaptability of modern object detection architectures to single-channel infrared data, and (3) providing insights for developing robust HCI systems that can operate across diverse environmental conditions.

## 2 Literature Review

Hand gesture recognition has been an active area of research in computer vision for several decades, with applications ranging from sign language interpretation to human-computer interaction. Traditional approaches can be broadly categorized into vision-based and sensor-based methods. Vision-based methods rely on camera systems to capture hand movements, while sensor-based approaches utilize specialized hardware, such as data gloves or wearable devices. Vision-based methods are generally preferred due to their non-intrusive nature and lower cost.

The majority of hand detection and gesture recognition research has focused on RGB cameras. Deep learning methods, particularly Convolutional Neural Networks (CNNs), have achieved remarkable success in this domain. MediaPipe, developed by Google, represents one of the most widely adopted frameworks for real-time hand tracking on RGB images. It employs a multi-stage pipeline that first detects hand regions and then estimates 21 3D hand landmarks with high accuracy. Recent hand perception systems rely heavily on RGB-based detectors and trackers, spanning one-stage detectors (YOLO variants), two-stage RPN models, keypoint pipelines and segmentation backbones, with extensive benchmarking on public RGB datasets that emphasize either egocentric or exocentric views, hand-object interactions, or whole-body annotations. YOLO-based pipelines have been adopted from YOLOv2/v3 to YOLOv8 for left/right hand detection, egocentric manipulation, and multi-view industrial HRI, often paired with keypoint extractors (OpenPose, MediaPipe) for downstream gesture analysis and intent prediction in real time. Two-stage models (Faster/Mask R-CNN) support pixel-level hand masks and multi-task training with object or action labels, while U-Net-like decoders remain strong for hand segmentation under clutter and gloves, highlighting the breadth of RGB-first literature that motivates domain-specific adaptation to infrared sensing.

Prominent RGB-D hand datasets commonly used for detection, segmentation, and tracking in HRI include Oxford-Hand [9] (exocentric bounding boxes), COCO-Hands and COCO-WholeBody (bounding boxes and 42 hand keypoints), Epic Kitchens [3] (large-scale egocentric hand/object boxes), H2O (egocentric RGB-D with 3D hand/object annotations), and MECCANO (egocentric industrial assembly with hands/objects), among others such as EgoHands/Ego2Hands for pixel-level hand masks and industrial HADR/HAGS segmentation corpora. These RGB datasets underpin many state-of-the-art pipelines surveyed for hand detection, segmentation, and tracking in HRI; however, their spectral assumptions limit direct transfer to single-channel infrared, motivating the dedicated ToF-IR dataset and benchmarks presented in this work.

However, RGB-based methods face several inherent limitations. They are highly sensitive to lighting variations, with performance degrading significantly in low-light or high-contrast environments. Despite advances in hand detection and gesture recognition, several gaps remain in the literature. First, there is a notable absence of large-scale, publicly available datasets specifically designed for hand detection and gesture recognition using infrared cameras [10]. Second, most existing studies focus on either RGB or depth data independently, with limited exploration of infrared intensity images. This work addresses these gaps by creating a custom dataset of infrared hand images captured with a ToF camera and developing a specialized hand detection model optimized for this sensing modality. Our approach provides a foundation for future research in touchless control systems that leverage the unique advantages of ToF infrared imaging.

## 3 Dataset Details

In this section, we describe the details of the system we consider for the creation of the dataset.

### 3.1 Data Acquisition and Hardware Setup

All data was captured using a Cube Eye I200 ToF camera [2]. This device operates by emitting infrared light and measuring the phase shift of the reflected signal to calculate depth. For this study, we focus exclusively on the 8-bit, single-channel infrared intensity images, as they provide strong contrast for the hand against most backgrounds and are less susceptible to the multi-path interference artifacts that can affect ToF depth data. The camera was mounted on a stable tripod for all data collection sessions.

### 3.2 Dataset Creation and Annotation

Recognizing the lack of a suitable public dataset, we undertook a two-phase creation process to develop a comprehensive ToF infrared hand gesture dataset.

Figure 1 shows the setup used to capture the infrared images of the participants performing distinct hand signs. The setup includes the ToF camera, a desktop machine, monitor, and green background. Participants were asked to sit in front of the camera and perform hand gestures. The images are recorded and stored in the desktop machine memory.

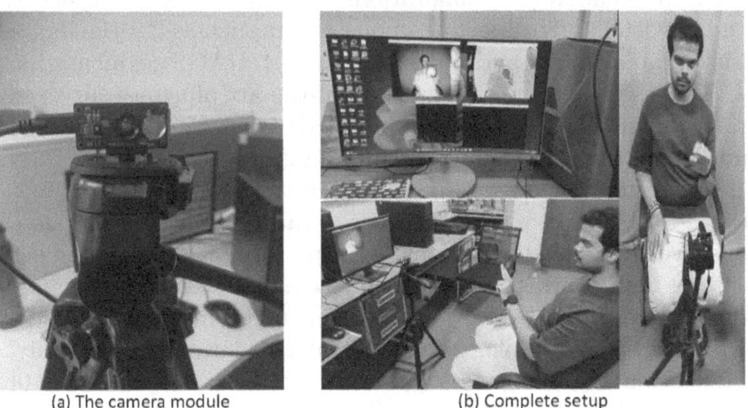


**Fig. 1.** The complete setup for creating the dataset.

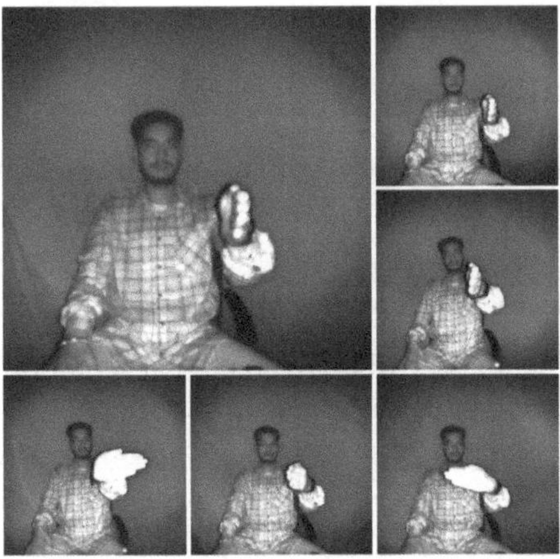

**Fig. 2.** A collection of sample images from our custom dataset.

**3.2.1 Phase 1: Initial Dataset Creation** The initial phase focused on creating a small but diverse dataset to train a baseline model. We collected data from 6 different subjects performing 59 distinct hand signs. For each sign, we captured 15 frames, with a controlled green screen background. This resulted in an initial dataset of 5,310 images. We used the popular LabelImg [14] tool to draw bounding boxes around every hand, treating them all as a single "hand" class and saving the labels in the YOLO format. Annotators were instructed to capture the entire hand, from the fingertips down to the wrist, but to exclude the forearm whenever it was clearly separate. For blurry or partially-hidden images, we made sure the box covered all visible parts of the hand. Figure 2 shows sample hand images from the custom dataset.

**3.2.2 Phase 2: Large-Scale Dataset with Semi-automated Annotation** Manually annotating tens of thousands of images is just a prohibitive bottleneck. So, to scale our efforts, we adopted a semi-automated workflow. First, we used an initial YOLOv11n [7] model, which was trained on 5,310 images, to generate some preliminary bounding box predictions. Then, we had to manually verify and correct each prediction where necessary, using LabelImg. We also manually annotated all thge false negatives (the hands it missed) entries and removed all the false positives entries. As a final step, all the bounding-boxes were adjusted for an optimal fit.

The semi-automated annotation approach dramatically accelerated the annotation process. We then collected an additional 17,601 images from more than 20+ subjects in a controlled green screen background. The trained initial model was used to run inference on these unlabeled images, generating preliminary bounding-box predictions. The human annotator's task then shifted from drawing new boxes to simply verifying and correcting the model's suggestions. The final compiled dataset consists of high-quality annotations for approximately 22,911 images, comprising 18,328 training images and 4,583 test images from 20+ subjects performing 59 distinct hand signs. The key specifications are summarized in Table 1.

**Table 1.** Specifications of the ToF infrared hand dataset. The final dataset combines the initial and large-scale sets for training and evaluation.

| Feature | Initial Dataset | Final Dataset |
|---|---|---|
| Total Images | 5,310 | 22,911 |
| Number of Subjects | 6 | 20+ |
| Number of Hand Signs | 59 | 59 |
| Annotation Method | Manual | Semi-Automated |

# 4 Methodology

## 4.1 Experimental Setup and Training

All experiments were conducted on a workstation equipped with an NVIDIA GeForce RTX 3090 GPU with 24 GB of memory, enabling efficient training of deep learning models. The system utilized CUDA 12.2 for GPU acceleration. The software environment was built on Python version 3.10.18, with all necessary deep learning libraries and dependencies installed.

## 4.2 Overview of YOLO Model

YOLO, introduced by Redmon et al. [12], is a framework that considers the entire detection a regression problem to predict the bounding box coordinates. The model directly predicts bounding box coordinates, confidence scores (objectness) and class probabilities.

**4.2.1 Basic Architectural Overview** YOLO models usually consist of the following 3 parts:

1. **Backbone:** It represents feature extractors in the context that it basically detects the edges, textures, semantic structures and patterns. It switched from having custom Darknet architectures earlier to CSP-based Darknet variants and NAS-selected backbones which trade representational power vs FLOPs/latency.
2. **Neck:** It is an optional module that connects the Backbone to the Heads which basically perform cross-scale feature aggregation in order to efficiently tackle and detect even small objects with lower resolution. It leverages Feature Pyramid Network (FPN) and Path Aggregation Network (PAN) to combine features from multiple layers (high level + low level) for local and global semantic feature understanding.
3. **Heads:** It is the final predictor which gives the output as: bounding box coordinates, objectness (confidence) and class probabilities. It also contains anchor boxes which are essentially templates of various shapes in order to capture objects of different shapes and sizes and properly fit them into the bounding boxes.

**4.2.2 YOLOv8** [6] is a model introduced by Ultralytics in 2023, it offers anchor-free split Ultralytics head along with fairly optimized Neck and Backbone architecture. It leverages the SPPF (Spatial Pyramid Pooling Fast) in order to divide the image into grid and pool features from each grid cell in order to tackle the size variations in different images. The novelty introduced in YOLOv8 includes an anchor-free head to not rely on predefined anchors and starting from center, regresses on all directions to find bounding box coordinates. It also includes decoupled head which basically separates the anchor-free regressor head, which predicts bounding box coordinates, and the classifier head, which then predicts the object class of given bounded object.

**4.2.3 YOLOv9** [16] is a significant step forward in the direction of real time object detection, which showcased a lot of unique novelty discussed below which revolutionized the YOLO object detection framework and very efficiently handled the inference speed-accuracy tradeoff. It significantly improves the model's learning capacity and retention of crucial information.

1. **Programmable Gradient Information (PGI):** It is a mechanism that acts like a supervised information pathway providing the most reliable gradient path directly from output back to the shallow layers bypassing the uncertain and possibly lossy gradient passing neural paths. It adequately counters the information loss caused by data propagation through progressive layers of deep neural networks.
2. **Generalized Efficient Layer Aggregation Network (GELAN):** It is the de-facto neck and backbone of YOLOv9, it has evolved from previously known CSPNet and ELA. GELAN allows programmable connectivity between layers and multi-path feature aggregation which can benefit greatly from the division of data into groups, apply group convolutions and channel shuffling to reduce parameters for efficient fusion.

**4.2.4 YOLOv10** [15] developed by researchers at Tsinghua University specifically addresses the shortcomings of the previous versions and delves into the territory of non-NMS architecture. The novelty of this version includes non-NMS dual assignment heads which includes one-to-many head to generate multiple predictions per object during training, providing hard discrimination for better learning and one-to-one head to return the best prediction per training object to compensate for NMS all while reducing training latency. It also has a holistic model design which is the optimization within spatial-channel decoupled downsampling and rank-guided block design with large kernel convolutions and partial self-attention modules make this model lightweight whilst still retain high predictive strength.

**4.2.5 YOLOv11** [7] is a cutting-edge real-time object detection network whose innovation lies largely in its optimization of YOLOv10 and other previous variants, which briefly are:

1. **C3k2 Block Inclusion:** Replaces the previously used C2f block with the C3k2 block as part of the neck and backbone architecture which uses smaller kernels or split convolutions, to reduce the FLOPS and increase efficiency.
2. **C2PSA Attention Module:** Introduces a Cross-Stage Partial Spatial Attention block that enhances feature representation by focusing on important regions, improving small-object detection and robustness in dense scenes.
3. **Improved Loss Balancing:** Optimization of classification loss and Distribution Focal Loss (DFL) improves localization precision and reduces false positives, especially at higher IoU thresholds.

**4.2.6 YOLOv12** [13] introduces an attention based mechanism while retaining the real-time inference speed. It achieves state-of-the-art detection accuracy through novel architectural modifications. It includes:

1. **Area Attention Mechanism:** A novel self-attention mechanism which divides feature maps into $l$ equal-sized regions (default $l = 4$) horizontally or vertically to increase receptive field while parrying heavy computations.
2. **Residual Efficient Layer Aggregation Network (R-ELAN):** An evolution of ELAN designed for attention-heavy architecture which introduces block-level residual connections with scaling, bottleneck-style feature integration, and improved gradient flow for stable optimization in large models.

### 4.3 Model Fine-Tuning Conditions

The models were fine-tuned on a custom curated dataset, as discussed in Sect. 3, under specific constraints. YOLO models, which were pretrained on the COCO dataset (with various versions referenced in Sect. 4 and Table 3), were used as the baseline. Fine-tuning was performed for 100 to 200 epochs with the optimizer set to auto. The batch size ranged from 8 to 32, and the models were saved in Torchscript format. Throughout training, the input image size was set to 640.

## 5 Results and Discussion

To evaluate the effectiveness of our approach, we trained and compared multiple YOLO-based detection models on our custom infrared hand dataset. Table 3 presents a comprehensive performance comparison across different model architectures, evaluated on the test set of 4,583 images.

**Table 2.** Comparative analysis of YOLOv8n model using input images of different resolutions

| Model | Image resolution | mAP@50 | mAP@50-95 |
|---|---|---|---|
| YOLOv8n | 320 × 320 | 0.99491 | 0.95244 |
| | 480 × 480 | 0.99494 | 0.95748 |
| | 640 × 640 | 0.99491 | 0.96249 |
| | 1024 × 1024 | 0.99489 | 0.96187 |
| YOLOv11n | 320 × 320 | 0.99491 | 0.95024 |
| | 480 × 480 | 0.99493 | 0.95787 |
| | 640 × 640 | 0.99491 | 0.9613 |
| | 1024 × 1024 | 0.99487 | 0.96138 |

The results demonstrate that all tested models achieved high performance on our infrared hand dataset across all different models variants. This indicates that training on domain-specific infrared data successfully addresses the domain mismatch problem observed when applying RGB-trained models like MediaPipe to infrared images. Upon reviewing Table 3, we can see that the number of parameters vary from 1.9M (YOLOv9t) to 68.12M (YOLOv8x) and the variation denotes the heaviness of each model. Along with number of parameters, we must also look at the number of GFLOPS (Gigabyte-Floating Point Operations per Second). This parameter is also directly correlated to the inference speed. It has varied within the range [6.3, 257.4], denoting YOLOv11n and YOLOv8x, respectively. As per the relationship established above, when we look at the inference times, we can observe that YOLOv11n and YOLOv8n have the lowest inference time of 0.9 ms which is expected due to the low number of GFLOPS and the highest inference time belongs to YOLOv12x with 14.4 ms which demonstrates that the inference time not only depends on GFLOPS but also the number of parameters. mAP (mean average precision) is the mean of precision at different thresholds. mAP50 scores of most models are well above 99.5% which showcases the true performance level of YOLO on our custom dataset. It is also important to note that mAP50-95 is a far more critical indicator of the performance of the model because it is measured against the IoU threshold [0.5-0.95]. Now, considering our model's minimum mAP50-95 is 95.8% (YOLOv12n) is a statement to the robustness in classification of our model and it can go as high as 96.4% which 7 out of the 26 trained YOLO models have demonstrated as mentioned in Table 3.

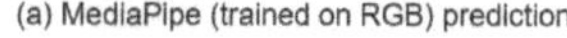
(a) MediaPipe (trained on RGB) prediction

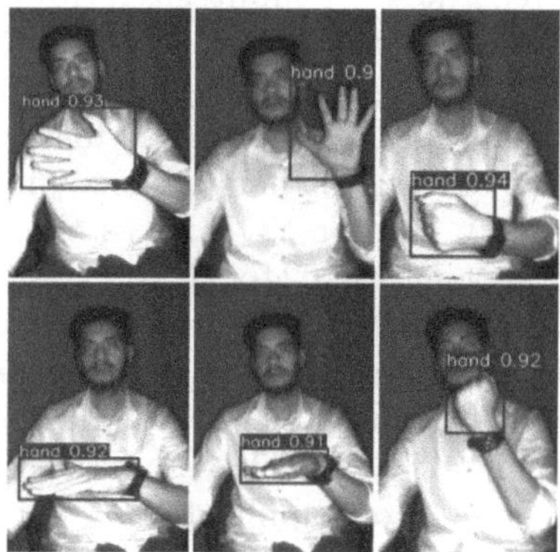

(b) Our model (trained on infrared) prediction

**Fig. 3.** Illustration of the efficacy of the RGB-trained hand detection model on ToF infrared images.

It is very clear from Table 3 that YOLO11n and YOLOv8n have the least inference time of 0.9 ms and YOLO8m, YOLO8l and YOLO11l all three have the highest mAP@50-90 score of 96.40%. Upon further inspection, non-NMS based architectural innovation in YOLOv10 performed worse than the likes of

YOLOv8, YOLOv9 and YOLOv11. The non-NMS dual assignment seems comparatively unreliable when it comes to the IR input characteristics of the single channel. Although YOLOv11 inherits the same non-NMS dual assignment policy, it also introduces C3k2 and SPPF attention modules which increase efficiency of small-object detection and multiscale contextual aggregation which bumps up it's mAP50-95 average (>0.962). Surprisingly, the strong area-attention based YOLOv12 performs the worst in terms of mAP50-95, averaging just around 0.961, which demonstrates that the area-attention and R-ELAN are better suited for multi-channel large-scaled textural RGB images instead of single-channel IR images.

We evaluated an RGB-optimized hand pipeline (MediaPipe) on ToF amplitude frames and observed frequent misdetections and missing landmarks due to spectral and textural domain shift, as illustrated in Fig. 3(a). In the same scenes, our YOLO model fine-tuned on a 22,911-image ToF amplitude dataset produced stable, high-confidence detections across diverse poses Fig. 3(b), demonstrating that ToF-domain training is essential for reliable infrared hand localization.

We conducted a comparative experiment to quantify the effect of input image resolution on the performance of these two models. Both YOLOv8n and YOLOv11n were evaluated on four distinct input resolutions: $320\times320$, $480\times480$, $640 \times 640$, and $1024 \times 1024$. As shown in Table 2, the mAP@50 metric shows performance saturation for both models, with scores remaining nearly identical (approx. 0.9949) across all resolutions. This indicates that for a lenient IoU (Intersection over Union) threshold of 0.5, both models perform exceptionally well regardless of input size. However, the more stringent mAP@50-95 metric, which averages mAP across IoU thresholds from 0.5 to 0.95, give a clearer distinction. We saw a big impact from resolution. For both models, increasing the resolution from $320 \times 320$ made a substantial improvement in mAP@50-95. For YOLOv8n, the performance jump from 0.95244 to 0.96249 when moving to $640 \times 640$, and for YOLOv11n the performance jump from 0.95024 to 0.96138 when moving to $1024 \times 1024$.

Based on this data, we can conclude that while YOLOv8n is the superior model in terms of accuracy, increasing its input resolution beyond $640 \times 640$ does not provide a noticeable benefit and would unnecessarily increase computational overhead. The $640 \times 640$ resolution appears to be the optimal choice for YOLOv8n in our application.

## 6 Conclusion

In this research paper, we aimed to expand the scope of research in the domain of hand gesture detection using a ToF-based 3D vision camera. Initially, we had the idea of using MediaPipe hand detection models for hands localization, but due to the lack of an RGB sensor in the Cube Eye I200 ToF camera that we used because of it's high maximum measurable depth of 7 meters with 15 FPS, we had to switch to custom IR dataset trained YOLO based hand localization methodology, which proved worthwhile. For retraining, the custom IR dataset

**Table 3.** Performance comparison of different YOLO detection models. The highlighted ones are the one with the least inference time.

| Models | Parameters(M) | GFLOPs | mAP@50 | mAP@50-95 | Inference(ms) |
|---|---|---|---|---|---|
| YOLOv8x [6] | 68.12 | 257.4 | 0.995 | 0.962 | 12.4 |
| YOLOv8s [6] | 11.13 | 28.4 | 0.995 | 0.964 | 1.9 |
| YOLOv8n [6] | **3.01** | **8.1** | **0.995** | **0.963** | **0.9** |
| YOLOv8m [6] | 25.84 | 78.7 | 0.995 | 0.964 | 4.7 |
| YOLOv8l [6] | 43.61 | 164.8 | 0.995 | 0.964 | 7.6 |
| YOLOv9t [16] | 1.97 | 7.6 | 0.995 | 0.96 | 1.7 |
| YOLOv9s [16] | 7.17 | 26.7 | 0.995 | 0.963 | 2.4 |
| YOLOv9m [16] | 20.01 | 76.5 | 0.995 | 0.964 | 5.7 |
| YOLOv9e [16] | 57.38 | 189.1 | 0.995 | 0.964 | 13.2 |
| YOLOv9c [16] | 25.32 | 102.3 | 0.995 | 0.963 | 6.1 |
| YOLOv10x [15] | 29.39 | 160.0 | 0.995 | 0.962 | 10.2 |
| YOLOv10s [15] | 7.22 | 21.4 | 0.995 | 0.963 | 2.0 |
| YOLOv10n [15] | 2.27 | 6.5 | 0.995 | 0.961 | 1.0 |
| YOLOv10m [15] | 15.31 | 58.9 | 0.995 | 0.961 | 4.2 |
| YOLOv10l [15] | 24.31 | 120.0 | 0.995 | 0.960 | 6.6 |
| YOLOv10b [15] | 19.00 | 91.6 | 0.995 | 0.961 | 5.2 |
| YOLOv11x [7] | 56.83 | 194.4 | 0.995 | 0.964 | 10.5 |
| YOLOv11s [7] | 9.41 | 21.3 | 0.995 | 0.963 | 1.9 |
| YOLOv11n [7] | **2.58** | **6.3** | **0.995** | **0.962** | **0.9** |
| YOLOv11l [7] | 25.28 | 86.6 | 0.995 | 0.964 | 5.8 |
| YOLOv11m [7] | 20.03 | 67.6 | 0.995 | 0.960 | 4.2 |
| YOLOv12l [13] | 26.34 | 88.5 | 0.995 | 0.961 | 8.0 |
| YOLOv12x [13] | 59.04 | 198.5 | 0.995 | 0.962 | 14.4 |
| YOLOv12s [13] | 9.23 | 21.2 | 0.995 | 0.960 | 2.5 |
| YOLOv12n [13] | 2.56 | 6.3 | 0.995 | 0.958 | 1.4 |
| YOLOv12m [13] | 20.10 | 67.1 | 0.995 | 0.961 | 5.4 |

consisted of a total of 22911 samples, from which we used 18,328 images to fine-tune the COCO pre-trained YOLO models. Subsequently, we evaluated the performance of the fine-tuned YOLO models on a separate test set comprising 4,583 images. Based on the evaluation results of different YOLO variants, we can conclude that for our needs, YOLOv11n was the best in terms of inference speed, and YOLOv8m was the best in terms of mAP@50-95 score. YOLO has proven to be the state of the art (SOTA) in multiple domains, and this research clearly demonstrates that all, while also showcasing the quality of the Custom Dataset we have created, enabling us to draw out the YOLO detector to its utmost potential. The dataset, along with the YOLO model, is highly capable in the domain of hand gesture detection, which, in turn, will greatly benefit the advancement of research in this specific domain. The study demonstrates that the convolution-based YOLOv8-YOLOv11 have better results compared to the attention-based YOLOv12 highlighting the case-specificity of this dataset. Since the ToF-infrared image showcases textural invariability and robust edges, CNN-based architectures are generally performing better than the heavy-attention-based models.

Future work will include optimizing the YOLO model for real-world use cases and integrating the models for edge devices using embedded platforms. Additionally, we will work to upgrade the models to include advanced features such as hand gesture recognition and develop human-computer interaction-based advanced applications using 3D cameras.

## References

1. Choudhary, S., Saurav, S., Saini, R., Singh, S.: Benchmarking yolo object detectors for component detection in power line infrastructure: dataset and results. In: International Conference on Computer Vision and Image Processing, pp. 396–410. Springer (2024)
2. Cube-Eye: Cube-Eye | ToF camera | 3D depth camera (2025). https://www.cube-eye.co.kr/old/en/#/spec/product_I200.asp. Accessed 30 Sept 2025
3. Damen, D., et al.: The epic-kitchens dataset: collection, challenges and baselines. IEEE Trans. Pattern Anal. Mach. Intell. **43**(11), 4125–4141 (2020)
4. Deng, J., Dong, W., Socher, R., Li, L.J., Li, K., Fei-Fei, L.: Imagenet: a large-scale hierarchical image database. In: 2009 IEEE Conference on Computer Vision and Pattern Recognition, pp. 248–255 (2009). https://doi.org/10.1109/CVPR.2009.5206848
5. Jalayer, R., Jalayer, M., Orsenigo, C., Tomizuka, M.: A review on deep learning for vision-based hand detection, hand segmentation and hand gesture recognition in human-robot interaction. Robot. Comput.-Integr. Manufact. **97**, 103110 (2026)
6. Jocher, G., Chaurasia, A., Qiu, J.: Ultralytics yolov8 (2023). https://github.com/ultralytics/ultralytics
7. Jocher, G., Qiu, J.: Ultralytics yolo11 (2024). https://github.com/ultralytics/ultralytics
8. Lin, T., et al.: Microsoft COCO: common objects in context. CoRR abs/1405.0312 (2014). http://arxiv.org/abs/1405.0312
9. Mittal, A., Zisserman, A., Torr, P.H.: Hand detection using multiple proposals (2011)
10. Rahman, M.M., Uzzaman, A., Khatun, F., Aktaruzzaman, M., Siddique, N.: A comparative study of advanced technologies and methods in hand gesture analysis and recognition systems. Expert Syst. Appl. **266**, 125929 (2025)
11. Redmon, J., Divvala, S., Girshick, R., Farhadi, A.: You only look once: unified, real-time object detection. In: 2016 IEEE Conference on Computer Vision and Pattern Recognition (CVPR), pp. 779–788 (2016). https://doi.org/10.1109/CVPR.2016.91
12. Redmon, J., Divvala, S., Girshick, R., Farhadi, A.: You only look once: unified, real-time object detection. In: Proceedings of the IEEE Conference on Computer Vision and Pattern Recognition, pp. 779–788 (2016)

13. Tian, Y., Ye, Q., Doermann, D.: Yolov12: attention-centric real-time object detectors (2025). https://github.com/sunsmarterjie/yolov12
14. TzuTa Lin: labelimg (2025). https://viso.ai/computer-vision/labelimg-for-image-annotation/. Accessed 30 Sept 2025
15. Wang, A., Chen, H., Liu, L., Chen, K., Lin, Z., Han, J., et al.: Yolov10: real-time end-to-end object detection. Adv. Neural. Inf. Process. Syst. **37**, 107984–108011 (2024)
16. Wang, C.Y., Liao, H.Y.M.: Yolov9: learning what you want to learn using programmable gradient information (2024). arXiv preprint
17. Zhang, F.: Mediapipe hands: on-device real-time hand tracking. arXiv preprint (2020)

# A Hybrid Multimodal Approach to Emotion Recognition with Spiking Neural Networks and Transformers

Ashika Babydasan(✉), Aadit Khanolkar, and Sakshi Indolia

STME, SVKM's NMIMS, Navi Mumbai, India
ashikababydasan@gmail.com

**Abstract.** The performance of emotion recognition models based on single modality such as electroencephalography (EEG) signals is limited due to noise and non-stationary nature of the data. To address this, we present a multimodal framework that fuses EEG and eye-tracking signals. In this paper, we propose a framework where EEG features are processed by a convolutional spiking neural network (CSNN), while eye-tracking signals are modeled via a transformer encoder. Thereafter, the resultant embeddings are fused through a late-fusion technique for emotion classification. Performance of the proposed framework is evaluated with leave-one-subject-out (LOSO) cross-validation. The proposed model achieves a mean accuracy of 75.8%, with a peak per-session accuracy of 91.67%—surpassing single-modality baselines by over 8% on SEED-IV dataset. These results demonstrate that the combination of CSNN and attention-based architectures outperform the unimodal emotion recognition frameworks.

**Keywords:** Emotion recognition · Electroencephalogram (EEG) · Eye tracking signals · Convolution Spiking neural networks (CSNN) · Brain-Computer Interface (BCI) · Deep learning

## 1 Introduction

Emotion recognition has emerged as a critical component for understanding human behavior and their emotional states. It's vast applications range from healthcare, education, human–computer interaction (HCI) to driver safety systems. Detecting emotions accurately and classifying them facilitates the creation of real-time responding intelligent systems, ultimately enhancing the user experiences and improving their outcomes across these domains.

Electroencephalography (EEG) has a high temporal resolution and capacity to measure neural activity, and has demonstrated shown strong potential for emotion recognition [9]. EEG captures electrical activity across brain regions, with frequency bands alpha, beta, gamma, theta and delta related their with distinct emotional states. Emotion models, like dimensional (valency, arousal) provide systematic frameworks for the classification of these neural patterns.


A. Shastri et al. (Eds.): IHCI 2025, LNCS 16437, pp. 450–461, 2026.
https://doi.org/10.1007/978-3-032-26352-0_37

Unimodal (Single-modality) approaches face many limitations, even if EEG captures temporal dynamics effectively it is also susceptible to noise and inter-subject variability. In recent research has shown that multimodal solutions offer better performance in comparison [5,17,26]. Other modalities like eye-tracking that contain features that include fixations, pupil dilations and saccades can be integrated with EEG to enhance the accuracy of emotion recognition.

In recent years the evolution of these emotion recognition models have significantly evolved. Machine Learning approaches like Support Vector Machines (SVMs) and Random Forests require hand-crafted features, and were limited in capturing complex temporal patterns. The rise of deep learning enabled automatic feature extraction with superior performance. Methods like Convolutional Neural Networks (CNNs) [2], Recurrent Neural Networks (RNNs) [10] demonstrate promising results by learning multi-level patterns directly from raw inputs.

Although emotion recognition has seen numerous advancements, neuromorphic approaches are still largely underexplored. Spiking Neural Networks (SNNs), the third generation of neural networks allow biologically inspired and even-driven processing [11]. These simulate a neuron's function by processing information in form of discrete spikes instead of continuous values [14,23]. This nature of SNNs is highly suitable for EEG signals where their temporal dynamics and low-energy requirements naturally align with brain's activity.

Some critical gaps still remain, despite the significant progress in both multimodal emotion recognition and neuromorphic computing:

1. Limited multimodal SNN architectures: Most SNN research focuses on singlemodality processing [14,22,23], with few attempts at integrating multiple physiological signals within spike-based frameworks.
2. Lack of hybrid architectures: Not many studies bring together the brain-like processing of SNNs and the strong attention capabilities of transformers, even though they could work well together [8,23].
3. Underexplored modality-specific architectures: Specialized neural architectures may be beneficial for different signal types (like spatial EEG versus sequential eye movements) rather than uniform processing approaches [12,17].

To address these gaps, we propose a hybrid multimodal framework for emotion recognition that combines EEG and eye-tracking signals through biologically inspired and attention-based architectures. We develop a topography-aware CSNN that processes EEG signals while preserving the spatial arrangement of brain electrodes, leading to more informative feature extraction. Develop a transformer encoder that excels at modeling long-range temporal dependencies, that are crucial indicators of emotional states. And demonstrate that combining these two modalities can significantly outperform unimodal approaches in the SEED-IV dataset, a widely recognized benchmark in emotion recognition research.

The remainder of our paper is organized into six sections. Related works, where we review existing emotion recognition methods, EEG-based approaches, eye-tracking approaches, and multimodal frameworks. Methodology, that contains the dataset description, preprocessing of EEG and eye-tracking data, Convolutional Spiking Neural Network (CSNN) architecture for EEG signals, transformer model for eye movement data, fusion strategy, and training/evaluation setup. Results and Discussion, containing the experimental setup, performance metrics, comparative results with baselines, analysis of multimodal fusion effectiveness, and discussion of limitations and insights. Conclusion with the summary of contributions, key findings, and future research directions. And references, which include cited works supporting the study.

## 2 Related Works

### 2.1 Existing Methods for EEG Based Emotion Recognition

Early approaches to emotion recognition primarily relied on hand crafted features extracted from EEG signals, including power spectral density, asymmetry measures, and statistical features computed across various frequency bands [1]. These features were typically classified using traditional machine learning algorithms such as Support Vector Machines (SVMs), k-nearest neighbors (k-NN), and Random Forests. While these methods established standard performance levels, they suffered from various critical limitations:-heavy dependence on domain expertise for feature engineering and not being able to effectively capture complex temporal pattern. Classification accuracies for multi-class emotion recognition tasks generally ranged from 85% to 90% [1]. The introduction of deep learning fundamentally transformed EEG based emotion recognition by enabling automatic feature learning. Convolutional Neural Networks (CNNs) allow topographic EEG representations, treating electrode arrangements as 2D images. CNNs achieved accuracies in the range of 75 to 90% on benchmark datasets [2,9]. In recent years, transformer architectures have gained significant attention in EEG emotion recognition as well [3,4,7,8,13,24]. Research has shown that attention based models can effectively capture both spatial relationships between electrodes and temporal dynamics of emotional states [2,3,8]. Hybrid architectures combining transformers with CNNs have been developed to learn spatial temporal features [4,20], achieving accuracies exceeding 85%, demonstrating the effectiveness of hybrid deep learning approaches. Wang et al. proposed an attention-based convolutional transformer network that effectively integrates spatial and temporal information [20], while Chen et al. developed a transformer-CNN hybrid specifically designed for EEG spatial-temporal feature learning [2], achieving state-of-the-art results across multiple emotion recognition benchmarks.

### 2.2 Spiking Neural Networks for Emotion Recognition

Spiking Neural Networks (SNNs) mimic brain activity by using spike patterns. Unlike ANNs that have continuous activation functions, SNNs employ discrete, event driven processing, making it suitable for temporal signals like EEG. Lillicrap et al. [11] highlighted SNN advantages including improved energy efficiency and biological validity. Zhang et al. [23] initiated the work of SNNs for EEG emotion recognition which demonstrated competitive accuracy while maintaining neuromorphic advantages. Liu et al. [14] developed convolutional SNNs for EEG-based stress detection, achieving 80–85% accuracy with potential energy savings. Xu et al. [22] introduced EESCN, a specialized SNN architecture incorporating custom encoding schemes for emotional brain signals. Zhang et al. [25] proposed FusionSense for multimodal data fusion, demonstrating effective information integration. Wang et al. [19] explored dynamic vision-based emotion recognition using SNNs. Poisson encoding has proved particularly effective in generating spikes stochastically based on signal intensity while preserving temporal and amplitude information. However, pre-existing SNN-based systems predominantly focus on single-modality EEG processing, with limited exploration of multimodal integration or hybrid architectures embodying transformers. This represents a significant opportunity for advancing both performance and computational efficiency.

### 2.3 Multimodal Emotion Recognition

Multimodal fusion strategies have been increasingly explored by researchers for emotion recognition. Using eye-tracking data with EEG has provided us with effective results [5,6,17]. Early studies employed feature-level or decision-level fusion with traditional classifiers. Soleymani et al. [17] demonstrated techniques that combine eye movements with EEG resulted in improved accuracy. Recent deep learning architectures learn joint representations across modalities, yielding substantial gains. Li et al. [8] introduced an Emotion Transformer Fusion approach modeling complementary properties of EEG and eye movements. Liu et al. [12] developed a Multimodal Adaptive Emotion Transformer with flexible modality inputs. Smith et al. [16] achieved high accuracy combining EEG and eye tracking through deep neural networks. However, most multimodal approaches rely on conventional artificial neural networks, which process information fundamentally differently from biological neural systems, motivating exploration of neuromorphic computing approaches.

## 3 Methodology

### 3.1 Dataset Description

We utilize the SEED-IV dataset [26], which is a widely-used dataset for EEG-based emotion recognition. Recordings from 15 subjects (9 females and 6 males, aged 20–24 years) were collected by presenting them with emotion-eliciting film clips on three different days/sessions. Every session contained 24 trials (2–3 minutes each), making it 72 trials per subject and 1080 trials in total. This dataset comprises of four distinct emotional states, happiness (labeled 1), sadness (labeled 2), fear (labeled 3), and neutral (labeled 0). The dataset provides both EEG recordings and eye movement data collected simultaneously during emotion elicitation.

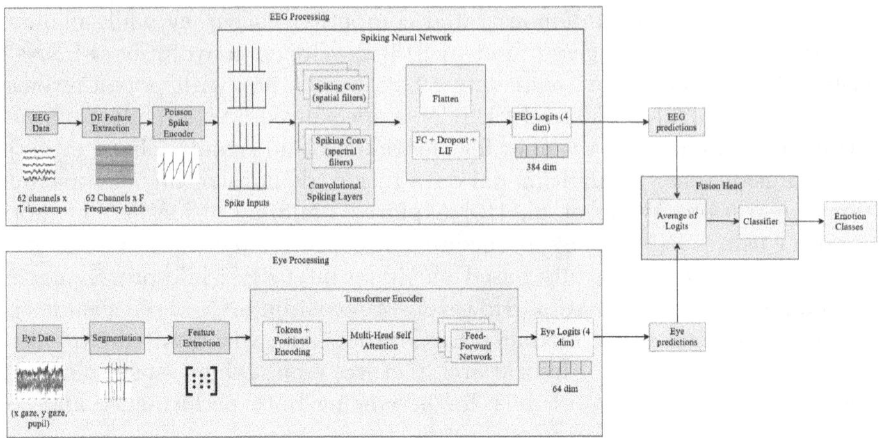


**Fig. 1.** Overview of the proposed multimodal framework combining CSNN for EEG and Transformer for eye data

The EEG signals and eye signals were recorded using 62-channel ESI NeuroScan system and SMI ETG eye tracker at 60 Hz respectively. With a sampling rate of 1000 Hz and a 0.05–100 Hz bandpass filter for EEG signals. The eye tracking data included various features like fixation duration, saccade amplitude, pupil diameter, and blink frequency. Each trial produced 31 temporal segments, with each segment containing 64 features [26].

### 3.2 Data Preprocessing

As depicted in Fig. 1, we utilized the pre-extracted differential entropy (DE) features provided with the SEED-IV dataset. The dataset creators computed DE features using 1-second windows, and applied temporal smoothing. [26]

**EEG Data Processing:** The 62 EEG channels were mapped onto a $8 \times 9$ 2D grid based on their scalp locations following the 10–20 system, with missing positions zero padded. The structure of trial was (5,8,9,5) which represents temporal frames, grid height, grid width, and frequency bands. We also clipped the values at the 1st and 99th percentiles to reduce artifacts. This resulted in features ranging from 0 to approximately 29.5.

**Eye Tracking Data Processing:** We replaced missing or infinite values were with zeros to maintain dimensionality. All trials were standardized to a fixed size of (31, 64) through zero-padding where needed. Extreme values were clipped to the 1st and 99th percentiles to mitigate measurement artifacts, and features were z-score normalized using statistics computed separately for each cross-validation fold to prevent data leakage.

**Data Alignment and Subject-Session Filtering:** Both modalities were synchronized using subject ID, session ID, and trial index metadata. For EEG, the five temporal frames per trial were treated independently during training (generating 5,400 training samples from 1,080 trials) but averaged during testing to produce trial-level predictions.

### 3.3 EEG Model Architecture

Our multimodal framework consists of three main components: a convolutional spiking neural network with spatial feature extraction for EEG processing, leveraging combined benefits of: CNNs' effectiveness in capturing spatial patterns from topographic EEG representations [23], SNNs' neurobiologically inspired temporal processing aligned with neural signals [11,14,23], and 3D convolutions' ability to jointly learn spatial-temporal-spectral features from the $(8 \times 9 \times 5)$ input structure.

**Spike Encoding.** EEG features are converted to binary spike trains using Poisson encoding, which generates spikes probabilistically based on normalized input intensity, as shown in Table 1. For each input frame, we generate $T = 20$ time steps of binary spike matrices by sampling from Bernoulli distributions with probability proportional to the min-max normalized feature values (scaled by maximum firing rate $r_{\text{max}} = 30$ Hz). This encoding preserves both intensity information through firing rate and maintains event-driven processing characteristics.

**Network Architecture.** The network comprises of four sequential processing blocks that transform raw EEG signals into emotion classifications.

- **Block 1** is a spatial convolutional layer wherein a 3D convolution is performed over 1 input channel and yielding 16 channels using a kernel with padding. Then 3D batch normalization with Parametric Leaky-Integrate-and-Fire (PLIF) neuron is utilized, this introduces parametric leakage that allows adaptive temporal dynamics. The $(3 \times 3)$ spatial kernel models neighborhood interactions between electrodes while padding preserves the spatial dimensions. The hyperparameter details are listed in Table 1.
- **Block 2** is a temporal-spectral convolution Layer, designed to learn cross frequency dependencies across the 5 frequency bands. We implement a 3D convolution Layer that produces 32 output channels from 16 channels (from Block 1). This is followed by an average pooling layer, so the frequency is reduced and the frequency dimension comes to 2 bands from the original 5 bands. We also employ an LIF neuron that provides both feature compactness and frequency invariance. The hyperparameter details are listed in Table 1.
- **Block 3** consists of feature embedding and integration. We first flatten the feature maps and then apply temporal averaging over T spike steps. The flattened features are then linearly mapped from 9216 dimensions to 384

dimensions. Then a normalization layer with residual connections is applied. Dropout (p=0.4) and a PLIF neuron complete this block, producing a 384-dimensional embedding that integrates spatiotemporal features. The hyperparameter details are listed in Table 1.
- **Block 4** is a classification head with a linear layer that maps the 384 dimensional embedding to 4 output logits corresponding to the emotion categories, thus giving the final emotion classification decision.

**Spiking Neuron Dynamics:** We employ Parametric LIF neurons with learnable time constants (initialized to $\tau = 2.0$), allowing the network to adapt temporal integration windows during training. The neurons use standard reset-by-subtraction dynamics with threshold $V_{\texttt{thresh}} = 1.0$. For gradient computation through the non-differentiable spike function, we use the Sigmoid surrogate gradient with smoothness parameter $\alpha = 4.0$ [11]. Multi-step processing (`step_mode='m'`) makes efficient parallel computation possible across time steps.

### 3.4 Eye Movement Model: Transformer Architecture

**Design Rationale:** The eye-tracking data consists of 31 sequential segments that capture the temporal gaze dynamics. This type of data is suitable for transformer based processing because, relationships between early and late fixations, saccade patterns, and attention shifts provides us with information that can be critical for emotion recognition.

**Network Architecture:** The proposed network architecture for eye transformer consists of three main blocks:

- **Input Embedding Layer** The 64-dimensional feature space is maintained by linear projection and the fixed sinusoidal positional encodings introduce temporal order information.
- **Transformer Encoder Stack** The model employs 2 transformer encoder layers with 4 attention heads per layer. Each layer has a model dimension (d_model) of 64 and feedforward dimension (d_ff) of 256. This allows the model to focus on multiple representation subspaces, capturing diverse temporal patterns in eye movements. Each layer includes multi-head self-attention with scaled dot-product attention, followed by residual connections and layer normalization, then a position-wise feedforward network ($64 \rightarrow 256 \rightarrow 64$) with another residual connection and normalization. Dropout ($p = 0.3$) is applied for regularization, and ReLU activation is used in feedforward layers.
- **Classification Head** Adaptive average pooling aggregates information across the 31 temporal steps. After flattening, dropout ($p = 0.3$) and a linear layer project features to 4 emotion class logits.

**Table 1.** Model architecture and hyperparameter settings for EEG CSNN, Eye Transformer, and fusion strategy.

| Component | Layer/Block | Parameters/Settings |
|---|---|---|
| EEG CSNN | Spike Encoding | Poisson, T = 20, r_max = 30 Hz |
| | Block 1 | 3D Conv (1 → 16, k = (1,3,3), p = (0,1,1)), BatchNorm3d, PLIF |
| | Block 2 | 3D Conv (16 → 32, k = (3,1,1), p = (1,0,0)), AvgPool(2,1,1), BatchNorm3d, LIF |
| | Embedding | Flatten → Linear(9216 → 384), LayerNorm, Dropout(0.4), PLIF |
| | Output | Linear(384 → 4) |
| | Neuron | PLIF/LIF, $\tau = 2.0$ (learnable), $V_{th} = 1.0$, Sigmoid surrogate ($\alpha = 4.0$) |
| | Optimizer | AdamW (lr = $1 \times 10^{-3}$, wd = $1 \times 10^{-3}$), Cosine annealing ($T_{max} = 30$), batch = 32 |
| Eye Transformer | Input | (31, 64) → Linear proj + sinusoidal pos enc |
| | Encoder | 2 layers, 4 heads, d_model = 64, d_ff = 256, ReLU |
| | Regularization | Dropout = 0.3 |
| | Output | AdaptiveAvgPool → Linear(64 → 4) |
| | Optimizer | AdamW (lr = $1 \times 10^{-3}$, wd = $1 \times 10^{-4}$), $T_{max} = 40$, batch = 64 |
| Fusion | Strategy | Fixed-weight logit averaging (Eq. 1) |

### 3.5 Multimodal Fusion

We employ a late fusion approach that combines predictions from both modalities at the decision level after training each modality independently. This strategy offers several advantages: each network specializes in extracting discriminative features from its input domain without interference, modality-specific architectures can be optimized independently, the approach is modular allowing easy component replacement, and it avoids the complexity of joint training which may be dominated by one modality. During inference, predictions are combined as follows:

- **EEG Processing:** The 5 temporal frames per trial are independently processed through the SNN, producing 5 sets of logits that are averaged to obtain trial-level predictions: $\mathbf{z}_{\text{EEG}} \in \mathbb{R}^4$.
- **Eye Movement Processing:** The 31-segment sequence is processed through the transformer to produce logits: $\mathbf{z}_{\text{Eye}} \in \mathbb{R}^4$.
- **Fusion:** Final predictions are computed by arithmetic averaging of the logits from both modalities:

$$\mathbf{z}_{\text{fused}} = \frac{\mathbf{z}_{\text{EEG}} + \mathbf{z}_{\text{Eye}}}{2} \tag{1}$$

The predicted emotion class is determined by argmax over the fused logits. This equal-weight averaging treats both modalities as equally important. Although alternative strategies such as learned weighted averaging or attention-based fusion could potentially improve performance, they would require additional validation data for hyperparameter tuning.

## 4 Results and Discussion

Our proposed CSNN for EEG-based emotion recognition was evaluated under LOSO cross-validation protocol on the SEED-IV dataset. The EEG-only CSNN

**Table 2.** Per-Session and Per-Subject Accuracy (%) on SEED-IV under LOSO Protocol

| Session/Subject | 1 | 2 | 3 | 4 | 5 | 6 | 7 | 8 | 9 | 10 | 11 | 12 | 13 | 14 | 15 | Mean |
|---|---|---|---|---|---|---|---|---|---|---|---|---|---|---|---|---|
| Session 1 | 75.00 | 79.17 | 79.17 | 79.17 | 87.50 | 91.67 | 83.33 | 83.33 | 79.17 | 79.17 | 75.00 | 83.33 | 70.83 | 83.33 | 83.33 | 81.11 |
| Session 2 | 79.17 | 91.67 | 79.17 | 70.83 | 79.17 | 79.17 | 83.33 | 79.17 | 79.17 | 83.33 | 83.33 | 70.83 | 83.33 | 87.50 | 75.00 | 80.56 |
| Session 3 | 70.83 | 62.50 | 58.33 | 54.17 | 75.00 | 62.50 | 70.83 | 54.17 | 62.50 | 66.67 | 66.67 | 66.67 | 66.67 | 66.67 | 54.17 | 63.33 |
| **Mean (Subject)** | 75.00 | 77.78 | 72.22 | 68.06 | 80.56 | 77.78 | 79.17 | 72.22 | 73.61 | 76.39 | 75.00 | 73.61 | 73.61 | 79.17 | 70.83 | **75.00** |

*Note: Accuracy (%) per session across 15 subjects under LOSO. Row "Mean (Subject)" shows average across three sessions per subject. Overall mean (75.00%) is the grand average across all 45 subject-session pairs.*

achieved a mean classification accuracy of 72.04% ± 8.94% across all 15 subjects with individual subject performance ranging from 68.06% (Subjects 6–8) to 80.56% (Subjects 2 and 12). This demonstrated that spike-based encoding and topographic convolutions can effectively capture spatial-spectral emotion patterns.

The transformer based eye model achieved a mean accuracy of 80.74% ± 0.0797% across the 15 subjects. Individual subject performance ranged from 70.83% (Subject 5) to 88.89% (Subjects 2 and 8), reflecting the inter-individual variability in gaze dynamics and attention patterns.

Both the model achieved stable training dynamics, typically converging within 20–30 epochs, with no signs of overfitting, suggesting effective regularization. This shows effective generalization that was made possible by the combination of multi-head attention, layer normalization, and dropout. As shown in

Table 2, the fusion results achieved a mean accuracy of 75.00% ± 9.26 % across 15 subjects. Individual accuracies ranged from 70.83% (Subjects 1 and 4) to 83.33% (Subject 2) highlighting individual differences in how neural and gaze signals interact. As summarized in Table 3, the proposed model outperforms existing SNN-based approaches, achieving higher accuracies across both unimodal and multimodal settings.

The results highlight how multimodal fusion effectively captures both neural and behavioral aspects of emotion, showing that combining SNNs with transformer-based models can improve emotion classification. Inter-session variability remains a key challenge, likely due to participant fatigue, electrode drift, or task engagement changes. Our approach also treats the 5 temporal EEG frames independently (averaging predictions), missing sequential dependencies that recurrent SNNs could capture.

### 4.1 Computational Efficiency & Real-Time Feasibility

Our proposed model achieves high throughput suitable for real-time affective computing, with latency values of 13.84 ms and 1.12 ms for EEG and Eye models respectively, making a latency of 16.84 ms for the hybrid model. This enables a stable throughput of over 66 FPS. The CSNN contains 56.6 million parameters while the Eye transformer uses 0.10 million parameters. The hybrid model

**Table 3.** Performance Comparison with SNN State-of-the-Art (SOTA)

| Method | Modality | Architecture Type | Accuracy (%) | Std Dev (%) |
|---|---|---|---|---|
| EEGSNet [15] | EEG | Spiking Neural Network | 63.64 | N/A |
| Fractal-SNN [9] | EEG | Spiking CNN (Multi-scale) | 68.33 | N/A |
| FusionSense [25] | EEG + Other | SNN-based Multimodal Fusion | 73.15 | N/A |
| **Proposed (Eye-only)** | Eye-tracking | Transformer Encoder | **80.74** | 0.79 |
| **Proposed (EEG-only)** | EEG | CSNN (SNN) | **72.04** | 8.94 |
| **Proposed (Multimodal)** | EEG + Eye | CSNN + Transformer Fusion | **75.00** | 9.26 |

**Table 4.** Ablation Study: Per-Session and Per-Subject Accuracy (%) on SEED-IV using Rate Encoding

| Session/Subject | 1 | 2 | 3 | 4 | 5 | 6 | 7 | 8 | 9 | 10 | 11 | 12 | 13 | 14 | 15 | Mean |
|---|---|---|---|---|---|---|---|---|---|---|---|---|---|---|---|---|
| Session 1 | 70.83 | 87.50 | 70.83 | 75.00 | 70.83 | 75.00 | 83.33 | 70.83 | 79.17 | 62.50 | 83.33 | 75.00 | 62.50 | 75.00 | 79.17 | 74.31 |
| Session 2 | 70.83 | 70.83 | 75.00 | 79.17 | 83.33 | 87.50 | 79.17 | 70.83 | 75.00 | 75.00 | 70.83 | 70.83 | 83.33 | 70.83 | 75.00 | 75.69 |
| Session 3 | 62.50 | 54.17 | 58.33 | 66.67 | 70.83 | 66.67 | 54.17 | 62.50 | 62.50 | 45.83 | 66.67 | 75.00 | 66.67 | 62.50 | 66.67 | 62.78 |
| **Mean (Subject)** | 68.06 | 70.83 | 68.06 | 73.61 | 75.00 | 76.39 | 72.22 | 68.06 | 72.22 | 61.11 | 73.61 | 73.61 | 70.83 | 69.44 | 73.61 | **71.11** |

combining both modalities with 56.7 M parameters. By achieving spike rates below 5%, the CSNN maintains high efficiency and it also remains compatible with neuromorphic hardware. It requires approximately 3.2 GB of GPU memory and trains in approximately 1 h for 40 epochs under the LOSO protocol. The Eye Transformer is computationally lighter, requiring 0.8 GB of memory and takes 40 min for 40 epochs under the same protocol. The hybrid configuration consumes about 4.0 GB GPU memory.

### 4.2 Ablation Study

We conducted an ablation study to validate our design choices under the same LOSO protocol. As shown in Table 4, the model achieved an accuracy of 71.94% across all 15 subjects. Session 2 yields the highest performance 77.22% and Session 3 generates the lowest accuracy 63.89%, this reflects the inherent variability in emotional elicitation. The robustness across individuals is depicted by per-subject mean accuracy that ranged from 68.06% (Subject S10) to 76.39% (Subject S5). We can confirm that our rate-based spiking representation preserves the discriminative features for emotion recognition using the consistent performance under the LOSO cross-validation protocol.

## 5 Conclusion

We have presented a hybrid multimodal framework for emotion recognition that combines EEG and eye-tracking signals through biologically inspired and attention-based architectures. By encoding EEG DE features into spike trains and processing them using a Convolutional Spiking Neural Network (CSNN), while modeling temporal eye-tracking sequences with a Transformer encoder, our system achieves 75.0% mean accuracy on SEED-IV under strict LOSO evaluation [1,18,21].

Our results demonstrate the feasibility of integrating neural and behavioral modalities through simple late-fusion strategies. Our approach achieves accuracy parity with existing SNN bases multimodal systems.

Despite these promising results, challenges remain in inter-session generalization and modality imbalance. Future work will explore confidence-weighted fusion, domain adaptation, and on-chip neuromorphic implementation to enhance robustness and efficiency, moving toward practical deployment of hybrid neuromorphic-transformer systems for real-world emotion recognition applications.

## References

1. Alhalaseh, R., Alasasfeh, S.: Machine-learning-based emotion recognition system using EEG signals. Computers **9**(4) (2020). https://doi.org/10.3390/computers9040095. https://www.mdpi.com/2073-431X/9/4/95
2. Chen, S., Wang, Y., Zhao, Z.: Emotion classification based on transformer and CNN for EEG spatial–temporal feature learning. Brain Sci. **14**(3) (2024). https://www.mdpi.com/2076-3425/14/3/268
3. Chen, Z., et al.: Attention based multiple dimensions EEG transformer for emotion recognition. arXiv preprint (2022). https://arxiv.org/abs/2212.12134
4. Ding, Y., et al.: EMT: a novel transformer for generalized cross-subject EEG emotion recognition. arXiv preprint (2024). https://arxiv.org/abs/2406.18345
5. Guo, J.J., et al.: Multimodal emotion recognition from eye image, eye movement and EEG. In: International Conference on Affective Computing and Intelligent Interaction (2019)
6. Iacono, P., Khan, N.: Multi-modal emotion recognition using EEG and eye tracking features. Sensors (2024). Evaluated on SEED-V dataset
7. Li, M., et al.: A spatial and temporal transformer-based EEG emotion recognition in VR environment. Front. Hum. Neurosci. (2025)
8. Li, R., Deng, L., Huang, Y.: Emotion transformer fusion-complementary representation properties of EEG and eye movements on recognizing anger and surprise. In: BIBM (2021). https://bcmi.sjtu.edu.cn/home/lirui/pdf/BIBM_2021.pdf
9. Li, W., et al.: Fractal spiking neural network scheme for EEG-based emotion recognition. IEEE Trans. Neural Netw. Learn. Syst. (2023). Includes SEED-IV evaluation
10. Li, X., et al.: Transformer-based spatial-temporal feature. arXiv preprint (2021). https://arxiv.org/abs/2106.11170
11. Lillicrap, T.P., Memisevic, F.Z., et al.: Deep learning in spiking neural networks. arXiv preprint (2018). https://arxiv.org/pdf/1804.08150
12. Liu, B., et al.: Multimodal adaptive emotion transformer with flexible modality inputs on a novel dataset with continuous labels (2023). https://bcmi.sjtu.edu.cn/~blu/papers/2023/2023-4.pdf
13. Liu, R., et al.: Ertnet: an interpretable transformer-based framework for EEG emotion recognition. Front. Neurosci. (2024)
14. Liu, Y., et al.: Advancing EEG based stress detection using spiking neural networks and convolutional spiking neural networks. Sci. Rep. **15** (2025). https://www.nature.com/articles/s41598-025-10270-0

15. Shi, J., et al.: Eegsnet: a novel EEG cognitive recognition model using spiking neural networks. Sci. Rep. (2025)
16. Smith, M., et al.: Multi-modal emotion recognition using EEG and eye tracking features. PubMed (2025). https://pubmed.ncbi.nlm.nih.gov/40039466/
17. Soleymani, A.: Combining eye movements and EEG to enhance emotion recognition. In: IJCAI Proceedings (2015). https://www.ijcai.org/Proceedings/15/Papers/169.pdf
18. Valderrama, C.E., Sheoran, A.: Identifying relevant EEG channels for subject-independent emotion recognition using attention network layers. Front. Psychiatry **16**, 1494369 (2025). https://doi.org/10.3389/fpsyt.2025.1494369
19. Wang, H., et al.: Spiking emotions - dynamic vision emotion recognition using spiking neural networks. In: CEUR Workshop Proceedings, vol. 3331 (2023). https://ceur-ws.org/Vol-3331/paper08.pdf
20. Wang, Y., et al.: EEG emotion recognition using attention-based convolutional transformer neural network. Neurocomputing (2023). https://www.sciencedirect.com/science/article/abs/pii/S1746809423002689
21. Wu, X., Ju, X., Dai, S., Li, X., Li, M.: Multi-source domain adaptation for EEG emotion recognition based on inter-domain sample hybridization. Front. Hum. Neurosci. (2024). www.frontiersin.org/journals/human-neuroscience/articles/10.3389/fnhum.2024.1464431
22. Xu, F., Zhang, M., Hu, C.: Eescn: a novel spiking neural network method for EEG-based emotion recognition. Neurocomputing (2024). https://www.sciencedirect.com/science/article/abs/pii/S016926072300593X
23. Zhang, F., Chen, Y., Fang, Y.: EEG-based emotion classification using spiking neural networks. In: Proceedings of IEEE (2020). https://ieeexplore.ieee.org/document/9024211
24. Zhang, J., et al.: Transformer-based self-supervised learning for emotion recognition. arXiv preprint (2022). https://arxiv.org/abs/2204.05103
25. Zhang, S., Li, Y., Wang, H.: Fusionsense: emotion classification using feature fusion of multimodal data and deep learning in a brain-inspired spiking neural network. Sensors **20**(18) (2020). https://www.mdpi.com/1424-8220/20/18/5328
26. Zheng, W., Liu, W., Lu, Y., Lu, B., Cichocki, A.: Emotionmeter: a multimodal framework for recognizing human emotions. IEEE Trans. Cybern. 1–13 (2018). https://doi.org/10.1109/TCYB.2018.2797176

# EnMod-DP: An Adaptive Framework and Benchmark for Dynamic Evacuation Pathfinding in Cyber-Physical Systems

G. Balaji[1](✉), Sadanand Venkataraman[1], M. Mahendravarman[1], Santhi Natarajan[1], and G. Ravi Prakash Iyer[2]

[1] Cognition Lab, Shiv Nadar University, Chennai, India
{balajig,sadanand23120023,mahendravarman24120016, santhinatarajan}@snuchennai.edu.in

[2] Krea University, Sri City, India
raviprakash.iyer@krea.edu.in

**Abstract.** Real-time evacuation guidance is a critical safety function for intelligent Cyber-Physical Systems (CPS) in smart buildings and other large-scale physical infrastructures. The core challenge lies in executing complex, multi-objective pathfinding algorithms under stringent real-time constraints. We present EnMod-DP, an accelerated and adaptive framework for evacuation navigation based on a semicontractive Abstract Dynamic Programming (ADP) model. The framework intelligently switches between model-based Dynamic Programming (DP) planners and model-free Reinforcement Learning (RL) policies based on real-time threat assessments, creating a robust hybrid system. We implemented and compared a suite of static, dynamic, and hybrid solvers, including state-of-the-art heuristic approaches like D*-Lite and RL-enhanced A*, in a C++ simulation environment featuring dynamic hazards. Through extensive simulations on grids up to $35 \times 35$, our results demonstrate that the EnMod-DP hybrid approaches achieve the same optimal path quality as computationally expensive dynamic planners while offering significant improvements in execution time and outperforming several dynamic heuristic methods in path quality. We further validate our framework with a multi-agent Cyber-Physical System (CPS) simulation, demonstrating its applicability to real-world, multi-agent evacuation scenarios. These findings establish EnMod-DP as a viable and efficient solution for intelligent, scalable, and adaptive evacuation routing systems.

**Keywords:** Cyber-Physical Systems · Evacuation Navigation · Dynamic Programming · Reinforcement Learning · Hybrid Systems · Multi-Agent Simulation · Abstract Dynamic Programming

## 1 Introduction

The increasing density of urban populations has led to the development of complex Cyber-Physical Human Environments (CPHEs), such as smart buildings


A. Shastri et al. (Eds.): IHCI 2025, LNCS 16437, pp. 462–472, 2026.
https://doi.org/10.1007/978-3-032-26352-0_38

and transportation hubs [1,2]. In the event of an emergency like a fire, providing real-time, optimal evacuation guidance is a life-saving necessity [3]. Traditional pathfinding models often fail to account for the highly dynamic and partially deterministic nature of such crises, where hazards spread and safe exits may change [4,5]. Dynamic Programming (DP) offers a powerful theoretical method for solving such multi-objective optimal control problems [6]. However, its direct application is hampered by the "curse of dimensionality," rendering it computationally intractable for the large state spaces inherent in real-time CPS applications [7]. While Iterative DP (IDP) variants like Forward IDP (FIDP) and Backward IDP (BIDP) offer potential solutions, their computational intensity remains a significant barrier to real-time deployment [8]. Conversely, model-free Reinforcement Learning (RL) excels in environments with unknown dynamics but often requires extensive training and may lack strong optimality guarantees during online adaptation [12].

This paper introduces and validates **EnMod-DP**, a novel framework that addresses these challenges through a hybrid, situation-aware approach grounded in Abstract Dynamic Programming (ADP) principles [6]. The framework employs adaptive policy selection, conceptually aligning with semicontractive ADP models where policy updates depend on the current state (threat level), offering a pragmatic balance between optimality and responsiveness. EnMod-DP functions as a meta-controller that adaptively selects the best planning algorithm in real-time. It leverages the global optimality guarantees of DP in stable conditions and the fast, reactive nature of pre-trained Reinforcement Learning (RL) policies when the agent is in immediate danger. We present a comprehensive C++ simulation environment that implements and compares a wide range of algorithms, from static planners (DP, RL, A*) and dynamic planners (re-planning DP, RL, D*-Lite) to our advanced hybrid models. Our results show that the EnMod-DP framework achieves optimal pathfinding with superior computational efficiency compared to pure dynamic re-planning and often better path quality than dynamic heuristic methods like RL-enhanced A*, making it a practical solution for next-generation safety-critical systems.

## 2 The EnMod-DP Framework

### 2.1 Evacuation Model

We model the evacuation environment as a 2D grid where an agent must navigate from a starting position to a safe exit [9]. The environment is dynamic, with hazards (fire, smoke) that can appear and spread over time, influenced by factors like hazard propagation rate and evacuee distribution [10]. The cost of traversing the grid is multi-objective, considering:

- **Distance**: The number of cells traversed.
- **Time**: The number of time steps taken.
- **Smoke Exposure**: A penalty for moving through cells with smoke, weighted differently based on the agent's current threat level in adaptive models.

The cost function adapts based on the `EvacuationMode` (detailed later) to prioritize safety (avoiding smoke) in ALERT/PANIC modes and speed/distance in NORMAL mode.

### 2.2 Core Planning Algorithms

The EnMod-DP framework integrates and compares several planning algorithms.

**Iterative Dynamic Programming (IDP).** IDP methods compute optimal policies by iteratively updating value functions based on the Bellman equation [6,8]. We implement:

- **Backward IDP (BIDP)**: Computes the optimal cost-to-go from every state to the nearest exit. Efficient for fixed goals.
- **Forward IDP (FIDP)**: Computes the optimal cost from a start state to all others. Useful for path exploration.

Dynamic versions ('DynamicBIDPSim', 'DynamicFIDPSim') recompute the DP solution at each step. We also include solvers based on Asynchronous Value Iteration ('DynamicAVISim') and Asynchronous Policy Iteration ('DynamicAPISim') [11].

**Reinforcement Learning (RL).** Model-free RL algorithms learn policies ($\pi(s) \rightarrow a$) through interaction, suitable for environments with unknown dynamics [12]. We implement:

- **Q-Learning**: Off-policy temporal difference learning.
- **SARSA**: On-policy temporal difference learning.
- **Actor-Critic**: Maintains separate policy (actor) and value function (critic).

These are used both statically (pre-trained) and dynamically (online learning after pre-training).

**Heuristic Search.** We include A* and its dynamic variants for comparison:

- **A*** (`AStarSolver`): Classic heuristic search for static environments.
- **Dynamic A*** (`DynamicAStarSim`): Re-runs A* at each step.
- **D*-Lite** (`DStarLiteSim`): An incremental heuristic search algorithm efficient for dynamic environments.
- **RL-Enhanced A*** (`RLEnhancedAStarSolver`): Uses Q-values from a pre-trained Q-learning agent as heuristics for A* search.

Additional heuristic methods like Anytime Dynamic A* (`ADASolver`) and Hierarchical Pathfinding A* (`DynamicHPASolver`) were also implemented and tested.

### 2.3 The Hybrid, Situation-Aware Approach

The core innovation of EnMod-DP is its adaptive planning strategy, implemented primarily in the **HybridDPRLSolver**. A meta-controller executes a three-stage process at each time step. This approach aims to balance optimality and computational cost based on perceived threat.

**Stage 1: Threat Assessment.** The agent's local threat level is assessed using the `assessThreatAndSetMode` function by analyzing proximity to active fire hazards and adjacent heavy smoke. This determines the current **Evacuation Mode**:

- **NORMAL**: No immediate threats (default state).
- **ALERT**: Agent is within a defined radius of a fire (small: radius = 1, medium: radius = 2, large: radius = 3) or adjacent (Manhattan distance = 1) to "heavy" smoke.
- **PANIC**: Agent's Manhattan distance to a fire cell is $\leq 1$.

The cost function weights change based on the mode, prioritizing smoke avoidance in ALERT/PANIC.

**Stage 2: Adaptive Planner Selection.** Based on the current mode from Stage 1, the `HybridDPRLSolver` selects the algorithm:

- **In NORMAL or ALERT modes**: The system uses a **Dynamic BIDP planner**. This involves running the BIDP algorithm on the current grid state to compute the cost-to-go map. The next move is then determined by selecting the neighboring cell with the minimum cost according to the computed map. The adaptive cost function handles the different priorities between NORMAL and ALERT modes.
- **In PANIC mode**: The system switches to the pre-trained **Q-Learning policy**. The next move is determined by querying the learned Q-table for the current state (agent position) and choosing the action (direction) with the highest Q-value ($\epsilon$-greedy exploration is typically turned off during deployment/simulation after training).

Algorithm 1 outlines this selection logic.

**Stage 3: Action Execution.** The chosen planner's recommended action is executed, and the agent's state is updated for the next time step. This hybrid strategy embodies the principles of a semicontractive Abstract Dynamic Programming system [6]. In ADP, a model is considered semicontractive if applying its mapping operator brings the value function closer to the optimal value function, potentially non-monotonically. Our EnMod-DP framework aligns with this concept: the meta-controller selects a policy (either DP-derived or RL-derived) based on the current state's threat assessment (`EvacuationMode`). Let $J^*$ be

**Algorithm 1** Hybrid DP-RL Control Logic (getNextMove)

**Require:** Current agent position *pos*, current grid state *grid*
**Ensure:** Next move direction *dir*

```
mode ← assessThreatAndSetMode(pos, grid) {Determine NORMAL, ALERT, or PANIC}
Set cost function weights based on mode
if mode = PANIC then
    dir ← rl_solver.chooseAction(pos) {Use pre-trained RL policy}
else
    {Mode is NORMAL or ALERT}
    bidp_planner ← BIDP(grid)
    bidp_planner.run() {Compute cost-to-go map}
    cost_map ← bidp_planner.getCostMap()
    min_cost ← cost_map[pos]
    best_dir ← STAY
    for each neighbor n of pos do
        if grid.isWalkable(n) and cost_map[n] < min_cost then
            min_cost ← cost_map[n]
            best_dir ← direction_to(pos, n)
        end if
    end for
    dir ← best_dir
end if
return dir
```

the optimal cost function and $T_{\pi}$ be the Bellman operator for a policy $\pi$. In our hybrid system, the policy $\pi$ changes based on the state $s$. We apply either the DP operator ($T_{DP}$) in NORMAL/ALERT modes or the RL policy operator ($T_{RL}$) in PANIC mode. The selection depends on the state $s$, denoted $\pi(s)$. The update can be conceptualized as applying a state-dependent operator $T_{\pi(s)}$. While standard DP iterations using $T_{DP}$ alone exhibit monotonic contraction properties under standard conditions (e.g., discounted cost problems), the switching between $T_{DP}$ (globally optimal for the current state snapshot) and the potentially suboptimal but reactive $T_{RL}$ means the overall mapping may only be semicontractive. It aims to drive the system towards $J^*$ by leveraging the strengths of each approach under different state conditions (normal vs. panic), without strict guarantees of monotonic cost reduction at each step [6]. Such state-dependent policy switching is common in ADP formulations designed for complex, real-time control problems where a single monolithic policy may be intractable or suboptimal across the entire state space. While a formal proof of the semicontractive properties and convergence guarantees under these adaptive switching conditions is complex and deferred to future work, the conceptual alignment motivates the architecture designed for real-time adaptability. The `HybridDPRLSolver` also validates the chosen move against the current grid to ensure it's walkable; if not, the agent stays put. This cycle repeats.

## 3 Experimental Setup

To validate our framework, we conducted a comprehensive set of experiments using our C++ simulation environment. We compared 24 different solvers (including static, dynamic, and hybrid variants of DP, RL, and heuristic methods) across scenarios on $20 \times 20$, $25 \times 25$, $30 \times 30$, and $35 \times 35$ grids featuring dynamic fire and smoke hazards designed to test adaptive responses. Solvers were categorized as:

1. **Static Planners (DP, RL & Heuristic)**: Plan once on the initial grid (e.g., BIDP, QLearning, AStar).
2. **Dynamic Simulators (DP, RL & Heuristic)**: Re-plan or adapt at every time step using a single strategy (e.g., DynamicBIDPSim, DynamicQLearningSim, DynamicAStarSim, DStarLiteSim, ADASolver, DynamicHPASolver).
3. **EnMod-DP Hybrid Approaches**: Our new adaptive solvers, including:
   - **HybridDPRLSim**: The core hybrid model switching between DP and RL.
   - **AdaptiveCostSim**: A DP-only model adapting its cost function based on threat level.
   - **InterlacedSim**: Re-plans with BIDP at every step.
   - **HierarchicalSim**: Re-plans a global path periodically.
   - **PolicyBlendingSim**: Blends DP and RL policies based on threat level.
   - **RLEnhancedAStar**: Uses RL Q-values as heuristic for A*.

Performance metrics were the final weighted evacuation cost (smoke * 1000 + time * 10 + distance * 1) and total execution time in milliseconds.

### 3.1 Implementation Details

**Reinforcement Learning Parameters.** The base Reinforcement Learning (RL) agents (`RLSolver`) are configured with the following parameters, defined in `RLSolver.h`:

- **Learning Rate** ($\alpha$): 0.1.
- **Discount Factor** ($\gamma$): 0.9.
- **Exploration Factor** ($\epsilon$): 0.1 (used for $\epsilon$-greedy action selection in Q-Learning and SARSA).

The number of pre-training episodes for static and hybrid solvers varies:

- `HybridDPRLSolver`: 5000 episodes.
- `QLearningSolver`, `SARSASolver`: 5000 episodes (default static training).
- `ActorCriticSolver`: 10000 episodes.
- `RLEnhancedAStarSolver`: 2000 episodes.

**Switching Criteria in Hybrid Solvers.** Adaptive switching is controlled by the `assessThreatAndSetMode` function, implemented consistently across hybrid solvers. The `EvacuationMode` is set based on hazard proximity:

- **PANIC Mode**: Agent's Manhattan distance to an active fire cell $\leq 1$. `HybridDPRLSolver` uses the Q-Learning policy.
- **ALERT Mode**: Agent is within fire radius (small: 1, medium: 2, large: 3) or adjacent to "heavy" smoke. `HybridDPRLSolver` uses Dynamic BIDP; `PolicyBlendingSolver` blends DP and RL. Cost function weights change.
- **NORMAL Mode**: No immediate threats; uses Dynamic BIDP planner.

**Policy Update Frequencies**

- **Static Planners**: Policy computed once initially.
- **Dynamic Simulators**: Re-plan/adapt policy at every time step. Dynamic RL variants include initial offline training (1000–2000 episodes) followed by online updates per step.
- **Hybrid Solvers**:
  - `HybridDPRLSim`, `AdaptiveCostSim`, `InterlacedSim`, `PolicyBlendingSim`, `RLEnhancedAStar`: Re-evaluate and adapt/re-plan every time step.
  - `HierarchicalSim`: Re-plans the global path using BIDP every 10 time steps.

## 4 Results and Discussion

The simulation results validate the EnMod-DP framework's effectiveness. Full results comparing all solvers across $20 \times 20$, $25 \times 25$, $30 \times 30$, and $35 \times 35$ grids are presented in Table 1.

### 4.1 Path Optimality and Efficiency

Key finding: **EnMod-DP hybrid approaches (HybridDPRLSim, AdaptiveCostSim, InterlacedSim, HierarchicalSim, PolicyBlendingSim) consistently found optimal paths** in terms of the weighted cost, matching the exhaustive re-planning 'DynamicBIDPSim' across tested scenarios (up to $35 \times 35$ grids). This confirms adaptive strategies maintain safety and path quality, achieving the same outcome as repeatedly solving the optimal control problem for the current state. Crucially, hybrid methods offer significant **speed advantages**. 'HybridDPRLSim' was consistently among the fastest dynamic solvers, substantially outperforming methods like 'DynamicAPISim' (which suffers from policy iteration overhead) and even baseline dynamic DP methods ('DynamicBIDPSim') in larger grids where the cost of full re-planning becomes prohibitive. The periodically re-planning 'HierarchicalSim' also achieved optimal results with top-tier efficiency.

**Table 1.** Performance Comparison Across Scenarios (Data from)

| Algorithm | 20x20 | | | | | 25x25 | | | | | 30x30 | | | | | 35x35 | | | | |
|---|---|---|---|---|---|---|---|---|---|---|---|---|---|---|---|---|---|---|---|---|
| | Smk | T | Dist | W.Cost | Exec(ms) | Smk | T | Dist | W.Cost | Exec(ms) | Smk | T | Dist | W.Cost | Exec(ms) | Smk | T | Dist | W.Cost | Exec(ms) |
| *Static Planners (DP-Based)* | | | | | | | | | | | | | | | | | | | | |
| BIDP | 0 | 34 | 34 | 374 | 0.36 | 0 | 44 | 44 | 484 | 0.58 | 0 | 54 | 54 | 594 | 0.85 | 0 | 64 | 64 | 704 | 1.16 |
| FIDP | 0 | 34 | 34 | 374 | 0.37 | 0 | 44 | 44 | 484 | 0.59 | 0 | 54 | 54 | 594 | 0.85 | 0 | 64 | 64 | 704 | 1.16 |
| API | 0 | 34 | 34 | 374 | 308.48 | 0 | 44 | 44 | 484 | 1021.80 | 0 | 54 | 54 | 594 | 2662.72 | 0 | 64 | 64 | 704 | 3470.75 |
| *Static Planners (Heuristic)* | | | | | | | | | | | | | | | | | | | | |
| AStar | 0 | 34 | 34 | 374 | 1.43 | 0 | 44 | 44 | 484 | 2.05 | 0 | 54 | 54 | 594 | 4.40 | 0 | 64 | 64 | 704 | 5.03 |
| *Static Planners (RL-Based)* | | | | | | | | | | | | | | | | | | | | |
| QLearning | 0 | 34 | 34 | 374 | 715.55 | 0 | 44 | 44 | 484 | 1135.99 | 0 | 54 | 54 | 594 | 1801.90 | 0 | 64 | 64 | 704 | 2655.93 |
| SARSA | 0 | 34 | 34 | 374 | 600.56 | 0 | 44 | 44 | 484 | 979.54 | 0 | 56 | 56 | 616 | 1802.93 | 0 | 64 | 64 | 704 | 2418.97 |
| ActorCritic | 0 | 34 | 34 | 374 | 2063.92 | 0 | 44 | 44 | 484 | 3328.50 | 0 | 54 | 54 | 594 | 6138.00 | 0 | 64 | 64 | 704 | 11479.10 |
| *Dynamic Simulators (DP-Based)* | | | | | | | | | | | | | | | | | | | | |
| DynamicBIDPSim | 0 | 34 | 34 | 374 | 33.81 | 0 | 44 | 44 | 484 | 66.24 | 0 | 54 | 54 | 594 | 128.83 | 0 | 64 | 64 | 704 | 206.56 |
| DynamicFIDPSim | 0 | 34 | 34 | 374 | 34.45 | 0 | 44 | 44 | 484 | 67.59 | 0 | 54 | 54 | 594 | 130.86 | 0 | 64 | 64 | 704 | 209.93 |
| DynamicAVISim | 0 | 34 | 34 | 374 | 347.57 | 0 | 44 | 44 | 484 | 904.77 | 0 | 54 | 54 | 594 | 2798.06 | 0 | 64 | 64 | 704 | 5388.54 |
| DynamicAPISim | 0 | 34 | 34 | 374 | 22494.80 | 0 | 44 | 44 | 484 | 95227.70 | 0 | 54 | 54 | 594 | 425622.00 | 0 | 64 | 64 | 704 | 659480.00 |
| *Dynamic Simulators (Heuristic)* | | | | | | | | | | | | | | | | | | | | |
| DynamicAStarSim | 0 | 34 | 34 | 374 | 29.29 | 0 | 44 | 44 | 484 | 56.35 | 0 | 54 | 54 | 594 | 98.24 | 0 | 64 | 64 | 704 | 148.54 |
| *Dynamic Simulators (Advanced Heuristic)* | | | | | | | | | | | | | | | | | | | | |
| DynamicHPAStar | 0 | 34 | 34 | 374 | 29.41 | 0 | 44 | 44 | 484 | 57.85 | 0 | 54 | 54 | 594 | 99.25 | 0 | 64 | 64 | 704 | 150.84 |
| ADASolver | Not Run | | | | | Not Run | | | | | Not Run | | | | | Not Run | | | | |
| DStarLiteSim | 0 | 34 | 34 | 374 | 32.28 | 0 | 44 | 44 | 484 | 60.74 | 0 | 54 | 54 | 594 | 101.17 | 0 | 64 | 64 | 704 | 162.04 |
| *Dynamic Simulators (RL-Based)* | | | | | | | | | | | | | | | | | | | | |
| DynamicQLearningSim | 1180 | 166 | 38 | 1181698 | 300.95 | 235 | 164 | 135 | 236775 | 605.53 | 0 | 171 | 171 | 1881 | 1025.29 | 445 | 240 | 164 | 447564 | 1585.38 |
| DynamicSARSASim | 80 | 49 | 38 | 80528 | 240.77 | 265 | 97 | 54 | 266024 | 454.28 | 500 | 290 | 206 | 503106 | 885.09 | 670 | 226 | 107 | 672367 | 1453.47 |
| DynamicActorCriticSim | 1170 | 161 | 34 | 1171644 | 823.39 | 245 | 85 | 44 | 245894 | 1685.85 | 80 | 67 | 56 | 80726 | 3663.02 | 3470 | 771 | 392 | 3478102 | 7266.39 |
| *Dynamic Simulators (Deep RL)* | | | | | | | | | | | | | | | | | | | | |
| DQN | 710 | 604 | 486 | 716526 | 764.91 | FAILURE / N/A | | | | | FAILURE / N/A | | | | | FAILURE / N/A | | | | |
| *EnMod-DP Hybrid Approaches* | | | | | | | | | | | | | | | | | | | | |
| **HybridDPRLSim** | **0** | **34** | **34** | **374** | **34.44** | **0** | **44** | **44** | **484** | **67.31** | **0** | **54** | **54** | **594** | **130.52** | **0** | **64** | **64** | **704** | **208.77** |
| AdaptiveCostSim | 0 | 34 | 34 | 374 | 33.62 | 0 | 44 | 44 | 484 | 66.01 | 0 | 54 | 54 | 594 | 129.31 | 0 | 64 | 64 | 704 | 205.56 |
| InterlacedSim | 0 | 34 | 34 | 374 | 33.62 | 0 | 44 | 44 | 484 | 66.21 | 0 | 54 | 54 | 594 | 128.82 | 0 | 64 | 64 | 704 | 205.93 |
| HierarchicalSim | 0 | 34 | 34 | 374 | 33.64 | 0 | 44 | 44 | 484 | 66.01 | 0 | 54 | 54 | 594 | 128.70 | 0 | 64 | 64 | 704 | 206.22 |
| PolicyBlendingSim | 0 | 34 | 34 | 374 | 33.65 | 0 | 44 | 44 | 484 | 66.50 | 0 | 54 | 54 | 594 | 128.70 | 0 | 64 | 64 | 704 | 207.55 |
| RLEnhancedAStar | 20 | 38 | 36 | 20416 | 149.30 | 10 | 45 | 44 | 10494 | 258.14 | 10 | 55 | 54 | 10604 | 431.74 | 10 | 65 | 64 | 10714 | 763.58 |

Comparisons with other state-of-the-art heuristic and adaptive methods further contextualize these gains. While dynamic heuristic methods like 'DynamicAStarSim' and 'DStarLiteSim' also found optimal paths in these specific scenarios. 'DStarLiteSim', designed for incremental updates based on detected environmental changes, performed well, although its computational cost can depend on the extent of changes. The EnMod-DP hybrids demonstrated comparable or slightly better speed than these full re-planning heuristics ('DynamicAStarSim', 'DynamicHPASolver'), particularly 'HybridDPRLSim' and 'AdaptiveCostSim'. This suggests that the hybrid switching mechanism can be more efficient than full A*-style re-planning in certain dynamic conditions. The 'RLEnhancedAStar' solver, which incorporates RL heuristics, yielded suboptimal paths with significantly higher costs (especially smoke cost). This highlights a potential limitation of purely heuristic guidance in dynamic hazard scenarios; the pre-trained Q-values, while informative, did not consistently lead the A* search to the dynamically optimal path as effectively as explicit re-planning or the DP-based components of the EnMod-DP hybrids. This shows that the EnMod-DP hybrid approaches effectively balance the optimality guarantees of DP with computational efficiency, achieving results comparable to or better than established dynamic heuristic methods in both path quality and speed for these scenarios, while offering a different architectural trade-off compared to incremental methods like D*-Lite.

This efficiency gain without sacrificing optimality is vital for real-time applications [4]. Static planners, while fast, failed in dynamic scenarios (data not shown but implied by the necessity of dynamic approaches), and dynamic RL methods often yielded suboptimal paths and higher costs due to exploration or convergence issues during the simulation. The Deep Q-Network (`DQN`) solver failed to converge reliably in these tests, likely requiring further hyperparameter tuning or architectural adjustments for this specific problem domain.

### 4.2 Multi-agent CPS Simulation

To demonstrate the framework's real-world applicability, we implemented a multi-agent CPS simulation. A central 'MultiAgentCPSController' manages five agents, receiving their positions and providing navigation commands from the 'HybridDPRLSolver'. To avoid collisions, the controller treats other agents as temporary dynamic obstacles (by marking their cells as unwalkable in a temporary grid copy) when planning for each agent. The entire simulation was rendered into a graphical, turn-by-turn HTML report using 'MultiAgentReportGenerator', providing a powerful visual validation of the framework's ability to manage complex, multi-agent scenarios. Figure 1 shows a snapshot from this simulation.

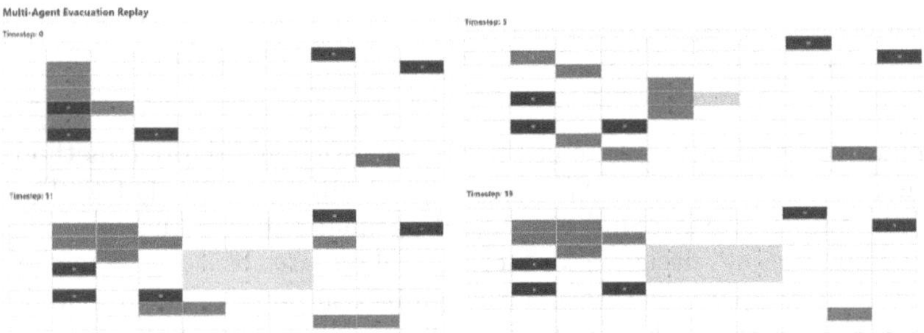


**Fig. 1.** A snapshot from the multi-agent CPS simulation on a $15 \times 15$ grid. Agents (A1-A5) are guided by the central EnMod-DP server, which treats other agents as temporary obstacles (walls) to ensure collision-free paths.

## 5 Conclusions and Future Work

In this work, we have introduced and validated EnMod-DP, a hybrid, adaptive framework for real-time evacuation navigation based on semicontractive ADP principles. Our extensive simulations show that by intelligently switching between model-based DP and model-free RL planners, the system achieves optimal path quality with superior computational efficiency compared to traditional dynamic planners and maintains optimality unlike some heuristic approaches. Based on our promising results, several avenues for future research remain:

- **GPU Acceleration and Parallelism**: To handle truly large-scale environments, the DP and RL algorithms should be ported to a GPU-accelerated platform like CUDA. The grid-based calculations are highly parallelizable and would see a dramatic speedup [13,14]. Further exploration of MPI-based parallelism can also lead to significant performance gains on distributed systems.

- **Real-Time Sensor Integration**: A crucial next step is to integrate the EnMod-DP server with real-world sensor networks (e.g., smoke detectors, thermal cameras, LiDAR for debris) and agent location data (e.g., from Wi-Fi or Bluetooth beacons) to create a true digital twin of the environment.
- **Advanced Reinforcement Learning**: For larger grids, the current Q-table could be replaced with a Deep Q-Network (DQN) or other deep RL methods to handle the vast state space more effectively, potentially improving scalability and performance beyond the limitations observed in our DQN tests [15,16].
- **Human-in-the-Loop Simulation**: Future experiments should include human behavior models to simulate how real people might deviate from suggested paths due to panic, herding behavior, or trust in the system [3].

These directions will help advance the development of intelligent, scalable, and life-saving evacuation routing systems for modern Cyber-Physical Human Environments.

## References

1. Lee, E.A.: Cyber-physical systems: design challenges. In: 11th IEEE International Symposium on Object and Component-Oriented Real-Time Distributed Computing (ISORC), pp. 363–369 (2008)
2. Rajkumar, R., Lee, I., Sha, L., Stankovic, J.: Cyber-physical systems: the next computing revolution. In: Proceedings of the 47th Design Automation Conference, pp. 731–736 (2010)
3. Kobes, M., Helsloot, I., de Vries, B., Post, J.G.: Building safety and human behaviour in fire: a literature review. Fire Saf. J. **45**(1), 1–11 (2010)
4. Hamacher, H.W., Tjandra, S.A.: Mathematical modeling of evacuation problems: a state of the art. In: Pedestrian and Evacuation Dynamics, pp. 227–266. Springer (2002)
5. Gelenbe, E., Gorbil, G., Wu, F.J.: Emergency cyber-physical-human systems. In: 2012 21st International Conference on Computer Communications and Networks (ICCCN), pp. 1–7 (2012)
6. Bertsekas, D.P.: Dynamic Programming and Optimal Control, 4th edn., Vol. I. Athena Scientific (2017)
7. Bellman, R.E.: Dynamic Programming. Princeton University Press (1957)
8. Kostreva, M., Wiecek, M.: Time dependency in multiple objective dynamic programming. J. Math. Anal. Appl. **173**(1), 289–307 (1993)
9. Cao, S., Fu, L., Wang, P., Zeng, G., Song, W.: Experimental and modeling study on evacuation under good and limited visibility in a supermarket. Fire Saf. J. **102**, 27–36 (2018)
10. Xin, J., Huang, C.: Fire risk analysis of residential buildings based on scenario clusters and its application in fire risk management. Fire Saf. J. **62**, 72–78 (2013)

11. El Baz, D., Spiteri, P., Miellou, J.C., Gazen, D.: Asynchronous iterative algorithms with flexible communication for nonlinear network flow problems. J. Parallel Distrib. Comput. **38**(1), 1–15 (1996)
12. Sutton, R.S., Barto, A.G.: Reinforcement Learning: An Introduction, 2nd edn. MIT Press (2018)
13. Mnih, V., et al.: Human-level control through deep reinforcement learning. Nature **518**(7540), 529–533 (2015)
14. Sanders, J., Kandrot, E.: CUDA by Example: An Introduction to General-Purpose GPU Programming. Addison-Wesley Professional (2010)
15. Kirk, D.B., Hwu, W.W.: Programming Massively Parallel Processors: A Hands-on Approach, 3rd edn. Morgan Kaufmann (2016)
16. Silver, D., et al.: Mastering the game of go with deep neural networks and tree search. Nature **529**(7587), 484–489 (2016)

# Body Landmark Dependent ANN Based Real-Time Yoga Pose Detection

Vaidehi Singh and Sandeep Saini(✉)

The LNM Institute of Information Technology, Jaipur, India
{21DEC010,sandeep.saini}@lnmiit.ac.in

**Abstract.** The proposed work introduces a real-time yoga pose detection system that relies on body landmark and joint angle data to classify yoga posture, its lightweight artificial neural network. Classifies eight static yoga poses, uses Mediapipe to extract body landmarks then computes angles, these angles are then scaled and are fed into the neural network as input and the output layer produces a probability distribution across the eight classes using softmax activation, the class with highest probability is the predicted posture. Based on ideal angles, feedback is generated in the form of text for angles where correction of pose is possible. The system is also deployed on raspberry pi hardware as it is an affordable hardware. The purpose of this project is to provide guidance to yoga practitioners so that they can practice yoga anywhere without the risk of injury.

**Keywords:** Tensorflow · Yoga pose estimation · ANN · Mediapipe · Opencv · raspberry pi · deep learning

## 1 Introduction

Yoga is considered a spiritual discipline that originated in India around 3000 years ago. The term 'yoga' is derived from the Sanskrit word 'yuj', which means unite or join [2].

It can be seen more as a way of life, consists of asanas, regulated breathing (pranayama), and awareness of yoga sutms (principles) that govern our mind. According to Patanjali, yoga consists of eight steps or limbs: Yama, Niyama, Asana, Pranayama, Pratyahara, Dharana, Dhyana, Samadhi.

There are several health benefits of yoga, such as improvements in maximum oxygen capacity, muscular strength, flexibility, blood cholesterol profile, and a lower level of perceived exertion at maximum exercise capacity. Several other benefits are improved respiratory and expiratory pressure and a better visual reaction time [18].

With its growing popularity and the number of practitioners, it is commonly observed that people tend to follow certain online tutorials for their practice, leading to the number of people who form incorrect yoga postures, leading to injuries.


A. Shastri et al. (Eds.): IHCI 2025, LNCS 16437, pp. 473–483, 2026.
https://doi.org/10.1007/978-3-032-26352-0_39

Research shows that spine, shoulders, or joint injuries are common among yoga practitioners. Like any other physical exercise, yoga is not without its adverse consequences in incorrect practice, as it has a large base of practitioners. Although it has some adverse effects in incorrect practice, it is found to be beneficial in several medical conditions and its practice is not discouraged, but it is highly recommended to practice yoga in an accurate way or with an experienced tutor. Certain practices such as voluntary vomiting and advanced breathing techniques such as Kapalbhathi are discouraged [7].

There are several people who still self-practice yoga, as we see the surge in online tutorials of yoga practice, in this case without supervision or guidance incorrect posture can lead to injuries. Rather than just copying from a tutorial, having a personal program to correct and guide you to a better or more accurate form can be really beneficial, and it can help reduce the risk of injuries.

Artificial intelligence based systems such as deep learning can help with this problem by providing real-time feedback to the practitioner. Locating the user and forming a skeleton-like structure twin for the user superimposed on the user's image, which is monitored.

This can provide insight about posture, its estimation, error in posture, corrective measures to improve posture, and percentage analysis or a confidence score of the performed asana.

The remainder of the paper is structured as follows. Section 2 describes the review of the literature on related work, Sect. 3 describes the proposed work, Sect. 4 describes the results and discussions, and Sect. 5 describes the conclusion.

## 2 Literature Review

Here we are going to look at related work for yoga pose estimation and raspberry pi hardware implementation.

In [16], the research methodology consists of three main steps: feature extraction, classification, and generating feedback. The data set includes six yoga poses, cobra, tree, mountain, lotus, triangle, and corpse, a total of 70 videos for the dataset. The key point extraction for pose estimation was done using Keras real-time multi-person pose estimation, in this key points for nose, ears and eyes were not collected, a total of 12 joints were recorded which are helpful for detection for example: left shoulder to the left elbow, left elbow to the left wrist, neck to the right hip, right hip to the right knee etc. Vectors for these keypoint coordinates are formed and $\cos\theta$ is calculated. The average values of these angles are calculated for each pose, and the images given as input to the model are classified into one of the six poses with which the values align, and feedback is generated based on the difference in the calculated and ideal values. The paper discusses a number of classification techniques, namely: SVM, CNN, CNN + LSTM, MLP, The accuracy achieved over training and testing datasets, respectively, are (0.9532, 0.9319), (0.9934, 0.9858), (0.9987, 0.9938) and (0.9962, 0.9958). With MLP performing better than the other chosen methods, neural networks (MLP) consist of 3 types of layers, namely, input layer, hidden layers, and output layer. There can be any number of hidden layers based on the complexity of the training data. MLP is a fully connected neural network, that is, every node is connected to every other node in consecutive layers in the neural network.

In [10] talks about the various tools they have used based on their literature survey, input is taken in real time, the output is the predicted or estimated pose along with benefits of that particular asana and cautions through display as well as speaker. This entire project is also deployed on raspberry pi hardware as well. TensorFlow is used as it provides the TensorFlow.js framework that enables the running of the machine learning model in the browser. Mediapipe is used for posture recognition/ keypoint extraction. Pyttsx (a Python library) is used for the text-to-speech functionality, It is used to provide voice feedback for guidance to users. OpenCV is used for image processing. Raspberry pi 4 model used, mini speaker for voice feedback along with Raspberry pi 5MP camera board module.

Paper [8] proposed a "sports co-creation" project which follows human pose recognition and is also deployed on raspberry pi, the work is divided into two processes: first the extraction of coordinates of human joints from the camera input image and secondly the pose estimation from extracted keypoints. PoseNet developed by Google-Coral is used to extract the key points from the input feed. The process involves feeding the image to a convolutional neural network to encode the RBG image, the model used for encoding was MobileNetV1, the keypoints are then obtained after going through the decoding algorithm for which a heatmap is generated, this is done for estimating the area around the key points, after estimating the area around the key points the final output(the keypoints) are obtained by going through the offset vector generated along side the heatmap to rule out the rough estimations caused by the lattice shaped subimage produced by it. The study involves the estimation of 10 human postures with postures like hand movements and leg movements along with shoulder movements, etc. The system was able to achieve semi-real-time estimation with accuracy of 70% for 3 postures and 2 movements. Although the accuracy for most postures and movements ranged from 13.3–73.6%, two postures (right hand up and left hand up) obtained the accuracy of 99.2 and 97.1%, respectively.

The study [6] used a variety of models, including random trees, logistic regression, randomized trees, gradient boosting and deep neural networks, it employed the Yoga-82 dataset. In their study, the highest accuracy was achieved by extremely randomized trees with a score of 91% for the test dataset and 92% for the training dataset. Other models like random forest, gradient boosting, extreme gradient boosting, and deep neural networks achieved accuracy of 90%, 89%, 90%, and 85%, respectively, while logistic regression underperformed, having the lowest accuracy. In their proposed work, the dataset used is Yoga-82 which was developed in [14], consists of 82 yoga pose classes with images downloaded from the Internet at various angles. MLKit Pose Estimation is used, which is a mobile software development kit from Google that provides APIs for machine learning assignments, it includes various features, and pose estimation is one of those. The X, Y coordinates from MLKit are used for calculating the angle between the body parts, however, the angel calculated using this method may vary based on the angle between the camera and the subject as well as the distance, Z coordinate may be used to overcome this; however, this is stated as one of the limitations for their research work. The pseudocode is provided within the paper for the calculation of angle: The vectors are computed on the basis of the coordinates, and then the dot product is computed to calculate the cosine angle converted to radians and then subsequently into degrees. One of the key advantages of this research is that it aims towards the future creation of a yoga pose classification app which can have a wide-spread positive impact and can be of important application in real world scenario.

In [3], an SYD-net architecture was proposed that integrates patch-based attention (PbA). SYD is an acronym for Sports, Yoga and Dance. PbA module, SYD-Net integrated spatial attention, and channel attention to standard CNNs. A patch-based approach is devised to learn contexts from various parts of the image at multiple scales, the aim is to integrate detailed information from several smaller overlapping image patches into a feature descriptor. It fuses where to focus and what to emphasize simultaneously in the feature maps F. Cross CA investigates the importance of feature maps (what) to enhance learning capability. In contrast, SA explores neighborhood structural interpretation for producing a spatial attentional mask (where) for further refinement of aggregated feature summarization. The dataset used for the classification of yoga postures is Yoga-82, available on the Internet along with Yoga-107 from Kaggle, the model is implemented using ResNet-50, DenseNet-201, NASNetMobile, MobileNet-v2, and Xception backbone CNNs. Yoga-82, using a variant for DenseNet-201 has attained 79.35% top-1 accuracy and 93.47% top-5 accuracy.

The paper [15] is a survey of the techniques, algorithms, and technologies which are used for yoga pose estimations; it is divided into several sections with topics ranging from pose estimation, keypoint detection methods, deep learning methods for classification, etc. Table 1 below states some of the methods used and some of the methods with higher accuracy in the input type of RBG.

**Table 1.** Some of the methods which achieve higher accuracy [15]

| Paper | Year | Method | Pose Classes | Accuracy |
|---|---|---|---|---|
| [9] | 2020 | OpenPose + ML, DNN | 6 | 99.38% |
| [12] | 2019 | OpenPose + CNN + LSTM | 6 | 98.92% |
| [11] | 2021 | 3-D CNN | 6 | 99.39% |
| [4] | 2021 | Mediapipe + Transfer Learning | 14 | 98.43% |
| [17] | 2020 | tf-pose estimation + ML | 10 | 99.04% |
| [1] | 2023 | PoseNet + MobileNet-SSD | 7 | 99.88% |
| [13] | 2022 | Multi-Layered Perceptron | 6 | 99.58% |

## 3 Proposed Architecture

Yoga pose detection comes with its own challenges, even after the advancement made in AI technology, detecting a person's posture is still a challenge in CV, they come from several different sources namely image size, resolution, lighting changes, clothing changes, surroundings, etc. Other challenges such as different physiological functions of different bodies built by different people, as well as the difference in the anatomy of men and women raise concern with inaccurate detection of the same postures among them. In addition to this, there can be a variation in the proportion of the human in the training data set and the yoga practitioner [15].

The proposed work is a real-time yoga pose estimator/detector, a lightweight body-landmark-based artificial neural network (ANN), it can overcome the issues raised above as it is based on the landmark detection rather than feeding and training on the entire image as we see in traditional CNNs. Conventional CNNs process entire image frames and are sensitive to irrelevant visual data, they suffer from challenges such as insufficient training data, occlusion, and ambiguity in depth and scale. The model focuses on the extracted landmarks, keypoint-based human pose representations have been proven to generalize better to unseen environments and are preferred for action recognition and posture correction [5], using Mediapipe, which in turn solves the issue of training separate models for men and women, by focusing on landmark detection and angle calculation. The model avoids gender or body-specific bias which makes it suitable for everyone, enhancing general application and robustness. This also leads to a lower complexity and lightweight model, with fewer parameters than traditional CNNs. We have used Mediapipe for the landmark detection (see Fig. 1), which gives 33 landmarks, but for the detection of yoga postures 12 joints are used, which are critical to determining the poses which are selected, which in turn further reduces the parameters and complexity of out model.

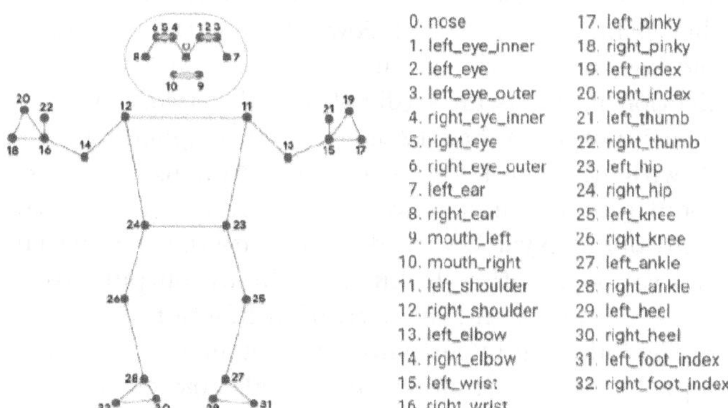


**Fig. 1.** Mediapipe Pose landmarks

The implementation of the proposed model utilizes MediaPipe to extract 33 human pose landmarks and OpenCV to handle image processing tasks, capturing camera feed, drawing landmarks, for feedback. In addition, commonly used libraries such as NumPy, Pandas, and Matplotlib were used. For the development and training of the neural network, Scikit-learn and TensorFlow were used as the main deep learning frameworks, for label encoding and feature scaling, and for designing the neural network. The model can detect 8 yoga postures, Ardhchandrasan (Half Moon Pose), Baddhakonasana (Butterfly Pose), Adho Mukha Svanasana (Downward Dog Pose), Natrajasana (Dancer Pose), Trikonasana (Triangle Pose), Utkata Konasana (Goddess Pose), Virbhadrasana (Warrior Pose), Vrikshasana (Tree Pose).

The pipeline of the proposed work is as follows. The system takes real-time input from camera feed, each frame is processed using Mediapipe Pose, which returns (x, y, z) coordinates and a visibility confidence score. These landmarks are the coordinates of crucial joints like the elbows, wrists, shoulders, hips, etc. Of the 33 landmarks, 12 specific joints are selected that are helpful in estimating the pose, the specific joints such as left elbow angle, right elbow angle, left shoulder angle, right shoulder angle, left knee angle, right knee angle, hand angle, left hip angle, etc.

The angle is calculated using the atan2 function, which provides stable angle measurements and is well aware of the quadrant to provide accurate results. The mathematical equation for angle calculation is as follows:

$$\theta = \tan^{-1}\left(\frac{y_3 - y_2}{x_3 - x_2}\right) - \tan^{-1}\left(\frac{y_1 - y_2}{x_1 - x_2}\right) \tag{1}$$

In implementation, this is computed using the `atan2` function as follows:

$$\theta = \texttt{atan2}(y_3 - y_2, x_3 - x_2) - \texttt{atan2}(y_1 - y_2, x_1 - x_2) \tag{2}$$

Each angle reflects the position of the joint with respect to the other two, along with these average visibility score is calculated if they are not clearly visibile, i.e., the visibility score falls below 0.6, and the corresponding angle is skipped to avoid incorrect classification.

The classification model is an artificial neural network built using Keras in TensorFlow. The input layer has 12 neurons corresponding to the 12 joints, hidden layer 1 with 64 neurons activation function used is ReLu, a dropout layer with dropout rate 0.2, hidden layer 2 with 32 neurons the same activation function, ReLu, dropout layer 2 with dropout rate 0.2, hidden layer 3 with 16 neurons and activation function ReLu, and finally output layer which has 8 neurons for the 8 yoga poses and the activation function is softmax. The model is trained using the following hyper-parameter settings: Adam optimizers, batch size as 16, 60 epochs, loss function as categorical cross entropy, validation split as 20% and training and testing split of data set as 80% and 20% respectively.

After the joints are extracted on the basis of the visibility confidence score, the angles are scaled using the standard scaling method to bring all angles into a common range. These angles are passed into the trained ANN, which produces a probability distribution across 8 defined yoga poses. The pose with the highest probability score is the predicted pose and taken as output of the classification process. The predicted pose is then displayed to the user along with a reference picture an "ideal image" for the predicted pose with the skeleton structure imposed onto them to increase the usefulness of the system and to benefit the user. The user's joint angles are then compared to the ideal angles based on the image to further improve the practitioner's pose. The system operates in real time, updating predictions and feedback while the practitioner is forming the pose.

The architecture is efficient, as it overcomes the limitations offered by traditional CNNs and full image classification systems. The limited number of input features keeps the model efficient, as it is also deployed on raspberry pi, which shows the lightweight and efficient performance of our model. The flow chart of the system can be seen in Fig. 2. Raspberry pi hardware is chosen for deployment due to its affordability, portability along with its compatibility with lightweight models, and availability of external device attachments such as webcams.

## 4 Results and Discussion

The hyperparameters selected to train this model are: Adam optimizers, batch size 16, 60 epochs, loss function as categorical cross-entropy, validation split as 20% and training and testing split of the data set as 80% and 20% respectively. See Fig. 5 for the confusion matrix of the test dataset. The model was able to achieve train and test accuracy of 99.48% and 95.88%, respectively. The system was also deployed on raspberry pi hardware; the hardware used is the raspberry pi 400, which consists of a 64-bit processor along with 4GB RAM, the camera used along with it has resolution of 2MP with USB interface. See Fig. 3 and Fig. 4 for the graphs of the performance of the model on the local system and Raspberry pi hardware, respectively.

The accuracy and efficiency of our model are comparable with the papers discussed in Sect. 2 (Literature Review) of this paper, the accuracy is higher than the papers discussed later on, the reason it is so is that the model was trained extensively on video dataset where as the proposed model was trained on image data set and is used for real-time detection. [8] aimed at human posture recognition; however, the accuracy ranged from 13-70%. [10] the accuracy or other parameter to measure efficiency are not stated, however, the feedback generation developed in this is innovative and interactive, as it uses audio along with display. [6] the accuracies attained by the models ranged from 85% to 91% with the highest accuracy obtained by extremely randomized trees.

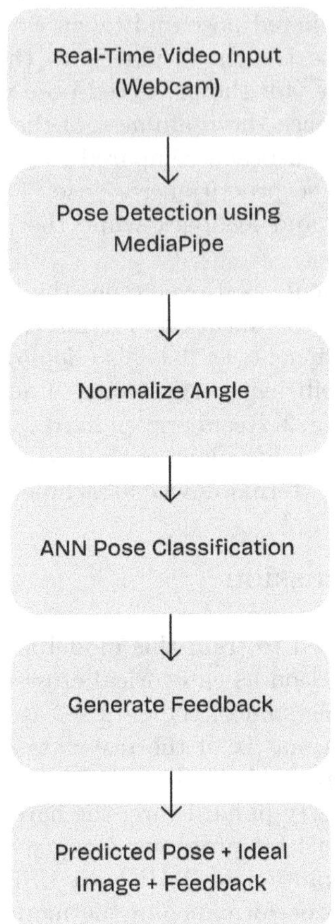


**Fig. 2.** Flow chart of the system

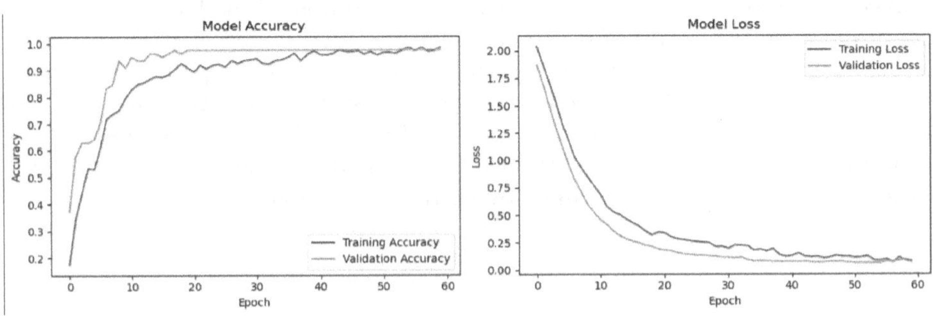


**Fig. 3.** In local system a) The epoch vs accuracy graph b) The epoch vs loss graph

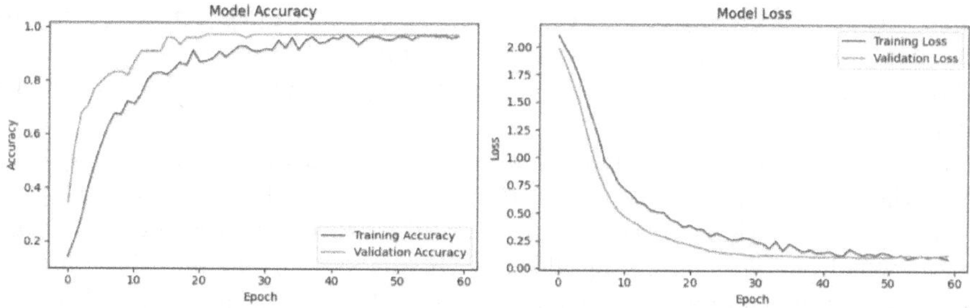


**Fig. 4.** In raspberry pi a) The epoch vs accuracy graph b) The epoch vs loss graph

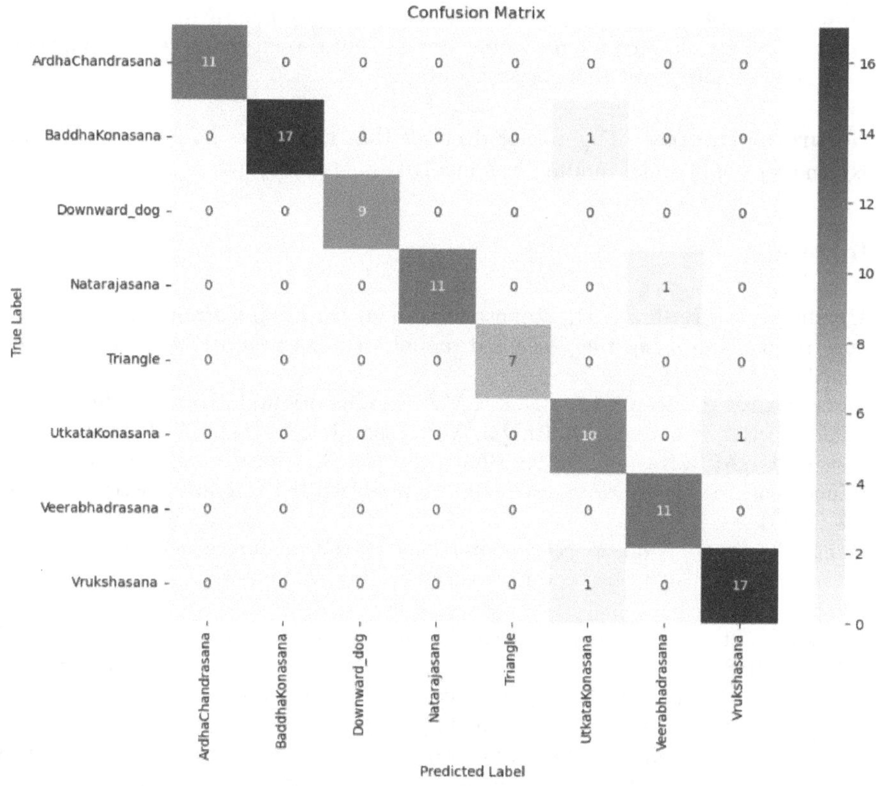


**Fig. 5.** Confusion matrix for test dataset

## 5 Conclusion

The proposed work presents a lightweight ANN model for real-time posture detection using body landmarks, which helps to keep the model comparatively simpler. As it is skeleton-based, it helps the model to work across a wide user base, regardless of background, clothing, and physical built.

The system successfully classifies 8 yoga poses and generates feedback if there is scope for improvement in the posture.

Future aspects for this project can be involvement of text-to-speech conversion of the feedback, as while performing a pose practitioner may not be able to read the instructions in this scenario, audio guides, increasing the number of poses which we are classifying along with their variations and dynamic yoga poses such as Suryanamaskar which consists of 14 poses, or addition of breathing cues can be helpful, as inhaling and exhaling in the correct postures in a given set of dynamic pose is essential.

**Acknowledgment.** The author gratefully acknowledges The LNM Institute of Information Technology, Jaipur, for providing the computational resources and infrastructure necessary to carry out this research work.

**Disclosure of Interest.** The author declares that they have no conflict of interest. No external or commercial funding was involved in this research.

## References

1. Upadhyay, A., Basha, N.K., Ananthakrishnan, B.: Deep learning-based yoga posture recognition using the ypn-mssd model for yoga practitioners. Healthcare **11** (2023)
2. Dubey, A.K., Pradeep Yadav, D.T.R.M.: Yoga: its origin, history and development. Swadeshi Res. Found. A Monthly J. Multidisc. Res. **10**(11), 67–70 (2023)
3. Asish Bera, Mita Nasipuri, O.K., Bhattacharjee, D.: Fine-grained sports, yoga, and dance postures recognition: a benchmark analysis. IEEE Trans. Instrum. Measur. **72** (2023)
4. Long, C., Jo, E., Nam, Y.: Development of a yoga posture coaching system using an interactive display based on transfer learning. J. Supercomput. **78**, 5269–5284 (2022)
5. Zheng, C., et al.: Deep learning-based human pose estimation: a survey. J. ACM **37**(04) (2018)
6. Borthakur, D., Paul, A., Kapil, D., Saikia, M.J.: Yoga pose estimation using angle-based feature extraction. Healthcare **11**(24) (2023)
7. Cramer, H., Krucoff, C., Dobos, G.: Adverse events associated with yoga: A systematicreview of published case reports and case series. PLOS ONE **08**(10) (2013)
8. Yamao, K., Kubota, R.: Development of human pose recognition system by using raspberry pi and posenet model. In: International Symposium on Communications and Information Technologies (ISCIT), Vol. 20, pp. 41–44 (2021)
9. Kothari., V.: Yoga pose classification using deep learning (2020)
10. Lavanya, Y.N., Rajalakshmi, N.N., Sumanth, K., Gowrishankar, S., Asha Rani, K.P.S.: A novel approach for developing inclusive real-time yoga pose detection for health and wellness using raspberry pi. In: International Conference on Computation System and Information Technology for Sustainable Solutions, Vol. 07 (2023)

11. Jain, S., Rustagi, A., Saurav, S., Saini, R., Singh, S.: Three-dimensional CNN-inspired deep learning architecture for yoga pose recognition in the real-world environment. Neural Comput. Appl. **33**, 6427–6441 (2021)
12. Yadav, S.K., Singh, A., Gupta, A., Raheja, J.L.: Real-time yoga recognition using deep learning. Neural Comput. Appl. **31**, 9349–9361 (2019)
13. Anand Thoutam, V., et al.: Yoga pose estimation and feedback generation using deep learning. Comput. Intell. Neurosci. (2022)
14. Verma, M., Kumawat, S., Nakashima, Y., Raman, S.: Yoga-82: A new dataset for fine-grained classification of human poses. In: Proceedings of the IEEE/CVF Conference on Computer Vision and Pattern Recognition Workshops, Seattle, WA, USA, 13–19 June 2020 (2020)
15. Chamola, V., Gummana, E.P., Madan, A., Rout, B.K., Coelho Rodrigues, J.J.P.: Advancements in yoga pose estimation using artificial intelligence: a survey. Current Bioinf. ResearchGate **19**(03), 264–280 (2024)
16. Anand Thoutam, V., et al.: Yoga pose estimation and feedback generation using deep learning. Comput. Intell. Neurosci. **2022**(01) (2022)
17. Agrawal, Y., Shah, Y., Sharma, A.: Implementation of machine learning technique for identification of yoga poses. In: 2020 IEEE 9th International Conference on Communication Systems and Network Technologies (CSNT), pp. 40–43. IEEE (2020)
18. Sharma, Y., Sharma, S., Sharma, E.: Scientific benefits of yoga: a review. Res. Rev. Int. J. Multidisc. **03**(08), 144–148 (2018)

# Audio Spectrogram Transformer for Automatic Speech-Based Depression Detection

Hitesh Arjunbhai Ramrakhiyani[1(✉)], Himashri Deka[1], Sandeep Kumar Pandey[2], N. S. Sreenivasalu[4], Hanumant Singh Shekhawat[1], and Ravi Jasuja[3]

[1] Indian Institute of Technology Guwahati, Guwahati, India
{ahitesh,h.s.shekhawat,h.s.shekhawat}@iitg.ac.in
[2] Acuity Knowledge Partners, Pune, India
sandeepandey456@gmail.com
[3] Brigham and Women's Hospital, Harvard Medical School, Boston, MA, USA
rjasuja@bw.harvard.edu
[4] XYonetx Therapeutics, Hyderabad, India

**Abstract.** This Research investigates the effectiveness of an Audio Spectrogram Transformer (AST) using a moderate negative mining technique to detect depression from speech automatically. Addressing the significant challenge of class imbalance in the DAIC-WoZ speech depression dataset, we implemented a moderate negative mining technique to selectively sample negative instances for balancing the dataset, thereby enhancing model learning and overall performance. The approach leverages transfer learning by fine-tuning a pre-trained AST model on the DAIC-WoZ dataset. Experimental evaluation demonstrates that the proposed method achieves robust classification results, attaining a macro F1 score of 0.7353 and a test accuracy of 76.43%. The findings indicate that integrating moderate negative mining with transformer-based audio models on imbalanced datasets provides a promising direction for improving automated, speech-based depression detection.

**Keywords:** Speech Depression Classification · Transfer Learning · Transformer Self Attention

## 1 Introduction

Depression is a widespread and complex mental health disorder that is characterized by an ongoing state of low mood, accompanied by a significant loss of interest or pleasure in daily activities. Individuals may also experience a spectrum of cognitive difficulties, such as impaired concentration and negative thought patterns, along with various physical symptoms, including fatigue and changes in appetite [1]. Depression is deeply linked with human emotions—disruptions cite bylsma2021emotionsuch as difficulty managing sadness or anhedonia (the


A. Shastri et al. (Eds.): IHCI 2025, LNCS 16437, pp. 484–492, 2026.
https://doi.org/10.1007/978-3-032-26352-0_40

inability to feel pleasure) [2], are core features of the condition. People with depression often experience emotional blunting, reduced emotional reactivity, and challenges in recognizing or expressing emotions.

According to the World Health Organization (WHO), depression is a leading cause of disability worldwide, affecting more than 264 million people and impacting individuals' thoughts, behaviors, emotions, and overall well-being. Depression can affect individuals of all ages and backgrounds, contributing significantly to the global burden of disease [2].

Recognizing depression is crucial because untreated depression can lead to severe consequences, including impaired social and occupational functioning and an increased risk of suicide. Early recognition allows for timely intervention and improved treatment outcomes. Depression can be recognized through various modalities:

- **Speech:** Depressed individuals may exhibit slower speech, monotone voice, reduced verbal output, and negative content.
- **Facial expressions:** Research shows that people with depression may have impaired ability to recognize or express emotions through facial expressions, often presenting with less expressive faces and difficulty recognizing happiness in others [3,4]
- **Text and Behavior:** In written communication, depression is often signaled by increased use of first-person pronouns, negative word choices, and expressions of hopelessness. Behaviorally, withdrawal from activities and social interactions is common.

AI models are increasingly used to recognize depression by analyzing data from different modalities, including speech, facial expressions (video), and written text. Each modality reveals unique signals associated with depressive states, and advanced AI techniques can leverage these features for reliable detection and monitoring. To use AI models, we need large, high-quality datasets labeled with depression severity or diagnostic information essential for training and validating models. Datasets related to clinical problems are facing the issue of imbalanced data because they have a good number of samples from healthy people, but have limited samples from depressed patients, resulting in learning models showing bias towards the majority class samples.

To evaluate depression severity, the PHQ-8 (Patient Health Questionnaire-8) is a widely used, self-administered tool for assessing depression severity in adults. It consists of eight questions—each addressing one of the core symptoms of major depressive disorder. The total score can vary from 0 to 24, with higher scores indicating more severe depression symptoms. The PHQ-8 evaluates key depressive symptoms such as low mood, loss of interest, sleep disturbances, fatigue, appetite changes, feelings of worthlessness or guilt, concentration problems, and psychomotor changes [5].

In this paper, we have used speech as a modality to classify depressive cues using a pre-trained audio spectrogram transformer model fine-tuned on the speech depression dataset Distress Analysis Interview Corpus - Wizard of Oz

(DAIC-WoZ) [6] and addressed issue of dataset imbalance using moderate negative mining method to enhance accuracy and other classification metrics, and further details of the conducted study are given in the subsequent sections.

### 1.1 Related Work

Automatic recognition of depression from speech has become a prominent research area owing to the prevalence of depression and advances in machine learning. Early studies primarily utilized handcrafted acoustic features with traditional classifiers such as SVMs and random forests, achieving moderate success on clinical datasets. With the advent of deep learning, more recent work has leveraged LSTM and CNN models to capture temporal and spectral nuances of speech, leading to improved performance. Publicly available datasets like DAIC-WOZ and MODMA have enabled benchmarking. Still, challenges remain in dataset diversity, robustness, and clinical adoption—the following review surveys key developments, representative methodologies, and the evolving landscape of speech-based depression detection.

Early works on depression detection in speech are devoted to extracting practical features from highly correlated problems with depression. Cummins et al. [7] studied the speech trajectory in acoustic space, which becomes smoother with increasing depression, and focused on tightly concentrated MFCC features. Ma et al. [8] proposed the DepAudioNet architecture, which had a 1-D CNN and an LSTM layer to classify speech depression cues, and the DAIC-WoZ dataset, which is imbalanced. To balance it, they used a random sampling technique to remove bias towards majority class samples, and they achieved 0.52 and 0.7 F1 scores on depressed and non-depressed samples, respectively. Sandeep et al. [9] proposed a novel tensor-based approach using mel-spectrogram features with multiple instance learning on a TFNN model with an F1 score of (0.7, 0.6) for (non-depressed, depressed) samples and an unweighted accuracy of 60%. W. Chen et al. [10] proposed a transformer-based SpeechFormer++ model on the speech depression dataset with handcrafted and HuBert features, with unweighted accuracy of 65.8%.

The study explores various models previously applied to classify depressed speech, highlighting their limitations. Traditional machine learning approaches like SVM and random forest rely on handcrafted features such as pitch, MFCC, jitter, and shimmer, which restrict their ability to model sequences effectively. In contrast, CNNs utilize spectrograms to learn the local context but fail to capture long-range temporal dependencies.

In the past, many researchers have proposed models that combine attention layers with convolutional neural network (CNN) layers to learn spatial and long-range global context. However, our study used a model entirely based on attention mechanisms without convolutional layers. This purely attention-based model can be directly applied to audio spectrograms, effectively capturing long-range global context even in the lowest layers. Additional details about the model will be provided in the following sections.

## 2 Methodology

This section outlines the experimental design and our strategy for fine-tuning the audio spectrogram transformer model [11]. The AST utilizes pre-trained weights from the data-efficient image transformer (DeiT), which has been trained using CNN knowledge distillation with 384 × 384 images and contains 87 million parameters. We fine-tuned our model by freezing the initial layers, which include the Distilled Vision Transformer (DeiT) module.

We updated the final classification layer (mlp_head) for two classes and trained it on the speech depression dataset. The pre-trained DeiT module is a core feature extractor trained on a large dataset, ImageNet, which enhances the model's ability to classify speech depression. In addition, we examine various classification metrics to ensure that the model is robust in identifying speech depression. The experimental framework is illustrated in Fig. 1 below.

### 2.1 Speech Depression Dataset

In this study, we used the Distress Analysis Interview Corpus - Wizard of Oz (DAIC-WoZ) [6] speech depression dataset to train our deep learning model, which contains a total of 189 speech audio recordings, along with text transcripts. Out of 189 participants, 132 were standard controls, and the remaining 57 were depressed participants. The audio recording is at a sampling rate of 16000 Hz. The data set was collected in a closed room with a participant and Ellie (a computer agent who is an interviewer and a human outside the room controls). In the interview, Ellie asked participants several questions about their past experiences, jobs, interests in activities, etc. With the dataset, Patient Health Questionnaire (PHQ-8) scores [5] were also given as a measure of depression.

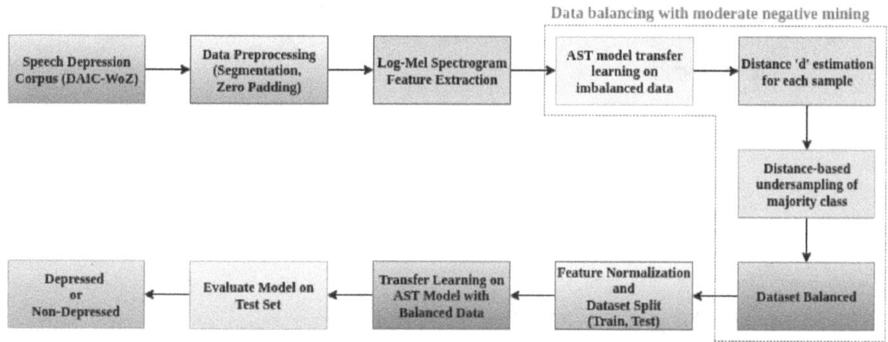


**Fig. 1.** Experimental framework of this study.

### 2.2 Data Preprocessing and Feature Extraction

In our study, we used audio recordings to classify participants as either depressed or non-depressed. We excluded segments of silence and the voice of the computer agent, Ellie, and focused solely on the participants' voices for further processing. As our pre-trained AST model was also trained on ImageNet and AudioSet dataset [12] (which contains audio recordings of 10 s), since the tapes varied in length, we needed to ensure uniform input sizes for training the model. To achieve this, we segmented the participants' voice recordings into 10-second chunks, assigning the same label to each chunk as the recording from which it was derived. Subsequently, we extracted the Log-Mel Spectrogram using the librosa library [13] from these 10-second segments to input the model. We extracted 128 dimensions of log-mel features computed with a 25 ms hamming window and hop length of 10 msec, and the input size of the mel-spectrogram feature to the model is $1024 \times 128$.

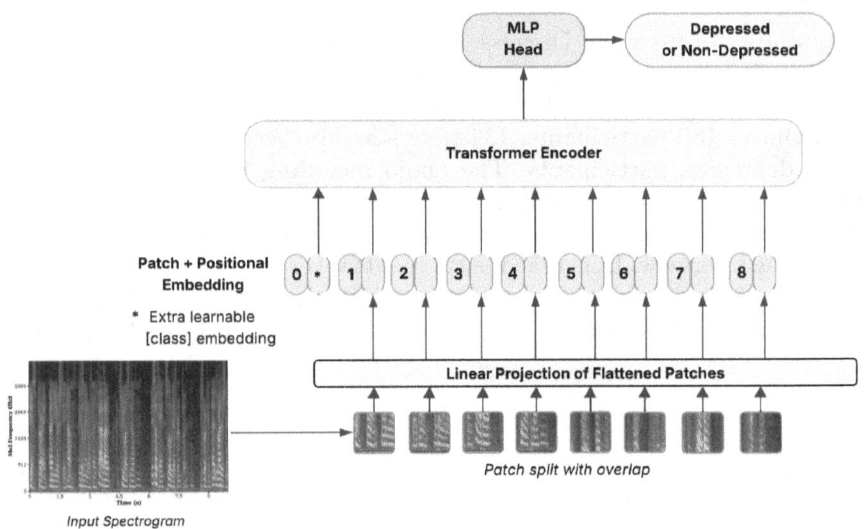


**Fig. 2.** Model architecture of AST model.

### 2.3 Moderate Negative Mining (MNM)

As we stated previously, the dataset used in this study is imbalanced, with the depressed class segments as the minority class and the non-depressed segments as the majority class. When we trained the model on this imbalanced dataset, it showed bias towards majority class samples, and its performance was uneven across the classes. The study by Song et al. [14] proposed a moderate negative mining (MNM), an under-sampling approach to balance the data set by identifying an essential factor contributing to the model's uneven performance. This factor is the distance between samples from the majority class and the classification boundary of the classifier model. This study used this factor to balance the dataset and improve the model's performance.

Since our model employs a softmax classifier in the final layer, we utilize the predicted probabilities to effectively assess the distance of majority class samples from the classification boundary. Here, we used 0.5 as the decision threshold in the softmax layer. Equation (1) shows the $i$th class probability using the softmax function:

$$p_i = \frac{e^{W_i^T \cdot x}}{\sum_j e^{W_j^T \cdot x}} \tag{1}$$

where $i$ is in $\{0, 1\}$, $W$ represents the learned weights of the softmax classifier, and $x$ denotes a data point in the embedding space. Thus, the classification hyperplane is:

$$(W_0 - W_1)^T \cdot x = 0. \tag{2}$$

For any data point in the majority class $x$, its signed distance to the classification hyperplane is:

$$\begin{aligned} d &= \frac{(W_0 - W_1)^T \cdot x}{||W_0 - W_1||} \\ &\propto (W_0 - W_1)^T \cdot x \\ &\propto \ln(p_0 \cdot \sum_j e^{W_j^T \cdot x}) - \ln(p_1 \cdot \sum_j e^{W_j^T \cdot x}) \\ &\propto \ln \frac{p_0}{1 - p_0} \end{aligned} \tag{3}$$

As per Eq. (3), the distance between majority class samples and the classification hyperplane is increasing concerning $p_0$ (probability of majority class samples). According to the MNM approach, we trained the model on an imbalanced dataset. Then we estimated the distance using the above equations by observing the probability of the majority class samples. Based upon which we selected samples, where the majority class probability $p_0$ lies in the range [0.39, 0.70], making both majority samples equal to the minority class to balance the data set. That balanced data set was used to train the AST classifier model.

### 2.4 Classification Model

Our Research employs the pre-trained Audio Spectrogram Transformer (AST) [11] to address these shortcomings to harness long-range global context for enhanced performance. This model was applied to the DAIC-WoZ dataset, where inputs are speech audio spectrograms categorized into depressed and non-depressed speech. The architecture of the AST model is illustrated in Fig. 2.

We fine-tuned the AST, which was pre-trained on ImageNet and the Audioset dataset, and examined classification metrics such as precision, recall, and the F1 score.

Our AST model adapts the Vision Transformer (ViT) architecture for audio tasks by converting audio signals into spectrograms. Here, AST has adapted concepts for patching images from ViT. A similar concept has been used by splitting the input audio-spectrogram of size $128 \times 1024$ into a sequence of $16 \times 16$ patches with an overlap of 6 in both time and frequency dimensions. These patches are projected linearly to create a sequence of one-dimensional patch embeddings. Each embedding includes a learnable positional embedding, and one classification token [class] is added at the start of the sequence.

The embedding is processed using a transformer encoder, with the classification token's output utilized for the final classification through a linear layer. The architecture of the transformer encoder includes an embedding dimension of 768, with 12 layers and 12 attention heads. The output of the [class] token represents the audio spectrogram, which is then mapped to classification labels using a linear layer with a softmax activation function having two output neurons, which output the probability of each class.

## 3 Results and Discussion

The AST model was fine-tuned on the DAIC-WoZ speech depression corpus for 20 epochs using the Adam optimizer with a learning rate 0.0005 and a batch size 16. The input features were mel-spectrograms of size $128 \times 1024$. Due to the DAIC-WoZ dataset's significant class imbalance—where non-depressed samples vastly outnumber depressed ones—the model tended to be biased toward the majority class, resulting in suboptimal performance on the minority class. We employed a Moderate Negative Mining (MNM) [14]technique to mitigate this.

In this approach, the AST model was initially trained on the imbalanced dataset, and the output probabilities for both classes were analyzed. Specifically, samples from the non-depressed class with moderate confidence scores—those neither classified with very high nor very low probability—were selected. These moderately complex negative samples are closer to the depressed class in the feature space and provide more informative training instances. By focusing on these samples during subsequent training and inference, MNM balances the effective training set and reduces the bias toward the majority class, improving the model's discrimination ability and generalization for depression detection.

After training, we tested the fine-tuned model on the test dataset, and due to the imbalanced dataset, we analyzed Macro Avg. The F1 score, the unweighted arithmetic mean of individual class F1 scores, treats all classes equally regardless of their size. It is a good choice for imbalanced datasets where all classes are considered equally important. We reported a Macro F1 score of 0.7353, test accuracy of 76.43%, precision of 0.8755, and recall of 0.7764. The confusion matrix and classification metrics are given in Fig. 3 and Table 1, respectively.

**Table 1.** Comparison of classification results with state-of-the-art methods: Depressed(Non-Depressed)

| Model | Precision | Recall | F1 Score |
|---|---|---|---|
| DepAudioNet [8] | 0.35(1.00) | 1.00(0.54) | 0.52(0.70) |
| TFNN MIL [9] | 0.54(0.62) | 0.67(0.8) | 0.60(0.70) |
| Speechformer-CTC [15] | 0.61(0.82) | 0.57(0.84) | 0.59(0.83) |
| CNN-LSTM [16] | -(-) | -(-) | 0.51(0.86) |
| AST-finetuned [proposed] | **0.58**(0.87) | 0.73(0.77) | **0.64(0.82)** |

According to the findings, the AST model performs well compared to state-of-the-art methodologies in capturing the global range context of the audio spectrogram. As per the results, our model performs well in terms of metrics accuracy, F1 score, and precision-depressed compared to other DepAudioNet and TFNN-MIL models.

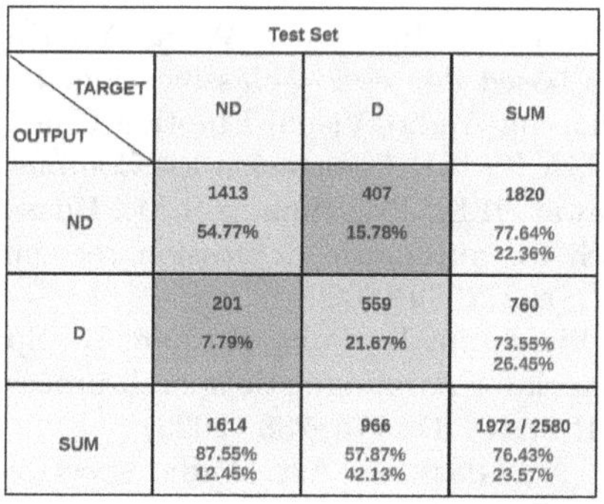

| Test Set | | | |
|---|---|---|---|
| TARGET / OUTPUT | ND | D | SUM |
| ND | 1413<br>54.77% | 407<br>15.78% | 1820<br>77.64%<br>22.36% |
| D | 201<br>7.79% | 559<br>21.67% | 760<br>73.55%<br>26.45% |
| SUM | 1614<br>87.55%<br>12.45% | 966<br>57.87%<br>42.13% | 1972 / 2580<br>76.43%<br>23.57% |

**Fig. 3.** Confusion Matrix on Test-Dataset.

## 4 Conclusion

In this study, we utilized a pretrained transformer-based AST model that was fine-tuned on a speech depression dataset to improve classification performance and capture global contextual information from log-mel audio spectrogram segments. We also utilized the Moderate Negative Mining strategy to balance the dataset by considering the distance between majority class samples and the classification boundary at the softmax classification layer. The resulting model, which was trained on a balanced dataset created using MNM, comprises approximately 87.73 million parameters and gave better and balanced performance on the test dataset.

## References


1. Joormann, J., Gotlib, I.H.: Emotion regulation in depression: relation to cognitive inhibition. Cogn. Emotion **24**(2), 281–298 (2010)
2. Christensen, M.C., Ren, H., Fagiolini, A.: Emotional blunting in patients with depression. part i: clinical characteristics. Ann. General Psychiatry **21**(1), 10 (2022)
3. Rutter, L.A., Passell, E., Scheuer, L., Germine, L.: Depression severity is associated with impaired facial emotion processing in a large international sample. J. Affective Disord. **275**, 175–179 (2020)
4. Akhapkin, R.V., et al.: Recognition of facial emotion expressions in patients with depressive disorders: a prospective, observational study. Neurol. Therapy **10**(1), 225–234 (2021)
5. Kroenke, K., Strine, T.W., Spitzer, R.L., Williams, J.B.W., Berry, J.T., Mokdad, A.H.: The phq-8 as a measure of current depression in the general population. J. Affective Disord. **114**(1-3), 163–173 (2009)
6. Gratch, J., et al.: The distress analysis interview corpus of human and computer interviews. In: LREC, vol. 14, pp. 3123–3128. Reykjavik (2014)
7. Cummins, N., Sethu, V., Epps, J., Schnieder, S., Krajewski, J.: Analysis of acoustic space variability in speech affected by depression. Speech Commun. **75**, 27–49 (2015)
8. Ma, X., Yang, H., Chen, Q., Huang, D., Wang, Y.: Depaudionet: aAn efficient deep model for audio based depression classification. In: Proceedings of the 6th International Workshop on Audio/Visual Emotion Challenge, AVEC '16, pp. 35–42. New York, NY, USA (2016). Association for Computing Machinery
9. Pandey, S.K., Shekhawat, H.S., Prasanna, S.R.M., Bhasin, S., Jasuja, R.: A deep tensor-based approach for automatic depression recognition from speech utterances. Plos One **17**(8), e0272659 (2022)
10. Chen, W., Xing, X., Xiangmin, X., Pang, J., Lan, D.: Speechformer++: a hierarchical efficient framework for paralinguistic speech processing. IEEE/ACM Trans. Audio Speech Lang. Process. **31**, 775–788 (2023)
11. Gong, Y., Chung, Y.-A., Glass, J.: Ast: Audio spectrogram transformer. arXiv preprint arXiv:2104.01778 (2021)
12. Gemmeke, J.F., et al.: Audio set: An ontology and human-labeled dataset for audio events. In: 2017 IEEE International Conference on Acoustics, Speech and Signal Processing (ICASSP), pp. 776–780. IEEE (2017)
13. McFee, B., et al.: librosa: Audio and music signal analysis in python. In: Proceedings of the 14th Python in Science Conference, vol. 8 (2015)
14. Song, J., Shen, Y., Jing, Y., Song, M.: Towards Deeper Insights into Deep Learning from Imbalanced Data. In: Yang, J., et al. (eds.) CCCV 2017. CCIS, vol. 771, pp. 674–684. Springer, Singapore (2017). https://doi.org/10.1007/978-981-10-7299-4_56
15. Wang, J., Ravi, V., Flint, J., Alwan, A.: Speechformer-ctc: sequential modeling of depression detection with speech temporal classification. Speech Commun. **163**, 103106 (2024)
16. Dumpala, S.H., Rodriguez, S., Rempel, S., Sajjadian, M., Uher, R., Oore, S.: Detecting depression with a temporal context of speaker embeddings. In: Proceedings of AAAI SAS (2022)

# Evaluating the Usability of an Intelligent Biodiversity Dynamics Assessment Dashboard

Nabila Wardah Zamani, Nurfadhlina Mohd Sharef(✉), Raihani Mohamed, Nurul Amelina Nasharuddin, Mohd Hafeez Osman, Razali Yaakob, and Syaifulnizam Abd Manaf

Faculty of Computer Science and Information Technology, UPM, Selangor, Malaysia
nurfadhlina@upm.edu.my

**Abstract.** Complexity of ecological data and the limited availability of intuitive analytical tools to support decision-making have posed a challenge to biodiversity monitoring effectiveness in tropical forests. Digital dashboards provide a way to visualize and integrate biodiversity information, but many remain underutilized due to insufficient attention to usability and interpretability. This paper presents a human-centered usability assessment of the *Biodiversity Dynamics Assessment Dashboard* developed for the Pasoh Forest Reserve, Negeri Sembilan, Malaysia. The dashboard functions as an intelligent augmentation system by transforming raw ecology data into cognitively supportive visualization for decision-makers and researchers by aggregating multivariate ecological data such as forest composition, species dynamics, and carbon indicators. Participants from environmental and governmental agencies evaluated the dashboard using the importance of ratings for key functions and metrics and System Usability Scale (SUS) score. The findings contribute to the design of human-centered biodiversity dashboards and offer design implications that enhance interpretability, transparency, and decision confidence in biodiversity monitoring systems.

**Keywords:** biodiversity dashboard · intelligent augmentation system · interface and usability · testing and evaluation · System Usability Scale (SUS) score · data visualization

## 1 Introduction

Interactive dashboards and visualization-based decision support systems have become powerful tools for transforming complex datasets into clear visual stories, serving not just to present data but also to enhance users' cognitive abilities [1–4]. They operate as intelligent mediators between ecological complexity and human reasoning, assisting users in interpreting multidimensional data, comparing results, and developing confidence in judgments drawn from data-driven insights [2, 3].

Earlier research has highlighted ongoing challenges in dashboard design, such as striking the right balance between analytical depth and simplicity, making information interpretable for users with varying levels of expertise, and accommodating the demands


A. Shastri et al. (Eds.): IHCI 2025, LNCS 16437, pp. 493–504, 2026.
https://doi.org/10.1007/978-3-032-26352-0_41

of dynamic datasets [5, 6]. Despite technological advances, biodiversity dashboards often fail to translate complex data into accessible, decision-relevant insights due to limited attention to usability and human-centered design. This imbalance, further exacerbated by fragmented datasets, inconsistent standards, and the absence of robust evaluation frameworks, limits both the effectiveness and accessibility of biodiversity dashboards [7]. As a result, biodiversity visualization tools often continue to be data-rich but insight-poor, which limits their ability to assist evidence-based environmental decision-making and widens the gap between data production and understanding.

To address this gap, this paper presents a human-centered usability evaluation of the Biodiversity Dynamics Assessment (BDA) Dashboard developed for the Pasoh Forest Reserve, Negeri Sembilan, Malaysia with eighteen samples as the pre-liminary assessment. The evaluation using SUS score and importance of rating for key function and metric. Therefore, the dashboard consolidates multiple biodiversity metrics and visualizes temporal changes in forest composition, species diversity, and carbon-related indicators to support data-informed monitoring and management. Eighteen participants from environmental and governmental agencies provided feedback on usability, interpretability, and cognitive engagement, revealing both strengths and design improvement opportunities. The findings contribute to a broader understanding of how human-centered and visualization-driven approaches can enhance the interpretive intelligence of ecological decision-support systems.

The remainder of this paper is organized as follows, Sect. 2 provides the related work, followed by Sect. 3 for BDA dashboard, and the discussion and results at Sect. 4. Section 5 for conclusion section that closes the paper.

## 2 Related Work

Biodiversity "dashboard" provides a visualization of biodiversity indicators that supports the tracking of biodiversity and conservation performance data in a user-friendly and clear format [8].

Existing works on biodiversity dynamics assessment dashboards highlight a rich but fragmented ecosystem of tools, the importance of robust and policy-relevant indicators, and the need for greater integration, standardization, and coherence across scales and sectors particularly in Southeast Asia, where the 4th and 5th national reports to the Convention on Biological Diversity (CBD) revealed disparities in data collection and reporting standards. Need mentation limits regional comparison and underscores the need for standardized visualization platforms that can harmonize indicators and facilitate cross-border biodiversity assessments [8]. International frameworks such as the Kunming–Montreal Global Biodiversity Framework further necessitate tools that enable coherent tracking of conservation targets at national, regional, and global levels [9].

While these dashboards are useful for many reasons, their limitations make them less useful: many biodiversity tools are static and do not offer actionable site-specific recommendations, but advances in AI and intelligent visualization are overcoming these limitations to develop dashboards as dynamic systems for real-time aggregation and visualization of multivariate ecological data, such as forest composition, species dynamics, and carbon fluxes, that can turn complex datasets into actionable insights [8, 10].

In addition, AI applications in biodiversity monitoring, such as image recognition for species identification, acoustic monitoring for detecting animal calls, and machine learning for habitat mapping, further increase the ability of dashboards to process, analyze, and visualize large ecological datasets efficiently [11–13]. Panigrahi et al., [14] and Panda et al., [15] presented frameworks using deep learning for real-time species recognition and ecosystem visualization, allowing early detection of ecological shifts. HoloFlora mixed-reality platform [16] takes this innovation further by providing an immersive visualization of biodiversity and carbon indicators.

Despite these technological advancements, usability and interpretability remain critical. As the author emphasized, dashboards often underperform in visual hierarchy and uncertainty communication [1]. The Marine Biodiversity Observation Network also addressed this by incorporating participatory design principles and modular visualization, linking regional indicators with species-level datasets to improve transparency and stakeholder trust [17].

This suggests that intelligent dashboards that incorporate dynamic analytics, uncertainty representation, and accessibility-focused design may serve as a bridge between ecological data and decision-making in biodiversity monitoring and sustainable ecosystem management in tropical and data-rich regions. Effective decision-support systems are not just about data analytics, but the cognitive and interpretive dimensions of how humans interact with information. Designing effective biodiversity dashboards that incorporate dynamic analytics, uncertainty representation, and accessibility-focused design is the challenge of the intelligent visualization challenge. This perspective frames usability not only as a measure of system efficiency but as an indicator of how well a visualization supports human interpretability, trust, and decision confidence.

Usability testing ensures that the dashboard is tailored to the needs of its users, enabling them to achieve their goals efficiently and effectively [18]. This aligns with current research in intelligent human–computer interaction, which views visualization systems as cognitive partners that support reasoning, exploration, and learning rather than passive information displays [19, 20].

## 3 BDA Dashboard

Human-centered visualization emphasizes designing systems that adapt to users' analytical goals, domain expertise, and interpretive behaviors. Such systems embody interactional intelligence augmentation enable users to guide attention, highlight salient patterns, and communicate data uncertainty transparently. The presented system is an AI-based tool that comprises of several data analytics, data science, machine learning and software design components. The scope of the work presented in this paper does not focus on the machine and deep learning algorithms used in the work. Instead, we focus on the human-AI tool interaction. Note that the current BDA dashboard version has much more features including visualization of the AI output.

We incorporated an approach in the BDA dashboard to cater users understanding on relationships between species composition, forest structure, and environmental factors through interpretable visual encodings and interactive exploration. The BDA Dashboard is designed following these principles. It consolidates multi-dimensional ecological indicators into an interactive interface that allows stakeholders to visualize forest dynamics and assess changes over time. Positioning the dashboard within this human-centered framework enables the usability assessment presented in this paper to be interpreted not merely as interface testing, but as an evaluation of how visualization design can amplify human interpretive capacity in complex environmental systems. In this study, we conducted a usability evaluation of the design and visualization and rating importance of function and metrics for the BDA dashboard.

### 3.1 BDA Dashboard Design

The BDA dashboard, developed using Power BI, provides a comprehensive and user-friendly interface for visualizing and analyzing biodiversity data. It is designed not only to generate insights but also to guide decision-making processes related to biodiversity conservation and management. The input to the dashboard is in the form of a comma separated values of tree diameters collected through standard tree census exercise conducted by a local forest management research institute. The data is ingested by loading into Power BI. Then, a series of data cleaning took place such as values imputation and decimal standardization. The dashboard encompasses five core modules:

- Module 1: Summary (presents the current status of biodiversity at a glance)
- Module 2: Trend (displays temporal changes in biodiversity metrics)
- Module 3: Insight (highlights analytical findings derived from historical biodiversity trends and projected future forest stand)
- Module 4: Explore (allows interactive exploration of datasets and related ecological indicators)
- Module 5: Simulator (what-if analysis according to manual and AI-prescribed forest management strategies, that considers predicted forest stand implications)

The BDA dashboard provides multiple layers of analysis through both core modules and by utilising eleven biodiversity metrics that represent fundamental aspects of forest and biodiversity dynamics as follows:

i. Carbon and AGB (Above-Ground Biomass): Indicators of forest carbon storage and productivity.
ii. Growth and Size Class: Capture population structure and forest regeneration dynamics.
iii. Age Class and Lifespan: Provide insights into demographic processes and species turnover.
iv. Degree and Type: Reflect ecological roles, structural diversity, and functional groups in the ecosystem.
v. Composition: Represents species richness and community structure.
vi. Mortality: Tracks species or tree loss, a critical signal for ecosystem stress or disturbance.
vii. Location: Grounds all metrics spatially, enabling mapping of biodiversity changes across different forest plots.

The value for each of the biodiversity metrics is calculated according to the formula provided by a local forest management research institute. BDA dashboard incorporates several interactive features as below:

1. Slicers and Filters: For selecting the year, filtering species, and metrics.
2. Tables and Matrix Visuals: For displaying tree lists, DBH values and so on.
3. Bar and Charts: For monitoring current and tracking growth trends.
4. Interactive Relationships: Connecting datasets for real-time updates when selections change.

Figure 1 represent the summary page of the BDA dashboard. The dashboard consists of the current status of the forest.

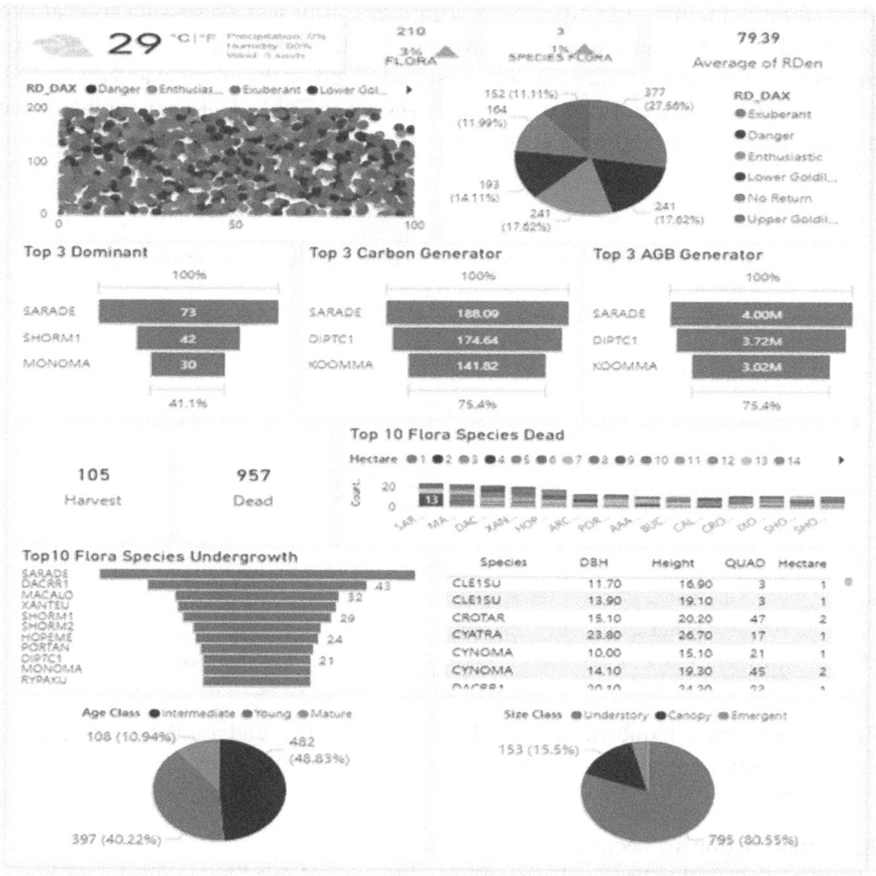


Fig. 1. Screenshot of the summary page of the BDA dashboard

## 3.2 Functions and Biodiversity Metrics Importance Rating

The questionnaire required respondents to rate the importance of key system functions and biodiversity metrics. This helped participants to identify features such as spatial distribution, biomass, composition, and growth to find most useful for understanding ecosystem health and supporting biodiversity monitoring and decision-making. The results also highlight areas that may need improvement or additional user training.

### 3.3 Usability Questionnaire

This study applied a mixed method assessment with SUS score and open-ended question to evaluate the usability of the dashboard. The study designs a set of qualitative and quantitative approaches with a section addressing evaluation using a modified SUS to adapt to the dashboard as the technology being targeted, and a section on functions and metrics importance ranking, followed by three open-ended questions. The purpose of these questions was to reveal deeper insights into participants' perceptions of the dashboard's likeability, the challenges they faced, and their suggestions for improvement.

The participants individually took part in a usability testing session to evaluate a dashboard. The participants were first introduced to the functionality of the dashboard. Then, a structured questionnaire was administered based on the adopted and revised SUS to gather feedback on the user experience as shown in Table 1. The participants were asked to rate the dashboard on a scale from 1 to 5, from strongly disagree to strongly agree [21].

**Table 1.** Questionnaire used to assess the usability of the dashboard

| No | Question |
|---|---|
| Q1 | I think that I would like to use this dashboard frequently |
| Q2 | I found the dashboard unnecessarily complex |
| Q3 | I thought the dashboard was easy to use |
| Q4 | I think that I would need the support of a technical person to be able to use this dashboard |
| Q5 | I found the various functions in this dashboard were well integrated |
| Q6 | I thought there was too much inconsistency in this dashboard |
| Q7 | I would imagine that most people would learn to use this dashboard very quickly |
| Q8 | I found the dashboard very cumbersome to use |
| Q9 | I felt very confident using the dashboard |
| Q10 | I needed to learn a lot of things before I could get going on this dashboard |

Three open-ended questions are administered at the end of the SUS questions to provide additional feedback on the dashboard in the form of suggestions or recommendations:

- I like this dashboard because…
- Usage of this dashboard is challenging (things you don't like about the dashboard) because…
- Any suggestions to improve the dashboard?

## 4 Discussion and Results

Three activities were conducted to the eighteen (18) participants to evaluate the functions, usability and metrics' importance and open-ended responses.

## 4.1 Functions and Metrics Importance

One of the main contributions of the reported work is the relevance of the incorporated biodiversity metrics in augmenting BDA for the users. Figure 2 presents a 100% stacked bar chart illustrating how participants rated the importance of the four core modules of the BDA dashboard: Summary, Trends, Insights, and Explore. The stacked bars display the proportion of responses across five levels of importance: not important, slightly important, moderately important, important, and very important.

The Summary and Trends modules achieved the highest perceived importance (94%), followed by Insights (84%), while Explore (77%) was the least prioritized. These results suggest users value modules that deliver clear, interpretable biodiversity information, whereas interactive exploration may benefit from usability enhancement or user capacity-building to increase adoption. The ANOVA result indicates a statistically significant difference among the perceived importance ratings of the four modules ($p < 0.01$), suggesting that users differentiate clearly between modules in terms of their value. Post-hoc (Tukey HSD) comparisons show that Summary and Trends modules have significantly higher importance ratings than Explore ($p < 0.01$). The Insights module, while also rated highly, shows a modest but significant gap compared to Summary and Trends ($p < 0.05$). No significant difference was observed between Summary and Trends ($p > 0.9$), confirming their comparable perceived utility.

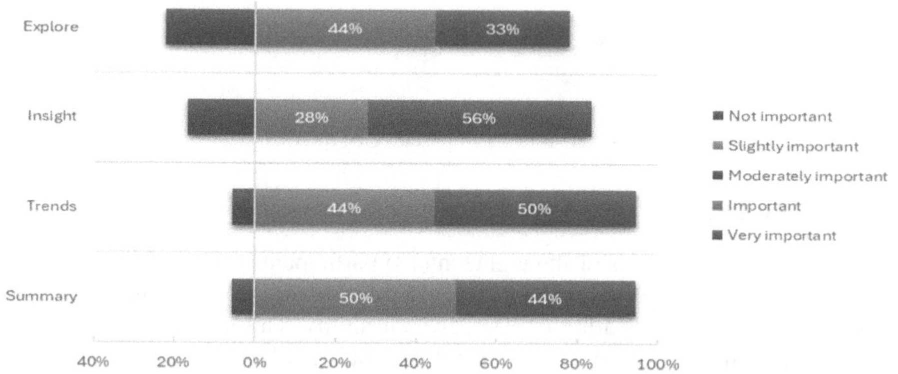


**Fig. 2.** Core modules importance rating

Figure 3 illustrates respondents' ratings of the importance of individual biodiversity metrics in the BDA dashboard. Overall, the results show strong support for most metrics, though the degree of perceived importance varies across categories:

a) *Growth* and *Location* (94%) are the top rated metrics, which emphasize the users' preference for indicators that represent dynamic ecological change and spatial context.
b) There is a high-consensus metrics (89%) across S*ize class, AGB, Type, Composition, Carbon Stock* which are structural and functional indicators seen as essential for assessing forest health and biomass.

c) *Mortality* (84%) and *Age class* (78%) are moderate important metrics, which are valued but with minor disagreement, suggesting interpretive variability.
d) *Degree* (73%) and *Lifespan* (72%) are the lowest important metrics, which show a greater divergence in perceived utility, possibly due to limited familiarity or contextual relevance.
e) A one-way ANOVA reveals a significant difference among the perceived importance of metrics where $F(10, N-11) = 6.84$, $p < 0.01$, $\eta2 = 0.41$ (large effect size). The post-hoc tests indicate that *Growth* and *Location* scored significantly higher ($p < 0.01$) than *Degree* and *Lifespan*, and there is no significant difference between *Size class*, *AGB*, *Type*, *Composition*, and *Carbon Stock* ($p > 0.05$), suggesting comparable perceived importance within this cluster.

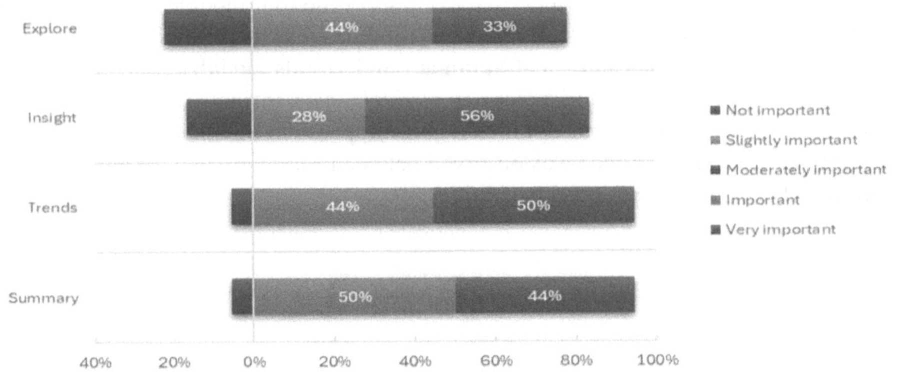


**Fig. 3.** Rate of importance of metrics

## 4.2 Usability Testing

Table 2 shows the responses of the eighteen (18) participants collected during testing. The preliminary usability evaluation of the BDA dashboard produced an average SUS score below fifty (50), indicating low perceived usability. This suggests that while certain features of the dashboard are functional, several usability challenges hinder overall user experience. According to usability literature, a SUS score of seventy (70) or higher is considered "passing" and reflects good usability, whereas a score below this threshold indicates "poor" usability [22, 23]. The relatively low score is expected for an early-stage prototype still undergoing refinement. The study involved limited number of participants due to preliminary scope aiming to gather formative rather than conclusive feedback. Despite the small sample size, participants provided valuable insights on improving learnability, navigation, and visual clarity. These findings will guide interface and functionality enhancements and support future large-scale evaluations to validate the dashboard's usability and effectiveness in biodiversity monitoring.

The average responses to the positive statements (Q1, Q3, Q5, Q7, and Q9) were around the mid-point, indicating that participants perceived the dashboard as moderately usable. This suggests that the dashboard was not particularly easy to use, and its functionalities were not seamlessly integrated. In contrast, participants' responses to the negative statements (Q2, Q4, Q6, and Q8) were below the mid-point, implying that they encountered difficulties in learning and understanding how to use the dashboard, as well as in navigating its complex features.

For Q4 and Q10, the question emphasizes the user learnability. The result showed with a score eight (8) indicates that the users need technical support and the necessity to acquire substantial prior knowledge before achieving proficiency with the dashboard. In this study, participants expressed difficulty in learning to use the dashboard, as reflected in the SUS responses for questions 4 and 10 in Table 2.

**Table 2.** SUS rate

| Respondent | Q1 | Q2 | Q3 | Q4 | Q5 | Q6 | Q7 | Q8 | Q9 | Q10 | Average | SUS Score |
|---|---|---|---|---|---|---|---|---|---|---|---|---|
| R1 | 4 | 3 | 4 | 5 | 3 | 3 | 3 | 3 | 3 | 5 | 3.6 | 50 |
| R2 | 3 | 2 | 4 | 4 | 5 | 1 | 4 | 2 | 2 | 5 | 3.2 | 62.5 |
| R3 | 4 | 4 | 3 | 4 | 4 | 3 | 3 | 3 | 4 | 4 | 3.6 | 52.2 |
| R4 | 4 | 3 | 4 | 4 | 3 | 2 | 3 | 3 | 4 | 4 | 3.4 | 57.5 |
| R5 | 3 | 3 | 4 | 5 | 3 | 3 | 1 | 3 | 2 | 5 | 3.2 | 45 |
| R6 | 3 | 3 | 3 | 4 | 3 | 3 | 1 | 3 | 2 | 4 | 2.9 | 45 |
| R7 | 3 | 4 | 2 | 4 | 3 | 3 | 2 | 4 | 2 | 5 | 3.2 | 37.5 |
| R8 | 4 | 3 | 3 | 4 | 3 | 3 | 1 | 4 | 2 | 3 | 3 | 45 |
| R9 | 4 | 2 | 3 | 3 | 3 | 2 | 4 | 2 | 3 | 2 | 2.8 | 60 |
| R10 | 2 | 2 | 2 | 4 | 3 | 3 | 3 | 4 | 2 | 5 | 3 | 40 |
| R11 | 3 | 4 | 4 | 4 | 5 | 3 | 2 | 4 | 3 | 5 | 3.7 | 50 |
| R12 | 3 | 3 | 3 | 4 | 3 | 3 | 3 | 3 | 3 | 3 | 3.1 | 47.5 |
| R13 | 2 | 4 | 2 | 1 | 2 | 3 | 4 | 4 | 2 | 4 | 2.8 | 40 |
| R14 | 4 | 2 | 4 | 5 | 4 | 2 | 2 | 2 | 3 | 5 | 3.3 | 60 |
| R15 | 5 | 4 | 4 | 5 | 5 | 1 | 2 | 4 | 4 | 5 | 3.9 | 60 |
| R16 | 4 | 3 | 3 | 4 | 3 | 3 | 3 | 3 | 3 | 4 | 3.3 | 50 |
| R17 | 3 | 2 | 3 | 2 | 4 | 2 | 4 | 2 | 3 | 5 | 3 | 62.5 |
| R18 | 2 | 4 | 2 | 1 | 2 | 4 | 3 | 4 | 2 | 5 | 2.9 | 37.5 |
| Average SUS Score | | | | | | | | | | | 3.22 | 50 |
| SUS Score | | | | | | | | | | | | 902.5 |

There was also one additional question on whether the dashboard is able to give depth of insight into the biodiversity dynamics. The results confirmed that most of the users agree that the dashboard can give depth of insight (17% stated Strongly Agree, 44% stated Agree). This indicates that the dashboard has been able to provide valuable intelligence.

When the evaluation session described in this paper was conducted, its primary objective was to assess user acceptance of the proposed innovation. To the best of our knowledge, this type of system had not previously been introduced to the respondents, who were accustomed to conventional methods for data analysis and forest management. During this phase, greater emphasis was placed on evaluating the functionality, relevance of metrics, and content scope of the dashboard rather than its aesthetic or interface design. Feedback gathered from this session serves as a baseline for future refinements, particularly in enhancing the user experience and visual appeal. Since then, several improved versions of the dashboard have been developed, following iterative cycles typical of data science project workflows.

### 4.3 Open-Ended Response

The thematic analysis of the open-ended responses revealed three major themes, positive aspects of the dashboard, challenges faced during its use, and suggestions for improvement. While participants appreciated the depth of insights provided by the dashboard, they highlighted the complexity and steep learning curve as significant barriers to effective use. This could be related highly to the dashboard being the first of its kind to be used in Malaysia and among the respondents. Suggestions for improvement focused on simplifying the user interface, enhancing the integration of functions, and providing better user support and documentation.

## 5 Conclusion

Although numerous biodiversity dashboards have been developed, most efforts remain focused on technical integration and indicator construction, with limited attention to usability testing and user experience. This gap is critical because a dashboard's effectiveness depends not only on analytical accuracy but also on its ability to transform multivariate ecological information into accessible, interpretable, and actionable insights for diverse stakeholders, including researchers, forest managers, and policymakers.

The findings demonstrate that the BDA Dashboard effectively consolidates and visualizes multivariate ecological data such as forest composition, species dynamics, and carbon indicators into interpretable visual narratives that aid monitoring and analysis. However, an average SUS score of 50 indicates moderate usability, with users emphasizing the need for improvements in learnability, visual hierarchy, and user navigation. These findings highlight the importance of iterative refinement guided by user-centered design principles to enhance dashboard adoption and trust. Since this evaluation is considered as pre-liminary assessment, there are many considerations that need to be taken for dashboard improvement to achieve intelligence augmentation system.

This research advances human-centered design in biodiversity informatics by stressing the need to balance analytical power with clarity and accessibility. Future work should test usability with more diverse users, include real-time data, and compare interface designs. These efforts will guide better ecological dashboard design to support effective conservation decisions.

**Acknowledgments.** This project is funded by a national flagship project on precision biodiversity, through 12th Malaysia Plan. The authors would like to acknowledge the substantial contributions of the Precision Biodiversity Task Force at Academy of Science Malaysia, staffs involved in this project from the Forest Research Institute Malaysia (FRIM), the Pasoh Forest Reserve research staffs, the representatives from Forestry Department of Peninsular Malaysia, the members of Precision Biodiversity Alliance and all PBD technical member. Special thanks extended to Universiti Teknologi Malaysia and Universiti Putra Malaysia for the support in this project.

## References

1. Riffat, M., Esmail, B.A., Wang, J., Albert, C.: Biodiversity and eco-system services dashboards to inform landscape and urban planning: a systematic analysis of current practices. Taylor and Francis Ltd. (2023). https://doi.org/10.1080/26395916.2023.2263105
2. Xu, H., Berres, A., Liu, Y., Allen-Dumas, M.R., Sanyal, J.: An overview of visualization and visual analytics applications in water resources management. Elsevier Ltd. (2022). https://doi.org/10.1016/j.envsoft.2022.105396
3. Al-Hajj, S., Pike, I., Fisher, B.: Interactive dashboards: using visual analytics for knowledge transfer and decision support. (n.d.)
4. Krsnik, G., et al.: Assessing the dynamics of forest ecosystem services to define forest use suitability: a case study of Pinus sylvestris in Spain. Environ. Sci. Eur. **36**(1) (2024). https://doi.org/10.1186/s12302-024-00956-z
5. Setlur, V., Correll, M., Satyanarayan, A., Tory, M.: Heuristics for supporting cooperative dashboard design. IEEE Trans. Vis. Comput. Graph. **30**(1), 370–380 (2024). https://doi.org/10.1109/TVCG.2023.3327158
6. Bach, B., et al.: Dashboard design patterns. IEEE Trans. Vis. Comput. Graph. **29**(1), 342–352 (2023). https://doi.org/10.1109/TVCG.2022.3209448
7. Savilaakso, S., Guariguata, M.R.: Challenges for developing Forest Stewardship Council certification for ecosystem services: how to enhance local adoption? Ecosyst. Serv. **28**, 55–66 (2017). https://doi.org/10.1016/j.ecoser.2017.10.001
8. Han, X., et al.: A biodiversity indicators dashboard: addressing challenges to monitoring progress towards the Aichi biodiversity targets using disaggregated global data. PLoS One **9**(11) (2014). https://doi.org/10.1371/journal.pone.0112046
9. Viti, M.M., et al.: Introducing the progress monitoring tools of the EU Biodiversity Strategy for 2030. Ecol. Indic. **164**, 112147 (2024). https://doi.org/10.1016/j.ecolind.2024.112147
10. Li, R., et al.: A cloud-based toolbox for the versatile environmental annotation of biodiversity data. PLoS Biol. **19**(11) (2021). https://doi.org/10.1371/journal.pbio.3001460
11. Willi, M., et al.: Identifying animal species in camera trap images using deep learning and citizen science. Methods Ecol. Evol. **10**(1), 80–91 (2019). https://doi.org/10.1111/2041-210X.13099
12. Stowell, D.: Computational bioacoustics with deep learning: a review and roadmap. PeerJ (2022). https://doi.org/10.7717/peerj.13152
13. Wäldchen, J., Mäder, P.: Machine learning for image-based species identification. Methods Ecol. Evol. (2018). https://doi.org/10.1111/2041-210X.13075
14. Panigrahi, S., Maski, P., Thondiyath, A.: Real-time biodiversity analysis using deep-learning algorithms on mobile robotic platforms. PeerJ Comput. Sci. **9** (2023). https://doi.org/10.7717/peerj-cs.1502
15. Panda, R.M., Dash, P., Roy, P.S.: A novel web-based approach for monitoring biodiversity. Ecol. Evol. **14**(10) (2024). https://doi.org/10.1002/ece3.70364
16. Fol, C.R., Zhao, J., Späth, L., Murtiyoso, A., Remondino, F., Griess, V.C.: Advancing forest biodiversity visualisation through mixed reality. Sci. Rep. **15**(1) (2025). https://doi.org/10.1038/s41598-025-00285-y

17. Villalobos, H., et al.: A practical approach to monitoring marine protected areas. UNESCO (2021). https://whc.unesco
18. Salvendy, G.: Handbook of Human Factors and Ergonomics. John Wiley & Sons, New York (2012)
19. Basole, R.C., Major, T.: Generative AI for visualization: opportunities and challenges. IEEE Comput. Graph. Appl. **44**(2), 55–64 (2024). https://doi.org/10.1109/MCG.2024.3362168
20. Reyes, J., Batmaz, A.U., Kersten-Oertel, M.: Trusting AI: does uncertainty visualization affect decision-making? Front. Comput. Sci. **7** (2025). https://doi.org/10.3389/fcomp.2025.1464348
21. Blattgerste, J., Behrends, J., Pfeiffer, T.: A web-based analysis toolkit for the system usability scale. In: Proceedings of the ACM International Conference Series, Association for Computing Machinery, pp. 237–246 (2022). https://doi.org/10.1145/3529190.3529216
22. Bangor, A., Kortum, P., Miller, J.: Determining what individual SUS scores mean: adding an adjective rating scale (2009)
23. Coe, A.M., et al.: Usability testing of a web-based decision aid for breast cancer risk assessment among multi-ethnic women (2017)

# Eye-State Classification for Smart Home Control: A Sub-Band CRV Approach to BCI

Ditsa Patel(✉), Neha Golani(✉), and Jyoti Maheshwari

Department of Electronics and Communication Engineering, School of Technology, Nirma University, Ahmedabad, India
{22bec042,22bec036,jyoti.maheshwari}@nirmauni.ac.in

**Abstract.** Brain Computer Interface (BCI) technology provides a communication link between the human brain and external devices, bypassing regular neuromuscular pathways and offering a wide range of smart home applications. This paper aims to develop a non-invasive and efficient BCI system that detects the user's eye-open and eye-close states using electroencephalogram (EEG) signals. In this direction, we have used sub-band characteristic Response Vector (sub-band CRV) based feature extraction method which represents the direction in which brain's static energy is concentrated. It captures the intricate inter-channel dependencies by computing a correlation matrix across EEG channels and applying eigenvalue decomposition to generate a low-dimensional description of brain activities. These sub-band CRV features are used to train a suitable classifier that distinguishes between the open and closed state of the eyes which are then mapped to control various smart home appliances. The results show that the proposed approach efficiently distinguishes between eye open and eye closed brain states, paving the way for a reliable and responsive BCI-driven home automation framework.

**Keywords:** Brain Computer Interface · Electroencephalogram · Sub-band Characteristic Response Vector (sub-band CRV) · Machine Learning

## 1 Introduction

Our thoughts, feelings, and interactions with the outside world are all reflected in our brain activity. This insight has inspired rapid advances in Brain–Computer Interface (BCI) research, where brain signals are decoded to control external systems without muscular movement. Because of its high temporal resolution, affordability, and non-invasive nature, electroencephalography (EEG) has become one of the most promising tools for BCI applications in the last

D. Patel and N. Golani—Equal contribution.


A. Shastri et al. (Eds.): IHCI 2025, LNCS 16437, pp. 505–511, 2026.
https://doi.org/10.1007/978-3-032-26352-0_42

ten years [5,11]. For communication, rehabilitation, and assistive control, EEG-based BCIs have been extensively investigated; they are especially advantageous for people with severe motor disabilities [12,13].

Among various EEG paradigms, the distinction between eyes-open (EO) and eyes-closed (EC) brain states has attracted significant research interest. These two conditions are known to exhibit distinct functional connectivity patterns, spectral power variations, and network topologies across frequency bands [5,11]. Several previous studies have analyzed these variations using graph-theoretical measures [5], inter-channel covariance matrices [6], or cross-correlation-based feature ensembles [7]. Although these methods effectively characterize neural behavior, many remain computationally heavy and are often restricted to offline experimental analysis rather than real-time implementation [8,10].

Smart home systems powered by EEG have drawn interest recently as a step toward useful, approachable BCI applications. Although they rely on voluntary muscular activity or external stimuli, existing systems based on eye-blink detection [9] or Steady-State Visually Evoked Potentials (SSVEP) [13,14] have demonstrated promising results. Their appropriateness for continuous or passive BCI systems intended for effortless control is limited by these dependencies. Therefore, methods that can use spontaneous EEG patterns without requiring visual or motor input to achieve dependable performance are needed.

The classified brain states are mapped into hardware-level commands through MATLAB–Arduino integration, enabling direct actuation of devices such as LEDs. This implementation bridges the gap between algorithmic EEG analysis and real-world BCI applications by validating real-time responsiveness, low-cost operation, and hardware feasibility. Ultimately, the proposed framework demonstrates a robust and efficient approach to enabling mind-controlled smart environments, paving the way for next-generation assistive technologies.

## 2 Methodology

The complete framework of the proposed BCI-based smart home automation system is depicted in Fig. 1.

### 2.1 Data Acquisition and Segmentation

A real-time EEG dataset from Texas Data Repository was utilized for this study, featuring 8 min of alternating eye-open and eye-closed states with one-minute interleaved intervals [3,4]. In our analysis, only 64 out of 72 channels were used, as the excluded channels did not contribute to relevant information.

Since EEG signals are non-stationary, i.e. they vary over time, a small segment of it can be assumed to be stationary and helps capture minute neural patterns corresponding to an event. An overlapping segmentation strategy was adopted to ensure that transitional dynamics between states are captured well, preserving critical information for robust feature extraction and analysis.

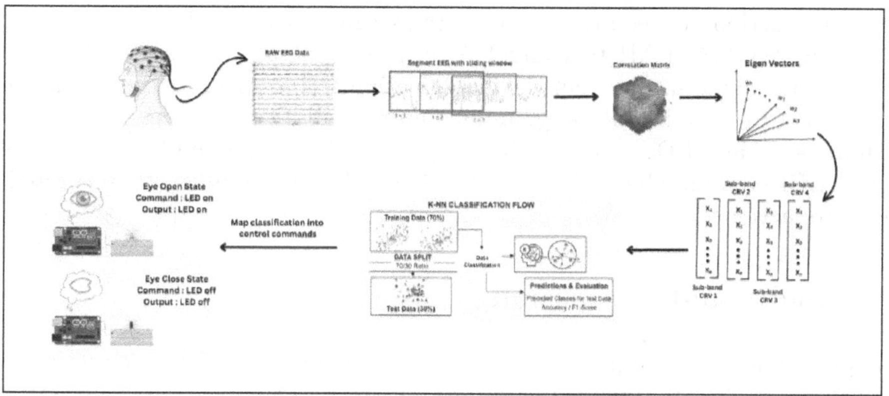


**Fig. 1.** Methodological workflow of the proposed BCI-driven smart home automation system.

### 2.2 Feature Extraction and Classification

After segmentation, Pearson correlation coefficient matrix for each segment is computed across all 64 channels. Eigenvalue Decomposition (EVD) is then applied to these matrices to generate eigenvalues and eigenvectors representing the dominant patterns of the inter-channel dependencies. Then, sub-band CRV is defined as the sum of product of eigenvalues and eigenvectors:

$$CRV = \Sigma_{i \in Q} \lambda_i w_i \tag{1}$$

where $w_i$ denotes $i$th eigenvector, $\lambda_i$ denotes the corresponding eigenvalue and $Q$ is a set of eigenvectors [2]. This approach effectively reduces the dimensionality of the data while preserving the most intricate neural information that encapsulates overall spatial co-activation of brain regions over time [1].

After extracting the sub-band Characteristic Response Vector (CRV), these were used to classify eye-open and eye-closed states, two cognitively distinct states, for controlling smart home devices. To identify the most effective approach for classifying these binary tasks, a range of machine learning algorithms were explored.

Both classical statistical models and modern machine learning algorithms were employed to find the most discriminative mapping between the sub-band CRV patterns and corresponding brain states. Comparing various performance metrics of the classifiers, we aimed to recognize the most reliable, generalizable and accurate classifier proficient for real-time brain-computer interface operation.

### 2.3 Hardware Implementation

For hardware implementation, an Arduino Uno microcontroller was utilized to establish real-time control of smart home devices based on the results of classification. The MATLAB Support Package for Arduino Hardware facilitated direct interaction between the software and Arduino via a USB serial connection and leveraged MATLAB to control Arduino's General-Purpose Input/Output (GPIO) pins dynamically from the classification script. MATLAB can send control signals to Arduino allowing immediate actuation of devices connected to Arduino such as LEDs or relays. This approach facilitates implementation of a simple BCI system, where classified EEG signals can be directly interpreted as hardware actions.

## 3 Results and Discussion

The performance of the proposed BCI system was evaluated by classifying eye-open and eye-closed states using sub band CRVs extracted from EEG signals. As the EEG data provided in the [3,4] is annotated at every 500 ms intervals and each state (eye-open or eye-closed) lasts one minute, each state corresponds to 120 consecutive events, and thus, we have defined segments of 120 samples in length, with an overlap of 80 samples of the previous segment.

The sub-band CRV features were obtained by splitting the 64 eigenvectors (calculated from the correlation matrix of the dimensions $64 \times 64$) into four groups, each containing 16 vectors. For each group of vectors, a sub-band CRV was computed as the weighted sum of the eigenvalues and eigenvectors. These four sub-band CRVs were stacked vertically to form a single feature vector of dimension $1 \times 256$ (no of groups x size of each vector) for each 120-sample segment.

Table 1 shows the comparative performance analysis of different machine learning algorithms on the sub band CRV features. All computations were performed in MATLAB. Each classifier model was trained and tested under multiple hyperparameter configurations. Highest accuracy of 92.35 % was achieved with the K-Nearest Neighbor classifier using cosine distance metric with well balanced F1 score for both classes indicating effective feature modeling and consistent and unbiased performance in classifying of both eye-open and eye-closed conditions. Support Vector Machine also showed competitive performance with accuracy of 90.51 % and higher F1 scores showing that it correctly detects most true cases while minimizing false detections. The F1 scores provided in Table 1 are reported in the format [Class 101 = eye-open, Class 201 = eye-closed]. The F1 score was chosen over other evaluation metrics as it provides a balanced measure of precision and recall, making it more reliable for assessing classification performance in slightly imbalanced datasets. Naive Bayes classifier showed comparatively lower accuracy due to its statistical assumptions. Overall, the comparative analysis highlights that distance-based classifiers such as KNN and SVM outperform probabilistic approaches for the sub-band CRV feature set, demonstrating the effectiveness of correlation-based feature modeling for EEG eye-state classification. The consistent F1 scores across classes further validate the robustness and reliability of the proposed framework for balanced and accurate brain-state detection.

**Table 1.** Classifier Performance Comparison

| Classifier | Model Configuration | Test Accuracy | F1 Score |
|---|---|---|---|
| LDA | Type: Standard | 82.54 % ± 0.85% | [0.81658 , 0.83341] |
| | Type: Regularized | 82.56 % ± 0.97% | [0.81659 , 0.83368] |
| | Type: Quadratic | 83.53 % ± 0.75% | [0.82638 , 0.84328] |
| Logistic Regression | Regularization: Ridge (L2) | 87.50 % ± 1.55% | [0.87192 , 0.87799] |
| | Regularization: Lasso (L1) | 84.71 % ± 2.05% | [0.84363 , 0.85047] |
| SVM | Kernel: Linear | 88.01 % ± 0.05% | [0.87761 , 0.88251] |
| | Kernel: Polynomial (Order 2) | 88.01 % ± 0.25% | [0.90456 , 0.90558] |
| | Kernel: Polynomial (Order 3) | 63.65 % ± 0.29% | [0.69784 , 0.54382] |
| | Kernel: RBF | 50.32 % ± 0.35% | [0.01164 , 0.66818] |
| Naive Bayes | Distribution: Normal | 74.42 % ± 3.43% | [0.70536 , 0.77397] |
| | Distribution: Multinomial | 50.02 % ± 1.03% | [NaN , 0.66687] |
| Decision Tree | LeafSize=1, NumSplits=10, SplitCriterion: gdi | 80.60 % ± 0.36% | [0.79846, 0.81295] |
| | LeafSize=1, NumSplits=50, SplitCriterion: gdi | 81.94 % ± 0.38% | [0.81841, 0.82036] |
| | LeafSize=1, NumSplits=100, SplitCriterion: gdi | 82.69 % ± 0.12% | [0.82323, 0.83049] |
| | LeafSize=20, NumSplits=100, SplitCriterion: gdi | 82.37 % ± 0.47% | [0.82001, 0.82724] |
| KNN | Distance: Cosine, k=7 | 92.35 % ± 0.13% | [0.86482 , 0.86208] |
| | Distance: Cityblock, k=7 | 86.70 % ± 0.28% | [0.86269 , 0.87106] |
| | Distance: Euclidean, k=7 | 86.50 % ± 0.21% | [0.86015 , 0.86953] |

Figure 2 illustrates the comparison between the manually annotated (actual) eye-state transitions and those predicted by the proposed sub-band CRV-based classifier.The LED turns ON for eye-open (class 101) and turns OFF during the eye-closed (class 201) condition.

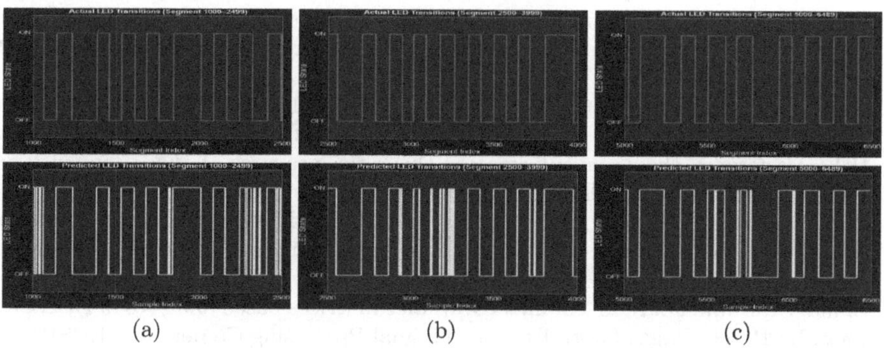

(a) (b) (c)

**Fig. 2.** Comparison between actual (upper row) and predicted (lower row) LED state transitions for segment groups: (a) 1000–2499, (b) 2500–3999, (c) 5000–6489.

The transitions observed exhibit strong concordance with the true sequence of ocular state transitions, substantiating the successful mapping of real-time hardware-level LED actuation via Arduino interface. The sharp binary transitions between logic-high and logic-low states of LED reflect precise temporal fidelity of the system, thereby establishing the feasibility of using EEG-driven KNN classification for ambient smart systems and assistive technology implementations [12,13].

## 4 Conclusion

A BCI-driven smart home automation system was successfully implemented that integrates EEG signal processing, feature extraction, classification of states and hardware deployment into a unified framework. This approach decomposes 64-channel EEG data into eigenspace representations and strategically groups eigenvectors into four sub-bands to capture multi-resolution neural dynamics. Using the stacked sub-band CRVs as features to distinguish eye-open and eye-closed conditions, K-Nearest Neighbor model with cosine distance metric provided accuracy of 92.35 % while MATLAB-Arduino interface expedited reliable translation of brain activity into device actuation commands, validating the system's practical feasibility as well as responsiveness for assistive BCI applications. Future enhancements may explore multi-class classification for diverse appliance control [14], deep learning architectures and adaptive segmentation to enhance robustness of the system in the real-world environments.

## References


1. Maheshwari, J., Joshi, S.D., Gandhi, T.K.: Tracking the transitions of brain states: an analytical approach using EEG. IEEE Trans. Neural Syst. Rehabil. Eng. **28**(8), 1742–1749 (2020). https://doi.org/10.1109/TNSRE.2020.3005950
2. Maheshwari, J., Joshi, S.D., Gandhi, T.K.: A novel spectral graph distance measure and its applications in biomedical signal processing. IEEE Trans. Signal Inf. Process. Over Netw. **11**, 114–123 (2025). https://doi.org/10.1109/TSIPN.2025.3536085
3. Trujillo, L.: Raw BFD data (2017). https://doi.org/10.18738/T8/EG0LJI
4. Trujillo, L.T., Stanfield, C.T., Vela, R.D.: The effect of electroencephalogram (EEG) reference choice on information-theoretic measures of the complexity and integration of EEG signals. Front. Neurosci. **11**, 425 (2017)
5. Tan, B., Kong, X., Yang, P., Jin, Z., Li, L.: The difference of brain functional connectivity between eyes-closed and eyes-open using graph theoretical analysis. Comput. Math. Methods Med. **2013** (2013)
6. Sinha, N., Babu, D.: Inter-channel covariance matrices based analyses of EEG baselines. In: Proceedings of 30th European Signal Processing Conference (EUSIPCO), Belgrade, Serbia, pp. 1303–1307 (2022)
7. Paranjape, P.N., Dhabu, M.M., Deshpande, P.S., Kekre, A.M.: Cross-correlation aided ensemble of classifiers for BCI oriented EEG study. IEEE Access **7**, 125 356–125 365 (2019)
8. Yan, W., Luo, Q., Du, C.: Channel component correlation analysis for multi-channel EEG feature component extraction. Front. Neurosci. **19**, 1522964 (2025). https://doi.org/10.3389/fnins.2025.1522964
9. Rabbani, M., et al.: EEG based real-time classification of consecutive two eye blinks for brain–computer interface applications. Sci. Rep. **15**, 21007 (2025). https://doi.org/10.1038/s41598-025-07205-0

10. Rabbani, M., et al.: EEG based real-time classification of consecutive two eye blinks for brain–computer interface applications. Sci. Rep. **15**, 21007 (2025). https://doi.org/10.1038/s41598-025-07205-0
11. Petro, N.M., et al.: Eyes-closed versus eyes-open differences in spontaneous neural dynamics during development. NeuroImage **259**, 119465 (2023). https://doi.org/10.1016/j.neuroimage.2022.119465
12. Drăgoi, M.-V., et al.: Real-time home automation system using BCI technology. Electronics **12**(10), 594 (2023). https://doi.org/10.3390/electronics12100594.
13. Yang, D., Nguyen, T.-H., Chung, W.-Y.: A bipolar-channel hybrid brain-computer interface system for home automation control utilizing steady-state visually evoked potential and eye-blink signals. Sensors **20**(19), 5474 (2020). https://doi.org/10.3390/s20195474.
14. Camilleri, T., Mangion, J., Camilleri, K.: Exploiting EEG-extracted eye movements for a hybrid SSVEP home automation system. In: Proceedings of BIOSIGNALS. vol. 4, pp. 1–8. Sliema, Malta, Jan 2022 (2022). https://doi.org/10.5220/0010783800003123

# Predicting Gaze Location in Dynamic Scenes Using Multimodal CNN-LSTM Network

Redwanul Haque Sourave(✉) and Javed I. Khan

Department of Computer Science, Media Communications and Networking Research Laboratory, Kent, OH, USA
rsourave@kent.edu, javed@kent.edu

**Abstract.** Human gaze contains a rich amount of information about the human attention on the scene. Thus, it is often used as a robust and rapid method of interaction with the computer. Predicting future gaze location in advance can provide an advantage in multiple use cases, including, but not limited to, human-computer interaction, designing efficient user interface, analyzing human behavior, image or video compression. However, prediction of gaze poses a unique challenge because of the dynamic nature of the human vision system and spatio-temporal nature of the data. We explore the applicability of multimodal CNN-LSTM network to predict future gaze location in videos. We compare the results of our model on the Coutrot and EGTEA gaze dataset against existing statistical models. The results show that modeling eye gaze with spatiotemporal model performs better than models that use per-scene analysis to predict eye gaze locations.

**Keywords:** Sequential Model · Machine Learning · Gaze Prediction · Computer Vision

## 1 Introduction

Human gaze plays a fundamental role in human–computer interaction, as it reflects attention, intention, and cognitive processes. Accurately predicting where people look in dynamic visual scenes is critical for a wide range of applications, including adaptive user interfaces, assistive systems, video content analysis, and immersive virtual environments. Gaze prediction in videos require modeling both spatial visual features and temporal dependencies among them, unlike predicting gaze location in static images. The possible applications make it an impactful but a challenging problem.

Eye gaze locations can be broadly classified into fixations and saccades [1]. Saccades are the rapid transition of fixation from one location to the other. Many research studies have been done to estimate both types of gaze. Most of these studies investigated prediction of a saliency map for single static images, where the most prominent location attracts the fixation. One of challenges in predicting eye gaze with statistical models is the well-known center bias in gaze


A. Shastri et al. (Eds.): IHCI 2025, LNCS 16437, pp. 512–523, 2026.
https://doi.org/10.1007/978-3-032-26352-0_43

[2]. Viewers tend to look center to the scene for multiple reasons. As a result of this, one can come up with a model which always predicts the center of the screen as the predicted gaze location, and, find that it performs better than some statistical approaches to predict gaze location. In contrast, predicting gaze in a dynamic scene requires more complex spatio-temporal modeling techniques.

Recent advances in deep learning have demonstrated significant progress in computer vision tasks, with convolutional neural networks [3] (CNNs) excelling at extracting spatial features. Recurrent neural networks such as LSTM [4] and GRU [5] have been proven effective for modeling temporal sequence. However, many existing approaches either rely heavily on only spatial information in image to predict gaze location, without considering the temporal relationship between frames in videos. Furthermore, most of the existing studies do not take into account the past gaze information on the frames that have already been viewed. The addition of past gaze record with frame sequence can assist the model in predicting gaze information on future frame. Without guidance from the gaze data, the model would make a decision based solely on the frame sequence, which might suffer from inaccuracy. Past eye gaze locations can impose additional constraints on the space. Incorporating past gaze data as an additional input with the video allows the model to learn about the spatial constraints on the future gaze along with the salient information in frames.

In this paper, we propose a deep learning model that integrates CNNs and LSTMs to handle both RGB frames in video and gaze location in video to predict eye gaze locations. The CNN component learns spatial representations from individual frames, while the LSTM component captures temporal dependencies across sequences of gaze locations. By combining these two architectures, our method is able to model both spatial saliency and temporal continuity, leading to improved gaze prediction performance compared to existing baselines. This is a continuation of our previous work [6], where we used only a CNN to extract salient features from the frames. Here, we extend our previous work by using LSTM to model the sequential gaze data, and evaluate the model on two different datasets. The main contributions of this work are as follows:

We present a CNN–LSTM based framework for eye gaze prediction in videos, specifically designed to capture spatiotemporal dependencies.

We evaluate our model on benchmark video gaze datasets and demonstrate improved accuracy over statistical methods.

The remainder of this paper is organized as follows. Section 2 reviews related work in gaze estimation and video-based attention modeling. Section 3 describes the proposed CNN–LSTM framework. Section 4 presents experimental results and evaluation. Section 5 discusses the findings and potential applications, and concludes the paper with directions for future research.

## 2 Literature Review

One of the first studies [7] theorized that human attention is guided by features, colors, and edges in the scene. Gradients, brightness, sharp edges contribute in creating salient areas in image, responsible for attracting human attention.

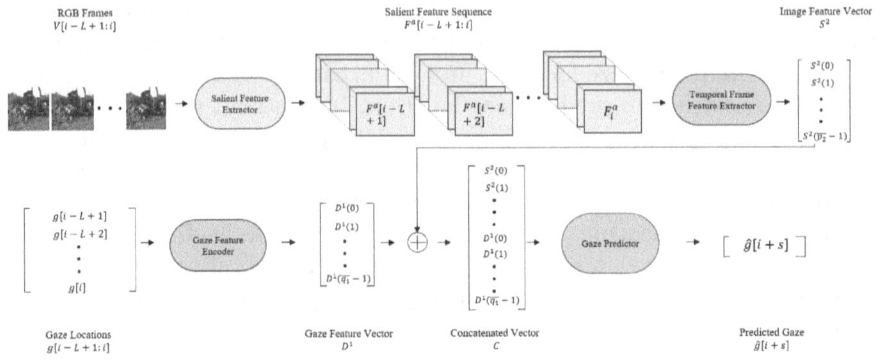


**Fig. 1.** Overview of Proposed Multimodal Gaze Prediction Model.

Itti et al. [8] proposed a feature extraction-based pipeline and merging multiple feature maps to a unified map to predict saliency from images. Bruce et al. [9] proposed a measure of saliency using Shannon's measure of self-information. The study explored creating a probability distribution by dividing the entire image into smaller image patches. Komogortsev and Khan [10] proposed using Kalman Filtering to mimic the mechanics of ocular muscles. Harel et al. [11] modeled each pixel in the image as a state in a Hidden Markov Model. They calculated the saliency map as the steady state of the HMM. Yanulevskaya et al. [12] used Weibul distribution to model image statistics.

The uprising success of machine learning, specially success of ML and DL in the field of computer vision has motivated researchers to study vision models for predicting image saliency. Kümmerer et al. [13] performed one of the earliest study to use pretrained CNNs to predict saliency map. Kruthiventi et al. [14] proposed a Fully Convolutional Network to predict saliency maps. Their CNN architecture was motivated from the VGG architecture. Pan et al. [15] proposed two end-to-end fully convolutional network to predict saliency map. They found that their deep convnet architecture is mostly better performing than shallow network counterpart. Pan et al. [16] used generative adversarial network to predict saliency maps. Their model achieved state of the art performance by learning to play against a discriminator. Assens et al. [17] also used a GAN to predict sequence of gaze locations on a static scene, also called a scanpath. Hu et al. [18] used CNN to predict gaze location in dynamic scenes rendered on a Head Mounted Display (HMD). Their setup uses the past gaze data along with the scene being viewed to predict gaze location. Feng et al. [19] used Hidden Markov Models to predict eye gaze locations in a video.

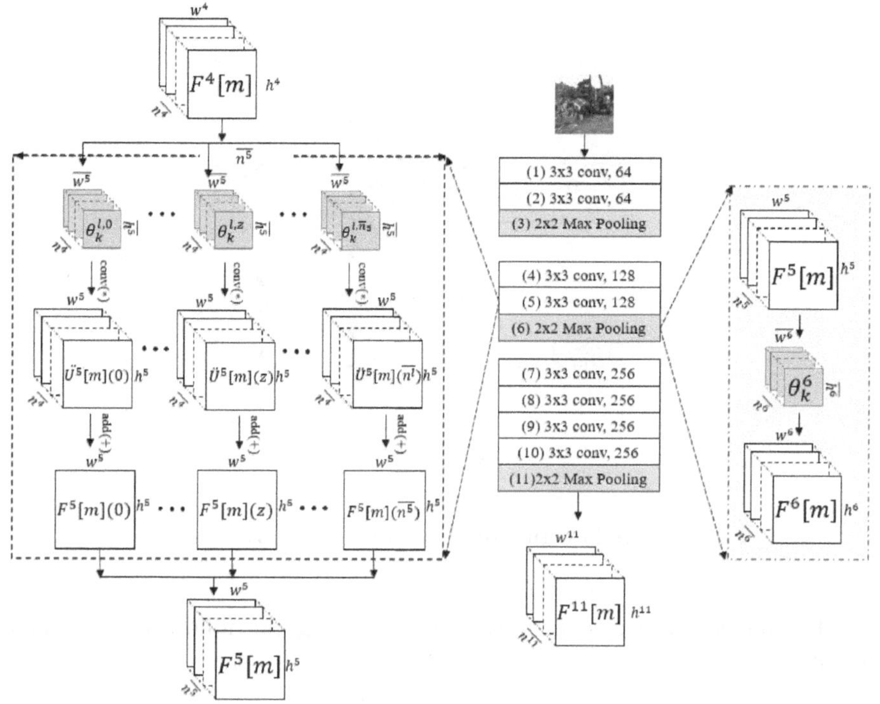


**Fig. 2.** Architecture of the Salient Feature Extractor

As seen from the literature review, many studies predict gaze locations for current scene in static images. There are very few studies which looks into predicting eye gaze location in videos.

## 3 Proposed Methodology

Figure 1 outlines the overall architecture of the model. The model consists of 4 modules which are described in their own subsections. We begin by defining the problem formally.

### 3.1 Problem Statement

Denote $V$ as a video consisting of $n$ frames. Also denote $V[i-L+1:i] \in \mathbb{R}^{L\times 3\times h\times w}$ as a continuous sequence of $L$ RGB-frames in the video. Furthermore, denote $g[i-L+1:i] \in \mathbb{R}^{L\times 2}$ the sequence of gaze on these $L$ frames. The objective is to learn a function $f_\theta : \mathbb{R}^{L\times 3\times h\times w} \times \mathbb{R}^{L\times 2} \rightarrow \mathbb{R}^2$ that outputs the gaze location $s$ frames into the future. The function $f$ is parameterized by $\theta$. The parameters $\theta$ are learned by minimizing a loss function $\mathcal{L} : \mathbb{R}^2 \times \mathbb{R}^2 \rightarrow \mathbb{R}$ that determines the distance between the predicted location and the ground truth.

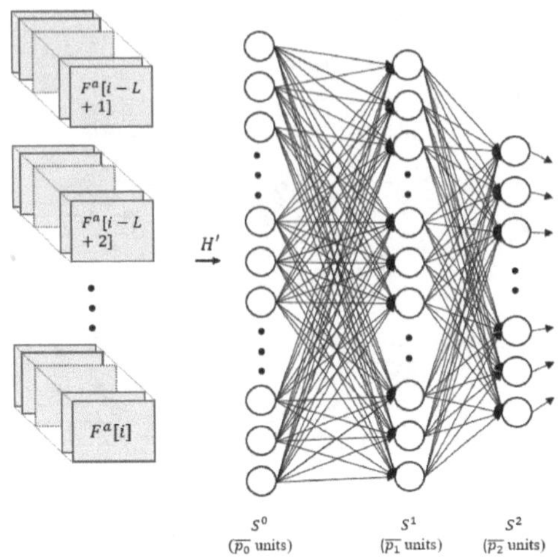


**Fig. 3.** Architecture of Temporal Feature Extractor.

Formally, the parameters $\theta$ are learned by solving the following optimization problem:

$$\arg\min_{\theta}\left(\mathcal{L}\left(f_\theta\right)\right) \tag{1}$$

### 3.2 Salient Feature Extractor

Features like edges, colors, and gradient in colors play an important role in attracting attention and guiding our gaze. Convolutional Neural Networks [3] have achieved state-of-the-art results in many computer vision problems [20–22]. Convolutional layers are robust in extracting spatial features. We used a pretrained CNN trained for object detection [23] and repurposed it to extract salient features from image. The module receives an RGB frame $V[i] \in \mathbb{R}^{3\times h\times w}$ and extracts features $F[i] \in \mathbb{R}^{256\times 28\times 28}$. The salient feature extractor is shown in Fig. 2.

Each image $V[i]$ is convolved by a set of convolutional layers and then downsampled by max-pool layers. Each convolution layer $l$ contains the convolutional kernel parameters $\theta_k^{l,z}$. The max-pool kernels only downsamples their input, they do not have any parameters, which is shown by $\theta_k^l$. The salient feature extractor implements the following set of equations:

$$\ddot{U}^l[m]\left(z_3, z_4, x, y\right) = \sum_{z_1=0}^{\overline{w^l}-1}\sum_{z_2=0}^{\overline{h^l}-1} F^{l-1}[m]\left(z_4, x - \lfloor\frac{\overline{w^l}}{2}\rfloor + z_1, y - \lfloor\frac{\overline{h^l}}{2}\rfloor + z_2\right) \times \theta_k^{l,z_3}\left(z_4, z_1, z_2\right) \tag{2}$$

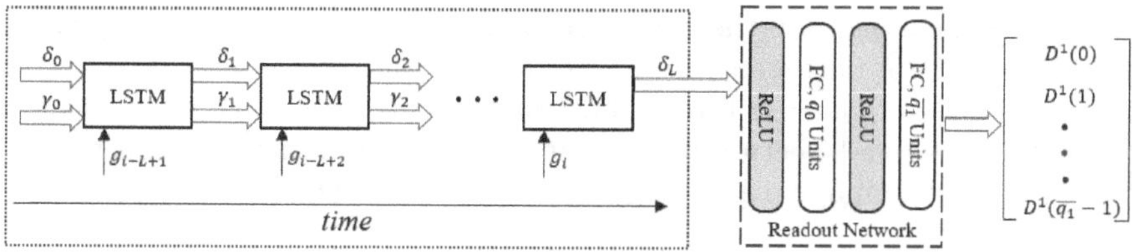


**Fig. 4.** Architecture of Gaze Location Encoder

$$F^l[m](f_{out}, x, y) = ReLU\left(\sum_{z_1=0}^{\overline{n^{l-1}}-1} \ddot{U}^l[m]\,(f_{out}, z_1, x, y)\right) \tag{3}$$

$$F^0[m] = V[m] \tag{4}$$

Equations 2–4 describe the operation of standard convolutional layer with *same* padding. Equation 4 states that the input to the first layer is an RGB frame from the video $V$. Equation 2 expresses the convolutional kernel at layer $l$, $\theta_k^l$ convolving its input $F^{l-1}[m]$ to produce a temporary output $\ddot{U}^l[m]$. The indexing variables in eq. 2–4 $z_3, z_4, x, y, m, l$ are constrained by the following:

$$\begin{gathered} 0 \leq z_3 < \overline{n^l} \\ 0 \leq z_4 < \overline{n^{l-1}} \\ 0 \leq x < h^l \\ 0 \leq y < w^l \\ 0 \leq m < l \\ l \in \{1,2,4,5,7,8,9,10\} \end{gathered} \tag{5}$$

For the sake of completeness, the max-pool layers operation can be specified by the following equation:

$$\begin{gathered} F^l[m](z, x, y) = \max_{z_1, z_2 \in \{0,1\}} F^{l-1}[m](z, 2x + z_1, 2y + z_2) \\ \text{for } m, z \in \mathbb{Z}, 0 \leq z < \overline{n^l}, 0 \leq m < L \end{gathered} \tag{6}$$

The VGG-16 uses $2 \times 2$ max-pool layers, which downsamples the input by a factor of 2 in both dimensions. Thus, between groups of convolutional layers, the dimension of the input image drops rapidly.

### 3.3 Temporal Frame Feature Extractor

The temporal frame feature extractor embeds the $L$ feature volumes into a smaller subspace. The sequence of maps is converted to a vector $S^2$. It also acts as a downsampler for the sequence of feature volumes. The sequence of feature maps, $F^a$ is flattened into a vector, and the vector is passed through a network of fully connected layers. The output is taken as the embedding $S^2$. Figure 3 shows the architecture of the temporal frame feature extractor.

The temporal frame feature extractor implements the following equation:

$$\begin{gathered} S^2 = \theta^2_{TF} * \theta^1_{TF} * S^0 \\ \theta^1_{TF} \in \mathbb{R}^{(L \times \overline{n^{11}} \times h^{11} \times w^{11}) \times \overline{p_0}}, \theta^2_{TF} \in \mathbb{R}^{\overline{p_1} \times \overline{p_0}} \end{gathered} \tag{7}$$

Here $*$ is the matrix multiplication operation.

### 3.4 Gaze Feature Encoder

The gaze encoder takes the past gaze locations $g[i - L + 1 : i]$ as input and encodes the future gaze feature in smaller subspace using a vector $D^1 \in \mathbb{R}^{\overline{q_1}}$. The sequence of gaze locations is processed by a Long-Short-Term-Memory(LSTM) [24] network. At each time step, the LSTM takes three inputs: 1. the gaze location $g[m]$, the last hidden state $\delta[j-1]$ and the last cell state $\gamma[j-1]$. The high level process of LSTM can be expressed as

$$\begin{gathered} \delta[j], \gamma[j] = LSTM(\delta[j-1], \gamma[j-1], g[k]) \\ \text{where } k = (i - L + 1) - j, 0 \leq j \leq L, \delta[j], \gamma[j] \in \mathbb{R}^u \end{gathered} \tag{8}$$

Figure 4 shows the gaze encoder. The last hidden state $\delta[L]$ is passed through a readout network which a multi-layered neural network. The output of the readout network $D^1$ is taken as the gaze embedding. The readout layer implements the following operation:

$$\begin{gathered} D^1 = \theta^1_{RO} * (\theta^0_{RO} * ReLU(\delta[L])) \\ \text{where } \theta^0_{RO} \in \mathbb{R}^{u \times \overline{q_0}}, \theta^1_{R0} \in \mathbb{R}^{\overline{q_0} \times \overline{q_1}} \end{gathered} \tag{9}$$

### 3.5 Gaze Predictor

The gaze predictor takes the gaze embedding $D^1$ and the temporal frame embedding $S^2$ and concatenates them into $C$. $C$ contains embedding from the data of both modalities. Then the module passes $C$ through a sequence of fully connected layers. Each layer downsamples its input vector and finally the last layer outputs the predicted gaze $\hat{g}$. The final layer outputs 2 values which is passed through a sigmoid activation, to restrict the output between $[0-1]$.

The gaze predictor implements the following equations:

$$\begin{aligned} \hat{g}[i+s] &= \sigma\left(\theta^5_{GP} * B^4\right) \\ B^a &= LN\left(ReLU\left(\theta^a_{GP} * B^{a-1}\right)\right) \\ B^0 &= C \end{aligned} \tag{10}$$

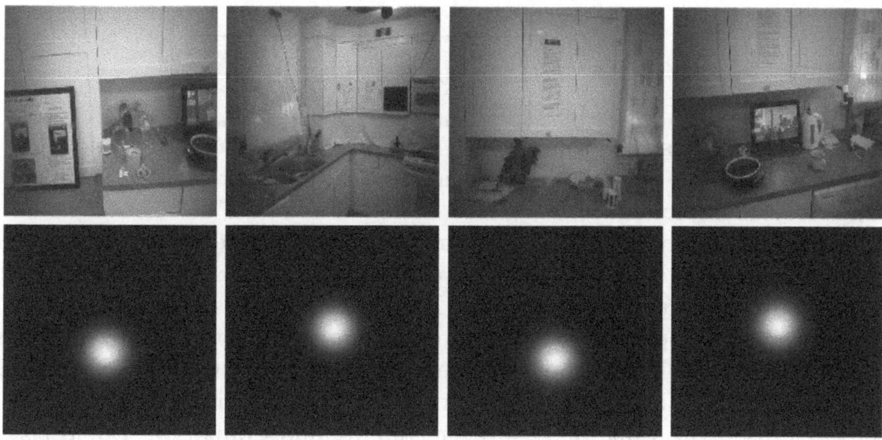

**Fig. 5.** Qualitative results of the model. The first row shows randomly sampled frames from randomly selected RGB videos. The second row shows the predicted gaze locations as a Gaussian centered around the predicted gaze.

The output of every layer except the last layer is passed through a layer normalization operation, which is specified in Eq. 10 as $LN$. Layer normalization helps the model to center the data after each layer. It prevents the output of the final layer from being too large or too small, which can push the sigmoid activation into saturation [25].

## 4 Implementation and Results

We used the Coutrot [26] dataset and the EGTEA [27] datasets to evaluate our model.

The Coutrot dataset consists of 60 videos of dynamic scenes. Each video contained 16 viewers. We used videos *clip-10, clip-11, clip-12, clip-18, clip-23, clip-28* as test dataset and the rest as the training dataset.

The EGTEA dataset consists of 86 egocentric videos of participants performing different types of cooking related tasks. We used *OP01-R03-BaconAndEggs, OP03-R01-PastaSalad, OP06-R04-ContinentalBreakfast, OP02-R03-BaconAndEggs, OP06-R02-TurkeySandwich, P21-R03-BaconAndEggs* as test videos and the rest as training videos.

We compared our model with 3 other models, i) Center: Always predicts the screen center as the future gaze location, ii) Itti: The Itti-Koch model [8] and iii) GBVS: The graph based visual saliency model. [11]

We used the L2 distance between the predicted location and the ground location to compare the results across models. The $(x, y)$ locations were normalized by the width and the height of the frames respectively. Equation 11 shows specifies the loss function for a single sample:

$$\mathcal{L}(g, \hat{g}) = \sqrt{\left(\frac{g[0]}{w} - \hat{g}[0]\right)^2 + \left(\frac{g[1]}{h} - \hat{g}[1]\right)^2} \tag{11}$$

Here, $g = (x, y)$ is the ground truth in pixels, $\hat{g}$ is the model's prediciton. $h$ and $w$ are the frame dimensions. In a minibatch, the average of $\mathcal{L}$ as taken as the loss for the minibatch.

During both training and evaluation, each frame of every video was resized to have dimensions $h = w = 224$. Every pixels were normalized using min-max normalization in the range $[0 - 1]$. Pytorch [28] was used to implement the model. Every layer, except the pretrained layers were initialized by randomly sampling Gaussian distribution with mean $= 0$ and std $= 0.02$. We used Adam [29] optimizer to optimize the parameters of the model with a learning rate of 0.0004. We used the value of $L = 3$ for training and evaluation. Batch size of 32 were used for training. We trained the model for 50 epochs. The model was trained on a server with Intel (R) Xeon (R) CPU, with NVIDIA A40 GPU with 48 GiB memory for processing batches in parallel. Additionally, the server had 32 GiB physical memory.

Table 1 summarises the result. Our model performs much better than the statistical approaches. Also Fig. 6 plots the $log(\mathcal{L})$ on y-axis vs. frame indices on x-axis. The reason for plotting $log(\mathcal{L})$ instead of $\mathcal{L}$ is scale. Our model cuts down the error by almost a factor of 10 and the difference is seen better in *log* scale. Figure 6 also shows another important detail, that is the center model has lower error than GBVS. The reason is the presence of center-bias in gaze datasets. Also, in statistical models, there are at least 2 jumps in error accross all three models, which can be hypothesized as a sudden eye movement, which the statistical models could not predict.

**Table 1.** Quantitative comparison of different saliency models on the EGTEA and Coutrot datasets. The best result for each dataset is highlighted in bold.

| Model | Center | Itti - Koch | GBVS | Our Model |
|---|---|---|---|---|
| EGTEA | 0.2170 | 0.4336 | 0.7587 | **0.0309** |
| Coutrot | 0.2169 | 0.4370 | 0.6033 | **0.0474** |

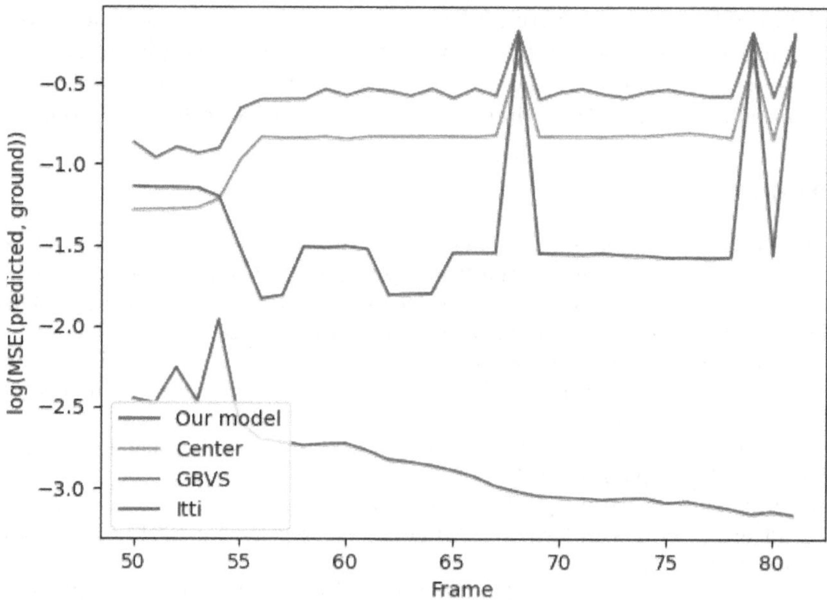


**Fig. 6.** Error of 4 models for 32 continuous frames.

## 5 Discussion and Conclusion

In this study, we designed and developed a multi-modal CNN-LSTM network to predict eye gaze location in videos. The goal of the study was to model spatio-temporal relationship in videos to predict eye gaze locations. Our model was compared with 3 other models on 2 different datasets. One of the dataset, had videos of different dynamic scenes. The other dataset, EGTEA, had egocentric videos of persons performing various food preparation activities.

The results demonstrate that spatiotemporal modeling can play a crucial role in predicting eye gaze in future accurately. Our approach models both spatial dependency and temporal dependency, which contributes to the improved results. One of the strong points of this study is the usage of 2 different datasets to evaluate the method, both datasets contain videos of very different categories. Gaze behavior of a viewer depends on the context of the video as well. For example, gaze behavior of a viewer will vary across egocentric, cinematic and surveillance style videos. Therefore, domain based fine-tuning can enhance performance in specialized settings.

There are multiple scopes of future work of this study. It remains to be seen on how model performs by learning with different type of loss metrics such as, AUC, NSS, KL Divergence etc. Training on different type of loss functions can improve the results further, or provide insights on the behavior of model on that particular loss metric. Another scope of future work is to use different architectures such as Conv-LSTM, GRU, Transformers to model spatio-temporal dependency of the data. Interpretability of the models under various loss function is also a future research scope. Future work will also explore multimodal research scope such as integrating audio cues, semantic understandic and task based gaze prediction, which will further align model predictions with human intent.

## References

1. Salvucci, D.D., Goldberg, J.H.: Identifying fixations and saccades in eye-tracking protocols. In: Proceedings of the 2000 Symposium on Eye Tracking Research & Applications, ser. ETRA '00, pp. 71–78. Association for Computing Machinery, New York (2000). https://doi.org/10.1145/355017.355028
2. Bindemann, M.: Scene and screen center bias early eye movements in scene viewing. Vis. Res. **50**(23), 2577–2587 (2010). vision Research Reviews. https://www.sciencedirect.com/science/article/pii/S0042698910004025
3. Dumoulin, V., Visin, F.: A guide to convolution arithmetic for deep learning. arXiv preprint: arXiv:1603.07285 (2016)
4. Sak, H., Senior, A., Beaufays, F.: Long short-term memory based recurrent neural network architectures for large vocabulary speech recognition (2014). https://arxiv.org/abs/1402.1128
5. Chung, J., Gülçehre, Ç., Cho, K., Bengio, Y.: Empirical evaluation of gated recurrent neural networks on sequence modeling. CoRR, vol. abs/1412.3555 (2014). http://arxiv.org/abs/1412.3555
6. Sourave, R.H., Khan, J.I.: Eye gaze prediction in videos using deep neural network. In: IECON 2024 - 50th Annual Conference of the IEEE Industrial Electronics Society, pp. 1–6 (2024)
7. Treisman, A.M., Gelade, G.: A feature-integration theory of attention. Cogn. Psychol. **12**(1), 97–136 (1980). https://www.sciencedirect.com/science/article/pii/0010028580900055
8. Itti, L., Koch, C., Niebur, E.: A model of saliency-based visual attention for rapid scene analysis. IEEE Trans. Pattern Anal. Mach. Intell. **20**(11), 1254–1259 (1998)
9. Bruce, N., Tsotsos, J.: Saliency based on information maximization. In: Weiss, Y., Schölkopf, B., Platt, J. (eds.) Advances in Neural Information Processing Systems, vol. 18. MIT Press (2005). https://proceedings.neurips.cc/paper_files/paper/2005/file/0738069b244a1c43c83112b735140a16-Paper.pdf
10. Komogortsev, O.V., Khan, J.I.: Eye movement prediction by oculomotor plant Kalman filter with brainstem control. J. Control Theory Appl. **7**(1), 14–22 (2009)
11. Harel, J., Koch, C., Perona, P.: Graph-based visual saliency. In: Schölkopf, B., Platt, J., Hoffman, T. (eds.) Advances in Neural Information Processing Systems, vol. 19. MIT Press (2006). https://proceedings.neurips.cc/paper_files/paper/2006/file/4db0f8b0fc895da263fd77fc8aecabe4-Paper.pdf
12. Yanulevskaya, V., Marsman, J.B., Cornelissen, F., Geusebroek, J.-M.: An image statistics-based model for fixation prediction. Cogn. Comput. **3**(1), 94–104 (2010)
13. Kümmerer, M., Theis, L., Bethge, M.: Deep gaze i: boosting saliency prediction with feature maps trained on ImageNet (2015). https://arxiv.org/abs/1411.1045
14. Kruthiventi, S.S.S., Ayush, K., Babu, R.V.: DeepFix: a fully convolutional neural network for predicting human eye fixations. IEEE Trans. Image Process. **26**(9), 4446–4456 (2017)
15. Pan, J., Sayrol, E., Giro-I-Nieto, X., McGuinness, K., O'Connor, N.E.: Shallow and deep convolutional networks for saliency prediction. In: IEEE Conference on Computer Vision and Pattern Recognition (CVPR), pp. 598–606 (2016)

16. Pan, J., et al.: SalGAN: visual saliency prediction with generative adversarial networks (2018). https://arxiv.org/abs/1701.01081
17. Assens, M., i Nieto, X.G., McGuinness, K., O'Connor, N.E.: PathGAN: visual scanpath prediction with generative adversarial networks (2018). https://arxiv.org/abs/1809.00567
18. Hu, Z., Li, S., Zhang, C., Yi, K., Wang, G., Manocha, D.: DGaze: CNN-based gaze prediction in dynamic scenes. IEEE Trans. Visual Comput. Graphics **26**(5), 1902–1911 (2020)
19. Feng, Y., Cheung, G., Tan, W.-T., Le Callet, P., Ji, Y.: Low-cost eye gaze prediction system for interactive networked video streaming. IEEE Trans. Multimedia **15**(8), 1865–1879 (2013)
20. Ronneberger, O., Fischer, P., Brox, T.: U-net: convolutional networks for biomedical image segmentation (2015). https://arxiv.org/abs/1505.04597
21. Dong, C., Loy, C.C., He, K., Tang, X.: Image super-resolution using deep convolutional networks (2015). https://arxiv.org/abs/1501.00092
22. Ren, S., He, K., Girshick, R., Sun, J.: Faster R-CNN: towards real-time object detection with region proposal networks (2016). https://arxiv.org/abs/1506.01497
23. Simonyan, K., Zisserman, A.: Very deep convolutional networks for large-scale image recognition. arXiv preprint: arXiv:1409.1556 (2014)
24. Sak, H., Senior, A., Beaufays, F.: Long short-term memory based recurrent neural network architectures for large vocabulary speech recognition. arXiv preprint: arXiv:1402.1128 (2014)
25. Ba, J.L., Kiros, J.R., Hinton, G.E.: Layer normalization (2016). https://arxiv.org/abs/1607.06450
26. Coutrot, A., Guyader, N.: How saliency, faces, and sound influence gaze in dynamic social scenes. J. Vis. **14**(8), 5–5 (2014). https://doi.org/10.1167/14.8.5
27. Li, Y., Liu, M., Rehg, J.M.: In the eye of the beholder: gaze and actions in first person video (2020). https://arxiv.org/abs/2006.00626
28. Paszke, A., et al.: PyTorch: an imperative style, high-performance deep learning library. In: Advances in Neural Information Processing Systems, vol. 32 (2019)
29. Kingma, D.P., Ba, J., et al.: Adam: a method for stochastic optimization, vol. 1412, no. 6. arXiv preprint: arXiv:1412.6980 (2014)

# Wearable Ear Device for Affective State Recognition in Human-Computer Interaction

Wan-Young Chung[1,2(✉)], Hika Barki[1], Ngoc-Dau Mai[1], and Fatima Ul Zahra[1]

[1] Department of AI Convergence, Pukyong National University, Busan 48513, Republic of Korea
{daljuhika,ngocdaumai95,fatimatzahra}@pukyong.ac.kr
[2] Department of Electronic Engineering, Pukyong National University, Busan 48513, Republic of Korea
wychung@pknu.ac.kr

**Abstract.** Affective computing enhances human–computer interaction by enabling systems to recognize and respond to emotional states. Ear-centered sensing offers a practical approach due to comfort, stability, and unobtrusiveness. This paper reviews advances in ear-based electroencephalography (EEG), ear-based photoplethysmography (PPG), and their integration with facial expression analysis for robust affective state recognition. We highlight contributions in on-device deep learning, time-frequency feature extraction, and multimodal pipelines for real-time stress, fatigue, and emotion monitoring.

**Keywords:** Affective computing · EEG · PPG · HCI · Emotion recognition · Stress monitoring · Drowsiness detection

## 1 Introduction

Affective computing, the interdisciplinary field merging artificial intelligence with psychology and neuroscience, has become a cornerstone of next-generation HCI. By enabling systems to detect and respond to human emotions, affective computing supports more natural, adaptive, and empathetic interactions. However, traditional approaches for emotion and stress recognition often rely on obtrusive methods such as scalp EEG, wrist-worn PPG, or full facial imaging that face challenges in comfort, stability, and user acceptance, limiting deployment in real-world HCI.

Recent studies highlight ear-centered biosensing as an unobtrusive yet powerful alternative. Behind-the-ear (BTE) EEG offers high-quality neural measurements in hair-free regions, while in-ear PPG provides robust cardiovascular dynamics with reduced motion artifacts compared to peripheral sites [1–4]. Research spans single-modality systems such as PPG-only stress detection or


A. Shastri et al. (Eds.): IHCI 2025, LNCS 16437, pp. 524–529, 2026.
https://doi.org/10.1007/978-3-032-26352-0_44

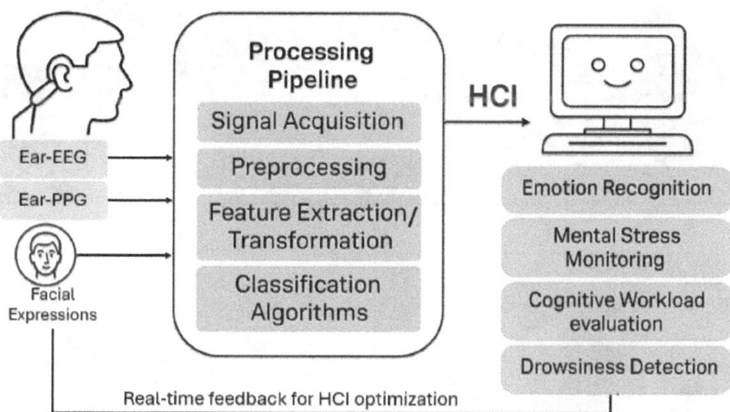


**Fig. 1.** Conceptual framework of wearable ear-based systems for affective state recognition in human–computer interaction.

EEG-only emotion monitoring and multimodal frameworks that combine ear-EEG with facial features or fuse in-ear PPG with ear-EEG for enhanced recognition [5–7].

Ear-based EEG, in-ear PPG, and facial expression analysis have been explored in both single- and multimodal systems. Advances in edge AI, including on-chip learning and time–frequency transformation, enable real-time processing with high accuracy and low latency. Figure 1 outlines a conceptual framework showing how these modalities individually or combined support applications such as emotion recognition, stress monitoring, workload evaluation, and drowsiness detection.

In summary, ear-centered sensing provides a practical and unobtrusive pathway for affective state recognition. While individual modalities such as ear-EEG or in-ear PPG have shown promise, a unified perspective that connects these approaches with multimodal integration and edge-AI implementation is still lacking. This paper addresses that gap by systematically reviewing advances in ear-based biosensing technologies, highlighting single- and multimodal systems, their applications in HCI, and the challenges and opportunities that shape the future of wearable affective computing.

## 2 Ear-Based Biosensing Technologies

Ear-centered sensing provides unobtrusiveness, comfort, and signal quality advantages over conventional approaches. Our research encompasses both single-modality and integrated multimodal systems.

### 2.1 Single-Modality Approaches

**Ear-EEG:** BTE-EEG electrodes achieve high correlation with scalp EEG while improving comfort and reducing setup complexity. Deep learning models applied

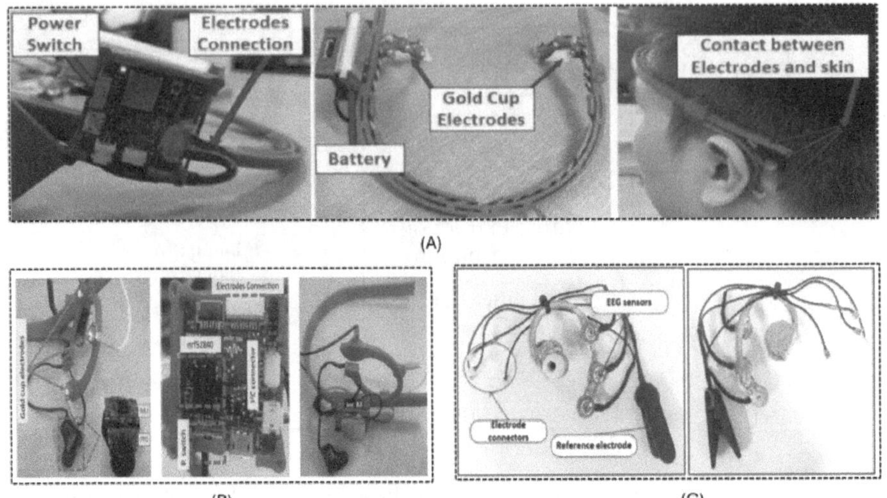


**Fig. 2.** Representative ear-based hardware systems from cited works: (A) Behind-the-ear EEG–based wearable driver drowsiness detection using embedded tiny neural networks [10]; (B) Optimized XGBoost for multimodal affective-state classification using in-ear PPG and BTE-EEG [7]; (C) Real-time on-chip ML–based wearable BTE-EEG device for emotion recognition [11].

to superlet-transformed ear-EEG signals achieved 92.39% accuracy for emotion recognition [5]. On-chip implementations enable real-time processing with 91.72% accuracy for stress detection using BTE-EEG Signals [8].

**In-ear PPG:** Unlike peripheral PPG, in-ear measurements provide stable cardiovascular signals with fewer motion artifacts. CNN-based frameworks for mental stress detection achieved 92.04% accuracy and 90.8% F1-score [1]. Vision Transformer models applied to PPG scalograms further improved classification to 97.78% accuracy [9].

### 2.2 Multimodal Integration

Integration with additional signals enhances robustness and contextual understanding. Ear-EEG combined with facial expression features achieved 95.33% accuracy for driver drowsiness detection [6]. The fusion of in-ear PPG and ear-EEG enabled multimodal emotion recognition, with Bayesian-tuned XGBoost achieving 97.58% accuracy, outperforming single-modality systems [7].

## 3 HCI Applications and Performance

Ear-based biosensing enables dynamic adaptation to users' emotional and cognitive states across multiple application domains. Hardware examples of the reviewed ear-based systems are shown in Figs. 2 and 3.

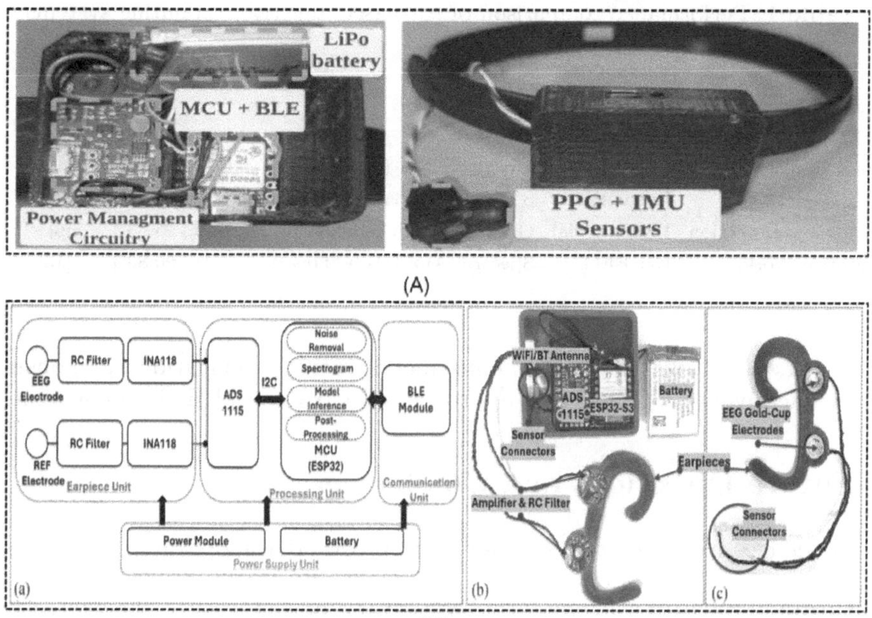


**Fig. 3.** Wearable prototypes for in-ear PPG and BTE-EEG: (A) Detection and classification of mental stress using in-ear PPG and a Vision Transformer [9]; (B) On-chip mental stress detection integrating a wearable BTE-EEG device with embedded tiny neural networks [8].

### 3.1 Emotion Recognition and Stress Monitoring

Ear-EEG with superlet transforms distinguished positive and negative affective states with 92.39% accuracy [5]. Real-time BTE-EEG implementation achieved 94.87% emotion classification accuracy [11]. Additionally, our recent work demonstrated that a variational quantum classifier applied to BTE-EEG features achieved 92.06 % accuracy in positive versus negative emotion classification, highlighting the promise of quantum machine learning for on-device emotion recognition [12]. For stress monitoring, in-ear PPG achieved 92.04% accuracy under motion-influenced conditions [1]. Vision Transformer approaches enhanced PPG-based stress classification to 97.78% accuracy [9].

### 3.2 Cognitive Workload and Fatigue Detection

Ear-EEG spectral features effectively tracked mental effort, enabling adaptive learning platforms and workload-aware AR/VR environments with 90.83% accuracy [13]. Selective auditory attention decoding from ear-EEG achieved a moderate accuracy using nonlinear models [14]. Driver drowsiness detection combining BTE-EEG with facial expressions achieved 95.33% accuracy [6], while embedded neural networks for drowsiness monitoring reached 91.31% accuracy [10].

**Table 1.** Performance comparison of ear-based affective computing systems

| Application | Modality | Method | Accuracy | Reference |
|---|---|---|---|---|
| Emotion Recognition | Ear-EEG | Superlet + DL | 92.39% | [5] |
| | EEG+PPG | Bayesian opt. + XGBoost | 97.58% | [7] |
| Stress Detection | In-ear PPG | CWT + CNN Framework | 92.04% | [1] |
| | In-ear PPG | STFT + Vision Transformer | 97.78% | [9] |
| Drowsiness Detection | EEG+Facial | GAN-based auto-denoising network | 95.33% | [6] |
| Cognitive Workload | Ear-EEG | Spectral Analysis + Tiny NN | 90.83% | [13] |

Table 1 summarizes key performance metrics across applications, demonstrating the effectiveness of ear-based approaches for real-world HCI deployment.

## 4 Future Directions and Challenges

Key challenges must be addressed for widespread HCI adoption:

- **Standardization:** Current prototypes vary in electrode placement, signal processing, and evaluation protocols. Interoperable platforms with subject-independent validation are essential [7,9].
- **AI Optimization:** While embedded neural networks show promise [8], improvements in power efficiency, memory usage, and adaptive personalization are crucial for continuous monitoring.
- **Privacy-Preserving Integration:** Combining ear signals with behavioral cues must balance recognition performance with user privacy and minimal intrusiveness [6].
- **Real-World Validation:** Extensive testing across diverse populations and environments is needed to ensure reliability in practical HCI applications.

## 5 Conclusion

Ear-based biosensing represents a promising direction for affective computing in HCI. BTE-EEG, in-ear PPG, and their multimodal integration demonstrate accurate, unobtrusive monitoring of emotional states, stress, workload, and drowsiness. These systems offer advantages over traditional approaches through improved comfort, stability, and real-time adaptability. Achieving accuracies up to 97.58% for emotion recognition and 95.33% for drowsiness detection, ear-centered devices show significant potential for transforming HCI through adaptive, emotion-aware systems. Future success depends on addressing standardization, subject-independent validation, and energy-efficient AI implementation for healthcare, education, safety, and immersive digital applications.

## References


1. Barki, H., Chung, W.-Y.: Mental stress detection using a wearable in-ear plethysmography. Biosensors **13**(3), 397 (2023). https://doi.org/10.3390/bios13030397
2. ul Zahra, F., Barki, H., Chung, W.-Y.: Emotion recognition from behind-the-ear photoplethysmography signal using continuous wavelet transform and deep learning. J. Inst. Convergence Sig. Process. **26**(1), 1–9 (2025)
3. Barki, H., Chung, S.H., Jafari, R., Chung, W.-Y.: Stress-ViT: in-ear plethysmography for mental stress classification with vision transformer. In: 2023 IEEE Biomedical Circuits and Systems Conference (BioCAS), pp. 1–4. IEEE (2023). https://doi.org/10.1109/BioCAS58349.2023.10389058
4. Ferlini, A., Montanari, A., Min, C., Li, H., Sassi, U., Kawsar, F.: In-ear PPG for vital signs. IEEE Pervasive Comput. **21**(1), 65–74 (2022). https://doi.org/10.1109/MPRV.2021.3121171
5. Mai, N.-D., Nguyen, H.-T., Chung, W.-Y..: Deep LearningBased wearable Ear-EEG emotion recognition system with SuperletsBased signal-to-image conversion framework. IEEE Sens. J. **24**(7), 11946–11957 (2024). https://doi.org/10.1109/JSEN.2024.3369062
6. Mai, N.-D., Nguyen, H.-T., Chung, W.-Y.: Multimodal driver drowsiness detection using facial expressions and EarEEGs With a lightweight auto-denoising network. IEEE Trans. Intell. Transp. Syst. **26**(6), 7819–7832 (2025). https://doi.org/10.1109/TITS.2025.3559098.
7. Barki, H., Mai, N.-D., Chung, W.-Y.: Optimized XGBoost for affective state classification using In-Ear PPG and behind-the-ear EEG signals. IEEE J. Biomed. Health Inform. (2025). https://doi.org/10.1109/JBHI.2025.3598354.
8. Mai, N.-D., Chung, W.-Y.: On-chip mental stress detection: integrating a wearable behind-the-ear EEG device with embedded tiny neural network. IEEE J. Biomed. Health Inform. **29**(3), 1872–1883 (2025). https://doi.org/10.1109/JBHI.2024.3519600
9. Barki, H., Nkenyereye, L., Chung, W.-Y.: Detection and classification of mental stress using In-Ear plethysmography and a vision transformer. IEEE Sens. J. **25**(2), 4015–4026 (2025). https://doi.org/10.1109/JSEN.2024.3512595
10. Nguyen, H.-T., Mai, N.-D., Lee, B.G., Chung, W.-Y.: Behind-the-Ear EEG-based wearable driver drowsiness detection system using embedded tiny neural networks. IEEE Sens. J. **23**(19), 23875–23892 (2023). https://doi.org/10.1109/JSEN.2023.3307766
11. Mai, N.-D., Nguyen, H.-T., Chung, W.-Y.: Real-Time on-chip machine-learning-based wearable behind-the-ear electroencephalogram device for emotion recognition. IEEE Access **11**, 47258–47270 (2023). https://doi.org/10.1109/ACCESS.2023.3276244
12. Mai, N.-D., Barki, H., Chung, W.-Y.: A wearable BTEEEG embedded device for emotion monitoring with quantum machine learning. In: 2024 Tenth International Conference on Communications and Electronics (ICCE), pp. 562–566 (2024). https://doi.org/10.1109/ICCE62051.2024.10634608
13. Mai, N.-D., Nando, Y.A., Chung, W.-Y.: End-to-end processing-on-chip wearable ear EEG device with tiny neural network for multilevel stress detection. In: Proceedings of the 2024 IEEE Sensors Conference (SENSORS), pp. 1–4 (2024). https://doi.org/10.1109/SENSORS60989.2024.10785105
14. Thornton, M.D., Mandic, D.P., Reichenbach, T.: Comparison of linear and nonlinear methods for decoding selective attention to speech from Ear-EEG recordings. IEEE Access **13** (2025). https://doi.org/10.1109/ACCESS.2025.3590490.

# Multivariate Pattern Analysis of Resting-State fMRI for the Classification of Osteoarthritis Patients and Healthy Controls

Khyati Dholariya[1], Shobha Sharma[2(✉)], and Tapan Kumar Gandhi[2]

[1] Computer Engineering, School of Engineering, RK University, Rajkot, India
kdholariya834@rku.ac.in

[2] Department of Electrical Engineering, IIT Delhi, New Delhi, India
sharma.shobha90@gmail.com, tgandhi@ee.iitd.ac.in

**Abstract.** This study explores the application of multivariate pattern analysis (MVPA) on fMRI data to classify osteoarthritis patients and healthy controls using functional connectivity from the middle frontal gyrus. The dataset, sourced from the paper "*Brain connectivity predicts placebo response across chronic pain clinical trials*", focused on placebo-only and treatment-only studies. Preprocessing steps included normalization, smoothing, and extraction of time-series data, followed by the use of tangent space embedding to compute connectivity matrices. Feature selection and classification were performed using models such as SVM and logistic regression. The middle frontal gyrus was selected based on prior evidence linking it to placebo response and chronic pain processing. Our models showed promising classification accuracy, particularly in the placebo group. The findings align with previous research demonstrating the capacity of MVPA to decode pain-related brain patterns and predict clinical outcomes. This study highlights the potential of using brain connectivity patterns as neurobiomarkers for chronic pain.

**Keywords:** fMRI · MVPA · Machine Learning · Chronic Pain · Brain Connectivity

## 1 Introduction

The human brain is a remarkably complex and dynamic organ, and decoding its structure and function remains a central goal in both neuroscience and clinical research. Magnetic Resonance Imaging (MRI) has emerged as a non-invasive and powerful modality for visualizing brain anatomy in detail. Taking this a step further, functional MRI (fMRI) captures fluctuations in blood oxygenation linked to neural activity, allowing researchers to examine how different brain regions communicate over time. Resting-state fMRI (rs-fMRI), in particular, has gained traction for its ability to measure intrinsic brain activity without requiring subjects to perform specific tasks [2]. This resting-state connectivity is vital for understanding the brain's default mode network and proves especially useful when comparing healthy individuals to those with clinical conditions.


A. Shastri et al. (Eds.): IHCI 2025, LNCS 16437, pp. 530–536, 2026.
https://doi.org/10.1007/978-3-032-26352-0_45

To analyze the complex functional connectivity patterns derived from fMRI data, Multivariate Pattern Analysis (MVPA) has become an increasingly popular approach. MVPA leverages machine learning techniques to detect distributed patterns across multiple voxels or regions, unlike traditional univariate methods that examine one voxel at a time [3]. This multivariate approach offers enhanced sensitivity in identifying subtle and widespread neural differences—making it especially powerful in the context of clinical neuroimaging and biomarker discovery.

Recent literature has highlighted the effectiveness of MVPA in decoding pain perception [3], identifying placebo responders [1], and distinguishing between psychiatric or neurological conditions [8]. For example, Wager et al. [2] demonstrated the ability of fMRI-based signatures to predict physical pain, while Vachon-Presseau et al. [1] showed how connectivity measures could predict placebo response in chronic pain trials. Marquand et al. [3] explored MVPA's strength in decoding pain experiences, further underlining its clinical relevance. However, despite these advancements, most existing studies remain focused on task-based fMRI paradigms, and relatively few have explored the potential of resting-state MVPA in understanding chronic pain or treatment outcomes.Furthermore, digital image processing plays a crucial role in fMRI studies. Preprocessing steps like motion correction, spatial normalization, smoothing, and noise filtering ensure that data used in subsequent analyses are clean and reliable [7]. When integrated with MVPA, these methods allow researchers to derive meaningful insights from high-dimensional neuroimaging data, improving both interpretability and predictive accuracy.

Clinically, such integrations are highly valuable. MVPA has been shown to distinguish healthy individuals from those with mental health or neurological conditions, offering promise in early diagnosis, prognosis, and personalized treatment planning [8]. However, as we reviewed prior studies involving our dataset of interest, we noticed a gap—no studies to date have applied a machine learning-based MVPA framework that includes hyperparameter optimization. This adds novelty to our work and opens new opportunities for improving classification and predictive modeling in the context of resting-state brain data.

Through this study, we aim to enhance the understanding of how brain connectivity differs between healthy and clinical populations and demonstrate how MVPA—combined with robust preprocessing and machine learning techniques—can uncover neural patterns that inform more personalized and effective treatment strategies in chronic pain and related disorders.

## 2 Methodology

### 2.1 Dataset Overview

This study uses a preprocessed neuroimaging dataset comprising 76 participants, including 20 healthy controls and 56 osteoarthritis patients. The patient group is divided into two cohorts: one that received a short-term placebo (Study 1) and another that underwent a 3-month placebo or duloxetine treatment (Study 2). Each participant's record includes resting-state fMRI, anatomical scans, demographic details (age, gender), and, for patients, clinical variables such as treatment type, response status, and changes in pain measured by VAS and WOMAC scores. This dataset supports both group comparisons and predictive modeling based on structural, functional, and clinical data (Table 1).

**Table 1.** Information on the Dataset

| Group | Count | Drug | Response Data | Study Type |
|---|---|---|---|---|
| Healthy Controls | 20 | N/A | N/A | No treatment |
| OA Patients (Study 1) | 17 | Placebo | Yes | 2-week placebo trial |
| OA Patients (Study 2) | 39 | Placebo/Duloxetine | Yes | 3-month RCT |

### 2.2 ROI Selection Based on Prior Literature

The middle frontal gyrus was selected as the region of interest (ROI) due to its consistent involvement in pain modulation and placebo responsiveness. This decision was guided by prior findings, particularly Vachon-Presseau et al. [1], who demonstrated that brain connectivity in this region can predict placebo responses across chronic pain trials. The ROI was anatomically defined using the Harvard-Oxford cortical atlas within FSLeyes to ensure reproducibility and anatomical accuracy.

### 2.3 Extraction of ROI Time Series and Whole-Brain Correlation

Resting-state fMRI data were used to extract the average BOLD time series from the selected ROI for each subject. These time series were then correlated with voxel-wise signals across the entire brain, generating subject-specific functional connectivity maps. This approach captures network-level interactions relevant to pain processing, in line with methodologies used in pain neuroimaging studies [2, 4].

### 2.4 Construction of Functional Connectivity Matrix

The resulting correlation matrices represent pairwise functional connections between the ROI and the rest of the brain. To reduce feature redundancy and dimensionality, only the upper triangular portion of each symmetric matrix (excluding the diagonal) was retained, similar to techniques described in prior fMRI pattern analysis studies [7, 8]. These matrices were then flattened into one-dimensional vectors, forming the input features for classification models.

### 2.5 Machine Learning Classification

Two machine learning models were employed: Support Vector Machine (SVM) and Logistic Regression. SVM is known for its ability to handle high-dimensional, non-linear data [11], while Logistic Regression provides interpretable linear decision boundaries. Both classifiers have been successfully applied in previous pain-related neuroimaging classification tasks [3, 6, 10].

### 2.6 Hyperparameter Optimization and Model Validation

Model performance was optimized using hyperparameter tuning via grid search, adjusting key parameters such as kernel type and regularization strength. To ensure generalizability, we used 5-fold cross-validation, which is a standard practice in neuroimaging-based predictive modeling [6, 10]. This approach reduces the risk of overfitting and provides robust performance estimates. Figure 1 illustrates the overall MVPA-based fMRI workflow, including ROI selection, time-series extraction, model training, and cross-validation with hyperparameter tuning.

**Fig. 1.** Methodology pipeline for MVPA-based fMRI

## 3 Results

The classification models applied to resting-state fMRI data effectively distinguished healthy individuals from OA patients. Using functional connectivity features extracted from the middle frontal gyrus, both SVM and Logistic Regression were trained on two study cohorts using 5-fold cross-validation.

The models were trained and tested separately for the two subsets of osteoarthritis patients: Study 1, which included only the placebo group, and Study 2, which included both placebo and duloxetine-treated participants. The classification performance, as measured by accuracy, is summarized in the table below:

**Table 2.** Classification Accuracy Results

| Study | Model | Accuracy (%) | AUC | Best Parameters |
|---|---|---|---|---|
| Study 1 (Healthy vs Study 1) | SVM | 98.57 | 0.986 | C = 1, gamma = 'scale', kernel = 'rbf' |
| Study 1 (Healthy vs Study 1) | Logistic Regression | 97.14 | 0.991 | C = 10, solver = 'liblinear' |
| Study 2 (Healthy vs Study 2) | SVM | 92.86 | 0.981 | C = 10, gamma = 'scale', kernel = 'rbf' |
| Study 2 (Healthy vs Study 2) | Logistic Regression | 92.86 | 0.955 | C = 0.1, solver = 'liblinear' |

Table 2 summarizes the classification performance of SVM and Logistic Regression models across two studies comparing healthy controls with osteoarthritis patients. In Study 1, which included only placebo-treated patients, SVM achieved the highest accuracy (98.57%), while Logistic Regression recorded the highest AUC (0.991). In Study 2, involving both placebo and duloxetine-treated subjects, both models performed equally well in terms of accuracy (92.86%), though SVM slightly outperformed in AUC. The optimal hyperparameters for each model are also listed.

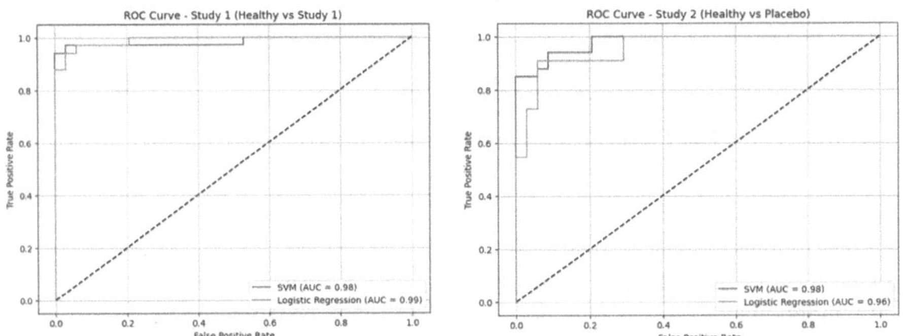


**Fig. 2.** ROC Curves Comparing SVM and Logistic Regression Performance for Two fMRI

Figure 2 shows ROC curves for SVM and Logistic Regression models applied to two fMRI studies. Both models show high classification performance. In Study 1 (left), Logistic Regression slightly outperforms SVM, while in Study 2 (right), SVM shows slightly better results. AUC values in both cases are close to 1, indicating strong model accuracy.

## 4 Discussion

This study demonstrates that functional connectivity patterns from the middle frontal gyrus can reliably differentiate osteoarthritis patients from healthy individuals through MVPA-based analysis. The choice of this ROI was informed by prior evidence identifying its role in placebo response and pain modulation [1].

Our classification models—particularly SVM and Logistic Regression—achieved strong accuracy and AUC, with Logistic Regression performing slightly better in the placebo-only group. These results support the hypothesis that the middle frontal gyrus contains meaningful neural signals related to chronic pain processing, echoing previous findings that fMRI data can capture subjective pain experiences [4] and that MVPA is effective for decoding such neural representations [5].

Unlike previous studies that used traditional machine learning approaches on chronic pain data, such as fibromyalgia and rheumatoid arthritis [16], this work is the first to apply MVPA techniques to osteoarthritis patients using this specific resting-state fMRI dataset. While [16] applied machine learning on functional connectivity, they did not explore OA nor utilize MVPA—an approach well-suited for capturing distributed brain activation patterns [3, 8].

Our study builds upon best practices in experimental design and multivariate modeling [5, 6] The successful application of MVPA in this context opens pathways for developing predictive tools for diagnosis and treatment response in OA.

## 5 Conclusion

This study provides compelling evidence that resting-state functional connectivity patterns from the middle frontal gyrus, analyzed through multivariate pattern analysis (MVPA), can accurately distinguish between osteoarthritis patients and healthy individuals. The use of machine learning classifiers—particularly SVM and Logistic Regression—demonstrated high performance, reinforcing the potential of combining MVPA and neuroimaging for pain-related biomarker discovery. Our findings support the relevance of the middle frontal gyrus in chronic pain processing and contribute to the growing body of research that leverages data-driven approaches for advancing pain diagnostics.

## 6 Limitations and Future Work

We used an open-source dataset for this study; however, the dataset itself was small. This limitation is largely due to the high cost and limited accessibility of fMRI scans—many patients are either unwilling or unable to participate in neuroimaging, which restricts subject recruitment. Additionally, the high dimensionality of neuroimaging data poses challenges in collecting large and balanced datasets, further affecting the scalability of our analysis.

## References


1. Vachon-Presseau, E., et al.: Brain connectivity predicts placebo response across chronic pain clinical trials. Nat. Commun. **9**, 3397 (2018)
2. Wager, T.D., Atlas, L.Y., Lindquist, M.A., Roy, M., Woo, C.-W., Kross, E.: An fMRI-Based neurologic signature of physical pain. N. Engl. J. Med. **368**, 1388–1397 (2013)
3. Marquand, A.F., Howard, M.A., Brammer, M.J., Chu, C., Coen, S., Mourão-Miranda, J.: Decoding the perception of pain from fMRI using multivariate pattern analysis. Neuroimage **49**, 2178–2189 (2010)
4. Wager, T.D., Rilling, J.K., Smith, E.E., Sokolik, A., Casey, K.L.: Placebo treatment can alter primary visual cortex activity and connectivity. Hum. Brain Mapp. **37**, 1664–1676 (2016)
5. Sørensen, T.A., Nielsen, F.Å., Hansen, L.K., Paulson, O.B., Hansen, A.K.: Optimizing fMRI experimental design for MVPA-based BCI control: combining the strengths of block and event-related designs. J. Neurosci. Methods **204**(2), 265–272 (2012)
6. Sundermann, B., Pfleiderer, B.: Multi-voxel pattern analysis of fMRI data predicts clinical symptom severity. NeuroImage: Clin. **5**, 111–118 (2014)
7. Smith, S.: Functional Magnetic Resonance Imaging (fMRI) processing and analysis. In: Neuroimaging in Psychiatry, 2nd edn. Springer, Heidelberg (2018)

8. Norman, K.A., Polyn, S.M., Detre, G.J., Haxby, J.V.: Multivariate pattern analysis of fMRI: the early beginnings. Trends Cogn. Sci. **10**(9), 424–430 (2006)
9. Bagarinao, E., et al.: Preliminary structural MRI-based brain classification of chronic pelvic pain: a MAPP network study. Pain **155**(12), 2502–2509 (2014)
10. Brodersen, K.H., et al.: Decoding the perception of pain from fMRI using multivariate pattern analysis. Neuroimage **63**(3), 1162–1170 (2012)
11. Chang, C.-C., Lin, C.-J.: LIBSVM: a library for support vector machines. ACM Trans. Intell. Syst. Technol. (TIST) **2**(3), 27, 1–27 (2011)

# A Self-Aware Generic Cognitive Architecture

Sabitra Sankalp Panigrahi and Romi Banerjee(✉)

Indian Institute of Technology, Jodhpur, India
{panigrahi.1,romibanerjee}@iitj.ac.in

**Abstract.** With availability of computing, memory and AI there is a surge in research related to cognitive science and cognitive architecture. This has led to increase in new design, development and deployment of cognitively enabled systems in the environment. The cognitively enabled system are deployed in the land, sea, air, outer space and cyber space in the form of autonomous systems or unmanned systems. Often human operators have to co-work with these autonomous systems such as unmanned ground vehicle, unmanned under water vehicle and unmanned aerial vehicles which in turn is increasing the cognitive load of the human operator in the loop. The increased use of cognitively enabled unmanned systems has fueled the research and development of a failsafe and robust cognitive architecture which meets both the safety critical and mission critical criteria. In this paper we propose a generic self-aware cognitive architecture for an autonomous system which answers two critical questions viz. Where am I? & what is my next state? The proposed architecture performs SLAM (Simultaneous Localization and Mapping) in a SWaP (Size weight, area and Power) constrained environment. Continuously meeting the mission requirements of a cognitive system in operation.

**Keywords:** Cognitive Architecture · Autonomous Systems · SLAM · SWaP

## 1 Introduction

Cognitive Architectures (CAs) [8] is a collaborative research area involving different technology domains and sub-disciplines. The prominent contributing domains are Cognitive Science, Artificial Intelligence, Robotics, Machine Learning, Navigation, Simultaneous Localization and Mapping (SLAM) etc. More recently, the advancement in computing science has contributed many solutions in the form of algorithms and concepts to design and develop autonomous systems which are performing to the expectation of human operators. Sub-disciplines such as Computational Neuroscience [9], Natural Language Processing, deep learning, etc. have given rise to many robust solutions used in autonomous systems. CAs have been historically introduced to capture (a) the computational level, the invariant mechanism of human cognition, including


A. Shastri et al. (Eds.): IHCI 2025, LNCS 16437, pp. 537–548, 2026.
https://doi.org/10.1007/978-3-032-26352-0_46

those underlying the functions of control, learning, memory, adaptability, perception and action and to (b) reach human level intelligence, also called General Artificial Intelligence, by means of the realization of artificial artifacts built upon them. During the last decade many cognitive architecture have been proposed and realized such as (ACT-R) [1,2], SOAR [3], OpenCog [4], KnowRob [5–7] etc. These CA have been widely tested in several cognitive tasks such as learning, reasoning, selective attention, multimodal perception, recognition, exploration and navigation etc. Despite the recent developments, however in the last decades the importance of the "knowledge levels" has been historically and systematically downsized by these research area, whose interest have been mainly based on the analysis and the development of mechanisms and processes governing humans and artificial cognition. The knowledge levels in CAs, however, presents several problems that may affect the overall heuristic value of such artificial general system and therefore needs more attention. How the CA addresses the key question of "Where am I?" and "Which is the next suitable state?" are two key research area useful in exploration and navigation. This paper proposes a generic CA which answers the above two questions and exhibits intrinsic motivation such that the architecture can be instantiate to different autonomous systems. Also discussed are the common functions exhibited by a systems built using the proposed CA. How the flow of data, control, logic and functioning is performed in the proposed CA is depicted in the form of a flow diagrams.

## 2 Architecture vs Cognitively Enabled Architectures

Before designing a cognitively enabled system the key question arise "What is Architecture?". Architecture is a meta-concept without any authentic definition. Often an architecture is described with some qualifier such as software architecture, hardware architecture, network architecture, temple architecture etc. Besides its objectification often architecture is described or qualified as robust architecture, agile architecture, fault tolerant architecture, reliable architecture etc. Architecture is always associated with an object, event or system describing its structure, shape, size, functioning, and aesthetics alone with or together. Cognitive architecture therefore is an architecture where cognition, cognitive computing, cognitive network and cognitive control is strongly associated with the system. A modern system constitutes of various systems, sub-systems, functional modules integrated through computing, control and communication mechanisms performing a specific objective. System architecture is the key artifact which describes to the designer, developer, and operator or for maintenance personnel the detail insight about the system. An information system or architecture can be thought of as a conglomeration of hardware architecture, software architecture [22], and information architecture, network architecture along with the cognitive architecture or neural architecture for computing. When we thought of software, hardware or distribute system the architecture comes to mind [23] through which we visualized various component of the overall system and interaction among various sub-systems and modules. In case of a software system it can be described through a context diagram [10], dataflow diagram [11], control flow graph [12] or a call graph [13]. This concept can be described as a context diagram or dataflow diagram and control flow diagram when software is in its inception stage or implementation stage therefore giving an idea for formulation of various software modules to a designer. Therefore a context diagram/dataflow diagram/control flow diagram and call graph are different abstract artifacts of the system design which gives different idea to a designer, developer and persons involved in maintaining and repairing the system. Cognitively enabled architecture is a special class of architecture which has inbuilt capability to exhibit human like cognitive capability. A cognitive architecture has applications in many domains especially in robotics, autonomous systems, decision support systems etc. Fig.- 1 depicts some domains which use CA as their basis to develop end applications.

Architecture can be viewed as enablers of some core functions of the system. Depending on the core functions different research groups have proposed and designed different cognitive architectures. These CAs differ based on their capacity to perform a set of core functions. Some of them are open source architectures and some of them are exclusive. Choice of a CA for system design depends on the capacity and capability to address some of the core functions of the system. Choice of CA by system designers depends on its functional capability and adoption to the OS and hardware architecture. During the last two decades many cognitive architectures have been proposed and realized. The prominent among them are Adaptive Control of Thought—Rational (ACT-R) developed byJohn Robert Andersonand Christian Lebiere [1,2], SOAR [3,24]., OpenCog [4], KnowRob [5,6]etc. Alan Newell's has enlisted some common functions which are exhibited by a cognitively enabled system. This can be treated as functional criteria for systems built with Cognitive Architecture (CA), 1.

From this table we can observe that most of the leading cognitive architectures available in open platforms exhibit cognitive functions such as learning, reasoning, selective attention, multimodal perception, recognition, exploration and navigation, sensing, navigation, mapping, NLP [15]. The common deficiencies of these architectures are that they do not have inbuilt self-aware support such as SLAM and SWAP.

## 3 Shortcomings of Open Source CA Systems

Handling a huge amount of knowledge, and selectively retrieve it according to the needs emerging in different scenarios, represent an important aspect of human intelligence known as episodic memory. For this task human adopts a wide range of heuristics due to their "bounded rationality". Currently, however, the Cognitive Architectures are not able, to deal with complex knowledge structures that can be even slightly comparable to the knowledge heuristically managed by humans. In other terms: CAs are domain specific structures without a general content. This means that the knowledge embedded and processed in such architectures is usually very limited, ad-hoc built, domain specific, or based on

**Table 1.** Function Compliance of Open Source Cognitive Architectures.

| Functions/Open Source CA | ACT-R | SOAR | OpenCog | KnowRob |
|---|---|---|---|---|
| Cognition Focus | simulates human thinking, decision making process | Focuses on human cognition, problem solving, and decision making. Emphasizes role of working memory | Designed for cognition-enabled robots, Focus is on Knowledge representation, reasoning in robotics systems | Designed for open source AGI (Artificial General Intelligence) |
| Knowledge Representation | Uses production Rule (if-then-else) Declarative Memory (facts and knowledge) | Also uses production rules and working memory (Temporary storage for processing information) Semantic memory (Facts and knowledge) Episodic memory (Captures, stores and temporarily indexes agent state) | Knowledge is stored in the form of Atoms (Nodes and Links) in Atmosphere | Employs ontologies (hierarchical knowledge structures) and semantic web technologies for knowledge re presentation. |
| Memory | Declarative memory (long-term storage) Working memory (temporary storage) | Long Term Memories Procedural Memory(Production rules) Semantic Memory Episodic Memory Short Term Memory Working Memory | Atmospace – in –Ram generalized hyper graph (meta graph) database. | Semantic memory (ontologies and knowledge graphs) episodic memory (robot experiences). |
| Reasoning | Forward and Backward chaining (rule-based reasoning). | Forward and backward chaining, plus working memory-based reasoning. | Graph based reasoning (AddLink, CondLink, GreaterLink, BindLink etc.) | Semantic reasoning (ontologies and inference), Plus rule based reasoning. |
| Learning | Learning through practice, reinforcement, and feedback. | Reinforcement Learning Chunking | MOSES (Meta-Optimizing Semantic Evolutionary Search)- machine-learning tool; it ia an "evolutionary program learner". | Learning through experience, feedback, and knowledge updates. |
| Applications | Human-computer interaction, cognitive modeling, education, and training | Human-computer interaction, cognitive modeling, decision-making, and expert systems | HCI, Expert System | Robotics, Artificial intelligence, knowledge representation, and cognitive architectures. |
| Strengths and Limitations | Strengths: flexible, adaptable, and human-like reasoning. Limitations: complex, computationally intensive | Strengths: efficient, scalable, and robust. Limitations: less flexible, more rigid than ACT-R | Strengths: flexible, adaptable, and Artificial General Intelligence Limitations: Many modules are obsolete | Strengths: robust, scalable, and knowledge-centric. Limitations: less focused on human cognition. |

the specific task they have to deal with. Thus every evolution of the artificial system relying upon them, is necessarily task-specific and do not involve not even the minimum part of the full spectrum of processes involved in the human cognition when the "knowledge" comes to play a role. As a consequence, the structural mechanisms that the CAs implement concerning knowledge processing tasks (e.g. that one of retrieval, learning, reasoning etc.) can be only loosely evaluated, and compared w.r.t. that ones used by humans in similar knowledge-intensive situations. Such knowledge limitation, in our option, does not allow to obtain significant advancements in the cognitive science research about how the humans heuristically select and deal with the huge amount of knowledge that possess when they have to make decisions, reason about a given situation or, more in general, solve a particular cognitive task involving several dimensions of analysis. With the advent of research and development in neuro-computing or biologically inspired computing the architecture of various systems are metamorphosed leading to the concept of cognitive architecture or architecture utilizing cognitive computing or cognitive systems. A cognitive system primarily constitutes of following concepts. (Human thinking mechanism through a NN, self-aware mechanism through as SLAM, motor control mechanism through sense-compute-control mechanism and overall thinking mechanism through means of computer vision sensing to computing to Decision to Control. These concepts put together are depicted in the sequence diagram (see Fig. 1). This concepts can be put in the form of vision modules/function modules and their interaction at various levels of abstraction. The overall sequence diagrams realized in a system leads to the description of a cognitive system architecture.

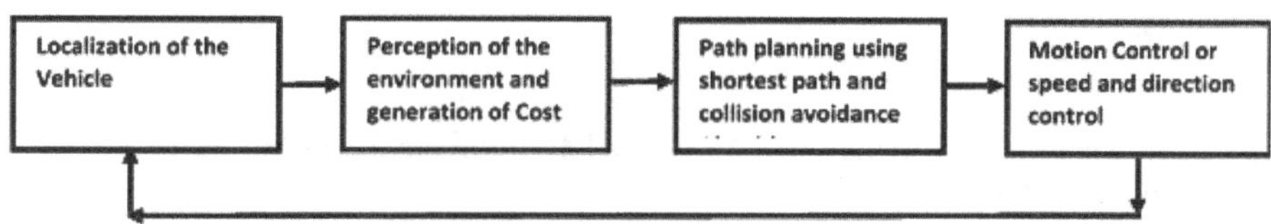


**Fig. 1.** Sequence diagram of Functioning of a cognitively enabled Autonomous vehicle

The above sequence diagram can be extended to describe the cognitive architecture of an overall system. Further the systems functional modules and sub modules and there interaction can be described and analyzed at various levels of abstraction and their relative importance can be discussed. The concepts of resilience, robustness, reliability (3R) with respect to the architecture are concepts which validate the time varying nature of a system. Therefore we tried to validate the above 3R wrt to the cognitive architecture.

## 4 A Generic Flow Diagram of A Cognitively Enabled System

To realize the list of cognitively enabled functions enlisted in Table-1, we have proposed a flow chart (see Fig. 2). This flow chart also enables the system to learn from its past actions by rewarding positive actions and by reprimanding negative actions leading to failure state. This action of rewarding actions which leads to improved realization of system objective is analogous to intrinsic motivation exhibited by human. This is implemented and realized as an AI agent [26] performing re-enforcement learning (RL).

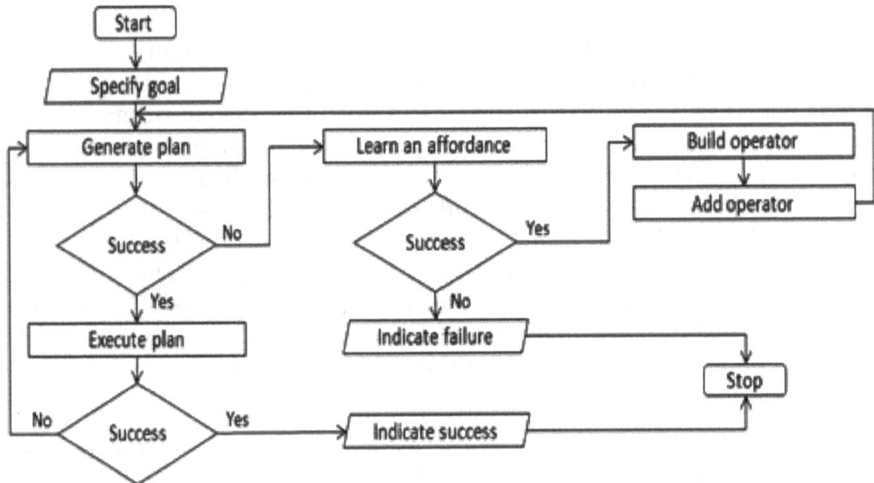


**Fig. 2.** Framework for Intrinsically Motivated Reinforcement Learning based Action Affordance Learning

Putting the functional criteria enlisted in Table-1 and the control flow in Fig. 3 a CA can be contextualized in the form of a model view and control (MVC) graph [14].

The above generic cognitive architecture can be modeled mathematically at various levels of abstraction such as functionally: Motor action, Memory, indexing, Decision, Retrieval, Self-aware, Sense and compute etc. The most common functional modules of any physical cognitive system should have (a) Cognitive action (b) Motor Action (c) Self-aware (d) Decision Action The overall cognitive architecture can be thought of as an conglomeration of MVC architecture Model to View to Control and sense to compute to Activate realized through a robot. But the above CA suffers from two critical functions that is where am I a? and what am I?. If the robot need to understand about itself (self-aware) in terms of its spatial location (Where am I ?) And what to do next (What am I ?) Then it should perform cyclically Sense to Compute to model to check to decide

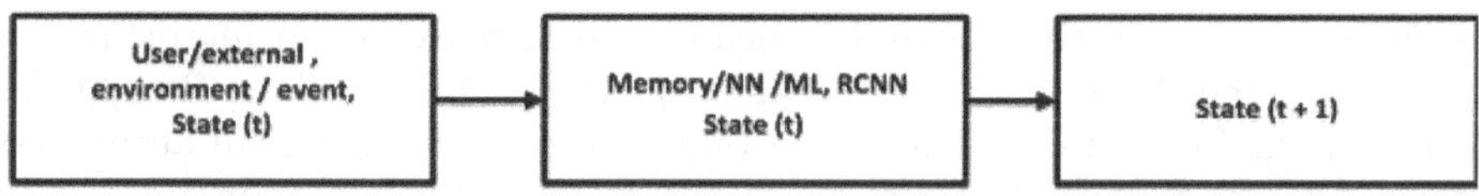


**Fig. 3.** Context Diagram of Cognitive Architecture

which can be described as DIKD (DatatoInformation to Knowledge to Decision) architectural pattern. This pattern is known as SLAM (Simultaneous Localization and Mapping). The knowledge about the environment in terms of the slope, aspect, temperature, almanac etc. can be obtained from its environmental sensing and decision can be taken accordingly so as where to move next is considered as a spatial cognitive ability. The decision is implemented through the control laws governing the robots physical actions [18,19] which takes care of all exceptional cases and forbidden cases of movement leading to catastrophic situations. To achieve this the system must save in its memory the event- action pair and index them to be retrieved and compared. This is known as episodic memory which forms a critical element of any CA. In the case of a cognitive architecture neuro-computing i.e. Computing using AI, NN, ML and other forms of modeling, classification and machine learning algorithms are employed at various stages of abstraction to achieve decision and episodic memory. This is described through the diagram below (Fig. 4).

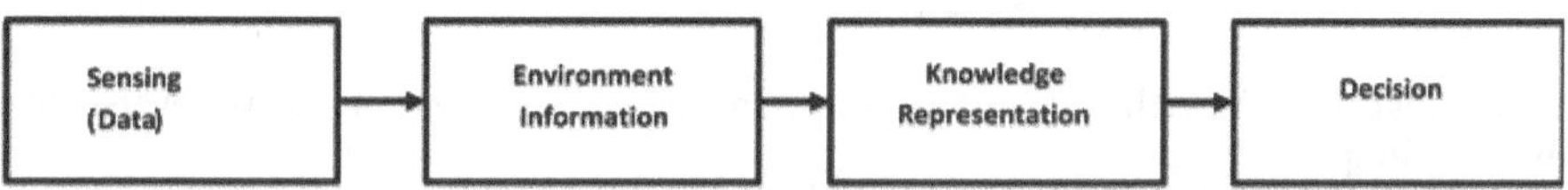


**Fig. 4.** The DIKD (data-Information-Knowledge-Decision) and MVC (Model-View-Control) Architecture of Cognitive Architecture

## 5 Self-aware CA with SLAM and SWAP

In this section we propose a self-aware CA which takes into account the shortcoming of the openly available CAs and addresses the two key questions through SLAM and SWAP. Sensing and computing of Spatial Location, time, direction, slope, aspect, speed, acceleration, distance, height and quantifying them in metric form as (x, y, z, t, x', y', z', x", y", z", require different types of sensors such as LiDAR, RADAR, SONAR, optical camera, day- night camera, thermal camera, GPS, INS, stereo-sensors [29] etc. The system need to store its current state, its past state in memory and compute on it using AI and ML techniques its next state or move. Therefore memory, ML and AI [25] algorithms impart the necessary cognitive capability to the autonomous system. This is exhibiting episodic memory. Continuous and judicious use of power is an important consideration of the AS (Autonomous System) making SWAP (Size Weight Area and Power) [27] constraint as an important factor for designing an autonomous system. Textual System Description in the form of Voice Command, Textual Command can be a MMI for autonomous system for human to interact with the system therefore should be an optional sub-system achieved through NLP [15]. Encompassing all the above factors a generic architecture for a CA is proposed and is depicted in the block diagram in Fig. 5.

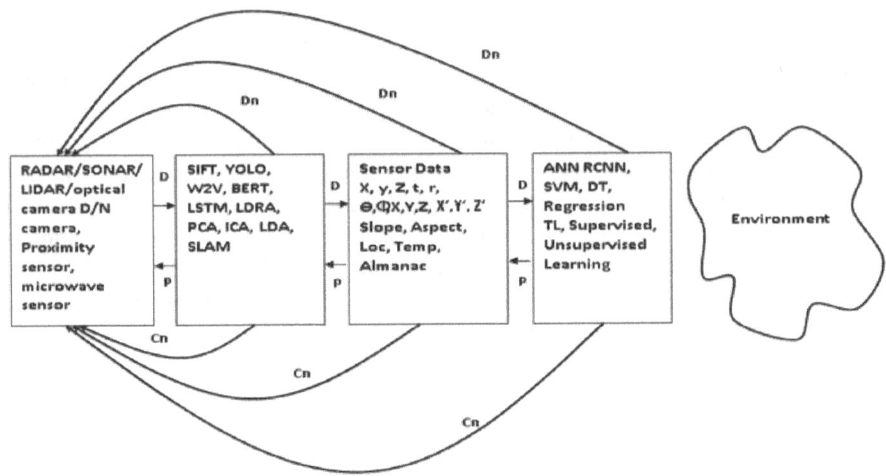


**Fig. 5.** Generic CA with 4 levels of abstraction and 4-cycles of data-power-control-command loops

This architecture can be validated against different class of physical systems such as a Radio/Radar, Sonar, Aircraft, Robot, Tracked /Wheeled Vehicle such as an autonomous car or armored carrying vehicle. The cognitively enabled system are often named as cognitive robot [18] cognitive Radio/Radar cognitive car, etc. making them a class of systems known as cognitive systems. Further in the next section we discuss the knowledge representation problem, SLAM, SWAP and locomotion in autonomous system.

sectionProblems of Knowledge Representation in CAs

Handling a huge amount of knowledge, and selectively retrieve it according to the needs of different situational scenarios, represent an important aspect of human intelligence. For this task humans adopt a wide range of heuristics due to their "bounded rationality ". Currently, however, the Cognitive Architectures are not able, de facto, to deal with complex knowledge structures that can be even slightly comparable to the knowledge heuristically managed by humans. In other terms: CAs are general structures without a general content. This means that the knowledge embedded and processed in such architectures is usually very limited, ad-hoc built, domain specific, or based on the specific task they have to deal with. Thus every evolution of the artificial system relying upon them, is necessarily task-specific and do not involve not even the minimum part of the full spectrum of processes involved in the human cognition when the "knowledge" comes to play a role. As a consequence, the structural mechanisms that the CAs implement concerning knowledge processing tasks (e.g. that one of retrieval, learning, reasoning etc.) can be only loosely evaluated, and compared w.r.t. that ones used by humans in similar knowledge-intensive situations. In other words: from an epistemological perspective, the explanatory power of their computational simulations is strongly affected. Such knowledge limitation [20], in our option, does not allow to obtain significant advancements in the cognitive science research about how the humans heuristically select and deal with the huge amount of knowledge that possess when they have to make decisions, reasons about a given situation or, more in general, solve a particular cognitive task involving several dimensions of analysis. This problem, as a consequence, also limits the advancements of the research in the area of General Artificial Intelligence of Cognitive inspiration.

## 6 Simultaneous Localization and Mapping of CA

Simultaneous localization and mapping(SLAM) [16,17] is the computational problem of constructing or updating a map of an unknown environment while simultaneously keeping track of anagent's location within it [26]. Motion planning and navigation of autonomous system is governed through SLAM. SLAM (simultaneous localization and mapping) is a method used for autonomous vehicles that lets it build a map of the environment and localize the vehicle on that map at the same time. SLAM algorithms allow the vehicle to map out unknown environments. Engineers use map information to carry out tasks such as path planning and obstacle avoidance and navigation. To build the map of the environment, the SLAM algorithm incrementally processes the LiDAR scans and builds a pose graph that links these scans. The robot recognizes a previously-visited place through scan matching and may establish one or more loop closures along its moving path. The SLAM algorithm utilizes the loop closure information to update the map and adjust the estimated robot trajectory. A map generated by a SLAM Robot. Simultaneous localization and mapping (SLAM) is the computational problem of constructing or updating a map of an unknown environment while simultaneously keeping track of an agent's location within it. Broadly speaking, there are two types of technology components used to achieve SLAM. The first type is sensor signal processing, including the front-end processing, which is largely dependent on the sensors used. The second type is pose-graph optimization, including the back-end processing, which is sensor-agnostic. The SLAM runs as cycle in the autonomous vehicle as described in the Fig. 6.

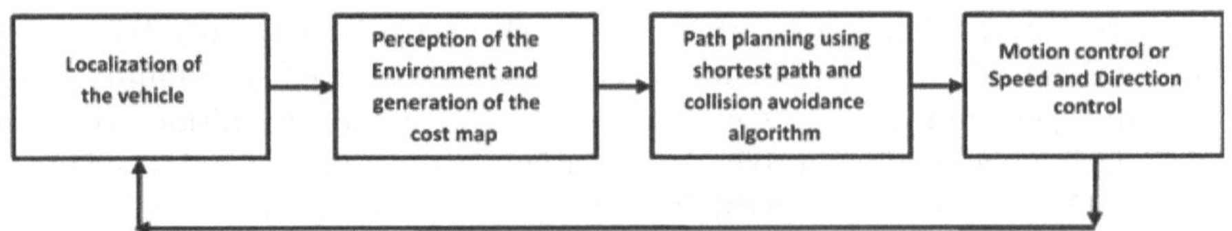


**Fig. 6.** SLAM cycle in a cognitively enabled autonomous vehicle

### 6.1 SWAP Constraints of CA

A system realized for operating in an aligned environment for exploration through sensing, learning, retaining the environment map and moving through locomotion require judicious use power and control throughout its operation. Therefore harnessing power from the environment, storing the energy in a suitable device such as battery and utilizing the energy to power all the modules and sub modules optimally is a critical design criteria of any CA. Often high endurance operation of autonomous vehicles such as UAV, UGV or under water vehicles are is an operation requirement. Therefore the design criteria must take into account the optimal use of power for high endurance operation. Therefore the size, weight and power consumption pattern of the modules need to be taken into consideration while designing efficient autonomous systems [15]. The constraints which make use of optimal power for long duration operation. Therefore the CA must take into consideration the power requirements must optimally be designed for size weight area of the modules and sub modules and this is known as the SWaP [27] Constraints of CA.

### 6.2 Locomotion Action of CA

Locomotion is most of the time considered to be the result of top-down control commands produced by the nervous system in response to inputs received via sensory organs from the environment. Locomotion may arise alternatively when attracting states are stabilized in the combined dynamical space made up by the brain, the body and the environment. Cognition is embodied in this case within the sensorimotor loop [29], viz. self-organized. Using a physics simulation environment one can show that self – organized locomotion may

result in complex phase spaces which include limit cycle corresponding to regular movements and both strong and partially predictable explorative behavior. Occurrence of self-organized embodiment in robots for which sensation is confined to propio-sensation.

## 7 Summary

The research on Cognitive Architectures (CAs) is a wide and active area of research involving a plethora of disciplines such as Cognitive Science, Artificial Intelligence, Robotics and, more recently, the area of computational Neuroscience. CAs have been historically introduced i) "to capture, at the computational level, the invariant mechanism of human cognition, including those underlying the functions of control, learning, memory, adaptively, perception and action" and ii) to reach human level intelligence, also called General Artificial Intelligence [21], by means of the realization of artificial artifacts built upon them. All the problems in architecting a cognitive system or autonomous system boils down to some key concepts such as MVC, DKID, SLAM and SWAP,. These concepts are realized differently in different autonomous system with varying combination of sensors, data representation, feature extraction, feature classification algorithms, knowledge representation and episodic memory [28]. This is described in the proposed cognitive architecture.

## References


1. Anderson, J.R.: How Can the Human Mind Occur in The Physical Universe? Oxford University Press, New York. This book provides a comprehensive overview and theoretical framework for ACT-R (2007)
2. Anderson, J.R., Bothell, D., Byrne, M.D., Douglass, S., Lebiere, C., Qin, Y.: An integrated theory of the mind. Psychol. Rev. **111**(4), 1036–1060 (2004). This influential paper details the core principles of ACT-R
3. Laird, J.E.: The Soar Cognitive Architecture. MIT Press (2012). ISBN 978-0262122962
4. Hart, D., Goertzel, B.: OpenCog: a software framework for integrative artificial general intelligence (PDF). In: Proceedings of the First AGI Conference. GBooks (2008)
5. Tenorth, M., Beetz, M.: KnowRob – knowledge processing for autonomous personal robots. In: IEEE/RSJ International Conference on Intelligent Robots and Systems, pp. 4261–4266. IEEE (2009)
6. Tenorth, M., Beetz, M.: Representations for robot knowledge in the KnowRob framework, artificial intelligence. Elsevier (2015)
7. Beetz, M., Beßler, D., Haidu, A., et al.: KnowRob 2.0 – a 2nd generation knowledge processing framework for cognition-enabled robotic agents. In: International Conference on Robotics and Automation (ICRA) (2018)
8. Lieto, A., Perrone, F., Pozzato, G.L., Chiodino, E.: Beyond Subgoaling: a dynamic knowledge generation framework for creative problem solving in cognitive architectures. Cogn. Syst. Res. **58**, 305–316 (2019). https://doi.org/10.1016/j.cogsys.2019.08.005.. hdl:2318/1726157. S2CID 201127492
9. Hesslow, G.: The current status of the simulation theory of cognition. Brain Res. **1428**, 71–79 (2012)
10. Jalote, P.: An Integrated Approach to Software Engineering, p. 372. Springer Science & Business Media (1997). ISBN 978-0-387- 94899-7
11. Uday, K., Amitabha, S., Bageshri, S.: Data Flow Analysis: Theory and Practice, p. 234. CRC Press (2009). ISBN 978-0-8493- 3251-7
12. Callahan, D., Carle, A., Hall, M.W., Kennedy, K.: Constructing the procedure call multigraph. IEEE Trans. Softw. Eng. **16**(4), 483–487 (1990). https://doi.org/10.1109/32.54302

13. Ryder, B.G.: Constructing the call graph of a program. IEEE Trans. Softw. Eng. SE- **5**(3), 216–226 ( 1979). https://doi.org/10.1109/tse.1979.234183. S2CID 16527042
14. Krasner, G.E., Pope, S.T.: A cookbook for using the model–view controller user interface paradigm in Smalltalk- 80. J. Object Technol. **1**(3) (1988). SIGS Publications: 26–49. Also published as Ä Description of the Model–View–Controller User Interface Paradigm in the Smalltalk-80 System
15. Guida, G., Mauri, G.: Evaluation of natural language processing systems: issues and approaches. Proc. IEEE **74**(7), 1026–1035 (1986). https://doi.org/10.1109/PROC.1986.13580. ISSN 1558-2256. S2CID 30688575
16. Jaulin, L.: Range-only SLAM with occupancy maps; a set-membership approach. IEEE Trans. Robot. **27**(5), 1004–1010 (2011). https://doi.org/10.1109/TRO.2011.2147110. S2CID 52801599
17. Cadena, C., et al.: Past, present, and future of simultaneous localization and mapping: toward the robust-perception age. IEEE Trans. Robot. **32**(6), 13091332 (2016). arXiv:1606.05830. Bibcode:2016arXiv160605830C. https://doi.org/10.1109/tro.2016.2624754. hdl:2440/107554. ISSN 1552-3098. S2CID 2596787
18. Vernon, D., et al.: Industrial priorities for cognitive robotics. Carnegie Mellon University Africa
19. Proceedings of Eucognition, Cognitive Robot Architectures - CEUR-WS, Rwanda, vol. 1855 (2016)
20. Lieto, A.: Representation limits in cognitive architectures. University of Turin, Department of Computer Science, Italy, ICAR-CNR, Palermo, Italy (2016)
21. Oltamari, A., Lebiere, C.: Pursuing artificial general intelligence by leveraging the knowledge capabilities of ACT-R, AGI. In: 5th International Conference on "Artificial General Intelligence", Oxford (2012)
22. Pressman, R.S.: Software Engineering, A Practitioner's Approach. McGrawHill Higher Education (2010)
23. Anderson, J.R., Bothell, D., Byrne, M.D., Douglass, S., Lebiere, C., Qin, Y.: An integrated theory of the mind. Psychol. Rev. **111**(4), 1036–1060 (2004). https://doi.org/10.1037/0033-95X.111.4.1036
24. Laird, J.E.: The Soar Cognitive Architecture. MIT Press (2012)
25. Newell, A.: The Knowledge level. Artif. Intell. **18**(1), 87–127 (1982)
26. Sun, R.: The CLARION cognitive architecture: extending cognitive modeling to social simulation. Cogn. Multi-Agent Interact., 73–99 (2006)
27. Panigrahi Sabitra Sankalp: Processing data acquired by a DRONE using a GIS: designing a size-, weight-, and power- constrained system. IEEE Consum. Electron. Mag. **7**(2), 50–54 (2018)
28. Pieters, R., Racca, M., Veronese, A., Kyrki, V.: Human-aware interaction: a memory-inspired artificial cognitive architecture. In: Proc. EUCognition, "Cognitive Robot Architectures" - CEUR-WS, vol. 1855 (2016)
29. Sandor, B., Martin, L., Gros, C.: The role of the sensori-motor loop for cognition. In: Proceedings of EUCognition "Cognitive Robot Architectures" - CEUR-WS, vol. 1855 (2016)

# Author Index





A. Shastri et al. (Eds.): IHCI 2025, LNCS 16437, pp. 549–551, 2026.
https://doi.org/10.1007/978-3-032-26352-0

Zeitfracht Medien GmbH
Ferdinand-Jühlke-Straße 7
99095 Erfurt, Deutschland
produktsicherheit@kolibri360.de